THE HOME DEPOT®

HOME IMPROVEMENT 1-2-3™

Meredith® BOOKS

Des Moines, Iowa

THE HOME DEPOT®

HOME IMPROVEMENT 1-2-3®

Meredith® BOOKS

Des Moines, Iowa

HOME IMPROVEMENT 1-2-3®

Meredith Book Development Team
Senior Editor: John P. Holms
Art Director: Tom Wegner
Contributing Art Director: John Eric Seid
Writer: Jeff Day
Graphic Designer: Tim Abramowitz
Copy Chief: Terri Fredrickson
Copy and Production Editor: Victoria Forlini
Editorial Operations Manager: Karen Schirm
Managers, Book Production: Pam Kvitne, Marjorie J. Schenkelberg, Rick von Holdt

Manufacturing and Inventory Control Manager: Mark Weaver
Contributing Copy Editor: Ro Sila
Contributing Proofreaders: Janet Anderson, Carol Boker, Julie Cahalan, Heidi Johnson, Barb Stokes
Illustrator: Jim Swanson
Contributing Illustrator: Gwyn Raker
Indexer: Donald Glassman
Electronic Production Coordinator: Paula Forest
Editorial and Design Assistants: Renee E. McAtee, Karen McFadden

Meredith® Books
Editor in Chief: Linda Raglan Cunningham
Design Director: Matt Strelecki
Managing Editor: Gregory H. Kayko
Executive Editor, Gardening and Home Improvement: Benjamin W. Allen

Publisher: James D. Blume
Executive Director, Marketing: Jeffrey Myers
Executive Director, New Business Development: Todd M. Davis
Director, Sales-Home Depot: Robb Morris
Executive Director, Sales: Ken Zagor
Director, Operations: George A. Susral
Director, Production: Douglas M. Johnston
Business Director: Jim Leonard

Vice President and General Manager: Douglas J. Guendel

Meredith Publishing Group
President, Publishing Group: Stephen M. Lacy
Vice President-Publishing Director: Bob Mate

Meredith Corporation
Chairman and Chief Executive Officer: William T. Kerr

Chairman of the Executive Committee: E. T. Meredith III

If you would like to purchase any of our home improvement, cooking, crafts, gardening, or home decorating and design books, check wherever quality books are sold. Or visit us at: meredithbooks.com

The Home Depot®
Marketing Manager: Nathan Ehrlich

Note to the Reader: Due to differing conditions, tools, and individual skills, Meredith Corporation and The Home Depot® assume no responsibility for any damages, injuries suffered, or losses incurred as a result of following the information published in this book. Before beginning any project, review the instructions carefully, and if any doubts or questions remain, consult local experts or authorities. Because codes and regulations vary greatly, you always should check with authorities to ensure that your project complies with all applicable local codes and regulations. Always read and observe all of the safety precautions provided by any tool or equipment manufacturer, and follow all accepted safety procedures.

The editors of *Home Improvement 1-2-3*® are dedicated to providing accurate and helpful do-it-yourself information. We welcome your comments about improving this book and ideas for other books we might offer to home improvement enthusiasts. Contact us by any of these methods:
Leave a voice message at: 800/678-2093
Write to: Meredith Books, *Home Depot Books*
     1716 Locust St.
     Des Moines, IA 50309–3023
Send e-mail to: hi123@mdp.com

HOME IMPROVEMENT 1-2-3

HOME IMPROVEMENT 1-2-3.

TABLE OF CONTENTS

HOW TO USE THIS BOOK   Page 8

1 PAINTING   Page 10

2 WALLPAPER   Page 58

3 PLUMBING   Page 84

ELECTRICAL   Page 148

 # WALLS AND CEILINGS   Page 222

 # FLOORING   Page 276

7 DOORS Page 330

8 WINDOWS Page 366

9 CABINETS, COUNTERTOPS, SHELVING AND STORAGE Page 384

10 INSULATION AND WEATHERPROOFING Page 420

11 EXTERIOR   Page 442

12 HEATING, VENTILATION, AND AIR-CONDITIONING   Page 486

13 MEETING CANADIAN CODE   Page 536

TOOL GLOSSARY   Page 544

INDEX, ACKNOWLEDGEMENTS, & RESOURCES   Page 552

How to use this book

People work on their homes for many reasons: To save money; improve their quality of life; provide a safe and attractive place for their families to live; feel the satisfaction of a job well done; and maybe, simply because they like doing it.

Whatever the reasons, there are four basic components of success:

● mastering unfamiliar skills

● using the right tools and materials

● working safely

● doing the job right the first time

Most homeowners need a little help balancing these components, so a home-improvement resource that's accessible, easy-to-use, and full of the right information can become one of the most valuable additions to a do-it-yourselfer's bookshelf. Here's how to get the most out of *Home Improvement 1-2-3*.

TRUST THE WISDOM OF THE AISLES. A genuine desire to help people say, "I can do that!" is what the associates at The Home Depot are all about. And, it's why these experts from around the country have contributed their years of on-the-job experience and wisdom of the aisles to this revision of *Home Improvement 1-2-3*. Their contributions have helped create a hardworking, accurate, and easy-to-follow guide for every aspect of home improvement, maintenance, and repair.

THE ORGANIZING PRINCIPLE. *Home Improvement 1-2-3* consists of 14 sections that provide detailed coverage of painting; wallpaper; plumbing; electrical; walls and ceilings; flooring; doors and windows; cabinets, countertops, and storage; insulation and weatherproofing; exterior; and HVAC(heating,ventilation, and air-conditioning).

There's also a special section that provides information about Canadian building codes and a comprehensive Tool Glossary.

DOING THE JOB—STEP-BY-STEP. All the projects include **complete instructions** along with detailed, **step-by-step photography** to make successful completion simple and easy. You've got everything you need to do the job right the first time following standards set by manufacturers and the trades—just like the pros.

SUPPORT YOUR LOCAL BUILDING INSPECTOR

Building codes are often confusing to the do-it-yourselfer; but they exist to enforce consistent methods of installation and, more importantly, to ensure the safety of your family. The National Electrical Code, which is written by the National Fire Protection Association, for example, says you can only put one wire under each screw on a receptacle or switch. It doesn't seem like two wires are more dangerous than one. But the NFPA has seen one too many fires caused by the second wire popping out from under the screw.

Fire Prevention Code says that if you're going to put in foam insulation (say in your basement) and then cover it with wood paneling, you have to put drywall over the foam first. Why? Foam insulation produces thick black smoke in a fire and drywall delays the spread of fire, giving you time to get out safely.

Sometimes the reason for code is common sense. Ever wonder why code requires outlets every 6 feet along walls, but every 2 feet along kitchen counters? It's because of the length of appliance cords—they're shorter on toasters than they are on lamps.

You must follow codes, so you should find out what's required and do it from the start. This book is written to meet the relevant national codes. But, codes change, and local codes can sometimes be more stringent than national codes. Legally, it's up to you to make sure the job you're doing meets code. The consequences of not meeting code are serious: You've potentially exposed yourself and your family to danger, an inspector who happens across your work can make you tear it out and start over (which can get expensive), and you may not be able to sell your house until you fix the violation.

You want to do a job you can be proud of, so follow through. Check with your municipality's building inspector to find out what local standards you need to meet. Get some advice on how to best go about the job. Get a permit, do the job right, and sleep soundly at night. For more general information on inspections that is common to both the United States and Canada see page 536.

MEETING CANADIAN CODE

While most Canadian building codes are compatible with those in the United States, there are differences, and some are significant. Because this edition of *Home Improvement 1-2-3* generally reflects relevant U.S. national guidelines; a section called **MEETING CANADIAN CODE** beginning on page 536 supplements the general information.

You'll also find the maple leaf symbol shown above appearing on pages and projects where there is a clear difference between code in the two countries. The symbol refers you to the **MEETING CANADIAN CODE** section.

Remember, codes in both the United States and Canada can (and do) vary greatly from locale to locale so it's impossible for any book to be comprehensive when it comes to code and code application. Always check with local authorities before you begin any projects that may require permits or inspections.

TIPS, TRICKS, AND TIMESAVERS. There's more on each page than just how to do the job. To help you plan your project and to schedule your time, we've asked the experts to tell us how hard a job is, how long it takes them, and how long it might take you.

Skill Scales fill you in on the skills you'll need, time involved, and variables that might complicate the job.

Stuff You'll Need at the beginning of each project provides a materials list along with commonly needed tools. Additional features on the pages are filled with specific information—**Safety Alert, Buyer's Guide, Good Idea!, Tool Tip, Trip Saver, Homer's Hindsight**, and **Work Smarter** are all there to help you work efficiently and economically. Whenever a project involves something special—whether it's safety or getting the right tool—you'll be prepared for whatever comes up.

AND THERE'S MORE. Introductory information at the beginning of projects will tell you what you need to know. **Real-World Situations** start each section and remind you that the world isn't perfect, so be prepared for what might be lurking behind your walls. **Tool Kits**, at the beginning of each section, show you the basic tools you'll need to do the projects that follow.

GET THE MOST OUT OF YOUR HOME IMPROVEMENT EXPERIENCE. To make the best use of what's inside, read through each project carefully before you begin. Walk yourself mentally through the steps from beginning to end until you're comfortable with the process. Understanding the scope of the job will limit unnecessary mistakes and spending the money to do things twice.

Take your time doing the job. If you're not a master plumber, don't expect to work like one. A little learning on the job will make it easier the next time. Expect problems, but also trust that you can solve them. If you can't, don't be afraid to ask the experts. There's no magic in home improvement: just a willingness to give it a try; a desire to learn how things work so you can fix them; and, finally, taking pride in what you can accomplish with a little elbow grease and good advice.

Tricks of the trade

Tips, insights, tricks, shortcuts, and even the benefit of 20/20 hindsight from the pros at The Home Depot are worth their weight in gold. Their years of experience translate into instant expertise for you. As you go through the book look for these special icons, which signal detailed information on a specific topic.

BUYER'S GUIDE
Select the best materials.

HOMER'S HINDSIGHT
Avoid common mistakes.

SAFETY ALERT
Prevent unsafe situations.

CLOSE LOOK
Understand all the details.

OLD vs. NEW
Find out new ways to work with old stuff.

TIME SAVER
Learn shortcuts that work.

Designer Tip
Design options to change your home.

OOPS!
Fix common mistakes.

TOOL TIP
Use specialty tools to their best advantage.

GOOD IDEA
Learn what you need to know before you begin.

🍁
Meet Canadian code.

A+ WORK SMARTER
Make smart work choices.

SAFETY ALERT

Some aspects of home improvement can be dangerous but it's hard to remember that when you're lying under the sink or bumping your head against a roof rafter. Being safe in potentially dangerous situations is not only a way of thinking, it's a way of working.

- Wear the proper safety gear including recommended gloves and clothing, safety glasses, and ear protection when working with power tools. A piece of flying debris can blind you or distract you long enough to create a disaster. Regular eyeglasses can shatter when hit.

- Wear a respirator or particle mask that's rated for the job you're doing. Breathing toxic fumes or inhaling particles can have serious consequences.

- Wear safety glasses when driving nails or working with hammers too. Nailheads are notorious for breaking off and flying off at odd angles.

- Always turn off the power at the circuit breaker when working with wiring. Also cut power when you're tearing down a wall or even drilling a hole in it. Live wires can cause serious injury.

- Choose the right tool for the job and know how to use it safely.

- Don't overreach. Move the ladder before you fall.

- Don't reach above your head to make a cut. Something is bound to fall on you. It may be the cutoff; it may be the saw.

- Ask questions. Store personnel can recommend the right tools and materials for the job; building inspectors can (and will) make sure you're doing the job right.

- Take your time. Read the directions carefully, look at the job at hand, and imagine what might go wrong. You don't do this kind of work every day, and short of having a pro in your house, the surest way to avoid trouble is to prepare properly.

1 PAINTING

PAINT IS ONE OF THE QUICKEST AND CHEAPEST FIXES. Your house is going to look better instantly, and if you're selling, you'll get back more money than you put into the paint. The question is, what paint to use?

OIL VS. LATEX. Latex has swept most of the market. It's water-based, durable, and easy to clean up. Oil (also called alkyd) is still available in most parts of the country. It's a little harder to work with and isn't as easy to clean up or dispose of, but still has its uses.

SHEEN (GLOSS). The glossier the paint, the easier it is to clean. The more flat (or less glossy), the more it hides mistakes. Use flatter sheens on most walls. Use glossier sheens on trim and in kitchens and baths, all of which get a lot of splatters, fingerprints, and other abuse.

COLOR. White is not the only color, and white on white is not the only color scheme. It may feel safe, and probably is, but you can do so much more. Check manufacturers' literature for recommended color schemes and see the color wheel on page 14. Then choose a color, buy a quart, and put it on a section of wall. Paint the trim too, and then live with it a few days. If it's a disaster, try again. If it works, do the entire room.

DECORATIVE PAINT. Sponging, dragging, stippling, and texturing add a lot to a room and are easy to master. Have some fun before you start: Get a sheet of drywall, prop it up in the garage, and try different techniques and color schemes. The practice will give you the confidence you need.

SECTION 1 PROJECTS

REAL-WORLD SITUATIONS

PAINTING RIGHT

Paint will not cover a multitude of sins. It will cover the wall, the door, or the trim, but that's about it. It will change the color of the bumps, nicks, dents, and cracks that are part of the wall, door, or trim, but it won't make the blemishes go away. That's your job.

Prep work or, to put it more simply, wall repair is the key to painting success. Plan on spending at least as much time repairing as you do painting.

Start by washing the wall. Wipe it down with trisodium phosphate (TSP) or one of its phosphate-free wall cleaning substitutes. Then rinse the wall with a sponge and clean water until the water runs clear.

Once the wall is dry, look for and repair each and every imperfection you find. Get suggestions from the staff in the paint department on the best products to use for your wall's problems, but count on using each of these:

Caulk. Caulk small cracks, caulk transitions from wall to molding, and run caulk down the corner of the room. Smooth it out with a wet finger so you have a nice transition from one surface to the next.

Surfacing compound. This compound is designed for repairing walls. Joint compound isn't (it's designed for drywall construction). Patch with surfacing compound. If you have holes, gouges, or wide cracks, patch with lightweight surfacing paste, which has more body and will fill and stay put easily.

Glazier's compound. Glazier's compound is the putty that holds windows in place. It's designed to stick in place and dry quickly so you can paint it, and it's perfect for filling nail holes.

Buy the best paint you can get, along with the best brushes and rollers. Cheap paint turns powdery after a couple of years. Cheap brushes and rollers leave fuzz and bristles on the wall.

Once you're ready to paint, protect any surface in the room you don't want stray paint on—especially floors, trim, and woodwork. (See Protecting Surfaces on page 19.)

Prime surfaces before you paint. On the molecular level, at least, primer is really sticky. It sticks to whatever is on the walls, as well as to whatever paint you're putting up. If the walls are stained, apply a primer sealer to keep the stain from bleeding through. (Water-based sealers may not be adequate—be sure you get the right product.)

Sand between coats. This doesn't take long—just wipe the wall down with a piece of 120-grit paper, and then brush off the dust with your hand or an old paintbrush. If you sand, the finished wall will feel like velvet. Don't sand, and the finished wall will feel like sand.

Test decorative techniques on a sheet of primed and base-coated drywall or poster board and practice until you achieve the look you want.

Paint during the day in strong light. Bare patches, drips, spatters, trapped brush fibers, and insects are easy to avoid when you can see what you're doing.

The homeowner's field guide to paint

The aisles in paint departments offer alkyd, enamel, latex, primer, stain blocker, gloss, semigloss, satin, and flat paint. When all you want is to redo the bathroom, it all seems pretty complicated. But actually, there's less to it than meets the eye. The world of paint is divided into two camps: latex and alkyd. Everything else is just a variation.

Eighty percent of the paint sold in the United States is latex. In the past, latex paint truly contained a naturally occurring rubber. These days it contains any number of manufactured resins, with acrylic being the best.

A good part of latex's popularity is convenience. It's a water-based paint, so drips and spills wash up with a wet sponge. Cleaning brushes can be done with soap and water, followed by a thorough rinse.

If you're applying a coat one day and another the next, however, you don't need to clean the brush in between. Wrap the brush in a plastic bag, leave it overnight, and it will be ready for work the next day. Though it's not strictly necessary, some people like to stick the wrapped brush in the freezer for good measure.

Few people like the smell of fresh paint. The fumes from latex aren't, however, nearly as strong as those from alkyd. (Stir in a few drops of vanilla to make the paint smell better.) Once dry, the latex paint is durable, washable, and as good as anything on the market.

Alkyd was once known as oil paint because of its linseed oil base. New formulations have led to its new name, but in simplest terms, alkyd is called oil paint. It isn't water based, and it isn't water soluble. If you spill it, you'll need to clean it up with mineral spirits (paint thinner). You'll need to clean the brushes with mineral spirits too, and rinse them with soap and water.

Professional painters still love alkyds, especially as a primer. Alkyd is better than latex at sealing in stains, and it provides a better vapor barrier too. Painters also like it because when they sand between coats, it leaves a powdery dust that wipes off with tack cloth or your hand. (Latex, because of its rubbery content, gums up a bit as you sand.) Be sure to sand between coats too: your surface will look better and feel satiny.

As with latex, you don't need to clean the brush while the paint dries overnight. Simply soak the brush, paint and all, in water. The next day, shake the brush vigorously to get rid of the water. (Do this outdoors, as it makes quite a mess.) Once the water is out, the brush is ready for the day's work.

Whatever else you wonder about—primers, stain blockers, enamels—know this much: Whatever it is, it comes in alkyd or latex.

THE PRIME DIRECTIVE. Whether working with alkyd or latex, always use a primer. Primers are specially formulated to stick well to whatever is underneath them, be it bare wall or paint. Likewise, whatever you put on top of a primer will stick well to it. It's like molecular hook-and-loop fasteners: The hooks in the primer grab the velvety layers of paint and hold them firmly.

Priming usually takes the place of a second top coat, so a coat of primer isn't really extra work. Just tint the primer with about half as much color as you will

---

BUYER'S GUIDE

READ THE LABEL ON THE PAINT CAN

Generally speaking, the quality of paint can be judged simply by the price.
It's one of the few products in the world where you actually get what you pay for. The more expensive the paint, the higher quality it is because more expensive ingredients are used in ratios that produce better color and adhesion.

The Four Basics:

- **Liquid** (water or mineral spirits) allows the paint to be applied and then evaporates.

- **Pigments** are finely ground, naturally colored solids that produce color when mixed. The higher the percentage of TiO_2 (titanium dioxide), the whiter and brighter the paint will be.

- **Additives** are chemicals added to the paint to enhance its mildew resistance, ability to stick, and ability to flow.

- **Binders** are 100 percent acrylic or vinyl acrylic. Generally, the higher the percentage of acrylic resin, the harder and more durable the finish.

The other things you see listed are largely filler. High percentages of filler tend to dull colors. If you are sensitive to chemical vehicles in paint or will have trouble ventilating the room as the paint dries, purchase a brand that is labeled low in volatile organic chemicals (VOCs).

The label provides more than instructions for use and drying times. It lists ingredients, general instructions for cleanup and disposal, and a toll-free number for help and advice.

use in the top coat (so you don't fill in all those molecular hooks) and apply the top coat.

Latex primers work well in most situations. Faced with a difficult wall, however, professionals will use alkyd. No matter what you've heard, you can apply latex over oil—painters do it all the time. Once they've solved the problem on the wall, they're just like anybody else: They prefer the convenience of latex. You can be pretty sure it sticks too. Having paint fall off a wall pretty much ruins a painter's reputation.

No matter how good—or expensive—the paint, however, some stains can bleed through a regular primer. Water stains, for example, are almost guaranteed to reappear once the paint has dried. If you're painting wood, the color of the knots bleeds through sooner or later. Smoke stains, oil stains, and the red chalk used in chalk lines are guaranteed to bleed through too—unless you use a stain-blocking primer.

Stain-blocking primers come in alkyd, latex, aerosol, and liquid. Shellac, which is neither alkyd nor latex, works as a stain blocker all by itself and is the base in some stain blockers. Get a stain blocker that's alkyd- or shellac-based; it's about the only stain-blocking primer that will seal in tough stains with a single coat.

CLOSER LOOK

ENAMEL PAINT

Real enamel is a mixture of quartz, silica borax, lead, and feldspar; it is the finish used on things like stoves. Enamel paint just looks like enamel—it forms a hard, shiny, easy-to-clean surface. Like other types of paint, it can be either latex or alkyd based and will have all the advantages and disadvantages of whichever base you choose. Either kind is thoroughly washable, making it a preferred paint for trim and doors. Once only available in a gloss sheen, it is now available as a flat enamel.

Casting a light on sheen

Once you've chosen between oil and latex, and once you've chosen your color, you still have five different sheens to choose from—flat, eggshell, satin, semigloss, and gloss. Each is a measure of how much light the paint reflects. A flat paint reflects perhaps 5 to 10 percent of the light that shines on it; a gloss reflects 50 percent of the light or more. With changes in sheen come changes in the appearance of both the surface and the color. A flat sheen looks duller and darker than the same color in a gloss.

Paint sheen comparison

Flat paint absorbs light and therefore hides many surface imperfections. Dents, dings, changes in texture, and undulations in the surface all tend to disappear behind the matte finish of a flat paint. Because it hides blemishes so well, you can often apply a single coat. On the down side, it tends to show dirt and doesn't stand up well to scrubbing.

Eggshell hides many imperfections but is a bit smoother than flat, meaning it reflects more light. It's also easier to wash and therefore more durable. Because of its washability, it has become a popular sheen for walls.

Satin. Think washability when you think satin— kitchens, bathrooms, hallways, kids' rooms, woodwork, and trim. Satin paint's silky finish looks good on walls but is smooth enough to stand up to dirt and cleaning.

Semigloss. Think shiny washability when you think semigloss. Semigloss reflects between 35 and 50 percent of the light that hits it, and most people find it too shiny on walls. It's extremely durable, however, and well suited to surfaces that get a lot of handprints—trim, woodwork, cabinets, and doors. For the same reason, it's also popular in kitchens and baths.

Gloss. For utility room or playroom walls, and for trim that gets a lot of abuse, the easy cleanability of gloss is a good call. Used on walls, however, the high shine may be discomforting. Minor surface imperfections suddenly look like glaring errors.

The color wheel

The biggest hurdle you'll face when painting—short of moving furniture—is choosing color. White is always safe; off-white is a bit wilder, while the more adventurous opt for ivory. Many people still seek cover at the mention of the color wheel, but if you ever want to paint your walls and woodwork something other than another shade of white, it's worth a look. Choosing a color scheme is nothing more than picking one color, and then choosing other colors to use with it based on their relative positions on the color wheel.

The primary colors—red, blue, and yellow—combine to form all other colors. You'll find them at about 12 o'clock, 4 o'clock, and 8 o'clock on the wheel. Combine any two primary colors, and you'll get a secondary color—secondary colors always fall midway between two primary colors on the wheel. Tertiary colors are the combination of a secondary color and a primary color.

You'll find them sandwiched between the secondary and primary colors on the wheel.

Now for the theory: Pick two colors that go together: red and green at Christmas; blue and gold football uniforms; or the blue and red spots on a brook trout. What do they have in common? Each is actually a color scheme found on the color wheel.

Designers long ago realized that most people don't want their houses looking like their favorite football team's uniforms, even during a winning season. Consequently, designers developed some shorthand approaches, using the color wheel, to find colors that work together. See Choosing a Color Scheme on the opposite page.

Colorful language

Color value: The lightness or darkness of a color.

Tint: A color that has been lightened with white. Pink is a tint of red.

Shade or tone: A color that has been darkened with black. Indigo is a shade of blue.

The color wheel illustrates the relationship between primary, secondary, and tertiary colors. The colors in the band between the white rings are pure colors. Colors closer to the center of the wheel are tints. Those closer to the edge are shades.

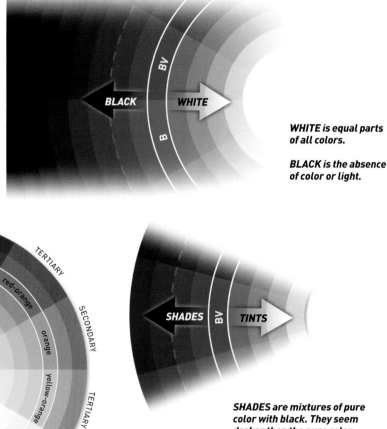

WHITE is equal parts of all colors.

BLACK is the absence of color or light.

BLACK / WHITE
BV / B

TERTIARY / PRIMARY
SECONDARY
red-violet / red
violet / red-orange
blue-violet / orange
TERTIARY / SECONDARY
blue / yellow-orange
PRIMARY / TERTIARY
blue-green / yellow
green / yellow-green / PRIMARY
TERTIARY / SECONDARY / TERTIARY

SHADES / TINTS
BV

SHADES are mixtures of pure color with black. They seem darker than the pure color.

TINTS are mixtures of pure color with white. They seem lighter than the pure color.

Choosing a color scheme

Any color scheme begins with a single color. You want a blue dining room. A red house. A yellow nursery. The question is, what next?

Look at the blue dining room. The simplest scheme would be a monochromatic approach: Do the entire room in shades of blue. You probably don't want dark blue walls, so go with a lighter tint, like powder blue. The trim could be a darker shade of the same color, or in what designers call an analogous scheme, the trim color could come from one of blue's adjacent slices of the wheel.

If blue-on-blue proves to be overpowering, you can look for a complementary color—one that falls opposite your first choice on the color wheel. Technically, in the blue dining room, this would be orange; however you might prefer to fudge just a little with a brass chandelier or a burnt umber finish on the furniture.

For more variety, you might choose triadic colors—those that are equidistant from each other on the wheel. Tints and shades of blue, red, and yellow are shown below. Garish? Not on an Oriental rug. Not convinced? Then keep it to two of the three colors.

Because it can be difficult to make these decisions in the abstract, paint manufacturers offer brochures that group colors in schemes they think you'll find attractive. Pictures in decorating and house magazines are also good sources for color combinations that work well together. If you see something you like, take it to a paint department and buy a quart of each of the colors. Paint a small part of the room, and live with it for a while. If it doesn't work, try another shade or tint. Keep trying until you find something you like.

Eventually, you may realize that no matter what you do, the golden trim you loved in someone else's country kitchen looks like yucky mustard in yours. Red, on the other hand, may add the warmth you want. Better to find out on a few square feet of the kitchen than on all four walls. If the complementary color scheme isn't working, try a variation of the triad.

MONOCHROMATIC COLORS

Shades and/or tints of a single color.

ANALOGOUS COLORS

Two colors adjacent to each other on the color wheel. One color dominates.

COMPLEMENTARY COLORS

Two colors opposite each other on the color wheel.

TRIADIC COLORS

Three colors equidistant from each other on the color wheel.

ANALOGOUS COLORS WITH COMPLEMENTARY ACCENTS

Two adjacent colors combined with a third that is opposite either of the first two.

THE PAINTER'S TOOL KIT

Below are some basic painting tools. For more information
see the Tool Glossary on page 544.

GOOD QUALITY TOOLS ARE ONE OF THE MOST IMPORTANT INVESTMENTS YOU'LL MAKE as you become more involved in home improvement projects. The tools on this page will help you achieve the best painting results possible. Some you may already have and some you'll need to purchase. When you're preparing for a project, fill out your tool list with the best products you can afford. Good tools save you time and effort.

1-QUART BUCKET	**BRUSHES**	**PAINT CAN OPENER**	**RAGS**	**ROLLERS**	**SPRAY BOTTLE**
5-GALLON BUCKET	**CAULKING GUN**	**PAINT CAN POURING SPOUT**	**ROLLER CAGES**	**ROUND-CORNERED SPONGE**	**STAINLESS WIRE BRUSH**
5-IN-1 TOOL	**DROP CLOTHS**	**PAINT MIXER**	**ROLLER GRID FOR 5-GALLON BUCKET**	**RUBBER GLOVES**	**STEPLADDER**
BRUSH AND ROLLER SPINNER	**EXTENSION POLE**	**PAINTER'S TAPE**	**ROLLER PAN**	**SAFETY GOGGLES**	**TAPE MEASURE**
BRUSH EXTENDER	**MASKS**	**PUTTY KNIVES**	**ROLLER PAN LINER**	**SANDING BLOCK**	**UTILITY KNIFE**

Brushes and rollers

When should you use a roller or brush? Use a brush when you need to paint narrow strips or to cut in (paint a sharp edge). (A roller has soft ends, so it cannot lay a sharp line of paint.) A roller lays down paint at least three times faster than the largest brush, and a good roller with beveled ends leaves no roller or overlap marks. A roller is the tool of choice for large, flat areas, such as ceilings and walls.

Most jobs will require both a roller and a brush. The key is to understand when to use each applicator and to know how to use each properly, including pouring out only as much paint as you are going to need for the job.

A good brush feels like a natural extension of your hand. There are many types of paint applicators available, but quality is the key. Bristle brushes are generally more expensive but will last longer and outperform their more inexpensive counterparts.

A good quality brush, properly cared for, will last for years.

THERE ARE TWO TYPES OF BRISTLES:

- Natural (usually hog) for solvent-based finishes.
- Synthetic (nylon or polyester) for water-based finishes. (Some can be used with alkyd-based finishes as well.)

THE ADVANTAGES OF BRISTLE BRUSHES:

- Versatility.
- Durability and reusability.
- Ability to apply a heavier coat.
- Fastest cleanup.

THE DISADVANTAGES OF BRISTLE BRUSHES:

- Slower application than a roller or pad.
- Can leave brush marks (require practice to use properly).
- Skill required to cover large areas.

Disposable brushes are the least expensive. They provide quick application of materials that are difficult to clean up, such as contact cement and fiberglass resin. Use low-cost foam brushes to apply smooth finishes to small areas.

PAINT ROLLERS are two-piece tools: There is a handle with a wire cage and threaded base, and a roller cover with a nap.

The handle will last as long as you clean it, so invest in the best you can afford. Look for these features:

Good quality roller cages with molded or wooden handles, used with good quality roller covers, make every painting job easier.

- A grip that molds to your hand.
- A heavy frame with minimum flex under pressure.
- Nylon bearings that spin easily.
- A cage with at least five wires and an antislip device.

Roller covers range in quality. Bargain roller covers with paper cores break down quickly and cannot be reused. Use them for small jobs. Look for these features in a high-quality roller cover:

- A resin core (or tube) that won't break down in water.
- Beveled ends to avoid leaving edge beads.
- Seams that cannot be felt through the nap.
- Heavy, uniform nap that sheds little lint.

Why quality brushes cost more

QUALITY	VS.	DISPOSABLE
Flagged (split) bristle ends for a smoother finish	BRISTLES	Unflagged bristle ends
Multiple wood spacer plugs to create paint reservoirs between bristle rows	DIVIDER	Single wood spacer plug
Reinforced, rustproof ferrule to hold bristles securely	FERRULE	Weak ferrule, allowing bristles to fall out more easily
Tapered end for better control	HANDLE	Blunt point

Protecting yourself: gloves, goggles, and respirators

You are vulnerable to particles and fumes when you are sanding, painting, or working with solvents.

TO PROTECT YOUR SKIN:

- Wear cotton gloves when using sharp or abrasive tools.
- Wear latex gloves when working with paint.
- Wear neoprene gloves when handling solvents, strippers, and harsh chemicals.

Neoprene gloves

TO PROTECT YOUR EYES:

- Wear safety glasses when working with tools.
- Wear goggles to protect against dust and aerosol droplets when sanding, spraying, or painting over your head.

Safety goggles

TO PROTECT YOUR LUNGS:

- Sand, paint, and strip outside, or cross-ventilate with at least two open windows or doors.
- If there is a danger of breathing dust, aerosols, or solvent fumes, filter the air with a respirator. Check product labels for the recommended type.

THERE ARE TWO TYPES OF RESPIRATORS: Dust masks, also called particulate respirators, filter out dry particles and most non-oil-based liquid droplets. Use a dust mask when sanding bare or painted wood (except lead-based paint), drywall, and rusted surfaces. Special-purpose particulate respirators are available for spraying latex paint and sanding (not burning) lead-based paint.

Cartridge respirators contain both particulate filters and chemically active canisters for absorbing solvent vapors. Use a cartridge respirator when spraying solvent-based paints and working with solvents and strippers.

Note: Unless specifically stated otherwise, no homeowner-type respirator protects against lead fumes, asbestos fibers, or sandblasting.

Cartridge respirator

FITTING RESPIRATORS:

A respirator must form an airtight seal around your nose and mouth. Respirators don't work with beards. So if you have a beard and you're going to be working with hazardous chemicals, consider shaving.

TO FIT A DUST MASK:

- Position the mask under your chin.
- Pull the top and bottom straps over your head and position them just above and below your ears.
- Mold the soft metal tab to fit your nose.
- Test the fit by covering the mask with both hands and drawing a sharp breath; it should be difficult to breathe.

TO FIT A CARTRIDGE RESPIRATOR:

- Place the respirator loosely over your face, low on the bridge of your nose.
- Fasten the straps for a snug but comfortable fit.
- Test the fit by covering the air inlets and breathing out gently. The mask should bulge slightly, and you should neither hear nor feel any leakage. If you smell fumes or feel dizzy, either the respirator doesn't fit or the canisters are the wrong type or are used up.

Always read the warnings on paint, solvent, and stripper containers, and compare them to the listed capabilities of the respirator canister.

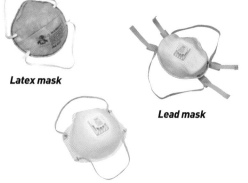

Latex mask

Lead mask

Sanding mask

SAFETY ALERT

ACCEPT NO SUBSTITUTES

To protect yourself from toxic fumes, wear the mask that's recommended by the manufacturer for the job. A garden-variety dust mask may look better and you may feel protected, but it's not made to block fumes. Asbestos and lead are potentially very dangerous, and sometimes even an organic respirator won't do the trick. If you're dealing with large amounts of either substance, get guidance from the EPA (Environmental Protection Agency) or consider hiring a professional removal company.

Protecting surfaces

Paint always ends up where you don't want it. You can stop and clean as you go, or you can protect vulnerable surfaces before you start, saving you time in the long run. Remove as much furniture as possible; protect floors, windows, doors, trim and baseboards, and light fixtures. Protect yourself with a long-sleeved shirt and pants, or purchase painter's coveralls and hoods.

Spatter-proof the room: To protect large surfaces and furnishings, invest in a good drop cloth. You will generally find three types:

1. **Polyethylene sheeting** (poly) is inexpensive but slippery (see "Buyer's Guide" at right).
2. **Canvas** is the toughest and most expensive, but it can leak water-based (latex) paints.
3. **Paper/poly** (fuzzy paper on one side and plastic on the other) is waterproof, less slippery than poly, and less expensive than canvas. It's a good solution for interior projects.

To protect trim and other margins, use blue painter's tape—a low-residue masking tape that won't mar or damage finished surfaces when you remove it.

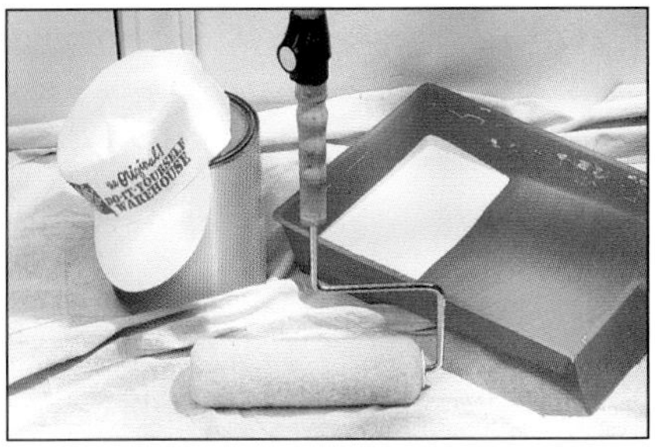

A PAINTER'S CAP keeps the spatters out of your hair when you're painting overhead.

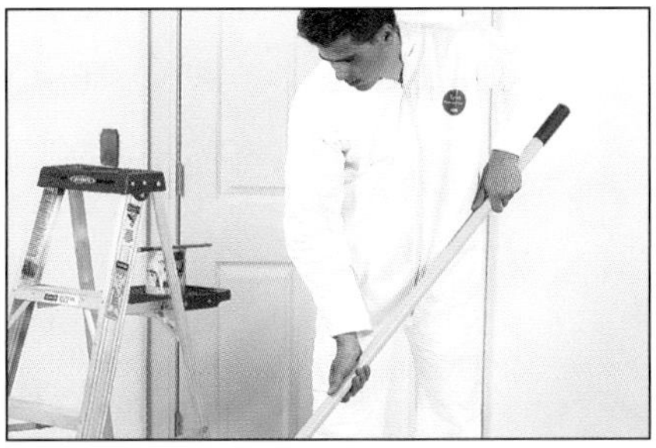

A PAINTER'S COVERALL offers neck-to-toe protection and "breathes" to keep you cool.

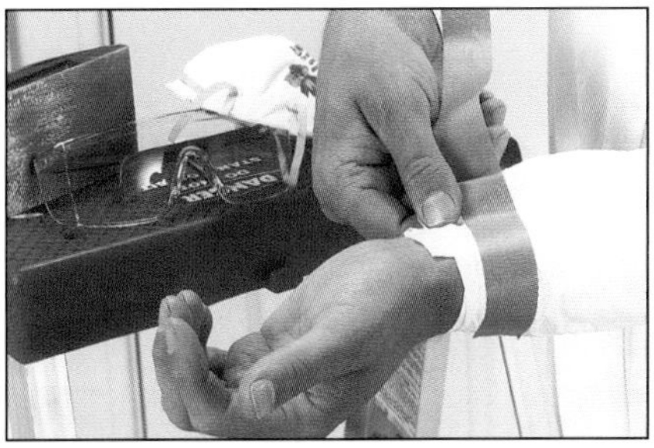

WHEN SANDING OR SPRAY-PAINTING, cinch your sleeves and cuffs with masking tape.

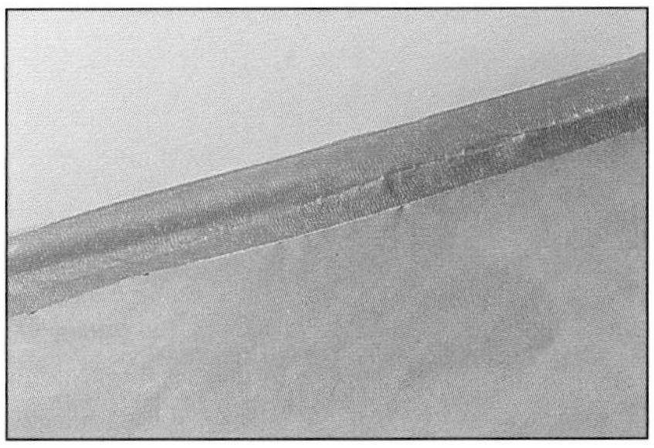

BLUE PAINTER'S TAPE can remain for up to a week while prepping but must be removed immediately after painting.

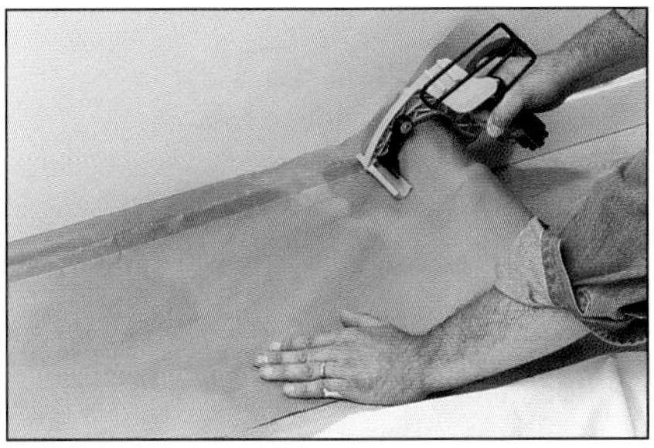

PAPER MASKING COMBINED with self-adhesive blue painter's tape is perfect for protecting baseboards and trim. Various widths are available.

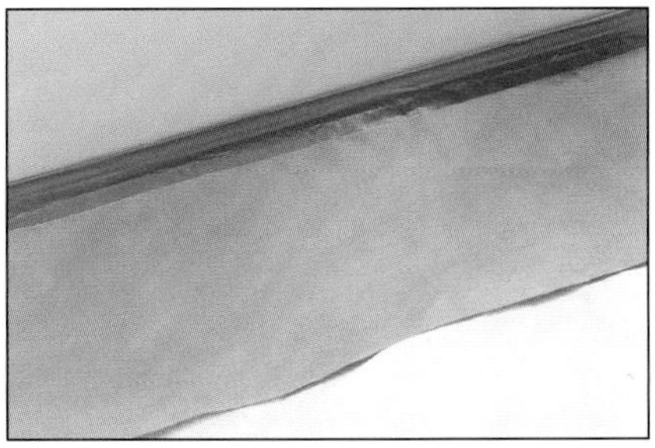

SLIP A PAPER/POLY DROP CLOTH under the baseboard masking for complete floor protection.

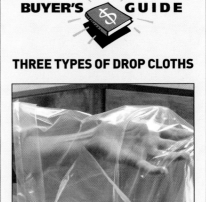

BUYER'S GUIDE

THREE TYPES OF DROP CLOTHS

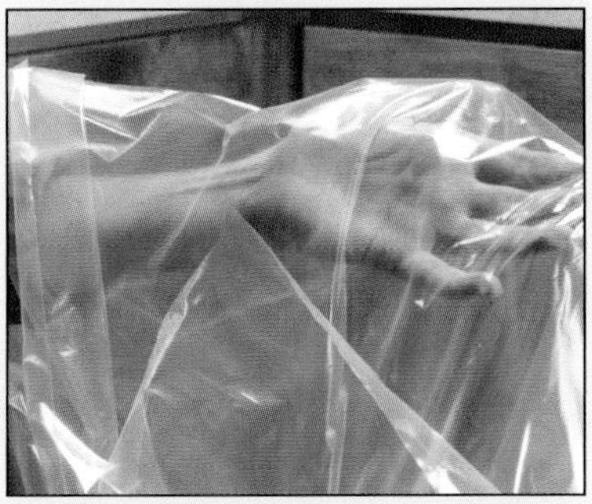

Poly sheeting, the least expensive, is waterproof. It's slippery underfoot but great over furniture.

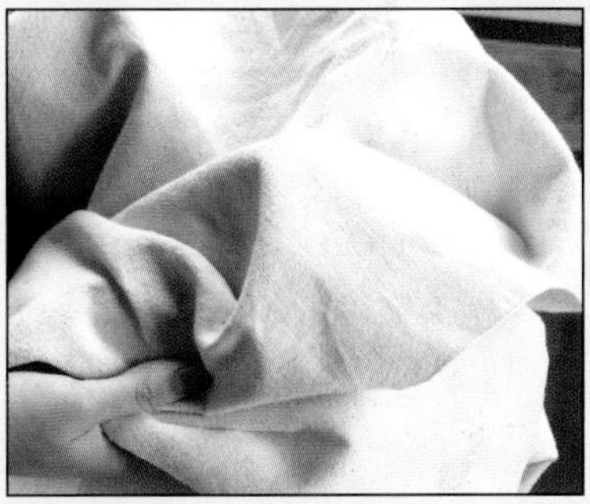

Canvas will last longest but is not waterproof; water-based (latex) paints will probably soak through it.

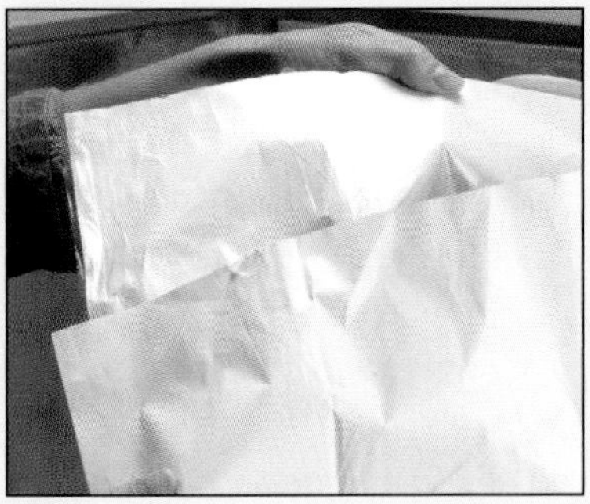

Paper/poly is a good compromise. It is waterproof and less slippery than poly sheeting.

Priming is essential

Priming helps ensure a professional-looking paint job. Primer is fundamental to good-looking walls, not a way to sell you one more paint product. It is a specially formulated product designed to:

- Increase adhesion.

- Help the finish coat develop maximum sheen.

- Give the finish coat a uniform appearance.

- Increase the finish coat coverage.

- Prevent blemishes on an old surface from bleeding through the new coat of paint. These might be stains from water, dirt, smoke, etc.; tannins from aromatic woods; or resins from knots and pitch pockets.

- Add to metal's corrosion resistance.

THE GOOD STUFF LASTS

Well, maybe not forever, but quality tools and materials will always provide a better result, especially if you're not a professional painter. Always buy the best equipment you can afford. It'll pay off in time saved and frustration averted. Plus, if you clean and store painting tools properly, good quality brands should last for years.

PRIME NEW DRYWALL to conceal the difference between taped and untaped areas.

PRIME NEW WOOD, old bare wood, and pressure-treated lumber with a stain-killing primer to block resins and tannins in the wood and create a smooth and seamless finished surface. Let the primer dry thoroughly according to the manufacturer's instructions before applying finish color.

PRIME OVER WALLPAPER using a high-adhesion wallpaper primer. Make sure the old wallpaper is firmly attached to the wall and that rips, gouges, nicks, indentations, bulges, and tears are repaired. Make sure the walls are clean and smooth before you roll on the primer.

Types of primer

1. **Just as primer is different** from finish paint, there are different primers for different problems and applications. Apply all primers in adequate ventilation.

2. **Polyvinyl acetate (PVA) latex primer** seals new drywall for painting. Both the paper face on drywall and joint compound are absorbent and would otherwise steal too much water from finish latex paint. PVA is not intended for trim or previously painted surfaces. Cleanup is with water.

3. **All-purpose primer** is a general term for any primer designed for maximum adhesion to impervious surfaces, such as metal, glass, tile, and thermoplastics such as laminated plastic and melamine. It is more difficult to work with than a conventional latex primer, but the results are well worth the effort. Cleanup is with soap and water.

4. **Latex, stain-blocking primer** stops most stains from coming through the paint. For difficult stains, such as washable markers, use oil-based or alcohol-based primer instead.

5. **Oil-based, stain-blocking primer** effectively blocks crayon, permanent-marker inks, grease, and water stains. Even though it is a bit harder to work with, the results are worth the effort—it's one of the rare ways to prevent an unremovable stain from bleeding through paint. Cleanup is with paint thinner.

6. **Alcohol-based, white-pigmented shellac** is impervious, exhibits excellent adhesion, effectively blocks smoke stains and all of the tannins and resins in wood, and inhibits pet odors. It is brittle and damaged by UV rays, however, so it is recommended only for interior use. The exception is spot-priming knots on pine trim and clapboards. Cleanup is with denatured alcohol.

7. **Enamel undercoat** contains a higher percentage of solids and is used when maximum effect is desired in satin, semigloss, or gloss. When hard, it can be sanded to produce the smoothest possible base for the finish coat. Cleanup is with soap and water.

HOMER'S HINDSIGHT

PRIME MISTAKE

Four coats of expensive designer color later, a friend finally asked me why he couldn't cover the stains on his wall. "You primed first, right?" I asked him. "Sure," he said, "I used up some leftover latex from the garage." I explained that regular latex paint isn't primer. Primer provides bonding and stain blocking. Paint provides durability and color. You need both to get a good job.

WORK SMARTER

PRIME INFO ON DARK COLORS

It seems logical that darker colors hide better, but it's not true. When painting a dark, rich color, you've got to use a tinted primer and at least two coats of paint to get a good look.

STAIN-BLOCKING PRIMERS AND SEALERS may still show the stain because they absorb, rather than cover, the stain. Use a stain blocker before you prime; allow it to dry thoroughly. This will help ensure that stubborn stains don't bleed through, ruining an otherwise perfect finish.

TINTING THE PRIMER CAN HELP WITH COVERAGE, especially when you make a dramatic color change. Ask a salesperson for advice. Remember that there are limitations on the amount of tint a primer can hold and still be effective. Follow the manufacturer's recommendations.

PREPARATION FOR PAINTING

SKILL SCALE

| EASY | **MEDIUM** | HARD |

REQUIRED SKILLS: General carpentry and repair. Using rollers and brushes.

HOW LONG WILL IT TAKE?

Experienced . . . . .Variable
Handy . . . . .Variable
Novice . . . . .Variable

VARIABLES: Prep time will vary depending on the condition the walls are in. Drying time between coats will depend on temperature and humidity.

STUFF YOU'LL NEED

✔ MATERIALS:
12-inch baseboard masking; bleach; water; lightweight crack filler; blue painter's masking tape; 220-grit sandpaper; latex or oil-based, stain-blocking primer; TSP solution

✔ TOOLS:
Bucket, rubber gloves, drop cloth, 4-foot stepladder, sponge, phillips screwdriver, 3-inch putty knife, sanding block, 2-inch nylon brush, 9-inch roller with ⅜-inch nap, roller tray, brass-wire brush

Prep and priming are so important that salespeople often wish they could go home with customers to make sure they do the jobs right the first time.

1 **MOVE FURNITURE AWAY FROM WALLS AND PROTECT FLOOR** and baseboards with 12-inch baseboard masking and a paper/poly drop cloth.

2 **SET POPPED NAILS OR SCREWS** (see page 226), repair cracks and holes (see pages 226–229), and fill dents with lightweight crack filler.

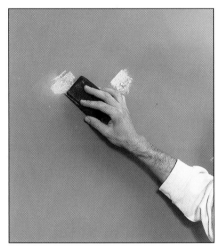

3 **LET THE CRACK FILLER DRY PER MANUFACTURER'S INSTRUCTIONS,** then sand the area using a sanding block with 220-grit sandpaper.

4 **TREAT ANY AREAS OF MILDEW** with a 3-to-1 water/bleach solution (see page 24). Protect your hands with rubber gloves.

TOOL TIP

WET-SANDING
One of the most annoying parts of sanding plaster and joint compound is the flourlike dust that is produced. To minimize the dust, use a drywall wet-sander—a sponge with coarse abrasive on one side and fine abrasive on the other side. Use the coarse side to level ridges and high spots; use the fine side to smooth.

CLOSER LOOK

TSP = SQUEAKY-CLEAN WALLS
Trisodium phosphate (TSP), a powerful, nonsudsing soap, is the painter's cleaner of choice. But phosphate also causes algae blooms in water bodies, so its use has been restricted in some areas. TSP substitutes are also available in box or bottle. TSP will prevent paint from bonding, so rinse the surface several times with fresh water to remove all residue. Always read the instructions.

5 **RINSE THE ENTIRE WALL SURFACE WITH CLEAN, FRESH WATER** and let the wall dry overnight. Clean with a TSP solution before you prime and paint.

6 **SPOT PRIME ALL OF THE REPAIRED AREAS** with a latex, stain-blocking primer. If stains are still bleeding through, use an oil-based primer.

7 **PRIME THE ENTIRE WALL** with the same stain-blocking primer for uniformity.

PREPARATION FOR PAINTING
Removing gloss

Use the edge of a quarter to "x" or circle spots on the walls that need attention and repair. That way you won't forget to do them, and the mark is easily covered.

Glossy paints dry to a hard, nonporous surface; therefore, it's almost impossible for new paint to adhere effectively. Glossy surfaces lack what painters call "tooth," or roughness, which gives the paint something to stick to. It doesn't take much to create tooth—a light sanding or use of a chemical deglosser will do the trick. When the surface has dulled and ceases to be reflective, it's ready to paint.

To detect gloss, use a bright light with a reflector to shield your eyes.

High-volume deglossing

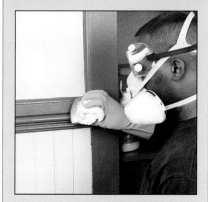

LIQUID DEGLOSSER
While roaming through the paint department, you may run into something called "liquid deglosser." It may sound a lot better than sanding, and it may be if you're repainting an office building.

Working at home, the drawbacks probably outweigh the advantages. It's caustic, and the fumes are strong and dangerous. If you use it, ventilate the area, wear neoprene rubber gloves, goggles, and a respirator recommended by the deglosser manufacturer.

1 **FILL GAPS IN TRIM AND BASEBOARD WITH PAINTABLE CAULK;** after drying, sand all glossy areas lightly with 220-grit sandpaper. Use a sanding block for flat surfaces, a brass-wire brush for fluted surfaces.

2 **REMOVE THE SANDING OR BRUSHING RESIDUE** with a damp rag or tack cloth.

Treating stains and mildew

It would be perfect if a fresh coat of paint, especially over a good primer, would cover stains, water marks, and mildew. In fact, when the paint is still wet, it may appear to cover. As it dries, however, these stains will seep through and you'll end up with a fresh coat of stained paint.

Before you prime or paint, remove stains and mildew. It takes elbow grease, but cleaning will save time in the long run because you won't have to repaint. Regular household bleach diluted with water is extremely effective in destroying the spores that cause mildew. Water stains need to be fixed at the source before you repair the wall or ceiling.

WATER LEACHES CHEMICALS FROM WOOD AND DRYWALL. When the mixture seeps through a wall or ceiling, it stains.

MILDEW IS A SPORE IN THE AIR. Given food (paper or paint) and moisture, mildew flourishes on walls.

STUFF YOU'LL NEED

✔ **MATERIALS:**
Water, household bleach, primer and paint, TSP solution

✔ **TOOLS:**
Bucket, rubber gloves, 4-foot stepladder, old clothes, safety goggles or glasses, large round-cornered sponge, rollers and brushes

WHAT'S THE REAL PROBLEM?
Anytime mildew or stains are present on your walls, it's a sign of a larger problem. Find the source of the moisture that's causing the staining and fix it.

SAFETY ALERT

BEWARE WHAT YOU BREATHE
Don't mix bleach with other household cleaners. Household cleaners often contain ammonia, which reacts with bleach to produce toxic fumes.

Inhaling such fumes can cause dizziness, nausea, cramps, or extreme illness. If you do breathe such fumes, get outside and breathe fresh air until your symptoms disappear.

1 MIX THREE PARTS WATER TO ONE PART LAUNDRY BLEACH in a bucket. If you are sensitive to bleach, protect your hands and eyes.

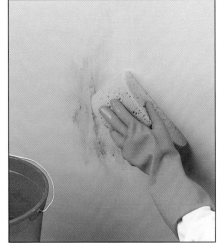

2 APPLY LIBERALLY WITH A SPONGE. Apply again after 20 minutes even if the mold has disappeared.

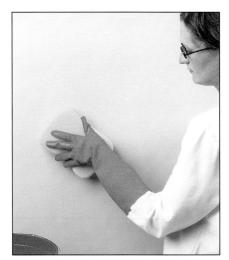

3 RINSE OFF THE BLEACH AND DEAD MILDEW WITH CLEAN, FRESH WATER. Allow it to dry thoroughly before cleaning with TSP or a TSP substitute (see page 22). Then prime with a stain-blocking primer, and paint.

PREPARATION FOR PAINTING
Removing wallpaper

REQUIRED SKILLS: Employing wallpaper removal tools and using basic wall repair techniques.

 **HOW LONG WILL IT TAKE?**

Experienced . . . . Variable
Handy . . . . Variable
Novice . . . . Variable

VARIABLES: Removal times will vary greatly depending on the type of wallpaper in place and the condition of the surfaces. Removal and prep could take several days.

Removing wallpaper is an inexact science—get the right tools and give yourself plenty of time. Removal is the only way to guarantee the best results but, if the surface is in good condition, professionals often paper or paint right over the old paper. (See page 26.) Make your decision about the condition of the wall objectively and honestly before you proceed. If you have any doubts, remove the paper. In any case repair and priming are essential. Remove nonvinyl papers—cleaning will do more damage than good. Clean vinyl and vinyl-coated papers the same way you clean painted walls.

Removing wallpaper goes one of two ways—incredibly difficult or unbelievably easy. Be prepared for a tough job and be surprised if it's not.

HOMER'S HINDSIGHT

WALLPAPER REMOVAL BLUES
I've decided there should be a law against putting wallpaper over unprimed drywall. Why? Because it just won't come off. Of course, that's never a problem until you decide to pull it down and redecorate. People I know not only removed the wallpaper, they also removed the paper facing on the drywall. I helped them put up wallpaper liner so they could paint. "Next time," I said, "try testing a small section first and maybe paint over the wallpaper rather than removing it."

STUFF YOU'LL NEED

✔ **MATERIALS:**
12-inch baseboard masking, blue painter's masking tape, wallpaper remover (white vinegar solution or chemical remover)

✔ **TOOLS:**
Screwdriver, wallpaper perforating tool, spray bottle or garden sprayer, rubber gloves, plastic bucket, 3-inch plastic scraper, sponge, moisture-proof drop cloth

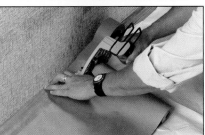

A+ WORK SMARTER

DO THE CEILING FIRST
If you're wallpapering the room and painting the ceiling and trim, do the ceiling and the trim first to avoid the inevitable drips and spills on the fresh paper.

① **TURN OFF THE POWER AT THE CIRCUIT BREAKER PANEL,** then remove all switch and outlet covers on the walls you are stripping. Cover switches and outlets with blue painter's masking tape.
COVER THE FLOOR WITH A MOISTURE-PROOF DROP CLOTH, then apply 12-inch baseboard masking and blue painter's masking tape to the baseboards. Allow it to overlap the drop cloth for complete coverage.

② **PERFORATE THE WALLPAPER FOR WATER PENETRATION.**
A perforation tool such as the one shown is fast and effective. Apply just enough pressure to perforate the wallpaper without damaging the underlying drywall.

PREPARATION FOR PAINTING
Removing wallpaper *(continued)*

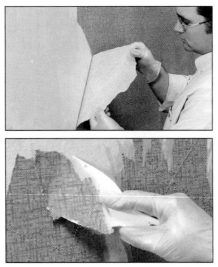

3 **APPLY WALLPAPER REMOVER TO AN ENTIRE WALL WITH A SPRAY BOTTLE,** or garden sprayer if you are removing paper from a large area. Both are available at garden shops or home centers. Mix the remover with water as hot as you are comfortable with to speed removal. (A solution of a cup of vinegar per gallon of water is an effective alternative to commercial wallpaper removers.)

4 **REMOVE THE WALLPAPER.** Wait 10 to 20 minutes or follow manufacturer's instructions. Then, wearing rubber gloves, peel off as much wallpaper as you can with your hands. Before turning to the scraper, spray on a second application of remover.
PEEL OFF REMAINING WALLPAPER. Use a 3-inch plastic scraper. Scrape lightly to avoid having to repair a damaged surface.

5 **AFTER REMOVING ALL OF THE WALLPAPER WASH THE WALL SEVERAL TIMES,** using fresh water and a sponge to remove paste residue. Residue will reduce bonding of the paint and cause it to peel.

Painting over wallpaper

Can you really paint over wallpaper? The short answer is yes, you often can. Some papers themselves are almost impossible to remove without damaging the surface. And, removing paper that has been applied to plaster walls or over unprimed drywall can be extremely difficult. If the surface is smooth and in good condition, professional painters will prime and paint over the existing paper. However, they do make sure the paper is securely on the wall and that all the seams are tight. They paint a test area to make sure the paper will hold, do any necessary repairs, and finally they prime with a tinted primer and then paint the room. So, if the old paper just won't come off, do what the pros do. If the paint sticks, and if the wallpaper remains securely attached to the wall and the seams don't show, painting over the old paper will probably look fine.

CLOSER LOOK

STAIN-BLOCKING PRIMERS
You may still see the blemishes you're trying to eliminate after applying a stain-blocking primer. It's doing its job, which is *blocking* the stain. Test with your finish color to see if the blocker is effective.

1 **RESIDUAL WALLPAPER PASTE IS INVISIBLE AND INTERFERES WITH PAINT ADHESION.** To remove it, wipe the wall thoroughly with a wet sponge. Repair any dings or dents with fast-drying surfacing compound. Remove dust and debris before continuing.

2 **APPLY A TINTED SHELLAC-BASED, STAIN-BLOCKING PRIMER ON A TEST AREA.** Wait 24 hours. Repair minor blisters or bubbles by slitting them with a utility knife and glue to the wall with a wallpaper adhesive. Apply the finish coat. If the coverage looks good, finish priming and painting the rest of the room.

Priming and painting walls

SKILL SCALE

EASY	**MEDIUM**	HARD

REQUIRED SKILLS: Using brushes and rollers. Applying masking and protection to nonpainted surfaces.

HOW LONG WILL IT TAKE?

Experienced . . . . 4 hrs.
Handy . . . . 6 hrs.
Novice . . . . 8 hrs.

VARIABLES: Time estimates assume a 10'×12' room and that surfaces have been properly prepared. Drying time between coats will depend on temperature and humidity.

STUFF YOU'LL NEED

✔ **MATERIALS:**
Primer and stain blocker, high-quality latex paint, wall repair materials, blue painter's masking tape, 120-grit sandpaper

✔ **TOOLS:**
Putty knife, brushes, rollers, spray bottle (for priming brushes and roller covers), extension pole, 5-gallon paint bucket with roller grid, small paint bucket, latex paint respirator (optional), safety glasses, drop cloth, ladder (if necessary), rags

A gray tint in the primer will produce a better final color in the finish coat, especially with darker colors such as red.

Although priming is vital to a lasting finish and a great-looking room, there are also sound economic reasons for a good priming job. If you spend $30 for a gallon of designer paint, you don't want to see stains or discoloration bleeding through because you didn't take time to prime and seal the wall.

Primer isn't just a watery paint. It is formulated to adhere well to a variety of surfaces and seals them to prevent stains and discoloration from bleeding through the final coat. The finish coat sticks more effectively to a primed surface than it does to plaster, wood, or an earlier coat of paint. Priming not only adds to the durability of the paint job, it may prevent you from having to roll on a second top coat—especially if you have the primer tinted the same color as the finish coat.

Prime and paint more efficiently by following a logical sequence: First apply stain and varnish to any new trim to protect it from paint. Next prime and paint the ceiling, proceed to the walls, and conclude with any trim that needs to be painted. Careful masking at each stage will allow you to work quickly and freely, saving time in the long run.

The first step to a good paint job is applying primer. It goes on like regular paint and can be tinted to match the finish coat. Primer makes applying the final coat easier and can reduce the number of top coats required.

WORK SMARTER

THE TRUTH ABOUT OIL (ALKYD) AND LATEX
If you've heard about the danger of putting latex over oil-based paint, forget about it. Once the paint is dry they're perfectly compatible. For the homeowner the larger issues are drying time and odor: oil takes longer to dry and has a stronger smell.

1 FIX THE DINGS. Examine all the surfaces, then carefully repair and sand any cracks, holes, or dents before you apply the paint.

2 TINT THE PRIMER. A percentage of the volume of a primer can be tinted with the final color to ensure good coverage with finish coats. Not all primers need tinting, so ask a salesperson and follow the manufacturer's recommendations.

Priming and painting walls *(continued)*

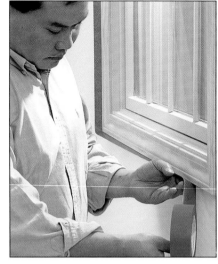

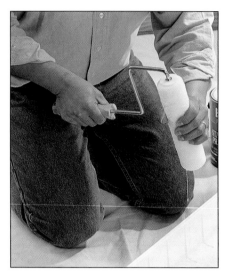

3 **MASK THE ROOM.** Determine the order for painting the room. Paint last the areas that are likely to get dripped on. Prime (and paint) the ceiling first, walls second, and trim last. If you plan to prime the trim with a different tint than you will use on the walls, mask the trim first. Mask the top of the walls if you are painting the ceiling; mask the ceiling and trim if you're starting with the walls.

4 **SPOT PRIME.** If using latex, dip the brush in water to help it absorb the primer. If using alkyd, dip the brush in mineral spirits. Brush out the liquid on a piece of cardboard to remove loose bristles. Brush primer on areas of walls and trim that need special attention: patches in drywall and plaster, areas of bare wood exposed by scraping and sanding, and any spots treated with stain blocker.

5 **PRIME THE ROLLER.** It's hard for a dry roller to absorb primer or paint, so "prime" the roller before you put it in the primer or paint. If the primer is latex, spritz the roller with a garden mister and squeeze off the excess water. Use mineral spirits for alkyd primer. Run the roller over the paint grid or roller pan several times to get an even amount of primer on the roller cover.

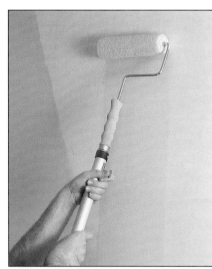

6 **PRIME THE CEILING.** Start on the short side of the room and "cut in" the edges about 2 inches wide and about 5 feet long along the edge of the ceiling. Then, wearing safety goggles and an old cap, roll paint onto the ceiling, working the roller into the cut-in area to remove as many brush marks as possible. Roll with diagonal strokes and move from the edge toward the middle of the room. Continue cutting in and rolling until you're finished.

7 **CUT IN A SECTION OF WALL.** Wait until the ceiling dries and mask it off with blue painter's masking tape. Mask off the trim if you haven't already done so. Starting in a corner, prime along about 5 feet of trim, 5 feet of ceiling, and from top to bottom of the corner.

8 **ROLL THE WALLS.** To minimize the wall area that will have a brush-stroke texture, run the roller over the strips you've primed during the cutting stage, getting as close as possible to the masked trim, ceiling, or adjacent wall.

Cheap roller covers are loaded with fuzz that ends up stuck to the wall. If you use such a roller cover, sand the wall to give it a "haircut."

9 **BEGIN ROLLING AT THE TOP SECTION OF THE WALL ALONG THE CUT-IN STRIP,** and work to the bottom in a series of Ws, as shown above, to avoid creating a visible pattern of vertical passes. Move along the wall in 3- to 5-foot sections, cutting in and rolling until the job is done. Work in sections small enough to cover with a single load of the roller, and always roll up on the first stroke. The key is to overlap areas of wet paint.

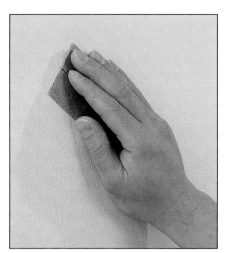

10 **SAND THE WALLS IF NECESSARY.** Wait until the primer is thoroughly dry and sand lightly with 120-grit sandpaper. Tear a piece of sandpaper in fourths, and then fold one of the quarters in thirds. Whisk the paper along the wall, removing bumps and other high spots. When the paper loads with paint dust, refold it to reveal a fresh face, and continue. An alternative is to drag the surface lightly with a 4- to 6-inch putty knife. Once you've finished, wipe the wall with a damp rag to remove dust and debris.

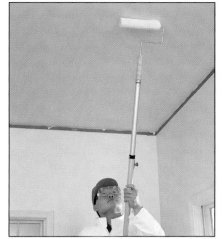

11 **ROLL THE CEILING WITH THE FINISH COLOR.** When the primer is dry, mask around the ceiling. After cutting in a section, start rolling. Protect your eyes with safety goggles and wear an old cap. A 5-gallon bucket with a roller grid requires filling less often and is less likely to tip than a paint tray. Use a relatively dry roller to reduce spattering. Roll diagonally, as you did to prime, to avoid creating visible rows across the ceiling. Extension poles allow you to reach more area without leaning dangerously from a ladder.

12 **CUT IN THE WALLS.** After you've painted the ceiling, remove the tape from the top of the walls and allow the ceiling to dry thoroughly. Then mask off the ceiling and trim to paint the walls. Start painting in a corner and cut in a few feet along the ceiling, a few feet along the baseboard, and the starting corner.

13 **ROLL CLOSE TO THE WALL PERIMETER.** The texture of brushed areas is different from rolled areas. Paint into the freshly cut-in areas with a roller, removing as much of the brush-stroke texture as possible. Cover as much of the cut-in as you can without getting paint on other surfaces. Starting with an up stroke, work from the ceiling toward the baseboard, rolling on large W-shape strokes. Back roll with a light load of paint to smooth things out.

14 **PRIME AND PAINT THE TRIM.** Remove the masking for the walls, allow the paint to dry thoroughly, and mask off for the trim. Control dripping by pouring the trim paint into a small bucket and dip the brush about halfway into the paint. Tap the brush against the sides (instead of scraping it around the rim) to remove excess paint in the tip of the brush; this will leave paint in the body of the brush.

Painting doors and trim

SKILL SCALE

| EASY | **MEDIUM** | HARD |

REQUIRED SKILLS: Removing a door, sanding, priming, and painting.

HOW LONG WILL IT TAKE?

Experienced . . . . 1 hr.
Handy . . . . 2 hrs.
Novice . . . . 3 hrs.

VARIABLES: Temperature and humidity will affect drying time.

STUFF YOU'LL NEED

✔ MATERIALS:
Four 3-inch drywall screws, white-pigmented shellac (if door has knots), latex wood putty, acrylic-latex caulk, lightweight crack filler (optional), 80- and 220-grit sandpaper, stain-blocking primer, latex paint (probably enamel), TSP solution, denatured alcohol or chemical deglosser, blue painter's masking tape

✔ TOOLS:
Screwdriver, two sawhorses, 2-handed paint scraper, pad sander or sanding block, 1½-inch polyester sash brush, 2-inch polyester trim brush, oval brush, plastic scrub pad, rubber gloves, lint-free rag, putty knife, caulking gun, sponge (optional)

Over time a fiberglass door will fade and need to be refinished. Strip it with a nonsolvent-based stripper. Finish with either a gel stain or primer and paint.

Painting doors, windows, baseboards, or moldings involves five key steps to success:

● Clean and prime to achieve maximum adhesion.

● Smooth the surface so that cracks, holes, dents, and chips don't show through the finish coat.

● Mask adjacent surfaces so you can paint quickly and confidently.

● Keep a wet edge to eliminate lap marks.

● Never overwork the paint. Brush it on, and then let it flow out to form a surface free of brush marks.

PAINTING DOORS. To minimize brush marks, paint your door in the order shown on the right. Painting sections from top to bottom will give you the time you need to feather each application of paint before it dries. Paint all the edges first and then areas 2 through 5 in each section of the door before you move on. Professionals often paint a door without removing it from the jamb, but laying the door out on sawhorses and following the painting order shown below is critical to avoid

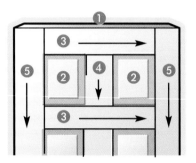

PAINTING ORDER:

① *All edges*

② *Panel bevels and flats*

③ *Rails*

④ *Stile middles*

⑤ *Stiles*

PAINTING DOORS

❶ **REMOVE THE DOOR.** Insert long screws in the top and bottom edges and suspend the door on sawhorses. Remove all hardware. Fill dings, spot prime knots, and sand the door as necessary with 80-grit sandpaper. Follow up with 220-grit sandpaper so the sanding marks won't show under the finish coat.

❷ **PRIME THE DOOR.** Use a tinted, stain-blocking primer to prime the door. Follow the painting order above. When the primer is dry, sand it lightly and then apply the finish coat following the same order.

drips that inevitably occur when you're painting vertically.

If the door has knots or strong variations in grain or color, it's a good idea to spot prime the offending areas with a stain-blocking primer to ensure even coverage with the tinted primer and the finish coats.

PAINTING TRIM. When you are painting trim, the critical tools are the paintbrushes. You will need:

- An angled sash brush for laying down sharp edges.

- A square-edged trim brush for laying down flat areas of paint.

- An oval brush for getting into tight areas.

PAINTING TRIM

1 WASH WOODWORK WITH A TSP SOLUTION and a plastic scrub pad to remove residue (wear rubber gloves). Rinse several times. Remove blistered or chipped paint with a paint scraper; be careful not to gouge the wood. Sand with 80-grit, then 220-grit sandpaper. Remove dust with a lint-free cloth.

2 FILL HOLES AND GOUGES WITH A LIGHTWEIGHT CRACK FILLER. Remove excess material and let dry per the manufacturer's instructions. Fill gaps and cracks between trim pieces with paintable caulk or glazing compound. Remove the excess and smooth with your finger.

3 SPOT PRIME ANY KNOTS OR RESIN POCKETS WITH WHITE-PIGMENTED SHELLAC PRIMER. Allow to dry. Wipe down the surface with denatured alcohol or a paint deglosser. Mask all adjacent surfaces with blue painter's masking tape. Seal the edges firmly.

4 PRIME THE ENTIRE SURFACE WITH A STAIN-BLOCKING PRIMER. After 24 hours, sand with 220-grit sandpaper. Wipe the sanded surface with a damp sponge or rag, then apply the finish with a 2-inch trim brush. Remove the masking tape while the paint is still wet.

Window painting basics

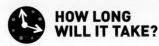
STUFF YOU'LL NEED

✔ **MATERIALS:**

TSP solution, wood putty, paintable caulk, primer, paint, sandpaper, blue painter's masking tape

✔ **TOOLS:**

Paint scraper, sash knife, tack cloth, wide putty knife or pry bar (for removing trim), 2-inch sash brush, utility knife, bucket, sponge

TOOL TIP

DON'T GET STUCK
A sash knife will open a window sealed with dried paint. You also can use a utility knife or a hacksaw blade.

Windows deserve a high-quality, smooth, and durable finish, but it's not an easy job. There are a number of delicate surfaces to paint—the casing, the ledge, and the sashes with delicate muntins (vertical wooden strips that separate the lights, or panes of glass)—and panes to avoid brushing. To make the job of painting or varnishing even more demanding, windows take a beating from sun, rain, and condensation, from potted plants, and from being opened and closed.

Prep work is essential before painting windows. Scuff and sand the existing finish so that the new finish will adhere. Chips and blistering are common with windows, requiring use of a scraper and sandpaper. Mask off both glass and the surrounding wall to decrease cleanup time.

Finally, reduce frustration and enjoy this somewhat finicky job by purchasing a good angled sash brush.

1 **SCRAPE AND SAND THE WINDOW.**
If either of the sashes is painted shut, free it with a sash saw. Slip the blade through the paint holding the window shut and work the blade back and forth to break the bond. Wash greasy or dirty areas with TSP solution. Remove loose paint with a scraper. Sand the wood, both to blend in scraped areas and to remove the sheen from glossy paints. Avoid scratching the glass when scraping and sanding. Go over the wood with a tack cloth to remove the dust.

2 **FILL HOLES AND CAULK GAPS.**
Use wood putty to fill in flaws in the wood. If gaps have opened between the wall and window frame, fill them with paintable caulk. Level the wood putty with a putty knife, and smooth the caulk with your finger.

③ REMOVE THE SASHES. If possible, remove the sashes from the frame and paint them on sawhorses; it's easier to contain runs. On many newer windows, the sashes pop out with little trouble. To remove those on older windows, carefully pry off the side trim. Use a wide, stiff putty knife before graduating to a pry bar. Some sashes just won't come out and you'll have to paint them in place.

④ MASK PANES AND THE SURROUNDING WALL. If the sash won't come out, as shown here, use blue painter's masking tape to avoid getting primer on the glass and wall.

Blue painter's masking tape is low-tack and therefore easy to remove.

⑤ APPLY TINTED PRIMER WITH A SASH BRUSH. If the window has snap-out grids of muntins and bars, remove them to paint. If it has actual muntins and bars, paint them first. Then paint the horizontal parts of the sash, followed by the verticals. Paint the sill last. Painting in this order will limit splashes and drips. To keep the sashes from sticking, do not paint the sides of the windows or the track in which they travel. If you paint the sashes in place, lower the upper one and raise the lower one to get to any surfaces that are inaccessible when the window is closed. Move the sashes as the paint dries to keep them from sticking.

⑥ APPLY ONE OR MORE FINISH COATS. Again using the sash brush, apply paint the same way you applied primer. If you used a tinted primer, one top coat may be enough. If the primer shows through or an edge didn't get painted, apply a second top coat.

⑦ REMOVE THE MASKING TAPE FROM THE GLASS AS SOON AS THE PAINT SKINS OVER to prevent pulling up dried paint later. Catch little leaks or blunders by drawing a sharp utility knife along the edges of each pane, leaving a narrow margin of paint on the glass; then push a window scraper toward this cut line to remove the excess paint.

Designer Tip

TRIM IS FOREVER
Use bold colors on the walls and neutral colors to paint the trim. You won't have to redo the trim if you change the color of the room or the fabric in the curtains.

Staining windows

PAINTING

SKILL SCALE

| EASY | MEDIUM | HARD |

REQUIRED SKILLS: Basic carpentry skills, repair and painting skills, masking panes and trim.

HOW LONG WILL IT TAKE?

Experienced . . . . 1 hr.
Handy . . . . 1.5 hrs.
Novice . . . . 2 hrs.

VARIABLES: Weather conditions will affect drying times. Window removal will vary in complexity.

STUFF YOU'LL NEED

✔ MATERIALS:
Paint and varnish remover, stain (optional), clear finish, 120- and 180-grit sandpaper, wood putty, painter's masking tape

✔ TOOLS:
rubber gloves, cartridge respirator, putty knife, utility knife, 2-inch sash brush, tack cloth or paper towel, window scraper, drop cloth, 000 steel wool

WORK SMARTER

PREP AND PRIME
The more complicated the painting or staining job, the more important it is that the surface beneath it is smooth and defect-free. Stain doesn't hide irregularities—they show through, interrupting the smooth look you're trying to create. Repair, sand, and seal before putting on the final finish.

A window takes a beating. Even if you remember to close it before every rainstorm and almost never overwater the plants parked on the sill, the finish degrades over time. Eventually, the effects of sunlight and moisture make it necessary to sand and strip the window.

Before the 1950s, most windows with clear finishes were shellacked. Lacquers followed, and now polyurethane is standard for homeowners who refinish their windows. Fortunately, it's not necessary to know what's on your windows because polyurethane does a good job of covering it. Either oil- or water-based poly works well, although water-based is easier to clean up. Be scrupulous with the prep work. If you won't be stripping the old finish, sand carefully to ensure that the new coats adhere well.

What about stripping a painted window and finishing it clear? You face the challenge of coaxing paint from the crevices of the trim, the window frame, and all the molding. It can be done, but it's difficult to do well. Take a good look at all the nooks and crannies to assess how much work you have ahead of you. Maybe you'll want to send the woodwork out to a dip-and-strip shop.

1 SAND OR STRIP THE EXISTING FINISH. If the window is in reasonably good condition, sand it to smooth the finish and dull the sheen. Cover your work surface with an inexpensive drop cloth. Begin with 120-grit sandpaper; once it's done most of the work, sand with 180-grit sandpaper for a smoother surface. If the finish is badly damaged or unattractively built up, remove it. On many newer windows the sashes pop out. To remove sashes on older windows, you may have to carefully pry off trim pieces. Brush paint and varnish remover onto the window sashes following the manufacturer's directions. (Provide good ventilation, and wear rubber gloves and a vapor respirator.) Scrape off the finish with a putty knife. Rinse with the solvent recommended for the remover.

2 FILL HOLES. Use wood putty to fill flaws. Spot-sand these areas when the putty dries. Go over the window with a tack cloth (if you'll be using an oil-based finish) or damp paper towel (before using a water-based finish). Unfortunately, no putty matches the wood exactly. If you stain the wood, a stainable putty absorbs the stain and comes close to a match, but it won't be perfect. Experiment with different brands to see which works best. If you're not going to stain, make your own putty. Gather a few pinches of fine sawdust from the type of wood you'll be patching, mix with five-minute epoxy, and fill in any holes. After the epoxy dries, trim off any bumps with a utility knife or sharp chisel and then sand. For a very smooth finish do a final sanding with 000 steel wool.

3 **MASK PANES.** Use masking tape to avoid getting finish on the glass. The new, low-tack tapes are easy to remove and leave less residue. They'll work well when you mask off trim too. Use white or blue rolls instead of brown—they stick better. There are several types of low-tack tape so read the label carefully and choose the one that best meets your needs. Make sure you mask the two side edges of the sash; they're traditionally left unfinished so that the finish won't stick when you open the window.

4 **APPLY THE STAIN AND FINISH.** If you have stripped the window and want to darken or warm its color, stain it now. The stain will take evenly only if you've been thorough in removing the old finish. If the window is made of soft wood—such as pine—you'll have an additional problem staining it. Soft woods absorb the stain unevenly, giving it a blotchy look. Avoid this by applying a gel stain, which won't blotch because it doesn't soak deeply into the wood. Apply at least two finish coats for greater durability; sills take the greatest beating and benefit from three coats. Sand lightly between coats, wiping up the dust with either a tack cloth or a damp paper towel.

5 **REMOVE THE MASKING TAPE.** Remove the tape from the glass as soon as the finish begins to dry to prevent adhesive residue. If you haven't taped off the glass (or if your masking job wasn't quite as good as you thought), draw a sharp utility knife along the edges of each pane, leaving a narrow margin of finish on the glass. Push a window scraper toward this cut line to remove the finish.

The more carefully you mask the window panes, the easier cleanup will be.

TESTING STAIN

Stain can look a lot different on your window than it does in the sample brochure. Test it first on the edges, top, and bottom of a door. On trim use the back of the molding or a scrap to test the color.

A clean cotton T-shirt is the best applicator. Dip the shirt in the stain, wipe it on the wood, and then wipe away the excess.

STICKY SASH

Troubled by sticking sashes? Mask off the surrounding wood and spray silicone along the channels in which the windows travel. Silicone will repel finish the next time the window needs refinishing.

EXTERIOR-GRADE VARNISHES

Marine spar varnish, originally designed for wooden masts, is still made for exterior applications. Because it's designed to withstand sun and moisture, it's ideal on windows. Even though it says "exterior," feel free to use it inside too.

Staining trim

PAINTING

SKILL SCALE

EASY	**MEDIUM**	HARD

REQUIRED SKILLS: Basic carpentry skills, repair and painting skills, masking panes and trim.

HOW LONG WILL IT TAKE?

Experienced . . . . 1 hr.
Handy . . . . 1.5 hrs.
Novice . . . . 2 hrs.

VARIABLES: Weather conditions will affect drying times. Window removal will vary in complexity.

STUFF YOU'LL NEED

✔ MATERIALS:
Water- or oil-based varnish, water- or oil-based stain to match varnish, denatured alcohol, stainable wood putty, wood conditioner or gel stain, 120- and 180-grit sandpaper

✔ TOOLS:
Sponge brush or paintbrush—natural bristle for oil-based finish, synthetic bristle for water-based finish; brush or sponge (optional); putty knife

WORK SMARTER

SAND BY HAND
Moldings made of soft woods like pine or poplar can lose their profile if you sand too heavily with a power sander. Hand sanding with a fine grit paper to prep for the finish is the safest way to go.

Compare the labels on a can of stain and a can of varnish—they're completely different products. Stain is full of dyes and pigments that changes the color of wood. Varnish is full of resins that protect it. Neither does both jobs. Although varnish can stand on its own, stain can't. You have to apply varnish over stain to give it shine and to protect it from grime. If you don't, the stain will look flat and grime will eventually work its way into the pores where you won't be able to get it out. If you stain the wood, also apply varnish.

It doesn't matter whether it's a door or trim under the finish; the application technique is the same. The condition of the door or trim does, however, matter. Stain will never look any better than what's under it. If you put up new molding, make sure it's stain grade. Paint grade is made of short lengths glued together. Using stain on paint grade will emphasize the joints and the different shades of wood.

To redo a varnished surface you do not have to remove the old finish. Modern varnishes adhere well to whatever is underneath. Clean the finish well by wiping it with denatured alcohol. Sand carefully with 180-grit paper, and wipe off the dust with a rag dampened in alcohol. Let it dry thoroughly before applying the new finish.

Staining and varnishing a painted surface is a larger challenge. Even a thorough dipping in stripper almost never removes all the paint, and whatever paint remains will show through. Plan to spend quality time with more stripper and a stout brush before you stain and varnish.

Spending the time to fill and sand will guarantee better results when you apply the final stain.

1 SAND THE TRIM AND CLEAN IT WITH ALCOHOL. Sand to remove dings, dents, and imperfections. Then sand all the trim to create a smooth surface, starting with 120-grit sandpaper. Follow with 180-grit to remove the marks left by the 120-grit, and finish with 220-grit. Between sandings wipe up the dust with a rag dampened with denatured alcohol. (Tack cloths, popular with painters, leave a residue that may interfere with the finish, especially if it's a water-based finish.)

CLOSER LOOK

STAINING PINE
Because pine density varies throughout a board, it stains unevenly, as shown on the left side of this board. Test stain on a scrap or the back of your wood. If you don't like the look, use wood conditioner, or stain the wood with a gel stain to get the even look shown on the right side of the board.

2 **REPAIR ANYTHING YOU CAN'T SAND AWAY.** Although patches will never match the rest of the wood perfectly, damaged wood looks far worse. Fill dents and gouges with stainable putty. Level them off with a putty knife or your thumb. Let the patches dry and, if any of them shrink while drying, patch again. Sand smooth and wipe with a rag dipped in denatured alcohol.

3 **APPLY A CONDITIONER.** Soft woods, such as pine, look blotchy when stained. Prevent this by brushing on a thinned finish sold as "wood conditioner." The directions usually advise to let it dry 15 minutes to 2 hours. Many painters admit they have better luck if they wait only 10 minutes, and most agree that you should not wait longer than 2 hours. At that point, the resins in the conditioner have dried out, and you can barely stain the wood. If this happens, sand the surface, and reapply the conditioner.

You can avoid the need for conditioner entirely by using gel stains, which don't penetrate deeply and therefore don't blotch.

Sponge brushes work well for staining wood and they're cheap enough that you can dispose of them instead of cleaning them.

4 **BRUSH ON STAIN.** Brush on the stain, let it soak in a bit, and then wipe it off, following the directions on the can. Old T-shirts, cheesecloth, or stain applicator pads are excellent for wiping. If the color isn't dark enough, wait the recommended time and apply a second coat. If you use a gel stain, apply it with a sponge. Take it off using a brush instead of a rag.

WORK SMARTER

STRIPPING TRIM
How you strip a finish depends on what you're stripping and why. An off-the-shelf liquid stripper will remove 90 percent of all clear finishes. Follow the directions on the can and sand when the wood is dry. If the wood is stained, you may need to apply a new coat of stain to even out the color the stripper leaves behind. If you're stripping paint—particularly if you suspect it's lead paint—use a peel-and-strip paste which removes the paint without fumes or chipping. Trowel on the paste, cover with the plastic sheet that comes with it, and a few hours later the paint and paste peel off like strips of putty. In the worst case—a project with lots of paint that probably contains lead—gently remove the trim, and have it stripped at a dip-and-strip store. Apply the new finish before reattaching the trim.

5 **APPLY THE VARNISH.** Brush the varnish onto a short section of trim. Go back over it quickly and lightly to brush out imperfections. Overbrushing leaves brush marks. Let the varnish dry according to the recommended time. Sand it with 220-grit sandpaper to smooth it. Once you sand, wipe down with a rag dipped in denatured alcohol, and apply another coat of varnish. Three coats are recommended for a durable and lasting finish.

CLOSER LOOK

VARNISH: STIRRED, NOT SHAKEN
You'll often see a layer of goo at the bottom of the can; it is a "flatting agent" designed to control the sheen. Mix the settling into the varnish before starting. Stir varnish, do not shake it. Shaking creates and traps bubbles that show up in the finish.

Painting interior brick

1 SCRUB THOROUGHLY WITH A TSP SOLUTION and a brush with firm, synthetic bristles. Wear goggles and protective gloves. Rinse at least twice. TSP is a suds-free cleanser; you may not see residue, but it will interfere with adhesion. Allow the surface to dry thoroughly.

2 REPAIR JOINTS WITH THINSET MORTAR AND A SMALL TROWEL, called a tuck pointer. Brush wet mortar off bricks with a stiff brush as you go. For a finished edge, smooth joints and corners with a tool called a jointer or with a copper pipe, as shown here. Allow to dry completely. Mask adjacent surfaces with painter's tape. Spread drop cloths to keep paint spatter off adjacent surfaces.

3 APPLY A LATEX PRIMER SPECIALLY FORMULATED FOR BRICK, masonry, and stucco using a roller with a 1-inch nap. Let the primer dry and roll on a semigloss or gloss latex paint. Touch up corners, cracks, and crevices with a 1-inch brush.

Painting interior concrete

1 TEST FOR MOISTURE IN OR UNDER THE CONCRETE BY TAPING A 4'x 4' POLY SHEET OVER THE FLOOR FOR 24 HOURS. If the sheet is damp or wet, there is too much moisture seeping through the concrete. Leave the surface unpainted. The moisture would cause the paint to blister.

If the sheet is dry, proceed to step 2.

2 SPRAY THE SLAB WITH WATER. If the water beads, scrub with a TSP solution to remove any grease; rinse and test again. If the water still beads, then scrub with a degreaser/concrete cleaner.

Once the concrete is clean, etch it with a solution recommended by the manufacturer of your chosen paint. Follow its safety recommendations carefully.

Rinse thoroughly. Cleaners may react with the paint or interfere with paint adhesion.

3 APPLY A CONCRETE PAINT USING A 9-INCH ROLLER WITH A ⅜-INCH NAP. Let the paint dry and apply a second coat.

Use a paint formulated to withstand hot-tire pickup, such as one-part epoxy, acrylic garage floor paint. Two-part epoxy is also available for particularly tough jobs. (Avoid using porch and floor enamel or ordinary epoxy on a garage floor: Hot tires will stick to it and lift it.)

Paint disposal

Paint is made of materials that are good for the wall but bad for the water and plants and animals. Due to studies showing the toxid effects of paint, clean-up methods have changed. The basics remain the same—clean up latex paint with water and alkyd paint with mineral spirits. The goal is to use as little of either as possible, and then to dispose of them wisely.

BASIC CLEAN UP

- Put as much paint as possible from rollers, brushes, and trays back into the paint cans. Begin by scraping the roller with the round section of a painter's 5-in-1 or 6-in-1 tool; scrape a brush with the flat end of the tool. Then put brushes and rollers on a brush and roller spinner, insert the roller inside a waste container, and spin. Let the paint dry and toss the container.

- Wash brushes and roller covers in as little water or mineral spirits as possible. See "Safe Cleaning" below.

Wash brushes or rollers where the liquids will not go down a drain. They pollute the water; even nontoxic solids inhibit aquatic life.

- When washing more than one roller tray, pour the water or mineral spirits from the clean tray into another tray to be washed.

- Place the water or mineral spirits used for cleaning into a covered 5-gallon (or larger) bucket, and let the solids settle. What you do next depends on whether the paint is latex or alkyd.

DISPOSAL OF LATEX WASH WATER AND WASTE

- According to the EPA you should "dispose of wastewater by tipping it onto a flat, grassy area or area of soil that can retain the liquid; put it in a place where it won't run into any sewer, stormwater drain, or natural waterway."

- Seal the solid wastes in a can and put the can out for a trash disposal service or take it to a licensed landfill.

DISPOSAL OF ALKYD WASTE

- Once the solids settle, pour the liquids into a sealable container. You will be able to use them next time you need to clean up alkyd-covered brushes, rollers, and pans.

- Seal the solid wastes in a can and put the can out for a trash disposal service that will take it to a licensed landfill.

- If the liquids are too old or too paint-laden to use again, do not dump them on the ground or pour them down the drain. Do not let the solvents evaporate and throw out the remaining solids. Solvents are prime sources of volatile organic compounds and are strictly regulated. Find a solvent recovery depot and take the solvents there for proper disposal.

Since requirements vary, always check with local authorities for approved disposal methods.

Safe cleaning

This 4-step process is one of the best ways to clean brushes; it's also environmentally friendly and cuts down on solvent use.

1. Half fill each of three cans with water (for latex paints) or paint thinner (for oil-based paints).

2. Clean the brush in the first can by moving it up, down, and sideways to remove most of the paint.

3. Repeat the process in can #2, and then again in can #3.

4. Dry the brush by slapping the ferrule on the heel of your hand, then pressing the bristles between newspaper or paper towels. Put the brush in its original cardboard holder to help it keep its shape. Hang it vertically to dry.

Allow the solids to settle into the bottom of the cans. Pour the thinner or water into clean cans for reuse. After the solids have dried, toss them.

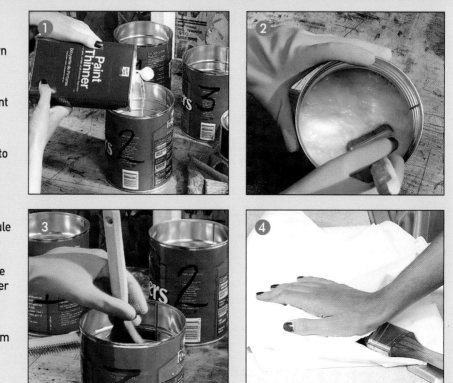

Sponging on and sponging off

SKILL SCALE

EASY **MEDIUM** HARD

REQUIRED SKILLS: Mixing glaze and paint. Using a roller and sponge.

 **HOW LONG WILL IT TAKE?**

Experienced . . . . 5 hrs.
Handy . . . . 6 hrs.
Novice . . . . 12 hrs.

VARIABLES: Paint drying time varies according to regional and seasonal climate conditions.

STUFF YOU'LL NEED

✔ MATERIALS:
Latex paint for base coat, second color latex paint for glaze coat, latex glaze, disposable latex gloves, blue painter's masking tape

✔ TOOLS:
Natural sea sponge, lint-free rags or coffee filters, measuring cup or paint bucket with marked measurements, stepladder, roller and pan for base coat, paper or ceramic plates

WORK SMARTER

PREP, PREP, PREP
Most faux techniques require a base coat that is well prepped and primed. Make sure you repair, fill, and sand as necessary, and then apply a primer before you do the base coat. The result will be worth the time spent.

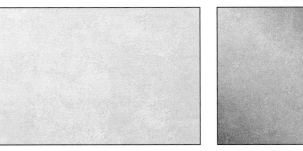

Sponging on leaves much of the base coat exposed. Sponging off leaves a much denser layer of the sponged color.

Sponging on and sponging off are methods of applying a second color to a wall. The first color is rolled on and the second color is either applied with a sponge, or rolled on and then sponged off. Sponging on focuses on the base color. Sponging off focuses on the second color.

CHOOSING THE RIGHT SPONGE.
A natural sea sponge works best—the random holes and varying texture create a more relaxed pattern than those of a synthetic sponge. Most paint departments carry sea sponges.

GLAZE IS THE KEY.
Glaze, sold in most paint departments, is a neutral finish to which no pigment has been added. Mix paint with the glaze to slow drying time and make it a bit translucent. Use latex paint and glaze for easy cleanup. Manufacturers usually recommend mixing one part paint with four parts glaze, a ratio that works on any wall, but you can experiment to create a different look.

PRACTICE MAKES PERFECT.
Prime and paint a scrap of drywall or hardboard with the base coat and let it dry. Mix varying proportions of paint and glaze and sponge them on or off to see how each looks over the base coat. Start by mixing different ratios in small disposable cups. A good variety of ratios to experiment with are: one part paint to eight parts glaze, one part paint to four parts glaze, and equal parts paint and glaze. Mark cups so you know each mix's proportions. Practice the technique with your selected ratio before you begin on the actual walls.

GOOD IDEA

EXPRESS YOURSELF
Faux painting is personal expression. Feel free to come up with your own vision.

SPONGING ON

1 **BEGIN WITH A BASE COAT OF PAINT.** What you apply depends on the wall. Prepare by masking the room's ceiling, trim, and adjacent walls so you can work freely and quickly. If the wall has never been painted, prime and apply at least one top coat. If the wall has been painted, wait for the first coat to dry and then look to make sure the color is solid. If it is not, apply a second top coat. While you're painting the wall, paint a scrap piece of drywall or hardboard so you can practice the technique.

2 **MIX THE SECOND COLOR.** Once the base coat is dry, mix your second color—the one you will sponge on—with glazing liquid. The standard ratio is one part paint to four parts glaze. The higher the proportion of glaze, the longer it takes the paint to dry, and the longer you have to work. Mix different proportions in disposable cups in order to see how proportions affect working time and the final result. Practice on a piece of drywall or hardboard first.

3 **USE A DAMP SPONGE.** Pour a small amount of the glaze mixture onto a plate. Before you dip the sponge in the glaze mixture, dampen it with water. Squeeze out as much water as possible, then dip the sponge into the glaze mixture.

4 **APPLY THE GLAZE.** Apply the glaze mixture by dabbing the wall with the sponge. Turn your wrist between each application and use different areas of the sponge to avoid repeating patterns. Work diagonally across the wall rather than straight up and down.

5 **CLEAN THE SPONGE.** If the holes in the sponge become filled with the glaze mixture, the finish will look blotchy. Periodically blot the sponge on a lint-free rag or coffee filter to keep the pattern crisp. When the sponge gets too loaded with glaze, dip the sponge in water to clean it. Wring it dry, dip it in the glaze mixture, and continue sponging.

6 **CONTINUE SPONGING.** Step back occasionally to look at your work. To clean up areas with too much paint, press a clean, damp sponge to the still wet paint and lift straight off.

Sponging on and sponging off *(continued)*

SPONGING OFF

STUFF YOU'LL NEED

✔ **MATERIALS:**
Blue painter's masking tape, latex paint, latex glaze

✔ **TOOLS:**
Measuring cup or paint bucket with measurements, roller, paint bucket and grid, natural sea sponge, lint-free rags or coffee filters

TOOL TIP

THINK SMALL
Don't try to wedge a huge sponge into corners and along trim. Cut off a small piece for hard-to-reach spots. For a final touch-up use a small artist's brush as necessary.

Sponging off—like ragging off (see page 44)—is a subtractive technique in which a base coat is applied to the wall and allowed to dry. Then a glaze mix is rolled on and removed by blotting it away with a sponge until the desired effect is achieved. Sponging off is a great way to work a delicate pattern across a wall. Practice on a sheet of drywall that has been primed and base-coated.

Remember, a hint of the base wall color will show through: This is a two-color or two-tone effect. Coordinate the two layers with some care. The closer the colors or shades of the base and top coats are to each other, the quieter the treatment. You can add more complexity and depth to the wall by lightly sponging on a second coat of glaze mix. Choose a third color or mix up a different shade of the same color by stirring in a different proportion of either glaze or white paint.

A base coat that has some gloss will give you more time to work. Prepare by masking the room's ceiling, trim, and adjacent walls so you can work freely and quickly.

WORK SMARTER

DON'T WORK TOO FAST!
If you sponge off a little too eagerly, the wall may end up with bald spots. Step back from the completed dry wall and look for spots that need paint. To fix the problem, lightly dab glaze on the areas with the same sponge you used to take off the glaze.

Sponge the second wall adjacent to the first so you can look over to see if your technique is consistent.

❶ TEST, PRIME, AND BASE. Prepare the glaze mixture. You'll get both translucency and a longer working time by mixing glaze in the second coat. Manufacturers usually recommend mixing one part paint to four parts glaze, but you can add more glaze to increase drying time. After the base coat has dried, begin by rolling glaze on a small floor-to-ceiling section of wall, covering no more area than you can sponge off before the glaze mixture dries.

❷ LIFT THE GLAZE WITH THE SPONGE. Begin removing glaze by pressing the sponge against it. Be sure to lift the sponge directly from the wall so that you don't smudge its distinctive effect. Turn the sponge between pressings by rotating your wrist to avoid creating a repetitive pattern. To reach into edges, use a torn piece of sponge to lift off glaze. Continue rolling and sponging off in sections. If a section starts drying out before you sponge it, mist the glaze with water from a spray bottle.

❸ CLEAN AND BLOT THE SPONGE. A glaze-saturated sponge is less effective at making a pattern. Blot the sponge frequently with a lint-free rag or coffee filter. Sponge off the glazed area, blot the sponge as necessary, and then roll more glaze into an adjoining area. Rinse the sponge as necessary.

Ragging on and ragging off

SKILL SCALE

EASY	**MEDIUM**	HARD

REQUIRED SKILLS: Mixing glaze and paint. Using rags and rollers.

HOW LONG WILL IT TAKE?

Experienced . . . . 5 hrs.
Handy . . . . 8 hrs.
Novice . . . . 10 hrs.

VARIABLES: Paint drying time varies according to regional and seasonal climate conditions.

STUFF YOU'LL NEED

✔ **MATERIALS:**

Latex base color, latex second color, latex glaze

✔ **TOOLS:**

Lint-free rags, measuring cup and container for mixing paint, roller, rubber bands, paint tray

WORK SMARTER

PRIME THE RAG

A slightly damp rag will absorb the glaze mix better than a dry rag. Dip the rag briefly in water and then roll it along the wall to remove excess water. (Do this on a section of wall that will be ragged last to allow that section of the wall to dry before ragging.) Put the roller in the pan and load it with paint the same way you would load a regular roller.

Ragging on leaves much of the base coat exposed. Ragging off leaves a much denser layer of the ragged color.

Ragging provides a great finish for hiding rough or uneven surfaces—though it doesn't hide bad prep work. Scrape, sand, and clean the walls as you would for any other paint job.

Ragging on is an additive technique, meaning that a rag is used to roll paint over a base to achieve an effect.

Ragging off is a subtractive technique and a traditional way of applying a two-color surface. The look is achieved by rolling a rag through a wet glaze to reveal the color underneath.

There are various techniques for both ragging on and ragging off. Instead of working the rag with your hands, wrap it around a paint roller, fix it with rubber bands, and work the rag and roller across the wall. To rag on, first paint the wall with a base color then coat the rag with the glaze mix and roll it along the wall—changing it when the rag becomes too wet. To rag off, apply a base coat and after it dries apply a second color. While the second color is still wet, move the roller across the surface, replacing the rag when it becomes saturated with glaze mix.

Any texture of rag will work, but a clean, lint-free cotton rag—an old T-shirt or cheesecloth—is the best choice.

Practice ensures even results. Before you commit to painting a large wall, experiment on several sheets of poster board taped together or an extra sheet of drywall or hardboard.

Ragging on and ragging off *(continued)*

RAGGING ON

1 **WRAP A T-SHIRT OR OTHER COTTON RAG AROUND A LOW-NAP ROLLER MADE FOR APPLYING CONTACT ADHESIVES.** Wet the rag and twist it as you wrap it around the roller, wrinkling it as much as you can. Slip rubber bands around the roller and rag, concealing them in the rag creases to keep them below the surface.

2 **MIX ONE PART PAINT TO FOUR PARTS GLAZE, AND POUR IT INTO A ROLLER PAN.** Dip the roller in the glaze. Similar to other special paint effects, the second coat—the ragged coat—consists of a glaze-thinned paint. The glaze makes the second color more translucent and slows the drying time of the paint.

3 **ROLL GLAZE ONTO THE WALL, WORKING FROM TOP TO BOTTOM.** To avoid painting stripes or columns, roll at a slight angle (shown above) and occasionally step back to look at the wall, making sure you do not create roller patterns.

RAGGING OFF

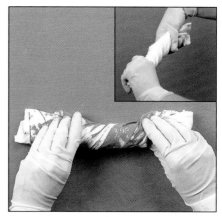

1 **BRUSH THE GLAZE MIXTURE INTO CORNERS.** Brush a 2- to 3-inch-wide strip in places where the roller will not reach—the corners, near the ceiling and along the woodwork, for example. Cut in about 5 to 10 feet at a time and then roll on the paint, as described in Step 2, so the cut-in area and the rolled area have the same effect. Rolling into a dry cut-in strip results in an obvious difference between the brushed and rolled sections.

2 **ROLL ON THE GLAZE.** Put some glaze in a paint tray, and using a short-napped roller, roll a 2-foot-wide section of wall from floor to ceiling. Work the roller into cut-in areas, removing as many brush marks as possible. The glaze can become too dry to work in as few as 15 minutes. For more efficient results, use two people—one to roll and one to rag.

3 **ROLL THE RAG ALONG THE WALL.** Loosely roll the rag into a cylinder, leaving it partially wrinkled. Practice on a scrap of painted and freshly glazed drywall to get the feel for handling the rag. Start at the bottom of the wall and roll the rag through the fresh glaze toward the top. The surface of the rag will fill with paint as you work. When the entire surface of the rag is wet, turn it inside out. When the rag becomes saturated, replace it. For more depth and texture, allow the first coat to dry and then apply a second glaze color over the first coat.

Stippling

Stippling produces a finely textured wall with hints of a second color peeking through.

Stippling is a subtractive finish. You apply glaze and then take some of it off—in this case by pouncing or bouncing the ends of a finely bristled stippling brush through wet glaze. It's in the same family as sponging off and ragging off but creates a more finely textured surface. It also requires more effort—pouncing the brush over every square inch of the freshly glazed wall.

A stippling brush has long bristles that cover a larger area than the end of a regular brush with each pounce. Stippling brushes can be expensive, but to get the right effect there is really no substitute. An edge stippler, another special-purpose tool, has a narrow design that makes it easier to pounce along the edges of the wall.

Stippling also can be an additive effect. A brush is dipped into the glaze mix and applied to the wall by lightly slapping the bristles against the palm of your hand, splattering tiny drops of paint on the base coat.

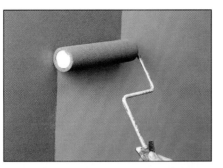

1 **PRACTICE AND PRIME.** Apply a semigloss base coat. For best results brush short sections and then roll out as many of the brush strokes as possible. Finish rolling the area and paint more of the edges with the brush. Allow the base coat to dry. Mix paint and glaze in a ratio of four parts glaze to one part paint. Roll a section of the wall with the glaze mixture, covering only as much area as you can stipple before the surface begins to dry. To create the effect, pounce or bounce the stippling brush on the glaze surface. Brush on the glaze near the edges. Apply it elsewhere with a ⅜-inch roller or with a foam roller. For a lighter finish, use less glaze and apply it in random swirls with a paintbrush.

2 **STIPPLE THE GLAZE.** Work from top to bottom of the wall, pouncing the brush so that you feel a rebound from the bending bristles. Push gently to finely freckle the existing layer of glaze. The overall effect on the wall should be even. Turn your wrist between each application of the brush to avoid creating a pattern. Remove excess glaze from the brush. A loaded brush won't leave a finely textured surface. Use a rag frequently to absorb excess finish from the bristles and to lighten the overall effect of the wall. Clean the brush after every five or six pounces. Stipple the corners. Move along the wall, rolling and stippling, section by section. When you get to the corners, use a small, stiff-bristled brush to stipple around the edges of the wall where the large brush can't reach.

Creating textured effects

Textured finishes are popular for covering drywall without the usual labor-intensive, three-coat painting. Application is simple, but repair can be tricky.

TEXTURE TYPES. Sand-texture paint is interior latex paint containing perlite—a sandlike additive available in fine, medium, and coarse particle sizes. The additive can be purchased separately, or premixed in 1- and 5-gallon sizes.

Orange peel is a slightly pebbly finish without the sharpness of sand. It's applied over primer with a spray gun, and covered with white-pigmented shellac primer and a satin or semigloss top coat. It's a good choice for both bath and kitchen because it is durable and scrubbable.

Knockdown is a two-step process. A rough ⅛-inch coating is sprayed on, followed 10 to 15 minutes later by a second person "knocking down" the high points with a mason's trowel. The result is a hand-plastered, old-world look popular in living rooms, bedrooms, and hallways.

Acoustic (also known as popcorn) is used on ceilings. It can be applied with a looped texture roller or sprayed on.

APPLICATION TOOLS. Sand-texture paint is applied with a thick-napped roller.

Orange peel, knockdown, and acoustic finishes may be applied by roller but are most often shot onto a primed surface from a spray gun with an attached hopper. You can use a hand-powered spray texture pump or you can rent or purchase an air-powered spray texture gun.

For touching up small areas (less than 10 square feet), all of the above textures are available in aerosol spray cans.

TOUCHY TOUCH-UPS. Regardless of the area involved, a seamless touch-up requires matching texture, color, and sheen.

Unless all three variables match those of the original finish, seams will be noticeable. Color is usually the most problematic—especially where a ceiling has been exposed to years of cigarette smoke.

Apply a stain-blocking primer, followed by a quality interior latex paint. The primer will block any smoke or water stains and provide maximum adhesion, while the top coat will provide uniform color and sheen.

TEXTURED REPAIR. Acoustic (popcorn) texture presents a special repair problem. It is heavy and loses adhesion when wetted by latex paint. It can slide or even fall off a ceiling. The solution is to first prime the entire ceiling with white-pigmented shellac, then apply the repair with an aerosol spray can. After the repaired area dries, prime it

YOU CAN'T ALWAYS TOUCH UP
So you touched up a spot on the wall and the touch-up is more visible than the problem was? Sometimes the paint has just been on the wall for too long to match what was left in the can. Smoke, grime, and general wear and tear may mean a corner-to-corner paint job is the only way to get a touch-up that actually works.

a second time. The shellac primer provides a uniform base color and makes the textured material far more water resistant. As the final step, apply a latex flat or eggshell top coat.

The extreme texture of acoustic finish requires a roller with an extreme nap. Some fiber roller covers are known as acoustic rollers. Better yet, purchase a split-foam roller. Even with a special roller, however, the rule is, "Get in and get out as fast as you can." Apply the primer and paint in 2×2-foot areas: two strokes one way, followed by just two strokes at a right angle. Do not try to stretch the paint and never go back.

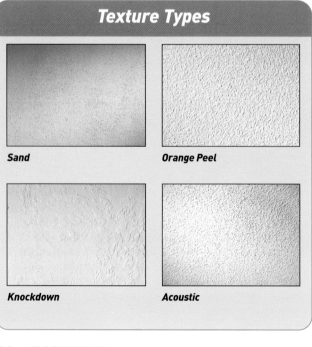

Texture Types

Sand

Orange Peel

Knockdown

Acoustic

BUYER'S GUIDE

USE THE RIGHT ROLLER FOR ACOUSTIC CEILINGS
Acoustic ceilings require special rollers that allow the paint to fill in properly. Depending on the thickness of the texture, use a thick-napped or split-foam roller. See the experts at your home center or paint store for information.

PAINTING EXTERIORS

EASY	**MEDIUM**	HARD

REQUIRED SKILLS: Prep, priming, and general painting skills are required.

HOW LONG WILL IT TAKE?

Experienced . . . . 2.5 hrs.
Handy . . . . 3.5 hrs.
Novice . . . . 4.5 hrs.

VARIABLES: Time of year, temperature, and general condition of the exterior walls will affect the length of the job.

LADDER SAFETY

Working with tall ladders can be tricky and sometimes dangerous unless you follow a few simple guidelines. Place the ladder so the feet are away from the building at a distance equal to one-fourth the height of the ladder.

Make sure the legs are on a level surface; on uneven surfaces, use wood shims to level them.

If the surface slopes away from the house, place a 2×4 across the base of the ladder and drive two 2×4 stakes into the ground to secure the ladder base.

Use ladder boots (see Step 1, page 50) or wrap a cloth around the top of the ladder legs to keep them from slipping or damaging the siding.

Remember, always be careful and be sure to get help when you need it.

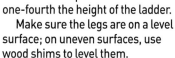

G ood preparation is probably the most important step in painting. You need to wash the surfaces, scrape off bad paint, and patch any rot or damage.

Until recently, scrapers and disk sanders were the only way you could get paint off your siding, and that's a lot of work. If the paint on your siding is in relatively good condition, a scraper is still the best bet. But if it's not, two new tools help solve the problem. One is a sander with a housing that fits around the disk. The housing rides on the surface you're sanding, letting you sand only so deep and no deeper.

The other tool is similar to a router—a large carbide bit spins at high speed to remove the paint. It's set in the housing in same way the sander is, so you can set it to take off the paint and no more.

Painting a house is a lot of work, so break the job down into a cycle of smaller jobs—a side a year, perhaps, then the trim, and then some time off before you start again.

STUFF YOU'LL NEED

✔ **MATERIALS:**

TSP/bleach solution (or a phosphate-free cleaner), wood filler, glazing compound, caulk, tape

✔ **TOOLS:**

Putty knife, broad knife, grinder, sander, wire brush, broom, caulking gun, hammer, screwdriver, garden hose garbage bags or tarps or drop cloths

DON'T BE STARTLED
Beware of hidden bee and animal nests when working at elevations. Sudden surprises can cause serious injuries from falls.

PAINTING EXTERIORS
Getting ready to paint

1 **COVER EXTERIOR HVAC UNITS.** Tie back or trim bushes and limbs. Cover plants in the work area with plastic garbage bags, drop cloths, or tarps. Turn off air-conditioning and exhaust fans. Cover and seal air-conditioning units and exhaust vents with plastic and tape as needed.

2 **REMOVE SHUTTERS AND HARDWARE AND CLOSE STORM WINDOWS.** Repair siding and trim as necessary and fill rotted or insect-damaged areas with wood filler.

PAINTING EXTERIORS
Getting ready to paint (continued)

③ REGLAZE WINDOWS AS NEEDED. Remove the old putty with a chisel or stiff putty knife; apply new glazing compound. When removing old putty be careful not to break the glass.

④ WASH THE SIDING AND TRIM WITH A TRISODIUM PHOSPHATE AND BLEACH SOLUTION OR A PHOSPHATE-FREE TSP SUBSTITUTE. Apply with a wire brush in sections about 8'×8' and let the solution do its work without any scrubbing on your part.

⑤ RINSE THE ENTIRE HOUSE WITH A GARDEN HOSE AND WATER UNTIL THE RUNOFF WATER IS CLEAR. Rerinse to ensure the solution is completely gone. Let the siding and trim dry completely, usually two days, before painting.

⑥ SOFFITS AND THE AREA UNDER PORCH ROOFS ARE NEARLY IMPOSSIBLE TO SAND UNLESS YOU CAN HANG UPSIDE DOWN. Power wash them with TSP/bleach solution instead. Set the spray to remove the loose paint, but don't set it so hard that it damages the wood.

⑦ SAND OFF LOOSE PAINT WITH A POWER SANDER MADE FOR THE JOB. Start with a coarse-grit—16, 24, or 36—disc. The sander cuts through the paint quickly, so be careful not to damage the siding. When you're done, resand with 60-grit to remove swirl marks, which will show through paint. Scrape off paint in unreachable areas. Sand the bottom edges of the siding even if the surface is alright.

⑧ REMOVE ANY DUST FROM THE SANDED AREAS AND THE AREAS AROUND THEM WITH A PAINTBRUSH. Prime any bare areas with an oil-based primer made by the manufacturer of the paint you'll use. Oil is the most durable primer, and contrary to prevailing wisdom, you can apply latex paint over it.

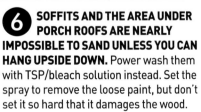

SAFETY ALERT

HANDLING A LADDER

Have a helper stand at the end of the ladder nearest the house, and put a foot on each leg. Grab the other end, lift the ladder up over your head, and hold it by a rung.

Take a step forward, moving your hand to the next rung as you do. Continue walking toward your helper, moving your hands and body forward one rung at a time.

When you get close enough, have the helper grab a rung too so that you are both holding the ladder as it approaches vertical.

Once the ladder is vertical, trade jobs with your helper. You become the anchor, placing your feet on the legs of the ladder.

The helper grabs the ladder and slowly backs up, sliding a hand up each side of the ladder until it is leaning against the house. Make sure both feet are level, and that the ladder is at the proper slope.

Reverse the process to take the ladder down. Put your feet against the base of the ladder as an anchor. Have your helper walk the ladder back toward you. Once it is vertical, let your helper act as the anchor while you walk backward to lower the ladder.

Painting exterior walls

REQUIRED SKILLS: Basic to intermediate painting and mechanical skills will be necessary.

HOW LONG WILL IT TAKE?

Experienced . . . . .Variable
Handy . . . . .Variable
Novice . . . . .Variable

STUFF YOU'LL NEED

✔ MATERIALS:

Exterior house paint, exterior trim paint, paintable caulk, disposable latex gloves

✔ TOOLS:

Paintbrush, trim brush, foam pad, extension ladder, stepladder, edge roller, wire brush, 2-inch putty knife, wide putty knife, soft-bristled brush

Painting exterior walls is quite different from painting interior walls because of the various siding types available and the equipment needed for working at higher elevations.

Siding material ranges from cedar lap, board-and-batten, and slate to masonite, stucco, and masonry. Each requires a slightly different technique: For example, the type of siding may dictate what you use to apply paint. But basics are basics and whatever you're painting, you'll follow the principles discussed here.

Be sure you have quality ladders and scaffolds in proper working condition to ensure a smooth and safe job. Remember, you are trusting your life to this equipment, so buy or rent the best available.

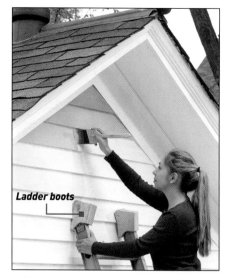

Ladder boots

1 START AT THE PEAK OF THE ROOF WITH THE LADDER CENTERED ON THE WALL. Paint three or four pieces of siding, working from one eave across to the other. Notice the boots that fit over the ladder tops to protect the siding and prevent the ladder from slipping on the siding. Called ladder boots, they cost only a few dollars and are available in most paint departments.

2 MOVE THE LADDER DOWN A COUPLE OF RUNGS, AND THEN WORK YOUR WAY ACROSS THE TOP OF THE WALL AGAIN. Be very careful not to overreach—tipping the ladder over or falling off it can cause serious injury.

3 LOWER THE LADDER ANOTHER COUPLE OF RUNGS, AND MOVE IT OVER TO ONE SIDE OF THE HOUSE. Paint two or three strips of siding, starting on the side, working across the top of the ladder, and painting the area you can reach comfortably on the other side. Lefties generally like to start on the left; right-handed painters generally like to start on the right.

4 MOVE THE LADDER SO YOU CAN REACH THE NEWLY PAINTED BLOCK OF SIDING. To eliminate lap marks, repaint the edges of the last area you painted as you start each stroke. Start at the side and paint across the top of the ladder to the other side.

Repeat the process, painting only the area you can reach until you finish the strips of siding you've been working on. Lower the ladder, and repeat until you've painted the entire side.

Exterior painting techniques

Wait until the surface is dry and check to make sure there is no rain in the weather forecast. Apply primer to any bare siding. Woods contain resins that bleed through water-based paints, so use an oil-based primer. Allow the primer to dry according to the manufacturer's recommendation.

If the wall is masonry, prime the entire surface. Masonry surfaces can usually be painted with a roller. Get one with a long nap, so that it will apply paint in all the nooks and crannies.

Paint roof trim and soffits first if they will be a different color from the walls. This prevents trim paint from dripping onto newly painted walls.

Mask the siding and paint the trim. Use a corner roller or trim brush to cut in these areas.

SPRAY GUNS

A spray gun speeds up the job immensely. If you're thinking of painting an entire house, don't let price be the deciding factor. A good spray gun is one you don't notice. It's comfortable to hold, doesn't clog, and puts out enough paint for the job. The shape of the mist coming out of the gun, called the pattern, is important too. Talk to your dealer about how to get the right pattern, and look for a gun that adjusts easily. You'll probably find that the gun the pros use is best—and expensive. Consider renting good equipment.

WORK SMARTER

PAINT PADS

If you're painting clapboard siding, ask your paint dealer about pads made for applying paint. You just dip them in the paint and slide them along the siding—it's easy compared to brushes because the pads cover the entire width of siding in one pass.

Painting exterior walls *(continued)*

PAINTING BOARD-AND-BATTEN

1 **PRESSURE WASH THE WALLS, STAYING AWAY FROM WINDOWS AND DOORS WHERE WATER CAN LEAK THROUGH AND STAIN THE INSIDE SURFACES.** Clean around doors and windows by scrubbing with a scrub brush. Once the wood is dry, caulk along the space between the batten and board with a 20- or 30-year paintable caulk. Smooth the caulk with a wet finger, or with a finger protected by a disposable latex glove.

2 **PRIME WITH A LATEX OR OIL PRIMER, TINTED TO A LIGHTER SHADE OF THE FINISH COAT.** Starting at an edge of the wall, prime face and edges of the battens. Work from the top down, and apply primer along the face of the board as you cover the battens. Prime the edges of the horizontal board above the siding (called the frieze) and the bottom kick board too, if there are any.

3 **ROLL THE FACE OF THE FIRST BOARD, WORKING FROM THE TOP DOWN** and then work your way across the building. Let the primer dry, and then cover with an acrylic-latex top coat.

PAINTING STUCCO

1 **SCRUB AROUND WINDOWS AND DOORS WITH WATER AND A WIRE BRUSH,** and then wash the rest of the surface with a garden hose. Clean away any remaining loose paint with a wire brush and with a putty knife if the surface is smooth enough.

2 **ROLL ON ACRYLIC-LATEX MASONRY PRIMER AND CHECK FOR CRACKS OR RUST MARKS ON THE STUCCO.** When the primer is dry, patch the cracks with vinyl concrete patch or elastomeric (synthetic rubber) stucco patch, applying it with a flexible 2-inch putty knife. While the patch is still wet, dip a wider knife in some water and skim over the face of the stucco to remove excess patch material. Caulk narrower cracks with concrete repair caulk.

3 **LET THE PATCH DRY AND SPOT PRIME THE REPAIRS,** as well as any discoloration. Roll on a finish coat of acrylic-latex paint. Read the label carefully, and get paint specifically designed for stucco.

PAINTING VINYL OR ALUMINUM SIDING

1 **REPLACE ANY DAMAGED OR CRACKED SIDING.** Pressure wash, but stay away from windows and doors, where water can leak through and stain the inside walls. Clean around doors by scrubbing with a soft-bristled brush.

2 **BRUSH ON A ACRYLIC-LATEX STAIN-BLOCKING PRIMER** that specifically states on the label that it will work on aluminum or vinyl—whichever surface you're painting.

3 **WHEN THE PRIMER HAS DRIED,** apply an acrylic-latex top coat, again choosing one designed for the surface you're painting. Don't choose a color darker than the original. It will absorb more heat and may cause the siding to warp.

PAINTING CONCRETE

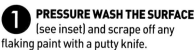

1 **PRESSURE WASH THE SURFACE** (see inset) and scrape off any flaking paint with a putty knife.

2 **PAINTED CONCRETE OFTEN SHOWS SHINY AND DULL SPOTS IF THE RIGHT PRIMER ISN'T USED.** Prime the entire wall with an acrylic-latex stain-blocking primer designed for masonry. (Some masonry paints double as primers, but usually leave shiny spots. Stick with a stain-blocking primer.)

3 **CAULK ANY CRACKS WITH MASONRY REPAIR CAULK.** Work the caulk in with a damp finger or damp rag, and wipe across the crack with a damp sponge to remove the excess. Once the caulk dries, roll on an acrylic-latex masonry paint. Although the paint will be dry to the touch in 24 hours, it takes 30 days to fully cure.

Painting windows

SKILL SCALE

| EASY | **MEDIUM** | HARD |

REQUIRED SKILLS:
Intermediate painting skills and minimum mechanical skills are needed.

HOW LONG WILL IT TAKE?

Experienced . . . . 20 min.
Handy . . . . 35 min.
Novice . . . . 1 hr.

VARIABLES: Time of year, temperature, and general condition of the exterior walls will affect the length of the job.

STUFF YOU'LL NEED

✔ MATERIALS:
TSP, primer, trim paint, putty, masking tape (optional)

✔ TOOLS:
Tapered sash brush, putty knife

- **Upper sash**: upper frame of a double-hung window.

- **Lower sash**: lower frame of a double-hung window.

- **Sash rails**: horizontal pieces of the frame that form the sash.

- **Sash stiles**: vertical pieces of the frame that form the sash.

- **Meeting rails**: rails that overlap each other in the middle of the window.

- **Windowsill**: piece of wood, metal, or plastic at the bottom of the window. Usually slanted.

- **Trim**: wood, metal, or plastic that frames the outside of the window.

- **Head**: piece of wood, metal, or plastic at the top of the window.

Windows get the worst of weather: rain, snow, blinding sun, hot humid weather followed in some parts of the country by freezing cold winters.

And they look it: flaked, chipping paint; broken putty, rotten wood, and dirt, dirt, dirt.

Prep work is a must. Wash everything down with TSP. Scrape off loose paint, and sand the rest. Prime bare wood.

To mask or not to mask? Putting masking tape along the line between the frame and glass eliminates the need to be overly neat with the brush. It also takes time. A lot of painters just let their brushes run across the glass whenever necessary, and then scrape off the paint with a razor blade. It's your call.

Once you've painted the windows, open and close them several times throughout the day. This keeps the paint from forming a bond between the parts and keeps you from dealing with a window you've painted permanently shut.

Someone is bound to have ignored this advice on at least one of your windows. You can free your windows in one of several ways. Sometimes a good sharp rap on the frame is all it takes. (Watch out for the glass.) If not, you can work around the seam between the sash and frame with either a utility knife or a special sash saw designed for the job. And before you get too frustrated, remember there are two sides to every window—yours could well be painted shut on the inside.

PARTS OF A BASIC DOUBLE-HUNG WINDOW

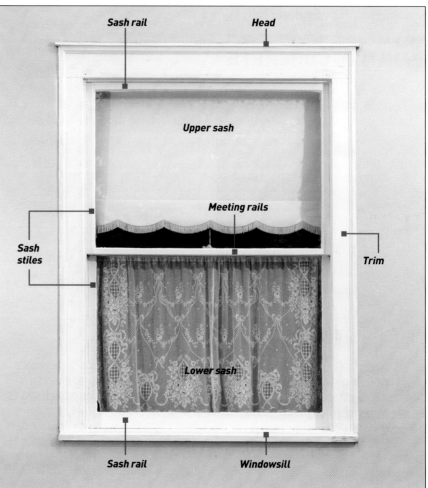

1 **SCRAPE ANY LOOSE WINDOW PUTTY FROM AROUND THE EDGE OF THE WINDOW AND BRUSH THE SASH CLEAN.** Brush the wood you exposed with linseed oil to help the new putty stick. Roll some new putty into a noodle and press it into the bare spots. Pull a putty knife along it to create a flat sloping surface. Slide a damp finger along the putty in the other direction to remove any small imperfections.

2 **LET THE PUTTY DRY FOR ABOUT A WEEK.** Then open the window and pull the top down until it's about 3 inches from the sill. Push the bottom sash up until it's about 3 inches from the top of the window frame.

3 **PAINT ALL THE PARTS OF THE SASH YOU CAN REACH.** Start with the pieces in the grid (called muntins) if there are any. Then paint the horizontal pieces, followed by the vertical. Following this pattern gives you a nice, neat job. Any brush strokes running across the grain are subsequently covered by strokes running with the grain.

4 **PUT THE SASHES BACK INTO THEIR REGULAR POSITIONS, BUT DON'T CLOSE THE WINDOW ENTIRELY.** Leave about a 1-inch gap at the top and bottom. Paint the parts of the sash you were unable to reach in Step 2. Move the sashes as the paint dries to keep them from sticking.

5 **PAINT THE STOPS AND JAMBS.** Don't paint the tracks the windows travel in—the paint buildup could cause the windows to jam.

6 **PAINT THE FACE OF THE WINDOW CASING.** Mask the siding unless you're going to paint it as well.

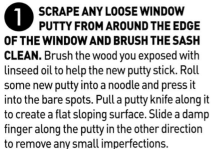

Priming and painting trim

| EASY | **MEDIUM** | HARD |

REQUIRED SKILLS: Priming and painting trim requires intermediate painting skills.

HOW LONG WILL IT TAKE?

Experienced . . . . 1 hr.
Handy . . . . 1.5 hrs.
Novice . . . . 2 hrs.

VARIABLES: Time is based on a 25' section of soffit and fascia.

STUFF YOU'LL NEED

✔ **MATERIALS:**

Exterior trim paint, appropriate primer for the surface

✔ **TOOLS:**

4" brush, 2" tapered sash brush, wire brush, corner roller

Once the trim has been prepared and is ready to paint, be sure to brush and wipe the trim just before applying primer. When the primer has dried thoroughly, paint the trim as soon as possible but no later than three days after priming. The longer you wait to paint, the greater the chances for chemical deposits and dirt to affect the surface.

Trim paint is specially formulated to withstand the extreme exposure and high traffic areas of roof trim, porches, railings, doors, and window trim. Trim paint is available in most popular finishes and can be custom blended for your specific color requirements.

USE THE RIGHT PRIMER. Most general-purpose primers can be used on any surface. For best results on metal use a metal primer with a rust inhibitor. Masonry primers are specially formulated to adhere to chalky surfaces.

PRIME AND PAINT WOOD STAIRS AND PORCH FLOORS AFTER ALL OTHER SURFACES HAVE BEEN PRIMED AND PAINTED. This prevents the need to touch up drips on the horizontal surfaces. Be sure to use specially formulated enamel floor paint that resists high volumes of traffic, and add an emulsifying bonder to the first coat to help the paint stick to chalky, powdery surfaces. Do not use the bonder in subsequent coats.

REMOVE LOOSE PAINT FROM METAL RAILING AND TRIM WITH A WIRE BRUSH. Rust can be brushed from iron or steel, but the surface must be primed right away to prevent further rusting. Finish with an enamel paint to ensure a long-lasting, protective finish.

AFTER THE WALLS AND TRIM ARE PAINTED, YOU MAY WANT TO PRIME AND PAINT THE FOUNDATION WALLS. Paint them the same color as the siding or choose an accent color. Paint around windows and doors first with a sash brush, then paint the broad areas with a 4-inch brush, working paint into the mortar lines.

PAINTING SOFFITS AND FASCIA

1 **PAINT THIS AREA FIRST SO THAT PAINT DRIPS WON'T RUIN THE WORK YOU'VE DONE ON THE SIDING.** Paint the overhang (soffit) first and then work your way onto the edges facing the soffit. If the soffit is supported by brackets (corbels), paint them once you've painted all the panels (see inset).

2 **AFTER THE SOFFIT AND TRIM HAVE BEEN PAINTED,** paint any moldings below the soffit.

3 **PAINT THE SURFACE ABOVE THE SOFFIT, CALLED THE FASCIA, NEXT.** If there is a cornice molding, paint both it and the fascia as you move along the wall.

PAINTING JAMBS, CASINGS, AND TRIM

1 **PAINT THE DOORS AS DESCRIBED ON PAGE 30, AND THE WINDOWS AS DESCRIBED ON PAGE 55.** Wedge the doors and windows open so they'll stay put while you paint them. Mask the floors underneath the doors, and mask the siding where it runs into the casing.

2 **AFTER THE DOOR OR WINDOW IS DRY, PAINT THE JAMB.** Start at the top on the inside with a moderate load of paint on a beveled sash brush. Paint the stop, then work outward. After the top, move to the inside edge (hinge side on doors and casement windows), saving the outside edge for last.

3 **PAINT THE CASINGS WHILE THE JAMBS ARE STILL WET.** Mask the siding along the outside edges or cut in with a brush. Feather the paint into the mitered joints; then angle your brush to match the miter line, and paint right up to it. Paint thresholds after the jambs and casings have dried.

THE HARDEST PART OF PAPERING IS BEING **PATIENT.** This is not a job you can rush, not a job you can muscle, not a job with any shortcuts. When you're wallpapering, you're better off taking your time until the job is finished.

Although you can't rush, you can enjoy yourself. Papering is a job that requires only a few basic skills like using a tape measure, a level, scissors, and a knife. It's a bit more expensive than painting, but cheap as home improvement projects go. And more than paint, more than furniture or carpeting, wallpaper sets the tone of your room. Victorian paper, combined with the right moldings, can transform the plainest tract house into a 19th-century classic. An Arts-and-Crafts print sets the stage for stained-glass lamps, mission furniture, and early 20th-century America.

But wallpaper does more than take you back in time. While it's dangerous to generalize, designers will tell you that light colors tend to open up a room and add a feeling of spaciousness. Striped papers pull the eye up and down, adding to the appearance of height. Small prints keep the eyes focused in the room, making it feel cozier. Dark colors can create a feeling of intimacy.

When choosing materials, however, don't decorate for the designer; decorate for the person living in the room.

SECTION 2 PROJECTS

REAL-WORLD SITUATIONS

PREPARATION IS KEY

The truth is that wallpaper you put up will never look better than the wall it's covering. Every bump, dimple, ding, dent, and crack will still be there and will still be visible. Paper hugs the wall as much as it covers it.

You can paper over old wallpaper, for example, but why would you? The surface will never be as firm as the wall itself, and new paper may actually pull the old paper off. Old seams will be visible under the new paper, especially if they're crooked or lapped. New liquid wallpaper removers work extremely well. For step-by-step directions, see pages 25–26.

● **After removing the old paper, clean the wall with TSP solution.** Dirt, grease, and grime keep the paper from sticking. When you're done washing, rinse with clean water until the water runs clear.

● **Prepare the walls.** Fill small cracks with surfacing compound. Buy it premixed, push the compound in place with a putty knife, and then run the knife over it so that the repair is flush with the wall. If the patch shrinks as it dries, repeat until the crack disappears.

Fill larger cracks and holes with spackling paste. Spackling paste has a consistency between that of cake frosting and grade-school paste. Apply with a putty knife, filling the hole entirely. Paste contains bubbles, so smooth out the top as you would with frosting.

If you've got big holes or loose plaster, the repair will be more extensive. On drywall, cut away the damage and screw drywall into the hole as described on page 226. Plaster patching compound works well for patching plaster over lath (see page 228), but it will take a couple of applications. Patching large areas can be a nuisance, but not as annoying as having the wall crumble behind your favorite wallpaper.

When patches are dry, lightly sand them so they are both smooth and level with the wall. Make a cleaner job of it by wiping the surfaces down with a damp sponge.

● **Seal, prime, and size.** This used to be three operations until paint companies managed to combine the liquids into one. Sealer keeps water, smoke, and other stains from showing through the paper. Primer provides a smooth surface for the paper to stick to. Sizing is thin wallpaper paste that seals the wall's pores to prevent paste from soaking into the plaster and provides extra adhesion. Primer/sealer can be clear or tinted to match the primary color of the wallpaper.

● **Put up the paper.** If you're using pasteless papers, brush a paste activator on the back. It's neater than soaking, makes the paper easy to adjust and align, and provides a better bond.

Wallpaper basics

STORES HAVE HUNDREDS OF WALLPAPER SAMPLE BOOKS. Most outlets will allow you to take several home to help you choose.

Wallpaper can establish the style of a room more thoroughly and more quickly than any other single element, including paint. If you're sure about the look you want, choosing the right paper is easy. If you're not sure or you find it hard to put your thoughts into words, open up a wallpaper sample book.

Sample books are available in most wallpaper outlets and are organized to help make the decision process easy. After a few minutes of browsing, you'll find yourself gravitating toward a look. If you're thinking about complex arrangements—perhaps a chair rail, with paper above and below, and maybe even a border along the ceiling—the books show combinations that work together.

Most wallpaper isn't just paper anymore. It's vinyl-coated to make removing dirt more efficient and to better resist scrapes and tears. It lasts longer and is easier to install than true paper.

If you're looking for historically accurate replicas, it's still possible to special order true paper. It's expensive and can be a challenge to hang. If you want a historical look without the problems, find a pattern in true paper and then search the vinyl books for a replica.

Before choosing a paper, ask to take the wallpaper book home to view the paper in your room. Once you've settled on a favorite, order a sample, tape it to the wall, and examine it night and day. Place it next to upholstered items and the carpet to see how they look together. Check it against the drapes. Tape samples of possible trim paint colors next to it. Be picky—if you don't love it, try again.

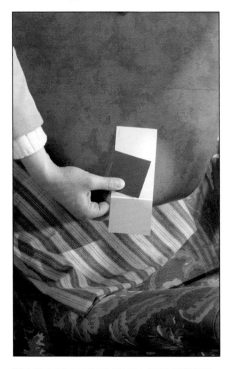

COLLECT SAMPLES OF ALL THE COLORS IN YOUR ROOM and use them to help select suitable wallpaper. Designers make books of samples of all the colors and textures in a room to help them make decisions.

ORDER A SAMPLE, TAPE IT TO THE WALL, AND LOOK AT IT under different lighting conditions and at different times of the day before you make your choice. Remember, you'll probably live with the paper for many years.

Tips from the pros

For the best wallpapering job, follow these guidelines from experienced paperhangers.

- Use a paste activator, as the pros do, instead of soaking prepasted papers. It's better to take time to brush on activator than to have wallpaper fall down later.

- Apply each strip from the top down.

- Choose patterns and match the seams well. Some seams match perfectly. Others, with a drop-match pattern, require the adjacent strip to be slid up or down to get a match. The amount, or drop, is listed in wallpaper books and on the package or roll.

- To get clean, straight cuts, you must use the right tool. Use a sharp blade and replace it often. Some pros advocate changing the blade after every cut. Pros often use single-edge razor blades in special handles.

- Wallpaper colors vary from batch to batch. Tell the supplier that you want paper from the same batch, and check label batch numbers to confirm. Save the labels from every roll.

THE PAPERHANGER'S TOOL KIT

Below are some basic wallpapering tools. For more information see the Tool Glossary on page 544.

1-QUART BUCKET	EXTENSION POLE	PLUMB BOB AND CHALK LINE	ROLLERS	STRAIGHTEDGE	WALLPAPER SCORING TOOL
3-INCH PUTTY KNIFE	GARDEN SPRAYER	RAGS	SANDING BLOCK	TAPE MEASURE	WALLPAPER SPONGE
5-IN-1 TOOL	LEVEL	ROLLER CAGES	SEAM ROLLER	UTILITY KNIFE	WATER TRAY
BROADKNIFE	PAINT CAN OPENER	ROLLER PAN	SMOOTHING BRUSH	WALLPAPER PASTE BRUSH	
CAULKING GUN	PAINTER'S TAPE	ROLLER PAN LINER	STEPLADDER	WALLPAPER SCISSORS	

Measuring and estimating wallpaper

Before you get too technical, remember one thing: You're estimating. **EASY ESTIMATING.** To estimate the number of double rolls you need, divide the square footage of the wall by 50. Round up to the nearest whole number and add 1.

NOW TO GET TECHNICAL. When you paper a room, you need to have enough paper to do the wall, plus about 10 percent extra to make up for trimming, matching, and mistakes. Because papers quickly go out of print, you also want to have a double roll on hand for subsequent repairs. At $20 or $30 a double roll, it's good insurance.

Start by figuring out the square footage of your room: Measure the height times the length of each wall in feet, and add up the total. Don't subtract for doors, windows, or obstructions because you can't use the pieces of paper you cut out.

Even though a double roll covers 56 square feet, the formula pretends it only covers 50 square feet, giving you the roughly 10 percent extra you need for trimming, matching, and mistakes.

Consider an 8×12-foot room with 8-foot ceilings. Two 12-foot walls with 8-foot ceilings account for 192 square feet (2×12×8=192). The two 8-foot walls total 128 square feet (2×8×8=128). Altogether the room has 320 square feet of wall (192+128=320).

Dividing the square footage by 50 and rounding up to the next whole number means you need seven double rolls (320÷50= 6.4, which rounds up to 7). Add a roll, and buy eight. Keep the extra roll for repairs. If you have more than one extra roll after you finish, return it.

WORK SMARTER

WALLPAPER TABLES

Professionals buy tables that are about as wide as a roll of wallpaper, but you can make your own. Cut a strip of plywood a little wider than your paper. Wrap the plywood in an old sheet to absorb activator and water and set it on two sawhorses or on an old table covered with newspapers.

Wallpaper as a foreign language

Like any craft, wallpapering has a language of its own. Here are a few terms you'll need to know:

Double Roll: A double roll is twice as long as the single rolls your grandparents bought. These are not twice as wide, however. A double roll covers 56 square feet of wall. A single roll covers 28 square feet. Virtually all rolls are double rolls these days.

Random-Match: If the pattern automatically aligns when you put one strip of paper next to the other, it is a random-match paper. Striped papers are random-match.

Straight-Match: The pattern on straight-match papers stops before it reaches the edge. When you hang a strip, make sure the pattern aligns with the pattern of the previous strip. If not, the pattern will zigzag as it crosses the wall.

Drop-Match: On a drop-match paper, the edge of the strip cuts through the pattern. The pattern runs diagonally— perhaps very subtly so—and meets the right edge of the strip at a point lower than on the left edge. If the edge of a drop-match paper cuts a flower in half, for example, you would have to align the edges of adjoining strips in order to get a complete flower. The amount of diagonal drop, called the **pattern repeat,** is printed on the back of the paper and is listed in wallpaper books.

Peelable: An easily removable paper. When you lift and pull off peelable paper, however, the backing remains on the wall. The backing was originally seen as a kind of liner that you could paper over. This idea largely has gone by the wayside.

Strippable: Lifting off the corner of strippable paper and pulling it will remove the entire strip of paper.

Vinyl: Vinyl refers to a pattern printed on solid vinyl, which is backed by paper or pulp. It is durable and scrubbable. Because of its cost, it's generally used in commercial settings.

Vinyl-Coated, Washable: A surface that you can occasionally wash with a sponge, mild soap, and water.

Vinyl-Coated, Scrubbable: A more durable surface that you can wash often with a sponge, mild soap, and water. No paper is up to the rigors of a scrub brush.

Finding the area if the walls aren't rectangular

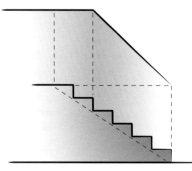

Stairs: Divide the wall into two triangles and a rectangle.

- To determine the area of a triangle, multiply the length of the triangle by its height and divide by 2. Repeat.

- To calculate the area of the rectangle, multiply the length by the height.
- Add the three areas together to get the total square footage.

Gable walls: Measure as though the surface were a square or rectangle. Measure the length and the height; multiply the two numbers to find the area.

WALLPAPERING WALLS

STUFF YOU'LL NEED

✔ MATERIALS:

Wallpaper, paste (for unpasted papers), wallpaper paste activator, vinyl-to-vinyl adhesive (for edges only of vinyl and vinyl-coated papers)

✔ TOOLS:

Tape measure, scissors, pencil, 2-foot level, water tray (for prepasted paper), paint roller or brush (for paste), wallpaper brush, seam roller, utility knife, trimming tool (also called a broad knife), sponge, wallpaper table or plywood on sawhorses

 WORK SMARTER

PRIMER/SEALER OPTIONS

Primers come in clear and white. Use a clear primer where you're worried about drips and spills—papering above wooden wainscoting, for example. If you're putting up a dark paper, tint either white or clear primer before painting. Tinted primer makes inadvertent gaps less visible.

Preparing the walls is as important as, or perhaps more important than, hanging the paper. Paper won't stick to a greasy surface, and irregularities in the wall may be visible on the paper's surface. So be prepared: Wash, patch, fix, prime, seal, and size before you paper.

Most of these chores are made easy by modern materials. Primers, sealers, and sizing are combined into a single product. Paint and plaster companies market many wall repair kits. For specifics on wall prep, see "Real-World Situations" on page 59.

Live with samples of a bold pattern for a few days before you make the decision to paper the whole room.

Wallpaper sets the tone of the room much more easily than paint.

Covering paneling and cement block

With the right preparation, and something called wallpaper liner, you can even put wallpaper over paneling or cement block walls.

Wallpaper liner is a heavy-duty, unprinted wallpaper that you apply before you put up the good stuff. It leaves a smooth surface that good paper can grip, and because it is thick, it hides a good deal of unevenness. Because it won't camouflage everything, however, you have to begin with good prep work.

On paneling, begin by nailing down any loose seams or panels. Pull out any nails that have popped loose and replace them with drywall screws.

Fill the grooves in the paneling and other imperfections with surfacing compound and a putty knife to create a flat surface. When the compound is set, sand the panel with 200-grit paper to create a good surface for the primer, sealer, and sizing.

On cement block, check for signs of mildew or efflorescence, a powdery residue that appears on walls. Either is a sign of excessive moisture, making the wall an unlikely candidate for wallpaper. Basement walls are poor candidates for papering. Fill any cracks or voids with surfacing compound. If the wall looks good, sand it the way you would any other paneling.

Whatever the surface, wash down the wall with TSP or with a 50-50 mixture of ammonia and water to remove the sanding dust and any grease or wax buildup. Rinse with a sponge and water until the water runs clear. Let the surface dry thoroughly for at least 24 hours.

Paint the wall with a combination primer/sealer/sizing; allow it to dry as recommended.

Now it's time to paper. Wallpaper liner contains no paste: Apply paste to the back before hanging. Put the strips up horizontally, so that the seams of the liner and the final paper will never fall in the same spot.

Let the paper dry, and inspect the wall for high and low spots. Hang the final paper as you normally would. Wallpaper liner also will make removing the final paper easier when you decide you're ready for a change.

Wallpapering the wall

① PATCH AND PRIME THE WALLS BEFORE YOU START. (See pages 18–29.) Primer can be white, clear, or tinted slightly to match the paper. Once you've primed, take a hard look at the paper you selected. The type of pattern determines how the strips are cut and glued on the wall. On straight-match and random-match papers, patterns along the left and right edges of the paper are the same, and installation is straightforward.

On drop-match papers, such as the one shown at right, the elements are staggered along both edges. Aligning the pattern results in an uneven top edge, which is trimmed. This takes more time and wastes some paper but results in a more interesting pattern.

Cutting alternating strips from two rolls of wallpaper will cut down on some of the wallpaper waste, but don't get too far ahead of yourself. You've got enough to think about without trying to organize 100 strips of paper.

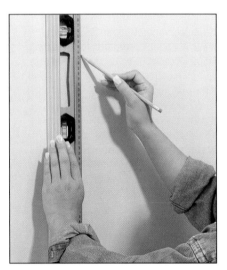

② BEGIN IN THE LEAST-CONSPICUOUS INSIDE CORNER OF THE ROOM. Position the first strip so that most of the paper is on the first wall to be papered, with about ½ to 2 inches of the strip wrapping around the corner onto the adjoining wall. (This hides cracks that may develop in the corner.) To lay out the strip, measure from the corner by the width of the paper minus the wrap. Draw a plumb line at this point, guided by a level.

③ CUT THE FIRST STRIP OF PAPER about 4 inches longer than needed so that it can temporarily overlap the ceiling and baseboard. Roll out the paper on a long work surface and cut the strip to length with scissors.

Change the blade in your knife often to prevent wrinkles and tears. Some paperers change the blade after every cut!

④ APPLY ACTIVATOR OR PASTE. Professional paperers and most wallpaper departments recommend applying a paste activator instead of soaking prepasted paper: The bond is stronger and drying time is longer so you can move the paper around the wall more. Brush or roll on the activator following the manufacturer's directions. (Make sure you've got paste *activator*, not paste.) If you use wallpaper without paste, brush on paste instead of activator.

5 GENTLY FOLD THE ENDS TOWARD THE MIDDLE, glued sides together with the patterned side out. (This is called booking the strip.) While it is sometimes unavoidable, try not to crease the paper. Wait one minute, or as directed, so the paste has a chance to activate before hanging. If you're called away from your project, tuck the paper in a plastic bag so that it stays wet.

6 HANG THE FIRST STRIP ALONG THE PLUMB LINE WITH A GENTLE BUT FIRM HAND. Start by positioning the middle of the strip, and work your way up to the top, sliding the paper to align it. Align the bottom and work it gently against the wall. Go back to the top and smooth—but don't stretch—the paper onto the wall with a brush or a flexible plastic smoother. Coax any bubbles out to the edges .

7 HANG THE SECOND STRIP AND THEN TRIM THE FIRST. Allow the glue to dry on the first strip while you hang the second strip, and then go back to trim the first. Trim as shown, placing a broad knife between the paper and the cutting knife, and guide the cut along the edge of the broad knife. A plastic smoother can also be used as a straightedge.

WORK SMARTER

PAPERHANGER'S SECRET
Wallpaper is printed in die lot batches, and the color can vary from lot to lot. Ask your retailer for rolls from the same lot, and check to make sure you get them. Write down the lot number so that if you need to repair wallpaper in the future, you'll be able to give the manufacturer the lot number, which they will try to match. It may not be perfect, but it's guaranteed to be better than if you didn't have the number.

8 BUTT SUBSEQUENT STRIPS AGAINST EACH OTHER. After you hang a few strips, go over the seams between them with a seam roller to fix the edges in place. Don't force too much paste out from under the strips or your seams will loosen. Sponge paste from the surface with clean, warm water. Foils and flocked or embossed papers may be damaged by rolling; instead, press along the seams with a smoothing brush.

9 PAPER OVER ELECTRIC SWITCHES AND OUTLETS. Cut away excess paper. Before cutting around an electrical box, shut off the power to the room. Make four diagonal slices, starting at the center of the box and working toward the corners. Avoid cutting into the outlet or switch. Trim to make a rectangular opening, leaving enough paper for the cover plate to conceal the edges.

EVERYBODY ACTIVATE
Prepasted papers seem simple: Just soak and hang. But at best it's messy work; glue-laden water drips everywhere. Wallpaper paste activator eliminates the mess and gives you longer working times and more "slip," which lets you slide the paper on the wall to position it. Activator also provides a better bond.

Wallpapering inside and outside corners

WALLPAPERING INSIDE CORNERS

1 **MEASURE DISTANCE BETWEEN THE CORNER AND THE LAST STRIP ON THE WALL.** These steps are designed to eliminate sloping paper caused by out-of-plumb corners. Measure in three places—from the edge of the previous strip to the corner at the top, middle, and bottom of the wall.

2 **ALIGN THE EDGES OF THE BOOKED STRIP.** Add one-half to 2 inches to the widest distance measured in Step 1. Mark that measurement at both folds of the booked strip. Hold a straightedge that is at least as long as the folded strip against the marks. Guide a razor knife against it to cut the strip to width. Save the cutoff.

3 **POSITION THE STRIP ON THE WALL SO THAT THE PATTERN MATCHES THE PREVIOUS STRIP AND OVERLAPS THE CEILING BY ABOUT 2 INCHES.** Align the edges so they butt against each other, and let any extra width go around the corner onto the next wall.

4 **USING OPEN PALMS** (and clean hands), **GENTLY SMOOTH THE PAPER** onto the walls and into the corner.

5 **MAKE SLITS FROM THE CORNER TO THE EDGE OF THE PAPER** at the top and bottom of the strip so that you can wrap the overlap around the corner without any wrinkles.

6 **FLATTEN THE STRIP WITH A SMOOTHING TOOL.** Trim the excess at the ceiling and baseboard. Be careful not to squish the glue out from behind the wallpaper by pressing too hard.

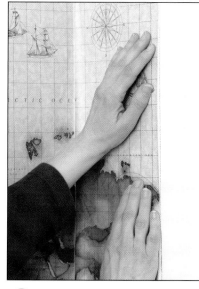

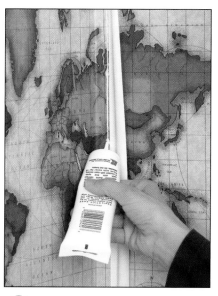

7 **MEASURE THE WIDTH OF THE CUTOFF FROM STEP 2.** Measure this distance from the corner onto the unpapered wall and make a pencil mark. Draw a plumb line through this mark from ceiling to floor, guided by a level.

8 **HANG THE CUTOFF ON THE WALL, WITH THE CUT EDGE TOWARD THE CORNER AND THE FACTORY EDGE AGAINST THE PLUMB LINE.** Align the pattern, overlapping the two pieces as necessary. Press the strip flat with a smoothing tool. Trim at the ceiling and baseboard.

9 **IF USING VINYL WALLPAPER, PEEL BACK THE EDGE AND APPLY VINYL-TO-VINYL ADHESIVE TO ANY PAPER THAT OVERLAPS.** Press the seam area flat. Let the strips stand for half an hour, or as directed on the package, and then roll the seams. Rinse excess paste off with a damp sponge.

WALLPAPERING OUTSIDE CORNERS

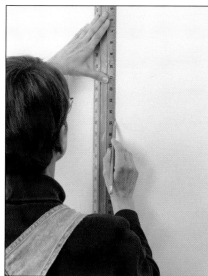

1 **DRAW A GUIDE LINE.** If the corner is out of plumb, the edge of paper you wrap around it will also be out of plumb. Lay out a plumb line that you can use as a guide. Start by measuring from the existing strip to the corner at the top, bottom and middle of the wall. Add ½ inch to the longest distance and subtract the total from a the width of a strip of paper. Draw a line this distance from the corner.

2 **MEASURE THE WIDTH OF THE CUTOFF.** Draw a plumb line on the wall that is this distance from the cut edge of the previous strip. Hang the cutoff. Align the leading edge with the plumb line, and smooth the paper against the wall. Slide the paper to match the pattern, overlapping the previous strip as necessary.

3 **CUT THE PAPER AT THE TOP AND BOTTOM USING WALLPAPER SCISSORS** so you can wrap it smoothly around the corner.

Wallpapering around windows and doors

Think of window and door openings as simply larger electrical outlets. Paper over them, at least in part, and then cut off the waste. Hang the strip as you normally would, right over the window or door casing. (A common mistake made when hanging wallpaper is to precut the strips to "fit" the shape of the windows and doors. Given Murphy's Law and the tendency of wallpaper to stretch, this inevitably fails.) Use a smoothing tool to smooth the strip before trimming the edges. Wipe any excess adhesive off casings with a wet sponge.

WORK SMARTER

BE STRIP WISE

If you're hanging short strips directly above and below an opening, draw a plumb line with your level to mark where the leading edge meets the wall. This helps to ensure a good pattern match with the full strip at the edge of the opening. Don't trim the short strips until you've hung the full strips and made sure they're plumb too. Leaving them long lets you jockey them into the correct position without creating gaps.

CLEANUP TIPS

Paperhangers aren't perfect, but the good ones have mastered a few tricks that make them look like they are:

- Club soda will break down dried glue without damaging the paper.

- If you have bubbles under the paper, smooth them toward seams. Don't cut the bubble unless the glue is dry. (See Fixing a Bubble, page 76.)

- Use clean water and change it frequently.

- Wipe excess glue from ceilings, cornices, and baseboard moldings before it dries or it will cause the paint to lift off the surface.

1 **PRIME AND SEAL THE WALLS.** (See page 59.) Position the strip on the wall, letting it cover the window or door casing. Butt the seam carefully against the edge of the previous strip. Smooth the flat areas of wallpaper with a smoothing tool. Press the strip tightly against the ceiling.

2 **HOLD YOUR FINGER AT THE CORNER OF THE TRIM** and cut diagonally toward it with wallpaper scissors. If you're hanging the paper around a window, make a similar cut in the bottom corner.

3 **PUSH THE PAPER TIGHT AGAINST THE TRIM** with a wallpaper knife or flexible smoother.

4 **USE WALLPAPER SCISSORS TO TRIM EXCESS WALLPAPER** to within about 1 inch of the outside edge of the window frame. Smooth the wallpaper and any bubbles as you work.

5 HOLD THE WALLPAPER AGAINST THE CASING WITH A BROAD KNIFE AND TRIM THE EXCESS WITH A RAZOR KNIFE. Trim the overlaps at the ceiling and baseboard. Then rinse the wallpaper and casings with a damp sponge.

6 CUT SHORT WALLPAPER STRIPS FOR THE SECTIONS ABOVE AND BELOW THE WINDOW. Draw a plumb line, guided by a short level, to mark the outside edge of the paper. Hang the strip, and double-check to make sure it's plumb. Work your way across the opening. Repeat below the window.

7 CUT AND PREPARE THE NEXT STRIP. No matter how careful you've been, the wallpaper will want to hang at an angle here. Snap a plumb line to guide placement of the outside edge. Hang the strip, aligning the edge with the line. If necessary, adjust the previous strip for a better match.

8 SNIP THE TOP AND BOTTOM CORNERS DIAGONALLY FROM THE EDGE OF THE PAPER TO THE CORNERS OF THE CASING. Trim any excess wallpaper to about 1 inch around the inside of the window or door frame.

9 ON WINDOWS YOU ALSO NEED TO MATCH THE SEAMS BELOW THE SILL. Use wallpaper scissors to trim any excess wallpaper to about 1 inch. Then flatten the strip with a smoothing tool.

10 HOLD THE WALLPAPER AGAINST THE CASING WITH A BROAD KNIFE AND CUT THE EXCESS WITH A RAZOR KNIFE. Trim the overlaps at the ceiling and baseboard. Rinse the wallpaper and casings with a damp sponge.

Wallpapering a recessed window

1 **HANG A STRIP OVER THE OPENING FOR THE WINDOW AS IF THE OPENING WEREN'T THERE.** Make two horizontal cuts—one slightly above the top of the opening, the other slightly above the bottom. Fold the flap formed by the cuts against the side walls of the recess. Fold the remaining paper over to form a flap on the sill and on the recessed wall above the window. Measure 2 inches to the right of the corner of the recess, and make a cut straight up and down from it to the ceiling. Remove paper at right of the cut.

2 **CUT A STRIP LONG ENOUGH TO REACH FROM THE CEILING AROUND THE TOP EDGE OF THE RECESS AND TO OVERLAP THE WINDOW SLIGHTLY.** Always make your cuts with a clean, fresh blade. Starting at the ceiling, hang the strip so it overlaps the entire width of the first strip. Align your straightedge with the edge of the window and cut along it to the corner of the opening. Fold the paper around the top edge of the recess and smooth it in place. Repeat below the window, as shown.

3 **YOU'RE ABOUT TO MAKE WHAT PAPERHANGERS CALL A "DOUBLE CUT," A PROCESS LESS FRIGHTENING THAN IT SOUNDS.** Align a straightedge with the left-hand edge of the recess. Cut along the edge, cutting through both layers of paper. Pull off the scrap to the left of the cut. Peel back the right-hand strip, and remove any paper underneath it. Put the right-hand strip back in place, smooth it, and roll the seam. Repeat below the window.

4 **IF THE REMAINING UNPAPERED SPACE ABOVE THE RECESS IS MORE THAN ONE STRIP WIDE,** hang the next strip, wrapping the paper around the top edge of the recess and across the upper recessed wall, trimming it at the window. Repeat below the window.

5 **POSITION THE NEXT STRIP SO THAT IT OVERLAPS THE PREVIOUS STRIPS COMPLETELY** and hangs from ceiling to floor. Cut vertically at the edge of the recess and fold the flap against the recess above the window and at the sill.

6 **ALIGN A STRAIGHTEDGE WITH THE EDGE OF THE RECESS AND DOUBLE-CUT BY GUIDING A KNIFE ALONG IT.** Peel back the top layer of paper as necessary to remove any scrap underneath.

Wallpapering inside an archway

① APPLY WALLPAPER ON BOTH SIDES OF THE ARCHWAY with strips hanging over the opening. Smooth the strips and trim the excess at the ceiling and baseboard.

② USE WALLPAPER SCISSORS TO TRIM THE WALLPAPER in the archway to about 1 inch below the arch.

Use vinyl-to-vinyl adhesive with vinyl and vinyl-coated wallpapers.

③ MAKE SLITS IN THE WALLPAPER ALONG THE CURVED PORTION OF THE ARCHWAY, cutting as close as possible to the wall edge. Cut carefully to avoid snipping into paper that will be covering the wall of the arch. The steeper the arch, the more slits you'll need to make.

④ WRAP THE CUT EDGES INSIDE THE ARCHWAY AND PRESS FLAT. If the adjacent room is being wallpapered, wrap the wallpaper around the edge of the archway from both sides.

⑤ MEASURE THE WIDTH OF THE ARCHWAY AND CUT A STRIP TO COVER IT FROM THE PAPER YOU'RE USING. The strip should be ¼ inch narrower than the inside surface of the archway.

⑥ COAT THE BACK OF THE ARCHWAY STRIP WITH VINYL-TO-VINYL ADHESIVE. Position the strip along the inside of the archway with a ⅛-inch space on each edge of the strip. Smooth the strip with a smoothing brush and rinse with a damp sponge.

Wallpapering around obstacles

Hanging wallpaper around sinks, pipes, and other obstacles requires careful cutting into the body of the wallpaper strips. Hold the strips so the patterns match, and cut from the edge closest to the fixture.

If possible, cut along a pattern line to hide the slit. At the end of the slit, cut an opening to fit around the fixture, cutting as close as possible to the fixture without damaging it.

Around wall-mounted sinks, tuck the small ends of the wallpaper overlaps behind the sink rather than cutting the wallpaper flush with the edge of the sink. This will provide a more professional and finished look.

SKILL SCALE

EASY	**MEDIUM**	HARD

REQUIRED SKILLS: Hanging wallpaper, measuring, and cutting.

HOW LONG WILL IT TAKE?

Experienced . . . . 30 min.
Handy . . . . 45 min.
Novice . . . . 1 hr.

STUFF YOU'LL NEED

✔ MATERIALS:
Wallpaper strips, wallpaper paste or activator, tube or strip silicone caulk

✔ TOOLS:
Wallpaper brush, razor knife, yardstick, wallpaper table, smoothing tool, chalk line, putty knife

A constant supply of fresh razor blades is essential. Change blades as often as every cut for best results.

WALLPAPERING AROUND A WALL-MOUNTED SINK

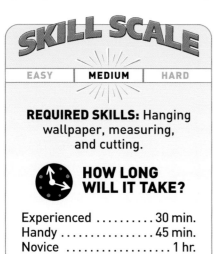

1 BRUSH THE WALLPAPER STRIP TO THE EDGE OF THE SINK. Cut from the edge about a third of the way toward the wall, and then cut back toward the upper and lower edges of the sink, stopping about ½ to 1 inch short of the edge of the sink. Use a smoothing tool to press the paper against the wall and into the edges of the sink.

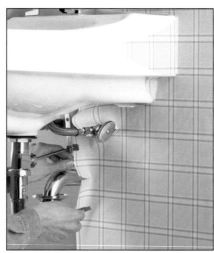

2 MAKE A SINGLE KNIFE CUT WHEREVER THE PAPER MEETS A PIPE, cutting from the edge of the paper past the obstruction. Put the paper against the wall, smoothing the excess so that it is against the pipes. Trim off the excess with a knife.

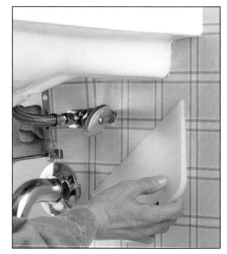

3 SMOOTH THE WALLPAPER WITH A SMOOTHING TOOL. Trim the paper off the side of the sink. Tuck the excess wallpaper along the top of the sink between the sink and wall, if possible. Otherwise, trim the overlap and caulk to cover the exposed paper edge.

WALLPAPERING BEHIND A RADIATOR

Electric baseboard heaters

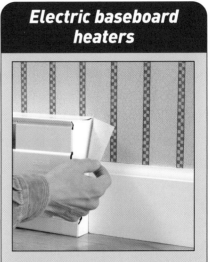

1 **UNFOLD THE ENTIRE STRIP AND POSITION IT ON THE WALL.** Smooth the strip from the ceiling to the top of the radiator. Use a flat, wooden yardstick to lightly smooth the strip down behind the radiator. Crease the wallpaper along the baseboard with the yardstick.

2 **PULL THE BOTTOM OF THE STRIP UP FROM BEHIND THE RADIATOR.** Trim the wallpaper along the crease line. Smooth the paper back down behind the radiator with the yardstick.

Electric baseboard heaters are wallpapered the same as other wall-mounted fixtures. Brush the strip up to the edge of the heater. Then trim the wallpaper around the heater, leaving a slight overlap, which you can tuck behind.

When good things come to an end: handling transitions

Wallpaper doesn't always wrap conveniently around a corner. Sometimes you want to end it mid-wall; sometimes it runs into and ends at ceramic tile; sometimes it reaches the corner but doesn't wrap around it.

The trick isn't in ending the paper—generally all that's required is not putting up the next strip. If you've picked a stopping point that doesn't fall at the edge of a strip width, measure carefully and cut the strip before you hang it. Attempting to cut it on the wall is a good way to 1) cut into the wall; 2) move the paper you've so carefully positioned; and 3) get a ragged seam. Instead of cutting on the wall, book the paper and cut it on the table. Cut it the same way you would when cutting a corner strip. (See Wallpapering Inside and Outside Corners, page 66.)

An unprotected edge is vulnerable to ripping and loosening, so once the glue has dried, you'll need to find a way to protect the edge. If the paper ends where it meets ceramic tile, cut it to width and then caulk it. Run a narrow bead of caulk along the transition (or use the new peelable strip caulk for a neatly finished edge). Get a silicone caulk, and pick a color that handles the transition well. On a light paper, white may be your best choice, but you also may be able to find a color that complements the tile or the paper and seems to disappear once you adhere it. Cut a hole about 1/8 inch in diameter in the tip of the caulk tube, break the seal in the tube, and run the bead along the edge of the tile. Wet your finger and run it along the caulk to create a smooth, narrow line of caulk. Wipe up the excess with a damp cloth.

If the paper ends at an outside corner it is vulnerable to peeling as people brush by. (In fact, you'll want to protect any outside corner in a high-traffic area,

whether the paper ends there or not.) One option is to use a clear plastic corner guard, either a nail-on or self-stick model. You can also use wooden trim such as a corner molding—an L-shaped profile with flat, unadorned surfaces. Nail it over the corner. Specialty houses sell Victorian corner molding that is turned to a simple but interesting shape on a lathe, then notched to fit over a corner.

If you've stopped the paper mid-wall, protect the edge with a decorative molding. Any molding, from simple half round to fancy baseboard or door trim, will do the trick. Find one you like, then paint or stain it before installation. Be sure you nail one edge of the molding over the paper edge. Stop the molding a couple of inches above the baseboard to avoid visual clutter where the profiles meet.

Wallpapering ceilings

Wallpapering a ceiling is always a two-person job, so collect a favor from someone. Use a heavy-duty adhesive and give yourself plenty of time to complete the job. If you are using the same paper on the walls, paper the ceiling first and make sure to match the seams from ceiling to walls.

| EASY | MEDIUM | **HARD** |

REQUIRED SKILLS: Covering an 8×10 foot ceiling requires basic wallpapering skills.

HOW LONG WILL IT TAKE?

Experienced . . . . 8 hrs.
Handy . . . . 12 hrs.
Novice . . . . 16 hrs.

VARIABLES: Set aside a weekend to complete wallpapering a ceiling.

Designer Tip

EMBOSSED PAPERS
If you like the look of tin, tooled leather, or ornamental plaster for your ceiling, try installing a vinyl embossed paper to save time and expense. This material can be painted and detailed by a brush or roller. Embossed papers will hide cracks and unevenness in plaster ceilings.

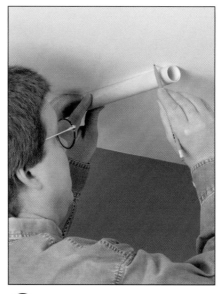

1 PRIME AND PATCH THE CEILING. Lay out the paper on the ceiling so that the strips will overlap the wall by about ½ inch. To lay out the strip, hold a roll of paper against the ceiling at one side of the room. Make a mark on the ceiling ½ inch from the end of the roll. Go to the other side of the room and make a similar mark.

2 SNAP A CHALK LINE CONNECTING THE TWO MARKS. Use blue chalk— red chalk will bleed through the paper. Cut a strip of paper to the proper length and then apply wallpaper paste activator.

3 WORKING IN SMALL SECTIONS, POSITION THE STRIP AGAINST THE GUIDELINE. Overlap the side wall by ½ inch and the end walls by 2 inches. Flatten the strip with a smoothing brush as you work. If the walls will be covered with matching wallpaper, trim the ceiling wallpaper so it overlaps the wall by ½ inch. On walls that will not be covered, trim the excess by holding a broad knife against the corner and cutting with a razor knife.

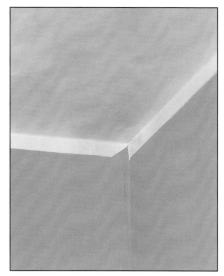

4 CUT OUT A SMALL WEDGE OF WALLPAPER IN THE CORNER SO THAT THE STRIP WILL LIE SMOOTH. Press the wallpaper into the corner with a broad knife.

Finishing touches

PAPERING COVER PLATES

1 REMOVE THE COVER PLATE AND REINSERT THE SCREWS. Place wallpaper over the fixture so the patterns match. Rub the surface of the wallpaper to emboss the outline of the fixture.

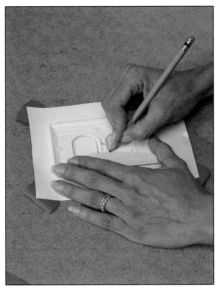

2 ALIGN THE COVER PLATE ON THE WALLPAPER WITH THE EMBOSSED MARKS. Mark the corners of the cover plate and the openings with a pencil. Trim the wallpaper ½ inch wider than the cover plate. Trim the corners diagonally, cutting just outside the corner marks.

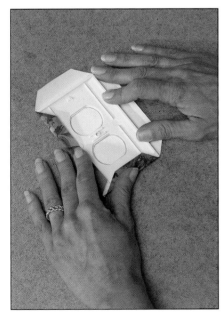

3 APPLY VINYL-ON-VINYL ADHESIVE TO THE COVER PLATE AND WALLPAPER. Attach the cover plate to the wallpaper and smooth out bubbles. Wrap the overlap around the cover plate and tape the edges in place.

4 CUT OUT THE COVER PLATE OPENINGS WITH A RAZOR KNIFE AND MOUNT THE PLATE IN PLACE. Open up the screw hole by gently pushing a finishing nail through it from front to back. Attach to the wall with a screw.

Checking your wallpaper job

How to get professional wallpapering results:
After you have finished wallpapering a room, check for final touch-ups while the job is still fresh.

- Pay special attention to the seams. If you rolled the seams too hard or rolled them before the adhesive set, you may have squeezed too much adhesive from under the edges of the covering. These edges will look tight while they are wet but will bubble after the wallpaper is dry.

- Stand close to the wall, looking down its length with a strong sidelight to check for imperfections.

- Use a strong sidelight to see any bubbles or loose spots in the coverage. See page 76 for fixes.

BUYER'S GUIDE

CLEAR PLASTIC COVER PLATES—THERE IS A BETTER MOUSETRAP!
Covering switchplates and receptacle plates takes less time to do than it does to explain. But if you're in a real hurry or just tired of messing with wallpaper, someone has come up with a quick fix. Check your paint and wallpaper department for a clear plastic cover made for wallpaper. It's really two pieces that snap together. Cut a piece of paper to fit, sandwich it between the two pieces, and then snap them together. You'll need to cut out a hole for the switch or outlets and poke a smaller hole for each screw. Finally screw the plate in place.

WALLPAPER

Repair and maintenance

FIXING A BUBBLE

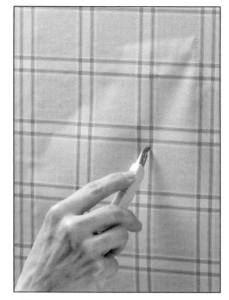

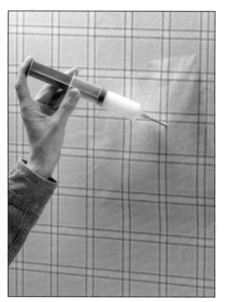

1 **CUT A SLIT THROUGH THE BUBBLE USING A RAZOR KNIFE.** If there is a pattern in the wallpaper, cut along a pattern line to hide the slit.

2 **INSERT THE TIP OF THE GLUE APPLICATOR THROUGH THE SLIT** and apply adhesive sparingly to the wall under the wallpaper. Sponge off excess glue.

Fixing Seams

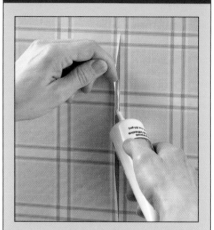

Dampen the wallpaper to make it easier to put back in position. Lift the wallpaper edge and insert the tip of the glue applicator. Squirt vinyl-to-vinyl adhesive onto the wall and gently press the seam flat. Let it stand for half an hour, smooth lightly with a roller, and wipe the seam lightly with a damp sponge.

PATCHING WALLPAPER

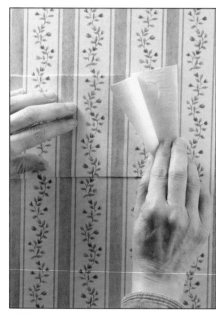

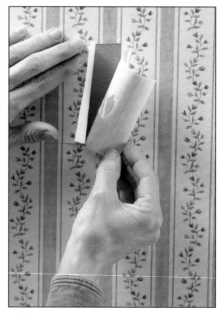

1 **FASTEN A SCRAP OF MATCHING WALLPAPER OVER THE DAMAGED PORTION** using blue painter's tape, aligning the scrap so that the patterns match.

2 **HOLDING A RAZOR KNIFE AT A 90-DEGREE ANGLE TO THE WALL,** cut through both layers of wallpaper. If the wallpaper has strong pattern lines, cut along the lines to hide the seams. With less definite patterns, you can cut irregular lines.

3 **REMOVE BOTH LAYERS OF PAPER.** Peel away the damaged wallpaper. Apply adhesive to the back of the patch and position it in the hole so that the pattern matches. Rinse the patched area with a damp sponge.

Hanging borders on painted walls

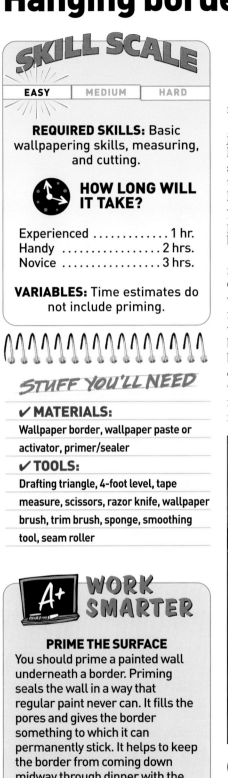
No matter where you put a border—along the ceiling, around a door or window, partway up the wall as a chair rail—installation is basically the same.

Start with priming and sizing—it's just as important for a border as it is for larger surfaces. Without priming and sizing, stains or paint may show through the border, and the paper is much more likely to peel off the wall within the first year. Get a combination wallpaper primer and sizing, and you can apply both in one step.

If you're applying the border as a chair rail, draw a layout line to guide you. Chair rails are typically one-third of the way up the wall, but there's no hard-and-fast rule. Look to see where the border will meet windows, for example. If the bottom of the trim would split the border in half, move the border up or down. Think too about how the border will look with furniture against it. If the furniture is going to hide all your work, move the border farther up the wall.

If the border will go along the top of the wall, the ceiling is your layout line. Tuck the border along the corner between the ceiling and wall. Because this is rarely perfectly straight, there are two things you should do to compensate. First, paint a strip of the ceiling color along the top ¼ inch of your wall. Secondly, keep your eye on the bottom edge of the border as you apply it to make sure it looks straight. If necessary, you can slide the border down the wall in spots to keep the edge straight. The ceiling paint you put on the wall will camouflage the resulting gap.

To figure out how much border you'll need, add up the length of all the walls. Add in the distance you'll need to go around any doors and windows, plus an extra foot for each turn you make. Plan ahead for waste. If the border is in 5- or 7-yard rolls, add at least ½ yard extra for each 5 yards you measure. If the border is in longer rolls, add 2 yards for each roll you use.

1 **LAY OUT A LINE MARKING THE TOP OF THE BORDER USING A PENCIL AND A LEVEL.** Draw a fine, faint line so that it won't show through once the border is up.

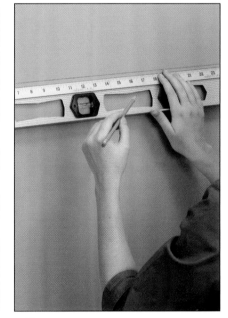

2 **YOU'LL NEED TO PRIME AND SIZE AN AREA SLIGHTLY NARROWER THAN THE BORDER.** To lay it out, draw a second line parallel to and ¼ inch below the first. To mark the bottom of the primed area, measure and draw a line ¼ inch above what will be the bottom of the border.

Hanging borders on painted walls *(continued)*

BORDER DISPUTE

Generally speaking, a chair rail goes about one-third of the way up the wall, but don't be a slave to fashion. If the room has windows, you may want to run the border so that it meets the bottom of the frame. If there's a sofa against the wall, you might want to position the border to run slightly above it. If you're trying to create an Arts and Crafts look, the molding might go as much as two-thirds of the way up the wall.

A plastic smoother is a good alternative to a straightedge.

3 **BRUSH A PRIMER/SEALER CAREFULLY BETWEEN THE LINES,** using a trim brush for better control. Let the primer dry according to the directions on the can.

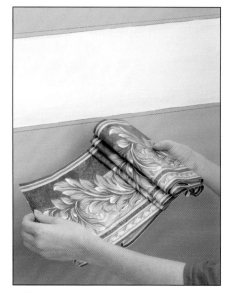

4 **BRUSH PASTE ACTIVATOR ONTO THE PAPER** (or paste if the paper isn't prepasted). To make the paper easier to handle, "ribbon-fold" the strip as shown so that the pasted sides face each other. Let the strip rest for a minute, or as directed by the activator manufacturer, so that the glue can reach full strength.

5 **HANGING ACTUALLY STARTS PARTWAY INTO THE LAST WALL YOU'LL PAPER.** Start the roll ½ inch from the corner on what will be the last wall. (Go as much as 4 inches for stiff paper.) Push the paper into the corner with a broad knife and continue along the wall, smoothing with a smoothing tool as you work.

6 **WHEN ONE ROLL RUNS OUT, JOIN IT TO THE NEXT WITH WHAT'S CALLED A "DOUBLE CUT."** Apply the end of the second roll so it overlaps the end of the first roll, and slide it until the patterns match. Cut through both strips, guiding the cut along a straightedge. Peel away the scraps and press the two pieces of border together. Smooth the paper. Roll the seam with a seam roller and sponge away excess paste.

7 **WHEN YOU REACH AN INSIDE CORNER, CUT THE STRIP SO THAT IT'S LONG ENOUGH TO RUN AROUND THE CORNER** and ½ inch onto the next wall. Place a dry strip over the first, align the patterns and make a crisp fold in the dry strip at the corner. Cut along the fold with a pair of scissors and hang the strip tight against the corner.

8 **IF YOU'RE TURNING AN OUTSIDE CORNER, THE BORDER WILL GO OUT OF LEVEL UNLESS THE CORNER IS PERFECTLY PLUMB.** To avoid this, cut the border so it's just 1 or 2 inches longer than the corner edge. Apply paste or activator to the cutoff and hang it so it just barely overlaps the paper on the wall. Align the new piece with the layout lines and continue down the wall.

9 **AS YOU FINISH THE LAST WALL, YOU'LL COME TO THE SMALL SECTION OF BORDER THAT STARTED THE JOB.** Lay the final strip over the small section, and push it into the corner with a broad knife, creating a crease. Cut along the crease with scissors and smooth the paper in place.

HOMER'S HINDSIGHT

ON THE (ALMOST) LEVEL
A lot of folks think that drawing lines across the wall with a level to put up a border is a bother. So they measure up from the floor at each end of the room and snap a line assuming the floor is level because it looks right. Well, the eye may accept a not-so-level floor but an out-of-level border looks like the mistake it is and will have to be replaced. If you're in doubt, tape your border in place first, and let your eye be the judge.

Make sure the pattern is right side up when adding the next strip.

MITERING BORDER CORNERS

1 **APPLY BOTH THE HORIZONTAL AND VERTICAL STRIPS SO THEY EXTEND BEYOND THE CORNER.** The extra length should be equal to the width of the border, plus at least 2 inches.

2 **CHECK THE POSITION OF THE BORDER STRIP TO MAKE SURE IMPORTANT PATTERN DESIGNS WILL REMAIN INTACT AT DIAGONAL CUTS.** Remove and adjust the strips if necessary. Then make a diagonal cut, guided by a broad knife, that goes through both layers of wallpaper.

3 **REMOVE THE CUT PIECES.** Press the border back in place, and let it stand for half an hour. Lightly roll the seams and clean off excess glue with a damp sponge.

Combining a border with wallpaper

REQUIRED SKILLS: Measuring, cutting, and hanging wallpaper.

HOW LONG WILL IT TAKE?

Experienced . . . . 6 hrs.
Handy . . . . 7 hrs.
Novice . . . . 8 hrs.

VARIABLES: Time is based on an 8×10 foot room. Rooms with damaged walls or additional doors and windows will take extra time. Time does not include priming.

STUFF YOU'LL NEED

✔ **MATERIALS:**

Primer, wallpaper paste or paste activator, wallpaper, companion border

✔ **TOOLS:**

Tape measure, 4-foot level, scissors, wallpaper smoothing tool, seam roller, single-edge razor blades with handle, sponge, chalk plumb tool

WORK SMARTER

APPLYING BORDERS OVER PAPERED WALLS

Applying a border over a papered wall is much like applying one to a painted wall. Don't prime or size, but make sure you use the right adhesive: vinyl-to-vinyl for vinyl papers and paste activators for most others. Lightly draw a single layout line marking either the top or bottom of the border. Cover the pencil mark by about 1/16 inch when you hang the border.

A paper chair rail can act as a border for wallpaper wainscoting or be used as trim for the bottom edge of wallpaper that covers the top two-thirds of the wall. Use a paper chair rail as a transition between patterns or textures.

It takes a little engineering to get everything to come out perfectly but not so much that you'll need a degree in mathematics. You'll need a sharp razor, a good straightedge, and patience.

The method shown will give the best results because it will eliminate shadow lines or ridges where the wallpaper and the border meet. It also will make matching complex patterns easier but will require a little practice and careful cutting. An advantage to this process is that you can change either the border or the paper without having to redo both sections. Two alternative applications are shown on page 81.

1 **DRAW A LEVEL PENCIL LINE ON THE WALL MARKING WHERE THE BOTTOM OF THE BORDER WILL BE.** Draw lightly, so that the line won't show through the border. Apply a primer/sealer between the pencil lines if you're putting border over paint.

2 **HANG THE BORDER THE SAME WAY YOU WOULD ON A PAINTED WALL.** Start in the corner with about ½ inch of the border overlapping the adjacent wall. Hang the paper along the wall using the line as a guide. Clean off your work with a damp sponge as you go.

3 **CHOOSE THE TOP OF THE FIRST STRIP OF WALLPAPER CAREFULLY.** Hold a scrap of border over the paper, sliding the border up and down to see how it looks on different parts of the paper. Choose a position that doesn't block out parts of the lower pattern such as the top of a flower or the head of a statue. When you find the right spot, cut the wallpaper a few inches above it. Then cut the paper to length, measuring from where the border will cross it and adding 3 inches for trimming.

4 DRAW A PLUMB LINE TO MARK WHERE THE EDGE OF THE PAPER WILL BE ON THE WALL. Draw it with the help of your level and position the line so that about ½ inch of paper goes around the corner and onto the adjacent wall. Hang the first strip of paper along the line, and position the top so it crosses the border as planned.

5 YOU'LL BE ABLE TO SEE A SLIGHT RIDGE IN THE PAPER WHERE IT CROSSES THE BOTTOM OF THE BORDER. Put a straightedge along the ridge and, with a new blade in your knife, cut along the straightedge through to the wall. Trim the bottom of the paper where it meets the baseboard.

6 GENTLY PULL BACK THE CUTOFF AND CLEAN UP ANY EXCESS GLUE WITH A DAMP SPONGE. Continue along the wall. Check each piece for plumb as you hang it. Smooth it with a smoothing tool, trim the top and bottom, and then hang the next piece. Continue until you've hung paper below the entire border.

PAPER AND BORDER INSTALLATION OPTIONS

LAY OUT A LINE FOR THE WALLPAPER WITH A STRAIGHTEDGE (see step 1, page 80). Apply the wallpaper around the room, following the line. Activate and book the border strip and apply it over the wallpaper, using the top of the wallpaper as a guide.

LAY A LINE FOR THE TOP AND BOTTOM OF THE BORDER WITH A STRAIGHTEDGE. Hang the wallpaper so it slightly overlaps the bottom border line. Hang the border following the top trim line once you've installed the wainscoting.

HOMER'S HINDSIGHT

CHALK IT UP TO EXPERIENCE
My wife, who loves to paint and paper, was snapping lines on the wall for a new project when she ran out of chalk. The store didn't have any blue so she bought red and went ahead with the job. Chalk is chalk, right? Well, when fuzzy red lines kept bleeding through the paint, we realized we had a problem. I did a little research and found out that red chalk is considered permanent and will bleed through paint and sometimes wallpaper unless you apply a special sealer. Blue (or yellow) washes off easily and won't bleed. We primed and sealed the walls, which solved the problem, but we'll use blue chalk from now on.

Combining wallpapers

Wallpaper, borders, and chair rails can each stand on their own, but they also can reinforce one another. The Victorians in particular loved to combine papers. Below the chair rail would be a paper with a dominant image. Above the rail a contrasting paper gave way to a wide ceiling border. Ceilings were papered. Sometimes ceiling borders and corner molding were layered on regular paper.

The current approach to wallpaper combinations is somewhat simplified in comparison, but most wallpaper pattern books do contain bold paper and border combinations designed to work well together. Homeowners can combine pattern books and their imaginations to suit their sense of style and taste.

The border snugs up against crown molding (above).

Coordinating wallpaper, fabric, and painted surfaces provides dynamic decorating options (left).

In the dynamic Victorian scheme (above), the border offers a bold break from the rest of the paper, framing the wall like a frieze and dramatically separating the walls and ceiling.

A wallpaper chair rail repeats as a border at the ceiling (above), and both chair rail and border are framed between wooden chair and crown molding.

Matching the curtains and wallpaper presents a lush, sensual effect (above).

CLOSER LOOK

WONDERFUL EXCESS

A well-appointed Victorian room took wallpaper to its zenith. Across the top of the wall would be a wide border called a **frieze**. Below it, the paper ran two-thirds or more of the way down the wall. It was usually printed with a small, repetitive pattern called **fill**. Below the fill was a **border** applied at chair-rail height. A bold-patterned paper, called the **dado**, ran down from the chair rail.

Just above the baseboard, the dado met yet a third border, distinct from but complementary to, the frieze and chair rail. This lower border ran along the baseboard and around the doors and windows.

Sometimes a wallpaper corner block would be applied wherever the border turned a corner. Sound complicated? This is precise work where mistakes easily can be made. But if you've mastered a border with two complementary papers and actually liked doing it, you may be a candidate for the full Victorian treatment.

Ask your wallpaper dealer (or check renovation magazines) to find makers of reproduction papers. You'll find a world of papers you never dreamed possible. Start small. Look at some dados that include both the chair rail and baseboard borders, making the job much easier.

3 PLUMBING

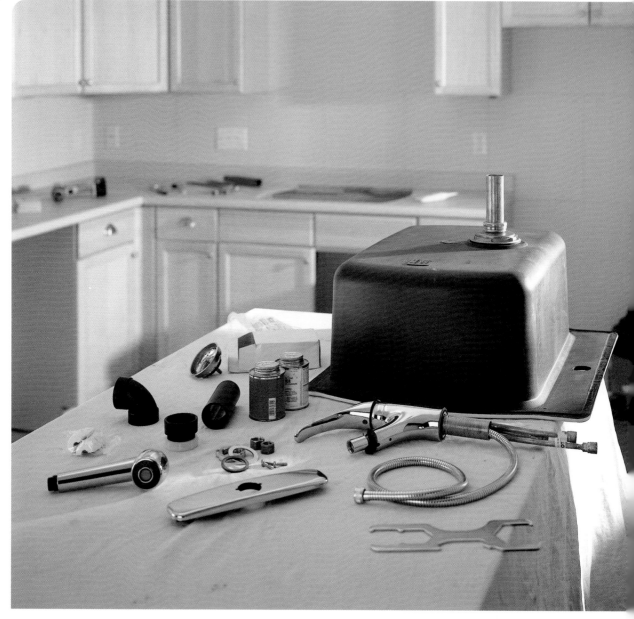

PLUMBING PROJECTS ARE OFTEN **UNPREDICTABLE.** Failures and leaks can happen at any time and have to be dealt with quickly and efficiently.

You do have choices when you're remodeling or upgrading; you can pick projects within your skill level. The key to success is common sense. Do your homework. Make a good plan. Become familiar with the materials and equipment needed for the job. Ask yourself: "Can I do this and do I have the time?" If the answer is yes, get started!

A working knowledge of your plumbing system will help you understand why something isn't working properly. Make a map showing how the plumbing in your home is installed. Know where the water meter and the main shutoff valve are located. Find out where water comes into the house and where the drainpipes and traps flow out.

Begin with easy projects. Most repair and maintenance jobs are fairly simple. Check throughout the house to see if repairs are needed. Does a faucet drip? Is the toilet acting up? Once you've mastered basic skills, you'll be ready to move to more complicated projects such as new installations and remodeling jobs.

SECTION 3 PROJECTS

REAL-WORLD SITUATIONS

MOM, THERE'S A SWIMMING POOL IN THE BASEMENT!

Plumbers will tell you two things about their trade: Water is tricky stuff, and there aren't any standard sizes. Here are some sure-fire plumbing tips from the professionals:

● **Leaks happen.** That's why plumbers have jobs. The first rule is that there are no easy fixes. Magic powders, pastes, and incantations won't solve the problem. Get some advice from a knowledgeable salesperson and do the job right the first time.

● **If you're working in plastic, clean and prime it before you cement it.** With copper, the only solid joint is a clean joint: Polish the surface with emery cloth, deburr the inside of the fitting with a wire brush, and brush on plenty of flux to further clean the surfaces. (You can never apply too much flux.)

● **If the joint has a compression fitting—a little metal sleeve that squishes tightly against the fitting to prevent leaks—you won't need solder.** But, you can only use the sleeve once and will have replace it every time you disconnect the fitting. Sleeves are cheap and the job is easy, but eventually the pipe will become too short to use.

● **Don't apply logic to plumbing sizes.** A faucet supply line and a toilet supply line are different diameters, for example. Kitchen faucets won't fit in a bathroom sink, and toilets are one of three different distances from the wall. There are at least a dozen kinds of toilet flappers and countless faucet washers.

Fortunately, a good salesperson can often look at a faucet stem and tell you the manufacturer and which part you need to fix it. While they can often recognize a part, they are seldom able to look across town and see inside your kitchen. Bring the piece in—or as much of it as you can. If it's too big, bring a photo. Call ahead to find out what else you need to know or bring. It's the best chance you'll get of walking out of the store with the right part.

How the plumbing system works

Understanding your home's plumbing system: Water enters your house through a main supply line. It passes through a water meter and a portion of the incoming water is then branched off to enter your water heater. The heated water and the remaining cold water are then piped to fixtures throughout the house. Toilets need only cold water. Waste water travels by gravity, but first it must pass through a trap located below each fixture. Traps allow water to flow through but prevent sewer gas from drifting up the drain. Vents on the roof let in air. This allows waste water to flow freely to the waste and vent stack and out the sewer line.

MULTISTORY CONSTRUCTION

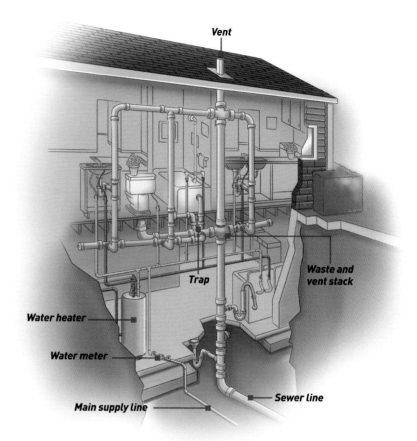

Vent

Waste and vent stack

Trap

Water heater

Water meter

Sewer line

Main supply line

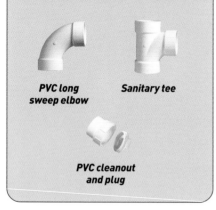
SLAB CONSTRUCTION

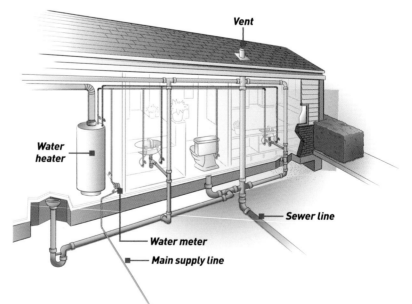

Vent

Water heater

Water meter

Main supply line

Sewer line

Qualify yourself for plumbing projects

Assess your basic skills, accurately and honestly, to pick projects that you can complete successfully and with confidence. Store associates at home centers qualify customers for plumbing projects by asking some basic questions to get a sense of their abilities.

QUALIFYING QUIZ

- **Do you mind getting wet? How about dirty?** Some plumbing projects can get messy; that's just the nature of the job.

- **How about doing physical labor?** Tubs, toilets, and water heaters are heavy. The ability to do physical labor is an important part of the job.

- **Do you have the time?** Once you take something apart, you have to live without it until you finish the job. Check out the time estimates we give, and make sure you have the time you need.

- **Are you a tinkerer?** If you're good at taking things apart and putting them back together, you can learn plumbing skills.

- **Are you willing to research projects and make a plan?** Doing your homework to develop an understanding of the process and scope of a project is essential. Learn the skills you'll need and explore all the safety issues before you start.

- **Do you enjoy working on your house?** If you don't enjoy maintaining and improving your home, you may not want to replace a sink or fix a leak.

- **Do you know your limitations?** It's OK to admit that a particular project is a little beyond your current skill level. It's better to pay a professional to do a job you're not comfortable with than to pay one even more to fix your mistake.

    OK, YOU'RE QUALIFIED. Once you've answered these questions and qualified yourself, you're ready to choose your projects.

"REPLACING A CARTRIDGE FAUCET," (See page 112.)

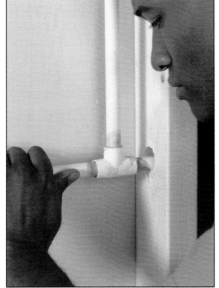

"CONNECTING CPVC," (See page 91.)

TIME SAVER

KNOW WHEN TO CALL A PLUMBER!
Homeowners often like to take on new challenges, but when it comes to home repair, sometimes it's best to be cautious. Flooding your basement or having to tear down a finished project because you didn't do the installation properly can be an expensive lesson. Don't be afraid to call a plumber when there's an emergency or if you're just not sure how to proceed with a project.

WORK SMARTER

GROWING YOUR SKILLS

The key to growing your skills is learning to do things correctly from the start. Looking for shortcuts before you understand the basics can lead to costly mistakes. Plumbing is a process. It helps to know how something works before you try to fix it. Pick a project you're comfortable with, assemble all the tools and materials you'll need, and review the entire process by reading all of the instructions before you start. Once everything is in place, all you have to do is follow the step-by-step instructions until project completion.

Your skills will grow in proportion to your willingness to do things right.

THE PLUMBER'S TOOL KIT

Below are some basic plumbing tools. For more information
see the Tool Glossary on page 544.

4-IN-1 COMBINATION TOOL

CORDLESS REVERSIBLE ⅜-INCH DRILL

HAND AUGER

PLASTIC PIPE PRIMER

SELF-ADJUSTING PLIERS

SPUD WRENCH

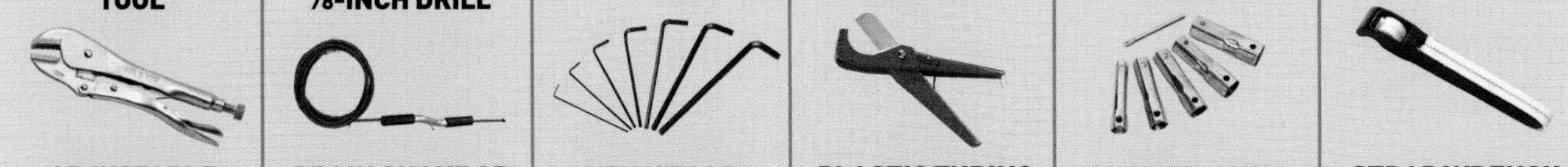

ADJUSTABLE LOCKING PLIERS

DRAIN SNAKE OR DRAIN AUGER

HEX KEY OR ALLEN WRENCH SET

PLASTIC TUBING CUTTER

SHOWER-STEM SOCKET

STRAP WRENCH

ADJUSTABLE WRENCH

EMERY CLOTH

LEAD-FREE FLUX AND SOLDER

PLUMBER'S PUTTY

SILICONE GREASE

TAPE MEASURE

BASIN WRENCHES

FAUCET HANDLE PULLER

MAPP TORCH

PUTTY KNIVES

SLIP PLIERS

TEFLON PASTE

BASKET STRAINER WRENCH

FLANGED PLUNGER

NEEDLE-NOSE PLIERS

RATCHET-TYPE PVC CUTTER

SLOTTED AND PHILLIPS SCREWDRIVERS

TEFLON TAPE

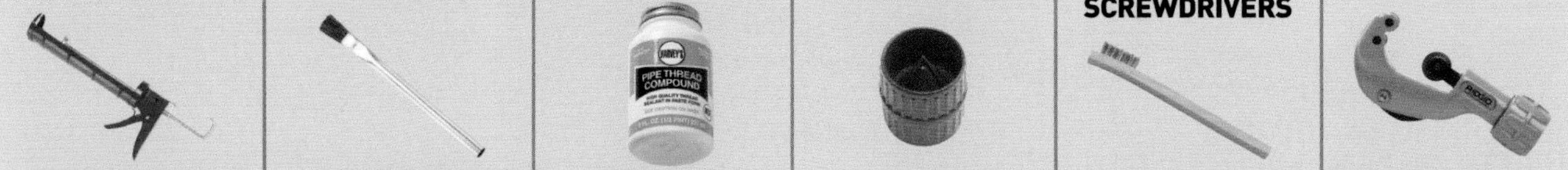

CAULKING GUN

FLUX BRUSH

PIPE JOINT COMPOUND

REAMER (PVC)

SMALL WIRE BRUSH

TUBING CUTTER

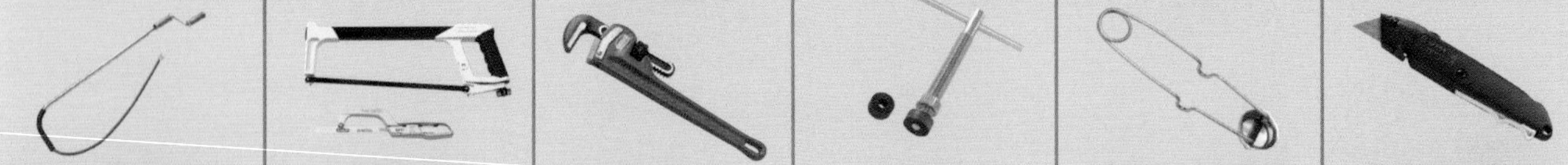

CLOSET AUGER

HACKSAWS

PIPE WRENCH

SEAT DRESSING TOOL

SPARK LIGHTER

UTILITY KNIFE

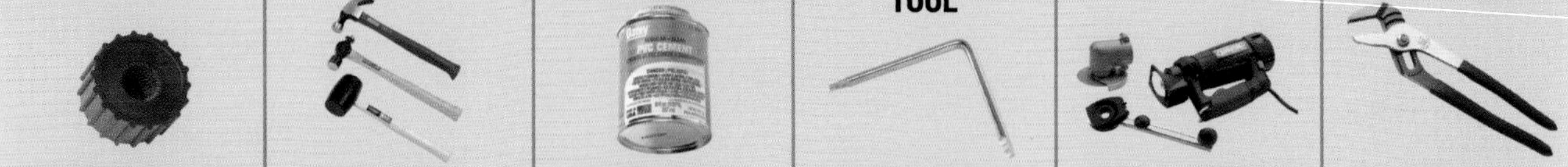

COPPER TUBING DEBURRER

HAMMERS

PLASTIC PIPE CEMENT

SEAT WRENCH

SPIRAL CUTTING SAW

WATER-PUMP PLIERS

CONNECTING RIGID PLASTIC PIPE

REQUIRED SKILLS: Cutting rigid plastic pipe and connecting plumbing fittings.

HOW LONG WILL IT TAKE?

Experienced .... 10 min.
Handy .... 20 min.
Novice .... 25 min.

VARIABLES: Time is for cutting and assembling a single joint. Complicated runs take longer.

BUYER'S GUIDE

USE THE RIGHT PRIMER

If you want your work to pass inspection—and not leak—use the right primer. Purple-tinted primer is required by code for drainage lines and will also work on supply lines. Clear primers are fine on supply lines but won't pass inspection when it comes to drain lines. Save yourself some grief—buy the purple primer and use it everywhere.

Rigid plastic pipe was developed to replace cast iron and galvanized steel in plumbing supply and waste systems. Plastic pipe is cost-effective and easy to install. Use rigid plastic PVC (or ABS if codes allow) for drain, waste, and vent systems. Use CPVC or PEX for hot and cold water supplies. Plastic pipe is available with inside diameters (ID) of $1\frac{1}{4}, 1\frac{1}{2}, 2, 3$, and 4 inches.

● Use $1\frac{1}{4}$-, $1\frac{1}{2}$-, and 2-inch ID PVC for sink drains and lavatories.

● Use $1\frac{1}{2}$- and 2-inch ID pipe for tubs and showers.

● Use 3- or 4-inch ID pipe for toilets. New 1.6-gallon flush toilets work best with a 3-inch fitting.

● Drain lines and vent stacks can use 2-, 3-, or 4-inch ID pipe.

ASSEMBLE QUICKLY. Plastic pipe is joined with fast-acting solvent cements. Once you glue a fitting in place, it can't be removed—you have to cut it apart and start over. You can't twist fittings apart, and fine-tuning is impossible. Cut sections to length and test-fit the entire run before cementing the lines in place.

DRY-FIT ALL THE CONNECTIONS BEFORE THE FINAL ASSEMBLY. Dry-fit the connections before applying primer and cement—once you've cemented the pipe, it can't be changed. Check the fall with a level. There should be a $\frac{1}{4}$-inch fall, or slope, for each lineal foot of run.

WORK SMARTER

TIPS FOR CONNECTING RIGID PLASTIC PIPE

❶ Use the correct pipe cleaners, primers and cements for the pipe you're installing. CPVC, PVC, and ABS are not interchangeable without transition fittings or special glue.

❷ Cure time depends on the cement used, the size and tolerance of the pipe and fitting, and the air temperature. You will weaken the bond by trying to speed or retard the cure.

❸ Keep lids on cements and primers when not in use.

❹ Stir or shake cement before using.

❺ The size of the adhesive and primer applicator, called a "dauber," depends on the size of its container. You'll want a $\frac{1}{4}$-inch dauber on small-diameter pipes; a $1\frac{1}{2}$-inch dauber for pipes up to 3 inches; and a natural-bristle brush, swab, or roller half the pipe diameter for pipes 4 inches or more. Try to buy a can that has a dauber that matches the job at hand.

❻ Do not mix primer with cement. Do not use thickened or lumpy cement. Cement should have the consistency of syrup or honey.

❼ Do not handle joints until they are fully cured.

❽ All colored cements and primers will leave a permanent and recognizable stain.

CONNECTING RIGID PLASTIC PIPE
Connecting PVC

STUFF YOU'LL NEED

✔ **MATERIALS:**
PVC pipe and fittings, cleaner, primer cement

✔ **TOOLS:**
Tubing cutter, hacksaw or miter saw and box, deburring tool, knife, emery cloth, rags

CLOSER LOOK

LOOKS CAN BE DECEIVING
Each type of plastic pipe is composed of different materials and requires its own blend of cleaners and cements to make a proper bond. If you have to join PVC to ABS, you'll need a special glue transition fitting to make the connection. Ask at the store, and check local codes.

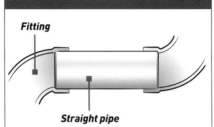

A tight fit

Fitting

Straight pipe

For a PVC joint to be effective the pipe must seat itself fully into the fitting. Without the adhesive as a lubricant, it's often hard to see if the pipe is seated properly.

1 A STRAIGHT, SQUARE CUT IS NECESSARY FOR A GOOD CONNECTION. PVC tubing cutters are made for both small- and large-diameter pipes. If you don't have a cutter, you can cut the pipe with a miter saw, hacksaw, or power miter saw. Take your time and make sure you get a clean, square cut. Deburr the inside and outside edges of the pipe, and test-fit before final assembly. Clean the pipe with the manufacturer's recommended cleaner, and use the correct primer and adhesive to ensure a solid joint.

2 DEBURR THE CUT. After each cut, deburr the pipe with a deburring tool, knife, or emery cloth to remove rough edges that could interfere with the flow of water or the fit of the joint. Sand the section of pipe that will be housed by the fitting too. If you don't, the pipe won't travel as far into the fitting as it will once you apply glue. The run will be slightly short as a result.

3 APPLY PRIMER TO THE CONNECTIONS. The primer softens the ends, preparing them for application of the cement. An inspector will often look for the permanent purple stain at the joint to make sure primer was used to help make the connection.

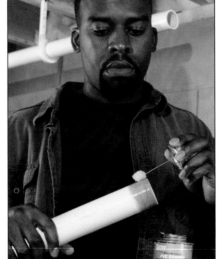

4 COAT THE PIPE AND FITTING WITH CEMENT. While the primer is still damp, quickly apply a thin, even coat of cement to the surfaces. Too much cement can weaken the pipe and destroy the fitting.

5 WORK QUICKLY TO CONNECT THE PIECES. Insert the pipe into the fitting with a quick push and a quarter-turn to seat. Hold the connection for 30 seconds to prevent the heat produced by the cement from pushing the connection apart. The cement melts the surfaces and forms a secure bond. With a rag, wipe away excess cement, which can weaken the joint.

Connecting CPVC

STUFF YOU'LL NEED

✔ **MATERIALS:**
CPVC pipe and fittings, primer, dauber cement

✔ **TOOLS:**
Tubing cutter, hacksaw or miter saw and box, deburring tool, knife, emery cloth, rags

SAFETY ALERT

DANGEROUS FUMES
Fumes from primers and cements can lead to loss of consciousness. Work in a ventilated area. The fumes are also highly inflammable and explosive. DO NOT smoke or use torches or electric tools that spark (such as power drills) near areas where there may be fumes.

TOOL TIP

JOINING CPVC TO COPPER
You may run into a situation where copper pipe is in the walls and you don't want to remove it but you want to run CPVC for the hot and cold water supply for your new sink. No problem! A special transition fitting available at your home center or hardware store can join CPVC to brass or copper.

Deburring (removing debris left from cutting the pipe) is essential. Chips and chunks, both inside and outside, affect the final bond.

CPVC is used for hot and cold water supply. It is less expensive than copper but just as durable, and it withstands high temperatures and pressure in the supply system. It cuts easily with a tubing cutter or hacksaw, connections are easy, and assembly is quick.

One-step cements are available for CPVC and eliminate the need to use purple primer, but one-step cements may not meet local code in many areas. Check local codes carefully to determine if primer is required. In some localities, you will fail inspection if you don't use it. Purple primer leaves a permanent and recognizable stain on the pipe, so inspectors will know whether you've used it. It's a lot easier to do the job up to code the first time to avoid the hassle of redoing it when the inspector fails your installation.

1 **DEBURR THE PIPE.** Removing burrs ensures even coverage with the primer and cement. Once you've deburred, sand *lightly* with emery cloth, so that the pipe will seat in the bottom of the fitting.

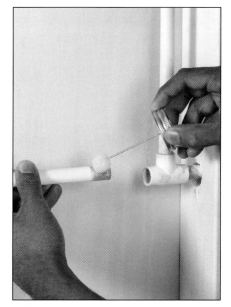

2 **COAT THE SURFACES WITH PRIMER IF REQUIRED.** Apply an even coat of primer to the pipe and the fitting. Primer softens the pipe to help seat it and reacts with the cement to make a permanent bond. Using a purple primer is essential in areas where priming is required by code. The resulting stain tells the inspector the joint has been properly treated prior to connecton.

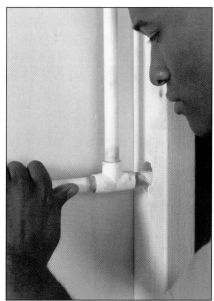

3 **APPLY CEMENT AND ASSEMBLE THE PARTS QUICKLY BUT CAREFULLY.** Use a dauber to apply an even coat of cement to the pipe and fitting and insert the pipe all the way into the fitting until it stops. Twist a quarter of a turn to spread the cement evenly. Hold the pipe together for 30 seconds to prevent the heat generated by the cement from pushing the connection apart. With a clean rag, wipe off excess cement between the fitting and pipe.

PLUMBING

Connecting ABS

STUFF YOU'LL NEED

✔ **MATERIALS:**
ABS pipe and fittings, cleaner, primer cement, dauber

✔ **TOOLS:**
Tubing cutter, hacksaw or miter saw and box, deburring tool, rags

PLUMBING

The first rigid plastic pipe approved for use in drain, waste, and vent systems was ABS. It is inexpensive, easy to cut, lightweight, and very rigid. However, it becomes brittle over time and therefore is susceptible to cracking and breaking.

Before purchasing ABS pipe, check your local plumbing codes. Some communities forbid the use of ABS.

❶ CUT AND DEBURR THE PIPE. Removing burrs ensures even coverage with the primer and cement. Sanding can change the diameter and cause a poor fit. Test-fit the pipe to the fitting; it should seat snugly in the fitting.

❷ APPLY CEMENT AND ASSEMBLE THE PARTS QUICKLY BUT CAREFULLY. Hold the connection for 30 seconds. Don't puddle the cement on—too much cement can weaken the pipe wall. Push the connections together with a twisting motion until properly seated. The solvent produces heat that may cause the connection to push apart. Wipe away excess cement with a rag to prevent weakening of the ABS pipe walls.

CLOSER LOOK

PEX (FLEXIBLE PLASTIC PIPE) (cross-linked polyethylene) is a flexible plastic pipe used for hot and cold supply lines. While it is gaining wider national acceptance, PEX is primarily used in the southern United States and in parts of southern California. In these areas it can also be used to run the main supply line from an outside water meter into a slab home.

Resistance to deterioration, heat, and the high pressure required for supply, plus ease of assembly, make PEX an ideal choice for do-it-yourselfers where it's use is approved. (Check local codes.)

The system uses two types of fittings:

● Plastic compression-type fittings, which are tightened by hand and then given one full turn with pliers until snug. No tape or pipe compound is required.

● Brass ribbed fittings, which are permanently sealed to the pipe with a crimping tool and crimp ring (usually a professional installation).

The pipe, available in rolls of 50 to 100 feet, is cut with a utility knife or a tubing cutter. It is flexible enough to turn corners that would require new connections and fittings with other types of plumbing. (Follow the manufacturer's instructions for maximum bends.)

Both the compression and crimped fittings are required by code to be accessible for inspection and repair and cannot be sealed in walls or ceilings. In

order to make the fittings accessible, they are often grouped in manifolds behind conveniently located access panels.

Plastic compression-type fitting

HOMER'S HINDSIGHT

A FITTING STORY

I was really busy at work so my cousin and his buddy (who said he was a plumber) offered to help me out by installing a new drain line. They got it in no problem, but they used a straight vent tee, instead of a sanitary tee, which is required by the plumbing code. I know they just wanted to help but the inspector failed the job and we had to start over. Plumbing codes can be tricky so don't be afraid to ask questions.

Soldering copper pipes

SKILL SCALE

EASY	MEDIUM	HARD

REQUIRED SKILLS: Operating a torch. Connecting plumbing fittings.

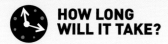

HOW LONG WILL IT TAKE?

Experienced .... 10 min.
Handy .... 20 min.
Novice .... 30 min.

VARIABLES: Good soldering technique requires practice.

Cut and test-fit all the pieces of the puzzle before you begin soldering. Solder fittings with pipe already set in both ends. There's enough heat to make both joints at the same time.

Soldering copper pipe fittings isn't difficult, but you'll need to practice to make perfect. Gather some scraps of copper and solder a few joints until you get the hang of it. Once you've mastered the skill, you'll see why copper plumbing is appreciated for its professional look. Copper is a durable, clean, and functional connecting system.

Make sure you get type L pipe. (Type M pipe is for heating systems and has a thinner wall that may leak under the greater pressure of a water supply system.)

TOOL TIP

THE RIGHT COMBINATION

Wire brushes work well for cleaning fittings, but the 4-in-1 cleaning tool is a solderer's friend. It's a combination deburrer and cleaner for preparing ½- and ¾-inch copper pipe.

STUFF YOU'LL NEED

✔ **MATERIALS:**
Type L copper pipe, copper fitting, lead-free soldering paste (flux), water, lead-free solder, bread

✔ **TOOLS:**
Tubing cutter, MAPP torch, spark lighter, emery cloth, round wire brush or 4-in-1 combination tool, flux brush, fire extinguisher, fiberglass flame barrier, bucket, rags

GOOD IDEA

NO-FREEZE SOLUTION
In colder climates, run supply lines at a slight slope so they will drain easily. Add bleeder caps at the low points to get rid of excess water.

① PREPARE THE INSIDE OF THE FITTING. Ream the inside of each fitting with a round wire brush and sand the end of the fitting with emery cloth. Clean connections ensure a good seal.

Don't apply heat directly to the solder. It will melt away and you'll never seal the joint.

② CLEAN THE OUTSIDE OF THE PIPE with emery cloth or steel wool. Use a deburring tool or the handle of a pair of pliers to deburr the inside of the pipe. (A burr can cause an obnoxious hum once water starts running through the pipe.) Work carefully—the edges may be sharp!

③ APPLY FLUX TO THE PIPE. Apply a layer of lead-free soldering paste (flux) to the end of the pipe using a flux brush. The paste should cover about 1 inch of pipe. Insert the pipe into the fitting, making sure the pipe is tight against the bottom of the fitting. Twist the fitting slightly to spread the flux.

Soldering copper pipes (continued)

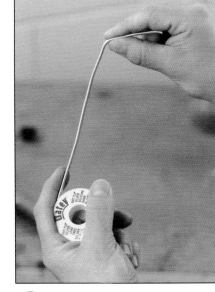

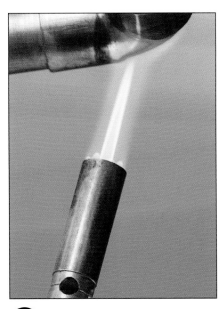

④ UNWIND THE SOLDER WIRE. You will need 8 to 10 inches of the wire extended from the spool. Bend the first 2 inches to a 90-degree angle.

⑤ HEAT THE FITTING. Put pipe in both sides of the fitting so that soot from the torch won't contaminate the joint. Light the torch. Hold the tip of the flame against the middle of the fitting for 4 to 5 seconds or until the soldering paste begins to sizzle.

⑥ TOUCH THE SOLDER TO THE PIPE. Move the flame to the low end of the fitting. (Some of the heat you apply will migrate to the upper end, where you'll be working next.) Remove the flame, and touch the solder against the pipe. If the solder melts, the pipe is ready to solder.

TOOL TIP

KEEPERS OF THE FLAME

Use MAPP gas cylinders for plumbing. MAPP comes in a yellow cylinder and is a combination of propane and methylacetylene-propadiene. It burns hotter and solders better than the pure propane that comes in the blue cylinders.

A+ WORK SMARTER

KEEP YOUR COPPER DRY

Whether you're adding fittings to a system or starting from scratch, water in the line will keep the pipe from getting hot enough to make a secure solder joint.

❶ Drain the line and open a faucet down the run to release steam.

❷ Stuff bread into the pipe to absorb moisture; it will dissolve later when you run water.

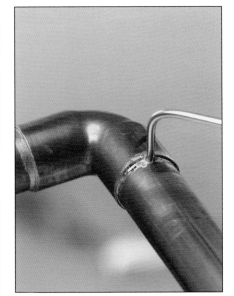

⑦ APPLY MORE HEAT, IF NECESSARY. Once the solder melts when touched against the pipe, remove the flame and quickly melt ½ to ¾ inch of solder into the joint. Capillary attraction will draw the liquid solder into the joint. A properly soldered joint should show a thin bead of solder around the fitting.

⑧ CLEAN THE FITTING. At this point, some plumbers reapply flux and briefly heat the pipe to clean it further. Always wipe away the excess solder with a rag. The pipe will be hot, so be careful while handling it. Cool the pipe and fitting with a damp rag, and then turn on the water and check for leaks. If the joint leaks, take it apart and resolder it.

Emergencies—quick fixes for frozen or leaking pipes

TIME SAVER

A QUICK FIX FOR A LEAKING PIPE

Plumber's epoxy is a good quick fix for a small leak at a pipe joint. Turn off the water supply upstream of the leak. Tear off two pieces of the claylike ribbon. Knead enough plumber's epoxy putty to cover the surface around the leak, and apply the putty according to the manufacturer's instructions. Turn on the water and inspect for leaks. Remember, this is only a temporary fix, so be sure to permanently repair the line.

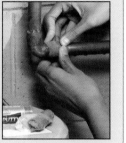

Finding a leak is only half the battle. Water can travel across joists and other surfaces long before reappearing to ruin a wall or ceiling. You may have to cut into walls and ceilings to find the source, but most leaks occur at pipe fittings. Temporary fixes are only that; permanent repairs should be made quickly. Never make a quick fix behind a wall.

Fractures, on the other hand, result from corrosion, dents, or freezing. Water expands when it freezes, fracturing pipes and valves. Bury pipe below the frost line outdoors. Prevent pipes from freezing by not running supply lines in exposed areas or against exterior walls, wrapping pipes with sleeve-type foam insulation, or protecting them with an insulation wrap such as heat tape. Be careful when using heat tape, however. It can deteriorate over time and pose a fire hazard. Inspect it occasionally and replace it if worn.

PIPE INSULATION

A Fiberglass insulation **B** Synthetic rubber insulation for copper **C** Foam and fiberglass insulation **D** Pipe tape **E** Foam insulation for CPVC that won't soften or damage pipe

PLUMBING

BUYER'S GUIDE

PATCHING THE LEAK

Small leaks and wet surfaces can be fixed quickly with **A** plumber's epoxy putty. More serious leaks require more drastic measures, but solutions abound. Try 1/16-inch-thick neoprene rubber or a bicycle tube patch with **B** hose clamps, **C** sleeve clamps, or **D** dresser couplings.

CLOSER LOOK

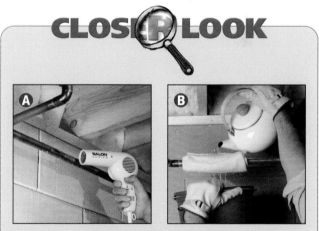

THAWING FROZEN PIPES

Turn off the water from the main shutoff valve. Inspect the pipe for damage. Look for ruptures that may have been caused by expansion of the freezing water. If the pipe does not appear to be fractured, drain the line by opening a downstream faucet. Then, use **A** a hair dryer or heat lamp to thaw the pipe. Or **B** place a bucket under the pipe, wrap the pipe with an old towel, and pour hot water over the towel to thaw out the pipe. After thawing, turn on the water supply while you inspect the pipe for leaks and damage. Repair ruptures.

Running new supply lines

SKILL SCALE

EASY	MEDIUM	HARD

REQUIRED SKILLS: Carpentry skills and connecting plumbing fixtures.

HOW LONG WILL IT TAKE?

Experienced . . . . 6 hrs.
Handy . . . . 8 hrs.
Novice . . . . 12+ hrs.

VARIABLES: Time doesn't include demolition that may be required.

WORK SMARTER

KEEP YOUR EYES ON THE BALL
Plumbing code doesn't allow either compression fittings or flexible line fittings inside the wall. Both must be accessible for repair and inspection.

STUFF YOU'LL NEED

✔ MATERIALS:

Copper supply pipe, copper fittings, integral stops, copper tube straps and anti-vibration pads, brass screws, faucet assembly, shower tee, solder, flux, PVC P-trap, tub overflow and drain assembly, PVC primer and adhesive, bathtub, galvanized nails, 2×4 blocking, 1×3 ledger strips, silicone caulk

✔ TOOLS:

Electric drill, spade bits, tape measure, carpenter's level, pencil, hammer, MAPP torch and striker, tubing cutter, soldering kit, fiberglass flame barrier, hammer, screwdriver, saber saw, PVC cutter, gloves, safety glasses

Running new supply lines requires planning in order to choose the best route for the pipes and break the job down into manageable phases. Hot and cold supply lines can be either copper (as shown here), CPVC, or, if code allows, PEX.

You must decide the most convenient point to break into existing service and then track the pipe runs to the point of the new installation (in this case, a control riser for a new bathroom). The closest point may not be the best choice—remember pipe is cheap.

The idea is to plan a run that does the least damage to existing walls and installations and therefore requires the least patching and repair. (Once you've planned the run, you may find it easier to install the system in the bathroom first and then connect the supply lines downstairs.)

ORDER OF WORK

- Plan ahead. Make a sketch of the installation.

- Create a tools and materials list.

- Purchase all materials and make everything you'll need accessible before you begin work.

    (NOTE: The diameter of the pipe you're installing must be the same as the existing supply line.)

- Turn off the water supply and drain the pipes you are cutting into to install the new lines.

GOOD IDEA

INTEGRAL STOPS

Integral stops are set screw-operated shutoff valves that can be installed as part of the valve body assembly. The advantage of using an integral stop is that you can access it by removing the escutcheon plate that covers the valve assembly.

- Mark the location of the new supply lines on the wall studs. Space the hot and cold water supply lines approximately 8 inches apart.

- Cut out sections of the existing supply lines and install T-fittings for connecting the new pipes.

- Cut and test-fit all the pipes and fittings before you solder the connections.

- Going through studs: Drill holes for the supply lines in the center of the studs, making the holes at least ¼ inch larger than the diameter of the pipe you are running. Code may require larger holes in earthquake zones.

- Attaching to floor joists: Secure the pipes to the joists with hangers as you go to prevent stress. (See Step 5 on the opposite page.)

Standard showerhead height is 6'6" from the floor, but you can place it wherever you choose.

Standard spout height is 28", but it must be at least 6" above the finished top of the tub. Center both the spout and showerhead over the drain.

If local code requires an inspection, make sure it is done before you close up the walls.

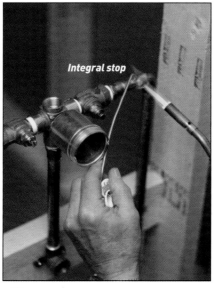

1 **DRILL HOLES FOR THE RISERS.**
Drill riser holes through the stud wall into the basement. The diameter of the holes should be at least ¼ inch larger than the diameter of the riser to allow some flexibility when hooking up the supply lines. The type of faucet you're installing will determine the spread and placement of the riser holes.

2 **INSTALL THE VALVE BODY.** Make sure the faucet controls are centered and level. Do a dry assembly to make sure everything fits. The heat of soldering may damage the valve's internal parts; to prevent this, remove them if possible. If the valve attaches to a screw-in fitting, solder the first piece of pipe to the fitting before screwing the fitting to the valve. (See Soldering Copper Pipes, pages 93–94.)

3 **INSTALL THE TOP BLOCKING.**
Blocking for a tub spout should be centered 6 inches above the top of the tub. Faucets installed more than 6 inches above the spout need separate blocking. The blocking should be level, at the correct depth inside the wall, and toenailed firmly to the studs. Blocking for the showerhead is usually about 6½ feet above the floor, but you can adjust the height to suit your needs.

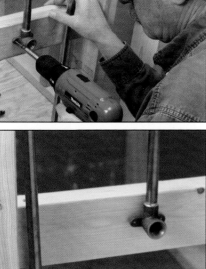

4 **SECURE THE SPOUT AND SHOWER RISER TO THE BLOCKING.** Connect all the pipes and fittings. Screw any brass fittings to the framing with brass screws to prevent the corrosion that occurs when dissimilar metals are in contact with each other. (See pages 93–94 for soldering copper pipe and page 91 for connecting CPVC pipe.)

5 **RUN SUPPLY LINES TO THE RISERS. CUT PIPE LENGTHS.** Test-fit each supply line, and mark adjustments on the piping. Take the runs apart and make the changes. Anchor the pipes securely to the joists as you make the runs, and solder in place.

GOOD IDEA

PIPE DOWN IN THERE!
Believe it or not, water running through pipes can make a lot of noise. To isolate it, slide plastic or felt fittings around the pipes wherever you attach them to the framing. Foam insulation designed to prevent frozen pipes will also minimize noise inside the wall.

TOOL TIP

WATER HAMMER
The banging caused by water pounding against a valve when you shut off the water is called water hammer. If it's a problem in your house, buy a commercial water hammer arrester, a small pipelike device that absorbs the shock.

Installing shutoff valves and supply tubes

SKILL SCALE

EASY	MEDIUM	HARD

REQUIRED SKILLS: Connecting plumbing fittings.

HOW LONG WILL IT TAKE?

Experienced .... 25 min.
Handy .... 45 min.
Novice .... 1 hr.

VARIABLES: Look at the pipes carefully. They may unscrew from the wall. If you must cut, don't cut close to the wall.

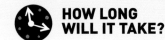

STUFF YOU'LL NEED

✔ **MATERIALS:**
Compression valve, compression fittings, flexible supply tubing

✔ **TOOLS:**
Mini-pipe tubing cutter or minihacksaw, emery cloth, two adjustable wrenches

Shutoff valves let you turn off the water near your fixtures so that you don't have to shut off water to the entire house every time you make a repair. They attach in different ways: by soldering, threading, or compression fittings. Compression fittings are easy to install and don't require pipe dope or compound—a metal sleeve makes the fitting watertight, as long as it's properly installed.

Turn off the water before you start. Open the faucet you're working on and another one somewhere below it in the house so that the water will drain from the line.

Escutcheon plate

1 DISCONNECT THE SUPPLY PIPE.
Turn off the main water supply. Unscrew the supply pipe at the wall. If it's soldered in place, cut with a mini-pipe tubing cutter or, as a last resort, a minihacksaw. (Cut carefully. If the tube is out of round, the compression fitting will leak.) Leave enough room between the escutcheon plate and the cut to install the fitting. Deburr the pipe with emery cloth. Slide the compression nut over the supply pipe as far back as possible.

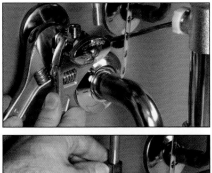

3 TIGHTEN (BUT DON'T OVERTIGHTEN) THE COMPRESSION VALVE TO THE NUT. Use one wrench to hold back the valve and keep it square and another to turn the nut. Follow the same procedure you used to install the valve to attach the supply lines. Turn the water on briefly (and let it flow into a bucket) to flush the lines before installing any new fixtures.

2 PLACE THE COMPRESSION RING OVER THE END OF THE SUPPLY PIPE. The ring should completely cover the end of the supply pipe.

Thread the compression valve into the compression nut. The valve should slide squarely and snugly over the ring. Hand-tighten. If the nut doesn't turn easily, add a tiny drop of oil to the threads. Don't use pipe compound; the fitting doesn't require it, and it can actually make the fitting leak.

BUYER'S GUIDE

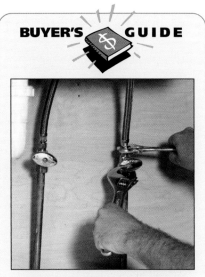

BRAIDED FLEXIBLE SUPPLY TUBING IS EASY TO INSTALL
Braided flexible supply lines are stronger and last longer than straight chrome tubing. Some are actually made of stainless steel, but most are heavy-duty braided plastic. Use two adjustable wrenches to attach the compression fittings.

Repairing or replacing a sink strainer

SKILL SCALE

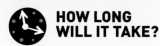

EASY	**MEDIUM**	HARD

REQUIRED SKILLS: Removing and installing pipe fittings.

HOW LONG WILL IT TAKE?

Experienced .... 20 min.
Handy .... 40 min.
Novice .... 1 hr.

VARIABLES: Chrome pipe often breaks during repairs and may take longer to replace.

STUFF YOU'LL NEED

✔ **MATERIALS:**
Plumber's putty or silicone caulk, gaskets and washers

✔ **TOOLS:**
Water-pump pliers, hammer, basket strainer wrench, plastic putty knife, mini hacksaw, screwdriver

---

WORK SMARTER

DIFFICULT NUT TO CRACK?
You may find the locking nut is difficult to loosen. If all else fails, cut a groove in the nut at about a 30-degree angle with a minihacksaw. Insert a screwdriver into the groove and twist or tap with a hammer until the nut breaks off.

The sink strainer assembly connects the sink to the drain line. To fix a leak, you'll need to take it all apart. Remove and clean the sink strainer basket, then replace any worn washers and gaskets. If the seal where the strainer basket meets the lip of the drain line was not properly installed, it may leak.

Repairing does not mean replacing every part. If you don't mind reusing old parts, don't replace them. The sink drain body may be usable even though it may not shine like a new one; reuse it or any of its metal parts. The drain locknut can be reused because it is hidden below the sink. The only parts you should not reuse are washers and gaskets; they may not provide a proper seal. (They're also the least expensive parts to replace.)

If possible, replace chrome drainpipe with plastic. Chrome pipes corrode on the inside. As a result, they'll leak sooner and are more likely to break during minor repairs.

1 **GIVE YOURSELF ROOM TO WORK.** Inspect the area below the sink and remove any obstacles.

2 **DISCONNECT THE SLIP NUTS.** Use water-pump pliers to loosen the slip nuts and slide them out of the way. Remove the tailpiece.

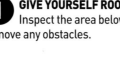
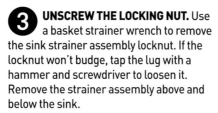

3 **UNSCREW THE LOCKING NUT.** Use a basket strainer wrench to remove the sink strainer assembly locknut. If the locknut won't budge, tap the lug with a hammer and screwdriver to loosen it. Remove the strainer assembly above and below the sink.

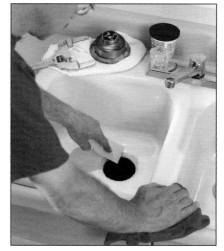

4 **SCRAPE OFF THE OLD PUTTY WITH A PLASTIC PUTTY KNIFE.** If you reuse the old strainer, clean it as well. Always replace gaskets and washers.

Repairing or replacing a sink strainer *(continued)*

Plumber's putty

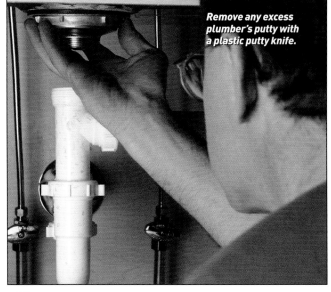

Remove any excess plumber's putty with a plastic putty knife.

5 **COAT THE FLANGE.** If the sink is cultured marble or stainless steel, coat the bottom rim of the flange with silicone caulk. If the sink is enamel, use plumber's putty instead. Roll the putty between your hands to create a "rope" about ⅜ inch in diameter. Apply the putty to the underside of the flange rim. Insert the drain unit into the sink.

6 **REASSEMBLE THE STRAINER.** Install a new rubber gasket and friction ring. Hand-tighten the new locknut. Connect the tailpiece to the assembly body with slip nuts. Test by filling the sink with water and then draining. Tighten the nuts if you see any leaks.

SINK STRAINER ASSEMBLY

- Sink strainer basket
- Drain unit
- Drain gasket
- Drain seal (friction ring)
- Drain locking ring
- Tailpiece washer
- Slip nut

OOPS!

EASY DOES IT!
Even experienced plumbers sometimes break plastic fittings. That final turn with the pliers may seem like a good idea, but it can result in a cracked fitting and a trip to the home center. Hand-tighten all fittings, then a quarter-turn at a time with the pliers until the leaking stops.

GOOD IDEA

TWIST AND SHOUT
If the drain unit turns every time you try to give the locking ring a final twist, you need a helper. Put a couple of screwdrivers between the crosspieces in the drain unit. Have a helper hold them firmly while you tighten the locking ring.

Installing a single-bowl PVC P-trap

SKILL SCALE

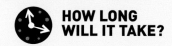

EASY	MEDIUM	HARD

REQUIRED SKILLS: Connecting plumbing fittings.

HOW LONG WILL IT TAKE?

Experienced	20 min.
Handy	40 min.
Novice	1 hr.

VARIABLES: Installing a trap is easy, but be prepared to cut the pieces for a proper fit.

STUFF YOU'LL NEED

✔ MATERIALS:
PVC P-trap (United States),
ABS P-trap (Canada), slip-joint tailpiece

✔ TOOLS:
Felt marker, PVC pipe cutter,
water-pump pliers

CANADA WATCH
DWV systems in Canada use black ABS (acrylonitrile butadiene styrene) for running drain lines instead of white PVC. Techniques for cutting, connecting, and cementing ABS are similar to PVC. (See Connecting ABS, page 92.)

Drains in the United States must have either a P-trap or an S-trap, depending on code requirements. (In Canada, you may only use a P-trap.) The trap serves as a safety device by preventing noxious gases from backing up the sewer pipe and entering the house. Sewer gases not only pose a health hazard, they can also be explosive.

Here's how a P-trap works: The curved portion of the trap is filled with standing water, which prevents sewer gas from leaking into the room. Every time the drain is used, water is flushed through the trap and is replaced with fresh water. Over time, solids will adhere to the trap and may eventually clog the drain or possibly damage the trap—which means it's time to install a new one.

BUYER'S GUIDE

WHAT'S A SLIP JOINT ANYWAY?
Slip joints allow fixtures such as strainer baskets to be joined to drainpipes without making permanent connections. This means parts can be replaced easily. A smaller pipe with slip nuts at each end is inserted into a larger pipe, and the seal is made by the pressure that results from tightening the slip nuts to the threaded ends of the larger pipe.

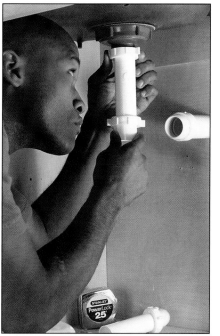

1 **CONNECT THE TAILPIECE TO THE SINK DRAIN.** Hand-tighten the slip nut.

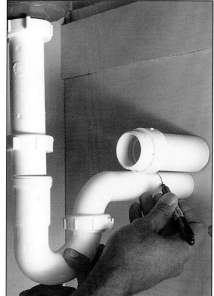

2 **MEASURE THE PIPE.** Test-fit the P-trap. Mark the P-trap inlet so it will seat inside the end of the drainpipe. Remove the P-trap. Cut the inlet of the trap to length using PVC pipe cutters. Insert the inlet into the pipe socket. Slide the slip nut over the end of the inlet and tighten by hand.

Hand-tightening is usually sufficient for a pressure connection. Use pliers gently to stop leaks only if necessary; too much pressure on the fitting can crack or weaken it.

Installing a single-bowl PVC P-trap *(continued)*

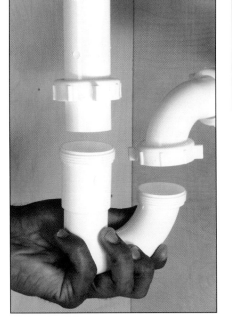

3 **ALIGN THE TRAP.** Make sure the trap will set flush against the outlet and inlet pipes. Adjust the pipe if necessary.

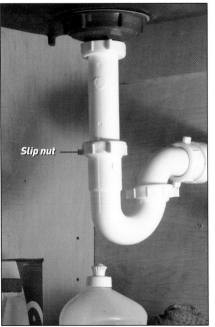

Slip nut

4 **TIGHTEN THE SLIP NUTS.** Turn the nuts until they are hand-tight. Fill the sink with water and then drain it, inspecting for leaks as the sink drains. Tighten if necessary.

GOOD IDEA

ESCUTCHEON PLATES HELP TO FIGHT BUGS!

Escutcheon plates fit flush around the pipe where the drain line enters the wall or floor. They add a finishing touch where plumbing is visible, such as under a wall-hung lavatory. Escutcheon plates also seal the drainpipe hole and can prevent drafts or unwanted insects from entering your home.

◄ *Split-ring escutcheon plates fit around a pipe that is already in place.*

◄ *Solid-ring escutcheon plates slip onto the pipe before the drain is assembled.*

CLOSER LOOK

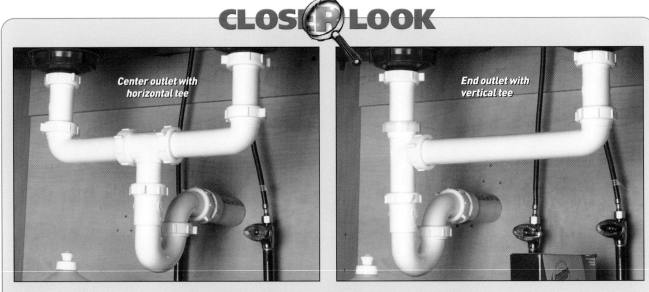

Center outlet with horizontal tee

End outlet with vertical tee

CONNECTING OPTIONS FOR DOUBLE-BOWL SINKS

Two bowls can be served by one P-trap. Conversion kits are available at your local home center. One style has the P-trap centered between the bowls with a connecting tee and separate lengths running to the sink drains. Centering the P-trap does not meet code in Canada or California. Another style has the P-trap aligned beneath one of the drains with a vertical tee connecting to the second bowl. Though the installation procedure is the same as for a single-bowl sink, make sure the horizontal run has a fall of ¼ inch per linear foot toward the tee connector. Otherwise, solids will settle along the horizontal pipe and eventually stop or impede the flow of wastewater.

See page 538

UNCLOGGING THE CLOGS

Stopped or slow-moving drains are seldom the result of collapsed or defective pipes. Blockage in the lines caused by the accumulation of solid waste such as small objects, hair, or clumps of soap and grease is usually the culprit.

ISOLATING THE PROBLEM. If one fixture seems to drain slowly or not at all, first check to see if other fixtures have the same problem. If only one fixture is affected, fill the sink with water. If the water drains for two seconds or less before clogging, the problem is in the trap. If two or more fixtures are clogged, the clog may be in the branch line, the main line, or the vent stack. If more than one fixture is affected and all are on the second level of the house, the blockage may be high in the main line or in a vent stack. Isolating the affected area will help you decide how to clean out the line—and whether you need to hire a professional.

DRAIN LINES ARE FRAGILE—more fragile than you might expect, especially because of all the fixtures attached to them. Be careful when using chemicals and augering—some chemicals can weaken the walls of the drain lines, and augers can shatter porcelain fixtures. Try using a plunger first. If that doesn't solve the problem, move on to snakes and augers, but work carefully and slowly.

THE RISKS OF USING CHEMICAL CLEANERS. In general, it's best to avoid using chemical cleaners, but if you do, follow the directions carefully and always let other people (like plumbers) know if you've put chemicals in a drain they may be working on. Never use a drain cleaner on a clogged drain or in a toilet, and never pour acid in standing water. It will probably make matters worse. Use cleaners only on sluggish drains, and be skeptical of cleaners that claim to be safe on pipes and gaskets.

GOOD IDEA

KNOCK, KNOCK. WHO'S THERE?

If your pipes are exposed, as in a basement or crawlspace, here's a tip to speed up the search. From the clog to the drain, the pipe will be full of water. From the clog to the street, the pipe will be empty. Tap along the pipe from the side nearest the street, using a broomstick or a piece of scrap lumber. (Don't use a hammer or piece of metal.) A ringing or hollow sound means a clear pipe. When you hear a thud, you've found the clog. Open up the nearest clean-out and put the auger to work!

You can learn from the pros at a local rental center.

CLOG REMOVERS

For almost every clogged drain you'll encounter, a tool solution exists, including: **A** Common household plunger **B** Closet auger for toilets (won't damage porcelain) **C** Hand snake **D** Power drill auger attachment, and **E** Hand spinner. Use the right auger for the right job. It's easy to damage pipes or scratch fixtures.

MAYBE IT'S TIME FOR A HEAVY-DUTY SOLUTION. Sometimes it's easier to get to a blockage in the main line through the vent system. If that's the case, you'll need to rent a commercial auger to remove the blockage. This might be the time to bring in a pro; but if you want to do it yourself, get some lessons from a rental center, take every precaution, and work carefully while on the roof.

Unclogging drains and waste lines

SKILL SCALE

| EASY | MEDIUM | HARD |

REQUIRED SKILLS: Connecting plumbing fittings and using a hand auger.

HOW LONG WILL IT TAKE?

Experienced .... Variable
Handy .... Variable
Novice .... Variable

VARIABLES: Stubborn, hard-to-reach clogs, and pipes that don't come apart take longer.

Most clogs that result from buildups of grease or hair can be removed by opening the drain line and using an auger to clear the blockage. Small objects, such as toys or toothbrushes, can be difficult to snag and remove. Sometimes the best solution is to remove the drain trap and push the blockage further down the drain line system to a clean-out, or to flush the line with water once the blockage has been jarred loose.

Pushing an object farther down the system can cause a clog that's difficult to auger. You might have to call in a plumber or a drain service. If you don't have accessible clean-outs in your home and can get the blockage into the main drain line, it can sometimes be removed through the roof stack vent.

STUFF YOU'LL NEED

✓ **TOOLS:**
Water-pump pliers, bucket, hand auger, rags for cleanup

A+ WORK SMARTER

PLUMBERS HAVE SPECIALTIES TOO
Don't be surprised if your plumber isn't interested in going after a tough clog. He may suggest a drain cleaning service to handle the job instead.

Using a hand auger

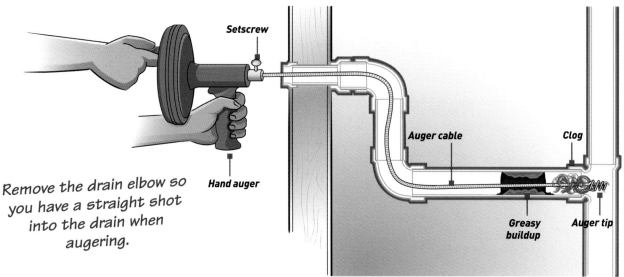

Remove the drain elbow so you have a straight shot into the drain when augering.

Labels: Setscrew, Hand auger, Auger cable, Clog, Greasy buildup, Auger tip

Ⓐ Disconnect the drain trap. Place a bucket under the drain trap to catch wastewater. Loosen and slide back the slip-nut couplings with water-pump pliers. Remove the trap and clean out any debris stuck in it. Look for cracks in the pipe or sediment buildup in the trap; in either case it means you'll have to replace the trap (see Installing a Single-Bowl PVC P-Trap, page 101).

Ⓑ Loosen the auger setscrew and pull out about a foot of cable. Push the cable through until it meets resistance which is probably a bend in the pipe. It's often difficult to tell the difference between a bend and the clog. Be patient. The auger will either push the blockage out of the pipe or snag it so you can pull it out.

Ⓒ Tighten the setscrew and turn the handle clockwise until the cable moves forward again. Loosen the set screw and feed cable until you meet resistance again. Repeat this process until you feel the obstruction is removed or that you've snagged the blockage. Remove the cable and clean the tip.

Ⓓ Test by running water through the drain and waste line. If the line is still blocked, the clog may be in the main drain. If that's the case call in a professional.

Unclogging sink drains

STUFF YOU'LL NEED

✔ TOOLS:

Flange plunger, bucket,
water-pump pliers, sink auger, rags

Plunging is the best option for removing a clog because it's the easiest and least likely to damage pipes. Fill both basins with 4 inches of water. Have a helper hold a rag or a closed strainer over the opening of the disposer drain. Use a plunger to vigorously plunge the drain in the other sink. A dozen times should be enough for most clogs. If the drain is still clogged, switch positions with your helper and plunge the drain in the other basin.

While plunging is the best option, you may have to use a sink auger for stubborn clogs. To use the auger, remove the trap and elbow below the sink and send the auger down the line to locate and remove the clog.

A+ WORK SMARTER

PREVENTATIVE MEASURES TO AVOID CLOGS

1. Disposers grind food into a paste that can collect in the drain line and eventually form a clog. Avoid oily or dense matter and flush the lines thoroughly with cold water after each use.

2. Hair and food clogs can be difficult to clear. Clean tubs and sinks regularly.

3. Don't pour grease down the drain unless you have a grease trap.

4. Also, don't put dental floss, sanitary napkins, or paper towels down the toilet.

Unclogging jammed disposers

STUFF YOU'LL NEED

✔ TOOLS:

Flashlight, ¼-inch allen wrench, a
disposer wrench or adjustable wrench,
broom handle

Disposers without hex sockets have a special wrench that comes with the disposer. Keep it in a location you'll remember. If it's already lost or isn't working, buy a replacement in the plumbing department of your home center.

Turn off the power to the jammed disposer and unplug it. Look inside the opening with a flashlight to see what is jamming it. Remove the waste and restore power. If it's still jammed, try the following:

● Check the bottom of the unit; press the reset button. Turn on the power. The disposer should run freely. If it's still stuck, turn the power off.

● Insert a broom handle into the drain opening and try to free the impellers.

● Next, insert a ¼-inch allen wrench into the hex socket on the bottom. The socket is connected to the impellers that crunch up the waste. Using the hex key turns the impellers in both directions to free them.

SAFETY ALERT

WORK SAFELY!

Before reaching into a disposer, disconnect the power. Unplug the unit from the outlet. If there is no outlet, turn off the circuit breaker. Never stick your hand into a connected disposer.

Unclogging bathtub and shower drains

SKILL SCALE

EASY	**MEDIUM**	HARD

REQUIRED SKILLS: Operating a hand auger and removing plumbing fittings.

HOW LONG WILL IT TAKE?

Experienced . . . . .Variable
Handy . . . . .Variable
Novice . . . . .Variable

VARIABLES: Time depends on the nature and location of the clog.

STUFF YOU'LL NEED

✔ **TOOLS:**
Screwdriver, flange plunger, hand auger

The drains in sinks and shower stalls work hard, and not just to drain away soap, grease and oil, hair, and the occasional hairpin or ring. We use these fixtures to wash the dog and the leaves of our plants. A shower is the perfect place to scrub miniblinds. When the weather is too cold to hose things down outside, we use the shower stall to clean dirty boots. It's no wonder the drain clogs.

Plunge the drain vigorously with a flange plunger to unclog it. For stubborn clogs, try a hand-driven auger. Try both options before calling a plumber or a drain cleaning specialist to do the job.

TOOL TIP

PLASTIC TO THE RESCUE
If you don't have a plunger, try out a plastic drain tool, which has barbs at one end. Slip it in the pipe; the barbs grab the clog and pull it out.

WASTE AND OVERFLOW DRAINS

1 REMOVE THE POP-UP DRAIN ASSEMBLY. Flip the drain lever up and pull out the drain plunger. Remove the screws from the overflow cover plate with a screwdriver, then lift out the linkage. If you're going to set tools and parts in the tub, protect it from scratches by using an old towel.

2 AUGER THE DRAIN. Insert the end of the hand auger into the overflow drain. Turn the handle clockwise, feeding out the cable until you meet resistance. Slowly withdraw the auger to dislodge or remove the blockage. Repeat until the tub drains normally. Insert the linkage back into the overflow drain and install the cover. Flip the lever up and insert the stopper.

Don't use a power-driven auger in a bathtub drain; the assembly is too fragile and can be easily damaged.

FLOOR DRAINS

1 USE A PLUNGER. Remove the screws from and lift off the shower strainer. Fill the shower pan to a depth of 1 inch. Plunge forcefully about a dozen times. Remove the plunger and see if the water drains freely. If not, repeat.

2 AUGER THE DRAIN. Tougher clogs require a tougher approach. Feed a hand auger into the drain until it meets resistance. Turn the auger handle clockwise and slowly withdraw the auger. Repeat until the shower drains normally. If the blockage refuses to clear, call a plumber or a drain service.

Unclogging a toilet

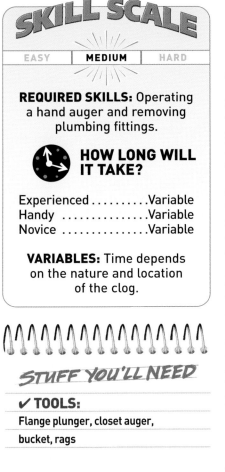

SKILL SCALE

EASY	**MEDIUM**	HARD

REQUIRED SKILLS: Operating a hand auger and removing plumbing fittings.

HOW LONG WILL IT TAKE?

Experienced . . . . .Variable
Handy . . . . .Variable
Novice . . . . .Variable

VARIABLES: Time depends on the nature and location of the clog.

STUFF YOU'LL NEED

✔ **TOOLS:**

Flange plunger, closet auger,

bucket, rags

WORK SMARTER

HOW TO TAME A CLOG
This recipe for a clog buster really works. Add 3 tablespoons of dishwashing soap to the bowl. The soap will lubricate the interior of the drain and help to loosen the clog when you plunge. Wait a few minutes for the soap to do its work, then plunge vigorously.

TOOL TIP

AUGER MAINTENANCE
When you're done with the auger, rinse it in warm water. Then spray on an aerosol lubricant to keep rust from forming on the tool.

Toilets have built-in traps. Objects stuck in the trap cause slow draining or clogged toilets and usually can be dislodged by plunging.

DON'T USE A COAT HANGER TO UNCLOG A TOILET—you will scratch the bowl. If the bowl is scratched, try removing the black marks with a heavy-duty powder-type cleanser containing bleach.

NEVER USE CHEMICAL DRAIN CLEANERS IN A TOILET. If there is no water in the bowl, pour some water into it. Water helps seal the plunger flange, creating a vacuum and allowing you to apply pressure to dislodge the blockage. **A** Plunge forcefully about a dozen times. Remove the plunger to allow the toilet to drain. If it doesn't drain, or drains slowly, repeat plunging.

IT'S AUGER TIME. You may need an auger to remove stubborn objects, such as small toys. Never use a hand auger on a toilet. The force of the auger when turning the crank may shatter the porcelain bowl. A closet auger is designed specifically to be used on toilets. It has a long handle with a crank, and the bend in the handle is covered with a protective sleeve to prevent scratching the porcelain. **B** Turn the crank clockwise and push. The auger can shove the blockage forward into the drain system. If the auger catches on the object, continue turning the crank as you pull out the cable until you can retrieve the object.

REMOVE THE TOILET. When plunging or augering doesn't work, your only option will be to remove the toilet (see Removing an Old Toilet, page 136) and try to fish out the object from the other end.

WORK SMARTER

KEEP IT PRETTY
Some augers, like the one shown here, have a protective rubber sleeve. Those that don't will leave noticeable scratches. Protect the surface by lining it with a towel.

A *Common household plunger*

B *Closet auger*

REPAIRING FAUCETS

SKILL SCALE

EASY	MEDIUM	HARD

REQUIRED SKILLS: Assembling plumbing fittings.

HOW LONG WILL IT TAKE?

Experienced . . . . 20 min.
Handy . . . . 40 min.
Novice . . . . 1 hr.

VARIABLES: The fancier the faucet, the longer it will take to fix.

WORK SMARTER

LOOK BEFORE YOU LEAP

It's easy to lose track of the assembly order and even easier to lose faucet parts themselves. Read instructions carefully before you begin. Always cover the drain to keep pieces from escaping and arrange the parts on a flat surface as you remove them.

TIME SAVER

REMOVAL MAY BE THE HARDEST PART

The hardest part of almost any plumbing job is removing the old stuff. Corrosion and inaccessibility can make the job more difficult than you might expect. Be patient and budget a little extra time. That way you won't be unnecessarily frustrated.

FAUCET ASSEMBLIES

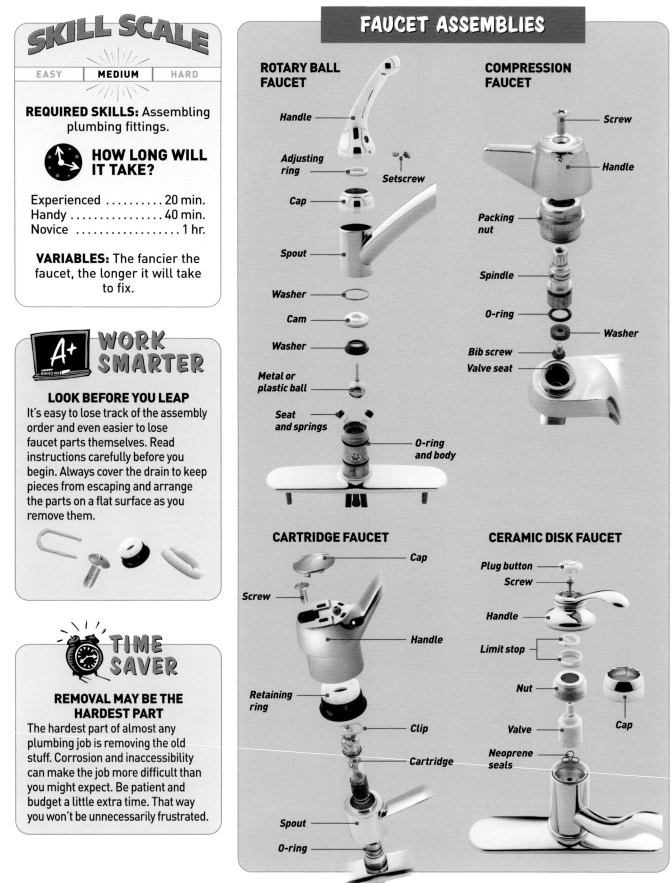

ROTARY BALL FAUCET

- Handle
- Adjusting ring
- Setscrew
- Cap
- Spout
- Washer
- Cam
- Washer
- Metal or plastic ball
- Seat and springs
- O-ring and body

COMPRESSION FAUCET

- Screw
- Handle
- Packing nut
- Spindle
- O-ring
- Washer
- Bib screw
- Valve seat

CARTRIDGE FAUCET

- Cap
- Screw
- Handle
- Retaining ring
- Clip
- Cartridge
- Spout
- O-ring

CERAMIC DISK FAUCET

- Plug button
- Screw
- Handle
- Limit stop
- Nut
- Valve
- Cap
- Neoprene seals

Repairing a compression faucet

STUFF YOU'LL NEED

✔ **MATERIALS:**
Universal washer kit, O-ring, silicone grease

✔ **TOOLS:**
Screwdriver, water-pump pliers

OLD VS. NEW

PACKING STRING VS. O-RINGS
You may find packing string rather than an O-ring in some compression assemblies. If so, you'll need to replace the packing string before you reassemble the faucet.

1 TURN OFF THE WATER SUPPLY AND UNSCREW THE STEM ASSEMBLY. Pry off the handle cap. Remove the handle screw with a screwdriver. Lift it up and off the handle. To remove corroded handles, you may have to use a handle puller (see Closer Look, below). Unscrew the packing nut from the faucet body with water-pump pliers.

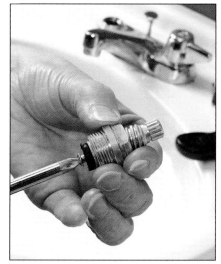

2 TAKE OFF THE WASHER. Use a screwdriver to remove the bib screw that holds the washer in place. If the screw is stuck, tap on it gently for about 30 seconds to loosen the rust. Remove the screw, pry out the worn washer, and discard it. While the valve is out, examine the valve seat by touch. If you feel any roughness, replace it. (See Replacing a Worn Valve Seat, page 110.)

3 REMOVE THE STEM FROM THE RETAINING NUT. Inspect the threads for damage and replace the stem if necessary.

Never reuse an old washer, no matter how good it looks!

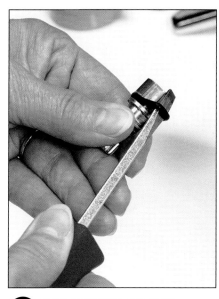

4 PEEL OFF (DON'T CUT) THE O-RING. Slip the O-ring from its groove and peel it from the housing. It's important to keep the ring whole so you can find an exact replacement at the store. Use the tip of a screwdriver to help release it if necessary. If you can't peel it off, get an O-ring remover to help you with the job.

CLOSER LOOK

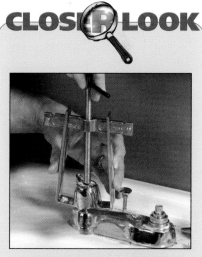

REMOVING A STUBBORN HANDLE
A handy tool to remove corroded handles is a handle puller. Clamp the side extensions of the handle puller beneath the handle. Thread the puller into the faucet stem. Continue to tighten the puller until the handle is free.

Replacing a worn valve seat

Only compression valves have valve seats. When repairing a compression valve, check to see if the valve seats need to be resurfaced. Poke your finger down into the faucet body to feel if the valve seat is rough. A rough seat will quickly damage a new washer. You should either replace or resurface the valve seat at the same time you are replacing the faucet washer. (See "Closer Look," below.)

STUFF YOU'LL NEED

✔ **MATERIALS:**
Valve seat, silicone grease, pipe dope

✔ **TOOLS:**
Screwdriver, water-pump pliers,
seat wrench, seat cutter

❶ TURN OFF THE WATER SUPPLY AND DISASSEMBLE THE FAUCET VALVE. Lower the sink stopper and cover it with a cloth to prevent loose parts from falling into the drain. Pry off the handle cap, and remove the handle with a screwdriver.

REMOVE THE VALVE. Loosen the compression valve with water-pump pliers and remove it. Keep any washers or O-rings with the valve and set them aside.

❸ REPLACE THE SEAT. Install the new seat into the faucet. Apply pipe dope to the seat threads to seal them; insert the end of the seat wrench into the seat, and set the seat in place. Screw the valve into place. Assemble the compression valve, faucet handle, and handle cap. Turn on the water supply and check for leaks.

❷ BACK OUT THE SEAT. Use a seat wrench to remove the valve seat. Select an end that fits snugly into the seat. Insert the end of the wrench into the seat and tap the top to seat it firmly. The valve seat may be stuck, so the first turn should be quick and firm to release it without stripping the threads. Once it's loose, turn the wrench counterclockwise and remove it. Take the old seat to your local home center to be sure you replace it with the correct part.

WORK SMARTER

REPAIR OR REPLACE

Compression faucets can be repaired up to a point. When too much of the seat is ground away, you're better off replacing the assembly.

HOMER'S HINDSIGHT

FLUSH OUT THE FAUCET BODY

Resurfacing the valve seat is actually an easy job but you've got to remember to clean the debris from inside the faucet body or it'll ruin that swell new washer you just put on. Flush the system before you reassemble the faucet. Cover the faucet hole with a rag and turn on the water gently to remove any debris or other gunk. You'll make a longer-lasting repair.

GOOD IDEA

LEAK PREVENTION

If you're replacing one valve seat, you might as well do the other. And because you've already got the assembly apart, replace the washers, bib screws, and O-rings on the valves.

CLOSER LOOK

RESURFACING A WORN VALVE SEAT

Worn valve seats can be resurfaced using a seat cutter, which can be purchased at a home center or hardware store. Select a seat cutter that will fit snugly inside the retaining nut. Slide the cutter and retaining nut over the threaded end of the valve seat dressing tool. Attach the locknut and cutter head to the shaft of the tool. Carefully screw the retaining nut into the faucet body. To resurface the seat, lightly press down on the handle while turning it clockwise two to three complete turns. Remove the tool and inspect the seat by feeling it to make sure it's smooth. If not, repeat the procedure. When smooth, reassemble the faucet.

PLUMBING

REPAIRING FAUCETS
Repairing a ceramic disk faucet

STUFF YOU'LL NEED

✔ **MATERIALS:**

Ceramic disk faucet replacement kit

with seals, abrasive pad, silicone grease

✔ **TOOLS:**

Screwdriver or hex key set

 GOOD IDEA

MAKE IT EASIER NEXT TIME
No shutoff valves below the sink? Think about installing them now. Shutoffs make all repairs easier because you don't have to run to the basement to shut off the water. They're handier in emergencies too. See Installing Shutoff Valves and Supply Tubes, page 98.

1 **TURN OFF THE WATER AT THE SUPPLY OR MAIN SHUTOFF.** Loosen the setscrew with a hex key. Lift off the handle and dome housing. Unscrew the disk cartridge screws with a screwdriver. Lift the disk up and out. Inspect the disk for cracks—replace it if damaged.

2 **TAKE OUT THE SEALS.** Take the disk and seals to your local home center to find the correct replacement parts.

3 **CLEAN THE SEAL SEATS** with an abrasive pad.

4 **INSTALL NEW SEALS.** Coat them with silicone grease to prevent them from drying out, making them easier to remove.

5 **ASSEMBLE THE FAUCET.** Install the escutcheon cap and handle, and tighten the setscrew. Remove air from the line before fully opening the supply valves. (See "Work Smarter," below.)

Keep the instructions that came with your faucet so you can easily order replacement parts.

 **A+ WORK SMARTER**

DON'T CRACK THAT CERAMIC DISK!
Air rushing through a ceramic disk can crack it. First, open the faucet in the center position to balance the flow of water, then gradually open the shutoff valves to bleed out the air. Don't turn off the faucet until water flows freely and all the air is out.

PLUMBING

Replacing a cartridge faucet

STUFF YOU'LL NEED

✔ **MATERIALS:**
New cartridge, O-ring, silicone grease

✔ **TOOLS:**
Screwdriver, water-pump pliers,
needle-nose pliers

GOOD IDEA

DIAL 1-800-ETC
Check with the manufacturer before
you buy replacement parts. Some
faucet parts are guaranteed for life,
and you can get replacements just
by asking.

1 **TURN OFF THE WATER SUPPLY AT THE SHUTOFF VALVE OR THE MAIN VALVE.** Pry off the handle cap. Unscrew the faucet handle screw using a screwdriver. Lift the handle from the faucet assembly.

2 **UNSCREW THE RETAINING NUT AND REMOVE THE RETAINING CLIP.** Spin the faucet out of the way and use water-pump pliers to remove the plastic retaining nut. Pull out the retaining clip that is just beneath it with needle-nose pliers. Lift the faucet spout straight up from the faucet body and remove.

3 **PEEL OFF (DON'T CUT) THE O-RING.** Slip the O-ring from its groove and peel it from the housing. It's important to keep the ring whole so you can find an exact replacement at the store. Use the tip of a screwdriver to help release it if necessary. If you can't peel it off, pry it out with a screwdriver and cut it with a utility knife.

4 **PULL OUT THE CARTRIDGE STEM.** Grip the exposed end of the cartridge stem with a cartridge puller. Pull it straight up and out of the faucet body. Some replacement cartridges may come with a cartridge puller designed for the job. Others require a tool you'll have to buy separately. In any case, don't use pliers to remove the cartridge or you might damage or destroy it.

5 **CLEAN AND REASSEMBLE THE FAUCET.** Clean the faucet body with vinegar to remove debris. Coat the new O-ring with silicone grease to lubricate it, then seat it into the faucet body O-ring groove. Insert the new stem cartridge. Replace the faucet spout and reassemble. Turn on the water. Check the hot and cold water to make sure they are not reversed. If reversed, disassemble, turn the stem 180 degrees, then reassemble.

Repairing a rotary ball faucet

STUFF YOU'LL NEED

✔ MATERIALS:

Silicone grease, rotary ball repair kit, rotary ball faucet replacement ball if necessary, masking tape

✔ TOOLS:

Hex set key wrench, water-pump pliers, tweezers, utility knife

GOOD IDEA

KEEP THOSE OLD PARTS!
Don't throw away any old parts until you're finished with the job; you may want them for reference. Take the old parts with you when you shop for replacements so you find exactly what you need.

1 SHUT OFF THE WATER AND UNSCREW THE CAP. Use a pair of water-pump pliers to remove the cap. Wrap the jaws of the pliers with masking tape to prevent damage to the cap.

2 REMOVE THE CAM. Lift off the cam housing, seal, and ball. Inspect each part for damage and replace damaged parts.

3 LIFT OUT THE SEATS. Use tweezers to remove the valve seats and springs. The springs are cone-shaped, with one end larger than the other. **NOTE HOW THE SPRINGS ARE INSTALLED BEFORE YOU LIFT THEM OUT**—you must install the replacement springs in exactly the same order you remove them or the faucet won't work properly. Remove the spout by twisting and lifting at the same time.

4 PEEL OFF (DON'T CUT) THE O-RING. Slip the O-ring from its groove and peel it from the housing. It's important to keep the ring whole so you can find an exact replacement at the store. Use the tip of a screwdriver to help release it if necessary. If you can't peel it off, pry it out with a screwdriver and cut it with a utility knife.

5 REASSEMBLE THE FAUCET. Coat the new O-ring with silicone grease and seat it in the faucet housing groove. Push the spout over the O-ring and faucet housing. Install the new valve seats and springs, making sure they are installed correctly. Fit the cam ball into the notch in the body. Screw on the cam housing using the wrench included in the kit. Screw on the cap and install the handle. Turn the water on and check for leaks. Tighten the adjusting ring firmly to prevent leaks.

Repairing a two-handle tub and shower faucet

STUFF YOU'LL NEED

✔ **MATERIALS:**

O-ring, cartridge replacement kit, silicone grease, white vinegar or lime-dissolving solution

✔ **TOOLS:**

Screwdriver, plastic putty knife, shower stem socket kit, pliers, utility knife, flashlight

If you see a mineral buildup on the assembly, soak parts in a white vinegar or lime-dissolving solution before you reassemble the faucet.

1 TURN OFF THE WATER SUPPLY AND REMOVE THE HANDLE. Pry off the handle cap. Use a screwdriver to remove the handle. If there is caulking around the escutcheon plate, use a plastic putty knife to remove the caulk. Slide the escutcheon plate off the stem.

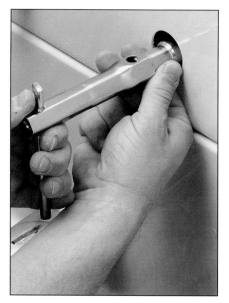

2 UNSCREW THE RETAINING NUT. Use a shower stem socket (available at home centers and hardware stores) to remove the retaining nut.

3 REMOVE THE CARTRIDGE. Grasp the end of the cartridge with a pair of pliers and pull it straight out. If the hole in the tile is too small, enlarge it by chipping with a screwdriver and hammer.

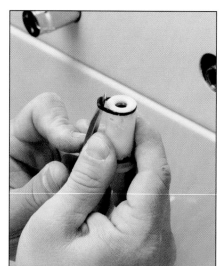

4 PEEL OFF (DON'T CUT) THE O-RING. Slip the O-ring from its groove and peel it from the housing. It's important to keep the ring whole so you can find an exact replacement at the store. Use the tip of a screwdriver to help release it if necessary. If you can't peel it off, pry it off with a screwdriver and cut it with a utility knife.

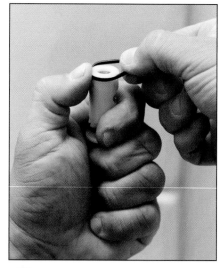

5 SLIDE ON THE NEW O-RING. Apply silicone grease to the new O-ring. Slide it over the cartridge, seating it into the O-ring groove. Reassemble the faucet. Turn on the water and test for leaks.

Repairing a tub diverter valve

STUFF YOU'LL NEED

✔ **MATERIALS:**

Compression replacement kit,

white vinegar solution, plumber's putty,

silicone grease

✔ **TOOLS:**

Screwdriver, stem socket set,

utility knife, water-pump pliers,

toothbrush

Replacing one cartridge? Replace them all; you'll save time and effort. If the stem is damaged, take it with you to the store to buy a replacement.

Place a blanket or a towel in the tub and cover the drain to prevent damage and lost parts.

1 **REMOVE THE HANDLE AND ESCUTCHEON CAP.** Shut off the water supply. Pry the cap off the diverter handle. Remove the screw and slide off the handle. You may have to unscrew the escutcheon to remove it. If so, wrap the jaws of the pliers with masking tape.

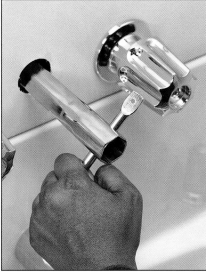

2 **DISCONNECT THE BONNET NUT.** Use a shower stem socket set to remove the bonnet nut and stem. If the handle keeps hitting the tub or another faucet, put a stem socket over the one you're using as an extension.

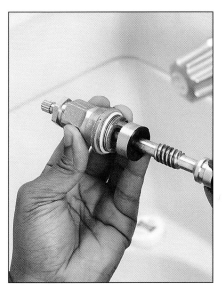

3 **UNSCREW THE STEM FROM THE BONNET NUT.** Hold the bonnet nut with one hand. Use your other hand to remove the stem from the bonnet nut with water-pump pliers. Inspect the threads of the stem for damage. If there is evidence of damaged threads, replace the stem. Check the valve seat with a flashlight to make sure it's OK. It may need resurfacing or replacement. (See "Closer Look," page 110.)

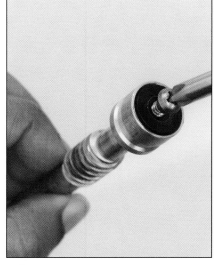

4 **REMOVE THE BIB SCREW.** Clean mineral deposits on the stem with a white vinegar solution, or buy a solution to dissolve mineral deposits at your local home center. A toothbrush easily removes deposits.

Look carefully at the replacement washer. If it has markings on one side, put that side into the stem.

5 **REPLACE THE OLD WASHER.** Seat the new washer in the stem. Apply silicone grease to the washer so it seats properly. Replace the bib screw with a new one. Reassemble the faucet, sealing the escutcheon in place with a bead of plumber's putty. Turn on the water supply and check for leaks and drips.

PLUMBING

REPAIRING FAUCETS
Installing a tub spout

STUFF YOU'LL NEED

✔ **MATERIALS:**
New spout, pipe compound,
silicone caulk

✔ **TOOLS:**
Small screwdriver or allen wrench,
water-pump pliers, rags or towels

Tub spouts come in two basic types—screw-on and set-mounted. Examine the underside of the spout. If there is a hole in the bottom, it's mounted with a setscrew. Slide the fitting over the pipe until it's snug with the wall. Then tighten the setscrew with a small screwdriver or allen wrench. If there is no hole under the spout, screw it hand-tight. Spouts with setscrews are easier to install because they're easier to square up than the threaded variety.

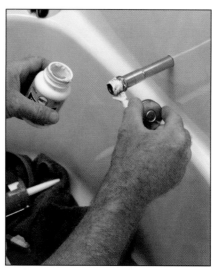

1 DISCONNECT THE OLD SPOUT. Check the underside of the spout to see if there is a setscrew. If so, loosen the screw and slide off the spout. If there isn't a setscrew, use a pipe wrench to unscrew the spout from the threaded pipe. Twisting too hard can potentially bend the spout nipple, especially if it's copper. Apply joint compound to the nipple threads.

2 INSTALL THE NEW SPOUT. Slide the new spout over the pipe and snug to the wall. If it has a setscrew, tighten it. If the pipe is threaded, screw on the spout hand-tight. If further tightening is required, put tape over the teeth of water-pump pliers to prevent scratching, and tighten until the spout is snug. Run silicone caulk around the spout or escutcheon plate if there is one.

REPAIRING FAUCETS
Cleaning a showerhead

Showerheads, like faucet aerators, in areas with hard water will eventually become clogged with mineral deposits. Not all showerheads break down the same way, but what's shown here is a common example. Newer showerheads come with a water-conservation device, called a flow restrictor, that cannot be removed.

- **Unscrew the swivel ball nut and remove the showerhead.**

- **Disassemble the internal parts.**

- **Soak overnight** in white vinegar or a lime-dissolving solution.

- **Reassemble the showerhead.** Apply silicone grease to the shower arm threads and install the showerhead. Turn on the water and inspect for leaks.

- **Use a small wire brush** to clean mineral deposits.

- **Use a paper clip** to remove mineral deposits from holes in the disk. Inspect for damage and replace components if necessary.

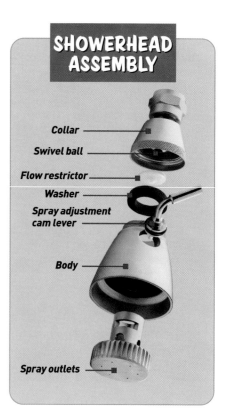

SHOWERHEAD ASSEMBLY

- Collar
- Swivel ball
- Flow restrictor
- Washer
- Spray adjustment cam lever
- Body
- Spray outlets

REPAIRING TOILETS

Fix a leaking toilet immediately. An unrepaired leak may become more than an annoyance. It can develop into structural damage not only to the floor, but also to the ceiling below the toilet. Both may require hiring a contractor for a repair that can be extensive and expensive.

TROUBLESHOOTING. Troubleshooting a toilet to locate a leak is easy. No tools are required, just food coloring (red is recommended) and paper towels. The food coloring added to the tank or bowl will make the leak easily visible so you can see what repairs are needed.

If the base is leaking see Installing a New Toilet, page 137.

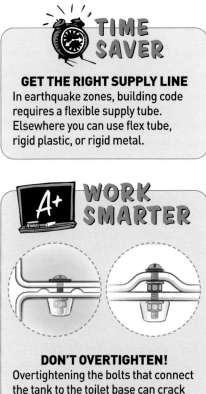

TIME SAVER

GET THE RIGHT SUPPLY LINE
In earthquake zones, building code requires a flexible supply tube. Elsewhere you can use flex tube, rigid plastic, or rigid metal.

WORK SMARTER

DON'T OVERTIGHTEN!
Overtightening the bolts that connect the tank to the toilet base can crack the base, the tank, or both. Tighten gently until snug and alternate from side to side to seat them evenly.

Toilets are heavy and a little awkward to handle but installation and repair is usually very easy.

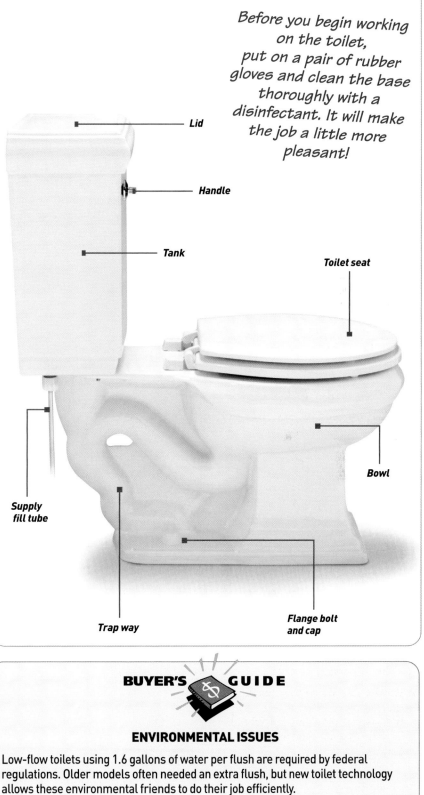

ANATOMY OF A TOILET

Before you begin working on the toilet, put on a pair of rubber gloves and clean the base thoroughly with a disinfectant. It will make the job a little more pleasant!

Lid

Handle

Tank

Toilet seat

Bowl

Supply fill tube

Trap way

Flange bolt and cap

BUYER'S GUIDE

ENVIRONMENTAL ISSUES
Low-flow toilets using 1.6 gallons of water per flush are required by federal regulations. Older models often needed an extra flush, but new toilet technology allows these environmental friends to do their job efficiently.

Adjusting the tank handle and water level

The sound of water bubbling from a fountain may be relaxing. But if it's coming from your toilet, it's just adding to the water bill. Quick fixes include shortening a chain, bending a wire, or adjusting a float clip. Each solution is easy and requires little time.

The tank handle uses what are called left-handed threads to help keep the handle assembly tight. Tighten them counterclockwise.

1 **ADJUST THE TANK HANDLE.** If the handle has too much play or binds, use an adjustable wrench to tighten the nut inside the toilet. Unlike other nuts and bolts, the threads on a tank handle are left-handed, so you'll tighten counterclockwise.

GOOD IDEA

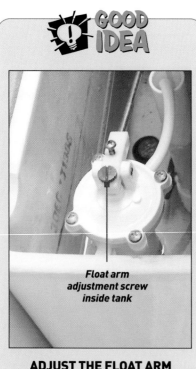

Float arm adjustment screw inside tank

ADJUST THE FLOAT ARM

Before you resort to more complicated measures, first try adjusting the float arm to change the water level. Turn the screw on top to lift or lower the float.

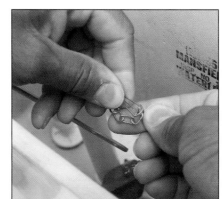

2 **SHORTEN THE CHAIN.** This will help if you have to hold the handle down to flush all the water from the toilet tank.

3 **BEND THE UPPER WIRE.** If the tank doesn't have a chain, it has a wire you can bend.

4 **BEND THE FLOAT ARM.** The water level should be just below the overflow. To adjust the water level in the tank, bend it up for a higher water level or down to lower the water level.

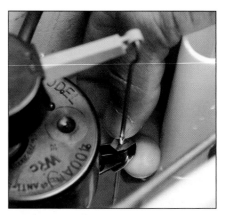

5 **SLIDE THE FLOAT CYLINDER.** Squeeze the float clip to release the float cylinder, which can be raised or lowered to adjust the water level in float-style toilets.

Repairing a leaking tank

SKILL SCALE

EASY	MEDIUM	HARD

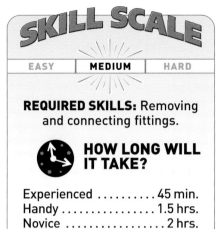

REQUIRED SKILLS: Removing and connecting fittings.

HOW LONG WILL IT TAKE?

Experienced . . . . 45 min.
Handy . . . . 1.5 hrs.
Novice . . . . 2 hrs.

STUFF YOU'LL NEED

✔ **MATERIALS:**

Flush valve gasket, fill valve, gaskets, spud washer

✔ **TOOLS:**

Two adjustable wrenches, screwdriver, small wire brush, spud wrench

WORK SMARTER

TRACKING LEAKS

If there is a leak along the supply valve, tighten the fittings an additional quarter-turn. If the leak is around the base of the tank, check the washers in the tank to make sure they're seated properly. If the washers appear to be properly seated, tighten the tank nuts another quarter-turn.

Sometimes it's easier to have a friend help lift the tank off the toilet base.

1 **IF THE FILL VALVE IS LEAKING** turn off the water supply valve. Flush the toilet. Disconnect the supply line from the tank and sponge the inside of the tank until it's dry. Use two adjustable wrenches to remove the fill valve. Remove the old fill gasket. If you're not replacing other parts, install the new fill valve and gasket. Turn on the supply line and check for leaks. If necessary, tighten a quarter-turn. Otherwise, proceed to Step 2.

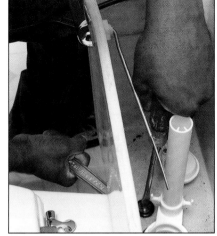

2 **IF THE TANK IS LEAKING:**
A screwdriver and adjustable wrench will remove most tank bolts. Remove the tank bolt, nut, and gasket. Clean the bolt and nut with white vinegar and a small wire brush. If you aren't replacing the spud washer, reinstall bolts and nuts with new gaskets. Alternate the tightening of the nuts to evenly draw the tank tight. If you need to replace the spud washer, continue to Step 3.

3 **IF THE SPUD WASHER IS LEAKING REMOVE THE BOLTS AND LIFT THE TANK STRAIGHT UP AND OFF THE TOILET BASE TO REMOVE IT.** Make sure you have a helper; toilet tanks are usually in an awkward place and are heavier than they appear to be. Set the tank upside down on the floor. It's best to set it on an old towel or rug because it may contain some water.

4 **REPLACE THE SPUD WASHER.**
Take the spud washer to your local home center to find the correct replacement. Place a new spud washer over the flush valve tailpiece. Lower the tank onto the base so the tank bolts go through the holes. Reinstall the tank bolts, gaskets, and nuts. Alternate tightening the nuts so they tighten evenly. Reinstall the supply tube coupling and fill valve. Turn on the water supply and check for leaks.

Replacing a toilet fill valve

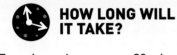

EASY	**MEDIUM**	HARD

REQUIRED SKILLS: Connecting and disconnecting fittings.

HOW LONG WILL IT TAKE?

Experienced .... 20 min.
Handy .... 40 min.
Novice .... 1 hr.

PLUMBING

Old toilet fill valves can develop leaks. If water continues to run after you have made the adjustments on page 118, you may need to remove and replace the fill valve. You may also have to replace the supply line so that the new valve fits.

Know the locations of the main water shutoff valve or the supply valves for each fixture in your home.

STUFF YOU'LL NEED

✔ **MATERIALS:**
Fill valve, fill valve gasket

✔ **TOOLS:**
Adjustable wrench

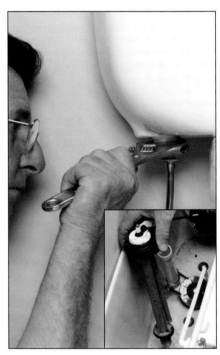

1 **SHUT OFF THE WATER** and drain the tank. Disconnect the fill valve nut and remove the old fill valve. (See inset.)

TOILET FILL VALVE COMPONENTS

Ⓐ Ⓑ Ⓒ Ⓓ Ⓔ Ⓕ Ⓖ

◀ **FILL VALVE COMPONENT NAMES**

Ⓐ Float with float arm

Ⓑ Refill tube

Ⓒ Fill valve assembly

Ⓓ Flapper

Ⓔ Plastic washers and nuts

Ⓕ Overflow tubes

Ⓖ Fill valve assembly with refill tube

2 ADJUST THE HEIGHT OF THE VALVE so that the marking on the top of the valve is at least 1 inch above the overflow tube.

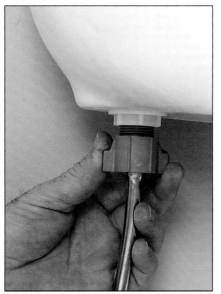

3 POSITION THE VALVE IN THE TANK. Push down on the valve shank and tighten the locknut a half-turn beyond hand-tight. Connect the supply.

4 ATTACH THE REFILL TUBE AND ANGLE THE ADAPTER TO THE OVERFLOW. Trim the tube if necessary to get rid of any kinks.

5 FLUSH THE SYSTEM. Remove the top valve. Hold a cup over the uncapped valve and turn on the water supply to flush the system of rust and debris. Turn off the water.

6 REPLACE THE TOP VALVE by engaging the lugs and rotating one eighth-turn clockwise. Make sure it's firmly locked into position.

7 ADJUST THE WATER LEVEL by squeezing the adjustment clip and moving the float cup up or down.

BUYER'S GUIDE

THREE VALVE TYPES—ONE WAY TO REPLACE

Three basic types of fill valves exist: the plunger valve, the diaphragm, and the float cup. Replace all three the same way. It may not be necessary to replace the fill valve with the exact same type that you remove, but it may be easier for you because the installation process is the opposite of the removal sequence.

Replacing a flapper

SKILL SCALE

EASY	MEDIUM	HARD

REQUIRED SKILLS: Removing the flapper and adjusting the chain.

HOW LONG WILL IT TAKE?

Experienced .... 5 min.
Handy .... 10 min.
Novice .... 15 min.

STUFF YOU'LL NEED

✔ **MATERIALS:**
Flapper or tank ball

✔ **TOOLS:**
Bucket, sponge, scrub pad

WORK SMARTER

FLAPPER TIPS
Have about a half inch of slack in the chain that connects the flush lever to the flapper. Most replacements have side tabs or a ring that slides over the overflow tube so that they can work with any system. Make sure the flapper moves up and down freely.

TIME SAVER

SQUARE PEGS, ROUND HOLES
While universal replacement flappers are available, they still may not fit exactly. Take the old flapper with you to get an exact replacement.

If you have hard water, you will probably need to change the toilet flapper occasionally. Minerals in hard water build up around the base of the flapper and the opening of the toilet. The sediment will eventually destroy the flapper, causing the toilet to leak.

HOMER'S HINDSIGHT

CHEMICAL REACTION
I was replacing toilet flappers and washers on a regular basis until my plumber friend told me those tablets I was putting in the tank contained chlorine and were eating away at the rubber. Just when you think you know everything, you learn something new.

1 **TURN OFF THE WATER SUPPLY SHUTOFF VALVE AND FLUSH THE TANK.** If there isn't a shutoff valve, turn off the water at the main valve; this is also a good time to install a shutoff valve for future use. (See page 98.)

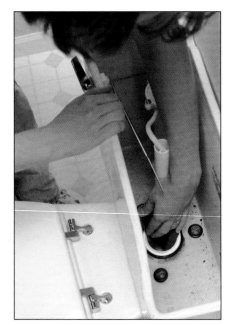

2 **REMOVE THE OLD FLAPPER.** Pull the flapper from the pivot arm. For ball-style toilets, grip a loop of lift wire and unscrew the old tank ball. Clean the surface area of the opening with a scrub pad to remove sediment.

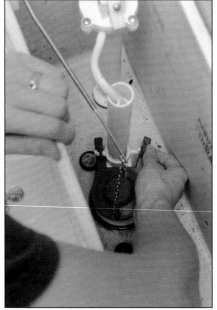

3 **INSTALL A NEW FLAPPER.** Line up the flap or ball with the valve seat by straightening the lift wire or adjusting the guide arm. This will provide a sufficient seat and keep the tank from leaking.

PLUMBING

INSTALLING AND REMOVING SINKS

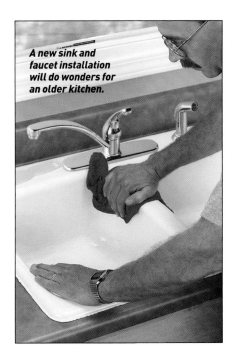

A new sink and faucet installation will do wonders for an older kitchen.

New colors, shapes, and features create a wide range of options in the world of sinks and faucets. Materials for sinks include porcelain, fired clay, porcelain-coated cast iron and steel, stainless steel, and more. Other alternatives include quartz-acrylic and solid-surface drop-in sinks. Quartz-acrylic sinks are popular among many homeowners and designers because they are attractive, durable, and heat resistant. Solid-surface drop-in sinks are popular for their longer warranties and a seamless look.

Clean up debris and tools as you go. It makes the installation easier and faster, plus you won't bruise your knee on a pipe wrench you forgot was there.

GOOD IDEA

USING ESCUTCHEON PLATES

Split-ring escutcheon plates, available in metal or plastic, fit around the drainpipe covering the hole where the drain line enters the wall or floor. Where plumbing is visible, such as under a wall-hung lavatory, they add a finishing touch. Using escutcheon plates inside cabinets isn't required, but they do help seal around the hole to avoid drafts and insects.

A+ WORK SMARTER

INSTALLATION TIPS FOR SINKS AND FAUCETS

A Do as much work above the counter as possible. Install the faucets and drain on a single sink before you set it in place. It will make the job easier because space to work is scarce when connecting fittings from beneath a counter.

B The drain holes on a double sink make perfect handholds for setting the sink into the countertop opening. Install the drain system once the sink is in place.

C Square up the faucet body on the sink top before you go below and tighten it.

D Flexible, braided supply line is a great alternative to copper because of its ease of installation. Carefully follow the instructions for hooking up compression fittings to prevent leaks.

E Avoid using pipe compound on compression fittings; it keeps the fitting from connecting tightly, which can cause leaks.

F Pipe compound and Teflon tape act as sealants, but they also lubricate the threads so you can fully tighten the connections. Don't use too much—no more than one pass with compound or two wraps of tape—or you may not get a good connection.

G PVC is light, easy to use, and more flexible to work with than steel pipe for drain systems.

H Joint compound is available with and without Teflon. Compound with Teflon is better for general use because it can be applied on plastic, brass, copper, steel, PVC, ABS, and CPVC. Joint compound without Teflon can damage plastic pipe.

I Avoid using plumber's putty on cultured marble or plastic sinks or fittings; it can discolor surfaces and weaken fittings. Follow the manufacturer's instructions and/or use silicone products.

J Metal strainer basket assemblies are superior to the plastic kind; they last longer and are less prone to leaking.

K If the drain isn't exactly where you need it to be, you can usually combine 90-degree and 45-degree elbows and short pieces of straight pipe to make the connection. P-traps and extensions with flexible sections may also help.

L If the stub coming out of the wall or floor for the drain is metal or an incompatible plastic and you want to install PVC or ABS, use rubber transition fittings to make the connection.

Installing a countertop sink

SKILL SCALE

EASY	**MEDIUM**	HARD

REQUIRED SKILLS: Carpentry and connecting plumbing fittings.

HOW LONG WILL IT TAKE?

Experienced .... 1 hr.
Handy .... 1.5 hrs.
Novice .... 2 hrs.

VARIABLES: Unforeseen problems can arise when you start cutting holes in countertops. Give yourself plenty of time to deal with the unexpected.

STUFF YOU'LL NEED

✔ **MATERIALS:**
Countertop sink, fixtures, cardboard template, silicone caulk, masking tape

✔ **TOOLS:**
Tape measure, scissors, carpenter's pencil, power drill and bits, saber saw, caulking gun, putty knife, screwdriver, utility knife, rags

TOOL TIP

CUT IT SHORT
High-speed cutting tools make short work of cutting holes in drywall and are a perfect alternative to using a saber saw for cutting out a countertop.

1 CREATE A TEMPLATE. If the sink doesn't come with a template, create one by laying the sink facedown on a sheet of cardboard and drawing a line around the edge. Lift off the sink and draw a second line ¾ inch inside the first line. Cut along the inside line with scissors.

MARK THE CENTER OF THE CABINET FROM BELOW. Drill a hole large enough to fit a finishing nail.

3 DRILL A ¾-INCH HOLE INSIDE THE CUTOUT LINE. Use a power drill and spade bit to make a starter hole for the saber saw.

INSTALL BRACES BENEATH THE COUNTERTOP. The braces will support the section to prevent it from binding while cutting.

2 MARK THE CENTER OF THE TEMPLATE. Push a nail through the center of the template into the hole. Center the template and square the edges so the rim will lie entirely on the surface.

TRACE THE OUTLINE ON THE COUNTERTOP. Remove the template and place tape along the edge. Replace the template and draw the outline of the sink on the tape. Remove the template.

4 CUT OUT THE OPENING. Use a saber saw with a blade designed to cut countertops without chipping the surface. Remove the masking tape. Test-fit the sink and trace the rim lightly on the countertop.

APPLY A BEAD OF SILICONE CAULK INSIDE THE LINE. Apply a steady, continuous bead between the mark and the opening.

PLUMBING

Installing a self-rimming sink

⑤ PLACE THE SINK IN THE OPENING. Press the sink firmly into the silicone caulking, then level and clean. Connect the faucets and the drains. Test for leaks.

CLEAN AWAY EXCESS SILICONE. Trim silicone caulking with a plastic putty knife for a professional look.

① INSTALL THE SINK. Follow the steps for installing a countertop sink through the first part of Step 4, check for fit, then caulk the rim and lower the under-mount sink into place.

② TIGHTEN THE CLAMPS BENEATH THE SINK. Align the clamps over the countertop; stagger-tighten with a screwdriver as you would the lugs on a tire, alternating so that the clamps tighten evenly.

Removing an old sink

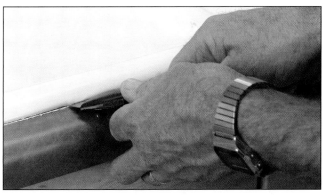

OUT WITH THE OLD. Like many plumbing projects, removing the old sink can be the toughest part of a replacement job. Fittings may be rusted or fused tight, and getting around under the counter can be tricky. If it's a cast-iron sink, it will be heavy, so get help for removal.

❶ Before you begin, make sure the new fixture will fit properly into the old hole.

❷ Turn off the water supply valves to the hot and cold water faucets. Place a bucket beneath the drain trap. Loosen the slip nuts and remove the trap. Support the bottom of the trap with your hand while loosening the nuts.

❸ Remove the bucket and place a shallow tray or rags beneath the sink supply lines to catch remaining water.

❹ Remove the coupling nuts connecting the supply tube to the faucet tailpiece.

❺ Disconnect additional plumbing for disposers (see pages 140–141), dishwashers (see page 142), and sink sprayers.

❻ Slice through the caulking around the rim using a utility knife.

❼ Lift the sink from the countertop using the drain hole as a handhold.

❽ Look for water damage to the countertop and clean any excess caulking from the rim before you install the new sink.

Call your local waste removal service for instructions on disposing the old sink.

PLUMBING

Installing wall-hung and pedestal sinks

STUFF YOU'LL NEED

✔ MATERIALS:

Wall-hung sink, mounting bracket, anchor bolts, 2×10 wood blocking, water-resistant drywall scrap, drywall tape and compound, paint, faucets and fittings, drainpipe and fitting, 2×4 brace, silicone caulk

✔ TOOLS:

Keyhole saw, hammer, tape measure, carpenter's pencil, power drill and bits, ratchet wrench and sockets, caulking gun, screwdriver, utility knife, rags

Measure the opening in the display model to make sure the new drain lines will meet the ones already in the wall.

INSTALLING WALL-HUNG SINKS

1 CUT AWAY A 16x16-INCH SECTION OF DRYWALL AND NAIL OR SCREW THE BLOCKING INTO PLACE. Use a keyhole saw to remove the drywall. Nail the 2×10 between the studs so that it's flush with the leading edge of the studs. Cut a piece of water-resistant drywall to cover the hole. You may be able to use the piece you cut away. Finish the drywall and paint it. Once dry, attach the mounting bracket.

2 PREPARE TO SET THE SINK. Attach the faucet and drain before mounting the sink. Run the supply line with stop valves. Install the drain line and P-trap. Set the sink on the bracket, securing it to the bracket with anchor bolts. Connect the supply line to the faucet, and the drain to the P-trap. Open the valves. Check for leaks. Tighten leaking fittings if necessary. Legs for most wall-mounted sinks are optional.

INSTALLING PEDESTAL SINKS

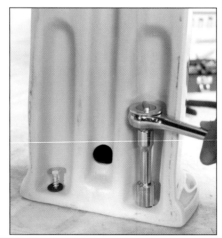

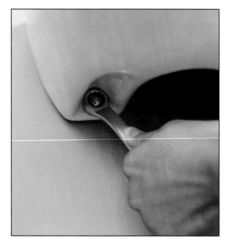

1 SET THE BASIN AND PEDESTAL IN PLACE. Install the fixtures and plumbing. Brace the basin with a 2×4. Outline the base of the pedestal on the floor with a pencil. Mark the floor with the location of the holes for the lag screws. Set the basin and pedestal aside. Drill holes in the floor for the lag screws.

2 INSTALL THE PEDESTAL LAG BOLTS, MAKING SURE THEY'RE SNUG. Don't overtighten; you could crack the base. Apply a bead of silicone caulk around the base. Install the faucet, then connect the supply lines and drain before you attach the basin to the wall so you'll have some play to make the hookup.

3 CONNECT THE BASIN TO THE WALL. Predrill a small hole through to the blocking, then insert and alternately tighten the lag screws until just snug—don't overtighten. Caulk the back of the basin with silicone caulk. Remove the brace and test the system for leaks.

Installing faucets

SKILL SCALE

EASY	**MEDIUM**	HARD

REQUIRED SKILLS: Connecting plumbing fittings.

HOW LONG WILL IT TAKE?

Experienced . . . . 40 min.
Handy . . . . 1 hrs.
Novice . . . . 2 hrs.

VARIABLES: Time does not include removing the old faucets.

Have someone hold the faucet in position while you tighten it.

STUFF YOU'LL NEED

✔ **MATERIALS:**

Widespread faucet, gaskets, pipe compound, Teflon paste or Teflon tape, plumber's putty

✔ **TOOLS:**

Plastic putty knife, adjustable wrenches, basin wrench

A+ WORK SMARTER

AVOIDING CLOGGED FAUCETS

Working on the pipes can dislodge old grime or rust. If this gets in the lines, it can plug the faucet and actually stop water from flowing. To prevent this, unscrew the aerator at the tip of the faucet. Turn on the water and let it run for a minute or so to remove any dirt. Once you turn off the water and replace the aerator, the faucet should work well without clogging.

WIDESPREAD FAUCETS

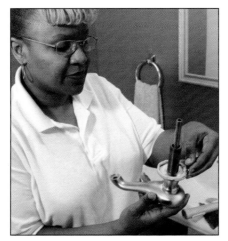

1 **SEAL THE SPOUT BASE.** Form plumber's putty into a rope and place it on the base of the spout. Press the putty against the base, and set the spout in place.

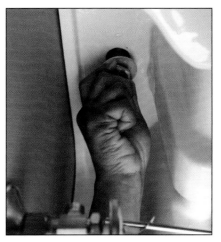

2 **HAND-TIGHTEN THE BASIN NUT** just enough to hold it in place. Don't overtighten, because you will need to center the spout on the sink in Step 4.

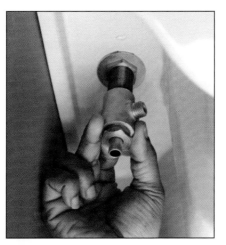

3 **THREAD THE TEE ON THE SPOUT.** Center the tee so that the outlets are approximately parallel to the back wall and line up with the faucets on either side. (See Step 7.)

4 **CENTER THE SPOUT** and tighten it from beneath the sink using a basin wrench.

GOOD IDEA

OUT WITH THE OLD IS THE HARDEST PART

As opposed to other home improvement jobs, such as installing cabinets or hanging doors, the hardest part of almost any plumbing job is usually removing the old stuff. Corrosion and inaccessibility can make taking out an old faucet a real pain in the neck. Give yourself extra time to remove old fixtures—it will save on frustration and bruised knuckles.

Installing faucets (continued)

WIDESPREAD FAUCETS

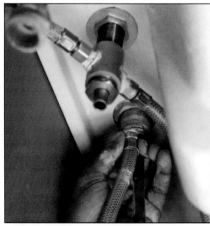

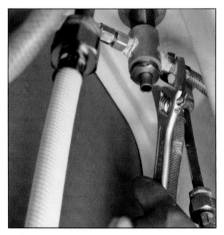

5 **PLACE THE FAUCET VALVES IN THE SINK.** Slide the washers over the threads from beneath the sink. Tighten the valve nuts until snug.

6 **CONNECT THE FAUCET VALVE LINES TO THE FAUCET VALVES.** Apply Teflon paste or Teflon tape to the threads of the valve lines, connect to the faucet valves, and hand-tighten. Apply pipe compound or Teflon tape to the other end of the valve lines and hand-tighten onto the spout tee.

7 **FINISH THE ASSEMBLY AND TIGHTEN THE CONNECTIONS.** Apply Teflon paste or tape to the threads of the water supply tailpieces and connect the hot and cold water supplies to the hot and cold supply valves. Tighten the connections with an adjustable wrench and connect the faucet handles to the valves. Turn on the water and test for leaks

CENTER-SET FAUCETS

STUFF YOU'LL NEED

✔ **MATERIALS:**
Center-set faucet, gaskets, plumber's putty or silicone caulk

✔ **TOOLS:**
Putty knife, adjustable wrenches, basin wrench

A+ WORK SMARTER

CULTURE IS IMPORTANT
Use silicone caulk instead of plumber's putty on cultured marble or other composite sinks. Putty will discolor the sink.

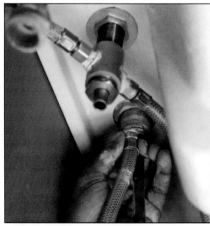

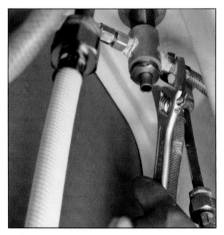

1 **SET THE FAUCET.** The tailpieces should fit into the hole spacing in the sink. Apply a bead of silicone caulk (or plumber's putty if the sink isn't cultured marble) around the faucet openings.
PLACE THE FAUCET GASKET. The gasket will set over the faucet tailpieces and set the faucet in the holes.

2 **CENTER THE FAUCET BODY.** Measure or visually center the faucet body on the lavatory.
HAND-TIGHTEN THE BASIN NUTS UNTIL THEY'RE SNUG. Install the pop-up drain. (See Installing a Pop-Up Drain on the opposite page.) Connect the water supply lines, turn on the water, and test for leaks.

PLUMBING

Installing a pop-up drain

A pop-up drain requires a special faucet fixture. If your current faucet doesn't accept a pop-up, you'll have to replace it with one that does. Installing a pop-up is a little like solving a jigsaw puzzle—a lot of little parts have to come together in the right order for it to work. Use plumber's putty with cast-iron sinks, or silicone caulk on composites or cultured marble, to hold the flange in place. Read carefully the installation instructions for your particular pop-up before you begin.

As with any plumbing job, visualize the steps from start to finish and anticipate the parts of the installation that may cause problems. Clear out a work space in the bathroom and lay out all the tools and materials you'll need for the job before you begin. Heading for your home center late on a Friday night because you forgot something important isn't the best way to start the weekend.

1 **APPLY PLUMBER'S PUTTY.** (Use a 2×4 to support a wall-hung sink while you're working.) Cover the bottom of the flange with a rope of putty.
THREAD THE LOCKNUT ONTO THE DRAIN BODY. Then add the friction washer and beveled gasket.

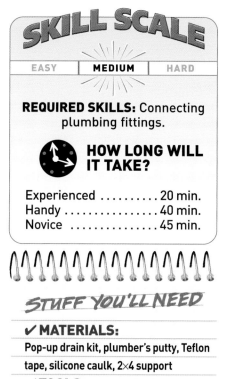

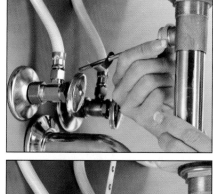

2 **INSTALL THE DRAIN BODY.** Push the drain body up through the lavatory hole from underneath.
HAND-TIGHTEN THE DRAIN BODY TO THE FLANGE. Turn the drain body and the flange to tighten the connection and line up with the linkage.

3 **INSTALL THE DRAIN PLUNGER.** Slide the plunger into the drain opening. Under the counter insert the ball into the opening. The ball should fit snugly into the opening in the drain tailpiece.

4 **THREAD THE BALL NUT HAND-TIGHT.** Slide the ball nut over the arm and screw it onto the threads of the drain tailpiece. Set the pop-up arm. Slide the arm through the nearest hole in the lever strap and fasten it with a clip. Connect the P-trap and adjust the arm if necessary.

Removing an old bathtub

SKILL SCALE

EASY	**MEDIUM**	HARD

REQUIRED SKILLS:
Removing and reinstalling simple pipe fittings with basic plumbing tools. Installing replacement gaskets.

HOW LONG WILL IT TAKE?

Experienced . . . . 1 hr.
Handy . . . . 1.5 hrs.
Novice . . . . 2 hrs.

VARIABLES: Time involved depends on the tub type.

STUFF YOU'LL NEED

✔ **MATERIALS:**

1×4 boards

✔ **TOOLS:**

Safety glasses, leather gloves, hammer, tarp, sledgehammer, reciprocating saw, pry bar

GOOD IDEA

WATER HAMMER ARRESTER

Though not generally required by code, it's a good idea to install a water hammer arrester when plumbing a bath. Pipes often make a loud bang, called water hammer, when you turn off a faucet. Water hammer arresters absorb the increase in pressure caused by turning off the water, keeping everything quiet in the walls.

Make sure you have plenty of room to work before you tackle tub removal. You'll need a clear space at least 3 feet deep when pulling the tub straight out from the wall. You need to be able to work around the tub when it's away from the wall. It's a good idea to remove other plumbing fixtures such as the sink or vanity and toilet.

MAP YOUR ROUTE. Measure the width of all door openings and the hallway along the path for removing the tub. Not only is this important for removing the old tub, it's essential for bringing in the new one. Tearing up your bathroom to remove the old tub, then discovering that the new one won't fit through the halls or doorway is not a pleasant way to spend the weekend.

THE ORDER OF BATTLE:

● **Turn off the water at the main water shutoff.** Drain the water supply lines by opening a faucet below the tub level.

● **Remove the faucet handles, spout, and drain.**

● **Cut away at least 6 inches of drywall above the tub on all sides.** Remove the screws or nails holding the tub flange to the studs. If you find a galvanized strip along the tub flange, use a flat bar or pry bar to remove it.

● **Lift up on the front edge of the tub** with a pry bar and slide a pair of 1×4s beneath it.

● **Pull the tub away from the wall using the 1×4s as a skid.** You'll need help carrying the tub, especially if it's cast iron. If you're not saving or reusing a cast-iron tub, cover it with a tarp and break it into pieces with a sledgehammer. Wear safety glasses when hammering, and put on gloves when you're picking up pieces of the tub: they're sharp—very sharp. Cut fiberglass and polymer tubs into pieces with a reciprocating saw.

Give yourself plenty of room to work when you're removing a tub. Cut away at least six inches of drywall above the tub.

PLUMBING

Installing a bathtub in an alcove

Place a blanket or piece of old carpet in the bottom of the tub to protect it while you're working. Dropped tools can easily crack or chip the finish.

I nstalling a tub isn't rocket science, but it does require solid plumbing, carpentry, and sometimes, tiling skills. Before installing a tub, review everything that affects the project. Make sure you've qualified yourself for the job and are comfortable attempting it. Measure the width of doors and passages. Make sure you not only can get the old tub out, but also that the new one fits into the bathroom. Rather than have a contractor take over a halfway-completed project, it's better to consider hiring one before you begin. This is also one job where it's great to have a helper to hold and haul.

Install an access panel behind the faucets and supply pipes so you won't have to remove the wall to work on them. Include shutoff valves or integral stops on the supply plumbing run. They isolate the plumbing from the rest of the house. Check local codes regulating installation of scald guards. They prevent someone from being scalded in the shower when cold water pressure changes, such as when a toilet is flushed. Bathtubs are heavy. Have someone help with the installation.

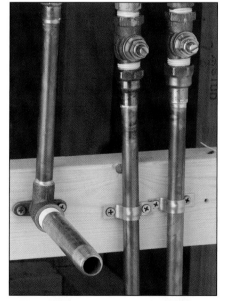

1 FRAME THE WALLS AND RUN THE SUPPLY CONTROL RISER. Frame the walls so that the alcove opening is just large enough to slide the tub into place. Leave a gap of ⅛ inch or less at the head and foot of the tub. Install plumbing for the risers, faucet, and showerhead (see page 96). Place 2×4 blocking as needed to secure the faucets, spout, and showerhead.

WORK SMARTER

MAKE A BED FOR MODERN TUBS

A cast-iron tub is plenty strong on it's own, but tubs made of enameled steel, acrylics, fiberglass, and similar materials flex when you fill them with water. Give them some extra support with a bed of sand mix. (Check the warranty to make sure the mix and the tub are compatible.) Sand mix is similar to concrete mix without the stones. Mix according to directions, and pour on the floor directly beneath the tub before you position it. Cover the wet mix with 6 mil. plastic sheeting to prevent any possible reaction with the tub.

Place 2x4 blocking behind the spout and the fixture to securely mount them to the wall.

2 MEASURE THE OPENING. Before you buy a tub, measure the alcove's width and length, and buy a tub to fit. Once you've run the supply lines and cut the access hole, slide the tub into the alcove for a test fit. See "Work Smarter," above.

Installing a bathtub in an alcove (continued)

3 **CHECK FOR LEVEL.** Lay a carpenter's level on the tub to check for level. If you are not setting the tub in a bed (see page 131), you will need to shim the tub to level it. Because wood shims will rot when exposed to moisture, use flattened copper tubing or plastic shims. Once level, mark the top of the nailing flange at each stud.

4 **DETERMINE THE LEDGER BOARD MOUNTING HEIGHT.** Ledger boards are required for fiberglass and polymer/acrylic tubs. Measure the distance from the top of the nailing flange to the underside of the tub rim inset. Subtract that figure—about 1 inch—from the marks on the wall studs and mark the ledger board mounting height.

5 **CONNECT THE P-TRAP.** Install the drainpipe and P-trap if they have not already been roughed in (see pages 101–102). Cut an access hole into the subfloor. Make it 4 to 9 inches wide and extending 12 inches from the center of the end wall. Connect the 1½-inch P-trap below the floor level so that the slip nut fitting is centered directly under the overflow and drainpipe on the tub.

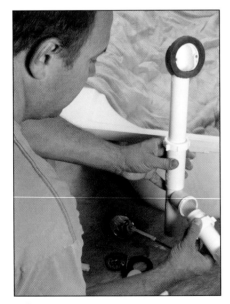

6 **DRY-FIT THE TUB DRAIN AND OVERFLOW.** Following the manufacturer's instructions, assemble the drain system so that you can measure and trim the drain tailpiece to connect with the P-trap. (See "Tub Drain Assembly," page 133.)

7 **TRIM THE DRAINPIPE.** The tub drainpipe will slide into the pressure fitting on the P-trap. It may be necessary to trim the pipe to fit smoothly. Check the manufacturer's instructions for installation.

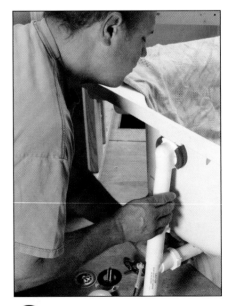

8 **CONNECT THE OVERFLOW** and drain to the tub and set the tub in place.

PLUMBING

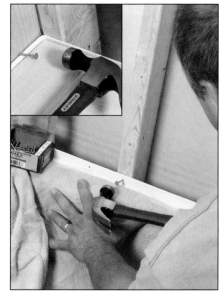

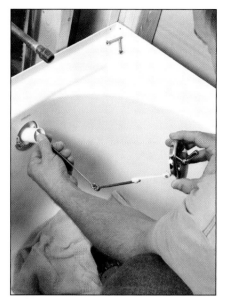

9 **INSTALL LEDGER BOARDS.** Cut the ledger boards to fit the alcove. Then use wood screws or galvanized nails to attach them to the studs following the marks you made in Step 4. Install the boards in sections if necessary to make room for any structural braces at the ends of the tub. Double-check for level.

10 **SET THE TUB INTO PLACE.** Seat the tub on the ledgers. The tub must sit firmly on the ledger strips and the drain must fit smoothly into the P-trap. Nail through the predrilled holes using galvanized nails. (If there are no holes, drive the nails so that the nailhead anchors the tub to the studs; see above inset.) Protect the tub with cardboard placed underneath a towel or rag.

11 **INSERT THE DRAIN PLUG LINKAGE.** Install the drain linkage through the overflow opening. Attach the overflow cover plate to the mounting flange with screws. Test the system for leaks and schedule a city inspection, if necessary, before you finish the walls and tile.

BUYER'S GUIDE

TILING THE WALLS
Planning to tile the walls? Tiles need a solid surface that can support their weight. Also, moisture may get behind the tiles, so the surface needs to withstand moisture damage. Use cement backerboard for the substrate; it's typically required by code.

Installing the drain assembly can take a little fiddling before you get it exactly right—be patient and take your time. Limit frustration by test-fitting everything before you do the final installation.

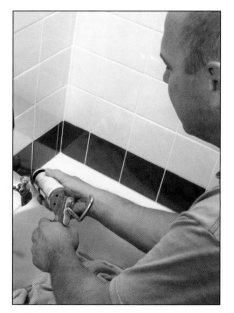

12 **CONNECT THE FAUCET HANDLES AND TUB SPOUT.** Use tub-and-tile caulk to seal around the faucet handles and tub spout. Apply a bead of caulk around the edge of the tub. Turn the water on and check for leaks.

TUB DRAIN ASSEMBLY

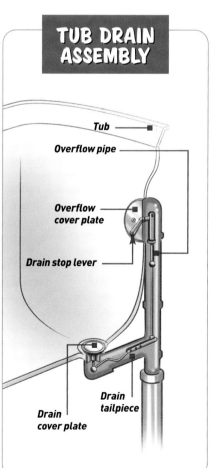

Tub

Overflow pipe

Overflow cover plate

Drain stop lever

Drain cover plate

Drain tailpiece

Installing a shower surround

Shower surrounds are quick and easy to install and have built-in soap and shampoo caddies. Surrounds can be installed directly over securely fastened ceramic tile. Loose ceramic tiles—and any plastic tiles—must be removed and the walls sanded smooth before installation. In new installations the enclosure should be applied over waterproof backerboard.

SKILL SCALE

EASY	MEDIUM	HARD

REQUIRED SKILLS: Using cutting tools, applying adhesive, and installing panels.

HOW LONG WILL IT TAKE?

Experienced . . . . 3 hrs.
Handy . . . . 5 hrs.
Novice . . . . 8 hrs.

STUFF YOU'LL NEED

✔ **MATERIALS:**
Tub enclosure, detergent, cardboard for template, double-stick tape, tub surround adhesive, silicone caulk, expanding foam

✔ **TOOLS:**
Tape measure, pipe wrench, screwdriver or hex wrench set, bucket, sponge, hole saw, utility knife, carpenter's pencil, caulking gun, rags

WORK SMARTER

THE RIGHT STUFF
Use only an adhesive made specifically for shower surrounds. Other adhesives may melt through the plastic.

① PREPARE THE ENCLOSURE. Shut off the main water supply. Remove all fittings. Clean film and dirt from the wall surface and dry thoroughly. Prep cement backerboard with a stain-blocking primer to create good bonding. Allow the surface to dry completely before installing the surround.

③ APPLY ADHESIVE TO THE PANEL using a caulking gun. Apply dots of the adhesive at intervals of no more than 12 inches along the vertical length of the panel. Rows of adhesive near the edge should be set back from it by 3 inches.

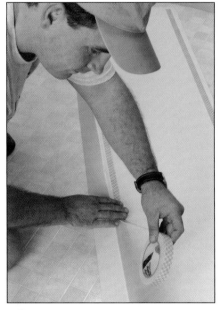

② SELECT A CORNER PANEL. It doesn't matter which corner you start in. Select a corner panel and test-fit it. Remove the panel and lay it on the floor with the surface that goes next to the wall facing up. Apply a pressure-sensitive, double-sided, 1-inch tape along the vertical edges of the panel.

BUYER'S GUIDE

PROVIDING VENTILATION
Bathrooms are the wettest places in the house and, therefore, need adequate ventilation to keep the buildup of moisture at a level that won't make the paint peel and the floor warp. A new shower surround will often cover a window that is the primary source of ventilation for the bathroom. If that's the case, you'll need to install a vent fan or make a cutout in the surround to allow access to the window.

Kits contain all the materials you'll need to do the framing job, or you can trim it out with a primed, painted, and sealed wooden frame.

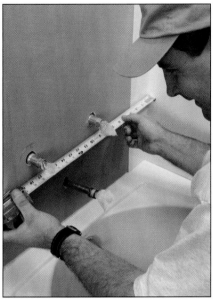

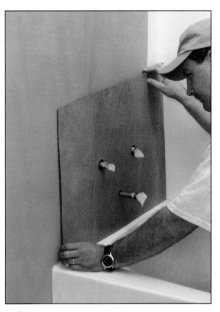

4 **INSTALL THE FIRST CORNER PANEL.** Position the panel. Press it firmly onto the wall, then pull it back about 6 inches for a few minutes (or per the manufacturer's instructions) to let the adhesive set up. Push the panel back in place. Firmly apply pressure, up and down, and side to side, making firm contact with the wall. Repeat in the opposite corner.

5 **MEASURE THE OUTLETS.** Create a cardboard template for the openings into one end panel for the faucet and spout piping. Determine the height from the bottom of the panel and the distance of each fitting from the inside edge of the panel.

6 **TEST-FIT THE TEMPLATE** by laying it against the wall, making sure the template openings line up with the pipe outlets. If they don't, remeasure them and make a new template.

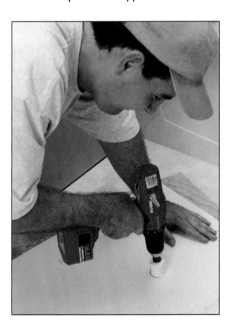

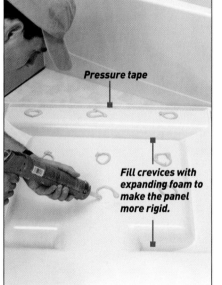

Pressure tape

Fill crevices with expanding foam to make the panel more rigid.

7 **CUT THE OPENINGS IN THE PANEL.** Mark the positions of the openings on the back of the panel with the template—drilling from the back will minimize chipping. Placing a piece of scrap wood beneath the panel will produce a cleaner cut. Test-fit a final time and use a hole saw to cut the openings.

8 **APPLY PRESSURE TAPE AND ADHESIVE.** You can fill the crevices in the panel with expanding foam to make them more rigid. Apply carefully; too much foam can expand and crack the panel. Position the panel onto the wall. Apply pressure by hand—side to side—to mount. Install the remaining panels.

9 **SEAL WITH A BEAD OF CAULK.** Use a caulking gun to apply a quality tub-and-tile sealant. Seal along the outside edges of the panel and around the fixtures. To get a "perfect bead," use a small spoon dipped in soapy water to smooth the caulk line. Avoid using the shower for at least 24 hours, or follow the manufacturer's instructions.

Removing an old toilet

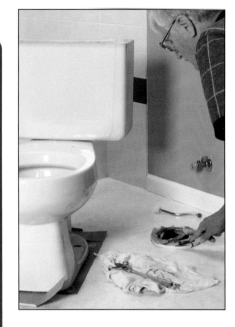

The biggest challenges in removing a toilet are getting the job done without creating a watery mess and not filling the house with sewer gases.

1. **Turn off the water supply at the shutoff valve.** Flush the toilet until the tank is empty. Wipe up excess water with rags and a sponge. Disconnect the supply tube.

2. **Remove the tank bolts** with a ratcheting socket wrench.

3. **Lift the tank off the bowl.** Be careful—most toilets are made of porcelain, which is easily damaged.

4. **Remove the toilet base.** Remove the floor bolt caps and then the nuts from the floor bolts. Rock the toilet from side to side to break the wax seal; lift it off the bolts and set it on an old towel. Plug the drain opening with a rag to keep sewer gases in the pipes.

5. **Scrape the old wax from the toilet flange** with a putty knife.

SAFETY ALERT

POTENTIAL BIOHAZARD!
The water in the toilet bowl may contain harmful bacteria. Wear rubber gloves when cleaning or removing the bowl. Avoid splashes. Wash your hands thoroughly with an antibacterial soap afterward.

A+ WORK SMARTER

CONNECTING OLD DRAINS TO NEW TOILETS

Before buying a new toilet, make sure it matches the location of the drain ("rough-in") on the bathroom floor.

Measure from wall to the toilet floor bolts, which are centered on the floor drain. In newer bathrooms, the distance is 12 inches from the wall. Most new toilets are designed to fit these specifications. If you live in a house built before the mid-1940s, however, the outlet may be 10 or 14 inches from the wall. You can get some toilets with a 10- or 14-inch rough-in, but not in all models, styles, and colors.

If you have your heart set on a toilet with a 12-inch rough-in, but your rough-in is 10 or 14 inches, it can be fixed. It's a big job, but you can install what's called an offset flange, then connect the new toilet's drain to the floor outlet.

CLOSER LOOK

GOT SOME TOUGH NUTS TO CRACK?

Nuts and bolts on toilet bowls can become so corroded that an adjustable wrench won't budge them, or the wrench will round the corners of the nut, making removal next to impossible. You may expand your vocabulary, but you won't budge the nut without applying some special techniques.

1. Before you attack the nut in the first place, assume it may be seized; squirt on some penetrating oil. Let the oil soak in thoroughly before you try removing the nut.

2. Try a minihacksaw. Protect the toilet base with masking tape and cut the nut at a slight angle (about 30 degrees) until you have a deep groove. Insert a screwdriver into the groove and twist to break the nut.

3. As a last resort (or first resort if you have one in your toolbox), you can use a nut splitter, which is a tool often found in the automotive section of your hardware store. The splitter fits over the nut. Hold it in position with an adjustable wrench and tighten it with a socket wrench that closes the jaws of the nut splitter against the nut and cuts it in half.

Installing a new toilet

If you're installing a new toilet in a new location, you'll need to run (or have someone run) a water supply line and a drainpipe, which must be connected to the drain/vent system in compliance with code. If the toilet is in the basement, you'll need an upflush toilet. Talk with your plumbing supplier to see what's involved.

SOME PARTS ARE EXTRA. Most of the parts you need to install the new toilet will come with it—except the toilet seat, which is a separate item on almost every model. The wax ring—which comes in several sizes—is also not part of the package. The manual that comes with the new toilet will tell you the correct size to buy.

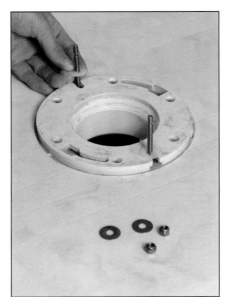

① SET THE MOUNTING BOLTS. If you're reusing the old flange, replace the 3½-inch flange bolts. Purchase two 3½-inch-long closet bolts at your local home center. If you're replacing the flange, it must be screwed into a wooden floor. Use self-tapping concrete screws for concrete. Closet bolts often tip over when you're trying to place the toilet. Put an extra nut on each bolt, and tighten it against the flange to hold the bolts in place.

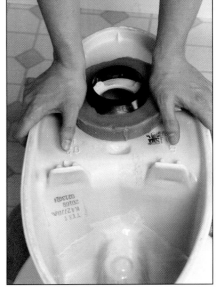

② PLACE THE WAX RING ON THE TOILET. The "no-seep" wax ring size will vary with the size of the flange. Be sure to purchase the proper size. A 3-inch neck will fit a 3-inch closet elbow, and a 4-inch neck will fit a 4-inch closet elbow. If the closet elbow is 4 inches and the neck is 3 inches in diameter, purchase a 4×3 reducer. If the flange is positioned below floor level, buy a double-thick ring.

Installing a new toilet *(continued)*

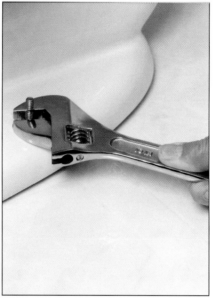

3 **SET THE TOILET BOWL.** Straddle the toilet bowl and lift, using your legs—not your back. Toilets are heavy, so get some help. Set the toilet over the anchor bolts and sit on the toilet, rocking it back and forth to seat the wax ring. Slip a washer over the closet bolt.

4 **TIGHTEN THE NUTS** against the washer by hand. With a wrench, tighten each nut a half-turn. Alternate tightening each side a half-turn until the toilet fits snugly. Tightening either side too much will cause the toilet to crack. If the toilet rocks or isn't level, shim it with plastic toilet shims, and cut the ends off, so they won't be seen.

5 **CUT THE FLANGE BOLT TO SIZE.** Use a minihacksaw to cut the flange bolt so only ¼ to ½ inch extends above the bolt. This will allow the cap to fit snugly. Most bolts have snap-offs every ½ inch or so, but you should still cut through so you don't bend the bolt.

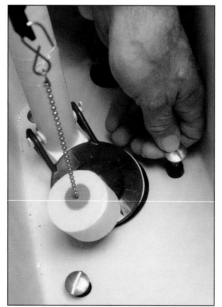

6 **INSTALL THE BOLT CAP.** Some types of caps will snap over the bolt. Others have to be filled with plumber's putty and seated over the anchor bolt.

7 **SET THE TANK ANCHOR BOLTS.** Place the tank anchor bolts in the holes of the tank to help guide the tank onto the bowl.

8 **PLACE THE TANK ON THE BOWL.** Lift the tank and place it over the bowl. You may need some help with this. Guide the tank bolts into the corresponding holes on the toilet bowl.

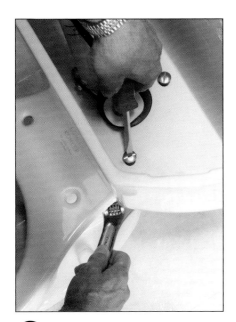

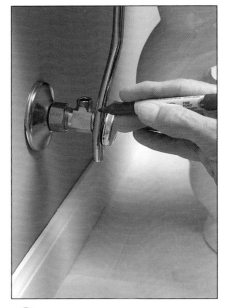

⑨ TIGHTEN THE TANK BOLTS. Hold an adjustable wrench over the tank bolt nut while you tighten the bolt with a screwdriver. Don't overtighten; you can crack either the tank or the bowl.

⑩ INSTALL THE SHUTOFF VALVE. Set the valve over the compression ring and draw the nut to it. Tighten the nut until hand-tight. Use two adjustable wrenches to tighten until snug—one to hold back the valve and the other to tighten the compression nut.

⑪ ALWAYS REPLACE THE SUPPLY TUBE TO HELP PREVENT LEAKS. Screw flex tube in place. If you're putting in chrome tube, hold it in place with the extra pipe extending past the shutoff. Mark the pipe for cutting. Leave enough pipe so it will fit inside the shutoff valve outlet. Cut with a tubing cutter.

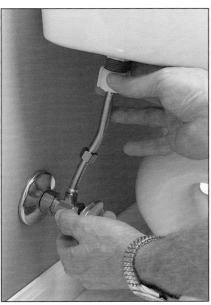

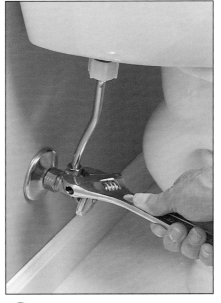

⑫ CONNECT THE SUPPLY PIPE TO THE TANK. Seat the end of the pipe against the tank. Draw up the tank nut, and hand-tighten until snug. Slide the compression nut over the other end, then place the compression ring over the end. Seat the end in the outlet of the shutoff valve.

⑬ TIGHTEN THE COMPRESSION NUT. Use an adjustable wrench to carefully tighten the compression nut. Don't overtighten. Turn on the water supply and check for leaks along the supply line, visually and by feel. Flush the toilet and check for leaks around the base of the tank. If there is a leak, tighten the connections a half-turn.

HOMER'S HINDSIGHT

GET THE RIGHT SIZE TOILET
Years ago I was browsing the plumbing aisle and saw the toilet of my dreams on clearance. Well, just because something's on sale doesn't mean it'll work. After I lugged it home I discovered the toilet didn't fit over the closet flange. Back then I didn't know the distance the drain is from the wall will determine the size of your toilet. Ninety percent of toilets are made for a drain opening 11 to 12 inches from the wall. The rest are either 9 to 10 or 13 to 14 inches away. On the plus side, I was lucky to pick a store that takes returns and I took home a valuable lesson about being an informed shopper.

Installing a garbage disposer

SKILL SCALE

EASY	**MEDIUM**	HARD

REQUIRED SKILLS: Connecting plumbing fittings and attaching electrical wires to terminals.

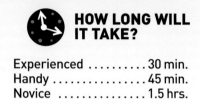 **HOW LONG WILL IT TAKE?**

Experienced .... 30 min.
Handy .... 45 min.
Novice .... 1.5 hrs.

VARIABLES: Time does not include installing a new circuit, if necessary.

A garbage disposer requires an electrical source for power. If you don't have one under the sink, you'll need to install one. Check with local codes before installation. Some communities have codes that don't allow disposers due to limits on sewer capacity. They may also require an air gap for a disposer and a dishwasher.

If you have a septic system, install a disposer specifically designed for use with a septic tank. Too much food waste can interfere with the normal decomposition of septic waste.

HOW MUCH HORSEPOWER?
In-home disposers with motors less than ½ horsepower are not recommended for households with more than two people. A 1-horsepower disposer is better. Not only is it more powerful, it has better sound insulation and may run more quietly.

STUFF YOU'LL NEED

✔ **MATERIALS:**
Garbage disposer, electrical cord, plumber's putty or silicone caulk

✔ **TOOLS:**
Screwdriver or disposer wrench, hacksaw or tubing cutter, water-pump pliers

TIME SAVER

SAVE THAT BRACKET
Are you replacing an existing garbage disposer with the same brand? You may be able to use the existing mounting bracket to make the job easier and quicker.

If the sink is made of cultured marble or a composite, use silicone caulk instead of plumber's putty to seal the flange.

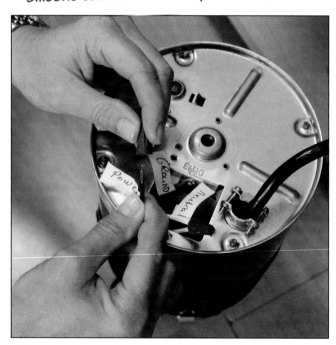

① WIRE THE DISPOSER. The disposer may come with the appliance cord attached. If not, you will have to connect one. Remove the cover plate beneath the disposer. Most cords and disposers have the same colored wires. Connect white to white, black to black, and the green wire to the disposer's ground screw. If the colors are different, read the manufacturer's instructions for wiring.

② APPLY PLUMBER'S PUTTY. Press a rope of plumber's putty onto the underside of the drain flange. Insert the flange into the drain hole and press down evenly. Install the backup ring, fiber gasket, and mounting ring from beneath the sink.

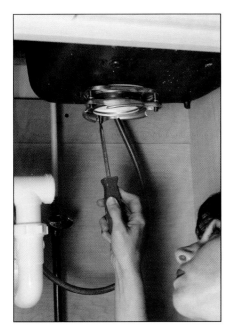

3 **INSTALL THE MOUNTING RING.** Tighten the mounting screws for the upper mounting ring. Alternate the tightening of the screws to pull the ring up evenly against the sink.

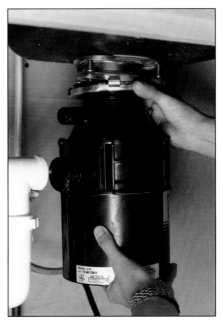

4 **MOUNT THE DISPOSER.** Place the disposer into the mounting ring, making sure the outlet of the disposer is facing the drainpipe connection. Turn the lower ring clockwise until the disposer is supported by the mounting assembly.

GOOD IDEA

CONNECT A DISHWASHER
Be sure the disposer you purchase has a knockout for a dishwasher. Remove the knockout for the dishwasher connection on the disposer. Connect the dishwasher discharge line to the disposer using hose clamps. If local codes require an air gap between the dishwasher and the disposer, see page 142 for instructions on installing one.

5 **CONNECT THE OUTLET TO THE P-TRAP.** Measure and then use a hacksaw or tubing cutter to cut the discharge pipe to length. Install the discharge pipe to the outlet of the disposer. Attach to the drain line with slip nuts.

6 **TIGHTEN THE MOUNTING LUG.** Insert a screwdriver or disposer wrench into the mounting lug on the lower mounting ring. Turn clockwise until the disposer is locked into place. Tighten all slip nuts snug using water-pump pliers. Run water into the sink. Turn on the disposer and check for leaks. Tighten fittings if necessary.

A+ WORK SMARTER

GETTING SOME LEVERAGE
Sometimes the trickiest part of mounting the garbage disposer is the moment when you lift it up and lock it into the mounting rings. The pros will stack a couple of thick telephone books under the unit so they won't have so far to lift. You can do the same thing, or use scrap lumber, a toolbox, or the box the unit came in.

Some disposers come with a special wrench that is used to turn the impeller when the disposer gets jammed. Keep it and the manual in an easy-to-remember location.

Replacing a dishwasher

SKILL SCALE

EASY	**MEDIUM**	HARD

REQUIRED SKILLS: Connecting plumbing fittings and attaching wire to a terminal.

HOW LONG WILL IT TAKE?

Experienced . . . . 1 hr.
Handy . . . . 1.5 hrs.
Novice . . . . 3 hrs.

VARIABLES: Time involved in running power, water, and drain lines for a new installation is not included.

STUFF YOU'LL NEED

✔ MATERIALS:

Air gap, drain hose, hose clamps, wire nuts, flexible copper tubing and compression fittings, drain tailpiece with inlet

✔ TOOLS:

Level, power drill, hole saw, screwdriver, adjustable wrench, tubing cutter

A dishwasher will clean your plates and glasses, and your countertop as well—by eliminating stacks of dirty dishes on display. Measure your space to find out what size you need. Most dishwashers are 18 or 24 inches wide.

Many dishwashers are designed to drain directly into the garbage disposer while others drain through an air gap that prevents a clogged drain from backing up into the dishwasher.

Take a look at the yellow Energy Guide label for the model's efficiency rating. The lower the number, the less energy the dishwasher will use over a one-year period.

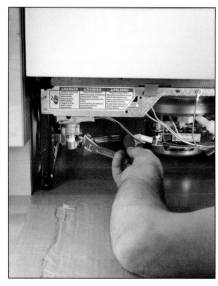

1 CONNECT THE LINES. Slide the dishwasher into place. Level it by adjusting the threaded feet. (Check the door. When level, it will open and close smoothly.) When level, tighten the locknuts. Align the mounting brackets with the counter. Follow the manufacturer's directions to connect the supply tubing to the dishwasher solenoid. Simplify the job by using braided, flexible tubing made for dishwasher supply.

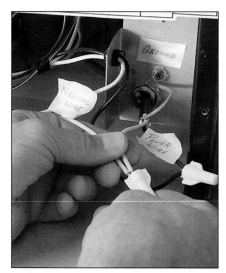

3 HOOK UP THE POWER. Match the wires: white to white, black to black, and connect the green to the ground screw. If the colors are different, read the manufacturer's instructions for connecting the wires. Connect the wires with wire nuts. Plug the power supply cord into an electrical outlet installed under the sink cabinet. Run the dishwasher through a test cycle to make sure it works properly.

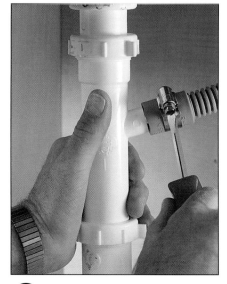

2 INSTALL THE DRAIN LINE. Connect the drain line to the dishwasher outlet using hose clamps. Measure the hose and cut it to length so that it connects to the tailpiece inlet under the sink. Connect the hose to the inlet with another hose clamp. If local codes require an air gap, install one using the manufacturer's instructions.

A+ WORK SMARTER

INSTALLING AN AIR GAP

Some local codes require an air gap between the dishwasher and the disposer. Mount the air gap in the countertop; if there is an extra hole available in the sink, mount it there. Connect a ⅝-inch drain hose to the ½-inch leg of the air gap with a hose clamp. Attach a ⅞-inch hose to the ¾-inch leg of the air gap. Make sure there are no low spots or kinks in either hose.

INSTALLING WATER HEATERS

Even with proper maintenance, your water heater will eventually need to be replaced. Either a gas or electric water heater will supply your hot water needs efficiently. Choosing one over the other is a matter of what kind of service is available to your home and what makes the most economic sense.

PAY ATTENTION TO THE WARRANTY. Warranties vary in length. Six to 12 years on the tank is the usual life span. Check the limitations of different manufacturers' warranties. The life of the water heater will depend on environmental factors; hard water shortens its life.

THE ENERGY FACTOR. Water heaters bear a yellow Energy Guide sticker that shows yearly usage for electricity and natural gas.

Rate of recovery is not listed on the tag, but ask about it. It reports how quickly the unit heats the water.

SIZE MATTERS—ELECTRICITY. A family of up to four in a home with two full bathrooms, a washing machine, and a dishwasher should have a 50- to 80-gallon tank with a 5,500-watt heating element. A family of five with the same appliances should have a 65- to 80-gallon tank and a 5,500-watt model.

SIZE MATTERS—GAS. A family of up to four in a home with two full bathrooms, a washing machine, and a dishwasher needs a 50-gallon tank with a 40,000-Btu burner unit. A family of six with the same appliances needs a 50- to 75-gallon tank and a 40,000-Btu model. A family of up to seven needs a 50- to 75-gallon, high-input 52,500-Btu unit.

SAFETY ALERT

CARBON MONOXIDE IS DANGEROUS

Colorless and odorless, carbon monoxide causes about 10,000 injuries a year. Symptoms of gas poisoning include headaches, fatigue, and nausea. Install a carbon monoxide detector and have gas appliances inspected once a year.

The tankless story

Electric or gas tankless "on demand" water heaters have recently been introduced in North America. While more expensive, they are more efficient than conventional water heaters. The savings in energy and maintenance could make up the difference in cost.

Tankless heaters save money because they don't need to heat a tank full of water. When you turn on the faucet, cold water flows through heating coils and is instantly heated to 105 to 115 degrees. When the faucet is turned off, the heating coils turn off as well.

Check details with your local home center. Large tankless heaters may require professional installation. Smaller "on demand" heaters can be installed in remote locations. (See page 147.)

PLUMBING

GAS

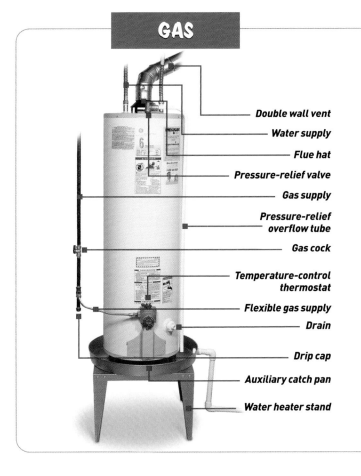

- Double wall vent
- Water supply
- Flue hat
- Pressure-relief valve
- Gas supply
- Pressure-relief overflow tube
- Gas cock
- Temperature-control thermostat
- Flexible gas supply
- Drain
- Drip cap
- Auxiliary catch pan
- Water heater stand

ELECTRIC

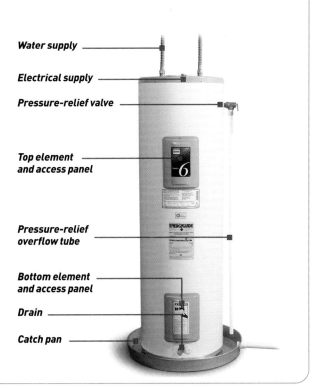

- Water supply
- Electrical supply
- Pressure-relief valve
- Top element and access panel
- Pressure-relief overflow tube
- Bottom element and access panel
- Drain
- Catch pan

Water heater installation basics

EASY	MEDIUM	HARD

REQUIRED SKILLS: Connecting plumbing fittings, stripping wire, and attaching wire to a terminal.

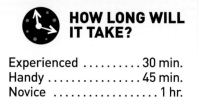

HOW LONG WILL IT TAKE?

Experienced .... 30 min.
Handy .... 45 min.
Novice .... 1 hr.

STUFF YOU'LL NEED

✔ MATERIALS:
Electric water heater, acid-free flux, Teflon tape or pipe compound, wire nuts, water heater heat trap fittings, 2×4 support, plastic shims, matches or grill igniter, masking tape

✔ TOOLS:
Hacksaw or tubing cutter, wire brush, carpenter's level, two adjustable wrenches, MAPP torch, screwdriver, rags

A+ WORK SMARTER

HEAVY WATER
Even empty water heaters are heavy and clumsy. Get the old heater out of the way first. If possible, leave the new heater in its box and slide it gently down the stairs. Stand it up and slide it to where it belongs before you cut off the box.

Installing a new water heater begins with the old heater. If you've got an electric heater, replace it with an electric heater, unless you're willing and able to run gas line and exhaust vents. If you've got a gas heater, stick with gas, unless your breaker box has room for (and you're willing to install) a new 240-volt circuit.

Whether the heat source is gas or electricity, make sure you shut it off before beginning work. Electric heaters can be cut off at the breaker box and may have an additional breaker closer to the heater. Gas heaters will have a cut off valve, usually with a red handle, along the line leading to the hot water heater.

Water and electricity are a dangerous mix. The power should be the first thing turned off and the last thing turned on during the installation process.

1 **REMOVE THE OLD WATER HEATER.** Turn off the water and gas supply valves and the power. Remove the electrical supply access plate at the top of the water heater. Check the connections with a continuity tester to make sure the power is off. Attach a garden hose to the drain valve and empty the tank. Using two pipe wrenches, disconnect the gas line at the union fitting if the pipe is galvanized, or at the flare fitting if the gas supply line is copper.

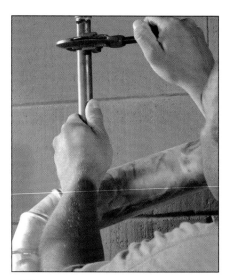

2 **DISCONNECT THE WATER LINES.** Using two adjustable wrenches or pipe wrenches, disconnect the piping above the tank. If the piping has been soldered into place, use a tubing cutter to cut it.

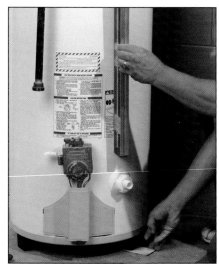

3 **SET THE NEW WATER HEATER.** Install the water heater in an area where it won't be cramped. Leave at least 6 inches of clearance around it for ventilation. Don't set it next to flammables. Turn the water heater so that access to the burner and controls is unobstructed. Place a level on the side of the water heater and plumb it with plastic shims.

4 **WRAP THE HEAT TRAP FITTING THREADS.** Use Teflon tape on the pipe threads. These fittings are directional and must be installed properly. Both have arrows showing the correct direction for installation. Attach the blue-coded fitting to the cold water inlet with the arrow facing into the water heater. Attach the red fitting to the hot water outlet with the arrow pointing away from the water heater. Tighten using two pipe wrenches or adjustable pliers.

5 **IF YOU REMOVED THE SHUTOFF VALVE, REPLACE IT.** Sweat solder the shutoff valve to the end of the cold water supply pipe. Use a MAPP torch and lead-free solder to connect the valve to the supply line. Solder with the valve in the open position to avoid overheating the parts.

6 **INSTALL THE WATER LINES AND PRESSURE RELIEF LINE.** Use two adjustable wrenches to connect the pipe from the pipe run to the water heater. Turn the main shutoff on and open all line valves. Open all the faucets in the house and run the water until it flows steadily from them. Close the faucets.

INSTALLING WATER HEATERS
Wiring an electric water heater

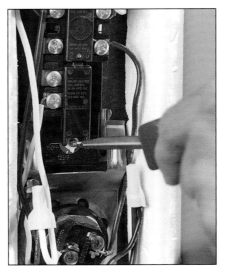

A+ WORK SMARTER

DON'T BLOW OUT THOSE HEATING ELEMENTS
Heating elements for electric heaters are extremely fragile. You'll burn them out in an instant if you power up the heater before it is full of water. To prevent this:

- Open the heater's cold water supply valve so that water can flow into the heater.

- Open the hot water faucet in the bathtub.

- When water starts flowing into the bathtub, the heater is full. Close the faucet, and turn on the electricity.

1 **REMOVE THE ELECTRICAL ACCESS PLATE.** Always turn off the power to the unit before you do any electrical work. Connect the electrical supply according to the manufacturer's instructions using wire nuts. Connect the bare copper or ground wire to the ground screw. Replace the electrical access plate. Remove the thermostat access plate.

2 **ADJUST THE THERMOSTAT.** Recommended settings are 120 to 125 degrees. Now open a faucet near the heater, turn on the water supply, and fill the tank until the faucet is flowing. The tank must be full before you restore power. When the tank is full, restore power and press the reset button on the panel.

Gas water heater installation

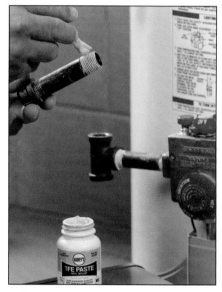

1 **INSTALL THE FLUE HAT VENT LINE.** Measure, cut, and assemble the vent pipe that runs from the flue hat to the roof vent stack. Make sure horizontal sections have a slope of ¼ inch of rise for every foot of length to efficiently carry fumes away from the house.

2 **ATTACH THE DUCTWORK.** Connect the ductwork by driving ⅜-inch sheet metal screws into the vent every 3 to 4 inches around the duct. You will need at least three screws per joint.

3 **CONNECT THE GAS SUPPLY LINE.** Clean all threads with a wire brush and rag. Apply pipe compound to the threads of the galvanized pipes as you connect them. Assemble and tighten each fitting with two pipe wrenches. Install the union fitting last because it connects the new line to the existing line. Once finished, open the gas supply valve.

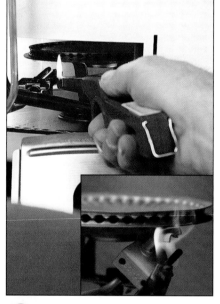

CHECKING FOR GAS LEAKS

Make sure the connections in your gas line are tight and that they don't leak any gas. Start by using plenty of pipe dope during assembly—it's cheap, and you can always wipe off the excess. When you turn the gas back on, check for leaks by brushing a 50-50 mixture of dishwashing soap and water on the joints. Leaks will show up quickly in the form of bubbles. Never test for leaks with a burning match. A small leak is enough to start a fire. A medium-sized leak can put enough gas into the air to cause a small explosion. And you never know—the leak you discover could be a large one.

4 **TEST THE GAS LINE FOR LEAKS.** Fill a sponge with liquid dishwashing soap and water. Apply it to the new fitting and look for bubbles. (The same process is used for finding a leak in a car tire.) If a leak is present, bubbles will form on the surface and you'll have to refit the joint. Test all connections.

5 **LIGHT THE PILOT.** Use a fireplace match or a grill igniter to light the pilot. Replace the burner access panel and set the control at 120 to 125 degrees.

Installing an on-demand water heater

EASY	MEDIUM	**HARD**

REQUIRED SKILLS: You will need basic carpentry, plumbing, and electrical skills.

 HOW LONG WILL IT TAKE?

Experienced . . . . 2 hrs.
Handy . . . . 4 hrs.
Novice . . . . 6 hrs.

VARIABLES: Make sure your breaker or fuse box has an extra circuit before starting. You'll need one free breaker for 120-volt heaters or two free breakers for 240-volt units. Time needed to run wire or pipe is not included in the estimate.

An on-demand water heater can easily be mounted under a kitchen sink or off to the side, in places where looks don't matter. When you turn the hot water tap on, the flow turns on a heating element that heats the water as it runs through copper tubes. When the faucet goes off, so does the heat. Because 20 percent of a home's energy use goes into heating water, an on-demand unit can save a lot of money.

To meet code, you will need a cutoff switch within sight of the unit, and cable must be flexible or housed in conduit.

STUFF YOU'LL NEED

✔ **MATERIALS:**
On-demand water heater, cutoff valves, solder, flux, Teflon tape, high-pressure flexible hose, cable, armored cable, junction box, cover and clamps, wire nuts, wire caps, electrician's tape

✔ **TOOLS:**
Pipe cutter, propane torch, wrench, drill and bits, screwdriver, wire cutter, needle-nose pliers

SAFETY ALERT
Turn off the power before you begin.

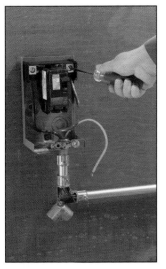

1 RUN POWER FOR THE UNIT. It will be either a 120- or a 240-volt circuit, and it must be a circuit wholly devoted to the heater. Either voltage requires 8-gauge wire, and the section exposed to the area under the sink must be armored cable. If the manufacturer's instructions call for a larger cable, the National Electrical Code says you must comply.

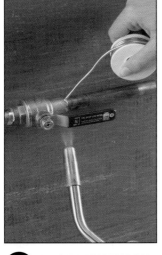

2 IF YOU'RE INSTALLING THE HEATER UNDER AN EXISTING SINK, turn off the water and cut through the water line. Drain the line by opening a faucet at a lower point somewhere in the house. Solder a cutoff valve onto the pipe stub that comes from the floor or wall. Solder a second valve onto what's left of the line that runs to the faucet, cutting the line as necessary to allow room for the heater. (For more on soldering, see page 93.)

3 SCREW THE UNIT TO THE WALL, following the manufacturer's directions. Connect the water supply line to the cold in-feed fitting with soldered copper pipe or high-pressure flex connections as shown here. Wrap Teflon tape around the threads before you make the connection and hand-tighen. Finish tightening with a wrench. Connect the line going to the faucet to the hot water outlet using the same materials.

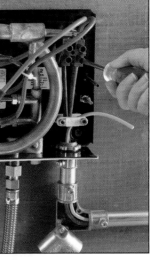

4 WIRE THE UNIT. On a 240-volt circuit, the white wire will attach to one of the hot terminals, and the black to the other hot terminal—they're often labeled L1 and L2. The ground will go to the grounding screw on the unit. On a 120-volt unit, twist the white supply wire to the white wire in the unit, and twist the black wire to the black. Cover with wire caps, and tape the caps in place.

4 ELECTRICAL

UPGRADING, REPAIRING, OR ADDING TO THE ELECTRICAL SYSTEM IN YOUR HOME is generally easier than most other major home improvement projects. It involves a minimum of heavy lifting, and most projects don't require expensive tools or costly materials. Electrical projects do, however, require working with electricity, and that scares many people away from repairs and installations they could do themselves. Following are some thoughts about working with what the fearful (or cautious) call Old Mr. Sparky:

1 Working on the electrical system is potentially dangerous. However, if you use common sense and approach projects with the same care and respect that a professional electrician does, you can perform electrical work safely and with confidence.

2 Electricians consult one another even when they're 99 percent sure they understand what's involved in the job, and you should as well. Proceed with a project, whether it's a simple repair or a major installation, only when you're sure you understand and can complete every step.

3 There are no "stupid" questions. The experts at home centers and hardware stores have years of experience in the business and are happy to share it.

4 Once you know what you're doing, electrical work is as simple as 1-2-3. Map the process, study the steps involved, get the necessary permits, schedule the required inspections, lay out all the tools and materials for the job, turn off the power, and get to work.

SECTION 4 PROJECTS

REAL-WORLD SITUATIONS

ELECTRICAL CODES MUST BE FOLLOWED!

Electrical codes are enforced to make sure electrical installations are safe and work properly, and inspectors don't kid around.

- When applying at your local building office for permits to do electrical work, present precise, easy-to-read drawings and include a complete list of materials for the project.

- Installations need to be seen to be inspected. Don't put up drywall or cover new wiring until the inspectors have signed off. If they don't approve the job, you'll do it over, and that can be expensive.

IMPORTANT NOTE: The projects in this section follow common national guidelines. Local codes can be stricter than national standards. Check local requirements carefully before you begin.

See page 536

How the electrical system works

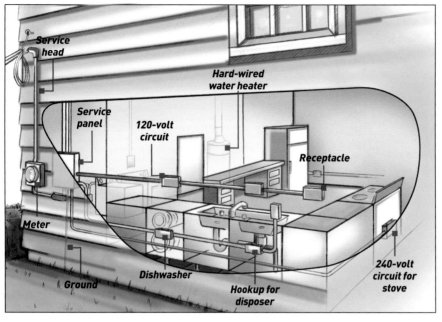

- Service head
- Hard-wired water heater
- Service panel
- 120-volt circuit
- Receptacle
- Meter
- Ground
- Dishwasher
- Hookup for disposer
- 240-volt circuit for stove

CLOSER LOOK

TECHNICAL ELECTRICAL

An **electrical outlet** is any place where electricity leaves the wires to perform a service—such as at a light fixture. A **receptacle** is an outlet where electricity exits the system through a plug. A **device** is something that carries, but does not use, electricity, such as a receptacle or switch. A **fixture** is an electrical outlet that is permanently fixed in place, and an **appliance** is a movable user of electricity. An overhead light is a fixture while a toaster is an appliance.

Electricity (current) is the flow of electrons through a conductor (usually copper or aluminum wire). The current travels in a loop, called a circuit, through a "hot" wire (usually black or red) to a fixture and returns through a "neutral" wire (usually white), completing the circuit. When the circuit is broken, the current ceases.

SAFETY ALERT

RESPECT YOUR BREAKER BOX

- Always know what's hot. The wires entering from the outside are always hot.

- Don't touch the bus bar; it remains hot even when a breaker has been shut off.

- Keep the cover on and closed (preferably locked) at all times.

- Post a circuit map on the door.

- Keep the area around the box clear and have a charged flashlight handy.

- Always wear rubber-soled shoes.

- Never clip temporary lines into the panel. (Welders and sanders will often want to clip temporary extension lines to the hot and neutral bars. Don't let them.)

The system is grounded to the earth to prevent a user from being shocked from damaged or defective wiring.

VOLTAGE AND AMPS. Voltage is electrical pressure exerted by the power source. Most household fixtures use 120 or 240 volts. Wires, appliances, and fixtures have different resistances to the voltage—the thicker the wire, the less resistance. Amperes and watts refer to the amount of electrical current used by devices in the system (such as a lightbulb).

POWERING YOUR HOME. Electricity flows from the utility provider through high-voltage wires to transformers that reduce the amount of power to 120 volts per wire. The wires enter your home through a service head, which attaches to a meter that records your power use. The wires then enter the service panel, which divides the power into circuits and then distributes power to outlets throughout your home.

Service to most homes is three-wire—two "hot" wires carrying power inside and one "neutral" wire completing the circuit. Two hot wires means that a home can run 120-volt and 240-volt circuits. Older homes with only one hot and a neutral are limited to 120-volt service.

KNOW YOUR LIMITS. Most repairs and installations can be performed safely inside the home. For any outdoor repairs or installations, including the service head and wires that feed the main shutoff in the service panel, call your local utility for service; that is its responsibility.

CIRCUIT BREAKER BOX

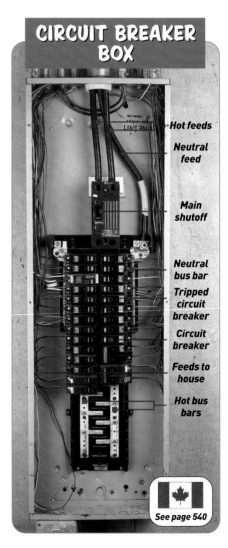

- Hot feeds
- Neutral feed
- Main shutoff
- Neutral bus bar
- Tripped circuit breaker
- Circuit breaker
- Feeds to house
- Hot bus bars

See page 540

Electrical safety

Electricity deserves your attention and respect. The wiring in a modern home should have safety features, such as grounding and ground fault circuit interruption. While both greatly reduce the possibility of dangerous shock, they fail to offer complete protection to a person working on exposed wires and devices. This danger is why professional electricians work very carefully; so should you.

SHUT OFF THE POWER. If there is no electrical current, you cannot receive a shock. A Always shut off power to the circuit on which you are working. Do this by flipping a circuit breaker or completely unscrewing a fuse. Then make sure you chose the right circuit by using a voltage meter to test the line: It should read zero.

TEST FOR POWER. Be aware that more than one circuit may be running in a box. B Test all the wires in an open box for power, not just the wires on which you will be working. Test everything twice.

STAY FOCUSED. Most electrical mishaps occur because of small, mental mistakes. Stories abound of someone turning off the power, only to have a family member or coworker turn it back on while work is in progress. C Post a sign telling others not to restore power; lock the service panel if possible. Remove all distractions. Keep others, especially children, well out of the way. Even after turning off the power, work as if the wires are live. Work methodically and double-check all connections before restoring power.

USE PROTECTIVE TOOLS AND CLOTHING. D Always use rubber-gripped tools. Grab tools by the handle, not the metal shaft. Don't touch any metal while working.

E Wear rubber-soled shoes and perhaps rubber gloves. Never work with wet feet or while standing on a wet surface. Do not wear jewelry or a watch—anything that could possibly get snagged on wires. Use a fiberglass or wooden ladder; an aluminum ladder conducts electricity.

ASK QUESTIONS. Never proceed with an installation or repair unless you are completely sure of what you are doing. Don't hesitate to ask "stupid" questions of electrical experts; they know there aren't any.

HOMER'S HINDSIGHT

SHOCKING STORY

A neighbor told me a potentially shocking story. He was doing some electrical upgrades while his family was out of town. He turned off the power at the breaker box just like you're supposed to but didn't put up a warning note. Lucky he was at the store and not connecting circuits when the family showed up early, found the lights out, and hit the breaker. Always put a warning on the box.

C Post a warning sign on the service panel.

A Shut off the power.

B Test for power.

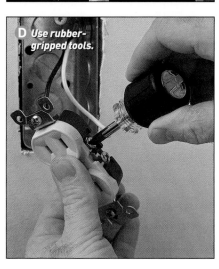

D Use rubber-gripped tools.

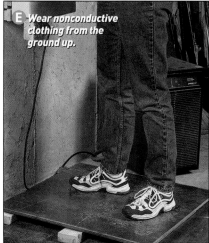

E Wear nonconductive clothing from the ground up.

THE ELECTRICIAN'S TOOL KIT

Below are some basic electrical tools. For more information see the Tool Glossary on page 544.

ELECTRICAL

2-PART CIRCUIT FINDER

CONDUIT REAMER

FISHING BIT

LEVELS

RUBBER-GRIP SCREWDRIVERS

TOOL BELT

4-LEVEL VOLTAGE TESTER

CONTINUITY TESTER

FLASHLIGHT

LINEMAN'S PLIERS

SABER SAW

TRENCHING SPADE

ADJUSTABLE WRENCH

DIGITAL MULTITESTER

FLAT PRY BAR

LONG-NOSE PLIERS

SIDE-CUTTING PLIERS

UTILITY KNIFE

ARMORED CABLE CUTTER

DRYWALL SAW

GFCI RECEPTACLE ANALYZER

MAGNETIC SLEEVE AND BIT

SPADE BIT

VOLTAGE DETECTOR

COAXIAL CRIMPER

ELECTRICAL TAPE

HACKSAW

NUT DRIVER

SPIRAL CUTTING SAW

WATER-PUMP PLIERS

COAXIAL STRIPPER

FIBERGLASS LADDER

HAMMER

POWER DRILL WITH ⅜" CHUCK

STAPLER

WIRE-BENDING SCREWDRIVER

COMBINATION STRIPPER

FISH TAPE

HOLE SAW

ROTARY SCREWDRIVER

TAPE MEASURE

WIRE STRIPPER/ CUTTER

Wires and cables

Use the right wire and cable to avoid creating a dangerous installation that you'll have to tear out and redo. Here are the basics:

WIRES. Wire is usually made of a single, solid strand of metal encased in insulation. For flexibility and ease of pulling, some wire is stranded (above right). Wire is sized according to American Wire Gauge (AWG) categories. Size determines how much amperage the wire will carry, and as of 2002, the color of the outer jacket tells you what gauge the wire is. Common household wires and their ratings and colors are:

- **#14 wire** (also called 14-gauge) carries 15 amps and is white.

- **#12 wire** carries 20 amps and is yellow.

- **#10 wire** carries 30 amps and is orange.

- **#8 wire** carries 30 amps and is black (as are all the gauges with numbers less than 8).

A wire that is overloaded to carry more amperage than it is rated for will dangerously overheat. Older wires have rubber insulation, which deteriorates after about 30 years. New wires have longer-lasting polyvinyl insulation. Insulation color often tells the function of wire: **Black, red,** or other colors indicate hot wire. **White** or **off-white** wire generally is neutral. **Green** or **bare** wire is ground.

See page 540

TYPES OF ELECTRICAL CABLE. Cable is two or more wires wrapped together and sheathed in plastic or metal. **Nonmetallic (NM) cable** is permitted inside wall, ceiling, and floor cavities. Special nailing plates must be added to the framing to protect the cable from puncture (see page 175). Printing on **NM cable** tells you what is inside: 12/3 means there are three #12 wires plus a ground wire. "G" means that there is a ground wire. For **underground installations and in damp areas use underground-feed (UF) cable.** UF cable encases the wires in solid plastic. **Telephone cable** is being supplanted by **CAT 5E cable,** suitable for telephones, modems, and computer networking. **Coaxial cable** carries television signals. **Armored cable** (see page 179) has a flexible, metal sheathing. One type of armored cable is **BX** (also called **AC**), which has no ground wire—the sheathing is used for grounding (the thin metal bonding strip cannot be used as a ground wire). The other armored cable is **metal-clad (MC) cable,** which has an insulated green grounding wire. (A similar material, Greenfield, or flexible conduit, is armored sheathing without wires. Install it, then pull wires through it.) **Conduit** is a solid pipe through which individual wires are run (see page 180). Metal conduit is often required in commercial installations. Most building departments require it only where the wiring is exposed (not behind plaster or drywall).

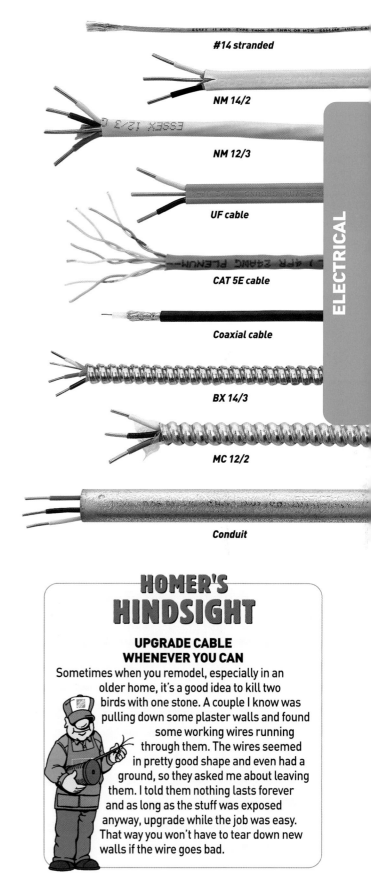

#14 stranded

NM 14/2

NM 12/3

UF cable

CAT 5E cable

Coaxial cable

BX 14/3

MC 12/2

Conduit

ELECTRICAL

HOMER'S HINDSIGHT

UPGRADE CABLE WHENEVER YOU CAN

Sometimes when you remodel, especially in an older home, it's a good idea to kill two birds with one stone. A couple I know was pulling down some plaster walls and found some working wires running through them. The wires seemed in pretty good shape and even had a ground, so they asked me about leaving them. I told them nothing lasts forever and as long as the stuff was exposed anyway, upgrade while the job was easy. That way you won't have to tear down new walls if the wire goes bad.

Wire nuts and tape

Wire nuts are required for all splices. The color of the wire nut indicates how many wires of a given size it can handle. Use **yellow** connectors for splices as small as two #14s or as large as three #12s. **Orange** nuts handle combinations ranging from two #16 wires up to two #14s. Use **green** wire nuts for ground wires only. The hole in the top allows you to make an instant pigtail (see page 160), with one wire poking out. **Red** wire nuts will grab splices as small as two #12s and as large as four #12s. **Black or blue** silicone wire nuts are waterproof once connected, though they should be protected by waterproof junction boxes.

Silicone wire nuts

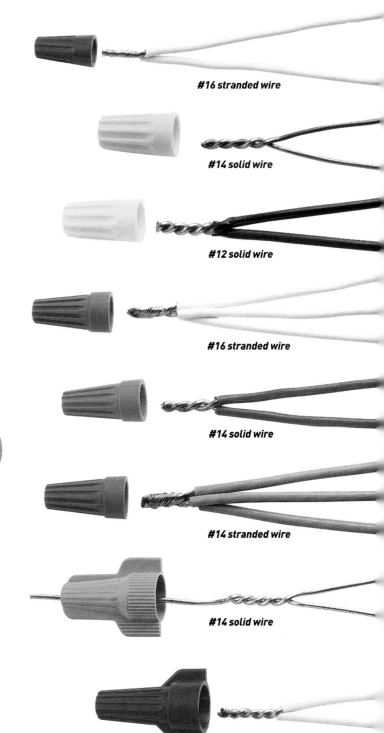

#16 stranded wire

#14 solid wire

#12 solid wire

#16 stranded wire

#14 solid wire

#14 stranded wire

#14 solid wire

#14 solid wire

#12 solid wire

HOMER'S HINDSIGHT

SPLICING WIRES

A guy I know makes his splices without twisting the wires together before he twists on a wire nut. "Just as strong and saves time," he said. "So, how much time will you save when one comes loose and you've got to take down an entire circuit to find the problem?" I asked. Believe me, you actually save time by doing the job right the first time.

Receptacles and switches

Most switches and receptacles in a home are designed to carry 15 amps. Look on the metal plate for the amperage rating. Any 15-amp device should be connected to #14 wire (see opposite page), which should lead to a 15-amp fuse or circuit breaker in the service panel.

Be sure that the amperage of a 240-volt receptacle is rated no lower than that of the appliance. If you are unsure as to which receptacle to use, check with your building department or ask an electrician.

See page 540

Switches

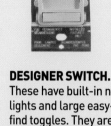

SINGLE-POLE.
This switch has two terminals for hot wires and a green terminal for ground. It is the most common household switch.

Ground terminal

Common terminal

Ground terminal

THREE-WAY.
Three-ways are installed in pairs—both switches control the same light(s) in either direction. There are no ON and OFF markings.

DESIGNER SWITCH.
These have built-in night lights and large easy-to-find toggles. They are available in single-pole and three-way.

240-volt receptacles

WALL-MOUNTED 240-VOLT RECEPTACLE.
Appliances using 240 volts have different plug designs to ensure that they are plugged into the correct receptacle. To be safe, check the information plate on the appliance to confirm that the amperage also matches that of the receptacle.

SURFACE-MOUNTED 120/240-VOLT RECEPTACLE.
Some heavy-duty appliances require receptacles with both standard voltage and high voltage. For example, a range commonly uses 240 volts for its burners and 120 volts for the light and the clock. A 120/240-volt receptacle provides both levels of power.

WALL-MOUNTED 120/240-VOLT RECEPTACLE.
This receptacle is typically used with a stove. Install it in a standard electrical box.

120-volt receptacles

UNGROUNDED 120-GROUNDED 15-AMP, 120-VOLT.
This is the most common household receptacle. It will overload if you plug in two items drawing more than 15 amps.

20-AMP, 120-VOLT.
This receptacle has a neutral slot shaped like a sideways T so that you can plug in large appliances or heavy-use tools. It should connect to #12 wires that lead to a 20-amp circuit or fuse in the service panel.

How a circuit works

Service panels, whether they have breakers or fuses, divide household current into several circuits. Each circuit carries power from the service panel via hot (usually black or red) wires to various outlets in the house, and then back to the service panel via a neutral (usually white) wire.

TYPES OF CIRCUITS. Most household circuits carry 120 volts; some may be 240-volt circuits. Circuits are rated according to amps. If the outlets on a circuit draw too many amps, the circuit overloads. When this happens, a fuse will blow or a breaker will trip (see pages 150–151), preventing an unsafe condition.

A 120-volt circuit usually serves a number of outlets. For instance, it may supply power to a series of lights, a series of receptacles, or some of each. A heavy-use item, such as a dishwasher or refrigerator, may have its own dedicated circuit. A 240-volt circuit is always dedicated to one outlet. A standard 120-volt 15-amp circuit uses #14 wire; a 20-amp circuit uses thicker #12 wire. Older 240-volt circuits use three wires; two hot and one neutral. Recent codes require four wires, as shown below; the added wire is for grounding.

Circuits provide convenience as well as safety. If you are making a repair or new installation, you can shut off power to an individual circuit rather than having to shut down power to the entire house.

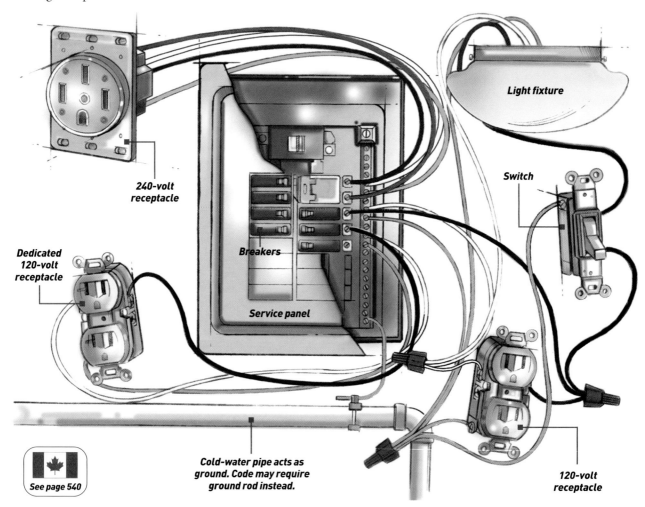

240-volt receptacle

Light fixture

Switch

Dedicated 120-volt receptacle

Breakers

Service panel

See page 540

Cold-water pipe acts as ground. Code may require ground rod instead.

120-volt receptacle

A SERVICE PANEL HAS 120- AND 240-VOLT CIRCUITS. Your service panel distributes power according to the needs of a circuit. For example, a 240-volt circuit is designed to supply electricity to a heavy-duty user of power, such as an electric range or a dryer. The single receptacle on a dedicated 120-volt circuit might feed a refrigerator or a large microwave, while another 120-volt circuit feeds a series of receptacles and overhead light fixture switches.

Grounding and polarization

Normally electricity travels through insulated wires and exits through a fixture such as a lightbulb. If a wire comes loose or if a device cracks, a short circuit (ground fault) results, releasing electricity where you don't want it. A short can occur, for example, if a loose wire inside a dryer touches the dryer's frame or if cracked insulation allows bare wire to touch a metal electrical box. If you touch electrified metal, you'll get a dangerous shock. Grounding and polarization protect against this. Here's how they work:

GROUNDING minimizes the possibility that a short circuit will cause a shock. A grounded device, fixture, or appliance is usually connected to a grounding wire—either bare or green— that leads to the neutral bar in the service panel. This bar is connected to the earth by a heavy-gauge copper grounding wire running to one or a combination of the following:

- cold-water pipe (If the water meter is installed on the cold-water pipe, the ground must be connected on the street side of the meter or the water meter must be jumped with a grounding wire tightly clamped to both sides.)

- grounding rods driven at least 10 feet in the ground

- metal plate sunk in a footing

Another method uses the metal sheathing of armored cable or conduit (see page 153) instead of a ground wire as the ground path to the service panel.

When a ground fault occurs, the ground path carries the power to the service panel. This extra path lowers resistance, causing a great deal of power to flow back to the panel. This in turn trips a circuit breaker or blows a fuse. At the same time, power is directed harmlessly into the earth.

Whether your system uses grounding wires or sheathing as the ground path, it must be unbroken. A single disconnected ground wire or a loose connection in the sheathing or conduit can make the grounding system useless. To check whether a receptacle is grounded, plug in a receptacle analyzer (see page 158).

POLARIZATION ensures that electricity goes where you want it to go. Because a polarized plug has one prong wider than the other, it can be inserted into a polarized receptacle only one way. If the receptacle is wired correctly and an appliance plug is polarized, the hot wire, not the neutral wire, will always be controlled by the appliance switch. If the receptacle or plug isn't polarized, the neutral wire might be connected to the appliance switch instead, and power would be present in the appliance even when it is switched off. For extra protection against shock, install GFCI protection (see page 164).

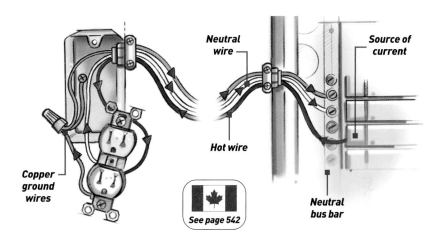

Neutral wire

Source of current

Hot wire

Neutral bus bar

Copper ground wires

See page 542

HOW A GROUNDED RECEPTACLE WORKS. To ground a receptacle, a ground wire (either **bare copper** or **green-clad copper**) is attached to the receptacle (and to the box, if it is metal) and leads to the neutral bus bar in the service panel. The panel itself is grounded. This receptacle is also polarized.

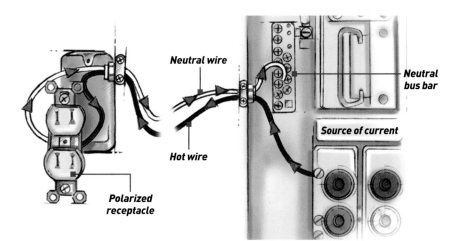

Neutral wire

Neutral bus bar

Hot wire

Source of current

Polarized receptacle

HOW A POLARIZED RECEPTACLE WORKS. The black wire is connected to the receptacle's brass terminal at one end and to the circuit breaker or fuse at the other end. The white wire runs from the silver terminal screw to the service panel's neutral bus bar.

Using testers

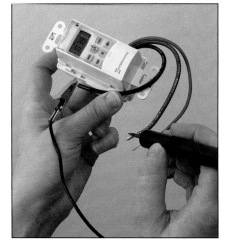

A CONTINUITY TESTER TELLS YOU WHETHER A DEVICE IS DEFECTIVE. Disconnect the device from all household wires. Attach the tester's alligator clip to one terminal and touch the probe to the other terminal. If the device switch is working, the tester light will glow when the switch is turned on and go out when the switch is turned off. To test the wiring in an appliance or lamp, touch both ends of each wire. The tester light will glow if the wire is unbroken. To test a fuse follow the same procedure.

A VOLTAGE DETECTOR SENSES POWER EVEN THROUGH WIRE AND CABLE INSULATION. This handy tester lets you check whether wires are live before you work on them. The probe doesn't need to touch a bare wire or terminal. Press the detector button and hold it on or near an insulated wire or cable to see if power is present. If it is, a light comes on.

TEST FOR VOLTAGE
Multitesters have negative and positive probes. Test for voltage by touching each probe to a wire, terminal, or receptacle slot. You also can touch one probe to the black wire and the other to a ground, such as a metal box. The display should show between 108 and 132 volts for a 120-volt circuit, and between 216 and 264 volts for a 240-volt circuit. Low-voltage circuitry can register as low as 4 volts.

A VOLTAGE TESTER INDICATES THE PRESENCE OF POWER. A four-level voltage tester is safer and more reliable than one-level versions. Always confirm that a voltage tester is working by trying it on a circuit you know to be live. Touch the tester's probes to a hot wire and a grounded box or to a hot wire and a neutral wire, or insert them into the slots of a receptacle. If the tester light doesn't come on, the circuit is shut off.

A RECEPTACLE ANALYZER TELLS YOU WHETHER YOUR RECEPTACLES ARE SAFE. When you plug this analyzer into a receptacle, one or more of three lights will glow, telling you whether the receptacle is working, grounded, and polarized (see page 157). Several styles are available, including some that vibrate or make noise to indicate which slot is hot. Red analyzers test ground fault circuit interrupter (GFCI) receptacles as well as standard receptacles. Yellow analyzers test standard receptacles only.

TEST FOR CONTINUITY
To test a switch with a multitester, shut off the power and disconnect the wires from the switch. Set the dial on the multitester to any ohms setting and touch a test probe to each terminal. Turn the switch on. Zero resistance shows the switch works; infinity means it is defective. The tester should indicate infinity when you turn the switch off.

Stripping and splicing wire

STUFF YOU'LL NEED

✔ **MATERIALS:**
Wire, wire nuts, electrician's tape

✔ **TOOLS:**
Combination stripper, lineman's pliers or side-cutting pliers

When splicing two wires together, strip off about 1 inch of insulation. If the wire will be joined to a terminal, remove about ¾ inch.

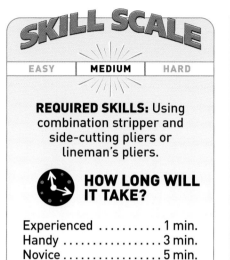

Combination stripper

1 STRIP WIRES WITH A COMBINATION STRIPPER. To use a combination stripper, slip the wire into the correct-size hole, squeeze, twist, and pull off the insulation. Yellow-handled strippers are for solid wire. Red-handled strippers are for stranded wire, like that found in lamp cords.

3 CUT THE END. Using the lineman's pliers or side-cutting pliers, snip off the end of the twist. Leave enough exposed metal so that the wire nut will just cover it—about ½ inch usually does it.

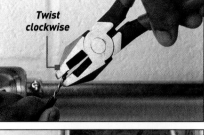

Twist clockwise

Lineman's pliers

2 TWIST WIRES TOGETHER. Hold the stripped wires side by side. Grab both with lineman's pliers. Twist clockwise, making sure that both wires turn. Twist them together like a candy cane to form a neat-looking spiral; don't overtwist or the wires may break.

SPLICING THREE OR FOUR WIRES. When twisting three or four wires together, hold them parallel and twist them all at once with lineman's pliers.

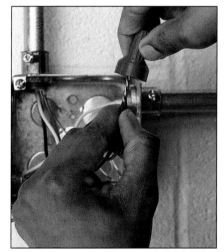

4 CAP WITH A WIRE NUT. Select a wire nut designed for the number and size of wires you have spliced (see page 154). Slip the nut on as far as it will go, then twist clockwise until tight. Test the connection by tugging on the nut; it should hold securely for dependable protection. Wrap electrician's tape around the bottom of the cap.

ELECTRICAL

Joining wire to a terminal

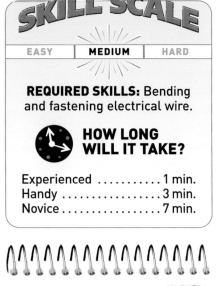

SKILL SCALE

| EASY | **MEDIUM** | HARD |

REQUIRED SKILLS: Bending and fastening electrical wire.

HOW LONG WILL IT TAKE?

Experienced . . . . 1 min.
Handy . . . . 3 min.
Novice . . . . 7 min.

STUFF YOU'LL NEED

✔ **MATERIALS:**
Wire, device with terminals

✔ **TOOLS:**
Long-nose pliers, side-cutting pliers, wire-bending screwdriver

Joining wire to a terminal is an important skill and a key step in most electrical projects. Do this step properly to ensure the device works and doesn't develop a short.

MAKING THE RIGHT CONNECTION. Electricians wrap the wire nearly all the way around the screw to make a connection that is completely reliable; with some practice, you can make joints just as strong. Bend a wire in a quarter circle, slip it under the screw head, and tighten the screw.

Many devices come with terminal screws unscrewed. Screw in any unused terminal screws so they won't stick out dangerously, creating a shock hazard should the terminal touch a metal box.

See page 540

When removing an old device, you may find spliced wire wrapped with rubberized tape covered with cloth friction tape. Slice the friction tape with a utility knife to remove.

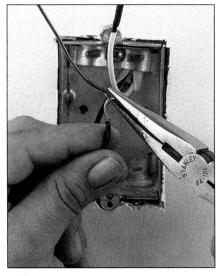

① **START A LOOP.** Check that the power is shut off. Strip about ¾ inch of insulation from a wire end. Using long-nose pliers or the tip of a combination stripper, grab the bare wire just above the insulation and bend it back at about a 45-degree angle. Move the pliers up about ¼ inch beyond the insulation, and bend again in the opposite direction, about 90 degrees.

WORK SMARTER

USING PIGTAILS
Codes prohibit attaching two wires to one terminal on a switch or receptacle. If you need to attach two wires to one terminal, use a pigtail splice. Cut a wire 6 inches long, and strip both ends. Splice the two original wires to the pigtail and join the pigtail to the terminal.

Pigtail

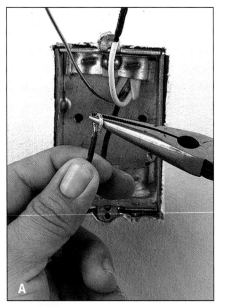

A

② **OPTION A: BEND A QUESTION MARK.** Use long-nose pliers to form a near loop with an opening just wide enough to slip over the threads of a terminal screw. Move the pliers another ¼ inch away from the insulation, and bend again to form a shape that looks like a question mark.

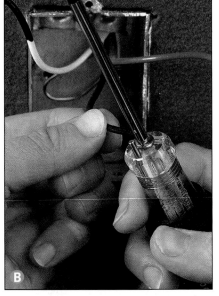

B

OPTION B: USE A WIRE-BENDING SCREWDRIVER. This simple tool makes perfect hooks every time. Just push the stripped wire between the screwdriver shaft and the stud at the base of the handle. Twist the handle to make a perfect loop.

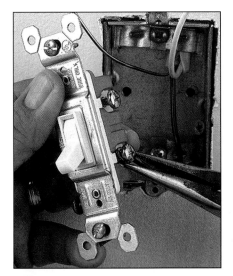

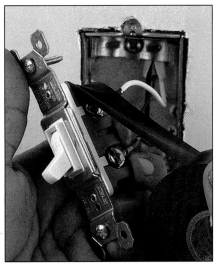

③ SQUEEZE THE LOOP AROUND THE SCREW. Make sure the terminal screw is unscrewed enough to become hard to turn. Slip the loop over the screw threads, with the loop running clockwise. Use long-nose pliers or a combination stripper to squeeze the loop around the terminal, then tighten the screw.

④ WRAP WITH TAPE. After all the wires are connected to a switch or receptacle, wrap electrician's tape around the body of the device to cover the screw heads and any exposed wires. The tape not only ensures that the wires stay attached, it keeps the terminals from touching the box and risking a short circuit.

Connecting to a 240-volt receptacle

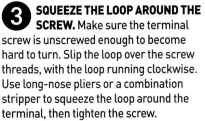

Be certain that power is shut off—there is a dangerous level of power here. Strip about ½ inch of insulation from the wire end. The wire should be straight, not looped. Loosen the setscrew, poke the wire into the hole, and tighten the screw.

SAFETY ALERT

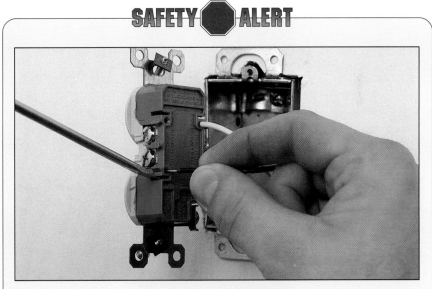

SKIP THE PUSH-IN OPTION
Many receptacles and switches have holes in the back for easy connection of wires. Once you've stripped the insulation (a strip gauge shows you how much), you poke the wire in. To remove a wire, insert a small screwdriver into a nearby slot. The wire releases.

The system works, but the resulting electrical connection is not as secure as a connection made using a terminal screw. Most professionals don't trust this method even though it saves time. Take the extra minute to do it right.

Receptacle and switch wiring

When you remove an electrical cover plate and pull out a switch or receptacle, you may find an arrangement involving a few wires going directly to the device. Or you may find a multicolored tangle of wires, some related to the switch or receptacle and some not. Here are some of the most common wiring configurations you'll find behind electrical cover plates.

See page 541

If your switches receive constant use in a particular area, consider paying a little extra for a device labeled "commercial" or "spec-rated." The contacts are stronger and the devices are sturdier.

Switches sharing a hot wire

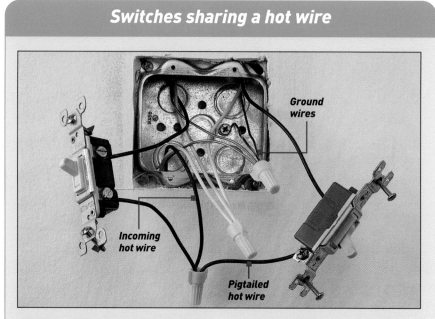

Ground wires

Incoming hot wire

Pigtailed hot wire

Switches that share a hot wire are on the same circuit. Two pigtails (see page 160) branch off from the incoming hot wire and connect to each switch. Another hot wire runs from each switch to a light. White wires are spliced.

A split receptacle

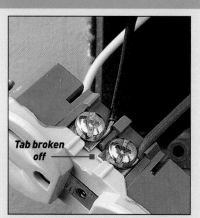

Tab broken off

Also known as a half-hot receptacle, this is connected to two hot wires. The brass tab joining the brass terminals has been broken off. With the tab broken, each hot wire energizes one plug. Some split-circuit receptacles have each plug energized by a different circuit so that you can plug in two high-amperage appliances without the danger of tripping a breaker. Others are wired so that half the receptacle is controlled by a wall switch, while the other half is hot all the time.

CLOSER LOOK

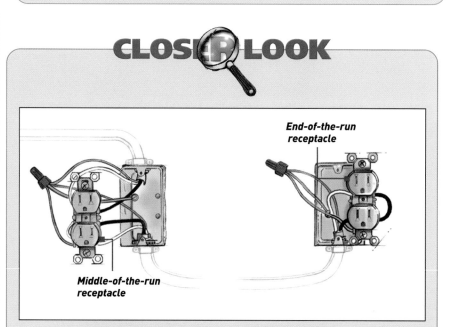

End-of-the-run receptacle

Middle-of-the-run receptacle

MIDDLE-OF-THE-RUN RECEPTACLE

A receptacle with one cable that carries power into the receptacle and one that carries it to another device is called a middle-of-the-run receptacle.

Usually two black wires are connected to the brass terminals and two white wires to the silver terminals. Sometimes the blacks and the whites may be joined, with a pigtail at each splice.

Each pigtail is attached to the receptacle. If only one cable enters the box, the receptacle is at the end of the run. The black wire is attached to the brass terminal, the white wire is attached to the silver terminal, and the ground wire is attached to the receptacle.

Installing or replacing a receptacle

SKILL SCALE

EASY	MEDIUM	HARD

REQUIRED SKILLS: Stripping wires and connecting to terminals.

 HOW LONG WILL IT TAKE?

Experienced . . . . 15 min.
Handy . . . . 20 min.
Novice . . . . 40 min.

STUFF YOU'LL NEED

✔ MATERIALS:

New receptacle, wire nuts, electrician's tape

✔ TOOLS:

Screwdriver, lineman's pliers, long-nose pliers, side-cutting pliers, receptacle analyzer, combination stripper, level

If a receptacle doesn't seem to work, first check that whatever is plugged into it works properly. Replace any receptacle that is cracked. Before buying a replacement receptacle, check the wiring. Usually the wires leading to a receptacle will be #14 and the circuit breaker or fuse will be 15 amps. In that case, install a 15-amp receptacle. Install a 20-amp receptacle only if the wires are #12 and the circuit breaker or fuse is 20 amps or greater.

 See pages 540–541

TOOL TIP

LOTS OF CONTINUITY

A simple continuity tester works fine on small jobs. If you're doing a lot of work, you may find one of the noncontact voltage detectors or even a professional-grade tool to be more handy.

1 **CHECK THAT THE POWER IS OFF.** Turn off power to the circuit. Test to confirm. If the tester shows current, check your service panel and turn off another likely circuit. Test again and proceed only if power is off. Remove the cover plate and unscrew the mounting screws. Being careful not to touch wires or terminals, pull out the receptacle.

2 **DOUBLE CHECK WIRES FOR POWER.** In a damaged receptacle, wires may be hot even though testing shows no power. Touch tester probes to the top pair of terminals, then to the bottom pair (see page 158). If you have old wiring and both wires are black, use a receptacle analyzer to check that the neutral wire is connected to the silver terminal and the hot wire to the brass.

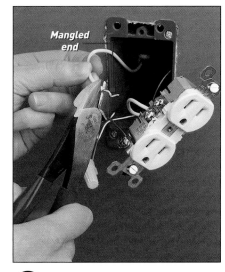

3 **SNIP AND RESTRIP DAMAGED WIRE ENDS.** Once you're sure the power is off, unscrew the terminals and pull away the wires, taking care not to twist them too much. If a wire end appears nicked or damaged or if it looks like it's been twisted several times, snip off the end and restrip it (see page 159).

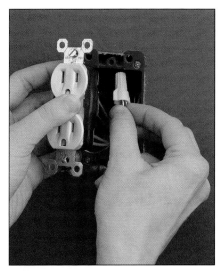

4 **INSTALL THE RECEPTACLE.** Wire the new receptacle as the old one was (each white wire connected to a silver terminal and each black or colored wire connected to a brass terminal). Wrap with electrician's tape to cover all terminals and bare wires (see page 161). Gently push the outlet into the box. Tighten the mounting screws and check that the receptacle is straight. Replace the cover plate, restore power, and test with a receptacle analyzer.

Installing GFCI receptacles

A ground fault circuit interrupter (GFCI) protects you against the kind of shocks that occur around water. It compares the current coming into a circuit with the current leaving it. If the GFCI detects a difference between the two—as would be the case if power were traveling through your arm into the water in the sink—it immediately cuts off the power. GFCIs are required in bathrooms, along kitchen countertops, and for outdoor outlets. A GFCI outlet can protect up to four receptacles, switches, or lights on the same circuit. A GFCI circuit breaker can protect an entire circuit . If your home has ungrounded receptacles (see page 157), installing GFCIs will provide protection but won't ground your circuits.

Check your GFCIs at least once a month by pushing in the test button while the power is on. (The reset button should pop out. Push it back in.) A GFCI may provide power even though it has lost its ability to protect.

Don't use a GFCI as a receptacle for a refrigerator, freezer, or any other appliance that must stay on all the time; the device may trip off without your knowing. Also do not attempt to control a GFCI with a switch.

 See page 540

See page 157

See page 540

SKILL SCALE

EASY	MEDIUM	HARD

REQUIRED SKILLS: Stripping and splicing wires, connecting wires to terminals.

HOW LONG WILL IT TAKE?

Experienced .... 20 min.
Handy .... 35 min.
Novice .... 45 min.

STUFF YOU'LL NEED

✔ **MATERIALS:**
GFCI receptacle, wire nuts, electrician's tape

✔ **TOOLS:**
Screwdriver, lineman's pliers, side-cutting pliers, combination stripper

Code requires that GFCI receptacles be installed in any exterior application. Include an in-use cover so you can plug into the device and still keep the cover down.

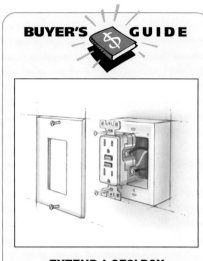
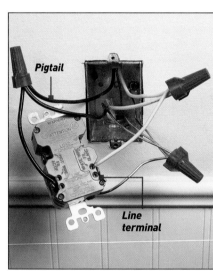
Pigtail · Line terminal

INSTALLING A SINGLE GFCI. Shut off the power. Make connections only to the LINE terminals. For an end-of-the-run box, connect the wires to the terminals. If the box is middle-of-the-run (shown), for each connection, make a pigtail by stripping either end of a 6-inch-long wire. Splice each pigtail to the wire(s) with a wire nut, then connect it to the GFCI terminals. Put the white wire on the silver terminal and the black or colored wire on the brass terminal.

Incoming connected to "line" · Outgoing connected to "load"

PROTECTING OTHER OUTLETS. Shut off the power. Connect the wires carrying power into the box to the line terminals marked on the outlet. Then connect the wires leading out of the box (to other receptacles or lights) to the load terminals marked on the outlet. If you're unsure which wires come from the service panel, pull the wires out of the box and position them so they will not touch each other, restore power, and use a tester to see which pair of wires is hot; connect these to the line terminals.

Installing an outdoor receptacle

These days houses are built with at least two outdoor outlets. If your house doesn't have them, you may want to add some. The sturdiest and simplest way to add an outlet is to screw a box built for outdoor exposure to the side of your house, put a receptacle in it, and put on a waterproof cover built to match the box.

You will, of course, need to install an outlet and run cable. To meet code, the outlet must be a GFCI outlet, which will keep any accidental shorts from running through the nearest human and into the ground. The best and easiest way to get cable to the GFCI is to drill through the rim joist, as shown. Power for the cable can either come from an existing circuit (see page 150), or by adding a new one to the breaker box, as shown on page 182.

To keep things watertight, make sure you caulk thoroughly, as described below, and install a gasket between the lid and the box. You also need to install a conduit bushing wherever cable leaves the conduit to protect the cable from fraying on rough edges.

STUFF YOU'LL NEED

✔ MATERIALS:
Rectangular metal watertight box, matching conduit nipple, conduit bushing, cover gasket, cover, GFCI, 12-2 NM cable, cable staples, silicone caulk

✔ TOOLS:
Drill, screwdriver, caulking gun, hammer

① CHOOSE THE SPOT FOR THE OUTLET FROM OUTSIDE THE HOUSE, and measure how far it is from a basement window, exterior cellar entrance, spigot, or other feature visible from inside the basement. Inside the house, measure and mark the spot on the rim joist, moving as necessary to avoid obstructions. Drill a hole slightly larger than the conduit nipple through the rim joist and through the siding. If the exterior of the house is brick, change to a carbide masonry bit once you hit it. If it's siding, drill through the entire hole with a spade bit. (See Step 2.)

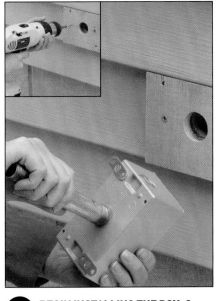

② BEGIN INSTALLING THE BOX. On wood siding, you'll need to make the surface behind the box flat by building it up. Do this by cutting a short piece of siding and putting it upside down over the existing siding. as shown. Screw the buildup to the siding (see inset). Attach the nipple into the receptacle box and slide it through the hole. Caulk around the nipple just before you push the box all the way in.

③ SCREW THE BOX TO THE WALL. From inside the house, put a conduit bushing on the nipple. Run cable from the fuse or breaker box, or from an existing outlet or junction box. Strip off about a hand's length of the outer jacket, and feed the wires through the nipple. Use cable staples designed for electrical work to secure the cable to the framing every 4 feet and within 1 foot of the nipple. (These staples are driven with a hammer, not a staple gun.) Install a GFCI following the directions on the box. Put a gasket over the box, and screw the cover in place (see inset).

ELECTRICAL

Adding a wall switch to a ceiling fixture

SKILL SCALE

EASY	**MEDIUM**	HARD

REQUIRED SKILLS: Cabling through walls and ceilings, stripping and connecting cable and wires.

HOW LONG WILL IT TAKE?

Experienced . . . . 2 hrs.
Handy . . . . 4 hrs.
Novice . . . . 6 hrs.

VARIABLES: If stud spacing is irregular or other systems such as plumbing risers are in the wall, fishing the cable may be tricky.

STUFF YOU'LL NEED

✔ MATERIALS:
Cable and clamps, remodeling box, staples, receptacle, wire nuts, nailing plates, electrician's tape

✔ TOOLS:
Drill, drywall saw or saber saw, fish tape, screwdriver, lineman's pliers, strippers

You can easily add a wall switch to a ceiling fixture currently controlled by a pull chain. The biggest challenge is planning the route and running cable from the fixture to the position for the new switch on the wall. If the wall is heavily insulated, push conduit through the insulation, and then feed wires or cable through the conduit.

See page 540

1 RUN CABLE. Shut off power to the circuit supplying the fixture. Plan a cable pathway that crosses as few studs or joists as possible. You may have to cut an access hole to run cable through framing (see page 171).

Pull cable here ...
... then here

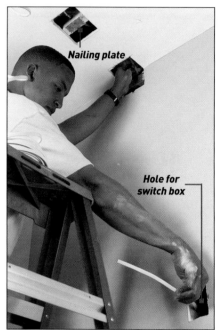

2 RUN CABLE TO THE SWITCH BOX. Add nailing plates where you bore holes in framing. Cut a hole for a remodel switch box and pull the cable through. Strip the wires.

Nailing plate
Hole for switch box

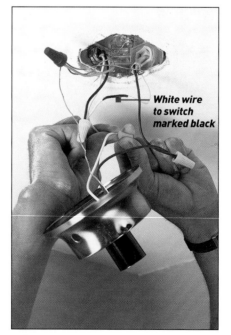

3 WIRE THE FIXTURE. Connect the ground (see page 157). Remove the black wire from the fixture lead, splice it to the new white wire to the switch, and mark it black. Splice the new black wire to the fixture's black lead.

White wire to switch marked black

4 CONNECT THE GROUND AT THE SWITCH. Attach both wires to the terminals and mark the white wire black. Restore power to the circuit and test. Repair the access hole in the drywall.

Controlling a single outlet with a switch

SKILL SCALE

EASY	**MEDIUM**	HARD

REQUIRED SKILLS: Running cable, stripping and connecting cable and wires.

HOW LONG WILL IT TAKE?

Experienced . . . . 1.5 hrs.
Handy . . . . 2.5 hrs.
Novice . . . . 4 hrs.

VARIABLES: Time depends on the difficulty of running cable.

STUFF YOU'LL NEED

✔ MATERIALS:

Cable and clamps, remodeling box, staples, switch, wire nuts, electrician's tape

✔ TOOLS:

Drill, saw, fish tape, screwdriver, long-nose pliers, combination stripper

When you assign one outlet of a duplex receptacle to a wall switch, you can control a floor or table lamp from a doorway. The second outlet will remain hot at all times and be available for general use.

See page 541

To run cable through finished walls and install a remodel box for the switch, see page 171. See page 157 for grounding methods.

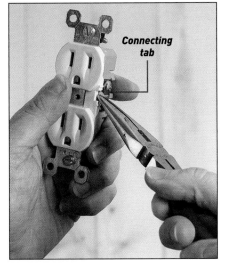

Connecting tab

MAKING OUTLETS OPERATE SEPARATELY. Shut off power. In order to make the two outlets of a receptacle operate separately, grasp the connecting tab between the two brass terminals with a pair of long-nose pliers. Bend the tab back and forth until it breaks off.

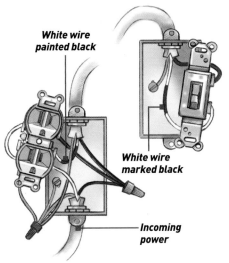

White wire painted black

White wire marked black

Incoming power

WORKING WITH AN END-OF-THE-RUN RECEPTACLE. Shut off power. Run two-wire cable from the switch to the receptacle. Paint both ends of the white wires black. Connect the grounds. At the receptacle, remove the old black wire and splice it to the new white wire (marked black) and a black pigtail. Connect the pigtail to the always-hot terminal and the other black wire to the other terminal. Attach both wires to the switch.

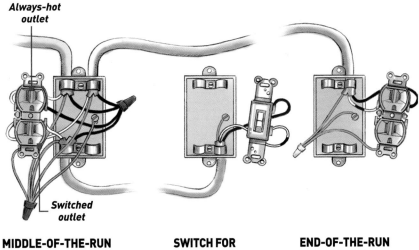

Always-hot outlet

Switched outlet

MIDDLE-OF-THE-RUN RECEPTACLE

SWITCH FOR LOWER OUTLET

END-OF-THE-RUN RECEPTACLE

WORKING WITH A RECEPTACLE IN THE MIDDLE OF A RUN. Shut off power. This project will be complicated if the receptacle you want to switch has wires attached to all four terminals. At the receptacle to be switched, remove both old black wires. Splice them with the new white wire and a black pigtail. Connect the pigtail to the always-hot outlet and the new black wire to the switched outlet. Wire the switch and connect the grounds.

Replacing a three-way switch

SKILL SCALE

EASY	MEDIUM	HARD

REQUIRED SKILLS: Stripping wire, connecting wire to terminals.

HOW LONG WILL IT TAKE?

Experienced . . . . 10 min.
Handy . . . . 20 min.
Novice . . . . 30 min.

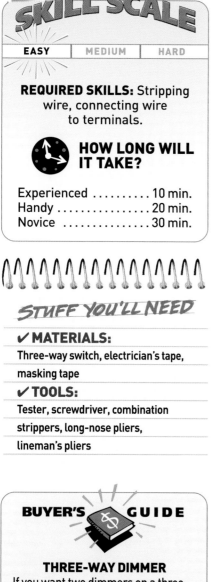

STUFF YOU'LL NEED

✔ **MATERIALS:**
Three-way switch, electrician's tape, masking tape

✔ **TOOLS:**
Tester, screwdriver, combination strippers, long-nose pliers, lineman's pliers

BUYER'S GUIDE

THREE-WAY DIMMER
If you want two dimmers on a three-way circuit, make sure you get special multilocation dimmers. Standard three-way dimmers can replace one but not both of the switches in a three-way circuit. (Fluorescent fixtures also require special dimmers.)

Replacing switches is easy as long as you get the correct replacement and label the wires for reassembly.

T hree-way switches work in pairs to control a light from two locations—handy for controlling a light from the top and the bottom of a stairway or from either end of a hallway. The toggle isn't marked OFF and ON. Either up or down can be ON depending on the position of the toggle of the other three-way.

Before you begin, shut off power to the circuit. Use pieces of tape to label each wire as you detach it from the old switch. At each switch, one of the wires goes to the common terminal, which is darker than the other terminals. The other two wires, called travelers, go to the lighter terminals. Restrip any damaged wires (see page 159). Most of the steps for replacing a three-way switch are the same as for a single-pole switch, but with three-ways, you must know which wire is which.

You can also control a circuit with three switches, but the wiring can be confusing. Consider hiring a professional electrician.

See page 541

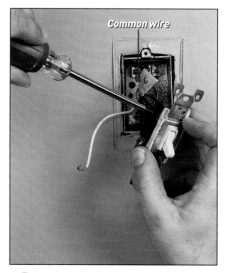
Common wire

1 **TAG THE COMMON WIRE.** Shut off power, remove the cover plate, and test to make sure there is no power in the box. Label the common wire with a piece of masking tape. The common terminal (see "Switches," page 155) is colored differently from the others (it's not the green ground screw) and may be marked "common" on the switch body.

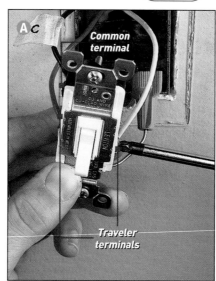
Common terminal
Traveler terminals

2 **OPTION A: WIRING ONE CABLE.** When only one cable enters the box, it will have three wires plus a ground. Identify the hot wire using a voltage detector (see page 154), or by touching one prong of a voltage tester to a ground and the other to each wire in turn. Attach the hot wire to the common terminal, which is a different color. Attach the other two wires to the traveler terminals. Connect the grounds.

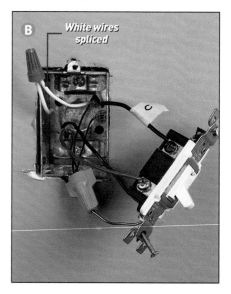
White wires spliced

OPTION B: WIRING TWO CABLES. If two cables enter the box, one cable will have two wires plus ground and the other will have three wires plus ground. Despite all the extra wires, you'll find only three wire ends. Proceed just as you would for a one-cable installation (left).

Replacing a dimmer switch

STUFF YOU'LL NEED

✔ **MATERIALS:**

Dimmer switch, wire nuts, electrician's tape

✔ **TOOLS:**

Screwdriver, side-cutting pliers, strippers

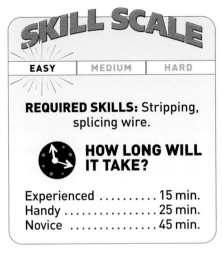

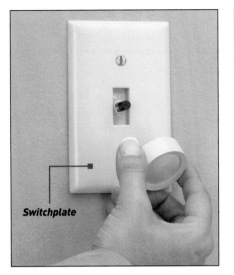

1 REMOVE THE DIMMER KNOB. Shut off power at the service panel. Pull off the rotary knob with firm outward pressure. Underneath is a standard switchplate. Remove it. Remove the mounting screws and carefully pull out the switch body.

Switchplate

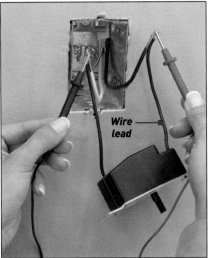

Wire lead

2 TEST FOR POWER. A dimmer has wire leads instead of terminals. Test for power by slipping the probes of the tester against the base of the wire nuts. If power is detected, shut off the correct circuit in the service panel. (To test for continuity, see page 158.)

ELECTRICAL

Make sure the new dimmer switch is rated for the total wattage of the fixture. A chandelier with eight 100-watt bulbs is too much for a 600-watt dimmer to handle. Don't use a standard dimmer for a fan or you will burn out the motor. Install no more than one three-way dimmer per receptacle; the other switch must be a three-way toggle. You can buy rotary dimmers (the least expensive), dimmers that look like standard switches (the toggle can be placed anywhere between on and off position), or rotary models with their own included ON-OFF switch so the dimmer will turn on at the level of your choice.

See page 540

The wide selection of dimmer switches at home centers and hardware stores gives you many control options.

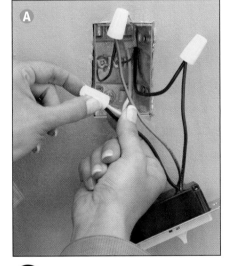

3 OPTION A: INSTALLING A STANDARD DIMMER. Attach the ground wire if there is one. Strip ¾ inch of insulation from each solid house wire and 1 inch from each stranded dimmer lead. Wrap a lead around a wire with your fingers so that the lead protrudes past the wire about ⅛ inch. Slip on a wire nut and twist until tight. Test the strength of the connection by gently tugging on both wires.

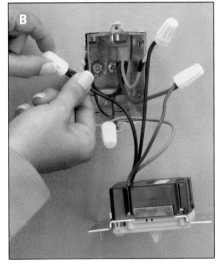

OPTION B: INSTALLING A THREE-WAY DIMMER. If you replace a three-way dimmer, tag the existing lead wires to connect the new dimmer in the same way as the old one. If only one cable enters the box, attach the black wire to the common terminal and the other two wires to the traveler terminals. If you replace a three-way toggle switch with a dimmer, tag the wire that leads to the common terminal. The other two wires are interchangeable.

Choosing electrical boxes

All electrical connections must be contained inside a metal or plastic box that complies with local codes. And all boxes, including junction boxes, must be accessible. Never cover a box with drywall or paneling.

Electrical codes specify the number and size of wires that each box can accommodate because crowding wires in a box is a potential hazard. Check codes carefully and, to be safe, install larger boxes than you need now so you have the option to upgrade. Compared to metal boxes, plastic boxes are easily damaged and should only be installed in a wall. Use metal boxes in exposed locations. Inspectors generally expect to see ¼-inch or more of wire sheathing inside the box.

See pages 540–542

METAL BOXES

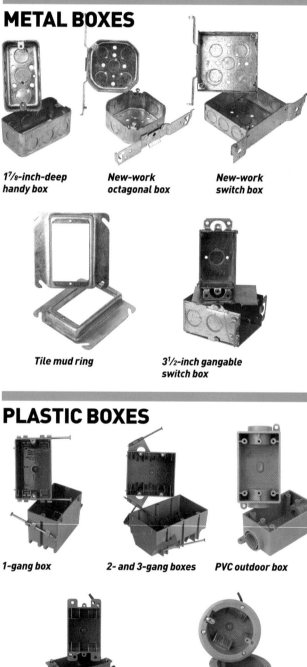

1⅞-inch-deep handy box

New-work octagonal box

New-work switch box

Tile mud ring

3½-inch gangable switch box

PLASTIC BOXES

1-gang box

2- and 3-gang boxes

PVC outdoor box

Remodel box with ears

Ceiling remodel box

CLOSER LOOK

FOUR WAYS TO ANCHOR NM CABLE TO A BOX

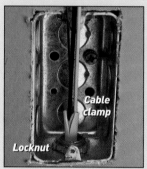

Cable clamp

Locknut

Push through flap

Cable clamp. Buy clamps made for NM cable. Remove the knockout. Screw the clamp to the cable, then slip it through the hole and screw on the locknut. Pinch the locknut by using a hammer to tap a screwdriver on it. Or attach it to the box first, slide the cable through the clamp, then tighten the screws.

Poke and staple. For many plastic boxes, to run cable you may need to push the cable past a plastic flap or knock out a plastic tab. Once you've inserted the cable into the box, staple the cable on a framing member within 8 inches of the box.

Built-in clamp

Built-in clamp. Plastic boxes large enough to hold more than one device have internal clamps, as do most remodel boxes. Tighten the clamp screw to firmly secure the cable.

Pop-in plastic connector. Remove the knockout and push this connector in place. Then push the cable through; if accessible, staple the cable within 8 inches of the box.

INSTALLING ELECTRICAL BOXES

✔ MATERIALS:
Remodeling (old-work) box, screws

✔ TOOLS:
Electronic stud finder, utility knife, drywall saw, saber saw or rotary cutter, screwdriver, drill

Floor-level receptacles are usually 12 to 15 inches off the floor. Rather than pulling out their measuring tape, electricians often set their hammer head down on the floor and use the length of the hammer to position the center of floor-level receptacles in the wall.

Installing electrical boxes is easy in new construction because the walls aren't in the way. You have more variables when working with existing walls. Self-attaching remodeling boxes make the job easier. All you have to do is cut a hole, run the cable, clamp the cable to the box, and install it in the wall.

Use a stud finder to make sure you won't hit a stud, joist, wiring, or anything else hiding in the wall.

Lay out the hole by tracing around the box, or ask the store for the layout template. (The templates are shipped with the electrical boxes but usually get separated from them by the time they reach the store shelf.)

Cut the hole carefully. The box should fit into the hole snugly, but not so tightly that you have to force it. If the hole is too wide, the box may not effectively attach to the drywall or plaster.

IN NEW CONSTRUCTION ATTACH ALL THE BOXES TO THE STUDS BEFORE RUNNING CABLE. Receptacle boxes are usually placed 12 inches above the floor, and switch boxes 45 inches above the floor. Hold a nail-on box with its front edge positioned out from the stud the thickness of the drywall, and nail it in place.

INSTALLING ELECTRICAL BOXES

Installing remodeling boxes

Remodeling (or cut-in) boxes are made to be installed in a finished wall. The first step is to cut a hole for the box in the wall. You have three options, depending on whether the wall is drywall or plaster. Installation for different types of remodeling boxes follows on page 172.

Ⓐ CUTTING A HOLE IN DRYWALL. Use a pencil to mark the location of the hole (check for studs) and score the paper surface with a utility knife. Cut along the inside of the knife-cut with a drywall saw. The resulting hole will be free of ragged edges. You also can cut drywall with a spiral cutting tool or a saber saw.

Ⓑ CUTTING A HOLE IN PLASTER WITH A SPIRAL CUTTING TOOL. Because of the motor's high RPMs, this tool won't rattle lath or loosen plaster. Set the base on the wall and tip the blade away from the surface while you let it come to full speed. Then tilt the blade gently into the wall. Have extra blades on hand; they dull quickly on plaster.

Ⓒ CUTTING A HOLE IN PLASTER WITH A SABER SAW. Cutting through a lath and plaster wall is difficult and often results in cracked plaster. Drill holes at each corner and score the face of the plaster with a utility knife. Cut with a saber saw equipped with a fine-tooth blade. Press hard against the wall to reduce lath vibration.

ELECTRICAL

Installing remodeling boxes *(continued)*

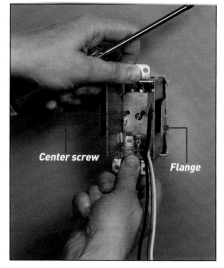

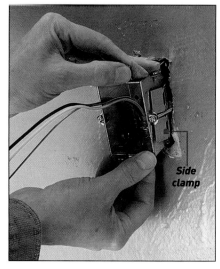

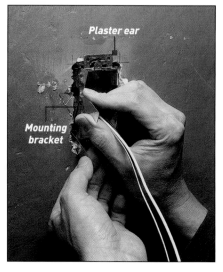

INSTALLING A BOX WITH SPRING FLANGES. If you buy this kind of box, make sure both flanges spring out firmly from the box. Push the box into the hole until the flanges are free to spring outward. As you tighten the center screw, the flanges should move toward you until they fit snugly against the back of the drywall or plaster.

INSTALLING A BOX WITH SIDE CLAMPS. After pushing the box into the hole, tighten the screw on each side. Each clamp extends behind the wall to hold the box in place.

USING MOUNTING BRACKETS. Push a metal box with plaster ears into the hole. Slip a bracket in on each side, pushing it behind the wall's surface. Pull the bracket toward you until it's tight, push the box tightly against the wall, then fold the tabs into the box with your thumbs. Tighten the tabs with pliers.

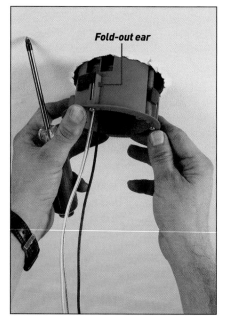

INSTALLING A BOX WITH FOLD-OUT EARS. These plastic remodeling boxes have ears that swing out behind the drywall or plaster. Push the box into the hole, then turn the screws clockwise until the ears clamp onto the back of the drywall or plaster. Switch boxes are also available with this same wall-grabbing mechanism.

CLOSER LOOK

INSTALLING METAL REMODELING BOXES

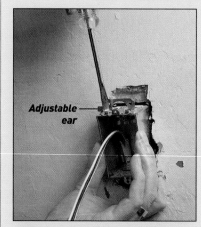

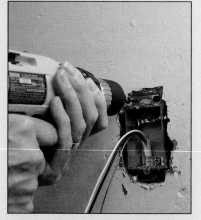

1 ADJUST THE PLASTER EARS. Many metal boxes have adjustable ears. Cut the hole and chip out the plaster above and below so the ears will fit. Loosen the two screws and adjust each ear so the face of the box becomes flush with the wall surface. Tighten the screws.

2 ANCHOR THE BOX TO THE LATH. Lath cracks easily, so work carefully. Drill pilot holes, and drive short screws to anchor the ears to the lath. Expect to do some wall patching after using this method.

Installing ceiling boxes

A+ WORK SMARTER

CEILING BOX HANGING OPTIONS

Ceiling joist box

Braced box

6½" Fiberglas Insulation

Ⓐ When framing is accessible, attach a ceiling box to a joist. Install this type of box in unfinished ceilings or ceilings with a large hole. Drill pilot holes and drive in 1¼-inch wood screws to attach it to joist.

Ⓑ Install a braced box from above. Buy a new-work box with a brace. Slide the box along the brace to position it. Tighten the clamp. Attach the brace to the joist by driving in 1¼-inch wood screws.

It's essential that the new ceiling box can carry the weight of the fixture you are planning to hang. Talk to a sales associate to make sure you're buying the right box and installing it properly.

Fan brace

① SLIP IN THE BRACE. Assemble the box on the brace to understand how it goes together, then take it apart. Push the brace in through the hole and spread it apart until it touches the joists on both sides. The legs of the brace at each end should rest on top of the drywall or plaster.

Adjustable wrench

Rotating the brace tightens it between the framing.

② TIGHTEN THE BRACE. Measure to make sure that the brace is centered in the hole. Position it on the joists at the correct height so that the box will be flush with the surface of the ceiling. Use an adjustable wrench or channel-type pliers to tighten the brace only until it is firm. Tightening beyond this point can cause the ceiling to crack.

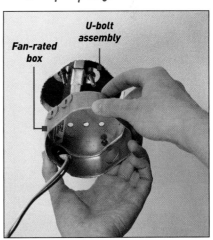

U-bolt assembly

Fan-rated box

③ ATTACH THE BOX. Attach the U-bolt assembly to the brace so that the assembly is centered in the hole and the bolts face down. Thread cable through the cable connector and into the fan-rated box. Slip the box up so the bolts slide through it and tighten the nuts to secure the box.

ELECTRICAL

Installing a junction box

SKILL SCALE

EASY	MEDIUM	HARD

REQUIRED SKILLS: Stripping and splicing wires, attaching a box.

HOW LONG WILL IT TAKE?

Experienced ....1 hr.
Handy ....2 hrs.
Novice ....3 hrs.

VARIABLES: Installing boxes on frame walls is faster than installing on masonry walls.

STUFF YOU'LL NEED

✔ MATERIALS:
Junction box with cover, wire nuts, screws

✔ TOOLS:
Combination tool, lineman's pliers, screwdriver, drill, voltage tester

Install a junction box wherever wires must be spliced. Keep the box accessible—never bury it in a wall or ceiling. Junction boxes are usually flush-mounted to walls or attached to attic, basement, or crawlspace framing. But you can set one inside a wall as you would a switch box. Cover the junction box with a blank plastic cover plate.

See page 540

Code requires that all splices be accessible for inspection and repair. Trying to take shortcuts here can be costly and dangerous.

1 ATTACH THE BOX. Shut off power to the wires that you will be splicing. Anchor the box with screws. To attach the box to a masonry surface, drill holes with a masonry bit. Drive masonry screws.

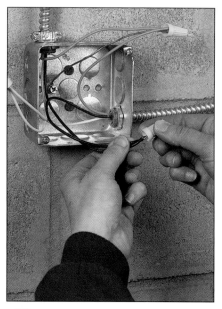

2 WIRE THE BOX. Strip cable sheathing and clamp the cable, or connect conduit. Strip wires and splice them with wire nuts. If the box is metal, make a grounding pigtail (see page 160) and connect it to the green grounding screw.

3 COVER THE BOX. Fold the wires into the box and attach the cover plate. To do so, loosen the screws at two opposite corners of the box, hook the cover plate on one screw first and then the other; tighten the screws.

A+ WORK SMARTER

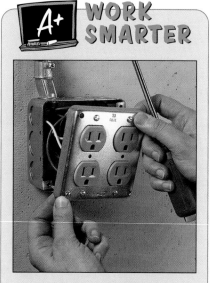

USE A METAL COVER PLATE IN UTILITY AREAS
If a receptacle or switch is in an exposed box, use a metal rather than a plastic cover plate. You may need to break off the device's metal ears. Attach the device to the cover plate first and then attach the cover plate to the box.

Installing NM cable in new walls

STUFF YOU'LL NEED

✔ MATERIALS:

NM or armored cable, electrical boxes, protective nailing plates, cable staples

✔ TOOLS:

Drill with ⅝-inch or ¾-inch bit, hammer, tape measure, level, long-nose pliers, utility knife, safety goggles

Nonmetallic (NM) cable is easy to cut and quick to install. Just be careful when you remove the sheathing so you don't accidentally slit the wire insulation. If you do, cut off the damage and start again; otherwise you will get a short or a shock. Whenever possible, strip sheathing before cutting the cable to length. That way, if you make a mistake you can try again.

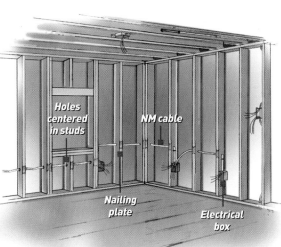

A TYPICAL CABLE ROUGH-IN. Run cable in a straight horizontal line, 1 foot above the receptacles (areas under windows are an exception) or according to local code. To keep cable out of the reach of nails, drill all holes in the center of studs and at least 1¼ inches up from the bottom of joists. Nail on protective nailing plates for extra safety. Even if you will only hang a light, install a ceiling fan box in case you choose to add a ceiling fan later.

Holes centered in studs

NM cable

Nailing plate

Electrical box

Spade bit

Framed corner

1 inch of play

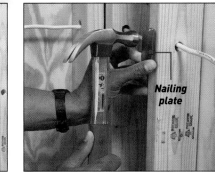

Nailing plate

Cable staple

① DRILL THE HOLES. Wherever possible, use a tape measure and level to mark studs and joists. Mark so holes will be in a straight horizontal line. Drill ⅝-inch holes for most NM cable and ¾-inch holes for three-wire cable or armored cable. A ⅜-inch drill works fine for small jobs, but give it a rest if it overheats.

PULL THE CABLE. To avoid kinks, keep the cable straight and untwisted as you work. When possible, pull the cable first and then cut it to length. If you must cut it first, allow plenty of extra length. Pull the cable fairly tight, but loose enough to have an inch or so of play.

② PROTECT THE CABLE WITH NAILING PLATES, which are inexpensive and quick to install. Be sure to nail one wherever the cable is within 1¼ inches of the front edge of the framing member. For added safety (and to satisfy some local codes), install nailing plates over every hole.

STAPLE THE CABLE AND RUN IT INTO THE BOXES. Staple cable tightly wherever it runs along a joist so it is out of the reach of nails. Staple within 8 inches of a plastic box and within 12 inches of a metal box. See page 170 for clamping methods.

Working with NM cable

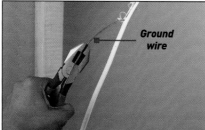
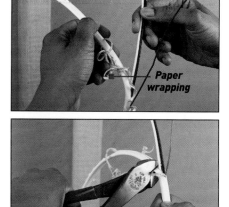

SKILL SCALE

EASY	MEDIUM	HARD

REQUIRED SKILLS: Careful cutting with a knife and side-cutting pliers.

HOW LONG WILL IT TAKE?

Experienced . . . . 5 min.
Handy . . . . 10 min.
Novice . . . . 15 min.

STUFF YOU'LL NEED

✔ **MATERIALS:**
Nonmetallic (NM) cable

✔ **TOOLS:**
Knife, lineman's pliers, side-cutting pliers, cable ripper

TOOL TIP

USING A CABLE RIPPER
Use this tool to strip cable that is already installed in a box. Practice on scrap cable first so you know how to make sure the ripper doesn't cut too deeply and damage wire insulation.

Ground wire

1 SLIT THE CABLE WITH A KNIFE.
One side of the cable has a slight valley. Insert the blade into the middle of the valley about 3 inches from the end so the blade just pierces the sheathing. Slit to the end of the cable. Be careful not to damage the ground or pierce the sheathing on the hot and neutral wires.

PULL THE GROUND WIRE. Cut or pull back the sheathing so you can grab the green or bare ground wire with lineman's pliers. Hold the cable end in the other hand and pull back the ground wire until you have a 12-inch slit in the sheathing. Pull carefully so you don't break the ground wire.

3 PULL THE CABLE INTO THE BOX.
Push the wires through the clip or clamp on the box. Pull the cable into the box so at least ¼ inch of sheathing is inside. Clamp the cable to the box (see "Closer Look," page 170).

Paper wrapping

2 REMOVE THE WRAPPING. Pull back the plastic sheathing. Peel back any protective paper wrapping or thin strips of plastic, and cut them off.

SNIP THE SHEATHING. Use side-cutting pliers, a combination stripper, or the cutting portion of lineman's pliers to cut the sheathing.

SAFETY ALERT

Corner framing

Longnose pliers

NEVER NOTCH
In a tight spot like this, you may be tempted to whip out the hammer and chisel and chop notches in the face of the studs so the cable runs easier. But the cable would then be dangerously exposed and severely bent at the corner. Instead, drill slightly larger holes, bend the cable before poking it in, and grab it with long-nose pliers.

Fishing and running cable

SKILL SCALE

EASY	**MEDIUM**	HARD

REQUIRED SKILLS: Basic carpentry and wiring skills.

HOW LONG WILL IT TAKE?

Experienced . . . . 6 hrs.
Handy . . . . 10 hrs.
Novice . . . . 14 hrs.

VARIABLES: Unexpected obstructions can slow work considerably.

STUFF YOU'LL NEED

✔ **MATERIALS:**

Cable, remodeling boxes

✔ **TOOLS:**

Electronic stud finder, drywall saw, saber saw, drill, hammer, screwdriver, fish tape, flat pry bar, safety goggles

TOOL TIP

FISH TAPE

Flexible wire fish tape comes on reels and is essential for running cable in existing walls. Feed the tape through the wall from the junction box to the receptacle box. Then attach the wire to the tape and pull the wire through.

You need the patience of a surgeon to run wiring through walls that are finished with drywall or plaster. At times you'll feel like grabbing a hammer and knocking big holes in the wall to get at that darned cable. But remember that wiring is more fun than patching and plastering, so any steps you can take to minimize wall or ceiling damage will pay off in the end.

FOLLOW THE EASIEST PATH. If you have an unfinished attic or a basement, run as much of the cable there as possible. If a basement or attic is finished, run armored cable instead of NM.

Use an electronic stud finder to locate joists and studs that may be in the way. You may be able to move a box a few inches to avoid an obstruction. Wherever possible, run cable parallel to studs or joists.

First, cut holes for the boxes (see page 171), then run the cable. If you're running cable horizontally, guide it with a fish tape. If you're feeding it up or down, drop a small chain from the upper opening to the lower and use the chain as a fish tape.

If you plan to use power from an existing receptacle for your new service, make sure the circuit can handle the new load.

If the attic isn't used for storage, you may be allowed to lay cable on top of the joists if you install 1x4 strips on either side of the cable.

RUNNING CABLE UP, OVER, AND DOWN. If the attic is accessible, drill a hole through the top plate above the outlet you'll tap into and another above the new outlet. Drop a chain down through the hole above the new box, and grab it through the opening you've cut for the box. Tape the cable to the chain and pull both up into the attic. Feed the cable over to the hole above the existing outlet. Drop a chain again, and grab it through a small opening you've cut above the box. Install cable clamps, tape cable to the chain, and use the chain to pull cable from the attic into the box.

Fishing and running cable *(continued)*

RUNNING CABLE THROUGH A FLOOR

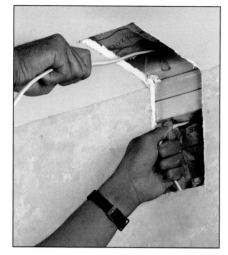

1 **WORK WHERE THE CEILING AND WALL MEET.** When there is no access from above or below, cut corner notches in the drywall or plaster, as shown. Drill a 1-inch hole up through the center of the top plate. Bend the cable, poke it up through the hole, and grab it from the other side.

2 **DRILL A LOCATOR HOLE.** Remove the shoe molding below the box that you will be taking power from. Drill a ¼-inch hole through the floor directly below the box and tight up against the wall. Poke a scrap wire down through the hole. Using the wire as a reference point, measure over to the middle of the bottom plate of the wall above (approximately 1¾ inches) and drill a 1-inch hole up into the wall.

3 **FEED THE CABLE.** Drop a chain through the hole you cut for the box, and jiggle it until it falls through the hole you drilled. Tape the cable to the chain and pull the cable through the wall. Put a cable clamp in a box, feed the cable through it, and mount the box in the opening.

RUNNING CABLE IN FINISHED WALLS

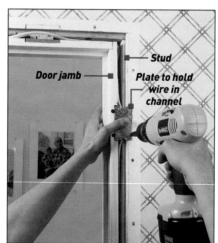

Stud

Door jamb

Plate to hold wire in channel

Channel

RUNNING CABLE THROUGH A WALL. Cut the hole for the remodel box (see page 171). Remove an existing receptacle and punch out a knockout in the back or bottom of its box. Run one fish tape through the existing box and one through the new hole. Hook them together. Pull tape back through the hole. Tape fish tape to cable, then pull cable from the hole to the box.

RUNNING CABLE AROUND A DOOR. If you have a slab floor and no access to the ceiling, this may be your only option, but check to see if this is OK with local codes. Remove casing from around a door opening and run cable around the door. You may be able to slip the cable between the jamb and the stud. Or, drill a hole and run the cable in the cavity on the side of the stud.

RUNNING CABLE BEHIND A BASEBOARD. Use a flat pry bar to remove baseboard molding. With a drywall saw, cut a channel in the drywall at least 1 inch shorter than the baseboard. Drill holes through the centers of the studs and run cable through the holes. Protect all holes with nail plates.

Working with armored cable

Armored cable is the middle ground between NM and conduit. It is easier to install than conduit and less flexible than NM. It protects wires better than NM but not as well as conduit. There are two types of armored cable. BX cable has no ground wire, the sheathing itself providing the ground. MC cable has a green-insulated grounding wire and is often required by code. Some codes call for armored cable instead of NM. Others require NM or conduit where the cable is exposed. Run armored cable inside walls, and protect it from nails as you would NM cable.

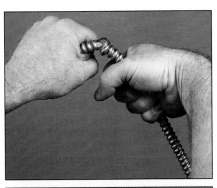

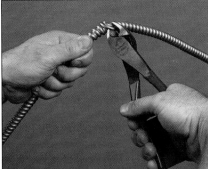

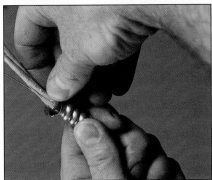

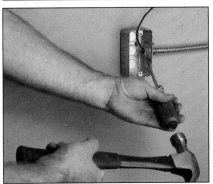

1 TWIST THE CABLE. Grasp the cable firmly on each side of the spot you want to cut. Twist the waste end clockwise until the armor comes apart far enough for you to slip in cutters. If you have trouble doing this with your bare hands, use two pliers.

SNIP AND REMOVE THE ARMOR. Cut through one rib of the armor with a pair of side-cutting pliers. Slide the waste arm off the wires, keeping your hands clear of sharp edges.

2 TRIM SHARP ENDS. Remove paper wrapping and plastic strips. Leave the thin metal bonding strip alone. Use side-cutting pliers to snip away pointed ends of sheathing that could nick wire insulation.

SLIP ON THE BUSHING. Slip a bushing over the wires. Slide it down into the armor so the bushing protects the wires from the sharp edges of the armor. If there is a bonding strip, ask your inspector what to do with it. Most inspectors want you to cut it to about 2 inches and wrap it over the bushing and around the armor, helping to ensure conductive contact between the armor and the box.

3 ATTACH THE CLAMP. Remove the locknut from an armored cable clamp. Slide the clamp down over the bushing as far as it will go, and tighten the setscrew. Double-check to make sure that none of the wires are in danger of being nicked by the armor.

CONNECT TO THE BOX. Remove a knockout slug from a metal box and poke the connector into the hole. Slide the locknut over the wires and tighten it onto the cable clamp. Use a hammer and screwdriver to tap the locknut tight. On BX cable, this connection serves as the ground.

Running conduit

REQUIRED SKILLS: Measuring and cutting conduit, assembling parts.

HOW LONG WILL IT TAKE?

Experienced . . . . 3 hrs.
Handy . . . . 5 hrs.
Novice . . . . 8 hrs.

VARIABLES: Time depends on the wall surface and number of turns in the conduit.

STUFF YOU'LL NEED

✔ MATERIALS:
Conduit and fittings, wire, PVC cement, lubricant

✔ TOOLS:
Screwdriver, lineman's pliers, hacksaw, conduit reamer, fish tape

Conduit is the most durable product for running wire. It's more expensive and time-consuming to install than cable, but it is no longer necessary to learn how to bend conduit. Ready-made parts make installation easier than ever. Use conduit on unfinished walls and ceilings where wiring will be exposed. Use electrical metallic tubing (EMT), or thinwall conduit, for most indoor installations. Use thicker intermediate metal conduit (IMC) above ground outdoors. Use plastic rigid nonmetallic conduit (PVC) for underground applications.

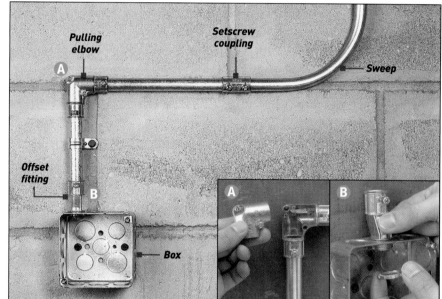

ASSEMBLING THE PARTS. Take a rough drawing of your installation to a home center or electrical supply store. Ask a salesperson to help you gather all the pieces you need. Generally use ½-inch conduit for up to five #12 wires or six #14 wires, and ¾-inch conduit for more wires. (Larger conduit will make pulling easier, so consider buying ¾ inch in every case.) Use a sweep to turn most corners. Use setscrew couplings and elbows for indoor installations (you'll have to use compression fittings outdoors). **A** At every four bends install a box or a pulling elbow (see inset above and "Closer Look," page 181). **B** If the conduit and the box are installed flush against a wall, you'll need an offset fitting.

Greenfield conduit

Greenfield. Also called flexible metal conduit, Greenfield is essentially armored cable without the wires. It is expensive, so use it sparingly for places where rigid conduit would be difficult to install.

PVC conduit

PVC conduit. In many areas PVC is acceptable for indoor and outdoor installations. Cut it with a backsaw or hacksaw and a miter box. Glue the pieces together using PVC cement approved by an inspector.

ELECTRICAL

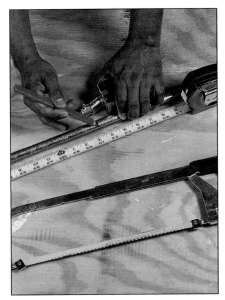

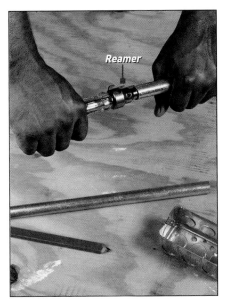

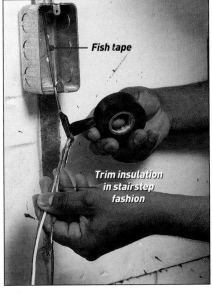

1 **MEASURE AND CUT.** Install the boxes first, then cut conduit to fit between them. At a corner, have a helper hold a sweep in place while you mark the conduit for cutting. Use a hacksaw with a fine-tooth blade to cut.

2 **REMOVE BURRS.** Ream out all burrs with a conduit reamer so the wires can slide smoothly past joints without damaging the sheathing.

Any tubing that carries electrical wires must be free from burrs and sharp edges that could damage the wire while it's being pulled.

3 **RUN FISH TAPE AND ATTACH THE WIRES.** Feed the fish tape through the conduit in the opposite direction from which you will pull the wires. Trim the insulation in a stair-step fashion (staggered exposure of wire) to make the wire easier to pull. Poke the wire ends through the fish tape's loop and bend them over. Wrap firmly and neatly with electrician's tape so the joint will not bind when it goes through a sweep.

4 **SQUIRT LUBRICANT.** To make pulling easier on long runs, pour a bit of pulling lubricant on the wires. (Avoid using substitute lubricants like dishwashing liquid or hand soap. Some can dangerously degrade wire insulation over time.)

5 **PULL THE WIRES.** Have someone feed the wires through one end while you pull the fish tape on the other end. Pull with steady pressure and keep the wires parallel to avoid twists that will jam in the conduit. Try to keep the wires moving, rather than starting and stopping. If they get stuck, back up a few inches to gain a running start.

CLOSER LOOK

INSTALL PULLING ELBOWS
If the conduit will make more than three turns between boxes, install a pulling elbow to make fishing easier. Don't splice wires here; just use the opening to pull the wires through.

Adding a circuit

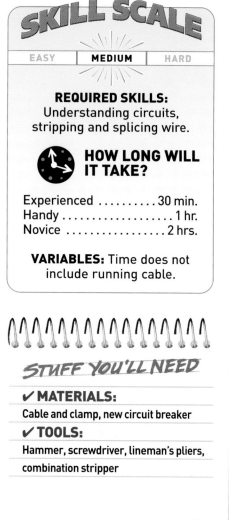

SKILL SCALE

EASY	**MEDIUM**	HARD

REQUIRED SKILLS:
Understanding circuits, stripping and splicing wire.

HOW LONG WILL IT TAKE?

Experienced . . . . 30 min.
Handy . . . . 1 hr.
Novice . . . . 2 hrs.

VARIABLES: Time does not include running cable.

STUFF YOU'LL NEED

✔ **MATERIALS:**
Cable and clamp, new circuit breaker

✔ **TOOLS:**
Hammer, screwdriver, lineman's pliers, combination stripper

If you're uncomfortable with the prospect of adding a new circuit on your own, get some advice from your home center or hire a pro.

SAFETY ALERT

FIRE PROTECTION
The NEC now requires the use of Arc Fault Circuit Interrupters (AFCI) for bedroom circuits. AFCIs provide greater fire protection than a regular breaker. Regular breakers trip for overloads and short circuits. AFCIs offer protection when arcing occurs because of frayed and overheated cords or from faulty wire insulation.

The physical work of installing a new electrical circuit is simple and calls for no special skills. Most of the work is completed outside the service panel. To get a breaker that will fit in your panel, jot down the brand and model number or bring a sample breaker to the store.

First determine whether your service panel can accommodate a new breaker, and then plan a circuit that will not be overloaded (see page 156). If the circuit will be in a bath or along a kitchen countertop, consider installing a GFCI breaker, so that you won't have to install individual GFCI outlets (see page 164). Install the new boxes. Run cable from the boxes back to the service panel. Electricians call this practice a "home run." Hook up the devices and fixtures. Now you're ready to energize the new circuit by installing a new breaker and connecting the wires to it.

Always buy breakers made by the same company that made the boxes they'll go in.

See page 540

① SHUT OFF MAIN POWER. Work during the daytime and have a reliable flashlight on hand. Turn off the main circuit breaker. All the wires and circuit breakers in the panel are now de-energized except for the thick wires that come from the outside and connect to the main breaker: Do not touch them.

CLOSER LOOK

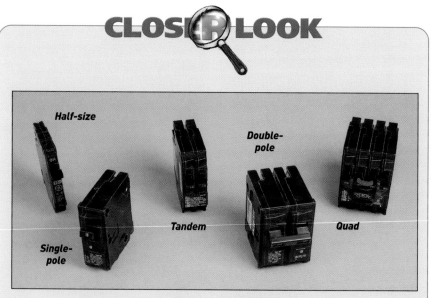

Half-size

Double-pole

Single-pole

Tandem

Quad

BREAKER OPTIONS

If the service panel has room, install full-size, single-pole breakers. If you're out of space, see if your panel can accommodate half-size or skinny breakers, or tandem breakers. In some panels, these breakers only fit in slots near the bottom.

You'll need double-pole breakers or a wafer breaker for 240-volt circuits. A quad breaker can supply two 240-volt circuits.

Your building code limits the number of breakers that can be installed. If you add too many, an inspector will require you to put in a new panel or a subpanel.

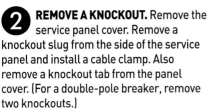

2 **REMOVE A KNOCKOUT.** Remove the service panel cover. Remove a knockout slug from the side of the service panel and install a cable clamp. Also remove a knockout tab from the panel cover. (For a double-pole breaker, remove two knockouts.)

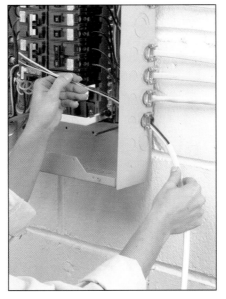

3 **CLAMP THE CABLE.** Determine how far the wires must travel to reach the breaker and the neutral bus bar. To avoid tangles, plan a path around the box's outside perimeter. Strip about a foot more sheathing than you think you will need. Thread the wires through the clamp and secure the cable. Don't overtighten.

4 **CONNECT THE NEUTRAL WIRE.** Run the neutral wire toward an open terminal in the neutral bus bar, bending the wire carefully so it will easily fit behind the panel cover. Cut the wire to length and strip off about ½ inch of insulation. Poke the end into the terminal and tighten the setscrew. Connect the ground wire to the ground bar (or neutral bus bar if there is no ground bar).

5 **WIRE THE NEW BREAKER.** Run the hot wire, bending it carefully so it will easily fit behind the panel cover. Cut the wire to length. Strip off ½ inch of insulation. Poke the wire into the new breaker terminal. If bare wire is visible, remove the wire, snip it a little shorter, and reinsert it. Tighten the setscrew.

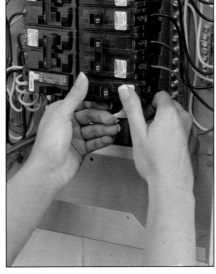

6 **SNAP THE BREAKER INTO PLACE.** Make sure the breaker is in the off position, and then slip one side of the breaker under a tab to the right or left of the hot bus bar. Push the other side onto the bus bar until the new breaker is flush with the other breakers. (Some brands of breakers may require a slightly different installation method; check the instructions.) Restore power, turn on the breaker, and try the switches or receptacles to see if they're getting power.

7 **INSTALLING DOUBLE-POLE BREAKERS.** Check to see if you have the two free spots you'll need for a 240-volt breaker. (A tandem breaker takes up only one spot and can be substituted as long as there are two lugs for it.) Shut off the power. Connect the black and red wires to the breaker terminals. Connect the white wire to the neutral bus bar and the ground wire to the ground bar (or neutral bus bar if there is no ground bar).

Planning kitchen lighting

Well-planned kitchen lighting will create cheerful and inviting spaces, increase the safety of food preparation, and highlight cabinetry and design features. Lighting serves three basic functions in the kitchen:

- **Ambient lighting produces a daylight effect.** Flush ceiling fixtures or track lights spread light more evenly than recessed can lights or pendants. (Ask for a kitchen/bath tube if using fluorescent lights in either of those rooms.) Windows and skylights are great sources of light during daylight hours, but they need help in the evening or during gloomy weather. A dimming system will make it easier to get the right amount of light.

- **Task lights under kitchen cabinets or in other strategic areas illuminate** common kitchen tasks like food preparation and dish washing. Can lights and track lights can both be aimed and provide good task lighting.

- **In-between lights illuminate kitchen work spaces** while providing generous amounts of ambient light. These lights include recessed can lights over a sink, pendant fixtures above an eating area, and track lights in a semicircle near cabinetry.

See pages
540–542

Ambient lighting

Task lights

In-between lights

Shaping up with track lighting

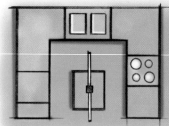

Single strip

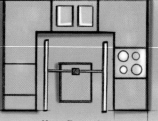

H configuration

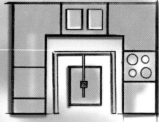

U configuration

Many kitchens feature a single strip of track lighting running through the center of the ceiling. This kind of light provides adequate illumination but can sometimes bounce off wall cabinets and produce an uncomfortable glare—especially if the cabinets are shiny or light in color. The lights can cast a shadow from a person over a food preparation area at the countertop, contributing to poor visibility. Instead of installing a single strip of track lighting along the ceiling, wrap the tracks around the room in an H or a U pattern.

Install the tracks about 3 feet out from the wall and 2 feet out from the wall cabinets. The lamps will then shine down over the shoulders of people working at counters, or toward the center of the room—providing both task lighting and ambient light.

Lighting a bathroom

An average-size bathroom needs a ceiling fan/light in the center of the main room, a moisture-proof ceiling light over the shower/bath, and lights over the sink.

- **Ambient lighting is typically provided by an overhead light combined with a vent fan.** Make sure the fan's blower is powerful enough to adequately vent your bathroom (see page 209). Spend a little more money to include a low-watt night-light or a forced-air heating unit. Some people prefer a heat lamp near the tub or shower for additional comfort while drying off after bathing.

- **Bathroom mirror lighting deserves careful thought.** A horizontal strip of decorative lightbulbs above the mirror provides lots of light but may shine in your eyes. A fluorescent fixture with a lens provides more even light, but make sure you choose a kitchen and bath tube with a warm tone similar to incandescent light. Sconce lights placed on either side of the mirror are the best source for lighting your face for shaving or applying makeup. When planning circuits, remember to install a ground fault circuit interrupter (GFCI) receptacle near the sink.

- **Shower lighting supplements what little light comes through the shower curtain or shower door.** Consider installing a recessed canister light with a watertight lens in the shower ceiling.

See pages 540–542

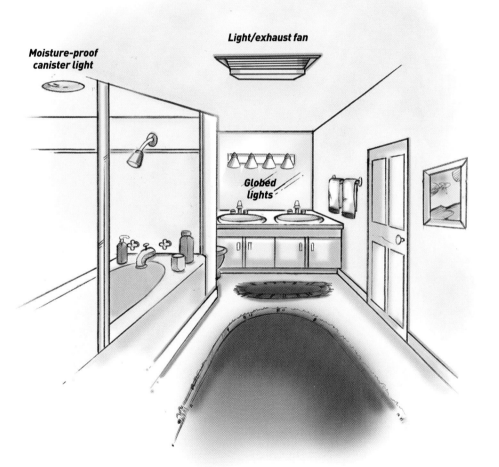

Moisture-proof canister light

Light/exhaust fan

Globed lights

LIGHTING UP YOUR BATHROOM. The darker the color of your bathroom walls and fixtures, the more light you need. Natural light from a window may be sufficient for daytime use. At night or in early morning, however, the shower in particular might need one or two moisture-proof canister lights. (Codes limit them to 60 watts each if the shower is enclosed.) Above the sink, install moisture-resistant globed lights that won't shine in your eyes. Overhead, install a single fixture that efficiently and stylishly combines a light and exhaust fan, with perhaps a night-light and/or a heater.

Lighting living areas

Living rooms, dining rooms, great-rooms, and large bedrooms all benefit from both ambient and task lighting. Rather than installing a single lighting component, think in terms of the total use of the room. Layering several types of lights makes a room more comforting and inviting by avoiding both glare and dark shadows. Your goal is flexibility so you can set a variety of moods by brightening or dimming the entire room or part of the room.

- **Highlight a piece of art or cabinetry, or accentuate wall texture,** with can lights to give the room warmth and interest. (If you don't want to install can lights, you can accent paintings with picture lights that attach to the frame.)

- **Put at least one of the components on a dimmer switch.** Install several lights that are optional but not necessary. Don't be afraid to install too many lights; you don't have to use all of them at the same time.

- **Install an in-between light such as a dining area chandelier** to brighten the dinner table and provide some ambient light.

- **Rope lights are strands of clear, flexible plastic** that you can drape around the inside of cabinets or behind fascia to provide accent lighting.

See pages 540–542

Fish-eye spot

Accent lights

In-between lights

Ambient lighting on dimmer switch

Lamp on switched receptacle

Task light on unswitched receptacle

SHOWING OFF A GREAT-ROOM WITH GREAT LIGHTING. The lighting plan for this large family room includes a grid of recessed canister lights for general lighting and a centrally located chandelier over the dining table. A recessed light with fish-eye trim spotlights a wall painting. The chandelier in the dining room creates ambient lighting when controlled by a dimmer switch. The task light on the piano offers movable light for specific needs. The table lamp and floor lamp are controlled by wall switches. Accent lights brighten shelves.

Planning for can lighting

Can lights vary in intensity and angle. The higher your ceiling, the more floor space a light will illuminate. In general, recessed cans should be positioned 6 feet from each other. Of course, most rooms are not sized to accommodate this, so you'll have to adjust your calculations. In the example below, most of the lights are 5 feet apart. Make a similar plan for your own installation, experimenting with several configurations. Take your plans with you to your home center for advice.

Lay out can lights using the templates that come with them, and mark the center point with a nail. You may have to move some lights a few inches one way or another in order to avoid hitting the ceiling framing. Fortunately, this will not make a big difference in the overall effect.

SPECIAL TECHNIQUES. In addition to providing general lighting, recessed can lights can enhance decorating strategies with:

- **Wall washing.** To light up a large wall area, install cans with wall-wash trims that are 24 to 30 inches apart and the same distance from the wall.

- **Accent lighting.** Spotlight a painting, fireplace mantel, or other feature with a can that has a fish-eye style trim. Place it 18 to 24 inches from the wall, centered on the object.

- **Grazing.** To dramatize an unusual vertical surface, such as a fireplace or a textured wall, place cans 6 to 12 inches from the wall and 12 to 18 inches apart. Wire them with a shared dimmer switch.

See pages 540–542

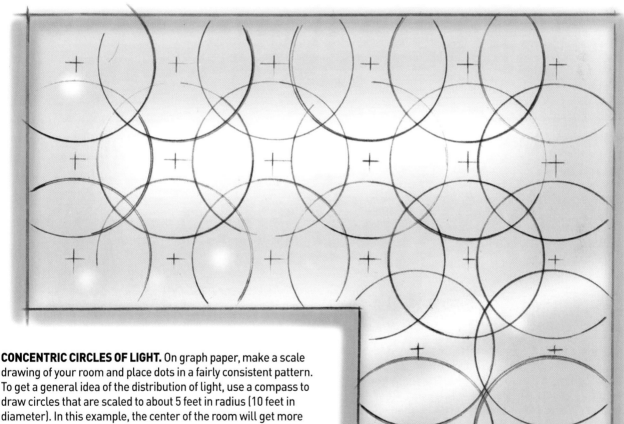

CONCENTRIC CIRCLES OF LIGHT. On graph paper, make a scale drawing of your room and place dots in a fairly consistent pattern. To get a general idea of the distribution of light, use a compass to draw circles that are scaled to about 5 feet in radius (10 feet in diameter). In this example, the center of the room will get more light than the perimeter—which is usually desirable. Generally, figure that a 65-watt floodlight in a room with an 8-foot ceiling will light up a circle that is 8 feet in diameter on the floor; if the ceiling is 10 feet high, it will illuminate a 10-foot circle.

Choosing ceiling fixtures

The broad range of overhead fixtures can be roughly divided into those with eye-catching decorative features (like the ones shown on this page) and those that are hardly noticeable but provide general illumination (like the flush ceiling fixtures shown opposite below). Track lights (opposite) fall in between. All come in a wide variety of styles. Here are the basic types and features to choose from.

PENDANT LIGHTS. Lights that hang down from the ceiling are called pendants. Use them for general lighting, to illuminate a dining room table, or to light up a work surface.

A chandelier or other type of pendant usually can't illuminate a large room on its own. A chandelier often hangs at eye level and would produce an unpleasant glare if it were bright enough to light an entire room.

- **Pendant shades.** Use a pendant shade to focus light on a specific space, such as a small table, a countertop, or a narrow work area. A pendant light with a glass shade will provide general lighting as well as directed light. A metal shade focuses light more directly. Older styles of pendant lights hang by decorative brass chains, with neutral-colored lamp cord running through the chain. Newer fixtures use a plain chrome-colored wire for support, with the cord running alongside.

- **Pendant lanterns.** These lights resemble the old glass lanterns that protected candles from wind. Use them in narrow areas like foyers and stairways. Hang these at least 6½ feet from the ground so that people can walk under them. Center a pendant lantern width-wise in a narrow room. If it is near a large window, place it so it will look centered from the outside.

- **Chandeliers.** Originally designed as candleholders, chandeliers usually have five or more lightbulbs. Look for a model that is easy to clean; complex designs can be difficult to dust or wash. Keep the fixture in scale; a chandelier that is too small will appear to be dwarfed by the room. When choosing a unit to hang over a dining room table, select one that is about 12 inches narrower than the table. If it is any wider, people may bump their heads on it when they stand up from the table. In an entryway, maintain proportion by installing a chandelier that is 2 inches wide for every foot of room width (for example, use a 20-inch-wide light in a 10-foot-wide room).

Get the height right. A common mistake is to hang a chandelier too low. A chandelier should hang about 30 inches above a tabletop. The length of the chain will depend on your ceiling height.

Pendant lantern

Pendant shade

Chandelier

Some lighting fixtures can be raised or lowered to perform different functions—raised for general room light or lowered to focus on a dining room table.

TRACK CEILING FIXTURES

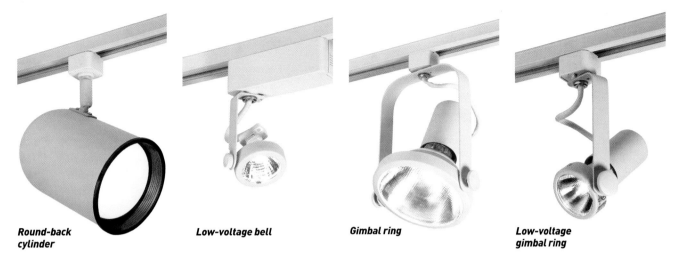

Round-back cylinder

Low-voltage bell

Gimbal ring

Low-voltage gimbal ring

CHOOSING TRACK LIGHTS. A single track lighting system can combine general lighting and accent lighting. When choosing a lamp, make sure it can handle the lightbulb of your choice and that it will fit onto your track. Incandescent lamps such as a **round-back cylinder** or a **gimbal ring** produce a broad, intense beam. Low-voltage halogen track lights such as a **low-voltage bell** or **low-voltage gimbal ring** produce a more intense, narrower beam

of light. Each has its own transformer, so it can attach to a standard-voltage track. (However, these low-voltage lights require a special electronic dimmer; a standard magnetic dimmer will damage the lamps.) A track that partially encircles a room at a distance of 6 feet or so from the walls will disperse light more effectively than a single track running through the middle of the room.

FLUSH CEILING FIXTURES

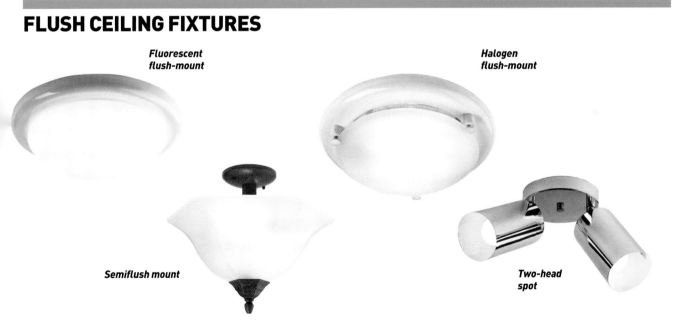

Fluorescent flush-mount

Halogen flush-mount

Semiflush mount

Two-head spot

CHOOSING FLUSH FIXTURES. A single flush fixture in the middle of the ceiling is the most common way to light a room. These fixtures usually produce enough light to adequately illuminate a 12'×12' room with an 8-foot ceiling or a 16'×16' room with a 10-foot ceiling (the higher the fixture, the broader the spread of its light). They hug the ceiling, consistently distributing light. Newer **fluorescent ceiling fixtures** with electronic ballasts look like

incandescents, save energy, and have tubes that rarely burn out. A **semiflush fixture** hangs down a foot or so from the ceiling. It diffuses light through the globe as well as upward, evenly illuminating a room. **Halogens** offer more intense light. **Two- or three-head spotlights** provide some of track lighting's versatility. Point the lights horizontally for general lighting, or angle them downward to highlight certain areas of the room.

Selecting bulbs and tubes

The color of a lightbulb or a light fixture globe or shade significantly affects the mood of a room. Lighting that is slightly red or yellow is considered warm, while blue-tinged light is cool. Incandescent bulbs produce warm light; many fluorescents are cool—if not downright cold.

Choose the color of your home's lighting according to the color of your furnishings. If you have pure white walls or cabinetry, warm lighting will make them beige. Cool light directed at brownish natural wood may give it a green tinge.

Fortunately, whether you have a fluorescent or an incandescent fixture, you can switch from cool to warm light, or vice versa, by changing the bulbs or tubes.

Ask your home center salesperson for advice on which bulbs or shades will work best in your setting.

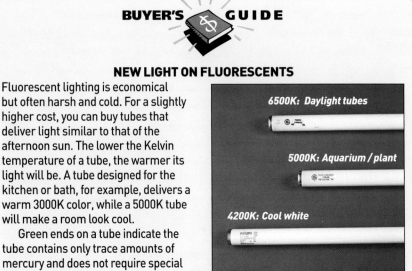

BUYER'S GUIDE

NEW LIGHT ON FLUORESCENTS

Fluorescent lighting is economical but often harsh and cold. For a slightly higher cost, you can buy tubes that deliver light similar to that of the afternoon sun. The lower the Kelvin temperature of a tube, the warmer its light will be. A tube designed for the kitchen or bath, for example, delivers a warm 3000K color, while a 5000K tube will make a room look cool.

Green ends on a tube indicate the tube contains only trace amounts of mercury and does not require special disposal. Recycle unmarked tubes at an approved facility.

T-8 tubes, like the one pictured below, are energy efficient.

6500K: Daylight tubes

5000K: Aquarium / plant

4200K: Cool white

3000K: Kitchen and Bath

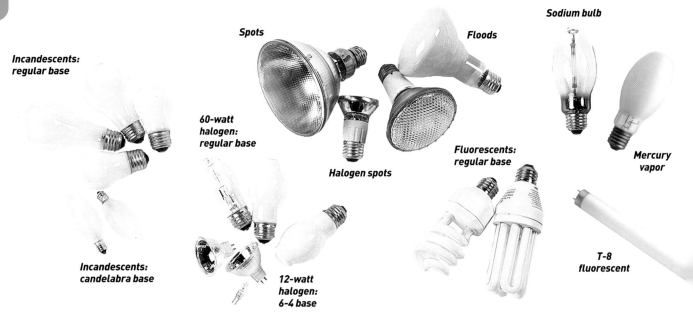

Incandescents: regular base

Spots

Floods

Sodium bulb

60-watt halogen: regular base

Halogen spots

Fluorescents: regular base

Mercury vapor

Incandescents: candelabra base

12-watt halogen: 6-4 base

T-8 fluorescent

LIGHTBULB OPTIONS

- **Incandescent bulbs** are the most common but have comparatively short lives and are not very energy efficient.

- **Low-voltage halogen bulbs** last longer than incandescents and use far less energy, but they burn hot. Halogens come in many styles so make sure the bulb base fits in your fixture.

- **Reflector bulbs** direct either a wide or narrow beam of light, depending on the bulb. A "spot" bulb projects a flashlight-like beam. A "flood" bulb illuminates a wider area. The second number on the stamped label indicates the degree of the beam spread.

- **Fluorescent tubes** that screw into incandescent sockets save money in the long run. Choose from among several shapes and degrees of warmth. Some fluorescents can be dimmed but require a special ballast and a special dimmer. T-8 tubes are energy efficient. Conversion kits are available for standard fixtures.

- **HID (High-Intensity Discharge) bulbs** such as sodium and mercury vapor produce bright, economical light outdoors.

Installing or replacing wall lights

SKILL SCALE

EASY	**MEDIUM**	HARD

REQUIRED SKILLS: Running cable, installing a box, stripping and splicing wires.

HOW LONG WILL IT TAKE?

Experienced . . . . 3 hrs.
Handy . . . . 6 hrs.
Novice . . . . 8 hrs.

STUFF YOU'LL NEED

✔ MATERIALS:

Wall sconces or bathroom wall fixture,
boxes, cable with clamps, staples,
wire nuts, electrician's tape

✔ TOOLS:

Drill, saw, fish tape, screwdriver,
lineman's pliers, combination
stripper, level

Wall sconces and vanity lights are lighting sources mounted on vertical surfaces. They are primarily used for ambient and task lighting. Most wall fixtures attach to a ceiling box with a swivel strap so you can easily adjust the fixture. A fluorescent fixture installed above a bathroom mirror may not require installing a box; read fixture instructions.

See pages 540–542

Try a swivel box

Swivel boxes are junction boxes that have an adjustable mounting strap that turns so that you can level the lighting fixture on the wall. They're available in the electrical department at your home center.

Installing a sconce

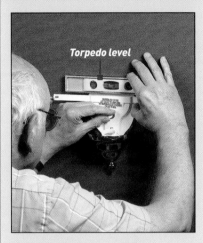

Torpedo level

Run cable from a nearby receptacle or other power source into a switch box and then to a box mounted on the wall. Get a box with a swivel strap to let you adjust the base until it is level. Depending on the sconce, use either a round or octagonal box. Wire as you would for a ceiling fixture (see page 173).

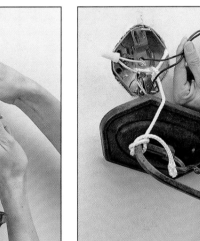

1 **REMOVE THE EXISTING FIXTURE.** Turn off the power to the fixture. Test with a voltage meter (see page 158). Remove the glass globe, shade, and bulb. Remove any nuts or screws holding the fixture in place. Carefully pull the fixture from the wall (pry if it has been painted in place); avoid yanking on the wires. After you remove the fixture, twist off the wire nuts that connect the wires.

Wiring a vanity light

Support heavy fixtures with a coat hanger.

Installing a light over a mirror or medicine cabinet calls for no special wiring techniques. Some fixtures require a box, while others can be wired and then attached directly to the wall. If you will be installing a mirror that reaches to the ceiling, give the glass company exact dimensions for cutting a hole in the mirror to attach the fixture to a box mounted in the wall behind the mirror.

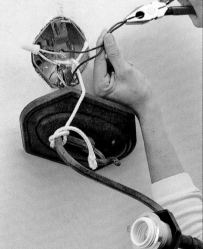

2 **INSTALL THE NEW FIXTURE.** Strip ¼ inch of insulation from wire tips. Twist and connect wires: white to white, and black to black. Twist on a plastic wire cap. If the cap doesn't cover all the bare wire, remove the cap, trim the wire a bit shorter, and reattach the cap. Fold the wires into the junction box, place the fixture over the studs or nipple, then attach with the ornamental nuts provided.

Installing a hanging fixture

| EASY | MEDIUM | HARD |

REQUIRED SKILLS: Running cable, installing a box, stripping and splicing wires.

 **HOW LONG WILL IT TAKE?**

Experienced . . . . 3 hrs.
Handy . . . . 6 hrs.
Novice . . . . 8 hrs.

VARIABLES: Adding a new box for the light takes considerably longer.

STUFF YOU'LL NEED

✔ **MATERIALS:**
Chandelier, wire nuts, electrician's tape

✔ **TOOLS:**
Ladder and support platform, screwdriver, wire stripper

SAFETY ALERT

EXTRA PROTECTION FOR WIRE CAPS

Once you've connected the wires with wire caps, wrap electrician's tape around the wire and the cap. This will help keep the wire from popping free and charging the metal parts of the chandelier with electricity.

Some form of chandelier illuminates most dining tables. Plan the placement of one as carefully as you would plan a good meal. To give off a pleasing light, a chandelier should be centered over the table and about 30 inches above it. If there is one socket, use a single 100-watt bulb. For two sockets, use two 60-watt bulbs. For three or more sockets, use 40-watt bulbs.

Lighting fixtures impact the ambience of a room, not only because of the quality of light they produce, but because of their appearance. This is especially true of chandeliers because they are prominent room features.

Although the term "chandelier" may bring to mind ornate lights with sparkling crystals, for practical purposes it includes any ceiling-mounted fixture that hangs from a chain or wire. This includes an incredibly wide range of hanging fixtures that complement any decor, from Early-American candle types to stained-glass Arts-and-Crafts designs.

All ceiling-mounted fixtures are installed similarly, regardless of style. Your biggest issue is determining if the electric box that houses the wiring connections in the ceiling will support the weight of the chandelier you have chosen. If you replace a hanging fixture with a fixture about the same weight, the existing box is probably fine. If the new fixture is heavier than the old one, you may need to replace the ceiling box with a fan box rated to hold more weight. If you put in a new box, make sure it's rated for a heavy fixture.

See pages 540–542

ELECTRICAL

1 **ASSEMBLE THE CANOPY AND HANGING HARDWARE.** Set aside any components that can be installed after the fixture is hanging (globes, glass panels, lightbulbs, etc.). Follow the specific instructions provided with the fixture. Remember to slide any necessary parts over the wiring and hanging chain.

Support the fixture close to the ceiling by screwing a platform to the top of a stepladder with a few drywall screws. This provides a good work surface and should put the chandelier close enough to the ceiling to allow you to do the wiring without having to hold the chandelier in midair. Having a second person on a second ladder may also work, but coordinating your movements can be difficult with a heavy fixture.

Fixtures usually come with a new mounting strap—a strip of metal that screws into the junction box in the ceiling. You can often use the existing strap, but if not, unscrew the old strap, and screw the new strap in place.

WORK SMARTER

NEED PARTS?

Break something while you were working on the chandelier? Many—but not all—parts of a chandelier or lamp are interchangeable. Take the broken part to an electrical department or a lighting store and show them what you need. Brass globes, threaded fittings, and brass stems almost always can be replaced with new parts.

FINDING NEUTRAL ON A LIGHT FIXTURE CORD

Light fixture cords don't have black and white cables, but it's still important to connect the neutral wire of the light with the neutral wire in the circuit. Look closely at the lamp cord: The plastic vinyl sleeve with the rib is the neutral wire. Connect it to the white cable coming into the junction box.

2 **CONNECT THE WIRING.** Check the supply wires for fraying or damage. If necessary, cut the wires and strip off about ¾ inch of insulation. On older fixtures, like this one, the wires aren't color coded. Connect one fixture wire to the black supply wire and the other fixture wire to the white supply wire. Newer fixtures have a black and a white wire. Twist the bare end of the black supply wire together with the bare end of the black fixture wire, then twist on a wire nut. Repeat with the white wires. Carefully tuck the wires into the junction box. Put a bulb in the fixture and check that connections work before finishing.

3 **HANG THE FIXTURE.** Thread the fixture's mounting stem into the mounting strap on the ceiling box. Although the fixture is now securely hanging from the ceiling, the box and mounting hardware are still visible. Slide the canopy up against the ceiling to cover the mounting hardware; tighten the locknut against the canopy.

Installing recessed lighting

ELECTRICAL

SKILL SCALE

EASY	**MEDIUM**	HARD

REQUIRED SKILLS: Installing cable, connecting to power, wiring a switch, and stripping and splicing wire.

HOW LONG WILL IT TAKE?

Experienced . . . . 8 hrs.
Handy . . . . 12 hrs.
Novice . . . . 16 hrs.

VARIABLES: Times are for installing six can lights.

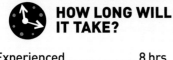

STUFF YOU'LL NEED

✔ MATERIALS:
Can lights and trims, switch box and switch, cable, cable clamps (if they're not built into the fixture), wire nuts, electrician's tape

✔ TOOLS:
Stud finder, drill with long bit, drywall saw or hole-cutting drill attachment, voltage tester or multitester, combination stripper, lineman's pliers, screwdriver, safety glasses

WORK SMARTER

POSITIONING LIGHTS
Can lights come with mounting templates that show you what size hole to cut. Tape templates to the ceiling to get an idea of where your lights should go and how they will look.

Can lights, also called "pot lights," are recessed lights that use 30- to 150-watt floodlight bulbs. They're ideal for task lighting, for highlighting artwork, or grouped to illuminate whole rooms. (See page 187 for tips on placement.) Cans get hot. Position them at least 1 inch away from wood and other flammables. Always follow the manufacturer's instructions.

If the joists are exposed, use a new-work can light (see page 196). For ceilings already covered by drywall or plaster and lath, buy a remodel can (below) that clips into a hole cut in the ceiling. (It's also called an old-work, or retrofit, can.) To install a remodel can, follow the steps beginning on the opposite page.

CHOOSING CANISTER LIGHTS. Can lights are designed to suit specific situations. Here's how to choose the right one:

● **If insulation is in the ceiling, buy IC (Insulation Compatible) lights.** Standard recessed lights will dangerously overheat when surrounded by insulation.

● **Tiny low-voltage can lights add sparkle.** They're stylish but expensive and are wired in the same way as standard can lights.

● **Use bulbs of the recommended wattage or lower.** Bulbs with too-high wattage will dangerously overheat. When putting a number of cans on a dimmer, add up all the wattage and make sure your dimmer is rated to handle the load.

● **If you have fewer than 8 inches of vertical space above the ceiling,** purchase a low-clearance canister.

See pages 540–542

ANATOMY OF A REMODEL CAN LIGHT

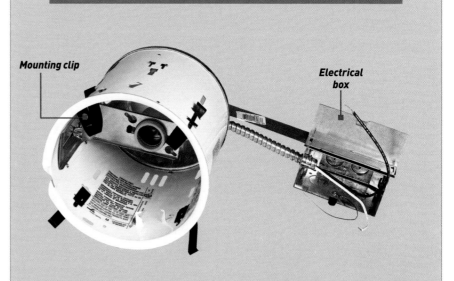

Mounting clip

Electrical box

A standard remodel canister fixture has an approved electrical box, suspended far enough from the light so it will not overheat. A thermal protector shuts the light off if it becomes too hot (for example, if you use a bulb of too-high voltage). If you have fewer than 8 inches of vertical space above your ceiling, purchase special cans designed to fit into this smaller space. Be sure the special cans are IC (Insulation Compatible) rated so there will be no danger of overheating.

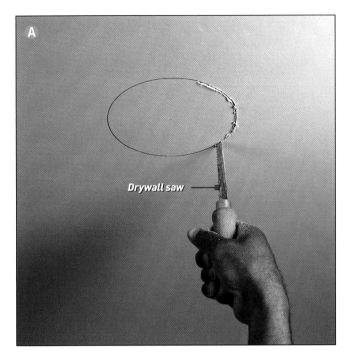

A

Drywall saw

B

Saw is made to cut a standard box diameter.

Arbor attaches to saw and fits in drill chuck.

① **OPTION A: CUT THE HOLE.** Lay out and mark all light locations with the help of the mounting template that comes with the light. Use a stud finder to make sure they will not overlap a joist, or drill a hole and poke a bent wire up into it to make sure the hole is entirely between joists. Draw and cut each hole precisely. If it is even a little too big, the can may not clamp tightly. Wearing safety glasses, cut the line lightly with a utility knife, then cut along the inside of the knife line with a drywall saw. Take care not to snag any wires that may be in the ceiling cavity.

OPTION B: USE A HOLE-CUTTING SAW. This tool saves time and cuts holes precisely. Instead of drawing the outline of the hole on the ceiling, just mark the center point shown on the mounting template. Check to see that you will not run into a joist. Check that the lights fit snugly without having to be forced into place.

NOTE: This tool is costly (the saw and the arbor are sold separately), but it's worth the price if you have more than six holes to cut through plaster. A less-expensive tool (see inset) is available for cutting through drywall only.

16 inches of extra cable

② **ROUGH-IN THE WIRING.** Run cable from a power source to a switch box, and then to the first hole, allowing at least 16 inches of extra cable to make wiring easy. (See page 177 for how to run cable.) Work carefully and use a drill with a long bit to avoid cutting additional access holes that will need patching later.

Designer Tip

Open

Fish-eye

Baffle

Reflective

CHOOSING CANISTER LIGHTS

Most can lights have two parts—the body and the trim. Choose both at the same time or install bodies with many trim options and choose later. Open trim is the simplest and least expensive option. Baffle trim diffuses light so it is more evenly distributed. Fish-eye (also called eyeball) trim swivels to highlight a decorative feature. Reflective trim offers maximum brightness.

Installing recessed lighting *(continued)*

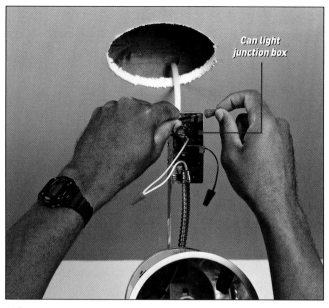

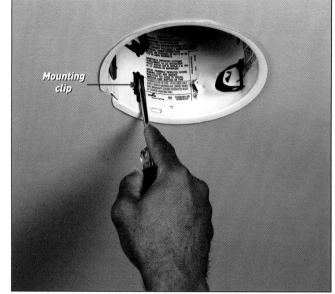

3 **WIRE THE LIGHT.** Open the light's junction box. Usually, a plate will pop off. Run cable into the box and clamp it. Strip insulation and make wire splices—black to black, white to white, and ground to ground (see page 159). Fold the wires into the box and replace the cover.

4 **MOUNT THE LIGHT.** Most remodel cans have four clips that clamp the can to the ceiling by pushing down on the top of the drywall or plaster. Pull the clips in so they do not protrude outside the can. Slip the can's box into the hole, then push the can body up into the hole until its flange is tight to the ceiling. With your thumb or a screwdriver, push each clip up and outward until it clicks and clamps the fixture.

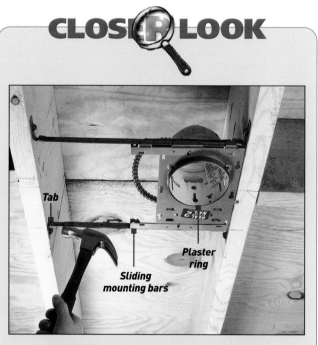

CLOSER LOOK

5 **ADD THE TRIM.** Most trims are mounted with coil springs or squeezable rod springs (as shown). If you have coil springs, hook each spring to its assigned hole inside the can (if it is not already there). Pull out each spring and hook it to the trim, then carefully guide the trim into position. If you have rod springs, squeeze and insert both ends of each spring into their assigned holes, then push the trim up. Different trims require different bulbs: The ones you'll need are marked on the inside of the trim.

MOUNTING A NEW-WORK CAN LIGHT

If ceiling joists are exposed, installation is easy. On a workbench, attach the plaster ring to the fixture. Adjust it to compensate for the thickness of the ceiling drywall that will be installed later. At the ceiling, slide the mounting bars outward so they reach joists on each side. Hammer the four tabs into the joists. Strengthen with 1¼-inch wood screws.

Installing halogen lighting

SKILL SCALE

EASY	MEDIUM	HARD

REQUIRED SKILLS: Attaching components with screws.

HOW LONG WILL IT TAKE?

Experienced . . . . 30 min.
Handy . . . . 1 hr.
Novice . . . . 2 hrs.

VARIABLES: Time does not include running power to the circuit.

To light counters or display shelves, consider a halogen puck light kit that plugs into a receptacle. A typical kit includes a transformer, cord, cord switch, several hockey-puck-shape lights that attach to the underside of shelves or cabinets, and detailed instructions. If you don't like using a cord switch, plug the kit into a receptacle controlled by a switch, or alter a receptacle and run cable so one outlet can be switched off and on (see page 167).

HALOGEN SAFETY TIPS. Halogens provide intense, almost glittering light, and they get hot. Position them where people won't brush against them. Don't attach them to particleboard that may scorch. Use halogens in a closet only if you are sure they will always be 18 inches or more away from clothing or boxes. If you use them in small, enclosed spaces, such as above shelves enclosed with glass doors, reduce the heat by replacing a 20-watt bulb with a 10-watt bulb. Drill ¼-inch air vent holes in the cabinet above the puck lights.

- **Halogens are very bright.** Position them so they will be out of sight.

- **Never use a halogen without the lens,** which filters UV rays.

- **Do not touch a bulb with your skin:** Natural oils will cause the bulb to burn out. Always handle halogen bulbs with a soft cloth.

See pages 540–542

STUFF YOU'LL NEED

✔ **MATERIALS:**
Halogen kit (wire, lights, terminal block, transformer, cord switch), insulated staples

✔ **TOOLS:**
Drill with screwdriver bit and ¼-inch bit, combination stripper, hammer

A round-top stapler (see page 214) makes it easier to attach the wires.

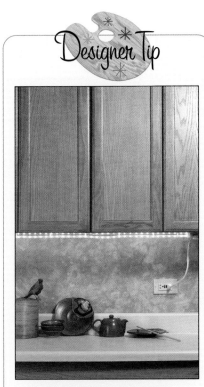

INSTALLING HALOGEN ROPE LIGHTS
To install rope lights, simply staple a rope into place and plug it in. It's bright enough to use as undercabinet lighting for the countertop and doesn't get as hot as puck lighting. Install rope lights in a straight line, or drape them in soft loops.

INSTALLING PUCK LIGHTING. Drill ½-inch holes to run wires, or plan to staple wires to the surface. Remove the covers from the lights, and mount the light bodies with screws. Most halogens are 120 volts, though some still run off low-voltage transformers. Wire the lights as directed, and snap on the trim rings, threading the wires through any holes. Run the wires to a switch box if they're 120 volts or to a transformer if they're low-voltage lights.

Installing fluorescent lighting

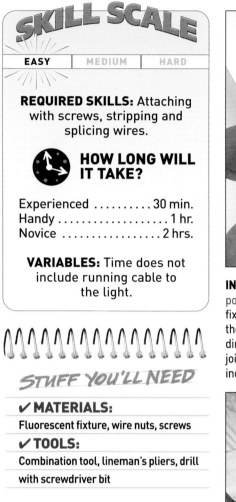

SKILL SCALE

EASY	MEDIUM	HARD

REQUIRED SKILLS: Attaching with screws, stripping and splicing wires.

HOW LONG WILL IT TAKE?

Experienced . . . . 30 min.
Handy . . . . 1 hr.
Novice . . . . 2 hrs.

VARIABLES: Time does not include running cable to the light.

STUFF YOU'LL NEED

✔ MATERIALS:
Fluorescent fixture, wire nuts, screws

✔ TOOLS:
Combination tool, lineman's pliers, drill with screwdriver bit

Fluorescent lights often are installed without a ceiling box: Cable is clamped to the fixture, which substitutes for a box. Some codes, however, require that fluorescent lights be attached to ceiling boxes. Suspend the fixture or set it in a suspended ceiling grid and make the connections. Square or rectangular fixtures with long tubes are the most common. Other fluorescent fixtures are shaped like incandescents and use circular or U-shape tubes. For directions on installing a longer fixture, see page 235.

See pages 540–542

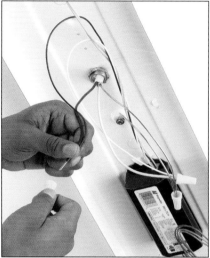

INSTALLING A FLUORESCENT. Shut off power at the service panel. Remove the old fixture. Clamp the cable to a knockout in the new fixture and attach the fixture directly to the ceiling by driving screws into joists. Splice the fixture's wires to the incoming wires. Attach the cover plate.

BUYER'S GUIDE

CONSIDER FLUORESCENT LIGHTING OPTIONS

● If an old fluorescent light needs a new ballast consider replacing the fixture. Newer fluorescents with electronic ballasts will be trouble-free for decades.

● Save money by buying fixtures for 4-foot tubes. Smaller tubes are more expensive.

● Fluorescent tubes offer a greater variety of light than ever (see page 190). A diffusing lens further softens the light.

INSTALLING FLUORESCENTS IN A SUSPENDED CEILING. Fluorescent fixtures fit into the ceiling grid, taking up the space of a 2'×2' (shown) or 2'×4' ceiling tile. For smaller fixtures, install additional metal grid pieces and cut ceiling tiles to fit on either side. Shut off power at the service panel; run a cable with ground wire for the lights (see pages 177–178 for how to extend the incoming line), screw the light to the grid, and then attach the cable to the fixture. Leave more than enough cable to reach the power source. Connect the wires to the power source before installing the tiles.

Installing track lighting

STUFF YOU'LL NEED

✔ MATERIALS:

Track system with lights, wire nuts, screws, plastic anchors

✔ TOOLS:

Combination tool, lineman's pliers, drill with screwdriver bit, tape measure, hacksaw or saber saw

A track system is the most versatile of all ceiling fixtures. You can configure it in many ways (see page 184), choose from several lamp styles (see page 189), and position the lamps to suit your needs. To begin installation, remove the existing ceiling fixture to locate the track. If you don't have an existing ceiling fixture that is switched, see pages 166 and 173 for how to install one. Be sure to get a fixture with a floating canopy—this lets you move the track back and forth a few inches in case you need to make adjustments.

 See pages 540–542

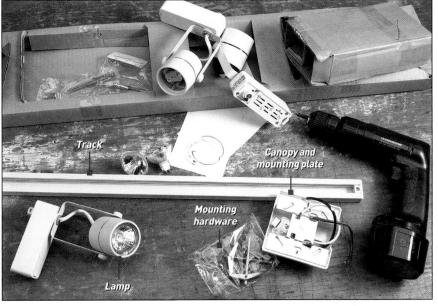

Track

Canopy and mounting plate

Mounting hardware

Lamp

PURCHASING A TRACK SYSTEM. Work with a salesperson; explain the size and configuration you want. Buy a kit that includes track, floating canopy mounting plate, end cap, and canopy. You also may have to buy additional track and end caps, as well as L- or T-fittings for the corners.

Choose the lights and bulbs when you buy the tracks. You can put different types of lamps on the same track, but be sure to purchase lamps made by the same manufacturer as the track—otherwise they may be incompatible.

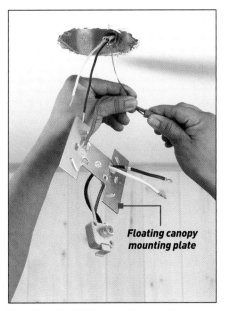

Floating canopy mounting plate

① INSTALL THE MOUNTING PLATE. Shut off power at the service panel. Use wire nuts to splice the house wires to the plate leads. Connect the ground wire to the plate and to the box if it is metal (see page 157). Push the wires into the box, and screw the plate to the box so it is snug against the ceiling.

② MEASURE AND MARK FOR THE TRACK. At the mounting plate, measure to see how far the side of the track will be from the nearest wall. Mark the ceiling so the track will be parallel to the wall. Use a framing square to draw lines if the track turns a corner.

Installing track lighting *(continued)*

3 **ATTACH THE TRACK TO THE MOUNTING PLATE.** Have a helper hold the track in place against the ceiling with it centered on the mounting plate. Drive the setscrews to anchor the track to the plate.

Floating canopy mounting plate

4 **TO LOCATE JOISTS IF THE TRACK IS MORE THAN 4 FEET LONG, HAVE A HELPER HOLD ONE END WHILE YOU USE A STUD FINDER.** Snap the track onto the plate and drive a screw into every available joist. If there are no joists, drill holes every foot or so, insert plastic anchors, and drive screws into the anchors.

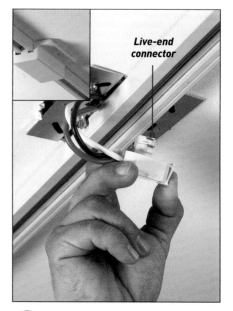

5 **TWIST ON THE LIVE-END CONNECTOR.** Insert the live-end connector and turn it 90 degrees until it snaps into place. Align the connector's two copper tabs with the two copper bars inside the track. Snap the plastic canopy over the track and mounting plate. (See inset.)

Live-end connector

6 **ATTACH A CORNER.** You can buy connectors to make 90-degree turns, T-shapes, or odd-angled turns. Slide the connector into the track that is already installed, slide the next track onto the connector, and attach that track to the ceiling. Cover all open track ends with end caps.

7 **TWIST ON A LIGHT.** This type of light twists into place in the same way as the live-end connector (see Step 5). Another type has a metal arm that is twisted to tighten. Restore power, turn on the switch, and swivel the lights to position them to meet your needs.

CLOSER LOOK

CUTTING TRACK

Tracks are available in standard lengths of 2, 4, 6, and 8 feet. If these sizes do not fit your needs, you can cut a track with a hacksaw or a saber saw equipped with a fine-toothed metal-cutting blade. Put electrician's tape around the track first to protect it, then clamp the track in a vise. Cut slowly and take care not to bend the track while cutting. Attach the plastic end piece as necessary.

Installing motion-sensor lights

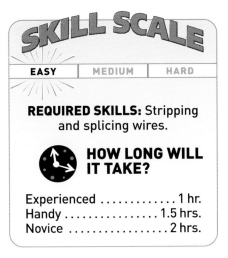

STUFF YOU'LL NEED

✔ MATERIALS:

Motion sensor light, wire nuts,

perhaps a mounting strap,

electrician's tape

✔ TOOLS:

Combination tool, screwdriver

HOMER'S HINDSIGHT

BE KIND TO YOUR NEIGHBORS

There's a place down the street where the family installed floodlights to ward off intruders. They adjusted the sensitivity so much that people walking on the sidewalk at night set off the floods. It felt like a prison break! After a few complaints they made adjustments. Sometimes you can have too much of a good thing!

Motion-sensor lights greet you when you come home at night, and they discourage potential burglars. If you have an existing floodlight, they are easy to install. (To install an exterior box for a new light, see page 165.)

Choose a fixture that lets you control the time and the sensitivity to motion. If the light is connected to a switch inside the house, you can override the motion sensor so the light stays on or off.

See pages 540–542

LOCATIONS FOR MOTION-SENSOR LIGHTS

Motion sensors should be installed in areas around your home where intruders are most likely to enter, such as near the front and back doors, above garage doors, and at the gate of a backyard fence.

1 CONNECT THE LIGHT. Shut off power at the service panel. Remove the old light. If necessary, install a swivel strap (also called an offset crossbar) so you can level the fixture after installation. Run the wires through the rubber gasket and splice them with wire nuts. While mounting the light to the box, position the gasket so it will keep the box dry.

2 POSITION THE LIGHT. RESTORE POWER. Loosen the locknuts and twist the light until it is directed where you want it. Tighten the locknuts. At night switch the light on by flipping the wall switch off, then on again.

3 MAKE ADJUSTMENTS. To activate the motion sensor, manufacturer's instructions will probably tell you to turn off the wall switch, wait a few seconds, then turn it back on. Choose how long you want the light to stay on (set ON TIME). There may be a control that keeps the light less bright for the amount of time you choose (set DUAL BRIGHT). Set the RANGE to the middle position and test how sensitive the motion sensor is by walking around near it. Adjust as necessary.

If you are using motion-sensor lights primarily to discourage intruders, position them at heights that will make it difficult to disable or knock them out. A safe height is usually above arm's reach, approximately 9 feet above the highest standing point.

Hanging a ceiling fan

EASY	MEDIUM	**HARD**

REQUIRED SKILLS: Removing an old box, installing a fan box, attaching a fixture, stripping and splicing wires, wiring a switch.

HOW LONG WILL IT TAKE?

Experienced . . . . 2 hrs.
Handy . . . . 4 hrs.
Novice . . . . 8 hrs.

VARIABLES: Running new cable adds significantly to the time involved.

STUFF YOU'LL NEED

✔ **MATERIALS:**

Fan, fan-rated box, downrod extender, light kit, fan/light switch (can be remote controlled), wire nuts, electrician's tape

✔ **TOOLS:**

Drywall saw, hammer, voltage tester or multitester, combination stripper, lineman's pliers, long-nose pliers, adjustable wrench, side-cutting pliers, screwdriver, reciprocating saw or metal-cutting keyhole saw

DOWNRODS

There are two broad options for hanging fans: close to the ceiling, or hung from a "downrod," an extension pipe that lets you drop the fan down lower. Get a downrod that puts the fan where you want it, but put it at least 10 inches from the ceiling and no fewer than 7 feet from the floor.

Ceiling fans circulate air downward to cool rooms in the summer and upward to evenly disperse heat in the winter. Observe the following guidelines to install a fan, and it will effectively circulate the air in your home without hissing, wobbling, or pulling away from the ceiling.

PLANNING FOR A FAN. Before installing a fan, consider these issues:

● **Decide whether to wire the switch** to control the fan and the light separately.

● **Buy a separate light kit if your unit doesn't include one;** some fans include lights, so check to be sure.

● **Plan how you'll cover the hole once you remove the old ceiling box.** Buy a light with a canopy that's wide enough to cover the hole or get a medallion to hide ceiling imperfections.

● **Measure the length and width of the room you want to cool** and talk to salespeople at your local home improvement center to find out what size fan(s) you need.

● **Avoid "ceiling hugger" fans**—they do not circulate air well. Fans should have downrods long enough (you can buy downrod extenders) to position fan blades at least 10 inches from the ceiling and at least 7 feet from the floor.

● **Use only a fan-rated speed control** if you install one; a standard dimmer switch will burn out the fan motor.

See pages 540–542

REMOVING AND REPLACING THE BOX

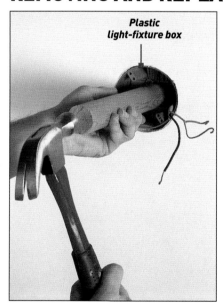

Plastic light-fixture box

Fan-rated pancake box

REMOVE THE CEILING BOX. Shut off power at the service panel. Sometimes you can remove screws or nails and pry out the box. You may have to carefully cut away drywall or plaster to get to fasteners. If the box is nailed to a joist, cut around the box to enlarge the hole and tap the box loose using a piece of wood and a hammer. You may be able to cut through fasteners or nails with a reciprocating saw or a metal-cutting keyhole saw. Take great care not to slice through any cable.

SCREW A FAN BOX TO A JOIST FROM BELOW. If you have a joist in the middle of the hole (as may be the case if you removed a thin pancake ceiling box), attaching a fan box from below will be easy. Buy a thin fan-rated box and clamp the cable to it. Hold it in place and drill pilot holes, then drive in 2-inch wood screws. (Avoid using drywall screws or all-purpose screws; they break too easily.)

ADDING A NEW CEILING BOX

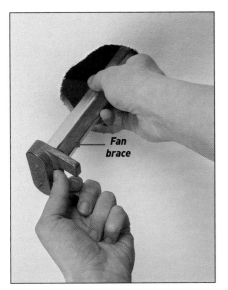

Fan brace

1 **SLIP IN THE BRACE.** Assemble the box on the brace to understand how it goes together, then take it apart. Push the brace in through the hole and spread it apart until it touches the joists on both sides. The legs of the brace at each end should rest on top of the drywall or plaster.

Rotating the brace tightens it between the framing.

2 **TIGHTEN THE BRACE.** Measure to make sure that the brace is centered in the hole. Position it on the joists at the correct height so that the box will be flush with the surface of the ceiling. Use an adjustable wrench or channel-type pliers to tighten the brace until it is firm. Tightening beyond this point can cause the ceiling to crack.

Fans come in all shapes and sizes. Consider them as viable design options and integrate them into your overall decorating theme as well as your air-circulation pattern.

ELECTRICAL

U-bolt assembly

Fan-rated box

3 **ATTACH THE BOX.** Attach the U-bolt assembly to the brace so that the assembly is centered in the hole and the bolts face down. Thread cable through the cable connector and into the fan-rated box. Slip the box up so the bolts slide through it and tighten the nuts to secure the box.

WORK SMARTER

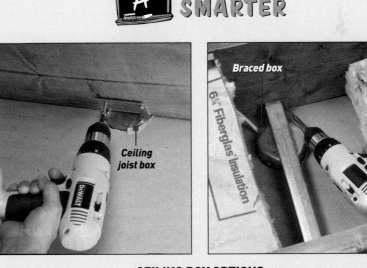

Ceiling joist box

Braced box

6½" Fiberglas insulation

CEILING BOX OPTIONS

When framing is accessible, attach a ceiling box to a joist.
Install this type of box in unfinished ceilings or ceilings with a large hole. Drill pilot holes and drive in 1¼-inch wood screws to attach it to a joist.

Or install a braced box from above.
Buy a new-work box with a brace. Slide the box along the brace into position. Tighten the clamp. Attach the brace by driving in 1¼-inch wood screws.

Hanging a ceiling fan (continued)

ADDING A NEW CEILING BOX

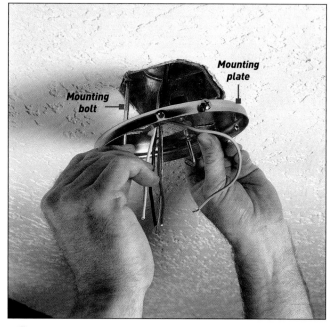

④ INSTALL THE MOUNTING PLATE. Thread the wires through the center of the mounting plate. If the box has mounting bolts that poke through the plate, fit the mounting plate over the bolts and fasten it with the nuts provided. If separate bolts are provided, push each one through the mounting plate as shown. When both bolts are in place, tighten the plate onto the ceiling.

Keep the box and packing for your fan until you're sure it's safely installed and working properly. It makes returning a damaged unit easier.

⑤ ASSEMBLE THE DOWNROD AND CANOPY. On a worktable, ready the fan for installation, following manufacturer's instructions. Run the fan leads through the downrod (or downrod extender), and screw on the downrod tightly. Remember to tighten the setscrews. Slip on the canopy, then install the bulb-shape fitting at the top of the downrod. It will rest in the canopy when the canopy is attached to the ceiling. Be careful not to mangle the wires. Wait to attach the fan blades.

See pages 540–542

SWITCHING THE FAN AND LIGHT

You probably have two-wire cable (not counting the ground wire) running into the ceiling fixture. If so, you have four options to control the fan and the light:

● Hook the fan to the two wires so the wall switch turns the fan and the light on or off at the same time. Use the pull chains on the fixture to control the fan and light individually. This is

convenient enough if you don't need to change fan speeds often.

● Purchase a fan that has a special fan/light switch that requires only two wires. These fans are expensive, however, and the switches have been known to turn the fan on by themselves— a dangerous situation if you're away for a few days.

● Install a remote-control switch, as shown on the opposite page. The receiver doesn't necessarily need to be inside the fan canopy. In some cases, you can put it in the attic.

● Run three-wire cable from the fixture to the switch and hook it up. You can conveniently control the fan and light separately by using a special wall switch.

6 **WIRE THE FAN.** Temporarily hang the fan from the hook on the mounting ring. Connect the copper ground wire to the green wire attached to the fan base. If you have only two wires, connect both the black lead (for the fan motor) and the blue or striped lead (for the light) to the black house wire, and the white lead to the white house wire. If you have three-wire cable, connect black to black, white to white, and red to the blue or striped light lead. Check the manufacturer's directions. You may choose to install a remote control unit (see below).

7 **ATTACH THE CANOPY TO THE MOUNTING PLATE.** Use a helper to support the fan motor while you drive the screws. Push the wires and wire nuts up into the box to keep them from vibrating against the canopy when the fan is running. Clip the canopy onto the mounting plate and tighten the screws.

BUYER'S GUIDE

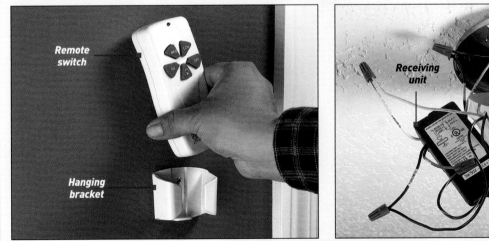

Remote switch

Hanging bracket

Receiving unit

WIRELESS REMOTE SWITCH

If you have only two wires running from the switch to the fan box, a remote control will let you control the fan and light separately. Before you install the canopy, hook up the receiving unit with both fan (black) and light (blue or striped) leads spliced to the remote's

black lead, and the receiver's white wire spliced to the white lead. Make sure the little dip switches are set the same on the remote switch unit and the receiving unit. Install the canopy as in Step 7 above. Put a battery in the sending unit, and attach a hanging bracket on a wall.

If the ceiling fixture was originally switched, the two wires sending power to the fan are still controlled by that switch. The sending unit controls the fan or light, or both, only when the wall switch is on.

Installing an attic fan

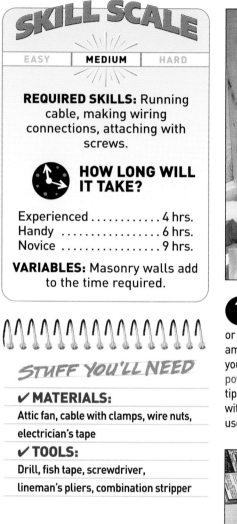

SKILL SCALE

EASY	**MEDIUM**	HARD

REQUIRED SKILLS: Running cable, making wiring connections, attaching with screws.

HOW LONG WILL IT TAKE?

Experienced . . . . 4 hrs.
Handy . . . . 6 hrs.
Novice . . . . 9 hrs.

VARIABLES: Masonry walls add to the time required.

STUFF YOU'LL NEED

✔ **MATERIALS:**

Attic fan, cable with clamps, wire nuts, electrician's tape

✔ **TOOLS:**

Drill, fish tape, screwdriver, lineman's pliers, combination stripper

Temperatures in an attic can reach 150 degrees in the summer, making it difficult (and expensive) to keep a home cool. An attic fan, a whole-house fan, or a roof fan slashes energy costs and reduces temperatures.

The manufacturer should provide a chart detailing how powerful a fan you need based on the size of your attic. Depending on the size of your house, you may require more than one fan.

See pages 540–542

If your attic doesn't have a louvered opening as shown in Step 2, you will have to install one. They can be purchased at home centers.

Pulling cable through a wall cavity

1 **BRING POWER INTO THE ATTIC.** Before tapping into a receptacle or junction box for power, check the amperage on your attic fan and make sure you will not overload the circuit. Shut off power to the circuit. See pages 177–178 for tips on running cable into the attic. Check with local codes to see whether you need to use armored cable instead of NM cable.

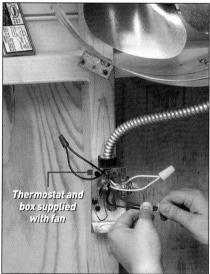

Thermostat and box supplied with fan

3 **MAKE THE ELECTRICAL CONNECTIONS.** The fan has its own thermostat switch. Mount the thermostat box to a framing member. Follow the manufacturer's instructions for connecting wires. Restore power and adjust the temperature control. Or, you can control the fan with a switch located in a downstairs hallway.

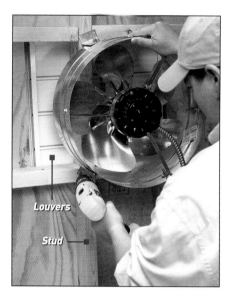

Louvers

Stud

2 **MOUNT THE FAN.** At a louvered opening in the attic, secure the fan by driving screws through its mounting brackets and into studs. If the studs do not allow you to center the fan in the opening, attach horizontal 2×4s that span between the studs. Attach the fan to the studs. You may choose to install louvers that close when the fan is not operating.

CLOSER LOOK

AN ATTIC MUST BREATHE

An attic fan, whole-house fan, or roof fan moves air efficiently only if the attic is properly ventilated. Usually a house needs vents near the bottom of the attic (usually under the eaves) and vents near the roof peak, such as turbine vents, gable vents, or a continuous vent running along the ridge. Check that eave vents are not clogged with insulation. If you are not sure that your attic is properly vented, have it inspected by a professional roofer.

A well-placed attic fan that ventilates effectively can reduce your overall cooling costs significantly.

ELECTRICAL

Installing a whole-house fan

STUFF YOU'LL NEED

✔ MATERIALS:

Whole-house fan, screws, junction box, switch box, cable with clamps, wire nuts, electrician's tape

✔ TOOLS:

Stud finder, drill, ladder, saw, combination stripper, lineman's pliers, screwdriver

Find a powerful yet quiet whole-house fan to pull up air through the house and into your attic. A whole-house fan is ideal for spring and fall cooling in hot climates; it may be the only method of cooling you need in moderate climates. For the fan to work, the attic must have adequate ventilation (see opposite page), and windows on the first floor must be open. Measure your home's square footage to choose the right size fan. It takes as much time and effort to put in wiring for an undersized fan that will not cool your house as it does to put in the right fan to be comfortable.

See pages 540–542

Finder hole

Cutout for louver

1 CUT A HOLE. Fans are designed to be positioned over one joist so you don't have to compromise ceiling framing. Use a stud finder, then cut a 1'×2' finder hole to confirm that the fan will center on a joist. Mark the cutout for the louver and cut through the drywall or lath and plaster. The fan manufacturer will specify dimensions for the hole.

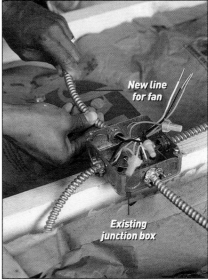

New line for fan

Existing junction box

2 BRING POWER TO THE FAN. After making sure that you will not overload a circuit (see page 156), shut off power to the circuit. Tap into a junction box or run cable up into the attic (see pages 177–178). Local codes may require you to use armored cable instead of NM cable (see page 179).

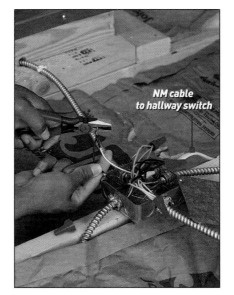

NM cable to hallway switch

3 WIRE FOR THE SWITCH. A fan-rated rheostat switch lets you vary the fan speed. Bring the two-wire switch cable to the box, marking the white wire black at both ends. Splice it to the black wires in the box. Splice the other switch wire to the fan's black wire and the fan's white to the white wires in the box. Connect the ground.

Add framing for fan base.

4 MOUNT THE FAN. With a helper, lift the fan up through the opening and into the attic. Add 2×4 framing as needed so that the fan is securely centered over a joist. Attach brackets to the fan frame and position them so they will slip over the exposed joist. Center the fan over the opening and secure the brackets with bolts.

Installing a whole-house fan (continued)

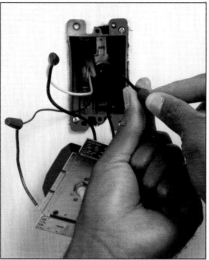

Louvers

5 **ENCLOSE THE FAN.** Pull back the insulation and cut pieces of 2×4 blocking to fill gaps at either side of the fan. At each side, cut two pieces to fit between the joists (shown) or one notched piece that fits over the joist. (Some manufacturers supply blocking.) Attach the wood to the joists by drilling pilot holes and driving 3-inch screws or 16-penny nails.

6 **WIRE THE RHEOSTAT SWITCH.** Install a fan-rated rheostat switch in the hallway, connecting it to the cable you have run through the wall from the attic junction box. Wire as shown or use the manufacturer's directions.

7 **ATTACH THE LOUVERS.** Hold the louver panel against the ceiling so it covers the hole. Attach the panel by driving screws into the joists and blocking. Restore power and test the fan.

CLOSER LOOK

A ROOF FAN WILL PULL THE AIR OUT OF YOUR ATTIC

If your attic does not have a vertical wall to accommodate an attic fan (see page 206), this is the next most efficient way to pull air out of an attic. The most difficult part of this installation is not the electrical work, but cutting the hole and properly sealing the roofing around the fan. The shingles must be laid correctly over the fan flashing or the roof will leak. Call a roofer if you aren't sure how to seal the fan. If you are uncomfortable working on the roof, hire a professional.

Choose a spot for the fan that is between rafters. Because they are structural elements, they must not be altered in any way.

1 **CUT THE HOLE AND ROOFING.** Follow the manufacturer's directions for cutting a hole through the roof and for cutting back shingles from around the hole. Carefully fold back the shingles.

2 **INSTALL THE FAN.** Slide the fan under the shingles and apply roofing cement as directed. Wire the fan as you would an attic fan (see page 206).

Installing a bathroom vent

DUCT THROUGH THE ROOF. You may have no choice but to run ductwork through an attic and out the roof. Choose a short, straight path and cut the roof and shingles correctly to avoid leaks. Moist air inside can condense on the ducts and drip onto insulation; you may want to wrap the duct with pipe insulation.

A vent fan considerably improves the atmosphere in a bathroom by pulling out moisture, odors, and heat. Codes require bathrooms to have vent fans if there is no natural ventilation, such as a window. When choosing a fan, use these guidelines:

● **Make sure the fan will move the air.** Unfortunately, many bathroom fans do little more than make noise. This happens when either the fan is not strong enough or the path through the ductwork is not free and clear. Measure your room and determine how far the ductwork has to travel. Then ask a home center salesperson to help you choose a fan and the ductwork to do the job. Keep in mind that air travels more freely through solid ducts than through flexible hoses.

● **Consider a fan equipped with a light.** Some units have a fan only, while others include one or more added features: a ceiling light, a low-wattage night-light, or a forced-air heating unit.

● **Consider the wiring options.** In some locations, local codes require that the fan activates whenever the overhead light is turned on. Given the choice, some people prefer separate switches for the fan and light.

● **Check local practices.** In hot, sunny climates, venting through the roof may be asking for leaks. If so, vent through the wall, as shown in installing a range hood (see page 212).

DUCTWORK AND VENT FAN INSTALLATION

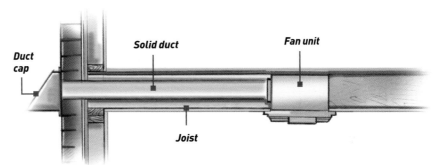

RUNNING DUCT THROUGH A WALL. Choose the shortest and straightest route. A wall vent is the easiest to install because no roofing is involved. However, it may be difficult to run ductwork between joists.

Installing a bathroom vent *(continued)*

ELECTRICAL

1 **CUT THE HOLE.** From the attic, hold the fan against a joist and mark its outline with a pencil. Cut out the opening. If there is no attic, from the bathroom use a stud sensor to locate a joist and cut the opening from below. Shut off power to the circuit and provide power if none is present (see pages 177–178).

2 **ATTACH THE FAN AND DAM OFF INSULATION.** Attach the fan to the joist with screws. Some models require a 6-inch gap between the unit and insulation. Cut or push back the insulation, then cut pieces of 2×4 lumber to fit between the joists, and attach the lumber with screws or nails.

Reciprocating saw

3 **CUT A HOLE IN THE ROOF.** On the underside of the roof, trace a circle just large enough for the roof cap tailpiece. Drill a hole large enough for the saw blade, then cut with a reciprocating saw, saber saw, or keyhole saw. (See page 209 for how to run the ductwork out the wall.)

4 **CUT AWAY SHINGLES.** Remove shingles from around the cutout without damaging the underlying roofing paper. The lower part of the roof cap flange will rest on top of the shingles, and the top part will slip under the shingles.

5 **INSTALL THE ROOF CAP.** Smear roofing cement on the underside of the cap flange. Slip the upper flange under the shingles as you insert the cap into the hole. Install the shingles on the side, smearing the undersides with roofing cement. Attach the flange with roofing nails; cover the nailheads with roofing cement.

BUYER'S GUIDE

NOISE CONTROL
A label on the fan packaging will indicate how many square feet of bathroom space the fan can successfully clear. If there's any doubt, or if your ductwork will be more than 5 feet long, get a slightly more powerful fan than you need. (However, don't overdo it. Keep the power of the fan appropriate to the size of the room.) Fans are rated by sones. The higher the sone rating, the noisier the fan will be; the lower the sone rating, the quieter it will be.

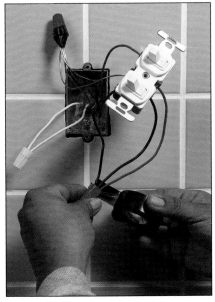

6 **CONNECT THE DUCTWORK.** At both the roof cap and the fan, slide a clamp over the flexible duct and slip the duct over the tailpiece. Slide the clamp back over the tailpiece and tighten the clamp. Wrap the joint with duct tape.

7 **WIRE THE FAN.** If wiring does not exist, run cable to the fan and to a switch. If you are installing a fan/light, run three-wire cable from the switch to the fan. Connect the wiring according to the manufacturer's directions. Plug the motor into the built-in receptacle.

8 **WIRE THE SWITCH.** For a fan/light switch that has power entering the switch box, splice the white wires and connect the grounds. Connect power to both switches through two pigtails (see page 160) spliced to the feed wire. Connect the red wire to one switch terminal and the black wire to the other terminal.

See pages 540–542

A+ WORK SMARTER

INSTALLING A WALL VENT

If a bathroom is not located directly beneath an attic, you must vent air out through a wall. Even if there is an attic above, it may be easier to run the vent out through a gable wall rather than through the roof. When running ductwork through a ceiling cavity, it is sometimes easier to shove a piece of solid ductwork through rather than snaking flexible ducting. From inside the attic, drill a locator hole through to the outside, then cut out the siding with a reciprocating saw, saber saw, or keyhole saw.

Duct pipe

Duct cap

1 **MAKE A TAILPIECE.** Press the duct pipe into the cap. Use sheet metal screws to attach a piece of solid duct to the cap, then caulk the joint or wrap it with duct tape. Apply a bead of caulk to the back of the flange so that it will seal against the siding.

2 **ATTACH THE VENT.** Caulk around the hole and push in the tailpiece. Secure it with four screws. Caulk around the edge of the vent. Complete the connection to the fan indoors using solid or flexible ductwork.

Installing a range hood

SKILL SCALE

EASY | **MEDIUM** | HARD

REQUIRED SKILLS:
Advanced electrical skills, carpentry skills.

HOW LONG WILL IT TAKE?

Experienced . . . . 6 hrs.
Handy . . . . 10 hrs.
Novice . . . . 14 hrs.

VARIABLES: Time is based on stud walls with wood, aluminum, or vinyl siding.

STUFF YOU'LL NEED

✔ MATERIALS:

Range hood, solid duct, wall cap, masonry screws, cable and clamps, wire nuts, caulk, electrician's tape

✔ TOOLS:

Drill, fish tape, saber saw or reciprocating saw, hammer and cold chisel, screwdriver, combination stripper, lineman's pliers, safety goggles

CLOSER LOOK

VENTING THROUGH A MASONRY WALL

Use a long masonry bit to drill the locator holes. Draw the outline and drill holes about every inch along the outline. Use a hammer and cold chisel to chip out the brick. To attach the duct cap, drill holes and drive masonry screws.

Be careful to avoid any existing wiring or plumbing in the wall when you cut through for the duct.

For the best range hood efficiency, run the duct through the wall directly behind the range hood, in as straight a line as possible. You can run the vents of most hoods out the back or the top of the unit.

If a wall stud is in the way of the ductwork, you could do carpentry work to change the framing. An easier solution is to purchase a hood with an extra-strong motor and run the duct around the stud.

Before you purchase a fan, check its CFM rating, which indicates the number of cubic feet of air it pulls per minute. Choose a fan with a CFM rating that is double the square footage of your kitchen.

If the location of your stove makes it impossible to run a vent outside, ask about a ductless vent. A ductless vent pulls the air through a filter that removes odors and grease. It won't work as efficiently as a fully ducted unit, but it will help remove odors, smoke, and grease. You will have to change filters frequently for best results.

See pages 540–542

2 **CUT THE SIDING.** Connect the dots between the holes on the outside to mark the outline of the hole. Cut out the opening. Remove any insulation or debris.

ATTACH THE DUCT CAP. Push the wall cap into the wall to see if the duct is long enough to reach the range hood. If not purchase an extension and attach it with sheet metal screws and duct tape. Apply caulk to the siding where the cap flange will rest. Push the cap into place and fasten with screws. Caulk the perimeter of the flange.

1 **MARK THE HOLES.** Remove the filter, fan, and electrical housing cover from the range hood. Remove the knockouts for the electrical cable and the duct. Hold the hood in place and mark the holes for the duct and the cable.

CUT OUT THE VENT HOLE AND DRILL A LOCATOR HOLE. Cut holes through the drywall or plaster. Drill holes at each corner all the way through the outside wall.

3 **RUN POWER TO THE HOOD.** Shut off power to the circuit. Run cable from a nearby receptacle or junction box through the hole in the wall. Strip the sheathing and clamp the cable to the range hood electrical knockout. Mount the hood securely by driving screws into studs or adjacent cabinets.

CONNECT THE WIRES. Splice the white wire to the white fixture lead, the black wire to the black lead, and the ground wire to the green lead. Fold the wires into place and replace the electrical cover. Reattach the fan and filter. Restore power and test.

Installing telephone and CAT 5 wiring

SKILL SCALE

EASY	**MEDIUM**	HARD

REQUIRED SKILLS: Attaching with screws; stapling, stripping and connecting thin wires.

HOW LONG WILL IT TAKE?

Experienced . . . . 2 hrs.
Handy . . . . 4 hrs.
Novice . . . . 6 hrs.

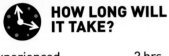

STUFF YOU'LL NEED

✔ **MATERIALS:**

Solid-core telephone cable,

phone jacks, staples

✔ **TOOLS:**

Drill, screwdriver, lineman's pliers,

combination stripper

BUYER'S GUIDE

GET CONNECTED

You can now buy faceplates that hold several interchangeable jacks along with distribution boxes that let you customize the phone, computer network, and cable services that go to each room in the house. Here's how it works: Run all of the incoming wires—such as phone, cable or satellite, and Internet—to the distribution box. Run cables to each room, and snap in and connect the jacks that match the services you want there. One room might have Internet, phone, and television, while another might have a different phone line and outlets for two computers. Connect the cables to the distribution box so that the appropriate service is going to the jack in the correct room (it's easier done than said), and the job is finished.

Adding a new telephone jack is straightforward work. Just run cable and connect wires to terminals labeled with their colors. The most difficult part is running, and then hiding, the cable.

Depending on your service contract, it may be cost-effective to have the phone company install new service for you. The lines they install will be under warranty—all future repairs will be free. Be aware that they may charge you a usage fee for the lines they run and maintain; this will appear on your monthly telephone bill.

Category 5 (CAT 5) cable and telephone wire are fragile. Don't bend, flatten, stretch, or otherwise compromise these wires. A damaged wire can result in a distorted connection, especially for computers.

Make all connections in a jack or junction box. Plan cable paths so as little of the cable as possible can be seen. For instance, going through a wall (see page 214) saves you from running unsightly cable around door moldings. Use these same techniques to run speaker wire.

1 OPTION A: **TAP INTO A PHONE JACK.** Unscrew the cover from a phone jack or a phone junction box. Strip about 2 inches of sheathing and ½ inch of insulation from each wire. (Standard phones use only two of the wires, but it doesn't hurt to connect all the wires.) Loosen each terminal screw. Bend the wire end in a clockwise loop, slip it under the screw head, and tighten the screw.

BUYER'S GUIDE

CAT 5 AND CAT 5E

Category 5 (CAT 5) cable consists of 4 pairs of cable and is used for computer networks, phone, audio, and video. CAT 5E has 4 twisted pairs of cable and is less subject to interference from outside sources. Because of their versatility, Cat 5 and 5E are excellent when wiring your house for entertainment/media systems. Both wire types come in several colors to help you identify which cable came from where.

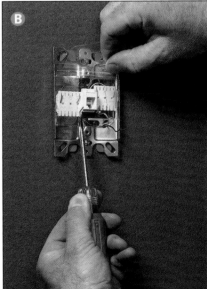

OPTION B: **USE PUSH-ON CONNECTORS.** Some jacks have terminals that clamp onto the wire so you don't have to strip it. Just push the wire down into the slot until it snaps into place.

2 OPTION A: **HIDE CABLE.** Use any trick you can think of to tuck away unsightly cable. Pry moldings away from the wall, slip the cable in behind, and renail the molding. Or pull carpeting back one short section at a time, run cable along the floor behind the tack strip, and push the carpet back into place.

OPTION B: **RUN CABLE THROUGH A WALL.** To go through a wall, drill a hole using a long, ¼-inch drill bit. Insert a large drinking straw through hole. Fish the cable through the straw. When you're finished, split and remove the straw.

OPTION C: **STAPLE EXPOSED CABLE.** When you have no choice but to leave cable exposed, staple it in place every foot or so along the top of the baseboard. Use a round-top stapler or plastic-shielded staples that hammer into place. (Square-cornered staples damage the cable sheathing.)

3 INSTALL A WALL BOX. A wall jack can attach to a low-voltage ring (as shown) or to an electrical remodel box. Cut a hole in the wall and install the ring. Tie a small weight to a string and lower it through the hole until you feel it hit the floor.

4 PULL THE CABLE. Drill a ⅜-inch hole just above the baseboard of the wall where you want the wire to go. Bend a piece of wire into a hook, slip it into the hole, and pull out a loop of the string. Tape the string to the cable and pull the cable up through the remodel box.

5 INSTALL A WALL JACK. Attach the base of the jack and make the connections. Install the cover plate.

Installing coaxial cable

Cable TV companies will run new lines and install jacks. Some do simple installations for free; for longer runs, they may charge and may not hide as much of the cable as you like. They also may increase your monthly fee after installing a second or third jack. Still, it's worth checking out the service options before deciding whether to do your own installations.

Purchase RG6 coaxial cable for all runs through the house. Don't use RG59; it has less-substantial wire wrapping. Coaxial cable is thick and ugly, so fish it through walls when possible.

If your cable signal is weak after adding new lines, install a signal booster to solve the problem. The booster attaches to the coaxial cable and plugs into a receptacle.

Be sure not to overbend, twist, or damage the cable during installation. Keep all splitters accessible for future repair or maintenance.

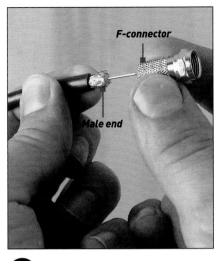

1 **MAKE A MALE END.** Use a combination stripper to remove ¾ inch of insulation from the end. Do not bend the exposed wire. With a knife, carefully strip ⅜ inch of the thin outer sheathing only: Do not cut through the metal mesh wrapping. Firmly attach screw-on F-connector. You also can purchase a coaxial crimping tool and attach a crimp-on F-connector.

2 **SPLIT A LINE.** Cut the line you want to tap into. Install male ends on both ends of the cut line and the end of the new line. Insert and twist all three male connectors onto a signal splitter. Anchor the splitter with screws.

3 **INSTALL A JACK.** Cut a hole in the wall and run cable to it using the technique shown on page 177. (A regular electrical box can be used, though a low-voltage ring is preferable. See opposite page.) Strip the insulation to make a male end in the cable. Clamp the mounting brackets in the hole. Connect the cable end to the back of the jack by attaching the F-connector. Tighten the connection with pliers or a wrench. Attach the jack to the wall by driving screws into the mounting brackets.

Troubleshooting a door chime

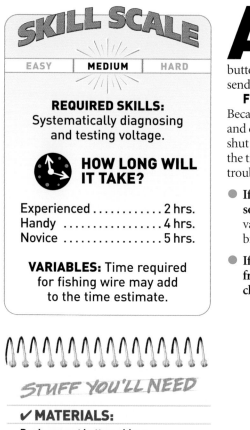

SKILL SCALE

EASY	**MEDIUM**	HARD

REQUIRED SKILLS:
Systematically diagnosing
and testing voltage.

HOW LONG WILL IT TAKE?

Experienced . . . . 2 hrs.
Handy . . . . 4 hrs.
Novice . . . . 5 hrs.

VARIABLES: Time required
for fishing wire may add
to the time estimate.

STUFF YOU'LL NEED

✔ **MATERIALS:**
Replacement button, chime,
transformer or bell wire,
electrician's tape

✔ **TOOLS:**
Screwdriver, multitester,
combination stripper

A doorbell or chime system is supplied with low-voltage power, between 8 and 24 volts, by a transformer. When the button is pressed, the circuit closes and sends power to the chime or bell.

FIXING COMMON PROBLEMS. Because the voltage needed by doorbells and chimes is low, there is no need to shut off power unless you are working on the transformer. Here's how to troubleshoot most problems:

● **If a bell or chime develops a fuzzy sound,** remove the chime cover and vacuum out any dust and debris and brush off the bell or chimes.

● **If you get only one tone when the front (or only) button is pushed, check the wiring in the chime** to see that the button is connected to the "front" terminal. On many two-button systems, the chime is supposed to dingdong when the front button is pushed and only ding when the rear button is pushed.

● **If the chime suddenly stops working at the same time you blow a fuse or trip a breaker,** restore power to the circuit supplying the transformer.

● **If the chime stops working altogether,** conduct a systematic investigation, moving from the simplest to the most complex repairs. First check out the button(s), then the chime, and then the transformer. If none of these reveals a problem, the wiring may be damaged.

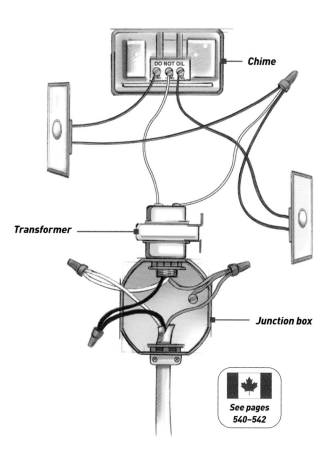

Chime

Transformer

Junction box

See pages 540–542

A TYPICAL TWO-BUTTON SETUP.
The transformer—usually located in an out-of-the-way spot such as the basement, crawlspace, or cabinet interior—sends low-voltage power to the chime, where one wire is connected to the chime. Another wire is spliced to two different wires, each of which travels through a button and back to the chime. When either button is pressed, the circuit is completed, power travels to the chime, and the chime rings.

ELECTRICAL

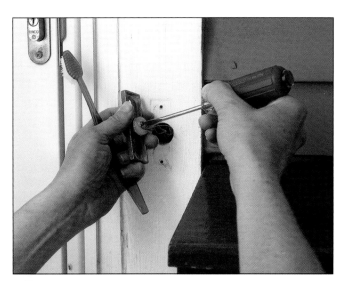

1 **EXAMINE THE BUTTON.** Remove the screws while holding the button in place, and gently pull out the button. (Make sure the wires do not slide back into the hole.) Use a toothbrush to clean away any debris, cocoons, or corrosion, and tighten the screws. If either wire is broken, restrip and reconnect it. Retest the button.

2 **TOUCH WIRES TOGETHER.** If the button still doesn't work, loosen the terminal screws and remove the wires. Holding each wire by its insulation, touch the bare ends together. If the chime sounds, the button is faulty and needs to be replaced. If you see or hear a tiny spark but the chime does not sound, the chime may be faulty (see Step 3). If there is no sound and no spark, check the transformer (see Step 4, page 218).

3 **TEST THE CHIME.** Remove the chime cover and ensure that all the wires are securely connected to terminals. Vacuum out any dust and scrape away any corrosion near the terminals. When you pull back a plunger and release it, the chime should sound. If not, clean any greasy buildup that may be gumming up the springs. If the chime still does not work, touch the probes of a multitester to the "front" and "trans" terminals, then to the "rear" and "trans" terminals. If power is present below 2 volts of the chime's printed voltage rating, then the chime is faulty and should be replaced.

Troubleshooting a door chime *(continued)*

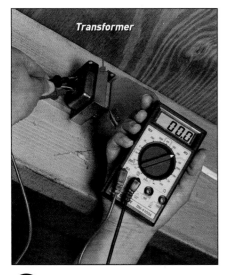

Transformer

4 **TEST THE TRANSFORMER.** Look for an exposed electrical box with the transformer attached. Tighten loose connections. Touch the probes of a multitester to both transformer terminals. If you get a reading of more than 2 volts below the transformer rating, the transformer is faulty and should be replaced.

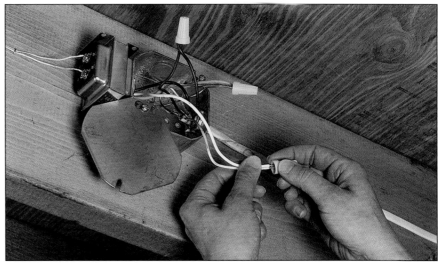

5 **REPLACING A TRANSFORMER.** Purchase a transformer with the same voltage rating as the old one. Shut off power to the circuit and open the adjacent junction box. Label the bell wires and disconnect them. Disconnect the transformer leads inside the junction box and disconnect the transformer. Thread the new transformer leads into the junction box, fasten the transformer to the box, and splice the leads to the wires. Connect the bell wires, turn the power back on, and test.

Installing wireless chimes

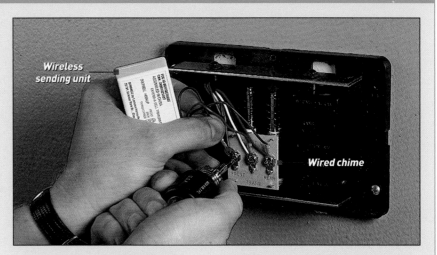

Wireless sending unit

Wired chime

Installing the chime. Rather than going through the trouble of replacing defective bell wire, buy a wireless chime system. Installation is simple: Plug the chime into a standard receptacle, power the button with a battery, and attach the button to the house.

Adding a wireless chime to an existing chime system. If you can't hear your door chime everywhere in your home, add a wireless chime to your wired system. Remove the cover from the existing chime and loosen the terminal screws. Take the leads of the wireless chime's sending unit and insert them under the screws. Tighten the screws. Using its double-sided tape, stick the sending unit to the chime housing. Plug the wireless chime into a receptacle. Depending on the model, it will have a distance limitation of 75 to 150 feet.

Troubleshooting a thermostat

The round, low-voltage unit featured in most of these pictures is the most common type of thermostat in use. Yours may be rectangular but its functions are the same.

If your furnace or air-conditioner fails to operate, check the thermostat for simple mechanical problems. The cover may be jammed in too far, disrupting the mechanism. A wire may have broken or come loose. Or the parts may be covered with dust, inhibiting electrical contact.

If cleaning and adjusting do not solve the problem, replacing a thermostat is a simple job. Consider installing a programmable unit for more control options and to save money. Remember that a thermostat contains mercury, so dispose of old units properly.

Cover the thermostat when you're painting or working in the room to keep dust and debris out of the workings.

CHECK THE ANATOMY OF A LOW-VOLTAGE THERMOSTAT. Thin wires come from a transformer and connect to the thermostat base. You'll probably find one wire for the transformer, one for heat, one for air-conditioning, and one for a fan. (A heat pump uses six or more wires and has a special thermostat. Contact a dealer for repairs.) To protect circuitry, shut off power before you start to work.

CHECKING A LINE-VOLTAGE THERMOSTAT. If your thermostat uses household current, always shut off power to the circuit before pulling it out. If it fails, disconnect it and take it to a dealer for service or replacement.

 **WORK SMARTER**

SEAL OFF DRAFTS

Even if your thermostat is on an interior wall, air coming through a hole behind it may throw its temperature readings out of whack, resulting in erratic heating. Remove the thermostat base from the wall and fill the hole with insulation or caulk.

Troubleshooting a thermostat *(continued)*

CLEAN THE CONTACTS WITH A BRUSH. Pull off the outer cover and use a soft, clean, dry brush to remove dust from the bimetal coil. Turn the dial to clean all the nooks and crannies.

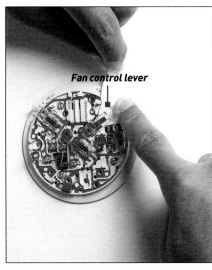

CLEAN THE SWITCH CONTACTS. Remove the screws holding the thermostat body and pull out the body. Gently pull back on the fan control lever, then slip a piece of white bond paper behind it and slide the paper back and forth to clean the contact behind the lever. Do the same for the mode control lever, if there is one.

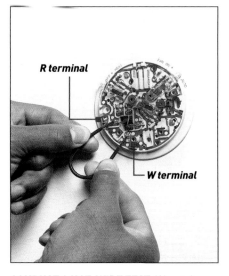

CONDUCT A HOT-WIRE TEST. If heat does not come on, test to see if power is getting to the thermostat. Cut a short length of wire and strip both ends. Holding only the insulated portion, touch the bare ends to the terminals marked R and W. If the heating system starts to run, replace the thermostat. If nothing happens, troubleshoot or replace the thermostat (as shown below).

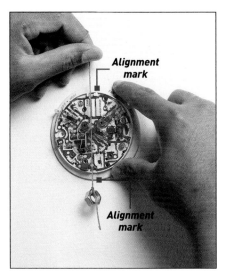

LEVEL THE THERMOSTAT. If the temperature is always warmer or cooler than the thermostat setting, the thermostat may be out of level. Hold a level or a weighted string in front of the thermostat to see if the two alignment marks line up. If not, remove the mounting screws, realign the thermostat, and drive new screws.

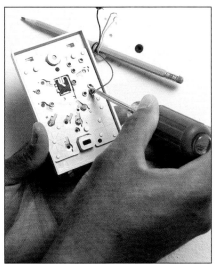

REPLACING A LOW-VOLTAGE THERMOSTAT. Loosen the terminal screws and pull out the wires. Remove the mounting screws and pull out the plate. Clip the wires so they cannot slide back through the hole. Thread the wires through the new thermostat and hook the wires to the terminals. Level and attach the base to the wall with screws.

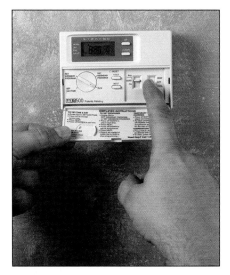

INVESTING IN A PROGRAMMABLE THERMOSTAT. Spend a little more and save money in the long run with a thermostat that adjusts heating or cooling several times a day.

Adding surge protection

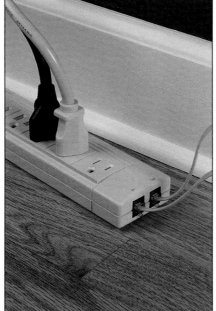

POWER STRIP SURGE SUPPRESSOR.
An inexpensive device like this not only protects against surges but makes it easy to organize all those cords in a home office. Just plug it into a wall receptacle. To protect a modem and computer, buy a device with a phone connection.

SURGE-PROTECTING CONSOLE.
Available at stores that sell computers, undermonitor devices protect electronic equipment and phone lines from surges. They also help you organize the tangle of cords behind your desk.

O nce in a while, power supplied by your utility company may suddenly increase for a few milliseconds. This surge does not affect most electrical components but it can damage sensitive electronic equipment such as computers and televisions. A surge on your telephone line can destroy your modem and damage your computer, so install surge protection. The higher a device's joule (a unit of energy) rating, the better the protection. A surge arrester or protector will work only if the electrical system is grounded.

A+ WORK SMARTER

Neutral bus bar

TWO-CIRCUIT ARRESTER IN BREAKER BOX

Shut off the main breaker. Remove two circuit breakers. Switch the breaker toggles to OFF. Push the breaker into place (see page 183). Transfer the black wires from the old breakers to the terminals of the arrester. Attach the curly white wire to the neutral bus bar (make sure there are no kinks). Restore power and switch the arrester breakers to ON. Another type of surge arrester protects the entire panel.

FEW PEOPLE WALK INTO A ROOM AND SAY, "NICE WALLS." Smooth, well-finished walls will usually go unnoticed but people will certainly see the dents, scrapes, and gouges of a poorly done job. For good results with wall and ceiling projects, think through the process first so you can create a detailed plan and materials list.

1 Projects involving walls and ceilings require general carpentry and drywalling skills.

2 Be comfortable with power tools such as circular saws, jigsaws, and drills and know how to use them safely.

3 Measuring and marking tools such as tape measures and combination and framing squares are essential.

4 You'll also need to be handy with a utility knife and a hammer.

5 You'll be spending part of your time on a ladder or scaffolding so you'll need to know how to work safely off the ground.

6 Wear a dust mask or respirator to keep airborne particles out of your lungs.

7 Eye protection in the form of authorized safety goggles is a must when hammering, drilling, cutting, or sanding, or when working above your head.

8 Wear gloves to protect your hands when handling lumber or materials with sharp edges.

SECTION 5 PROJECTS

REAL-WORLD SITUATIONS

EXPECT TO BE FOOLED

The thing to remember about walls is that something always lies behind them. Not just another room, but the entire infrastructure of your home: water pipes, drainpipes, live wires, gas lines, phone lines, and cable for the television or computer—to name a few items.

So before you start messing with walls, know what's behind them. Three tools will help: A stud finder beeps every time you pass it over one of the studs that make up the inside of the wall. A no-contact voltage detector lights up when you pass it over an electrical line. Both are musts if you're going to do so much as drive a nail.

The third tool is common sense. You know, for instance, that if there is a toilet upstairs, a drainpipe runs from it and a supply pipe runs to it. Plumbers like to run both of them straight up and down: If you're working on a wall below and behind the toilet, be surprised if you don't find them. Lines for faucets, bathtubs, and sinks probably run down through the wall behind them too, though in some cases they'll run through the floor for a short distance in order to reach the wall.

If a gas line runs to a stove or heater, trace its route back to the gas meter. The line most likely runs into the wall and then straight down, or through the floor and straight down. Once the line reaches the basement or crawlspace, it runs horizontally to the meter.

If you have a hot-air register in the wall, you also have a heating duct there. Most of the horizontal travel occurs where the vents come out of the heater. From there the vents run inside the walls with as little branching as possible. The same is true of pipes for hot-water heat.

Be prepared to check and double-check thoroughly for electrical lines with the no-contact voltage detector. Turn off the water and power if there is a faucet, tub, toilet, electrical outlet, or switch anywhere in the vicinity. Look for phone lines, cable TV lines, and anything else you can imagine. If you're doing major work on the wall, carefully remove part of it to get an idea of what's going on behind it. And if you're removing a wall, plan ahead. You need all the wires and pipes it conceals, and each will need a new home once the old wall is gone.

Wall and ceiling basics

WALLS AND CEILINGS

In the vast majority of homes built since World War II, interior walls and ceilings are wood frame finished with drywall. The drywall is nailed or screwed to the studs, and the seams are covered with reinforcing tape and filled with plasterlike joint compound. Repair is usually a matter of troweling on more compound, though repairing a hole may mean piecing a drywall patch into the wall.

In older houses, thin, closely spaced wood lath strips are nailed to the studs, then plaster is troweled over the lath. These walls tend to be thicker and may be more brittle because of age. Repair cracks with surfacing compound (which, unlike joint compound, is formulated specifically for plaster). Repairing holes usually involves removing the damaged plaster and troweling on a repair compound.

Paneled walls, wood wainscoting, and tile usually can be applied over existing drywall or plaster without repairing the existing wall. Suspended ceilings can cover up damaged plaster or basement joists.

A new surface changes the look of the room, though, and is seldom less work than repairing the original. This doesn't mean you shouldn't panel the study. It just means that at the start of the job, you need to decide whether you're repairing or remodeling. Once you know, choose the wall or ceiling treatment that meets your needs.

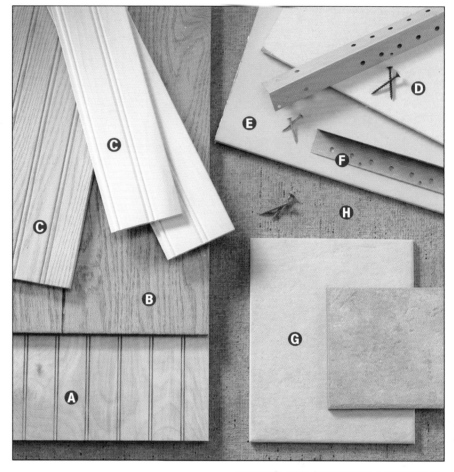

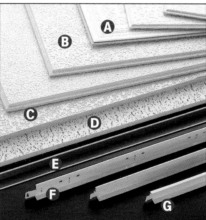

BUYER'S GUIDE

WHO'S ON FIRST?
Product names vary from region to region, company to company, and even contractor to contractor. If you're unsure what something is called, take a sample or picture to the store when you go shopping.

CEILING MATERIALS INCLUDE
A decorative 12-inch ceiling tiles and **B** decorative 24-inch ceiling tiles. Nail or staple them to a wooden grid built on the ceiling. **C** Insulated suspended ceiling panels and **D** acoustical suspended ceiling panels hang from **E** a metal grid made of wall angle, **F** suspended ceiling main tees (sometimes called runners), and **G** 2-foot and 4-foot cross-tees.

USING A AND B PLYWOOD PANELING IS ONE OF THE QUICKEST WAYS TO COVER A WALL. C Wainscoting is a tongue-and-groove solid-wood paneling that you piece together on the wall. You need to install it on a solid, flat surface. Installing **D** drywall is a matter of screwing it in place. In bathrooms, use **E** moisture-resistant "greenboard." Fill in seams between pieces of drywall with reinforcing tape and plasterlike joint compound, and protect the corners with corner bead. (Use **F** plastic corner bead in basements to prevent rust stains.) Applying tape and compound takes more patience, and often more time, than putting up the drywall itself. **G** Ceramic tile is an extremely durable wall surface. Install it over **H** cement backerboard, which comes in sheets. The mortar designed for use with backerboard comes ready to mix and is called thinset. Once the tile is in place, wipe grout over the surface to fill the gaps between the tiles.

THE WALL AND CEILING TOOL KIT

Below are some basic wall and ceiling tools that you can buy or rent as needed. For more information see the Tool Glossary on page 544.

3-LB. SLEDGEHAMMER

DRYWALL KNIVES

FOAM PAINTBRUSHES

LINE LEVEL

SANDING POLE

STUD FINDER

CAULKING GUN

DRYWALL MUD PAN

HACKSAW

NAIL PULLER

SANDING SPONGE

TAPE MEASURE

CHALK LINE AND MASON'S STRING

DRYWALL SANDING SCREEN

HAMMERS

PLIERS

SAWHORSE

TIN SNIPS

CLAMP

DRYWALL SAW

KEYHOLE SAW

RECIPROCATING SAW

SLOTTED AND PHILLIPS SCREWDRIVERS

TORPEDO LEVEL WITH MAGNET

DRILL

DRYWALL SQUARE

LADDER

SABER SAW

SPIRAL CUTTING TOOL

UTILITY KNIFE

DRILL BITS

EAR PROTECTION

LEVEL

SAFETY GLASSES

STRAIGHTEDGE

WIRE STRIPPERS

DRYWALL BUCKET

FLAT PRY BAR

LINE CLAMP

SANDING MASK

STUD DRIVER

Repairing drywall

WALLS AND CEILINGS

SKILL SCALE

EASY	MEDIUM	HARD

REQUIRED SKILLS: Basic carpentry and repair techniques. Using simple hand tools.

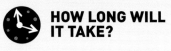

HOW LONG WILL IT TAKE?

Experienced . . . . 30 min.
Handy . . . . 45 min.
Novice . . . . 1 hr.

VARIABLES: Repairs are best made in thin layers. Each layer must be dry before continuing. Temperature and humidity will affect drying times.

STUFF YOU'LL NEED

✔ MATERIALS:

1×3 scrap lumber or ¾-inch plywood,
3-inch drywall screws, drywall scrap,
self-adhesive fiberglass drywall tape,
lightweight drywall compound,
fine-grit sandpaper

✔ TOOLS:

Framing square, drywall saw, utility
knife, electric drill with clutch and
phillips-head bit or drywall screw gun,
9-inch and 12-inch putty knives

WORK SMARTER

WALK AWAY

You'll get the best results from any drywall repair job by allowing the coats of joint compound to dry thoroughly before you proceed. Put up the mud and leave it for at least 24 hours. For a smoother finish, use water to thin the final coat of compound to the consistency of mayonnaise.

Traditional plastering was a messy, high-skilled job that required the house to dry out for weeks before painting. Then along came drywall, a thin manufactured sheet of gypsum sandwiched between two layers of paper. Although drywall sheets are notoriously vulnerable to breakage and crumbling, once you nail or screw them fast to studs and joists, they are largely out of harm's way. However the chalky material will get dinged with exposure. Fill small dents with lightweight drywall compound, then sand before repainting. Repairing larger problem areas involves cutting and fitting a drywall patch.

Fixing nail pops

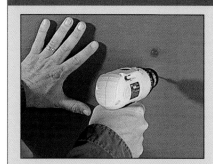

Nails pop out as the stud holding them dries out, revealing the head of the nail or appearing as if a small disk has been slipped under the drywall paper. If you can remove the nail without damage, do it. Drive a drywall screw an inch or so above and below the pop to secure the wall.

If the nail won't come out, drive it back in place, finishing with a slight dent in the drywall that doesn't tear the surface. Fill the dents or screw holes with joint compound. When dry, sand the patch, then prime and paint.

① OUTLINE THE DAMAGED AREA WITH A CARPENTER'S SQUARE.
The top and bottom of the rectangle should be an inch or so outside the damaged area. The sides should be centered over the studs on both sides of the hole.

For small, persistent cracks try paintable latex caulk. Apply it and smooth with a wet finger.

BUYER'S GUIDE

Lightweight surfacing compound is used for shallow dents and nail holes. It is easily sanded and dries in 15 to 30 minutes.

Spackling paste is for filling larger holes and dents and must be built up in layers ¼ inch thick. It dries in 10 to 40 minutes and can be sanded.

Wallboard joint compound is strictly for covering taped wallboard joints. It must be applied in thicknesses no greater than ¼ inch. It comes in containers as large as 5 gallons and is easily sanded.

Paintable latex caulk is the only filler that can handle unstable gaps and cracks on surfaces. Caulk cannot be sanded, so smooth it immediately after application.

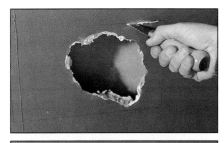

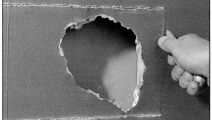

2 **CUT OUT THE SIDES.** When the saw blade runs into the studs, make a mark and measure over the stud ¾ inch. This is the center of the stud, and the edge of the patch should be directly over it so both the existing drywall and the patch will have support. Cut along the line with a utility knife using several cuts, each one slightly deeper than the previous one.

3 **CUT THE SUPPORTS, THEN THE PATCH.** Cut 1×3 or ¾-inch plywood scraps 2 to 4 inches larger than the patch is high. Screw these supports vertically behind the opening to keep the patch from cracking. Hold the support in place and secure it with drywall screws. Avoid driving the screws through the drywall. Cut the patch to size. Measure the opening and use the framing square to lay out the measurements on a scrap of drywall and cut out with a utility knife.

4 **INSTALL THE PATCH WITH 1¼-INCH DRYWALL SCREWS.** Position the screws as far as possible from the edges to avoid splitting or crumbling the drywall. Run strips of self-adhesive fiberglass drywall tape around the installed patch, centering the tape on the seam. Then use a 9-inch putty knife to spread drywall joint compound across the patch and tape to create a smooth, flat surface. Let the compound dry overnight, sand, and apply a second coat. For the smoothest patch, sand the surface to smooth out any irregularities; then spread a third coat with a 12-inch putty knife.

DRYWALL CRACK REPAIR

1 **WHEN YOU REPAIR DRYWALL, YOU HAVE TO MAKE THE SITUATION WORSE IN ORDER TO MAKE IT BETTER.** To fill a narrow drywall crack, widen it slightly. Brush off any loose pieces.

2 **FILL THE WIDENED CRACK WITH LIGHTWEIGHT SURFACING COMPOUND,** using your finger to apply it.

3 **SMOOTH THE AREA BY APPLYING ONE OR MORE THIN COATS OF THE SURFACING COMPOUND.** When the patch is dry, sand and prime it.

Repairing plaster walls

SKILL SCALE

EASY	MEDIUM	HARD

REQUIRED SKILLS: Basic carpentry and repair techniques. Using simple hand tools.

HOW LONG WILL IT TAKE?

Experienced . . . . 30 min.
Handy . . . . 45 min.
Novice . . . . 1 hr.

VARIABLES: Repairs are best made in thin layers. Each layer must be dry before continuing. Temperature and humidity will affect drying times.

STUFF YOU'LL NEED

✔ **MATERIALS:**

Patching compound, drywall scrap (optional), 150-grit sandpaper

✔ **TOOLS:**

Pocket can opener, paint can opener, or plaster scraping tool; spray bottle; plaster cup or plaster pan; dust respirator; 4-inch or 6-inch broad knife or putty knife; finishing nails; 10-inch or 12-inch broad knife

WORK SMARTER

DON'T STOP SHORT

A hole in a plaster wall may seem small until you actually begin removing all the loose plaster around it. The final repair may be much larger than the original hole, but you've got to be sure you get rid of all the plaster that's no longer attached to the lath.

The older your home, the more likely it is to have plaster walls. A plaster wall is actually three layers of plaster applied over wooden strips called lath. Plastering an entire wall is highly skilled work, but repairing a plaster wall is well within a homeowner's skill range.

Good tools and the right materials will make the job easier. For the best results use a powdered material called plaster patch, which has added adhesives that bond with the existing plaster. Surface and joint compounds are designed for other jobs and make a good plaster repair job next to impossible.

Plaster repair requires patience. Apply the compound in thin (⅛-inch to ¼-inch) layers and let each layer dry thoroughly before you add the next. This will keep the compound from cracking and make the repair permanent.

CLOSER LOOK

WHEN GOOD PLASTER GOES BAD

Cracks and broken plaster are often signs of other problems—usually a settling house. Settling is normal. If the house continues to settle after you patch the wall, the wall will crack again, probably in the same place. If so, basement floor jacks near or underneath the recurring crack may eliminate the problem. Ask for advice from a pro at your home center.

Brown spots or crumbly plaster usually indicate water damage—sometimes from the roof or a leaky pipe. Find and correct the problem before repairing the plaster to avoid it happening again.

When you repair a plaster wall, be prepared to remove all the loose material you find. Whatever is easily removed must be removed. This may mean removing a much larger section than you intended. If the hole is larger than the size of a broad knife (10 to 12 inches) fill it with a piece of drywall, as shown on page 229.

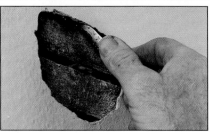

1 **REMOVE PLASTER FROM THE DAMAGED AREA.** Pry away most of the loose and cracking plaster with your fingers. Check to see if the remaining plaster is attached to the lath by trying to gently slip a 1-inch putty knife between the lath and plaster. If the knife slips under the plaster, pry gently to remove the plaster above it. Undercut the hole. Using a pocket can opener, paint can opener, or plaster scraping tool, undercut the edges of the hole to make it wider as it approaches the lath. This creates a void or notch under the good plaster, which will anchor the plaster patch when you apply it later. Remove dust and debris.

BUYER'S GUIDE

Patching plaster mixed from powder fills larger holes and cracks up to ¼ inch wide. Apply it in layers of ¼-inch maximum thickness. It dries in 90 minutes and can be sanded.

Plaster of Paris is mixed from powder and water. It's extremely durable but difficult to sand. A ¼-inch thickness hardens in 30 minutes.

Paintable latex caulk fills unstable gaps and cracks in walls and ceilings. It's paintable but not sandable. Smooth immediately after applying.

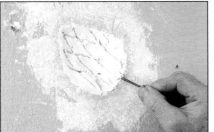

2 SPRAY THE AREA WITH WATER.
Plaster and lath will draw water out of the patching compound, leaving you with a crumbling mass that won't stick. Soak the lath and the surrounding area with water to keep the patching compound from drying too quickly. Mix the plaster patch wearing a respirator and safety glasses. If the hole is small, mix the compound in a cup. For larger holes mix the compound in a pan made for holding plaster or joint compound. Add the powder and stir in just enough water to form a paste. Stop stirring when the paste is smooth; overstirring causes the compound to set too quickly.

3 APPLY THE PATCH. Using a broad knife or putty knife, work the compound into the damaged area and press it through the spaces between the lath. Apply compound until the layer is about half as thick as the plaster. Cross-score the surface of the wet compound with a nail. The next coat will lodge in the grooves to create a mechanical bond in addition to the chemical bond that exists between coats. Let the patch dry thoroughly before applying the second coat.

Make sure a patch is thoroughly dry before you apply the next layer.

4 APPLY THE SECOND COAT. After the first coat is dry, mix another batch of compound. Apply a second coat, filling about half the space between the first coat and the wall surface, leaving no more than a ¼-inch recess. (See inset, above.) Let the second coat dry; then mix and apply a third coat. Smooth it with a 10-inch to 12-inch broad knife. Extend the edges of the compound beyond the edge of the original hole, feathering (tapering) and blending the edges flush with the wall. Wear a dust mask and sand lightly to complete the smoothing.

GOOD IDEA

PATCHING PLASTER WITH DRYWALL

Most plaster repair is a process of building up layers of plaster until the patch is thick enough to match the original wall. Work in layers ⅛ inch to ¼ inch thick. Borrow a technique from drywall repair for large holes: Square off the damaged area with a hammer and cold chisel. Tap gently to remove only the damaged area. In the example shown at right, the lath is missing because the patch will be applied over an outlet opening that is no longer used. Unless the lath is already missing, leave it intact to provide extra support for the patch.

Use a scrap of drywall as thick as the plaster. Lay out a rectangle that is larger than the opening in the wall by about 2 inches in each direction. Cut out the patch with a utility knife and snap it off.

Find the center of the patch and draw a rectangle slightly smaller than the opening in the wall.

Score along the line with a utility knife and pick away the gypsum, leaving a 2-inch paper flange around the edge of the patch.

Test-fit the drywall in the opening; make necessary adjustments. Lay plaster patch in the hole and trowel a layer on the wall larger than the flange on the patch. Put the patch in the hole and screw it in place with drywall screws. Trowel the flange tightly against the wall with patching compound. Feather the edges and sand smooth when the patching compound is dry.

Installing ceiling tile

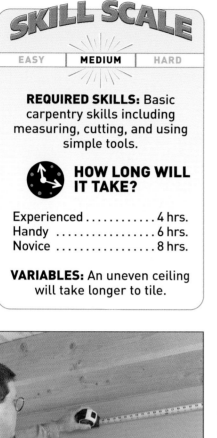

SKILL SCALE

EASY	**MEDIUM**	HARD

REQUIRED SKILLS: Basic carpentry skills including measuring, cutting, and using simple tools.

HOW LONG WILL IT TAKE?

Experienced . . . . 4 hrs.
Handy . . . . 6 hrs.
Novice . . . . 8 hrs.

VARIABLES: An uneven ceiling will take longer to tile.

Putting up ceiling tiles is a big job, but not necessarily a difficult one. You'll screw a grid of 1×3s to the ceiling, shim it to create a flat surface, and then staple the tiles to the grid.

The order in which you apply materials is designed to give you a balanced ceiling. This means that the center seam of the ceiling will run down the center of the room. It also means that the tiles (which have to be trimmed) running against the walls will be the same size on opposite ends of the room. Order 10 percent more tile than the ceiling area to account for trimming and replacement.

You'll start applying the grid in the center of the room, and you'll start applying tiles at the wall edges.

The ceiling here goes up over exposed floor joists. If you're applying the tiles over a finished ceiling, locate the joists with a stud finder. Drive a nail to make sure you're directly under the joist, and snap a chalk line to mark its location.

 MARK THE CENTER OF THE WALLS THAT RUN PARALLEL TO THE JOISTS. The visible edge of the tiles will be along this line. Measure over by the width of the tile's tongue—usually about ½ inch— to show where the tongue will be. Repeat the centering process on the two walls that are perpendicular to the joists. Snap chalk lines between the tongue marks so that two chalk lines cross each other on the ceiling.

Support blocks here (optional)

2 CENTER A 1x3 FURRING STRIP ON THE CHALK LINE AND SCREW IT TO THE CEILING JOISTS WITH #8 1⅝-INCH DRYWALL SCREWS. You'll find screws easier to use than the nails usually recommended, and if you have to back one of the 1×3s away from the joist later, you can simply loosen the screws. You may want to add support blocks to hold the edge of the furring strip against the joist. (See "Work Smarter," above right.)

GOOD IDEA

ADHESIVE AS ALTERNATIVE
If your ceiling is in good condition— flat and level—save time by applying the tiles directly to the ceiling with construction adhesive. But remember that any unevenness in the ceiling will be reflected in the tiles.

A+ WORK SMARTER

TO BLOCK OR NOT TO BLOCK
Although not necessarily required by manufacturers, blocking strips screwed to the joists to support the end of the furring strips may add stability to the finished ceiling. This is especially true in basements, where moisture can cause the supports to warp or sag, or when the furring strips themselves are warped or bowed.

Allow ceiling tiles and furring strips to acclimate to room conditions. Put materials in the room at least 24 hours (72 hours for a basement) before installing them.

3 **SCREW 1x3s TO THE REST OF THE CEILING,** spacing the centers so they are as far apart as the visible part of the tiles is wide, usually 12 inches. On the wall perpendicular to the joists, put a 1×3 right against the wall too.

4 **THE CEILING WILL ONLY BE AS FLAT AND AS LEVEL AS THE FURRING STRIPS.** Check by putting a level against the furring strip grid. If you see gaps between the level and the furring strips, back the screw out and slip in a shim. Tighten the screw until it is just snug, and check again with the level. Drive the shim in further or slide it partway out as needed.

5 **WHILE MOST TILES IN THE CEILING ARE FULL SIZE, THE BORDER TILES ARE TRIMMED TO FIT.** Lay out the full-size ones first—start at the lines you snapped in the middle of the ceiling and snap a new line every 12 inches.

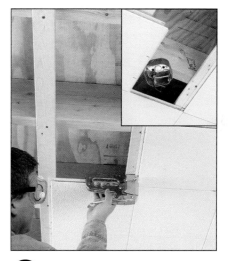

6 **MEASURE THE DISTANCE BETWEEN THE LAST LINE AND THE WALL AND CUT INDIVIDUAL TILES TO FIT.** Size them so that there is a ¼-inch gap between the tile and the wall—this leaves you room to maneuver the tile. It also means that you won't need to cut a tapered tile as long as one end is no more than ¼ inch shorter than the other. A molding will cover the gap later.

7 **STAPLE THE BORDER TILES IN PLACE, DRIVING THE STAPLES THROUGH THE TONGUE OF THE TILE.** On two walls, you'll be able to staple the tiles to the 1×3 furring against the wall, as shown here. On the other walls, nail the edge of the tiles into the joists, if possible. If you can't, the molding you'll apply later will provide adequate support.

8 **ONCE YOU'VE APPLIED THE BORDER TILES ON TWO ADJACENT WALLS, BEGIN APPLYING THE FULL-SIZE TILES.** Work your way across the room. Trim the border tiles against the remaining walls to the proper size and staple in place. If you need to make a cutout in a tile (see inset above), put it in place and mark each edge of the cut. Reposition it to mark the adjacent edge. Connect the lines on the back of the tile and cut the opening with a keyhole saw.

After all tiles are in place, cut molding to tightly fit against the ceiling and wall, and nail it in place, covering the gap left by the tiles.

You can use quarter round or cove molding to trim the ceiling and hide gaps. Cove is a little more decorative and will cover more minor errors.

WALLS AND CEILINGS

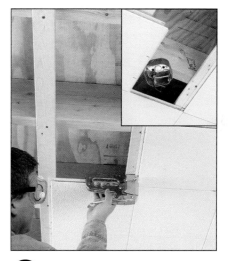

WALLS AND CEILINGS 231

INSTALLING A SUSPENDED CEILING

SKILL SCALE

EASY	MEDIUM	**HARD**

REQUIRED SKILLS: Suspended ceiling installation requires average carpentry skills.

HOW LONG WILL IT TAKE?

Experienced . . . . 3 hrs.
Handy . . . . 5 hrs.
Novice . . . . 7 hrs.

STUFF YOU'LL NEED

✔ MATERIALS:

Nails, wall angles, hanger screws, hanger wire, cross-tees, runners, suspended ceiling tiles, common nails, lights, translucent plastic panel, wire nuts, electrician's tape

✔ TOOLS:

Hammer, tape measure, chalk line and mason's string, line level, tin snips or hacksaw, screwdriver, 4-foot level, utility knife, straightedge, pliers

Suspended ceilings have two main features: a metal grid that provides a structure and lightweight panels that slip into the grid. The installation, which sometimes can be difficult depending on what the ceiling is suspended from, requires only common household tools.

You'll install the grid first, starting with the wall angles, which fasten to walls. Then come the runners (or main tees), which hang by wires from the ceiling and run perpendicular to the joists. Then come the cross-tees, which are installed between and perpendicular to the runners. Whichever way you install the runners, leave at least 4 inches of space above the framework (or 6 inches if you're installing lighting) to provide room to place the panels.

The loose ceiling panels sit on the flanges of the installed grid. They remove easily for access to ductwork, plumbing, or electrical circuits.

The secret to a successful installation is to measure, measure, measure, and then level. It's not hard, but unless you want a room with a sloping ceiling and a diagonal grid, make sure you do both.

Start by measuring the room. The ceiling will likely require some partial panels. For a balanced look, put in two equally sized partial panels, one on each side of the room. (See "Balancing the Ceiling," below.)

As you begin the actual installation, you'll be stringing lots of layout lines. Use mason's line because it won't sag as regular string will. Make sure the lines are level and double-check the grid with a 4-foot level as you build it. Correcting problems is easy, usually just a matter of tightening a screw.

BUYER'S GUIDE

HANDY HANGERS

The right hanger can make a job a lot easier. The simplest hangers are merely eye hooks, but the best are both easy to install and easy to adjust. One company makes a flattened bolt that you drive in with a socket that fits in your drill. Another company makes hanger wires with eyelets on one end: You run a drywall screw through the eyelet to attach the hanger and drive the screw in or out to level the grid. Check out the other options too, such as line clamps, which simplify attaching leveling lines to the grid.

Balancing the ceiling

Full 2' x 2' tiles

14'

¾ border tiles
(18 inches each)

11'

To balance the ceiling make the border tiles (next to the wall) the same size on opposite sides of the room. This example uses 2×2-foot tiles in a 11×14-foot room. First divide the width of the room by the width of the tiles. (11/2=5½ tiles.) Divide the fraction by two to determine the size of the border tiles. (½/2=¼ tile.) The border tiles would be ¼ tile wide, (6 inches) which would appear out of proportion to the other tiles. Add ½ tile to the size of the border tile, making it ¾ of a tile. Doing this means you use one less full tile. (4 full tiles and two border tiles of 18 inches each.) Repeat the process for the length of the room, if necessary.

WORK SMARTER

FINDING CEILING JOISTS

Some ceilings make it difficult to locate ceiling joists with a stud finder. If you have access, simply peek into the attic to see which direction the ceiling joists go and how far apart they are. If you don't have access you'll have to measure from below. Joist spacing is usually either 16 inches or 24 inches; once you determine the direction, measure from the end wall either 16 inches or 24 inches and drive a nail through the ceiling. If it doesn't hit a joist, move in either direction in ½-inch increments until you hit it, mark the joist position, and continue to measure across the ceiling.

Hanging a suspended ceiling

To put in a level ceiling you first need to draw a level line around the room marking where you will install the wall angles. The surest solution is to rent a tripod laser and follow the manufacturer's instructions. Generally you put it in the center of the room and level the legs. When you turn on the laser, it spins, tracing a level line around the room. Hang the wall angle along the lines.

If you'd rather not spend the rental money, count on spending more time doing layout. Start by driving a nail at one end of the wall to mark the height of the suspended ceiling. Tie mason's line to the nail—mason's line won't sag like regular chalk lines do—and rub it with a piece of chalk. Hang a line level on the line and stretch the line to the far end of the wall. Raise or lower the line until it's level and snap a line on the wall. Repeat on the remaining walls.

1 **LAY OUT THE BOTTOM OF THE WALL ANGLE 4 INCHES BELOW THE JOISTS,** or 6 inches if the ceiling will have a light in it. Nail or screw the wall angle along the line. Cut the wall angle as necessary with tin snips or a hacksaw. Butt the inside corners and miter the outside ones.

2 **SNAP A LINE ALONG THE JOISTS TO SHOW THE LOCATIONS OF THE HANGERS** for the wires that support the runners. Screw the hangers into the joists at 4-foot intervals along the chalk line.

Order 10 percent extra for trimming and replacement and allow the tiles to acclimate for at least 24 hours (up to 72 hours for a basement).

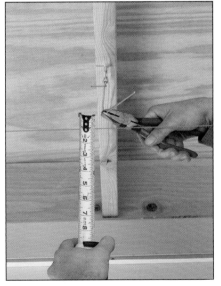

Mason's lines

3'

5'

4'

3 **TO LAY OUT A SQUARE GRID,** first run mason's line from wall angle to wall angle along the path of the runner nearest the wall. Then stretch mason's line along the path of cross-tees nearest the wall. To square up, mark one line 3 feet from the intersection and the other 4 feet from the intersection. When the distance between these marks is 5 feet, the lines are square. Slide the lines as necessary to square them.

4 **TO MAKE SURE THE GRID WILL BE LEVEL,** measure up from the lines to the hanger wires, and bend them at the point where they will slip through the hanging holes in the runners. The exact distance varies from brand to brand, but it's equal to the distance from the bottom of the runner to the center of the hole.

5 **CUT THE RUNNER TO SIZE.** Make the cut so that when you place the runner on the wall angle, the hole into which the cross-tee fits is directly over the line marking the path of the cross-tee.

INSTALLING A SUSPENDED CEILING
Hanging a suspended ceiling *(continued)*

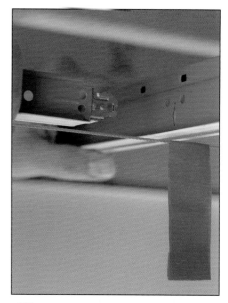

6 **REST ONE END OF THE RUNNER ON THE WALL ANGLE,** and slide the bent hanging wire through the hole. Snap sections of runner together as necessary to span the room, adding a hanger and wire to support the runner at any joints. If necessary, trim the last section of runner to fit.

7 **ONCE YOU'VE INSTALLED THE FIRST RUNNER, RUN LEVEL LINES MARKING THE PATHS OF THE OTHERS.** Measure up, bend the hangers, and hang each runner as before. Check with a 4-foot level to make sure each runner is level. Make any necessary adjustments by turning the hanger in or out of the joist.

8 **AFTER YOU'VE INSTALLED ALL THE RUNNERS, HANG THE CROSS-TEES.** Start in the middle of the room, put in a few cross-tees, and then install some ceiling panels to square up the grid. Then install the rest of the cross-tees.

9 **THE CROSS-TEES AROUND THE EDGE OF THE ROOM WILL PROBABLY NEED TO BE CUT TO FIT.** Measure, cut, and install them one at a time. To keep the grid uniform, alternate sides: Put a tee on one side of the room, follow the line of tees to the other side of the room, and then install the next tee.

10 **INSTALL ALL THE FULL-SIZE PANELS FIRST**. Install all the ceiling panels except for those around the edge of the room, which will need to be cut to fit.

11 **CUT THE TILES AROUND THE EDGE OF THE ROOM TO FIT.** Place the tiles face up on a flat surface, run a utility knife along a straightedge repeatedly, and then snap the panel in two. Once you've trimmed the panels, put them in their openings. **NOTE:** If your tiles have a rabbeted (grooved) edge you will have to cut a similar rabbet into the edges of the border tiles with a utility knife so they will fit flush in the grid.

Lighting a suspended ceiling

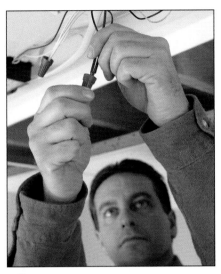

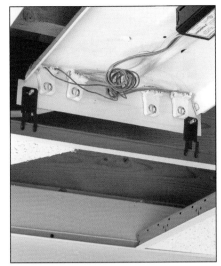

1 **MOST CEILING LIGHTS REQUIRE ASSEMBLY, WHICH CAN VARY SLIGHTLY FROM BRAND TO BRAND.**
Typically the fixture comes in several pieces: a reflector, which may (or may not) be part of the main housing; two bulb sockets per bulb; two end caps; and mounting brackets. Snap the sockets in place. Put the end caps on the housing and screw them in place.

2 **TO WIRE THE LIGHT, FEED CABLE THROUGH THE OPENING IN THE TOP.** Twist the light's black wire around the black cable wire, then twist the white cable and light wires together. Twist a wire nut over both and wrap electrician's tape around each nut and its wires. Screw the ground wire to the green screw in the fixture.

FOR LONG RUNS OF FLUORESCENT LIGHTING, SAVE TIME BY CONNECTING THE FIXTURES END-TO-END with special locknuts and connectors available where you buy the fixtures. It's more efficient to wire them in sequence than to have individual rows of lights connected to a single junction box.

BUYER'S GUIDE

THE RIGHT LIGHT

Ceiling grid fixtures like those shown here are the standard approach to lighting a suspended ceiling, but they're not the only way. Fixtures called "troffers" fit into the grid and cover the light with a hinged door that can have dressy slats, translucent panels, or a combination of the two.

Another option is to create a luminous ceiling with light fixtures running the width and breadth of the room and using translucent panels.

The best fixture to use in a luminous ceiling is a 4-foot long 40-watt rapid-start unit. To determine the number of lamps for the entire area, sketch out the dimensions of the ceiling. Plan for the lamps to lie in parallel lines between 18 inches and 24 inches apart. The narrower spacing provides more light but is more expensive. Allow about 8 inches between the ends of the lines and the wall.

3 **FASTEN THE REFLECTOR TO THE END CAPS, IF NECESSARY.** The mounting bracket varies from brand to brand, but the light shown here has a tee-bracket that attaches to each end cap. Attach the bracket ends to the fixture, lift the fixture into place, and attach the brackets to the ceiling grid. Install the bulbs in the fixture.

4 **INSERT THE COVER.** Slide a translucent plastic panel into place under the fixture. Angle the piece so you can position first one side and then the other on the grid. If the fit is tight, create flexibility by temporarily removing a ceiling panel next to the fixture.

WALLS AND CEILINGS

Removing a wall

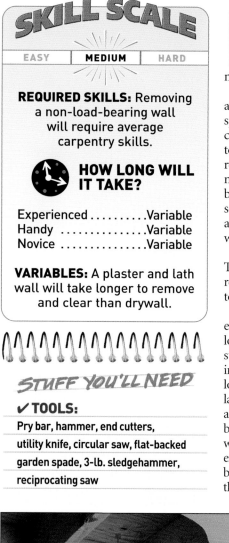

SKILL SCALE

EASY | **MEDIUM** | HARD

REQUIRED SKILLS: Removing a non-load-bearing wall will require average carpentry skills.

HOW LONG WILL IT TAKE?

Experienced . . . . .Variable
Handy . . . . .Variable
Novice . . . . .Variable

VARIABLES: A plaster and lath wall will take longer to remove and clear than drywall.

STUFF YOU'LL NEED

✔ **TOOLS:**

Pry bar, hammer, end cutters, utility knife, circular saw, flat-backed garden spade, 3-lb. sledgehammer, reciprocating saw

---

Removing a wall should appeal to the inner child in you. It's messy, it's fairly easy, and it reveals things that you might not otherwise see.

But before you start, take a good look at the wall. In addition to dividing a large space into smaller spaces, some walls—called load-bearing walls—are designed to hold up the house. Removing them requires some sophisticated carpentry, not to mention the approval of your local building inspector. By and large, it's something homeowners should stay away from. Hire a pro when you deal with load-bearing walls.

Partition walls are another matter. They provide no structural support, and removing them is one of the easiest ways to improve on an existing floor plan.

Fortunately the two types of walls are easy to tell apart. All exterior walls are load-bearing walls. Walls that sit on support beams, which are often visible in an unfinished basement, are load-bearing walls. Walls that support lapped joists are also load-bearing. These are also easiest to see in an unfinished basement. Instead of running the entire width of the house, a joist will start at an exterior wall and run to a middle, load-bearing wall. A separate joist runs from the wall to the second exterior wall. The surest way to know is to remove a little plaster or drywall. For strength, the top plate of a load-bearing wall is made of at least two 2×4s, as shown at bottom left. The plate on a partition wall is made of a single 2×4 as shown at bottom right.

Before you start swinging a hammer, try to figure out what might be behind the wall. Outlets mean hidden wires; nearby plumbing means water pipes; stoves or furnaces may mean gas pipes. Turn off the utilities before you start tearing down the wall and have plans for relocating whatever you find.

Completely removing a load-bearing wall can create a serious structural problem. Leave this job to professionals.

SAFETY ALERT

TURN OFF THE UTILITIES
Turn off the electricity, water, and gas at the main breaker or valves before removing any wall surfaces. Use an independent lighting source.

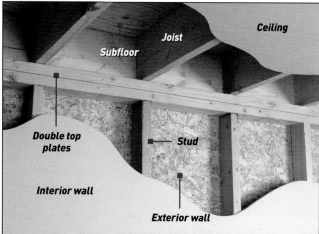

LOAD-BEARING WALLS CARRY THE STRUCTURAL WEIGHT of your home and can be identified by double top plates made from two layers of framing lumber. Load-bearing walls include all adjacent exterior walls and any interior walls that are aligned above support beams or that are positioned to support ceiling or floor joist lap joints.

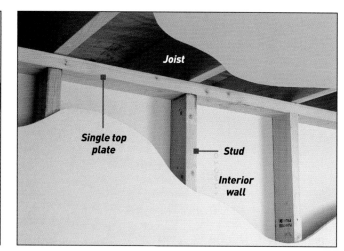

PARTITION WALLS ARE INTERIOR WALLS THAT ARE NOT LOAD-BEARING. Partition walls have a single top plate. Any interior wall parallel to floor and ceiling joists is a partition wall. A wall perpendicular to the joists can be either a load-bearing or partition wall. A load-bearing wall will be aligned above a support beam; a partition wall probably won't be. If you're not sure, consider it a load-bearing wall until you have a professional take a look at it.

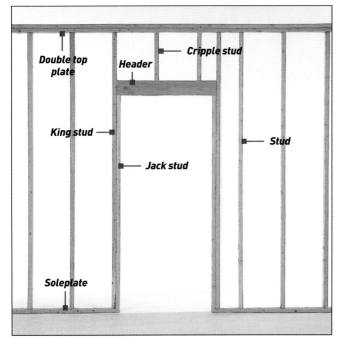

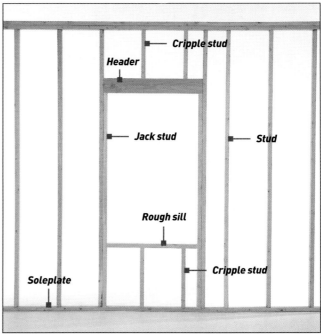

DOOR OPENINGS IN LOAD-BEARING WALLS NEED A HEADER TO PROVIDE ADEQUATE SUPPORT. Headers are a sandwich with 2×4 stock on the outside and plywood on the inside. The header is supported by jack studs that run down to the floor. Short studs called cripples run between the header and the top plate of the wall. All exterior doors are in load-bearing walls, as are some interior doors. Non load-bearing walls have headers made of single 2×4s mounted horizontally. (See page 342.)

WINDOW OPENINGS ALSO HAVE HEADERS. Because windows are in exterior walls, which are always load-bearing, they have built-up headers consisting of 2×4s sandwiched around a piece of plywood. The header is supported by jack studs; the rough sill below it is supported by cripple studs.

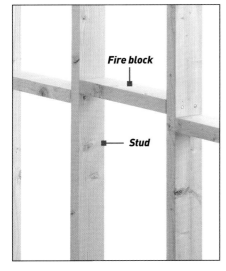

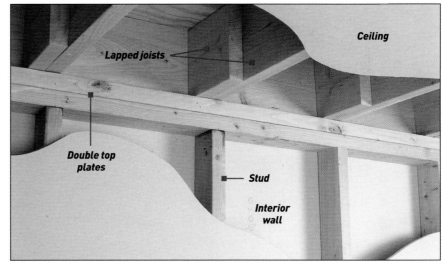

ALL WALLS TALLER THAN 8 FEET NEED FIRE BLOCKS, AND SOME LOCAL CODES REQUIRE FIRE BLOCKS ON SHORTER WALLS. Fire blocks prevent fire from traveling up the wall cavity. Cut 2×4s to fit between the studs and stagger them to make nailing easier.

FLOOR JOISTS SPAN THE ENTIRE WIDTH OF A HOUSE, and it's often impractical to make them out of a single length of wood. Lapping them, as shown here, solves the problem. The wall below the lap is always load-bearing, as is the wall above it.

Removing a wall *(continued)*

WALLS AND CEILINGS

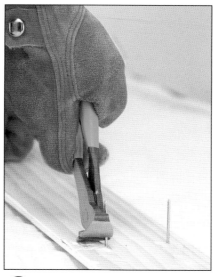

1 **REMOVE THE TRIM.** The baseboard has probably been nailed into the studs and floor plate. Start removing it at a doorway, driving a pry bar between a stud and the baseboard with a hammer. Work your way down the wall, prying at every stud, and then pull the board loose by hand. Door and window trim is nailed into the studs, usually with a double row of nails. Pry at each nail until the trim is loose and remove by hand.

2 **IF YOU'RE GOING TO REUSE THE TRIM, REMOVE THE NAILS.** In order to avoid splintering the board, pull the nails out from the back. End cutters remove nails quickly and cleanly. Pinch the nail at the board and roll the cutters sideways to pull the nail partway out. Repeat to remove. If you're throwing the trim away, bend the nails over so no one accidentally steps on one.

3 **OPEN UP THE WALL.** If you're removing part of a wall, start by drawing a line centered on the first stud that will remain on each side of the opening. On drywall, cut along the line with a utility knife. On plaster, cut the line with a circular saw, cutting through the lath but not into the stud. Break a hole in the wall with a 3-pound sledgehammer.

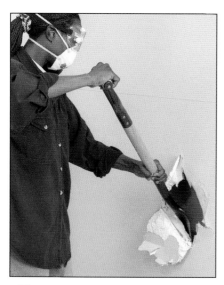

4 **REMOVE THE PLASTER OR DRYWALL.** If you try to remove the entire wall surface with a hammer, it will break the wall into small pieces, making it hard to remove a lot of wall quickly. Once you've made the hole in the wall with the hammer, make quick work of the rest of the job with a flat-back garden spade.

Behind the scenes

Removing a wall means removing the pipes and wiring in it too. Even if you're sure you've turned the power off double-check it after the plaster or drywall is off before you begin to remove or unhook outlets or switches. Pull the cable through the floor, wall, or ceiling as needed to remove it. Cap the wires with wire nuts and tape them in place with electrical tape. Cut any other cables and pull them out of the wall. Remove enough of the jacket to expose a couple of inches of wire; cap and tape them too.

You'll also need to cut and cap the pipes. Generally speaking, copper and smaller plastic pipes carry water; black iron pipe carries gas; and larger-diameter pipe is drainpipe. Follow the pipe back toward the meter. Double-check to make sure the gas and water are off. Cut copper or plastic and cap it

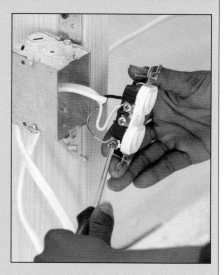

where convenient. Disconnect and cap gas pipe or drainpipe at the nearest convenient fitting.

238 WALLS AND CEILINGS

5 **TO REMOVE STUDS CUT THROUGH THE MIDDLE WITH A HANDSAW OR RECIPROCATING SAW.** Press them back and forth to pry them away from the soleplate and top plate. To remove the end studs, cut through them without cutting into the studs on the adjoining wall. Pry the studs loose as shown above.

Reusing the lumber

If you want to reuse the lumber, put a metal-cutting blade in the reciprocating saw. Instead of cutting through the middle of the stud, run the blade between the stud and the soleplate. Cut through the nails, and then cut through the nails between the stud and the top plate. Pull the stud free by hand.

6 **TO REMOVE THE TOP PLATE, FIRST MAKE TWO CUTS ABOUT 3 INCHES APART THROUGH IT,** using a reciprocating saw or handsaw. Knock the cut section away with the pry bar and hammer.

SAFETY ALERT

PLASTER DUST MAY BE DANGEROUS
Old plaster may contain anything from horsehair to asbestos. Protect yourself with goggles and a proper dust mask—a simple sanding mask won't do. Ask for a HEPA (high efficiency particulate arresting) mask. When you vacuum up the dust, use a shop vac with a HEPA filter. Aftermarket (replacement) filters are available at most home centers.

7 **PRY DOWN THE REMAINING LENGTH OF TOP PLATE WITH THE PRY BAR.** Work slowly to avoid damaging the ceiling beneath the plate, which will be visible in the new room.

8 **REMOVE A 3-INCH-WIDE SECTION OF SOLEPLATE** using a reciprocating saw or handsaw. Pry out the entire soleplate using a pry bar.

You can save a certain amount of cleanup and damage to the floor if you lay heavy-duty drop cloths down before you remove the wall.

Hang signs on utility shutoffs so someone doesn't turn them on while you're working.

BUILDING A PARTITION WALL

REQUIRED SKILLS: Building a partition wall will require average carpentry skills.

HOW LONG WILL IT TAKE?

Experienced . . . . 1.5 hrs.
Handy . . . . 2 hrs.
Novice . . . . 2.5 hrs.

VARIABLES: Time is based on a 10-foot partition wall.

STUFF YOU'LL NEED

✔ **MATERIALS:**

Framing lumber, 16d nails, metal connectors, 4d nails, shims

✔ **TOOLS:**

Drill and bit, combination square, plumb bob and line, chalk line, hammer, stud driver, ear protection, safety glasses for concrete floors, circular saw, 4-foot level

Partition walls define new living areas and are often used to create new rooms in unfinished basements. You can build a partition wall two ways: framing the wall in place, or building the frame on the floor and tilting it into place. If space permits, building the wall flat on the floor is easier. Before finishing the walls with drywall (see page 248), have the local building inspector check the construction. The inspector will also want to make sure that any required plumbing and wiring changes are complete. The electrical and plumbing sections of this book tell you how to make them.

Tape measures are not all created equal. Use the same tape from the beginning to the end of a project to ensure consistent measurements.

WORK SMARTER

MAKE WIDER WALLS TO HOLD LARGE PIPES

Interior partition walls are commonly built with 2×4 framing lumber, but in some situations it is better to frame with 2×6 lumber. Use 2×6 lumber to frame a partition wall that must hold large plumbing pipes, such as waste/drain pipes. In sections where the wall plates must be cut in order to fit pipes and other mechanical fixtures, use metal straps to join the framing members and tie them together.

If the intended use of the new room is a practice room for your teenager's new drum set, you may want to soundproof the new wall. You can easily accomplish this by filling the wall with fiberglass insulation (see page 244) before applying the wallboard.

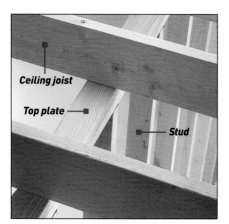

NEW WALLS THAT RUN PERPENDICULAR TO JOISTS are attached by fastening the top plate directly to the ceiling joists. The soleplate below will be fastened to the floor joists with 16d nails.

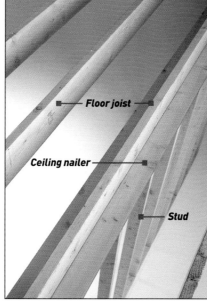

NEW WALLS THAT ARE PARALLEL TO THE JOISTS are attached by fastening the top plate directly to the ceiling joist and the soleplate to the floor joists using 16d nails. If the new wall won't be directly under a joist, consider moving it a few inches so that it is. Attaching it to the ceiling will be much easier if you do.

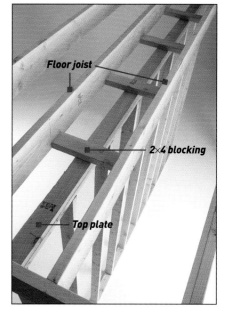

NEW WALLS THAT RUN PARALLEL TO THE JOISTS BUT AREN'T DIRECTLY UNDER ONE NEED ADDITIONAL BLOCKING. Install 2×4 blocking between the joists, every 2 feet, using 16d nails. The bottom of the blocking should be flush with the edges of joists. Unless you can install the block from above, you'll need to cut—and repair—holes in the ceiling.

BUILDING A PARTITION WALL
Attaching new walls to existing joists

1 **MARK THE LOCATION OF THE NEW WALL ON THE CEILING,** and then snap two chalk lines to outline the position of the new top plate. Locate the first ceiling joist by drilling into the ceiling between the lines, then measure to find and mark the remaining joists.

2 **MAKE THE TOP AND BOTTOM WALL PLATES BY CUTTING TWO 2×4s TO THE WALL LENGTH.** Lay the plates side by side and use a combination square to outline the stud locations at 16-inch intervals on center.

3 **DOUBLE-CHECK TO MAKE SURE THE LINES YOU SNAPPED ARE PARALLEL TO THE WALL.** Make any necessary corrections, and nail the top plate in place with 16d nails.

4 **DETERMINE THE POSITION OF THE SOLEPLATE BY HANGING A PLUMB BOB FROM THE EDGE OF THE TOP PLATE** so that the plumb bob tip nearly touches the floor. Mark the position on the floor. Repeat at the opposite end of the top plate, then snap a chalk line between the marks to indicate the location of the soleplate.

5 **ON WOOD FLOORS, ANCHOR THE SOLEPLATE WITH 16d NAILS DRIVEN INTO THE FLOOR JOISTS.** On concrete floors, attach the soleplate with a stud driver (inset), available at rental centers. A stud driver fires a small gunpowder charge to drive a masonry nail through the framing member and into the concrete. Wear hearing and eye protection when using a stud driver.

6 **THE FIRST STUD WILL BE INSTALLED TIGHT AGAINST THE WALL.** Measure the distance between the soleplate and the top plate at this point. Add ⅛ inch to ensure a snug fit and cut the stud to length.

WALLS AND CEILINGS 241

Attaching new walls to existing joists (continued)

7 **POSITION THE STUD AGAINST THE WALL, ALIGN IT WITH THE SOLEPLATE, AND NAIL IT IN PLACE WITH 16d NAILS.** Double-check to make sure the stud is aligned with the top plate, and then nail the top of the stud in place. Nail the rest of the stud to the wall with 16d nails every 2 feet. If there is no stud to nail to, attach the new wall to the old with construction adhesive.

8 **FASTEN THE STUD AT THE OTHER END OF THE WALL IN PLACE.** Once it's attached, measure and cut the stud next to it. Position the stud between the top plate and soleplate so the stud markings are covered.

9 **ATTACH THE STUDS TO THE SOLEPLATE** and top plate with metal connectors and 4d nails.

CLOSER LOOK

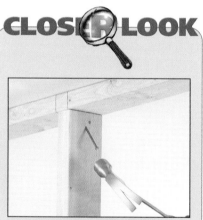

TOENAILING
Toenailing, once you get the hang of it, is faster, and as effective as using metal connectors. Begin with the stud ⅛ inch to ¼ inch in front of the layout lines, as shown. Drive the nail at an angle a bit steeper than 45 degrees so that at least half the nail will enter the plate. Support the 2×4 with your hand, foot, or body and drive the nail, knocking the stud into position with your final blows. Drive a second nail from the other side but not immediately opposite the first.

Framing partition wall corners

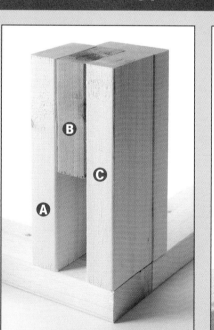

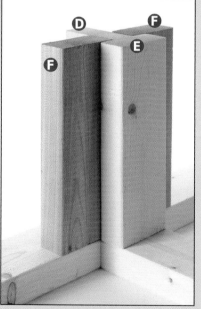

If you're adding more than one wall, you'll need a little extra framing to form the corner. Frame L-corners by nailing **A** an extra stud to the plates and to **B** 2×4 spacers that are nailed to the inside of the end stud **C**. Nail the new wall to the studs and spacer.

Frame T-corners by nailing D a stud in one wall to **E** a stud behind it in the other. Add **F** a 2×4 nailer to each side to provide a nailing surface for drywall.

BUILDING A PARTITION WALL
Framing a partition wall on the floor

Include the body of the tape measure in your calculations.

❶ SNAP A LINE ON THE FLOOR TO LAY OUT THE BOTTOM PLATE OF THE NEW WALL. Locate the line by measuring from an existing wall. It may not create perfectly square corners, but it's more important that the new wall and old wall be parallel, especially if you'll be installing tile or a suspended ceiling later.

❷ DETERMINE THE LENGTH OF THE WALL; CUT 2×4 TOP AND SOLEPLATES TO LENGTH. Place the 2×4s side by side and lay out the top plates and soleplates, spacing centers of the studs 16 inches apart (16 inches on center). Lay out doors and windows as described on page 237. Mark the edge of the plates too, so that the marks will be easy to see while nailing. See Sections 7 and 8, Doors and Windows.

❸ MEASURE THE DISTANCE BETWEEN THE FLOOR AND THE CEILING, OR THE JOISTS, at several locations along where the wall will be constructed. Take the shortest distance and subtract 3⅛ inches (1½ inches each for the top and soleplates and ⅛ inch for space to maneuver the wall into place). This will be the stud length. (For extra accuracy use a plumb bob.)

❹ COUNT THE LAYOUT MARKS TO SEE HOW MANY STUDS YOU'LL NEED, and cut them to length. Sight down the edge of each stud to see whether it's straight. If not, mark the edge to show which side has the crown (high spot).

❺ LAY THE SOLEPLATE ON EDGE ALONG THE FLOOR LINE. Take the best two studs you can find, and place them at each end of the wall with the crown up. Nail the soleplate and studs together with 6d nails.

❻ LAY THE TOP PLATE ON EDGE WITH THE LAYOUT MARKS FACING THE SOLEPLATE, and nail it to the end studs using 16d nails. Insert the remaining studs, crown up, and nail in place with 16d nails.

Framing a partition wall on the floor *(continued)*

7 **ONCE ALL STUDS HAVE BEEN ATTACHED TO THE TOP AND SOLEPLATES,** raise the wall and position the plates on the floor and ceiling lines.

8 **IF THE WALL FITS TOO LOOSELY, SHIM UNDER THE BOTTOM PLATE** to tighten the wall in the space. Nail the wall to the floor and ceiling joists with 16d nails.

Soundproofing a wall

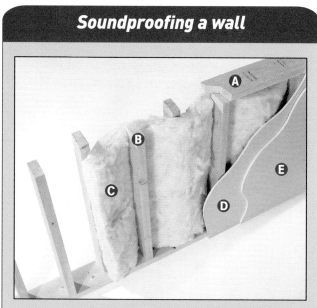

You can soundproof a room—at least partially—with regular fiberglass insulation. Start by using top and **Ⓐ** soleplates that are wider than the wall studs. Place the wall studs 8 inches on center, but stagger them so they alternate: Each stud should line up on the **Ⓑ** opposite edge of the plate from the previous stud. Weave **Ⓒ** fiberglass batt insulation between the studs along the entire wall, filling the full height of the studs. Apply a layer of **Ⓓ** soundproofing drywall to the wall studs, then cover that with **Ⓔ** regular drywall.

A+ WORK SMARTER

BUILDING FLOATING WALLS
In many areas of the country the soil beneath the slab in the basement expands and contracts with the changes in season. Sometimes the changes can be extreme and play havoc with basement partition walls. Improperly installed basement wall systems have actually moved houses off foundations. If these conditions exist in your area, you will have to build "floating" walls below grade in your basement to accommodate the changes in season. Floating walls are fixed to the ceiling joists and the wall is constructed to leave a gap at the bottom, which floats on pins in a plate anchored to the slab. This allows the slab to move up and down without affecting the partition wall. Bottom line? Check with your local building authority and local codes before you finish the basement.

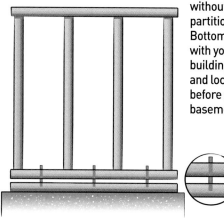

INSTALLING DRYWALL

Hanging drywall so that the seams are horizontal puts the seams at a convenient height for taping and actually cuts down on the taping you'll need to do.

At first, hanging drywall seems self-evident. You put the stuff up, and then drive screws through it. But, like most things in life, you have a choice between working longer and working smarter.

The smartest thing you can do *isn't* self-evident for most people. If possible, buy sheets the same length as the wall. (If necessary, buy sheets a bit longer, then trim them to length.) When you hang the sheets, position them with the longest edge parallel to the floor. Start at the top of the wall: If a sheet needs to be trimmed to height, it's at floor level and much easier to haul back to the sawhorses.

Plenty of good reasons exist for hanging the sheet parallel to the floor: To start with, it cuts down on the taping

and compound (also called mud by many) you have to apply along the seams. Because taping and mudding are the most miserable part of the job, horizontal seams are best. They cut taping by as much as 25 percent.

This installation is also stronger because each board ties more studs together and because the drywall's strongest dimension bridges irregularities like warped studs. When you are taping you'll find the seam is at a convenient height—you don't have to bend over to apply mud as you would for vertical seams.

Other hints: Center the short edge of the panels on the joists so that you have something to attach the next panel to. Screws hold better than nails, which tend to pop out as the wood expands and contracts with changes in humidity. Last but not least, avoid forcing a panel in place. Even if it survives without cracking, something is guaranteed to go wrong in the near future. A joint will pop open somewhere, or a section may break loose of its screws. To get the best fit, trim drywall with a utility knife. You can take small amounts off the edges with a coarse rasp.

DIFFERENT TYPES OF DRYWALL

Standard drywall panels come in 4×8 sheets (longer and wider panels are also available) and range in thickness from ¼ to ⅝ of an inch.

- Drywall is the standard wall covering panel, made of gypsum sandwiched between paper. Screw the panels to the wall. Fill the cracks between them with paper drywall tape, then joint compound.

- Greenboard is the water-resistant form of drywall and installs the same way. Do not put it on ceilings however; it is too heavy.

- Backerboard is a smaller panel, with a concrete core and fiberglass facing. It's used as a base underneath ceramic tile. Screw it to the wall with special backerboard screws.

Drywall cutting and screwing

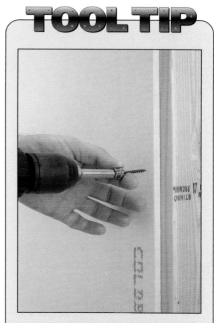

1 **TO MAKE STRAIGHT CUTS,** score the face paper with a sharp utility knife, using a drywall T square as a guide. Deepen the cuts into the gypsum with additional passes. Always make cuts so the knife is traveling away from the hand holding the square.

2 **COMPLETE STRAIGHT CUTS** by bending the panel away from the scored line until it breaks. Cut through the back paper with a sharp utility knife to separate the pieces.

To prevent rust stains in the basement or other damp areas, use galvanized screws instead of plain metal.

BUYER'S GUIDE

CHOOSING SCREWS

Drywall Thickness	Framing	Screw Length	Screw Spacing Walls	Screw Spacing Ceiling	Thread
3/8", 1/2", or 5/8"	Wood	1 1/4"	16"	16"	Coarse
1/2" or 5/8"	Steel	1"	16"	12"	Fine
5/8"	Steel	1 1/8"	16"	12"	Fine
3/4"	Steel	1 1/4"	16"	12"	Fine

NICE DIMPLES

When you're hanging a sheet, use screws instead of nails: Nails can work their way back to the surface as the studs expand and contract with the weather. Drive the screw deep enough to create a dimple without breaking the face paper—this significantly weakens the screw's holding power. Then fill the dimple with joint compound to cover the screw.

Professional drywallers use a special drill called a drywall gun to drive drywall screws. It looks much like a drill with a screwdriver in the chuck. The one important difference is that it has a clutch with an adjustable depth gauge. A pro will set the clutch so that the drywall screw will go just below the surface of the sheet and dimple—but not break—the paper. It makes a big difference to workers who get paid by the number of sheets they hang in a day.

Unless you're drywalling a whole house, however, you probably can get by with a drill. Get a "dimpler" bit (like the one shown above), which will set the screws just like a drywall gun.

INSTALLING DRYWALL
Drywalling a ceiling

Drywalling a ceiling is a challenge: You're constantly reaching over your head and more than once you'll find yourself holding something in place with the top of your head.

If you're doing an entire room, hang the ceiling first. Cut the panel so it stops about ¼ inch short of the wall studs. It's easier to hang, and the wall panels will give it some support when you install them. If you're installing a ceiling in a room that already has walls, leave a space of about ¹⁄₁₆ inch between the ceiling and walls so that you don't have to force panels in place.

Put up the longest panel you can handle. If you have to butt ends to span the room, stagger the panels so that the butt joints don't align.

Stand on something stable while you work—a sawhorse and some boards won't do. Use the scaffold set up as shown below.

Before you cover the walls, mark the floor to show where the studs are. This will make it easier to drive screws into the studs once you've covered them with drywall.

1 CUT A ⅜-INCH-DIAMETER HOLE in the tip of a tube of construction adhesive, and run a continuous bead of adhesive on the joists above the first panel you'll install. If you will be butting panels at the end, run the bead about ⅜ inch from the edge of the joist that supports the end. Run a new bead for the next piece.

TOOL TIP

HELPING HAND
Rent a cradle lift to help raise sheets into place quickly and safely. The lift allows you to load the drywall and lift the panel as high as 11 feet. The lift is on casters so you can roll it into position, set the caster brakes, and safely and securely place the panel into position. Most lifts can normally hold up to a full 4'×16' sheet of drywall and have a tilting platform feature that lets you easily install drywall on sloped ceilings.

As you install the subsequent sheets, leave a ¼-inch gap to ensure that the joint can be easily filled with joint compound.

SAFETY ALERT

BE CAREFUL WHEN WORKING ABOVE YOUR HEAD
Sheets of drywall are awkward and heavy, especially when working above your head. Always work with a helper, use a scaffold, and wear eye protection.

2 WORK WITH A PARTNER WHEN INSTALLING A DRYWALL CEILING. Build a 2×4 support for your helper to use to hold up the panel. Work together to lift the sheet against the ceiling in a corner of the room. Then support the sheet with your hand (or tuck a sponge inside your hat and use your head) while your helper supports it with the 2×4 T-support. Start at the end of the sheet, driving 1¼-inch drywall screws through the drywall into the joists. Drive the screws at 16-inch intervals into the joists. Push the sheet firmly along each joist to make sure it is embedded in the adhesive.

INSTALLING DRYWALL
Hanging drywall on walls

1 **MEASURE THE WALL** and cut the sheet so it's about ¼ inch shorter than the opening. Have someone help you position the sheet tight against the ceiling, and begin driving 1¼-inch screws in the middle of the panel at a convenient height.

2 **ONCE THE FIRST SCREWS ARE IN PLACE,** put in the rest, working your way from the center of the panel toward the outside. Drive the screws 16 inches apart into all of the studs.

3 **THERE SHOULD BE A SLIGHT GAP BETWEEN THE FLOOR AND THE DRYWALL SO THAT THE DRYWALL WON'T JAM AGAINST BUMPS IN THE FLOOR.** Baseboard will cover it later. If necessary, trim the sheet to leave about a ½-inch gap. Position the lower sheet of drywall by slipping a panel lifter under the bottom edge and stepping on the lifter, then screw the panel in place.

4 **A LONGER WALL MAY NEED MORE THAN ONE SHEET OF DRYWALL.** Start by hanging a full sheet as before. Tack it in place, and then drive screws every 16 inches into the studs.

Outlet options

The high-tech way to cut out for an outlet is to use a drywall router. The low-tech way is to use lipstick. If using a router, first note the height of the box, and draw marks on the floor to show where it is. Remove the wires, and then screw the drywall in place, covering the box and driving the screws just enough to keep the drywall in place. Find the inside edge of the box by plunging the router into the box and moving sideways. Guide the router counterclockwise to make the cutout. As far as the low-tech solution goes, rub the edges of the outlet box with lipstick, and then put the panel in place. Remove it, and cut along the lipstick marks on the back of the panel with a drywall saw.

IF THE SHEET COVERS A WINDOW THAT HAS YET TO BE INSTALLED, cover the window with drywall the same way you covered the outlet. Later, rout out the drywall and add drywall screws around the opening as necessary.

IF THE WINDOW IS ALREADY IN PLACE, TAKE OFF THE WINDOW TRIM AND CUT THE DRYWALL BEFORE YOU HANG IT. Lay out the cut by positioning the sheet along the floor and marking where it meets the edge of the windows. Measure from the ceiling to the window top to lay out the top of the cut.

5 **LAY OUT A DOOR CUT THE SAME WAY AS A WINDOW.** Remove the trim, lean the piece against the opening, mark the location of the studs, and draw a line for the top of the door opening. Make cuts for both doors and windows with a drywall saw, then screw the panels in place.

6 **CUT A PIECE OF DRYWALL TO FIT BETWEEN THE CORNER AND THE PIECE YOU JUST HUNG.** Cut it slightly undersized, leaving a ¼-inch gap in the corner. Screw the drywall in place. Where the panels meet, cut a V-groove with your utility knife (see inset); this will make hiding the joint easier when you're taping.

7 **BEGIN THE BOTTOM ROW WITH A SHORTER PIECE SO THAT THE SEAM IN THE TOP ROW WILL NOT BE DIRECTLY ABOVE THE SEAM IN THE BOTTOM ROW.** Position the piece, lift it with a panel lift, and screw it in place. When the small piece is in place, install the longer piece.

8 **WHEN FRAMING OUTSIDE CORNERS, CUT THE PIECE LONG SO THAT IT HANGS OVER THE CORNER.** Then trim it with a drywall router or saw after it's in place. Hang the abutting panel, leaving it long too, and trim it to create a tight, well-fitted corner.

9 **PROTECT THE CORNERS WITH METAL CORNER BEAD.** A bead that is a bit long will kink when you fasten it. To prevent this, cut the bead with tin snips, leaving it about ½ inch short. Hold the bead tight against the ceiling. Screws will distort the bead, so nail it in place, spacing the nails every 9 inches.

INSTALLING DRYWALL
Finishing drywall

SKILL SCALE

EASY	**MEDIUM**	HARD

REQUIRED SKILLS: Finishing walls will require average carpentry skills.

HOW LONG WILL IT TAKE?

Experienced . . . . 2 hrs.
Handy . . . . 3 hrs.
Novice . . . . 4 hrs.

VARIABLES: Time is based on finishing a 10-foot wall.

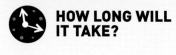

STUFF YOU'LL NEED

✔ **MATERIALS:**
Joint or drywall tape, joint compound, 200-grit sandpaper or sanding mesh

✔ **TOOLS:**
6-, 8-, and 10- or 12-inch drywall knives, pole sander

TOOL TIP

DRYWALL KNIVES
You put joint compound on in three coats, and you'll want a different knife for each. Get a 6-inch knife for the first coat, an 8-inch one for the second coat, and a 10- or 12-inch one for the final coat.

Before you start work, round over the corners of the knives with a file so they won't dig into the drywall. Specialty knives are made for inside and outside corners. Some people swear by them, some swear at them—but they're worth a look the next time you're browsing the drywall aisle.

Finishing drywall refers to taping and filling the seams between adjacent sheets. It's a three-coat process. The first coat, or bedding, is about 6 inches wide and holds a strip of paper or fiberglass tape over the seams. (The joint tape helps prevent cracks.) The second coat is about 8 inches wide and fills the imperfections of the first coat. The third is the smooth finish coat, about 12 inches wide. Allow each coat to dry overnight.

Inside corners, including those at the ceiling, are reinforced with the same tape you use on seams between sheets. Outside corners, because of the beating they get, are reinforced with a metal right angle called a bead.

The finish coat is either sanded or smoothed with a damp sponge. Use the sponge if you can. If you sand make sure you wear a dust mask.

BUYER'S GUIDE

DRYWALL TAPE
Drywall tape comes in two varieties: fiberglass mesh and thin paper. Fiberglass is self-stick, is easy to handle, and looks cool. Don't be seduced though.

Fiberglass mesh is designed for use with a strong, fast-drying compound that is mixed from a powder. Pros love it, but it's a bit tricky for homeowner use. Instead stick with a premixed joint compound that will give you plenty of time to work.

When used with a standard compound, fiberglass tape joints can crack at about half the stress it would take to crack a joint made with paper tape. If it does crack, you'll have to strip off everything, including the tape, and start from scratch.

APPLYING THE FIRST COAT

1 **COVER SCREW OR NAILHEADS WITH JOINT COMPOUND,** troweling it on with a 6-inch drywall knife. Add enough compound to fill the dimple left by the screw, and level the compound with the knife. If a screw missed the stud, it will eventually work its way out; so take it out now and fill the hole.

2 **PUT SOME DRYWALL COMPOUND ON THE 6-INCH KNIFE.** Starting at the top of the wall, rest one end of the blade on the raised part of the corner bead and the other end on one of the walls. Draw the knife along the wall toward the floor, applying compound to the corner. Repeat on the second wall.

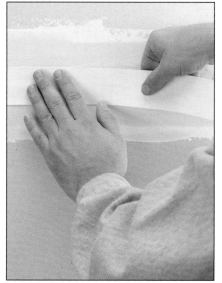

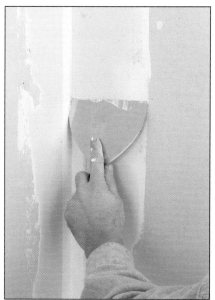

3 **WORKING WITH THE 6-INCH KNIFE, FILL THE TROUGH CREATED BY THE BEVELS WITH JOINT COMPOUND.** Pull the knife along the trough to create a smooth, continuous bed of compound.

4 **ONCE THE COMPOUND IS IN PLACE, COVER THE SEAM WITH A SINGLE PIECE OF TAPE.** (Multiple pieces are likely to slip and wrinkle when you embed the tape.) Push the tape into the compound every foot or so to hold it in place while you work.

5 **STARTING IN THE CENTER OF THE WALL, HOLD THE 6-INCH KNIFE SO THAT IT BRIDGES THE TAPE AND IS AT A SLIGHT ANGLE TO THE SEAM.** Draw it along the wall, applying enough pressure to embed the tape and also remove excess joint compound. Leave just enough compound under the tape edges to hold them in place—about $\frac{1}{32}$ inch. When you reach the corner, go back to the middle of the wall, and work toward the other corner.

APPLYING THE FIRST COAT IN CORNERS

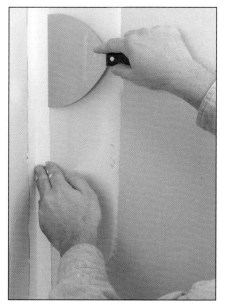

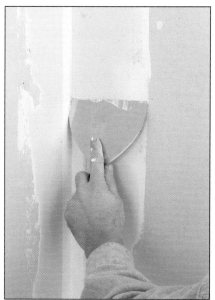

1 **APPLY A THIN LAYER OF JOINT COMPOUND** to both sides of the inside corner with the 6-inch knife.

2 **FOLD A STRIP OF DRYWALL PAPER TAPE IN HALF BY PINCHING THE STRIP** and pulling it between your thumb and forefinger. Position the end of the folded tape strip at the top of the corner joint. Press the tape into the wet compound about 12 inches.

3 **START AT THE TOP OF THE ROOM AND DRAW THE KNIFE ALONG ONE OF THE WALLS,** smoothing the tape. Repeat on the other wall. Move the knife a couple of inches away from the corner and pull from ceiling to floor, removing the excess compound left by the first pass.

Taping butt joints

Butt joints occur where the two narrow ends of a sheet meet. Unlike the long side, these ends aren't beveled to make taping easier. Open up the joints by cutting a 45-degree, ⅛-inch-deep bevel in the end of each panel with a utility knife. Fill the notch with compound, leaving a bed about ⅛ inch thick on the surface. Press the tape into the bed as you would with a tapered seam, and draw a knife along it to smooth the tape.

APPLYING THE SECOND COAT

1 LET THE FIRST COAT DRY THOROUGHLY. Apply a second coat of compound over the screws. Coat the outside corners and seams as before, using an 8-inch knife. Feather the edges so that they are about 2 inches wider than those of the first coat. Feather the edges of any butt seams so that they are about 4 inches beyond those of the first coat.

2 AT THIS POINT, FINISH THE INSIDE CORNERS ONE WALL AT A TIME. Apply a coat of compound on one wall, feathering it out 2 inches beyond the first coat. Let the compound dry, then repeat on the second wall.

APPLYING AND SMOOTHING THE THIRD COAT

1 APPLY A THIRD COAT (THINNED WITH WATER TO THE CONSISTENCY OF MAYONNAISE) TO THE SCREW HOLES, SEAMS, AND OUTSIDE CORNERS with a 12-inch knife, feathering the edges 2 inches beyond the second coat.

2 ONCE THE FINAL COAT HAS DRIED, SMOOTH OUT ANY IRREGULARITIES WITH A DAMP SPONGE. This works just as well as sanding—without creating dust.

Sanding high areas

Ceilings and some high areas may be easier to reach with a pole sander. Put 200-grit sanding mesh on the pad and run it back and forth along the seams. Sanding mesh is a piece of screen coated with abrasives; it won't clog when you sand with it.

Installing paneling

STUFF YOU'LL NEED

✔ MATERIALS:

Paneling, ringshank nails, construction adhesive, 4-mil vapor barrier, foam insulation, 1×3 furring strips, shims, masonry nails, ½-inch drywall screws

✔ TOOLS:

Hammer, saber saw with blade for plastic laminates, fine-tooth file, scribing compass, circular saw, chalk line, electronic stud finder, tape measure

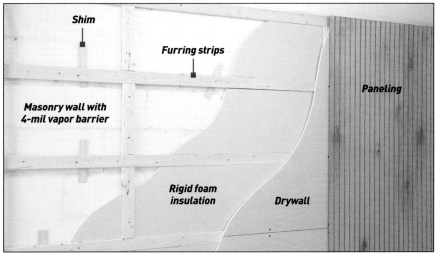

This cutaway view shows all the elements of a paneled basement wall.

(Labels: Shim, Furring strips, Paneling, Masonry wall with 4-mil vapor barrier, Rigid foam insulation, Drywall)

Outside of paint, 4×8 sheets of paneling are the quickest way to dress up a wall and a quick makeover for badly damaged drywall or plaster.

Panels expand and contract with changes in humidity. Give them time to come to the same moisture content as the room before you start nailing. Stack them on the floor with spacers in between. After 72 hours, the panels will have acclimated, and you can start nailing. As you unstack the panels, lean each against the spot on the wall where you think it will go. Reposition them as you go to get the most pleasing arrangement of grain and color.

Remove the baseboard before you start. Reapply it and add molding at the ceiling when you're done paneling.

YOU CAN PANEL MASONRY WALLS, including basements, but unless you want to void the warranty, you'll have to put up a 4-mil plastic vapor barrier and foam insulation. In order to meet fire code, you'll have to cover the foam with drywall—foam smokes heavily if it catches fire. Start by applying the vapor barrier and holding it in place with 1×3s nailed to the wall. Space the 1×3s so that your foam insulation fits snugly between them, and run them horizontally to bridge any dips in the wall.

Nail smaller vertical pieces to the wall to support the edge of the paneling. Shim as necessary to keep the 1×3s aligned.

Once everything is in place, cover it with ½-inch drywall in order to bring the wall up to fire code. Leave the joints alone—there's no need to apply tape and joint compound.

Double-check the rating of any paneling you're putting in a basement: Not all paneling is designed for use below grade.

Acclimate the panels for 72 hours before installation.

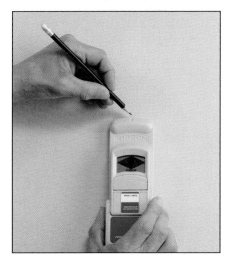

1 **FIND THE STUDS.** Studs are usually spaced 16 inches from center to center, so measure over from the corner to find the first one. Pinpoint its location with a stud finder or by driving nails through the wall until you hit something solid, then mark it. Measure over to find the next stud; pinpoint and mark it too. When you've found all the studs, snap vertical chalk lines along the center of each.

(Label: Scribe along wall if necessary)

2 **PUT THE FIRST PANEL AGAINST THE WALL IN THE CORNER.** Have a helper check with a level and help you hold the panel plumb. If any gaps greater than ¼ inch occur between the wall and panel, you'll have to cut the contour of the wall into the panel by scribing. (See Step 3, page 254.) Paneling on the adjacent wall will cover any smaller gaps.

Installing paneling (continued)

3 **TO SCRIBE A PANEL, SET A COMPASS TO A DISTANCE EQUAL TO THE LARGEST GAP.** Trace along the wall with the pointed end of the compass while drawing a line on the panel with the compass pencil.

4 **CUT ALONG THE LINE WITH A SABER SAW.** Most saber saw blades cut on the upstroke, which can splinter the panel, so use a blade designed for plastic laminates that cuts on the downstroke. Put the panel back on the wall to see how it fits. Use a fine-tooth file to make any minor adjustments.

5 **AFTER YOU'VE CUT THE SCRIBED LINE, CHECK THE FIT.** If the unscribed edge is not centered over a stud to allow for nailing, cut it to fit. Measure and mark the cut on the back of the panel to minimize splintering. Make the cut with a circular saw equipped with a fine-tooth panel-cutting blade and a straightedge. Allow for expansion by leaving a ¼-inch gap at both the ceiling and floor. You may have to cut the panel to allow for the gap.

TOOL TIP

CUTTING PANELS

To get a good, straight cut, guide the saw against a jig like the one shown. Make it by screwing a piece of 3-inch- or 4-inch-wide plywood, ¾ inch thick, to a wider piece. Before you trim the panel, trim the jig: Guide the saw against the narrow piece of plywood to cut off the wider piece. When you're ready to make the cut, align the cut edge of the jig with your layout line, clamp the jig to the panel, and make the cut.

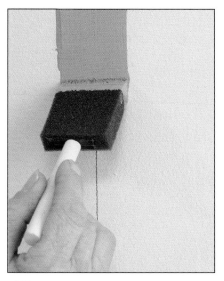

6 **PANELS EXPAND AND CONTRACT WITH CHANGES IN HUMIDITY.** To cover gaps that may appear, paint the wall behind the seam between panels with a strip of color that matches the grooves in the panel. To allow for expansion, use quarters on edge as spacers between panels when putting them up.

7 **PANELS MUST BE HELD IN PLACE BY BOTH NAILS AND CONSTRUCTION ADHESIVE.** Run adhesive in a zigzag pattern between the studs and around the perimeter on the back of the panels as well.

8 **PUT THE PANEL ON THE WALL AND DOUBLE-CHECK TO MAKE SURE IT'S PLUMB.** Nail it to the wall with 1½-inch paneling nails colored to match the paneling. Space the nails 6 inches apart along the panel edges. Space them 12 inches apart on the studs in between. Hang the remaining panels the same way, using quarters as spacers to create a gap between them.

Test on a scrap. If the panel splinters when cut, make the cuts from the back of the panel.

9 **WHEN YOU COME TO AN OUTLET, HOLD THE PANEL NEXT TO IT,** and mark the panel at the outlet box's upper and lower edge. Snap a line at each mark across the face of the board. Then measure the distance between the outlet and the last panel you installed. Measure this distance along each chalk line, and make a mark. Repeat for the other side of the outlet. Connect the marks to outline the outlet.

10 **TO CUT OUT FOR THE OUTLET, DRILL A ½-INCH-DIAMETER HOLE AT EACH CORNER OF THE OUTLINE.** Slip a plastic laminate blade mounted on a saber saw through one of the holes. Cut along the lines to remove the waste.

SAFETY ● ALERT

TURN THE POWER OFF!
Always turn off the power when working around electrical wires.

11 **TURN OFF THE POWER AND UNSCREW THE OUTLET FROM ITS BOX, BUT NOT FROM ITS WIRES.** Feed the outlet through the opening in the panel, and glue and nail the panel to the wall. Reattach the outlet. Before you tighten the screws, slip an extension ring over the outlet. Required by the fire code, this keeps the outlet flush with the paneling.

12 **AT DOORS AND WINDOWS TRIM THE PANEL SO THE SEAM IS MIDWAY OVER THE OPENING.** Then lay out the window cut the same way you laid out the outlet cuts. Make the cuts that begin at the edge of the panel first. Clamp the cutoff jig along the interior cut when you're done.

13 **SET THE BLADE TO CUT ABOUT ⅜ INCH DEEP.** Put the nose of the saw on the panel; hold the heel up so the blade clears the wood. Keep the side of the saw against the jig. Pull the guard back, start the saw, and gently lower the back onto the panel. Stop the cut ½ inch short of your earlier cut and finish by hand.

Tiling a wall

WALLS AND CEILINGS

SKILL SCALE

EASY	MEDIUM	HARD

REQUIRED SKILLS: Installing ceramic wall tiles requires intermediate carpentry skills.

HOW LONG WILL IT TAKE?

Experienced . . . . 8 hrs.
Handy . . . . 10 hrs.
Novice . . . . 14 hrs.

VARIABLES: The time is based on tiling a 10'×5' bathroom.

For information on installing a moisture barrier and backerboard see page 298.

Tile is what people see, but backerboard and thinset are what hold it up. Backerboard is sometimes called "mason's drywall". Depending on the manufacturer, it can be made of cement, fiber cement, gypsum, plywood, or plastic. Backerboard provides a sound substrate for setting tile and must be used as part of the installation procedure. Staple a plastic moisture barrier to the wall, screw the backerboard to the wall, and apply the tile over it.

Mortar for tile is called thinset. Mix it with a latex admix. Admixes make the thinset, stronger, and easier to work.

Grout is similar to thinset, but is used to fill the space between the tiles. A latex admix makes the grout watertight and thus more resistant to staining. If the tiles are less than ⅛ inch apart, use a sandless grout for a waterproof joint.

Grouted joints between the tub and floor or between adjacent walls will eventually crack, fill these joints with silicone caulk. The elasticity of the caulk will not only handle settling without cracking, it will prevent wall damage caused by moisture behind the tiles.

STUFF YOU'LL NEED

✔ **MATERIALS:**
Ceramic tile, thinset mortar, latex admix, wood spacers, plastic spacers, grout, grout sealant, silicone caulk

✔ **TOOLS:**
Combination square, tape measure, 4-foot level, tile cutter, rod saw, notched trowel, electric drill, mixing blade, tile-cutting bit, clamp, rubber grout float, plastic spacer remover, grout sponge, foam brush

You can't use tile-board panels in a shower even though they look like tile. Moisture will quickly destroy the panels.

❶ MAKE A TILE STICK TO SHOW THE SIZE AND SPACING OF THE TILES. Start by lining the tiles up on the floor, separated by commercially available plastic spacers the thickness of the grout line. With a square and pencil, mark a straight piece of wood showing the spacing between tiles.

❷ DRAW A REFERENCE LINE AROUND THE ROOM. In a bathroom, draw the line level with the top of the tub. In other rooms, draw a level line around the room that's halfway between the floor and ceiling. Draw a second horizontal line to lay out border tiles, if any. Also mark the location of recessed fixtures, such as soap dishes.

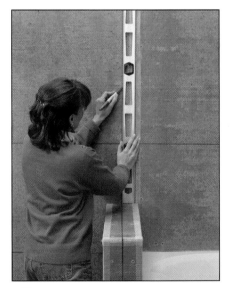

❸ IN A BATHROOM WITH A KNEE WALL, DRAW A LINE DOWN THE MIDDLE OF IT and transfer the line to the wall with a level. This vertical line will help center a grout line over the grout line in the knee wall.

Tile layout is always a compromise. This room is laid out so that there is a full tile immediately above the tub—something that wouldn't be the case if we had started with a full tile at the floor line. The room is also laid out so that the grout line that runs along the top of the knee wall aligns with the grout line on the wall.

As you'll see later, aligning the grout lines results in a very narrow tile in one corner of the room. It's a bit hard to put in, and some people don't like the look. If you're one of them, move the vertical reference line so that the width of the trimmed tiles is the same in the corners.

Likewise, if you want to put in cove tiles with an edge that curves to meet the floor, you'll start with a much lower horizontal reference line—one that marks the top edge of the cove tile.

In short, feel free to move your reference lines once you put them in. Move the vertical line left or right to control the size of the tiles that meet the wall. Move the horizontal line to control how the important element—be it tub, floor, or chair rail—meets the tile.

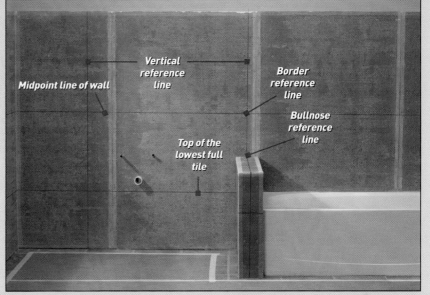

When you're finished drawing reference lines, the wall will look like this. The lowest horizontal line marks both the top of the tub and the bottom of a tile. The upper horizontal line marks the location of narrow border tiles that will run around the room. The vertical line marks the center of the knee wall and of a grout line on the wall.

4 **PUT THE TILE STICK AT THE INTERSECTION OF THE HORIZONTAL AND VERTICAL REFERENCE LINES.** Mark the horizontal line to show the edges of the tiles and the grout lines in between them.

5 **DRAW A VERTICAL LINE MARKING THE OUTSIDE EDGE OF THE LAST FULL TILE BEFORE THE CORNER.** Put the tile stick along it and mark the wall to show the location of the tiles and grout lines. When the time comes, you'll start tiling in this corner.

6 **MIX A BATCH OF MORTAR** following the manufacturer's instructions. If the mortar doesn't contain latex, stir in a separate latex additive sold in tile departments and tile stores. Latex strengthens the mortar and slows the drying rate, giving you more time to work.

Tiling a wall (continued)

7 **SPREAD MORTAR ON THE WALL FOR THE FULL TILE THAT WILL BE NEAREST TO BOTH THE CORNER AND THE FLOOR.** Spread the mortar with a notched trowel; the size and shape of the notch controls how much mortar gets on the wall. Be sure to follow the tile manufacturer's specifications.

8 **PUT A FULL TILE ON THE WALL** at the intersection of your reference lines.

9 **ONCE THE TILE IS IN PLACE, MEASURE THE GAP BELOW IT.** Subtract the width of a grout line from this measurement and use the combination square to mark a line on the face of a tile to get the right size.

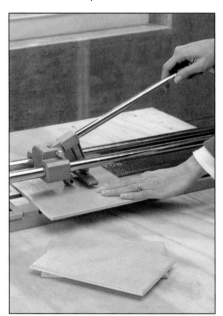

10 **TO CUT THE TILE, PLACE IT FACE UP IN A TILE CUTTER.** Align the cutting mark on the tile with the guide on the cutter. Put the cutting wheel down and pull the handle toward you, scoring the tile. Lift the cutting wheel, lower the pressing tee, and push the handle down sharply to snap the tile along the scored line.

11 **BACK-BUTTER TILES IN AREAS WHERE IT'S DIFFICULT TO APPLY MORTAR TO THE WALL.** Depending on the size of the space, it may be hard to put mortar in the area along the floor or near the corner. If so, apply mortar to the back of the tile, using the same notched trowel you used on the wall.

12 **PUT A TILE SPACER BETWEEN THE CUT TILE AND THE ONE ABOVE AND PUSH THE TILE INTO THE WALL.** (Mortar the wall first if you haven't back-buttered the tile.) Spacers are sold in tile departments and come in various widths. Make sure you get ones that match the width of the grout line recommended by the tile manufacturer.

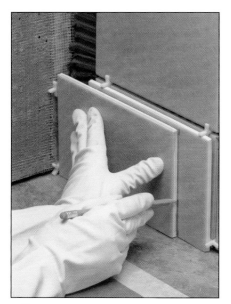

13 **TO LAY OUT CUTS ON CORNER TILES, PUT A TILE DIRECTLY OVER THE LAST FULL TILE INSTALLED.** Place another tile so the edge butts against spacers set against the wall. Trace along the edge of the top tile onto the middle tile to mark it for cutting. Cut the tile to size, and set it in the mortar.

14 **CONTINUE SETTING TILES, ALIGNING THEM WITH THE REFERENCE LINES** and using spacers to keep them the proper distance apart. See Step 15 to cut tile around pipe shown here (or other obstacles). See Step 16 for fitting obstacles at the edge of tile.

15 **CUT HOLES FOR OBSTACLES WITH AN ELECTRIC DRILL FITTED WITH A TILE-CUTTING TOOL.** Mark the center of the hole on the tile, then set the diameter of the cutter to the size of the hole. Clamp the tile to a piece of scrap wood on a flat surface and cut the hole, using slow speed on a variable-speed drill.

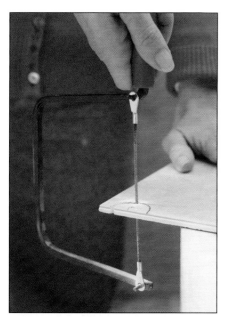

16 **MAKE NOTCHES AND CURVED CUTS IN TILE** by clamping the tile to a flat surface, then cutting it with a rod saw fitted with an abrasive blade designed for cutting tile.

17 **PUT THE TILE OVER THE OBSTRUCTION AS YOU WORK YOUR WAY ALONG THE WALL.** Make sure you keep the grout lines uniform so that this tile doesn't create problems for tiles you put in later.

18 **CUT TILES TO LEAVE SPACE FOR ACCESSORIES, SUCH AS SOAP DISHES, AS YOU'RE TILING.** Apply ⅛ inch of thinset mortar to the wall and to the back of the accessory. Set it into the space you left for it. Support it with masking tape until the mortar is dry. Grout the soap dish when you grout the tile joints.

Tiling a wall *(continued)*

⑲ INSTALL THE BORDER TILES WHEN YOU REACH THE LINES MARKING THEIR LOCATION. Border tiles dress up a wall and are no harder to install than regular tiles. Put the tiles in place with spacers between them and their neighbors. Follow the layout line carefully so that the border remains level.

⑳ INSTALL THE TRIM TILES, SUCH AS BULLNOSE EDGE TILES, at the upper edge of tile that stops before it reaches the ceiling. (Bullnose tiles have one or more edges rounded over for a finished look.) Tile going all the way up to the ceiling needs no trim. If necessary, trim regular tile to fit in the space above the last full tile.

㉑ TILE THE KNEE WALL WHEN YOU GET TO IT. Keep the grout lines aligned with those on the wall, and keep the tiles level. Tile the top and front edge with bullnose tiles that are only half as wide as the wall is thick. Start in the top front corner of the knee wall with a double bullnose, which has two edges rounded over. Install it first, and then trim a single bullnose to fit next to it.

Double bullnose

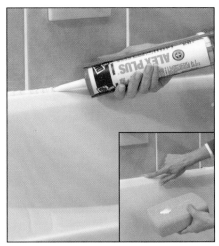

㉒ REMOVE PLASTIC SPACERS AND LET THE THINSET DRY. Mix enough grout to fill the joints. Working in 3-foot-square sections, apply grout in sweeping motions with a rubber grout float held at a 45-degree angle to the wall. Do not grout joints along the floor, the bathtub, or room corners.

㉓ ALLOW THE MANUFACTURER'S RECOMMENDED TIME FOR THE GROUT TO SET, then wipe joints with a barely damp grout sponge to remove most of the excess grout. Rinse the sponge frequently in clean water. Wait 2 hours, and sponge away remaining excess. After waiting the time specified by the manufacturer for the grout to fully dry, use a special applicator or small foam brush to apply a coating of silicone sealer to the joints to help prevent stains and mildew.

㉔ SQUEEZE A BEAD OF SILICONE CAULK INTO THE JOINT ABOVE THE TUB and all floor and corner joints to seal them against moisture. Run a wet finger along the wet caulk to create a smooth line of caulk. Once the caulk is dry, buff the tiles with a dry cloth.

Installing chair and picture rails

Chair and picture rails dress up a room and help define period and style. Originally used to protect plaster walls from damage, chair and picture rails also establish a border between two different wall treatments, such as a wallpapered lower section and a painted upper section. Chair rails also provide a transition between paneling below and paint or wallpaper above. (See Installing Beaded-Board Wainscoting, page 272.)

Even if a chair rail isn't intended to be functional, it should still be placed at a height that will protect the wall from damage from chair backs. Depending on the chairs in a room, the rail should be placed between 32 and 36 inches from the floor. Adjust the height as necessary to avoid awkward meetings with the bottom of window frames, as well as to suit rooms with ceilings that are unusually high or low.

Picture rails are usually installed from 10 to 16 inches below the ceiling line, depending on the height of the wall. Follow the same procedures for installing picture rails as you would for chair rails. Picture rails should be mounted securely to the wall whether they are intended to carry the weight of hanging objects or to be used as purely decorative elements.

Chair rails protect wallpaper and paint from damage done when the back of a chair slides against the wall. Picture rails can be used for hanging pictures or as a decorative detail.

You can apply any combination of paint and/or wallpaper you choose above and below the chair rail.

Installing picture rails

Picture rails protect walls as chair rails do. They allow pictures and other objects to be hung without hammering nails into the wall, and they add visual interest or historical pedigree to a room. Picture rails have a cove along the top edge to hold specialized hardware from which pairs of wires descend to support pictures. If the trim is purely decorative it can be nailed in place. If it will be used to hang pictures, however, screw it to the studs, countersink the screws, cover them with putty, and paint or stain to match the rail.

Installing chair and picture rails *(continued)*

1 **PRIME THE RAIL.** To prevent warping, paint, stain, or varnish both sides of the rail before installing it. If you plan to finish the trim after it is nailed on, apply a coat of finish to the back now.

2 **DRAW A LAYOUT LINE.** Determine the height of the rail. Mark the wall at that height, and use a level to extend a horizontal line for the top edge of the rail.

3 **MAKE MITER CUTS AT CORNERS.** Moldings with simple profiles can meet at 45-degree miter joints for both inside and outside corners. Complex moldings meet better at inside corners if joints are coped. (See Coping a Chair Rail, page 264.)

4 **MAKE SQUARE CUTS AT DOOR AND WINDOW CASINGS.** At doors and windows, end the molding with a square cut. If the molding is thicker than the casings, make a transition by cutting a bevel on the portion that protrudes. Along walls that can't be spanned with a single length of rail, scarf two or more pieces. (See "Work Smarter," page 266.)

5 **NAIL THE CHAIR RAIL.** Locate the studs with a stud finder or by tapping a nail through the wall where the holes will be concealed by the trim. Hold the chair rail in place and transfer the stud locations to the rail. Drill pilot holes at each mark and attach the molding with finishing nails. Countersink the nails, putty the holes, and smooth outside corners by sanding the exposed edges.

WORK SMARTER

WHAT YOU SEE IS WHAT YOU GET
When installing molding around a room, lay it out so that you start and end in the least conspicuous corner, such as above the entrance door. It will be easier to hide small errors.

GOOD IDEA

LEVEL ALL AROUND THE ROOM
Use your level to check that the layout line on one wall is level with the layout line on the abutting wall. Start a couple of feet from the corner and put one end of the level on the line. Put the other end of the level on the line on the other wall. It's OK that only the ends of the level touch the wall. If you get a level reading, the lines are level. If not, redraw one of the lines.

In most rooms, moldings go along the wall and end when they run into door or window trim. The termination looks neat and clean. But what do you do if there's no trim on the door or window? Or what if the molding is thicker than the trim it meets, leaving the end of the thicker molding partially exposed?

Sometimes you can solve the problem by rounding the end over with sandpaper or by slightly beveling the exposed end.

Professional carpenters, however, handle this situation by cutting what's called a molding return.

A return is a small mitered piece that allows the profile to turn (or return) back to the wall, much the way it wraps around an outside corner. This eliminates abrupt endings and exposed end grain.

1 **CUT A 45-DEGREE MITER ON THE MOLDING THAT RUNS ALONG THE WALL.** Cut it a bit short of the door or window. Nail the molding in place.

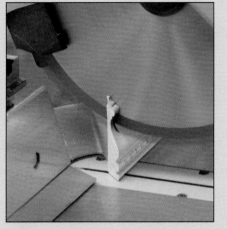

2 **CUT ANOTHER 45-DEGREE OUTSIDE MITER ON A SCRAP PIECE THAT WILL MATE WITH THE ONE ALREADY CUT.** When fit together, they will form a 90-degree angle. Make a square cut as shown above that frees just the mitered section of molding from the rest of the stock.

3 **DAB WHITE OR YELLOW GLUE ONTO THE MATING SURFACES AND PRESS THE PIECE INTO PLACE.** Do not use a nail. Hold it for a few seconds or wrap masking tape around it until the glue sets. Lightly sand as necessary to clean the joint.

TUNING UP A POWER MITER SAW

Having spent a few bucks on a miter saw, you may think it's ready to plug in and use. And it may be.

But it also may have spent a few weeks getting jostled during shipping. The saw that was perfectly aligned in the factory may now be slightly out of whack. If so, the problem is easy to fix, but do so before you begin your first project. Start by unplugging the saw and removing the guards so that you can get to the blade.

Put a speed square between the fence and the body of the saw blade. (Speed squares are the triangular ones that carpenters use and are more reliable than combination squares because they have no moving parts.) Turn the saw blade, or push the saw

down slightly, so that the square isn't resting against any saw teeth.

If you see a gap between the saw fence and the square anywhere along the length of the square, your saw is out of alignment and needs to be adjusted. The details vary from saw to saw, but it's usually a matter of adjusting a couple of screws. Check your owner's manual for exact directions.

If you have a compound miter saw, you'll also have to check the relationship between the saw blade and the saw bed: Is the saw cutting straight up and down? Put the square on the bed of the saw and slide it gently against the saw blade, turning the blade so the square doesn't hit any teeth. If any gaps exist between the saw and the square, you'll need to

adjust the stop that holds the saw in position. Follow the directions in your owner's manual. Once you've made any necessary adjustments, set the saw to 45 degrees and check against the sloping side of the square. Adjust the stops as necessary.

Coping a chair rail

SKILL SCALE

| EASY | MEDIUM | HARD |

REQUIRED SKILLS: Using miter and coping saws, measuring and fitting joints.

HOW LONG WILL IT TAKE?

Experienced . . . . .Variable
Handy . . . . .Variable
Novice . . . . .Variable

VARIABLES: The key to good coping is patience and refining the cuts until the joint fits cleanly.

STUFF YOU'LL NEED

✔ **MATERIALS:**
Chair rail, patching compound

✔ **TOOLS:**
Power miter box or miter box and miter saw, tape measure, pencil, clamps, coping saw and blades, round file, utility knife

Originally designed to protect plaster walls from damage, chair and picture rails give a room a colonial, Victorian or even a Mission look, depending on the molding you choose.

Whatever you select, the temptation when running molding around a room is to miter it. But if the room is out of square, if there is a buildup of drywall compound in the corners, or if the moldings are slightly different thicknesses, you'll get a gap that putty will only begin to fix. Worse yet, even a perfect joint will develop gaps when dry winter weather causes the wood to shrink.

Cope joints, in which you cut one joint to nest against the profile of another, are the only joints that will solve these kinds of problems.

No joint is perfect so carpenters install molding in a certain order for the easiest and best-looking job. Start on the wall opposite the door (1) and install a piece that's square at both ends. This presents the best (and easiest to cut) side of the joint to anyone entering the room. The molding on the second wall (2) is coped

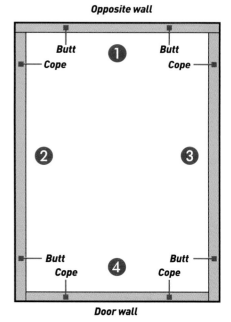

Opposite wall

Butt ❶ *Butt*
Cope *Cope*

❷ ❸

Butt ❹ *Butt*
Cope *Cope*

Door wall

where it meets the installed molding and square where it meets the other wall. The third wall (3) is treated the same way. The fourth wall (with the door) will have to be coped on both ends but it's the wall where tiny mistakes will be less noticeable.

❶ **CUT A MITER.** Start with a piece of molding a few inches longer than final length, and cut a miter in it as if you were mitering an inside corner.

❷ **FOLLOW THE OUTLINE WITH A COPING SAW.** The miter reveals a crisp profile of the molding. Cut along the profile, creating a socket that fits over the face of a similar piece of molding. Angle the saw as you cut, creating a gentle point that will be the only part of the joint to touch the neighboring molding.

❸ **CLEAN UP AND TEST THE CUT.** File the coped cut to clean up the profile. Check the joint by fitting it against a cutoff. Look for gaps, then sand and file high spots for a good fit. Once the fit is right, cut the molding to length by cutting the uncoped end square, and nail the molding in place. Proceed around the room in the order described above, cutting and coping as needed.

Creating custom moldings

EASY | **MEDIUM** | HARD

REQUIRED SKILLS: Using miter and coping saws, measuring and fitting joints.

HOW LONG WILL IT TAKE?

Experienced . . . . .Variable
Handy . . . . .Variable
Novice . . . . .Variable

VARIABLES: Size and complexity of installation will affect the time required.

STUFF YOU'LL NEED

✔ MATERIALS:

1×3 pine; twice room perimeter plus 8 feet, $^{11}/_{16}$×$2^5/_8$-inch chair rail (WM390), room perimeter plus 8 feet; $^{11}/_{16}$×$2^1/_2$-inch chair rail (WM298), room perimeter plus 8 feet; $1^{11}/_{16}$×$1^{11}/_{16}$-inch cove molding (WM100), twice room perimeter plus 16 feet; wood putty

✔ TOOLS:

Chalk line, 4-foot level, saw, hammer, #4, #6, and #8 finish nails, nail set, blue painter's masking tape, paint or stain, miter box or power miter saw, wood form

GO LONG

When you make a cut in a miter box, never try to cut right along the line on the first try. Make a cut that you know leaves the piece a bit long, and then edge the piece over to make another cut. Keep cutting and edging until the piece is the right length. If you want the piece to fit tightly between two walls, cut it $^1/_{32}$ to $^1/_{16}$ inch long, flex it into place, and nail it down.

Combining multiple chair rails can give your home a distinctive look.

While home centers and lumberyards carry what seem to be large selections of wood moldings, they usually have two or three choices with slight variations—mostly the same profiles in different widths. If it's variety you want, create custom molding by combining stock.

This chair rail is a combination of simple profiles. Each molding is identified by a number assigned by the Wood Moulding and Millwork Association. The upper rail, for example, is based on a $^{11}/_{16}$×$2^5/_8$-inch chair rail called WM390. The lower rail is built around WM298, a $^{11}/_{16}$×$2^1/_2$-inch chair rail. The rest of the stock is either 1×3 or cove molding.

If all this molding talk seems like a foreign language, ask an associate at your home center or lumberyard to take you on a tour of the molding and trim area.

You can combine molding creatively in lots of ways. Play with combinations in the molding aisle until you come up with something you like.

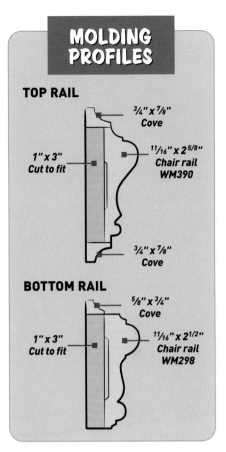

MOLDING PROFILES

TOP RAIL

$^3/_4$" x $^7/_8$" Cove

$^{11}/_{16}$" x $2^5/_8$" Chair rail WM390

1" x 3" Cut to fit

$^3/_4$" x $^7/_8$" Cove

BOTTOM RAIL

$^5/_8$" x $^3/_4$" Cove

1" x 3" Cut to fit

$^{11}/_{16}$" x $2^1/_2$" Chair rail WM298

1 MAKE A SAMPLE PROFILE.
Determine from the molding profiles above which molding you want to create. Sketch the molding and then make a full-size drawing to take to the store. Purchase samples—you may be able to buy 1-foot samples of the moldings—and use these to create short sample assemblies. Before you purchase the molding you need, hold a sample in place in the room to get a sense of the scale and fit.

Creating custom moldings *(continued)*

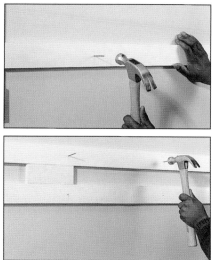

2 **DRAW A LAYOUT LINE ON THE WALL.** The base of the double chair rail molding is a pair of 1×3s. Determine the height of the chair rail; 30 to 40 inches from the floor is typical. Draw a level line where the bottom edge of the lower 1×3 will be.

3 **CUT THE LOWER 1×3 TO LENGTH.** Butt the 1×3s at the inside corners, and miter the outside corners. Nail the 1×3 to the wall with #6 or #8 finishing nails or fasten screws into the studs. Use a 1×3 spacer to position the second 1×3. Rest it on top of the piece nailed to the wall. Use the scrap as a spacer to keep the second 1×3 parallel to the first.

4 **NAIL ON THE ADDITIONAL MOLDINGS.** Before you nail the top trim in place, bevel the edges where the molding will fit window or door frames. This will provide a cleaner look. Nail moldings to the face and edges of the two 1×3s.

5 **MITER MOLDING AT INSIDE AND OUTSIDE CORNERS.** Use a miter box or power miter saw to cut all the inside and outside corners. Wherever possible miter the end of the first piece and nail it in place. Hold the second piece in place and mark it to meet the first piece. Miter at the mark and put the molding in place. It's faster and more reliable than measuring. Cut long, and trim it to fit. (See "Good Idea," page 265.)

6 **PRIME AND PAINT THE MOLDING.** Mask the wall at the top and bottom edges of the molding. Set all the nails and fill the holes with latex wood putty. Prime and paint the new molding. An alternative to painting in between the moldings is to run a strip of wallpaper that matches other decorative elements in the room.

A+ WORK SMARTER

SCARFING MOLDING TOGETHER

Although walls may be 12 feet long or more, moldings often come in shorter lengths. No problem. Just splice or scarf a shorter length onto the long one to complete the wall. Make a splice joint by mitering the end pieces and overlapping them. Be sure the splice will be over a stud. The angle is not crucial (although between 35 and 45 degrees is best). Cut the first piece, with the molding on one side of the box. Put the second molding against the other side of the box when you cut it. Overlap the first piece with the second piece to create a straight rail with no visible seam. Nail in place.

Installing crown molding

When joints are coped instead of mitered, you cut the profile of one molding into the end of another. The two nest together, creating the look of a miter without creating the problems miters cause.

WALLS AND CEILINGS

Designer Tip

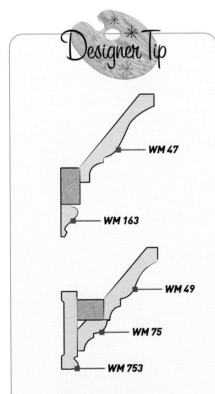

WM 47

WM 163

WM 49

WM 75

WM 753

BUILT-UP MOLDINGS
Crown moldings come in a few basic profiles, but you can create more than just a few basic styles. Combine moldings to achieve a fancier look. Typical solutions are shown here.

Like chair and picture rails, crown molding is coped rather than mitered together in the corners. The cope is a joint in which one molding is cut to nest against the profile of another. Coping overcomes out-of-square corners, wall irregularities, and problems caused by wood expansion. Because crown molding slopes from the wall to the ceiling, however, coping requires some fancy work at the miter saw. It's nothing so fancy that you can't do it, and once you've made the miter cut, the rest of it is no harder than coping baseboard or chair rail. (See Coping a Chair Rail, page 264.)

So far, no one has invented a nesting joint that works on outside corners, so the joint you'll use there is a good old-fashioned miter. It too is complicated by the slope of the molding but is simple to lay out and straightforward to cut. (See Mitering Outside Corners, page 270.)

To help visualize the cut, imagine that the base of the miter box is the ceiling and the fence of the box is the wall.

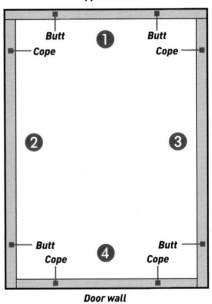

Opposite wall

Butt — Cope ... ❶ ... Butt — Cope

❷ ... ❸

Butt — Cope ... ❹ ... Butt — Cope

Door wall

❶ PLAN YOUR INSTALLATION. No joint is perfect so carpenters install molding in a certain order for the easiest and best-looking job. Start on the wall opposite the door (1) and install a piece that's square at both ends. This presents the best (and easiest to cut) side of the joint to anyone entering the room. The molding on the second wall (2) is coped where it meets the installed molding and square where it meets the other wall. The third wall (3) is treated the same way. The fourth wall (with the door) will have to be coped on both ends but it's the wall where tiny mistakes will be less noticeable.

Installing crown molding *(continued)*

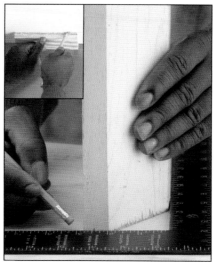

② MEASURE THE ROOM AND MARK THE STUD LOCATIONS. The molding will be nailed into the wall studs. Find them with a stud finder and make faint pencil marks high on the wall (where they won't be covered by molding) to guide the nailing.

③ PUT THE MOLDING AGAINST A FRAMING SQUARE TO SEE HOW IT MEETS THE WALL AND CEILING. Note the distance between the face of the molding and the corner of the square. Cut a scrap of lumber to the correct dimension and draw layout lines marking the distance on the wall and ceiling. (See inset.) When you install the molding, align it with the layout lines.

④ MEASURE THE WALL OPPOSITE THE DOOR, AND CUT A MOLDING TO THIS LENGTH. To prevent molding from splitting when you nail it in place, drill pilot holes the diameter of the finishing nails you'll use (see inset). Mark the locations of pilot holes by holding the molding in place and transferring the wall stud marks onto the molding.

NAILING MOLDING WHEN THE NAILS WON'T REACH THE CEILING JOISTS

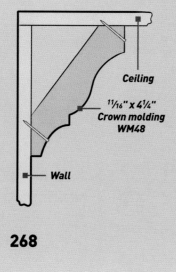

Ceiling

$^{11}/_{16}$" x 4¼"
Crown molding
WM48

Wall

On the two walls perpendicular to the ceiling joists, you'll nail the bottom edge of the molding into the studs, and the top edge into the ceiling joists. On the other two walls, there are plenty of studs, but the first ceiling joist is some 16 inches from the wall. Carpenters use one of two tricks to solve the problem. If they can, they'll predrill and drive a 16d nail at an angle to catch the framing at the top of the wall, as shown at left. If this doesn't work well enough, they'll cut infill blocks, such as the one shown at right. Nail the infills into the studs and into the plate at the top of the wall. When you install the molding, nail it to the infill.

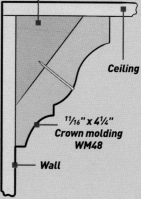

2" x 4" backing
cut at 38°

Ceiling

$^{11}/_{16}$" x 4¼"
Crown molding
WM48

Wall

268

5 **LAY OUT THE COPE JOINT.** Now that the first molding is in place, lay out the cope joint on a second molding. Start with a piece a few inches longer than finished length and flex it in place. At the end you'll cope, draw a line from the bottom of the molding up and away from the corner of the room at roughly a 45-degree angle. It's OK if the line isn't straight and if it isn't perfectly 45 degrees. This line is there to show you the general direction the saw will cut, not its precise path.

6 **SET UP THE SAW.** Put the molding on the miter saw so that the ceiling edge is flat on the bottom of the miter box. Lean the molding back so the edge that goes on the wall is tight against the fence. Turn the saw in the general direction of the line you drew in Step 1. (If the blade and line won't even come close to aligning, turn the molding upside down and try again.) Set the saw to cut at 45 degrees and cut a miter close to the end.

7 **CUT THE PROFILE.** When you look at the face of the molding, you'll see that the miter cut exposed the profile of the molding, outlined here in pencil. Cut along the profile with a coping saw to create a joint that will nest against a similar piece of molding. Tilt the coping saw back at a 45-degree angle to create a razor-thin edge where the two moldings will meet.

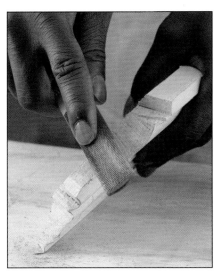

8 **TEST-FIT THE CUT.** Check the joint by fitting it against a cutoff. Be prepared for an imperfect fit. Even experienced carpenters fine-tune the joint.

9 **SAND AND FILE TO CREATE A TIGHT FIT.** Sand or file to remove high spots that keep the moldings from fitting properly. When the joint fits, measure the wall. Cut the molding ⅛ inch longer than measured by making a square cut on the uncoped end. Flex the molding in place—the extra length will help push the cope joint closed.

10 **NAIL THE MOLDING IN PLACE.** When the moldings fit together without any gaps, nail the molding to the wall and ceiling. If you're painting the molding, run a bead of caulk in the seam and wipe it smooth with a wet finger.

Mitering outside corners

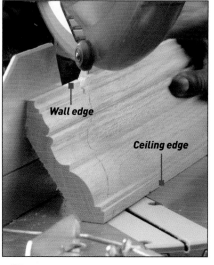

1 **LAY OUT THE JOINT.** Laying out an outside miter joint is much like laying out a cope joint. Start with a piece longer than needed. Hold it in place so that the extra length extends beyond the corner. Draw a line from the bottom of the molding up and away from the corner at about a 45-degree angle. The line shows you the general direction the saw should cut; it doesn't need to be straight or at a precise angle.

2 **PUT THE CEILING EDGE OF THE MOLDING ON THE SAW BED AND THE WALL EDGE ON THE FENCE.** Set the saw handle to 45 degrees in the direction indicated by the line. Position the cut so that the piece will be longer than needed, and make the cut. To cut the molding to length, set the saw to make a square cut. Measure and cut the piece to length by cutting the unmitered end square.

3 **REPEAT THE PROCESS ON THE OTHER PIECE OF MOLDING THAT FORMS THE CORNER.** Put the piece in place in the corner. Draw a layout line on the molding that starts at the bottom of the molding and travels away from the corner. Lean the molding back in the miter saw and cut a 45-degree angle in the direction of the layout line. Cut the other end square to cut the molding to length.

4 **NAIL THE MOLDING IN PLACE.** Test-fit the moldings first, trimming them to length by making a cut on the square end, if necessary. When the joint fits well, brush a little glue on the end grain of the mitered surfaces and nail the molding in place.

5 **DRIVE 4d FINISHING NAILS THROUGH THE TOP AND BOTTOM OF THE JOINT.** To help close any gaps in the joint, drill pilot holes, and drive a 4d nail perpendicular to one molding into the end of the other. Repeat on the other molding if necessary. If gaps persist, run the shaft of a screwdriver along the joint, forcing the fibers of the molding into the gap.

A+ WORK SMARTER

SCARF JOINTS
Where you need two or more strips of molding to span a wall, have them meet with an angled scarf joint. Mark the strips for 45-degree cuts that will position the joint over a stud. Make the cuts with a miter saw, leaning the piece against the fence the way you do when cutting a corner.

Installing no-miter/no-cope crown molding

When painted, polyurethane molding looks much like solid wood molding. Putting it up, however, is much easier. There are no finely fitted cope joints here. The corner is actually made from small blocks that screw in place. The outside edges of the blocks are square, and adjoining molding, which runs along the walls, butts against the corner blocks. The only cuts you'll have to make are simple square ones that cut the molding to length.

Unlike wood, polyurethane molding screws to the wall. Use trim-head screws, which are essentially drywall screws with a smaller head. The holes the screws leave are large enough to need filling. Use glazing putty by rolling some into a ball and packing it into the hole. Run your thumb along the molding and over the putty to create a patch that follows the shape of the molding.

While polyurethane won't take a stain, it paints nicely. The advantage of glazing putty is that you can paint over it almost immediately. See the manufacturer's directions on the back of the can for specifics.

STUFF YOU'LL NEED

✔ MATERIALS:
Inside and outside corners, straight moldings, latex adhesive caulk, trim-head screws, glazing putty

✔ TOOLS:
Electric drill, power miter saw or miter box, tape measure, pencil, framing square, caulking gun

1 **INSTALL THE INSIDE AND OUTSIDE CORNER BLOCKS.** Make sure they are square. Apply adhesive latex caulk. Align and screw blocks in place with trim-head screws.

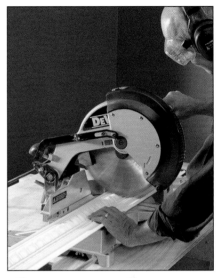

2 **CROSS-CUT THE MOLDING TO LENGTH.** Measure the distance between corner blocks. Mark the straight moldings across the face with a pencil and adjustable combination square. Cut the molding on a power miter saw or by hand in a miter box.

3 **INSTALL THE MOLDING.** Apply a bead of latex adhesive caulk to the edges of the molding that will contact the ceiling and wall. Once in place, snug it into position to equally contact the wall and ceiling. Then drive trim-head screws through the molding and into the wall studs and ceiling joists. Wipe away excess caulk. Fill gaps along the wall and ceiling with latex caulk. Fill the screw holes with glazing putty and paint the molding.

Designer Tip

INSTANT FORMALITY
Companies that make polyurethane molding also make rosettes that fit on the ceiling around light fixtures. They install quickly and create a formal-looking room. You'll want to screw the rosette to the ceiling joists, so position it on the ceiling before you install it, and trace around it in pencil. Using a stud finder, locate where the joists cross the pencil line and mark the position lightly. Put construction adhesive on the back of the rosette, put it in place, and drive trim-head screws into the joists.

Installing beaded-board wainscoting

SKILL SCALE

| EASY | MEDIUM | **HARD** |

REQUIRED SKILLS:
Intermediate carpentry skills, including using power tools, measuring, cutting, and attaching materials.

HOW LONG WILL IT TAKE?

Experienced ....Variable
Handy ....Variable
Novice ....Variable

VARIABLES: Installing wainscoting depends on the condition of the walls, the size of the room, and the type of beaded board you choose to put up. Finishing and drying times for paint or stain will also affect the time spent on installation.

STUFF YOU'LL NEED

✔ **MATERIALS:**
Tongue-and-groove beaded board, cap rail, baseboard (optional), varnish or paint, construction adhesive, #6 and #8 finishing nails, paintable caulk

✔ **TOOLS:**
Pry bar, 4-foot level, stud finder, miter box or power miter saw, saber saw, tape measure, pencil, notched trowel, hammer, caulking gun, hand plane (optional), nail set, rubber gloves, saber saw, combination square, paintbrush

Wainscoting provides an intimate, traditional feeling in dens, bedrooms, and bathrooms, as well as a somewhat formal look for dining rooms.

Installation is typically 32 to 36 inches off the floor, or roughly one-third of the room height. You can also create real drama in a dining room, as shown in this project, by reversing that proportion. Whichever proportion you choose, adjust the top edge to avoid running directly into windowsills or other trim in the room. Select wainscoting that is thinner than door and window casings to avoid building up the thickness of existing door and window trim.

The most common version is tongue-and-groove beaded board. The edges between boards have a ridge or bead. Wainscoting can also be built from a horizontal series of panels set in frames, similar to a row of traditional cabinet doors. There also may be a bead running down the center of each board so that a single board looks like a pair. Plywood wainscoting sheeting is a modern, easy-to-install alternative.

Designer Tip

PREFAB WAINSCOTING
Manufacturers offer easy alternatives to traditionally installed wainscoting. The wainscoting comes in prefabricated panels to which you will add baseboard and caps. The many options include the frame-and-panel style shown above as well as panels of beaded board. Check with your home center or search online.

Solid wood used as a wall surface is called wainscoting. Beaded-board wainscoting, like that shown here, is usually made of 2- or 3-inch-wide strips that are nailed and glued over the existing wall.

1 **PREFINISH ALL THE MATERIALS BEFORE YOU BEGIN THE INSTALLATION.** Remove the baseboard and outlet covers. If you are reusing the baseboard, carefully pry it from the wall. You may prefer to use new baseboards with a groove to hold the lower ends of the wainscoting boards. Install outlet box extension rings that allow you to bring the outlet to the wainscoting surface.

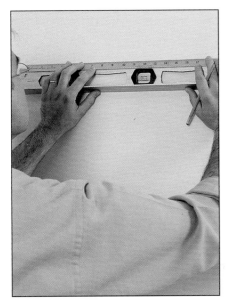

2 **DRAW A LINE FOR THE TOP EDGE OF THE WAINSCOTING.** Determine the height for the wainscoting, measure up from the floor, and with a level, extend a line around the room.

3 **LOCATE THE STUDS.** The top and the bottom of the wainscoting are held in place by a cap rail and a baseboard nailed into the studs. Locate the studs with a nail or stud finder and mark them both at floor level and just above the level line. (Don't drive nails near electrical outlets or switches.)

Installing baseboard

At this point you will either install the baseboard or the wainscoting. What you do depends on the wainscoting system and the baseboard material you're using.

● If the baseboard you use has a rabbet that houses the beaded boards, cut it to length and install it now. Nail it to the studs with #6 finishing nails and countersink the nailheads. When splicing two lengths of baseboard to span a wall, achieve an inconspicuous seam by overlapping them with a scarf joint, as shown on page 266 and 270.

● If the baseboard isn't rabbeted and it will be nailed on top of the wainscot boards, install the beaded board first, as described below.

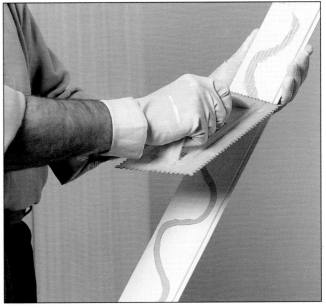

4 **CUT THE WAINSCOTING TO LENGTH.** Begin at either end of the wall, and measure to determine the length of the wainscot boards. If you have a rabbeted baseboard, measure from the bottom of the rabbet to the line marking the top of the wainscoting. If the baseboard will be attached after the wainscoting is installed, measure between the line and the floor. Don't cut everything all at once; the length of the boards may change as you move along because of uneven or unlevel floors.

5 **GLUE THE WAINSCOTING IN PLACE.** Butt the grooved end of a board into a corner and nail it in place. Run a wavy line of construction adhesive along the back of several boards. Spread the glue with a notched trowel as you slip the boards into place. Slide the tongues in the grooves, leaving a 1/16-inch space between the visible edges to allow for expansion in humid weather. Align the top edges with the level line; check the edge for plumb with a level. Press the boards with the heels of your hands to help bond the boards with the wall.

Installing beaded-board wainscoting *(continued)*

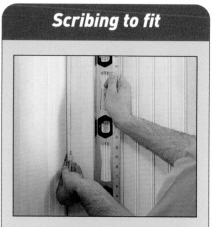

Scribing to fit

To scribe a board, hold it in the corner with its edge against the problem wall. Plumb the board with a level so that it is perfectly vertical. Lay out the cut with the help of a simple compass. Set the distance between pencil and point to the width of the gap. Run the metal point along the wall and the pencil along the board to lay out the cut. (Make sure the compass setting doesn't change while you do this.) Cut along the pencil line with a saber saw.

6 **ONCE YOU INSTALL THE BOARDS YOU'VE CUT TO LENGTH, MEASURE FOR THE NEXT TWO OR THREE BOARDS, AND CUT AND INSTALL THEM.** Whenever a board is over a stud, nail it in place. Hide the nail in the groove along the bead or drive it through the tongue if possible. Cut or plane as much of the last board as needed to make it fit. Install it by slipping it down from above.

7 **OUT-OF-PLUMB CORNERS.** Make adjustments several boards away. Measure between the last board and the corner at both the top and bottom of the wainscoting; divide the difference by the number of boards remaining to be installed. If the difference is within $1/16$ inch, install the remaining boards slightly out of plumb so the last one will be flush with the adjoining wall. If the gap is more than $1/16$ inch, scribe the last board to fit.

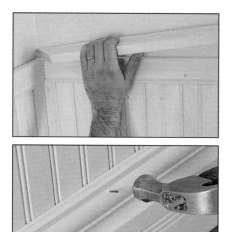

Cutting for outlets

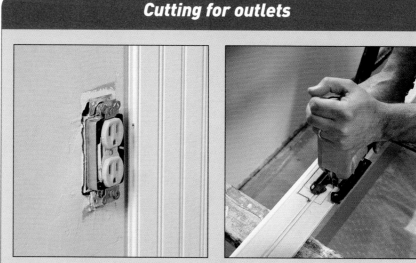

8 **INSTALL THE CAP RAIL AND BASEBOARD.** Nail the cap rail in place with #6 or #8 finishing nails. Miter inside and outside corners. If the rail is complex, cope inside corners. (See Coping a Chair Rail, page 264.) If the baseboards go on top of the beaded boards, nail them in place using #8 finishing nails. Countersink and fill all nail holes. If you paint the wainscoting, seal any gaps with paintable caulk.

To accommodate electrical outlets, cut rectangular notches in the beaded boards. Lay out the hole by rubbing lipstick or chalk onto the edges of the electrical box holding the outlet. Position the board on the wall and press it against the box. Put the board on a work surface and drill $1/2$-inch holes just inside each corner. Cut along the line with a saber saw to make the cut.

Hanging and arranging pictures

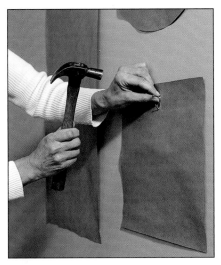

1 **GROUP THE PICTURES ON THE WALL.** Trace the outline of each frame on paper. Cut out the shapes, place masking tape loops on the backs, and experiment with grouping the pictures. For the security of anchoring heavy works and mirrors into wall studs, first locate the studs with a stud finder. To support especially large objects, drive hangers into adjacent studs.

If you're rehanging old pictures, check the screw eyes and picture wire before you put them back up on the wall.

2 **INSTALL EYES AND PICTURE-FRAME WIRE.** Screw eyes and braided wire are sold to handle different weights. To position the eyes, measure the height of the frame, and mark pilot holes one-third of the way down the frame. Drill a hole slightly smaller than the diameter of the threaded portion of the eye. Don't bore through the frame. Twist in the eyes. Determine the length of wire by measuring the picture width and adding 50 percent. Wrap each end around a screw eye and then around itself. The frame should not drop below the hanger.

3 **NAIL A HANGER TO THE WALL.** To determine the exact position for the hanger, poke a pencil point through the paper cutout at the spot where the picture wire will be when fully stretched by the picture weight. When you find the best location for the picture, tap a nail through the hole just enough to mark the wall. Select a picture hanger that will accommodate the weight. To help prevent plaster from chipping, apply a small cross of tape to the wall at the point where you are driving the nail.

Picture hanging hardware

In the hardware department you'll find a variety of picture hangers that will accommodate various weights. These common hangers work in almost every situation.

Ⓐ Traditional hangers have a nail that runs through the top, with a hook that acts as a hanger. They work in both drywall and plaster but may tend to chip plaster.

Hangers sold as **Ⓑ** "professional" picture hangers also work in plaster and drywall. They have a thin, sharp, hardened nail that is less likely to chip plaster. The nail is removable and reusable.

Ⓒ Wallboard anchors are large nylon screws that house metal screws. Drive the pointed end into the drywall with a hammer; then screw the anchor into the wall with a standard screwdriver. Drive in the metal screw and hang the picture.

Anchors are available with **Ⓓ** hooks to hang pictures and with special hooks to hang mirrors.

6 FLOORS

CHOOSING A FLOOR IS A BALANCING ACT. YOU BEGIN BY BALANCING WHAT YOU WANT WITH WHAT YOU NEED. Carpet, for example, a common choice for a living room or bedroom, quickly becomes dirty in high-traffic areas. Avoid carpet in the kitchen unless the kids are gone, cooking is at a minimum, and the thought of walking on hard ceramic floors makes your hips ache.

Next you balance the look of the floor against the appearance of the rest of the room. Is the floor the focal point? Think ceramic tile. Or should it disappear into the wallpaper? Think carpet. Do you want it to warm up a cool wall? (You're talking wood now.) Or is your goal to brighten up a plain room? (Think tile or sheet vinyl.)

Finally you're balancing what you want with what you can afford. Budget, of course, is a real factor. But so is location: Wood floors are a bad idea in a bath and impossible in the basement. Vinyl or ceramic tile may be perfect for a bath, and wood great for the family room. But if the floor beneath either is old vinyl, removing it may be an asbestos hazard. And how are you going to nail a wooden floor to the concrete in the garage-turned-family room?

Fortunately no act is impossible to balance. Take a look at "Real-World Situations" on the opposite page to see what goes where, and look at individual projects to see how to make the floor work in a given situation.

SECTION 6 PROJECTS

REAL-WORLD SITUATIONS

PUT THE RIGHT FLOOR IN THE RIGHT PLACE

If you install the right floor in the right place properly you will enjoy it for years. Check and double-check the manufacturer's instructions and recommendations before you begin. Following is a list of various types of floors and where you can install them.

- **Solid wood floors** can be installed above grade (ground level), but not below. The preferred subfloor is ¾-inch CD grade exterior (CDX) plywood. You can also use ¾-inch Oriented Strand Board (OSB) underlayment, ⅝-inch CDX, or tongue-and-groove subflooring.

- **Parquet floors** can be installed above grade, but not below. The preferred subfloors are ¾-inch CDX plywood or ¾-inch OSB. You can also apply parquet over ⅝-inch CDX or existing solid wood flooring.

- **Engineered wood** can be installed above or below grade. Recommendations on use in bathrooms varies by manufacturer. This cannot be installed on moist or damp floors. If it is applied over a crawlspace, there must be at least 24 inches between the bottom of the joists and the ground.

- **Laminate floors** can be installed above or below grade and over radiant heat. Recommendations on use in bathrooms varies by manufacturer. Laminate can go over almost any subfloor, including concrete slabs, ceramic tile, stone, vinyl sheet and tile, chipboard, particleboard, and terrazzo. If installed over a crawlspace, there must be at least 24 inches between the bottom of the joists and the ground.

- **Sheet vinyl** can be installed above or below grade over existing sheet vinyl, linoleum, tile, new plywood, concrete, ceramic tile, or marble. Do not apply over lauan. Some plywoods are made especially to be used as underlayments for vinyl.

- **Vinyl tile** is not recommended below grade. Install over smooth, single-layer vinyl floors that are firmly attached, dry concrete, and wood floors with a plywood overlay. Do not apply over lauan.

- **Ceramic and stone** can be installed above or below grade and over radiant heat. Suitable subfloors include cement backerboard, or concrete. They cannot be installed over moist or damp floors.

- **Carpeting** can go over almost any subfloor. If planning to use it below grade, make sure the carpet you have in mind is suitable.

Flooring materials

Flooring materials are available in a wide variety of colors, styles, sizes, types, and prices. Whether you choose ceramic floor tile, hardwood strips, vinyl tiles, carpeting, or sheet vinyl, each has many grades and costs.

Do your homework before you purchase your flooring. The real test of the cost-effectiveness of the flooring comes when the flooring is installed and used day after day. Inferior-quality flooring materials will become evident after a fairly short period of use; you'll just have to repeat the process—this time with a removal.

Professional flooring installers use a number of specialty tools, which will be introduced as they come up in various projects. You can use simpler and cheaper tools but for professional-grade results, use professional-grade tools. If this is the only time you'll ever need a pneumatic nailer, rent one instead of buying. But get one. If the pros have decided that tile cuts more cleanly and quickly with a power wet saw, trust them. While you're investing in the materials to put down a new floor, spend a few extra bucks to help yourself do it right.

COMMON FLOORING MATERIALS INCLUDE: Ⓐ adhesive-backed vinyl floor tiles, Ⓑ sheet vinyl, Ⓒ wide-plank flooring, Ⓓ parquet wood floor tiles, Ⓔ prefinished hardwood floor planks, Ⓕ unfinished hardwood flooring strips, Ⓖ prefinished hardwood flooring strips, Ⓗ carpeting, Ⓘ snap-together laminate flooring, Ⓙ bamboo flooring strips, Ⓚ ceramic tile, Ⓛ slate tile, Ⓜ marble tile, Ⓝ glue-together laminate flooring, and Ⓞ cork flooring.

Selecting the right materials

Material	Ceramic Tile	Carpeting	Vinyl Tiles	Sheet Vinyl	Parquet Tiles	Hardwood	Stone	Laminate
Installation	Labor-intensive	Somewhat difficult to handle and install	Easy to handle and install	Somewhat difficult to install	Relatively easy to handle and install	Relatively easy to handle and install	Labor-intensive	Relatively easy to handle and install
Durability	Extremely durable	Durability depends on grade	Fairly durable	Fairly durable	Fairly durable	Fairly durable	Extremely durable	Extremely durable
Water-Resistant	Yes	No	Yes	Yes	No	No	Yes	Yes
Cost	Moderate to high	Moderate to high	Low to moderate	Low to moderate	Moderate to high	Moderate to high	Moderate to high	Moderate to high
Maintenance	Easy; damp mop	Easy; vacuum, steam cleaning	Easy; use manufacturer's recommended products	Easy; use manufacturer's recommended products	Moderate to difficult; sweep and damp mop, refinish	Moderate; sweep and damp mop, refinish	Moderate to difficult; clean with damp mop; use sealer	Easy; sweep, damp mop

THE FLOORING TOOL KIT

Below are some basic flooring tools. For more information
see the Tool Glossary on page 544.

5-GALLON BUCKET

DRILL

FLOORING DRUM SANDER

NAIL PULLER

SABER SAW

TAPE MEASURE

CAULKING GUN

DRILL BITS

FLOORING EDGE SANDER

PAINTBRUSHES

SAFETY GLASSES

TROWELS

CHALK LINE

FILES

FLOORING VIBRATING SANDER

POWER MITER SAW

SCREWDRIVERS

UTILITY KNIFE

CIRCULAR SAW

FLAT PRY BAR

HAMMER AND NAIL SET

PUTTY KNIFE

SHOP VACUUM

WIDE-BLADE PUTTY KNIFE

COLD CHISEL

FLOOR NAILER

HANDSAW

ROTARY HAMMER

SLIDING T-BEVEL

WIRE BRUSH

COMPASS

FLOOR ROLLER

LAMB'S WOOL VARNISH APPLICATOR

ROUTER

STAPLER

WOOD CHISELS

COPING SAW

FLOOR SCRAPER

MIXING HOE

RUBBER MALLET

STRAIGHTEDGE

WOODEN GROUT FLOAT

FLOORS

Stopping squeaks

Floor squeaks are usually caused by the floor flexing. They could be floorboards rubbing against each other, bridging pieces rubbing against each other below the floor, or even water pipes or air ducts rubbing against floor joists.

Most often the root of the problem is a loose board, and the solution is a few well-placed ringshank nails or wood screws. When possible fix squeaks from underneath the floor or staircase. If the bottom of the floor or staircase is covered by a finished ceiling, work on squeaks from the topside. On hardwood floors drive finishing nails into the seams between planks to silence squeaking. Check pipe hangers, heating ducts, and bridging for rubbing and friction that can cause noise.

SQUEAKY FLOORS COVERED WITH LONGER-PILED CARPET CAN BE SILENCED by driving a nail or shooting drywall screw through the carpet and pad into the floor joist below. Drive the nail or screw head into the subfloor so that the carpet will lie flat.

HOMER'S HINDSIGHT

LAYING THE GROUNDWORK

We went next door to see the brand-new wood floor in my neighbor's living room. It was a beautiful thing, carefully installed, lovingly finished, in fact, it was perfect until you walked on it. The floor was a creaky, squeaky nightmare because they didn't make sure the subfloor was in good shape before they started. Took a lot of work to make it right. The subfloor would have been a lot easier to fix before the floor was down.

SHIMMING THE SUBFLOOR

IF FLOOR JOISTS ARE NOT TIGHT AGAINST THE SUBFLOOR IN THE AREA THAT IS SQUEAKING, shimming may solve the problem. Wedge shims in the gaps between the joist and subfloor and tap them into place. Don't drive the shims in any more than is needed to close the gap: Driving them further lifts the floor and causes more squeaking.

CLEATING THE SUBFLOOR

WHERE NEIGHBORING BOARDS ABOVE A JOIST ARE MOVING, A CLEAT IS MORE EFFECTIVE THAN SHIMMING THE BOARDS INDIVIDUALLY. A piece of 1×4, wedged against the subfloor and screwed or nailed to the joist and the flooring above, will keep the subfloor from moving.

FLOORS

REINFORCING JOISTS

SQUEAKING OVER A LARGE AREA MAY INDICATE THAT THE JOISTS BENEATH THE FLOOR ARE SHIFTING SLIGHTLY and providing inadequate support for the subfloor. Steel bridging, attached between joists, keeps the joists from moving side to side and stabilizes the subfloor.

DRIVING SCREWS

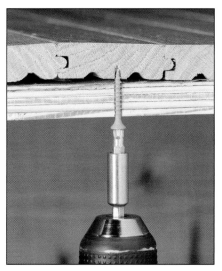

DRILL A PILOT HOLE THROUGH THE SUBFLOOR AND INTO THE FINISHED FLOOR. Have someone stand on the raised boards while you drive a deck screw through the subfloor to pull the loose boards down.

A TWO-BIT SOLUTION
If you're drilling pilot holes and driving screws with the same drill, changing back and forth between bits and drills can get old quickly. A multi-bit solves the problem. A magnetic socket that fits in your drill houses the screwdriver. The drills that come with the multi-bit also have an end that fits the socket. Changing from screwdriver to drill bit is a matter of popping one out and popping the other in.

Hardwoods are hard; that's why they last for years. That also means they're hard to nail through. Drill pilot holes to make the job easier.

FLOORS

SURFACE NAILING

NAIL DOWN FROM THE TOP WITH 16d FINISHING NAILS when you can't get access to the floor from below. Locate the floor joists and nail directly into them—nails will solve the problem only if they catch a joist.

ANCHOR STAIR TREADS BY DRIVING NAILS INTO THE RISERS AT OPPOSING ANGLES. If the stairs will be covered by carpet, use flooring nails. If not, use finishing nails. On hardwood treads, drill pilot holes for the finishing nails and then drive the nails into the risers. Drive the nails below the surface using a nail set, fill the holes with wood putty, then smooth even with the tread.

Patching concrete floors

FLOORS

SKILL SCALE

EASY	**MEDIUM**	HARD

REQUIRED SKILLS: Cleaning concrete and applying patches.

HOW LONG WILL IT TAKE?

Experienced . . . . 30 min.
Handy . . . . 45 min.
Novice . . . . 1 hr.

VARIABLES: Time involved depends on the nature and extent of the crack.

STUFF YOU'LL NEED

✔ MATERIALS:
Concrete cleaner, sand, crack sealer, repair caulk, vinyl concrete patch or sand mix, bonding adhesive for deep cracks, self-leveling floor compound for uneven floors

✔ TOOLS:
Wire brush, caulking gun, putty knife, hammer drill and bit, trowel, wooden float, paintbrush, bucket, wheelbarrow or mixing bin, mixing hoe, goggles and rubber gloves (optional)

WORK SMARTER

BIG CRACKS COULD MEAN BIG PROBLEMS

A big crack in a slab can mean that shifting and settling are going on below. Before you install a new floor over a big crack, find out what's causing it and make sure the shifting is no longer active, or the crack will reappear.

When a good floor goes bad, it can happen many ways. It can develop small cracks, large cracks, or pitting, or it can become uneven. The causes vary and usually have something to do with either the original mixture of concrete or a shifting surface below the concrete. But it's the size of the crack, not the cause, that determines the cure.

Fix small cracks with a crack sealer, usually a ready-mix material that trowels in place. It comes both in a caulklike form and as a liquid. Use the liquid on floors and pads and the caulk on walls.

Larger cracks require more work. Chisel away any weak spots and widen the bottom of the groove. Repair with a cement-and-sand mixture known as sand mix. (It's stronger than concrete, which also contains gravel.) Use sand mix to fill pitted surfaces too.

If the crack resulted from shifting of the material under it, the floor may also have shifted, leaving one part higher than another. If you're covering the floor with vinyl or laminate flooring, the floor will wear through at the crack. Start by using a self-leveling resurfacer, a mixture thin enough that it forms a smooth, level surface when you pour it on. This can be a lot of work, so find several helpers.

If the patching compound requires mixing, add a little water and mix compound with a garden hoe (or a mason's hoe, which has a couple of extra holes in it to help with the job). Add more water as needed.

REPAIRING SMALL CRACKS

❶ CLEAN OUT THE CRACK WITH A WIRE BRUSH to remove dirt and loose stones. Wash the crack with a concrete cleaner. Get a commercially available nonacid concrete cleaner made by the same company that makes your patching compound. It's more convenient and safer than the large bottles of muratic acid masons use.

❷ LET THE SURFACE DRY. If the crack is deep and it's in a floor, fill it partially with sand, leaving an opening about ¼ to ½ inch deep. Pour in the crack sealer until it forms a layer ¼ inch deep. Let it dry overnight and then apply another layer. Repeat until the surface is flush with the floor. Don't overfill—apply just enough patch material to bring the surface flush with the floor. If using caulk, smooth with a putty knife.

If you are using an acid-based cleaner, wear goggles and rubber gloves while you apply it.

FIXING LARGE CRACKS

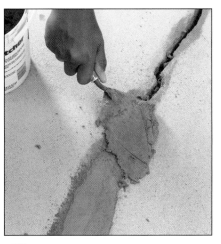

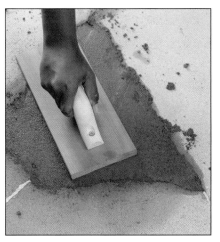

1 WITH A HAMMER DRILL, RESHAPE THE CRACK SO THE BOTTOM IS WIDER THAN THE TOP; this helps hold the patch in place. Chisel out any weak or crumbling spots too. If the crack is deeper than ½ inch, paint it with a bonding adhesive made by the company that manufactures the patch you're using. Let glue dry thoroughly before applying the patch.

2 ON CRACKS UP TO ABOUT ½ INCH DEEP, TROWEL IN A VINYL CONCRETE PATCH. Mix according to the directions on the bag or pail, and trowel a ¼-inch layer into the crack. If more layers are necessary, let the patch dry for several days before applying a new layer. Trowel the final layer flush with the surface and smooth.

3 ON DEEPER CRACKS, MIX SOME SAND MIX ACCORDING TO THE DIRECTIONS ON THE BAG. Trowel it into the crack, filling it flush with the surface. Initially, the patch on both deep and shallow cracks will have a watery sheen. When the sheen dries off, use a wooden float to smooth the surface and give it a texture that matches the rest of the concrete. If the existing concrete is very smooth, then smooth the surface with a metal finishing trowel.

LEVELING UNEVEN FLOORS

1 CLEAN THE ENTIRE FLOOR and patch any holes following the directions above. Nail a strip of wood across door openings to keep the patching material from pouring into the next room.

Be sure to work toward an exit when leveling an uneven floor.

2 MIX A THIN MIXTURE OF THE LEVELING COMPOUND and brush it on the floor as a primer. New concrete usually requires only one coat of primer; older concrete may require two coats. Follow the directions on the bag for both mixing and priming. Let the primer dry as specified by the manufacturer—usually for 1 to 2 hours.

3 MIX A THICKER CONSISTENCY OF COMPOUND, following the proportions on the bag. Starting in a corner on the narrow end of the room, pour the mixture on the floor. Pour the second batch next to it along the narrow wall. Repeat along the entire wall, and then work your way back across the room, pouring a new row of compound next to the old. Let the compound flow to level itself.

Measuring for flooring

To calculate the amount of material you'll need for a rectangular room: Multiply the length by the width, and add 10 percent. For example, a 10-foot-wide by 15-foot-long room will need 150 square feet of flooring material. Add 10 percent for waste to ensure you have enough material for the job. Some stores will take back unused material, but you may want to keep some extra for later repairs.

If the room has counters, protruding closets, or other obstructions, subtract the square footage they occupy from the overall footage of the room. Begin by taking the overall dimensions: Multiply the longest dimension of the room by the widest dimension. Then measure the length of each obstruction, and multiply it by its width. Subtract these amounts from the overall square footage of the room, add 10 percent for waste, and head for the store.

Note that adding a tile floor could add ¾ inch to 1 inch to the overall height of the floor. This may make it impossible to remove objects like dishwashers when the time comes. And whether you're putting in carpet, tile, wood, or vinyl, plan on having to trim the bottom of closet and room doors once the job is done.

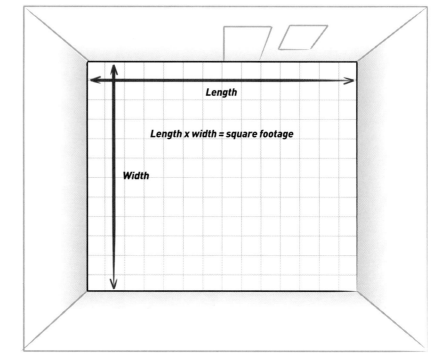

Length

Length x width = square footage

Width

IN A SQUARE OR RECTANGULAR ROOM, multiply the length by the width to get the total square footage. Add 10 percent for waste when you purchase the flooring.

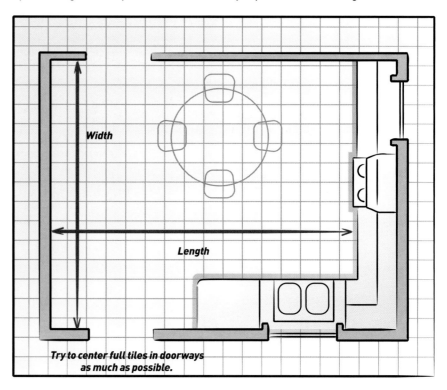

Width

Length

Try to center full tiles in doorways as much as possible.

MAKE A FLOOR PLAN. Draw the walls of the room as accurately as you can on a sheet of grid paper. Include doorways and floor obstructions such as cabinets and fixtures. Graph paper is available in ⅛-inch, ¼-inch, and ½-inch grid spacing.

REMOVING EXISTING FLOORING

SKILL SCALE

EASY	**MEDIUM**	HARD

REQUIRED SKILLS: Average carpentry skills will be necessary when removing existing flooring.

HOW LONG WILL IT TAKE?

Experienced .... 30 min.
Handy .... 45 min.
Novice .... 1 hr.

STUFF YOU'LL NEED

✔ **TOOLS:**

Pry bar, handsaw, utility knife, wide-blade putty knife, safety glasses, hammer, cold chisel, long-handled floor scraper, floor sander, circular saw, drill, bits, screwdriver

Before you install a new floor, you'll have to deal with the old one. In some cases, it's simple. Sheet vinyl can be installed right over old sheet vinyl unless the old vinyl is loose, more than one layer thick, or cushioned. New ceramic floors can go right on top of old ones. Products like laminated or engineered flooring often can go over the existing floor, no matter what material it is.

Old resilient floor coverings that are either cushioned or damaged are also straightforward: You must either remove them or cover them with a new layer of plywood underlayment. If the old flooring is embossed vinyl, you can either remove it or trowel on an embossing leveler, which fills the low spots in the surface.

Ceramic floor tile that is damaged or loose must be completely removed. It is easiest to break the tiles with a hammer and then pry up the pieces with a cold chisel and hammer. If the tile was set in

Sturdy pry bars make removing old flooring easier and quicker.

mortar, you'll also have to replace the subfloor. Cut the old subfloor into small sections with a circular saw. (You can count on ruining the blade and, depending on the size of the room, you may need several.) Remove the sections with a pry bar.

Sometimes it is easier to install new underlayment than it is to remove the existing flooring. Keep in mind that each layer of flooring and underlayment on a floor increases the height of the floor. Consequently, you'll have to undercut door jambs and door stops to make them fit properly. Also the kickboard on the cabinets will be shorter if the flooring and underlayment is installed around the cabinets. Your biggest problem may come in later years when you try to remove a built-in dishwasher. To remove the machine you'll have to lift the front edge, perhaps higher than the counter will allow, because of the now-higher floor.

HOMER'S HINDSIGHT

GIVE YOURSELF EXTRA TIME
My friend was jazzed to put down his new tile floor. "I've got pretty much the whole weekend to chip the old tile off the slab and lay the new ones," he said. "Might take a little longer than that," I warned him. He just laughed and said he was a fast worker. He started in with a hammer and cold chisel, then brought in his wife and two kids. After a weekend of the whole family chipping away by hand, he surrendered and rented a jackhammer to remove the remaining tiles.
I reassured him that installing the new floor would be a breeze compared to removing the old flooring. In the end they loved their new floor but they'll budget a little more time for the next project.

REMOVING EXISTING FLOORING
Preparing for removal

REMOVE THRESHOLDS BY PRYING THEM UP FROM THE FLOOR WITH A METAL PRY BAR. If the floor jambs were undercut to house the threshold, saw the threshold into two pieces and remove each piece separately. Since you're removing the old flooring you don't have to worry about the saw scarring the wood when you cut the threshold.

BASEBOARD OFTEN SITS ON TOP OF WOOD OR SHEET-VINYL FLOORS. If you need to remove the baseboard, pry it gently away from the wall with a flat pry bar. Protect the wall by putting a piece of wood between the bar and the wall.

Preparing for removal *(continued)*

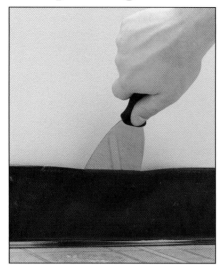

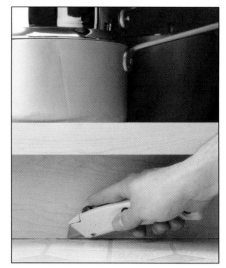

TO REMOVE COVE BASE FROM THE WALL, first run along the top with a utility knife to cut through any paint that may be holding it to the wall. Then loosen the cove base with a wide-blade putty knife and strip it away. Scrape the wall with the putty knife to remove any remaining adhesive.

CUT ALONG THE TOP OF WALL TILES WITH A UTILITY KNIFE. Pop each tile loose from the wall with a metal pry bar. If you are concerned about scratching or damaging your wall, place a scrap piece of wood behind the pry bar. Scrape the wall free of any remaining grout or adhesive.

REMOVE VINYL FLOORING AROUND CABINETS BY CUTTING WITH A SHARP UTILITY KNIFE along the base of the cabinets. If you have ceramic or hardwood flooring underneath the cabinets, you will probably have to remove the cabinets in order to pry up the flooring.

Removing carpet

Prying up carpet tacks

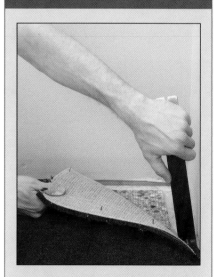

① TO REMOVE CARPET INSTALLED ON A TACKLESS STRIP, FIRST REMOVE ALL METAL EDGINGS, and the quarter round, if any, along the baseboard. Pry up the carpet corner and, working around the room, remove carpet from the strips along the walls. Then roll the carpet up and carry it out.

② THE PAD UNDER THE CARPET IS USUALLY STAPLED IN PLACE. To remove it, grab one end of the pad and pull on it as you cross the room. Roll up the padding and remove it. Check the floor for staples that didn't come up with the padding and remove them. If the padding is glued down, remove it with a long-handled floor scraper. Sand the floor smooth with a floor sander if necessary.

To remove carpet installed with carpet tacks, slide a flat pry bar under one edge of the carpet and pry up several tacks. Proceed until all tacks are removed.

Removing ceramic tile

1 PUT ON YOUR SAFETY GLASSES, AND CHIP OUT THE GROUT BETWEEN THE TILES WITH A HAMMER AND COLD CHISEL. Once you've removed the grout, continue using the hammer and chisel to break the tiles free.

2 OPTION A: FOR CERAMIC TILE SET IN MASTIC, use a long-handled floor scraper to scrape away tile fragments and any adhesive residue. Sand the floor smooth with a floor sander if necessary.

OPTION B: IF THE TILE WAS SET IN MORTAR, YOU WILL NOT BE ABLE TO SALVAGE THE SURFACE BELOW. Cut the old subfloor into small sections using a circular saw with an old carbide blade. Pry up the sections with a pry bar. If the tile was laid on underlayment, cut through the underlayment and mortar but not the subfloor.

Removing wood flooring

SAFETY ALERT

BETTER SAFE THAN SORRY
Wear safety glasses and hearing protection when running a saw.

1 BEFORE PRYING UP PLANK FLOORING, BORE OUT THE SCREW PLUGS—if any—and remove the screws that hold the floor in place.

2 SET THE BLADE ON YOUR CIRCULAR SAW TO CUT THROUGH THE FLOOR BUT NOT THE SUBFLOOR. In most cases this will be ¼ inch or ⅜ inch, but start with a shallow cut and adjust the blade until you just cut through the floor. When the setting is right, cut down the length of one of the floorboards.

3 PUT A PRY BAR IN THE SLOT LEFT BY THE SAW CUT AND PRY THE BOARD LOOSE. Put the bar under the next board and pry it free. Work your way across the floor, board by board. If the flooring has been glued down, drive a chisel under the board to break it free before prying it loose.

Removing wood flooring *(continued)*

SAFETY ● ALERT

ASBESTOS ALERT

Asbestos, which can cause cancer, can be found in linoleum, vinyl flooring, and mastics made before 1978. The long, thin fibers in asbestos were used to reinforce these materials. Enlarged under a microscope, however, the fibers resemble tiny swords. The shape of these fibers allows them to be breathed deep into the lungs, where they get trapped. Scar tissue develops around the fibers, causing irreversible damage that can lead to cancer. If you think your house has asbestos-

containing materials, don't panic. Undamaged (not cracked, gouged, etc.) asbestos is generally safe, and covering it usually eliminates the risk. (Engineered and laminate floors may be the perfect cover.)

If you decide the asbestos has to go, do not attempt to remove it yourself. Paint masks and standard respirators will not protect you from fibers, plus you're likely to track asbestos throughout the house, endangering your family too. Check with your state

department of environmental affairs or your local health department for advice. They can tell you how to find a certified professional to test the flooring material and do whatever needs to be done.

In the meantime, make sure you leave the material alone. Don't sand it, don't break any of it away, and don't cut it. Until you get a professional opinion on your old flooring's makeup, leaving it undisturbed is the safest thing you can do.

WORK SMARTER

LOOK BEFORE YOU LEAP

You have several options when removing old flooring. Analyze the condition of the existing flooring and determine the course of action. If the flooring is mildly worn or damaged, use an embossing leveler to smooth out the flooring surface to provide a stable base for the new flooring material. Remove the existing flooring if it is too badly damaged to resurface with the embossing leveler and is relatively easy to remove. If the surface is too rough for the leveler and too difficult to remove, cover the existing flooring material with new underlayment.

Choose the right underlayment for your job. Cement backerboard is best for ceramic tile, while plywood works well for carpet or wood.

UNDERLAYMENT OPTIONS

POUR EMBOSSING LEVELER OVER CLEAN EMBOSSED OR MILDLY ROUGH FLOORING. Then trowel the entire surface to smooth it out. Leveler must be applied on a clean floor. It won't work on all surfaces, so be sure to read the label. Hold the trowel at a 60-degree angle and use light pressure. After the leveler dries, sand or scrape away any ridges.

APPLY NEW UNDERLAYMENT OVER EXISTING FLOORING IF THE FLOORING MATERIAL IS TOO DIFFICULT TO REMOVE and too badly damaged for an embossing leveler. This raises the floor, so make sure that when replacement time comes you'll have enough clearance to remove appliances such as dishwashers from under the counter.

FLOORS

Replacing underlayment

Most manufacturers require a properly installed underlayment in order to honor warranties on their products. The most commonly approved underlayments for sheet vinyl and vinyl tiles are exterior plywood products grade BC or better, poplar or birch plywood with a fully sanded face and exterior glue, and lauan plywood, Type 1 (Exterior), grade BB or CC. The minimum thickness for underlayment is ¼ inch.

Before you install underlayment, nail down any loose subflooring with 6d ringshank nails. Set all nailheads below the flooring surface. Check the seams between boards or sheets of plywood on the subfloor. If a board is higher than its neighbor, sand with a flooring edge sander to create a smooth surface. Look for high spots and sand them too. Fill any low spots with liquid underlayment—a latex gap filler that you trowel on.

And if you don't do all this? Count on soft spots and squeaks. On vinyl, high edges will show through and will wear out the top flooring prematurely.

1 **IF YOU NEED TO REMOVE THE OLD UNDERLAYMENT, PRY THE EDGES LOOSE WITH A PRY BAR.** Underlayment is nailed in place every 6 inches and can be extremely stubborn. A 36-inch wrecking bar will give you extra leverage. In tough cases, you may want to pry with something longer, like an ice fisherman's spud.

2 **NAIL DOWN ANY LOOSE SUBFLOOR BOARDS WITH 6d RINGSHANK NAILS.** Replace warped, bowed, or damaged boards. If one edge of a board is higher than its neighbor, sand it flush with a flooring edge sander.

3 **MAKE SURE THE FINISHED HEIGHT OF THE NEW FLOOR WILL ALLOW ROOM FOR REPLACING APPLIANCES.** The countertop may need to be shimmed up, or the old flooring removed, to allow appliances to fit. Also remove any heating vents that will interfere with the floor. If necessary, relocate the vent, as described on page 531.

Replacing underlayment *(continued)*

FLOORS

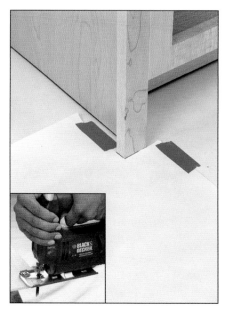

4 **REMOVE THE BASE MOLDING, THEN UNDERCUT THE BOTTOM EDGES OF DOOR CASINGS** to make room for the new underlayment and flooring. Use a piece of flooring and underlayment as a spacing guide. Rest a handsaw on the guide, and trim the casings. Use the same tile on each jamb as the saw may scratch the tile. If you have a lot of jambs, consider renting a power jamb saw.

5 **INSPECT THE SUBFLOOR FOR LOW SPOTS.** Fill any low areas with ready-mix latex underlayment. Trowel it on, let it dry, then sand it smooth with 80- or 100-grit sandpaper. Wrap the paper around a scrap of 2×4 when sanding to help ensure a flat surface.

6 **MAKE A CARDBOARD OR PAPER TEMPLATE FOR IRREGULAR EDGES,** then trace the template outline onto the underlayment. Cut the underlayment to fit, using a circular saw for long, straight cuts and a jigsaw for irregular-shaped cuts. (See inset.)

7 **PUT ON YOUR SAFETY GLASSES** and begin installation along the longest wall.

8 **DRIVE 6d RINGSHANK NAILS ON A 6-INCH GRID ALONG THE ENTIRE FACE OF THE PLYWOOD** and every 3 inches around the perimeter of the floor. Leave ⅛ inch between the underlayment sheets for expansion caused by changes in the temperature and humidity.

9 **COVER THE REMAINING AREAS, STAGGERING THE PLYWOOD SEAMS.** Fill the seams and any other irregularities in the subfloor with ready-mix latex underlayment. (Any irregularities will be visible through the finished floor.) Let it dry, then sand it smooth. Clean the surface thoroughly to remove debris and dust before installing the flooring material.

INSTALLING SHEET VINYL

Making a flooring template

Sheet vinyl is manufactured in 6- or 12-foot widths. Large areas may require that pieces of flooring be joined together. If you have to use two pieces of vinyl flooring, try to put the seams in inconspicuous areas.

To eliminate cutting errors, create a template of your room with heavy paper or with a template kit offered by some flooring manufacturers. A template allows you to trace an accurate outline of your room onto the new flooring. You'll need to find a large, level area to lay the flooring completely flat to transfer the template markings. Sweep it well before you put your vinyl on it.

Some vinyls require a slightly different installation than the one described here. Follow the manufacturer's directions closely.

1 **REMOVE THE QUARTER-ROUND MOLDING THAT RUNS ALONG THE BASEBOARD.** Remove doors. Undercut the door trim by cutting into it while the saw rests on a scrap piece of flooring.

2 **YOU CAN INSTALL VINYL OVER OLD VINYL FLOORING, PLYWOOD, CERAMIC FLOORS, OR CONCRETE.** Make sure old vinyl is firmly attached and wax-free. Fill embossed patterns with embossing leveler. For plywood nail down loose boards, then fill gaps and knotholes. Patch and fill concrete or ceramic to create a smooth surface. Prime the floor as directed by the manufacturer.

Making a flooring template *(continued)*

3 **MAKE A PATTERN FROM SHEETS OF HEAVY BUTCHER'S PAPER.**
Place the paper's edges against walls. (Some flooring requires a ¼-inch gap between the vinyl and the wall; follow the manufacturer's directions.) Cut triangles in the paper with a utility knife. Tape the template to the floor through the holes.

4 **WORK YOUR WAY AROUND THE ROOM, TAPING THE PAPER IN PLACE AS YOU GO.** At corners, overlap adjoining sheets of paper by 2 inches and tape them together. Continue taping pieces around obstacles that you couldn't remove. Mark the seams, as shown, so you can put the pieces back together if they come apart.

5 **TO FIT THE TEMPLATE AROUND PIPES, TAPE SHEETS OF PAPER ON EACH SIDE OF THE PIPE.** Measure the distance from the wall to the center of the pipe, using a framing square or combination square.

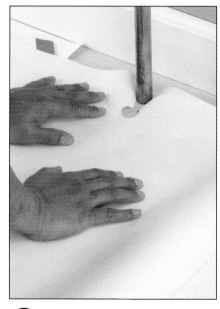

6 **TRANSFER THE MEASUREMENT TO A SEPARATE PIECE OF PAPER.**
Use a compass to draw the pipe diameter onto the paper and cut a hole with scissors or a utility knife. Cut a slit from the edge of the paper to the hole.

7 **FIT THE HOLE CUTOUT AROUND THE PIPE.** Tape the hole template to adjoining sheets.

8 **WHEN YOU'VE FINISHED MAKING THE TEMPLATE,** roll or loosely fold it and set it aside until you've unrolled the sheet vinyl.

FLOORS

Cutting and installing sheet vinyl

1 **ONCE YOU CUT THE VINYL, YOU'LL NEED TO INSTALL IT WITHIN 3 OR 4 HOURS,** as directed by the manufacturer. If you wait longer, the vinyl will lose its flexibility. When you're ready, unroll the flooring on any large, flat, clean surface—even one in another room. As you unroll it, it will be pattern-side down. When you've unrolled the sheet, turn it pattern-side up for marking.

2 **POSITION THE PAPER TEMPLATE ON THE VINYL SHEET AND TAPE IT INTO PLACE.** Trace the outline of the template onto the flooring with a ballpoint pen.

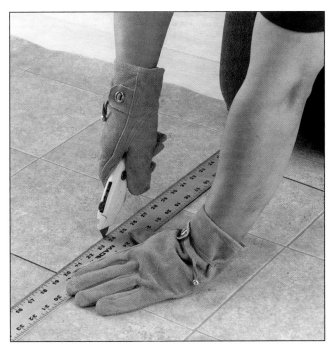

3 **REMOVE THE TEMPLATE.** Cut along the template marks using a sharp flooring knife guided by a straightedge. If you're working in the room the vinyl will go in, don't cut on the underlayment, as the scratches may show through. Cut on a piece of scrap instead.

4 **CUT HOLES FOR PIPES OR POSTS USING A FLOORING KNIFE.** Then cut a slit from the hole to the nearest edge of the vinyl. Make the cut on a piece of scrap underlayment to protect the surface below.

Cutting and installing sheet vinyl *(continued)*

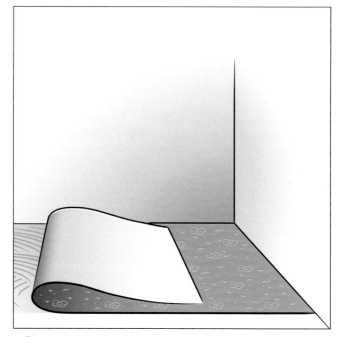

5 **IF YOU CUT THE VINYL SOMEWHERE OTHER THAN ITS FINAL LOCATION, ROLL IT UP LOOSELY AND TAKE THE ROLL TO THE ROOM IT WILL BE IN.** Be careful not to fold the flooring. Unroll and position the vinyl carefully. Slide the edges beneath the undercut door casings.

6 **FOLD THE MATERIAL BACK HALFWAY ACROSS THE ROOM.** Make sure the subfloor is clean, then apply adhesive with a notched trowel. The size of the notch depends both on the manufacturer and the application; follow manufacturer's directions carefully. Let the adhesive dry for 10 to 20 minutes. Then fold the floor down over it. Fold back the other half of the vinyl and repeat the process.

7 **FOR A FIRM BOND, ROLL THE VINYL WITH A HAND ROLLER OR AN OLD ROLLING PIN.** Start in the middle of the floor and work your way to the edges.

WORK SMARTER

MIXING BRANDS

Resilient flooring adhesive and seam sealer are made for specific types of flooring; adhesives are also made for specific types of subfloor. Read carefully the specifications that come with your flooring to make sure you're getting the right adhesive. Then double-check with the dealer just to make sure.

Not all flooring materials and supplies are compatible. Stick with the same manufacturer for flooring material, adhesive, seam sealer, and cleanup solution. You will have an easier time and it will protect your warranty. Also, you should have a floor covering that will stay where you put it.

GOOD IDEA

SEAM SEALER

If your floor requires a seam, be sure to use a seam sealer. It joins the two sheets into one, making the flooring stronger. Sealer comes in a package with a cleaner, an applicator, and two small bottles that you mix together to form the sealant. Start by cleaning the vinyl; then pour about half of each bottle into the applicator. Apply as directed. Leave any extra sealer that gets on the surface of the vinyl; it will wear away with use, leaving a level seam. Be sure to get a high-gloss sealer for high-gloss floors, and a low-gloss sealer for low-gloss floors. Ask your dealer for help.

Laying vinyl floors with seams

1 **IF YOUR FLOOR IS LARGE ENOUGH TO REQUIRE A SEAM,** tape the pieces together before you apply the template. Align the sheets so they overlap by at least 2 inches and so the patterns match. Tape the sheets together.

2 **CUT THE SEAMS USING A STRAIGHTEDGE AS A GUIDE.** Choose a line in the pattern and put a straightedge against it. Hold the straightedge tightly against the flooring and cut along the pattern lines through both pieces of vinyl flooring.

3 **REMOVE BOTH PIECES OF SCRAP FLOORING.** The patterns on the two sheets now match.

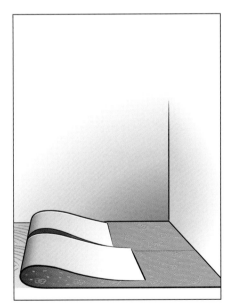

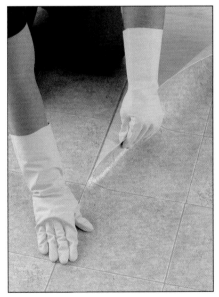

4 **PUT THE VINYL IN PLACE,** roll back one side, and draw a line on the floor showing where the seam is. Draw two guidelines, each 12 inches from the one marking the seam. Put the vinyl back in place, match the patterns, and tape across the seam.

Fold the vinyl back the same way you would with a one-piece floor, but make the fold perpendicular to the seam.

5 **APPLY ADHESIVE UP TO THE GUIDELINES,** and roll the vinyl back onto the floor. Fold back the second half of the vinyl and apply adhesive up to the guidelines. Put the vinyl in place and roll the floor with a heavy floor roller before you start work on the seam.

6 **FOLD BOTH PIECES OF VINYL BACK FROM THE SEAM.** Apply adhesive, then fold the vinyl back onto the floor. Roll with a hand roller and seal the seam.

Installing resilient vinyl tile

SKILL SCALE

EASY	MEDIUM	HARD

REQUIRED SKILLS: Average carpentry skills will be necessary when installing resilient vinyl tile.

HOW LONG WILL IT TAKE?

Experienced . . . . 4 hrs.
Handy . . . . 6 hrs.
Novice . . . . 8 hrs.

VARIABLES: Time is based on installing vinyl flooring in a 10'×15' room.

STUFF YOU'LL NEED

✔ MATERIALS:
Vinyl floor tile, floor tile adhesive, primer

✔ TOOLS:
Chalk line, paintbrush, floor roller, notched trowel, tape measure, framing square, flooring knife

R esilient vinyl tiles are relatively easy to install. Many have self-sticking adhesive backs, perfect for do-it-yourself projects. Others require flooring adhesive but can still be installed by the homeowner.

You can lay tile over dry concrete, underlayment, or sheet vinyl (but not vinyl tile). Tiles will eventually sag into any gaps below them, so fill all cracks as recommended by the manufacturer. If you're laying tile over an embossed tile floor, fill the embossing with embossing leveler. Make sure the floor is spotlessly clean and free of wax and oil first.

Resilient vinyl tiles don't require an expansion gap where the floor meets the wall. Mount them flush to the vertical surface or the tiles will eventually slide and separate from each other leaving an unsightly gap. If you have molding attached to the baseboard, remove it carefully before pulling up the old flooring so that you can replace it later.

Let the tiles adjust to the room temperature by placing them in the room to be floored at least 24 hours before installation.

Don't use adhesive with self-stick tile. It ruins the bond.

ESTABLISHING LAYOUT LINES

1 **PAINT THE FLOOR WITH A PRIMER MEANT FOR SELF-STICK TILE, IF YOU'RE USING THEM.** Then measure opposite sides of the room and mark the center of each wall. Snap a chalk line between the marks.

2 **MEASURE AND MARK THE CENTER OF THE CHALK LINE.** From this point, use a framing square to lay out a second line perpendicular to the first. Snap the new line across the room.

3 **CHECK FOR SQUARENESS USING A CARPENTER'S TRIANGLE, ALSO KNOWN AS A 3-4-5 TRIANGLE.** Measure and mark one layout line 3 feet from the center point, then measure and mark the perpendicular layout line 4 feet from the center point.

4 **MEASURE THE DISTANCE BETWEEN THE MARKS.** If the layout lines are perpendicular, the distance will be exactly 5 feet. Adjust the lines, if necessary, until they are square with each other.

FLOORS

INSTALLING VINYL TILE

1 **LAY OUT TILES ALONG THE LAYOUT LINES.** Check on opposite sides of the room to see if all the tiles against the wall will be the same size. If not, snap new layout lines so that they are. Double-check by laying the tiles along the new lines.

2 **BEGIN LAYING TILES WHERE THE LAYOUT LINES CROSS.** If the tiles have arrows on the back, make sure they all point the same direction. With self-stick tiles, remove the paper backing and apply the tiles to one quadrant of the floor. Lay the tiles in a stair-step pattern, as shown. Repeat for the remaining quadrants.

Using adhesive

If using tiles that need adhesive (rather than self-stick tiles), apply the adhesive recommended by the manufacturer with a notched trowel. Start with a section about 4×4 feet. When the adhesive is dry enough to touch without sticking to your hands, lay tiles in the same stair-step pattern used for self-stick tile.

3 **TRIM THE TILES THAT MEET THE WALLS.** Mark the cut so that the tile is flush to the wall or cabinet—don't leave an expansion gap. To cut a tile to size, place a cutoff against the wall. Place a loose tile **A** directly over the last full tile. Place another tile **B** against the wall or cabinet, over tile **A**. Mark as shown. Cut tile **A** with a flooring knife.

4 **AT OUTSIDE CORNERS, MARK THE TILE AS IN STEP 3, AND THEN USE A SQUARE TO DRAW A LINE AT THE MARK,** outlining the final shape of the tile. Cut with a flooring knife and a straightedge. At inside corners, mark as in Step 3, putting the loose tile first against one wall and then against the other.

5 **FORM A FIRM BOND BETWEEN THE TILE AND THE FLOOR BY ROLLING IT IN BOTH DIRECTIONS WITH A HAND ROLLER OR ROLLING PIN.** Then install baseboard, quarter-round molding, or both to cover the gap at the edge of the floor.

LAYING A TILE FLOOR

Tile is a layered floor. Underneath those fancy tiles that you so carefully chose is a dull gray base that carries all the weight. Without it, the floor would flex, the tiles would crack, and the grout between them would pop out.

The base is backerboard, a rigid panel that, depending on the manufacturer, is composed of cement, fiber cement, gypsum, plywood, or plastic that provides a sound substrate for setting tile. It sits in a thin coat of wet mortar and is screwed to the floor or wall underneath. It's sometimes referred to as "mason's drywall".

Some companies make a mastic that you can use to stick tiles to a plywood subfloor, but most tilers are against using it. When you're tiling, mortar over a recommended backerboard results in a far superior bond and a more rigid base. In short, the tiles stick better and won't crack.

Once the base is down, laying the tiles is a matter of spreading mortar and putting the tiles in place. The mortar is called "thinset" not because it's runny, but because you can use a thinner layer than with older products. Thinset mortar is plenty strong, so don't be tempted to use an epoxy mortar; epoxy is for pros who can work quickly and neatly.

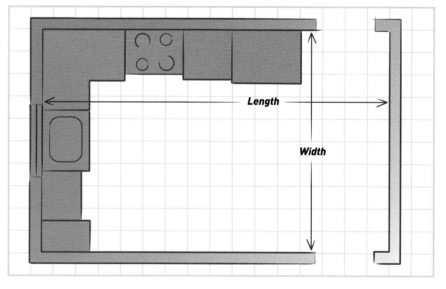

MAKE A FLOOR PLAN. Draw the walls of the room as accurately as you can on a sheet of grid paper. Include doorways and floor obstructions such as cabinets and fixtures. Grid paper is available with ⅛-inch grid spacing. For greatest accuracy, draw your plan as large as possible on the page. Mark dimensions and your scale.

Laying backerboard

1 CHECK TO SEE WHETHER THE FLOOR ON WHICH THE TILE WILL GO IS FLAT. To do this, put a straightedge on the floor, and look for gaps between it and the floor. Mark gaps on the floor; clean the area and paint it with a latex primer. Pour self-leveling mortar over the area (see inset), then feather the edges with a straightedge.

2 SNAP CHALK LINES ON THE FLOOR TO SHOW WHERE THE SHEETS OF BACKERBOARD WILL GO. Arrange the sheets so that the ends are staggered. If some sheets need to be cut to fit, lay out the cut on the backerboard. Score along the line with a carbide backerboard cutter guided by a straightedge. If recommended by the manufacturer, score both sides. Press down with your hand and knee on one side of the line, and lift the opposite edge to snap the panel.

WORK SMARTER

PRESETTING SCREWS MEANS FASTER DRIVING

Most of the time required to drive backerboard screws is taken up by fumbling in your work apron for the screws. Although the screws pull themselves into the panel once the threads engage, they have a hard time penetrating the rocklike surface. You will find it much faster to preset the screws by tapping them through the surface with a hammer. You can cut the time in half again by giving the presetting operation to a handy assistant.

3 A LAYER OF MORTAR UNDER THE BACKERBOARD HELPS TO KEEP THE BOARD FROM FLEXING and is an important part of the installation. Mix mortar according to the directions on the bag. Spread mortar on the floor where your first sheet of backerboard will go. Once it's spread, comb it out with the notched edge of the trowel, holding the trowel at about a 45-degree angle to the floor.

4 PUT THE FIRST SHEET OF BACKERBOARD IN PLACE AND SCREW IT DOWN with backerboard screws placed every 4 inches. (Use 1½-inch screws for ½-inch board and 1¼-inch screws for ¼-inch board. Do not screw directly into joists.) Spread mortar for the next sheet; put the sheet on edge against the previous sheet and pivot it down into the mortar. Leave a ⅛-inch gap between sheets, and screw each board as you go. At the corners, keep the screws 2 inches from the edge to avoid cracking it. (If directed by the manufacturer, use a screw gun with a clutch.)

5 LAY THE REST OF THE BACKERBOARD SHEETS. Fill the spaces between them with thinset mortar and a margin trowel. Reinforce by covering the gap with fiberglass tape, embedding it firmly in the wet thinset. Cover the tape with a second layer of thinset. Feather the edges with the trowel to create a flat surface.

Laying out the floor

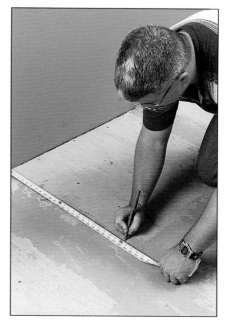

1 **MEASURE FROM BOTH ENDS OF THE LONGEST WALL OUT SEVERAL TILE SPACES** (allowing a ¼-inch gap at the wall) and mark with pencil.

2 **SNAP A CHALK LINE BETWEEN THE TWO POINTS JUST MARKED.** This line should represent the center of one of the tile joints.

3 **REPEAT STEP 1 FOR THE NEXT LONGEST ADJACENT WALL,** and snap a second chalk line. This line also will represent the center of a tile joint.

4 **CHECK THE ANGLE BY MARKING POINTS 3 FEET AND 4 FEET FROM THE INTERSECTION.** Measure the diagonal. If it is exactly 5 feet, your lines are squared. If not, repeat the first three steps.

Thanks, Pythagoras

The ancient Greek mathematician Pythagoras provided a useful rule of carpentry: A triangle with sides in the proportions 3-4-5 always forms a 90-degree angle. For larger triangles, use multiples of 3-4-5 (6-8-10, 9-12-15, etc.).

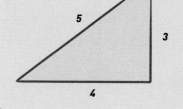

Before you snap chalk lines on the floor, shake the line to remove excess chalk. Too much chalk makes the line muddy and hard to follow.

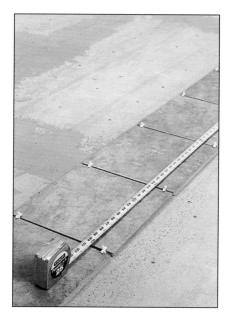

TEN TIMES MORE ACCURATE THAN MEASURING A SINGLE TILE AND SPACER IS MEASURING 10 TILES AND 10 SPACERS. Simply line up 10 in a row, measure the span, and divide by 10. See page 302 for spacer installation instructions.

LAYING A TILE FLOOR
Setting the tile

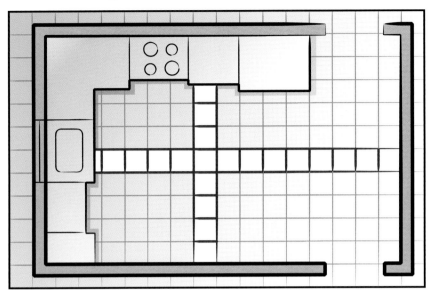

LAYING OUT THE TILES. Test-fit the tiles along the layout lines as shown above. The object is to make the most use of whole tiles and to cut as few as possible. Shift the layout lines as necessary to get maximum use of the tiles. Once you're satisfied with the look of the layout, you can begin installing the floor. (See Installing Resilient Vinyl Tile on page 296 for more information.)

1 **MIX THINSET MORTAR WITH A PADDLE** designed for mortar, not paint. Make sure the drill has enough power for the job, and mix at slow speed. Mix only what you can use before it hardens. Start by mixing enough to fill a 3½-quart bucket, then adjust the amount as you become more experienced.

Keep the mortar sticky. If the mortar doesn't stick to your fingers it won't stick to the tile. If the mortar on the tile is too dry, scrape it off and reapply.

2 **SPREAD ADHESIVE.** Press the mortar into the backerboard with the trowel at a shallow angle in order to make it fully adhere to the backerboard.

3 **COMB THE ADHESIVE OUT INTO STRAIGHT LINES, HOLDING THE TROWEL AT A 45-DEGREE ANGLE** to the floor and pushing the trowel teeth to the floor. Set the first tile in place, pressing it firmly into the mortar.

4 **LIFT THE FIRST TILE AND CHECK THE MORTAR ON ITS BACK.** Parallel rows show the bed isn't thick enough. Dry areas mean the mortar needs to be scraped and reapplied.

LAYING A TILE FLOOR
Setting the tile (continued)

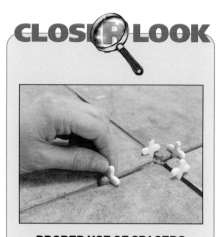

5 **SET REMAINING TILES BY BUTTING EDGE AGAINST EDGE,** hinging down, twisting slightly back and forth, placing spacers, and sliding into the final position.

6 **PLACE SPACERS ON END SO YOU CAN REMOVE THEM EASILY.** Although this requires more spacers, you can reuse them in another part of the project.

PROPER USE OF SPACERS
Spacers may be used flat, requiring only one per four-way intersection. However, removal requires use of a special tool and risks disturbing the set tile. It is better to place four spacers on end, as shown. Placed on end, the spacers are easily removed before grouting, allowing for a better grout seal.

LAYING A TILE FLOOR
Marking special cuts

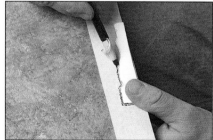

GAPS AT WALLS. Place the tile to be cut on the last tile set. Place a marker tile on top, against a spacer tile at the wall. Trace the edge of the marker tile onto the tile to be cut.
OUTSIDE CORNERS. Mark the first cutting line as above. To mark the second cut, mark the corner on the marker tile, allowing a ¼-inch gap.

AROUND PIPES. MARK THE WIDTH OF THE NOTCH ON THE EDGE OF THE TILE, with the tile to be notched lined up with the tile beneath and butted against the pipe.
MEASURE THE DEPTH OF THE NOTCH with a tape measure butted against a ¼-inch spacer held against the wall.

OTHER CONTOURS. Mark the outline of the cut on heavy paper stock or cardboard. Cut it out with scissors or a utility knife.
TRACE THE OUTLINE BY APPLYING MASKING TAPE TO THE EDGE OF THE TILE. Mark the outline with a grease pencil. Cut with a saw or nippers.

LAYING A TILE FLOOR
Cutting tile

USING A TILE CUTTER. Align the cutting wheel, raise the pressing bar, and then pull the wheel toward you with moderate pressure. Pull several times. Lift the cutting wheel, lower the pressing tee, and strike the handle to snap the tile.

USING A TILE CUTTING SAW. Adjust the fence (guide) so the cut mark lines up with the blade. Hold the tile with both hands; wear safety glasses. Advance the tile into the blade, guided by the fence. Avoid chipping the tile by cutting slowly.

CURVED CUTS WITH A NIPPER. Start at one end of the cut line, using one-quarter of the jaw to make the bite. Work from both ends toward the middle, taking small bits. **HOLE CUTS.** Mark the center of the hole on the tile. Break through the glaze with a center punch to keep the drill bit from wandering. Clamp the tile firmly to a table or workbench. Drill slowly and lightly to avoid breaking the tile.

LAYING A TILE FLOOR
Grouting tile

Do not damp cure tinted grout. Damp curing can dissolve the tint and leave an inconsistent color.

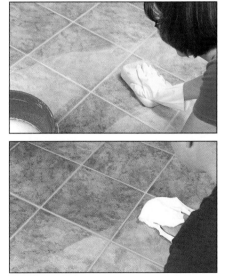

1 MIX THE GROUT PER THE MANUFACTURER'S INSTRUCTIONS. Spread grout in sweeping arcs with a rubber grout float held at a shallow angle. Press the grout into the joints, filling them completely. For joints wider than ⅜ inch, use a grout bag. **REMOVE THE EXCESS** with the grout float held at a steep angle. Sweep the float diagonally across the tiles to avoid dipping into the joints.

2 WIPE THE TILES WITH A DAMP SPONGE (wring dripless) to remove grout residue. If the residue resists, use a scrub pad, but avoid scrubbing the joints. **REMOVE THE HAZE** immediately; do not take a break. First wipe the haze with a damp cloth, then buff the tiles with a clean, dry cloth.

3 DAMP CURE THE GROUT by misting it twice a day for three days. Do not damp cure tinted grout, it will discolor. When grout is thoroughly dry, **APPLY TILE AND GROUT CLEANER** with a sponge, then scrub the surface with a stiff brush. Rinse thoroughly and let the floor dry before applying the penetrating sealer.

Installing parquet tile

SKILL SCALE

EASY	**MEDIUM**	HARD

REQUIRED SKILLS: Average carpentry skills will be required when installing parquet tile flooring.

HOW LONG WILL IT TAKE?

Experienced . . . . 4 hrs.
Handy . . . . 6 hrs.
Novice . . . . 8 hrs.

VARIABLES: Time is based on installing parquet tile flooring in a 10'×15' room.

STUFF YOU'LL NEED

✔ **MATERIALS:**

Parquet tile, adhesive, adhesive cleaner, plywood scrap

✔ **TOOLS:**

Tape measure, chalk line, notched trowel, saber saw, safety glasses, rubber or leather knee pads, rubber mallet, floor roller or rolling pin

Parquet tile is made of thin strips of solid wood glued together to make a pattern. Each tile is usually made of four smaller tiles glued together, measures 12"×12", and has a tongue on two sides and grooves on the others. Small strips of soft metal reinforce the tile, helping to keep it from breaking into smaller pieces. The metal is soft enough that you can safely cut through it with a saber saw, but not with a circular saw.

Because the tiles are wood, they expand and contract with changes in humidity. To allow for this movement, leave a ½-inch to ¾-inch gap between the tiles and the wall. Once the floor is in, install baseboard on top of it to hide the gap.

Be sure to follow the manufacturer's recommendations in caring for the floor.

1 REMOVE THE BASEBOARD, THE QUARTER-ROUND, OR BOTH, AND PREPARE THE SUBFLOOR AS NECESSARY. Undercut door trim by placing a saw on a parquet tile and cutting through the trim. When it comes time to install the tile, slip it under the trim.

2 TILE LAYOUT BEGINS AT THE CENTER OF THE ROOM. Find the center by measuring to the halfway point of opposing walls and snapping a chalk line between them. Measure and find the middle of the chalk line, and lay out a perpendicular line, using a square and the carpenter's triangle, as described on page 296.

3 TEST-FIT THE TILES ALONG THE LAYOUT LINES IN BOTH DIRECTIONS WITHOUT USING ADHESIVE. The tiles along the walls on opposite sides of the room should be the same width. If not, reposition the layout lines until the tiles are the same.

4 USE A NOTCHED TROWEL TO SPREAD ENOUGH FLOORING ADHESIVE FOR THE FIRST THREE TILES, following the manufacturer's directions. Take care not to cover the layout lines with adhesive.

The strips of wood bonded together to make parquet tiles are randomly colored and grained. This adds to the beauty and interest of the finished floor.

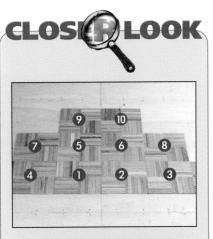

CLOSE R LOOK

LAY TILES IN A PYRAMID

Tiles can vary by as much as ³⁄₃₂ inch, making them hard to align. When you start laying them, place them in the pyramid pattern shown here. It helps solve the problem, because you fit most tiles into a corner made by their neighbors. They still won't align perfectly, but the variations won't throw you off. Once you've established the pyramid, work your way methodically along the outside edges until you've filled half the room. Then lay a pyramid to begin the other half of the room.

5 **LAY THE TILES IN A PYRAMID.** If you need to kneel on freshly laid tiles, put a piece of plywood over them to keep them from shifting. Sometimes the color in one of the strips that makes up the tiles contrasts sharply with the other tiles. Some installers like the look; others don't. Make your choice. Finish the first half of the room, then lay the second half of the floor.

6 **SET AND LEVEL THE TILES BY TAPPING THEM INTO THE ADHESIVE WITH A RUBBER MALLET.** Wipe up adhesive that seeps between the joints, using a solvent recommended by the flooring adhesive manufacturer.

7 **MARK THE BORDER TILES FOR CUTTING.** To allow for tile expansion, leave a ½-inch gap at the walls. Lay out the cut by placing a ½-inch spacer against the wall. Put a loose tile **A** directly over the last full tile. Place a tile or half tile **B** against the spacer and over tile **A**. Mark tile **A** as shown. Cut along the line with a saber saw. (If you used a circular saw the wires in the tile would get caught and ruin the cut.)

8 **AT OUTSIDE CORNERS, MARK THE TILE AS IN STEP 7.** Then slide the tile against the wall to mark the second cut. Use a square to draw a line at the mark, outlining the final shape of the tile. Mark the same way at inside corners, putting the loose tile first against one wall, then the other.

9 **SOME MASTICS REQUIRE YOU TO BED THE FLOORING IN THE ADHESIVE;** others do not. Follow the manufacturer's directions for the specific product you are using. Allow the recommended drying time before walking on the floor.

When you move appliances, slide them on sheets of fiberboard to protect the floor.

FLOORS

Sanding and refinishing a floor

Keep the sander in motion to avoid gouging the floor.

FLOORS

Hardwood floors typically last for the life of a home, but eventually they will need refurbishing or refinishing.

REFINISHING. If the floors are simply dirty from years of use but aren't worn through to bare wood, you can probably clean them with household detergent and elbow grease, or you can rent a floor-buffing machine with an abrasive pad. Remove all the dirt and wax from the floor but not the finish itself, then apply a new finish coat.

REFURBISHING. If your floors are deeply stained, discolored, or damaged, you can often sand them back to their original state. Solid-wood-strip floors can be sanded and refinished several times. Some wood-strip floors, however, are made from laminated wood products and can be sanded only once and with great care. Examine an edge of the floor—under a threshold, for example—to determine the floor's thickness. If the floor is laminated wood, leave the job to professionals.

If the floor is reasonably flat and free of dips and gouges, all you need to do is remove the finish with a vibrating sander. Vibrating sanders work on the same principle as handheld finishing sanders: A flat pad or plate with sandpaper on it vibrates and oscillates to remove the old finish. Floor models are bigger and heavier, of course, but work gently enough to control easily.

If the floor is uneven or has scratches or deep gouges, you need to use a drum sander. If you're not comfortable

Refinishing saves the character of an old floor while giving it the shine of a new one.

WORK SMARTER

TOO THIN TO SAND?
Wondering whether the floor is too thin to sand? Pull up the floor vents or take off the threshold or the baseboard to reveal the edge of a floorboard. How far can you sand? Down to the tongue and groove, but no deeper.

running the machine, call a professional to do the sanding, then do the finishing and staining yourself.

Renting floor sanders

Drum and vibrating floor sanders and edgers are rental items. The drum and edging sanders are powerful, aggressive tools and take some practice to operate properly. Many rental companies offer a training demonstration, so take advantage of the opportunity. After class you're on your own. To minimize potential damage to your floor, start by using fine sandpaper on a small area to become familiar with the machine. Later switch to coarse paper and start the real sanding. Sandpaper comes with the sanders but you pay per piece. Get more than you think you'll need—unused paper can be returned when you return the sander.

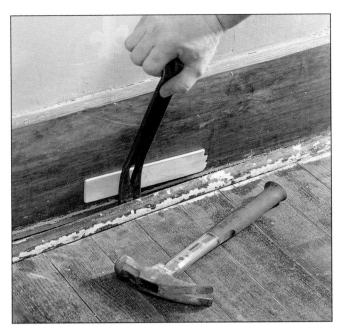

1 **REMOVE THE BASE MOLDING.** A floor sander may bang against base molding, so remove it. Usually all it requires is removing the shoe molding—the quarter round that runs along the floor. Pry it off as shown, protecting the baseboard with a piece of scrap wood. If there is no shoe molding, either remove the base molding or take care not to damage it with the sanders.

2 **CHECK FOR SQUEAKS AND NAIL LOOSE FLOORBOARDS.** The best approach is to nail into a floor joist, not just the subfloor, with #8 finishing nails. Set the nails and fill the holes with latex wood putty. Set protruding nails that would tear the sandpaper.

FLOORS

3 **CONTAIN THE DUST.** To prevent dust from sifting throughout the house, close off doorways with plastic sheeting. Stick strips of masking tape around the edges of closet doors. If possible, pull the dust toward a window or door with a box fan. Wear a dust mask when sanding.

4 **ROUGH-SAND WITH A DRUM OR VIBRATING SANDER.** If the floor itself is in bad shape, start with a drum sander. If refinishing is all that's necessary, use a vibrating sander (Step 6) instead. Get advice from the tool rental company. When drum sanding, start with the coarsest sandpaper grit—typically 36- or 40-grit—then switch to 60-grit. Finish with 80- or 100-grit. Move the sander so that it travels along the length of the boards, with the grain of the wood. Work the drum sander forward and back over 3-foot to 4-foot lengths of floor, overlapping the strokes by at least one-third of the belt.

Sanding and refinishing a floor *(continued)*

5 **SWEEP AND VACUUM BETWEEN SANDINGS.** The sanding dust eventually gets in the way of the sanding process and has to be swept and vacuumed. Always sweep and vacuum before starting with the next grit of sandpaper. It not only makes the floor cleaner, it picks up any grit that may have been left by the sandpaper—grit that would scratch the job of the finer-grit paper.

6 **FINE-SAND WITH A VIBRATING SANDER** (optional). These sanders level mino unevenness left by drum sanders. If you use both tools, use the um sander for the two coarse grits (36 and 60), then use the vib ting sander for the medium and fine grits (80 and 100). If you us nly the vibrating sander, start with 60-grit, then sand with 80- , and finally with 100-grit.

TOOL TIP

A DIFFERENT DRUMMER
A sander drum is usually made of rubber wedged between two discs held in place by a nut. To lock a roll of sandpaper in place, tighten the nut, squeezing the sides of the drum together. This increases the diameter just enough to prevent the sandpaper from slipping off. Loosen the nut to remove the sandpaper.

7 **SAND CORNERS AND EDGES WITH AN EDGE SANDER.** The edge sander usually comes as part of the rental. Use 80-grit paper to reach areas that the large sanders cannot reach: corners, under radiators, in small closets, etc. Edge sanders can be difficult to control; practice on a hidden area, such as the inside of a closet, until you get the hang of it.

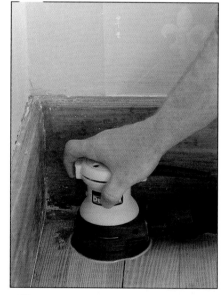

8 **A RANDOM-ORBIT SANDER IS EASIER TO CONTROL THAN THE EDGER.** Use it to finish tight places such as corners. Random-orbit sanders are less aggressive and less likely to gouge, and they do an excellent but slower job.

9 **APPLY A WOOD STAIN** (optional). When the sanding is done, clean up all the dust with a vacuum and tack cloth. Apply wood stain with a foam applicator pad. Work one manageable area at a time—4 square feet, for example. Always stain in the direction of the wood grain.

10 **WIPE OFF THE EXCESS STAIN AS YOU GO.** Most manufacturers recommend removing excess stain as you go—usually after a few minutes. Use clean cotton cloths or paper towels. Try wiping the floor with a cloth wrapped around a dry applicator pad.

GOOD IDEA

SANDING PARQUET

Parquet floors require a special technique or a special machine. Unless you're a pro, use the machine. To create a parquet pattern the tile is made of several strips with the grain running in different directions. As a result, sanding across the grain is unavoidable, and the sandpaper leaves noticeable scratches.

Rent an orbital floor sander, which has a pad that moves in a random semi-circular pattern that doesn't scratch the grain. Use a 36-grit sandpaper to remove the finish. Change to a 60-grit paper for a first pass over the floor. Make a second pass with 80-grit, and a final pass with a 100-grit sandpaper. Sand around the edges of the floor with a hand sander, using the same progression of grits.

11 **APPLY A CLEAR FINISH.** Allow the stain to dry as recommended before applying the first coat of varnish. Polyurethane, either oil-based or water-based, is a reliable finish for floors. Apply the finish with a lamb's-wool applicator. Sand the floor lightly with 220-grit paper, or #000 steel wool. Vacuum up the dust. Sand and apply three coats of oil-based finish, or four coats of water-based finish.

BUYER'S GUIDE

OIL-BASED VS. WATER-BASED POLYURETHANE

Oil-based polyurethane is reliable and has been around for years. It imparts warmth to most wood colors, darkening them slightly. Use a brand that is recommended for flooring and has a warranty. Some brands dry slowly, requiring a full day between coats. Others are fast-drying (4 hours is about the minimum), which allows you to get two, even three, coats on in a single day. Good ventilation is a must, and you should wear a ventilating respirator.

Water-based polyurethanes dry quickly and are nearly odorless. They're also virtually clear when dry, an advantage if you don't want the finish to darken the wood. Many professionals use commercial water-based polyurethane that holds up well, but reports are mixed on the water-based varnishes available to consumers. Quality seems to vary from brand to brand. Check warranties and discuss your choice with knowledgeable floor-finish experts.

SAFETY ALERT

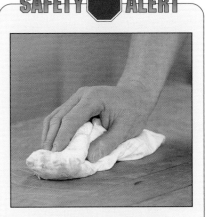

OIL-SOAKED RAGS ARE A FIRE HAZARD

The heat from dry, oily rags can set the rags on fire, especially if they are bunched together. Hang the rags outside, away from any structures, and allow them to dry thoroughly before you throw them out.

FLOORS

Installing a strip-wood floor

SKILL SCALE

EASY | **MEDIUM** | HARD

REQUIRED SKILLS:
Intermediate carpentry, measuring, and layout; sanding and finishing.

 **HOW LONG WILL IT TAKE?**

Experienced . . . . 8 hrs.
Handy . . . . 10 hrs.
Novice . . . . 14 hrs.

VARIABLES: Time estimates are for a 10'×15' room with a sturdy subfloor and do not include sanding, finishing, and drying time.

STUFF YOU'LL NEED

✔ MATERIALS:
Wood flooring, building paper, floor finish, #6 finishing nails, latex wood putty

✔ TOOLS:
Pry bar, hammer stapler, tape measure, chalk line, hammer, nail set, drill, ³⁄₃₂" drill bit, flooring nailer, miter saw, saber saw, table saw (optional)

TOOL TIP

PREDRILLING FOR NAILS

Nails seem to bend and wood seems to split in the most visible places on a floor—it's almost guaranteed. For finish carpentry, it pays to drill a pilot hole in the visible surface to keep the wood from splitting and help prevent the nail from bending over and marring the wood. A ³⁄₃₂-inch drill bit is about right for #6 finishing nails, but the best drill bit is an extra nail. Clip off the head, pop it in your drill, and use it as you would a standard drill bit.

All strip-wood floors require a stable subfloor. Materials such as ¾-inch plywood, tongue-and-groove pine, or oriented-strand board (OSB) are all typical and acceptable. Floorboards should be installed perpendicular to the floor joists. Parallel installation is acceptable in hallways if the subfloor is sturdy, but it may cause more spring in the floor and possibly more squeaks.

A strip-wood floor consists of solid strips of wood, typically ½ inch thick, with tongue-and-groove joints along the edges. The tongue-and-groove joints keep the surface of each board flush and conceal the nails, which are driven through the tongue and covered by the groove of the next board.

Oak strip flooring is available as a stock item in most home centers. For a slightly higher cost, you can choose from maple, walnut, cherry, and hickory. All will probably last the life of the house and will withstand sanding and refinishing several times.

You can buy strip flooring in 2¼-inch or 3¼-inch widths, sold in bundles of approximately 22 square feet. It's also sold in random widths to create less-formal floors. Buy it either unfinished or prefinished with a durable commercial

Solid-wood floors add warmth to a room.

finish. The higher cost of prefinished strip flooring is worth considering because you won't have to sand and finish after installation. Because prefinished boards can't be sanded flush the way unfinished flooring can, some prefinished strip flooring has a small V-groove along the length that conceals slight unevenness.

Prefinished flooring cuts installation time in half but doesn't allow options for stain and gloss. If you have a custom look in mind, go with unfinished flooring.

Flooring installation tips

● **Acclimating the flooring.** Wood expands and contracts with changes in moisture, and even kiln-dried boards will warp. To acclimate the wood to the moisture content of your house, put the bundles in the room where they'll be installed. Unpackage them, cut any binding, and leave the flooring for two weeks. The wood will gradually come to the same moisture content as the room, minimizing problems that might occur after installation.

● **Hallways.** In a large room, install the flooring perpendicular to the joists because it results in a stronger floor. In hallways, run the boards the length of the hall because it looks better.

● **Shuffling the deck.** As you unbundle the flooring, you'll see that all wood is not alike. Some boards will be dark; some will be light. Some will be highly figured; others won't. Professional floor installers don't try to group similar boards. Instead, they shuffle the boards, mixing them for a random-looking floor.

1 **REMOVE SHOE MOLDING OR BASE MOLDING, IF NECESSARY.** It's often easier to lay a floor if the trim isn't in the way. Removing it, however, can be tricky because it's easy to damage and will break. If necessary, remove the molding with a pry bar, wedging a scrap between the wall and the bar to avoid damage. Reinstall the molding after the new floor is installed.

2 **TACK DOWN BUILDING PAPER.** Building paper makes it easier to slide the flooring into place and provides somewhat of a vapor barrier. Roll it out and staple every 8 to 10 inches. At the seams, overlap the pieces about 3 inches.

3 **DETERMINE THE WIDTH OF THE STARTER STRIP.** Figure how many strips it will take to complete the width. The first and last strip should be relatively equal in width. Lay out flooring, or use a calculator and divide the room width by the width of an individual strip of flooring. Allow a gap the thickness of the flooring for expansion along both walls; the shoe or base molding will cover the gap.

4 **RIP-CUT THE STARTER-ROW STRIPS.** Use a table saw with a sharp rip blade to cut the starter strips of flooring. Because the tongue edge of the first strip must face into the room, you will cut off the groove edge.

Determine the width of the starter strip; add the thickness of the flooring. Measure this number from the wall at each end and mark the floor.

5 **SNAP A CHALK LINE FOR THE STARTER ROW USING THE MARKS ON THE FLOOR;** this will show where the edge of the tongue will fall. This line must be straight because the straightness of the starter row affects the entire installation. Don't guide along the wall as it may not be perfectly straight.

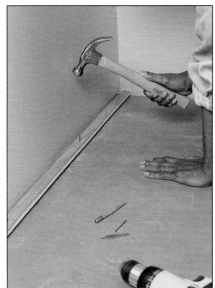

6 **FACE-NAIL THE FIRST ONE OR TWO STRIPS** (a flooring nailer can't be used). Align the first piece with the tongue edge on the chalk line. Drill holes every 12 inches along the length of the strip, drive #6 cement-coated finishing nails through the holes, and set the heads flush with the surface. Note the expansion gap between the first floorboard and the wall.

Installing a strip-wood floor (continued)

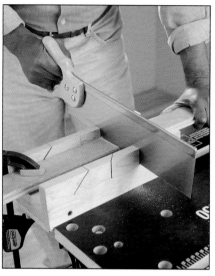

7 **NAIL SUBSEQUENT STRIPS WITH A FLOORING NAILER.** You can use a hammer, but nailers save a lot of time. (Both manual and air-powered models are available.) Position the nailer on the tongue edge of the board, and whack the plunger head with the heavy rubber mallet that's supplied with the nailer. After a little practice you'll nail down this skill.

8 **CROSSCUT END PIECES.** At the end of each row, the last piece needs to be crosscut to fit. Allow a small gap here to make getting the piece in place easier. Avoid using an end piece that's less than a foot long; instead, use two medium-length pieces to end the row.

9 **TIGHTEN SEAMS.** Some pieces will be bowed. If you have enough extra pieces, these may not be needed. If you have to use a piece that's bowed, screw a piece of scrap to the floor about an inch from the strip and tap a wood wedge into the gap, as shown. Also try wedging a pry bar edge into the subfloor and prying against the edge of the bowed strip. Then nail the strip in place.

10 **FIT PIECES AROUND OBSTACLES.** Where the flooring meets a jog in the wall or another obstruction, cut the pieces to fit. Position the piece of flooring as close to its destination as possible, then transfer the measurements for the cuts directly from the wall or obstruction to the flooring. Remember to allow a gap along the wall length.

11 **CUT AND FIT THE LAST ROW.** The last row, like the first, may have to be sawed to width. It also will have to be face-nailed. To tighten the joint between the final two pieces, use a pry bar between the wall and the edge of the last strip, with a scrap block of wood protecting the wall. Then nail the strip in place.

12 **APPLY BASE AND SHOE MOLDING.** If you use unfinished flooring, sand it and apply the finish before installing the base molding. (See Sanding and Refinishing a Floor, page 306.) If installing new baseboard, cut and fit it once the floor is completely finished. Rest the molding on a piece of paper when you nail it in place to allow the floor to expand and contract under it. Remove the paper when done.

Installing a decorative border

A decorative border frames the room and defines its shape. It can be a lavish assembly of inlaid wood (available from specialty suppliers) or a simple contrasting band of wood.

One option for a decorative border is to buy a small amount of flooring in a different wood species from the same manufacturer as the rest of the floor. This works whether you use finished or unfinished strip flooring. For example, if you use natural oak for the floor, use walnut for the border.

A border creates two distinct spaces: the perimeter area outside the border, and the main floor field inside the border. The floor strips outside the border as well as the border itself are either mitered at the corners or lapped one over the next for a "log cabin" effect. Either approach creates the framed look that visually distinguishes the border and perimeter from the floor field.

The space inside the border is treated the same as a regular strip-floor installation except that the end joints that

A decorative border is usually just a strip of regular flooring in a contrasting color. Install the border first, making sure that the corners are square and the sides parallel. Once the border is in place, fit the flooring on both sides of it.

meet the border have to be cut to fit precisely. Install the wood border first, then the perimeter area, and finally the main body of the floor.

1 **DETERMINE THE LOCATION.** A border can be located a few inches to a foot from the wall, depending on the size of the room. Lay out short lengths of the flooring across the whole width of the floor. Measure carefully, and then lay out a field composed entirely of full-width strips. Snap chalk lines to mark the inside edge of the inlay. (See page 311, Step 5.)

2 **CUT THE INLAY AND NAIL IT TO THE FLOOR.** If you use a piece of standard flooring for the inlay material, first cut off the tongue edge on a table saw. Rip the inlay piece to a narrower width at the same time. Miter the inlay at the corners, using a miter box and handsaw or a power miter saw. Predrill holes through the inlay and nail it to the subfloor with #6 finishing nails. With a framing square, check that the inlay is square in the corners. Countersink the nails and fill the holes with a matching latex wood putty.

3 **INSTALL THE PERIMETER FLOORING.** Cut and fit mitered pieces of the regular flooring at the corners. Because they are close to the wall, you won't be able to use a flooring nailer; face-nail them instead. You may be able to use the tongue-and-groove joint for the perimeter pieces, but you will have to cut off the tongue to fit the last piece against the wall. Install the field as if the borders were walls surrounding a standard strip floor.

Installing a decorative inlay

Decorative inlays are available in several thicknesses, finished or unfinished. Inlays match most off-the-shelf flooring from home centers, though you may have to special-order them. The installation procedure for an inlay depends on the manufacturer. Some provide a template with each inlay that requires a router to cut the recess into the surrounding floor. The special router bit is included in the installation kit. This approach, shown opposite, is nearly foolproof. It's also ideal if you want to install an inlay in an existing floor. The inlay will have to match the thickness of the existing floor. To measure the floor's thickness, remove a threshold or baseboard to expose an edge of the floor.

1 LOCATE THE INLAY ON THE FLOOR. Take time to position the inlay, placing it on the floor with straight edges parallel to floor strips to prevent awkward seams. When you have it where you want it, use a pencil to trace around its perimeter onto the floor.

2 NAIL THE TEMPLATE TO THE FLOOR. Lay the template on the floor so the inside edges line up with the pencil lines traced from the inlay. Nail each corner of the template to the floor with #4 finishing nails.

3 **ROUT AGAINST THE TEMPLATE EDGE.** Adjust the router to make a ⅛-inch-deep cut into the excess flooring. (The first cut should be deep enough to skim across the top of the tongues on the boards.) Start the bit about an inch away from the template, and cut clockwise around it. Set any exposed nails all the way down through the boards. Lower the bit ⅛ inch and repeat until you've cut all the way through the floor strips—three passes for ⅜-inch flooring. Remove the floor strips within the inlay area. Chisel out the corners, then check the fit of the inlay.

4 **APPLY ADHESIVE TO THE FLOOR.** Use high-quality construction adhesive available in tube form. Evenly spread the adhesive with a small notched trowel (the kind sold for applying base cove molding adhesive) over the entire surface of the inlay area.

Learn to use a router by installing a medallion. Kits make this easy to do.

5 **ATTACH THE INLAY TO THE FLOOR.** Drop the inlay into the recess and press it into the adhesive. Use a rubber mallet to tap it into place if it gets hung up on a corner. Then walk all around on the inlay to set it firmly into the adhesive.

6 **DRIVE 1⅝-INCH DRYWALL SCREWS** into the predrilled holes to secure the inlay to the subfloor.

7 **GLUE IN SCREW COVERS.** Apply yellow or white glue to the back of the loose pieces of the inlay that cover the screws. Set the pieces into the recesses; tap them down with a block of wood and hammer. Wipe excess glue. Let the glue dry before sanding the inlay.

Installing wide-plank flooring

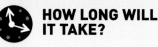
STUFF YOU'LL NEED

✔ **MATERIALS:**
Wide-plank flooring, cut nails.

✔ **TOOLS:**
Circular saw, quick square, hammer (Installation is similar to strip flooring; see page 310 for additional tools and materials necessary.)

Wide-plank flooring adds a touch of warmth and a hint of country to any room.

Wide-plank flooring provides an appealing country look. Installing wide-plank flooring has notable differences from installing regular wood flooring. You'll use from one-third to one-half as many pieces of wide-plank floor, which means the installation will go more quickly. Though the long edges in wide-plank floors are sometimes tongue and groove, the end joints are not. Wide-plank floorboards are face-nailed across the wide widths into the joists. Square-head cut nails (if they're really rectangular) hold well and mimic the look of older floors.

This flooring expands and contracts more than narrow boards, creating wider gaps or cracks along the seams, especially during heating season. Gaps and cracks are considered part of the look.

Predrilling for square nails will help make sure the board stays intact as you nail it home.

1 **MARK THE FLOOR JOISTS WITH A CHALK LINE.** Wide boards expand and contract, so they must be nailed into the floor joists. On plywood subfloors, the nailing pattern should reveal the joist locations. Typical spacing from center to center of joists is 16 inches. After you find one, move over and drive more nails to find the next joist.

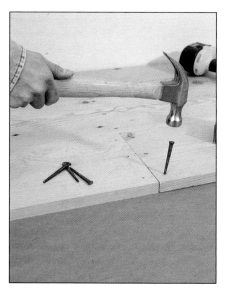

2 **NAIL DOWN THE BOARDS.** A power nailer can be used to start tongue-and-groove boards, but face-nailing is necessary as well. Cut nails, with square heads, hold well and provide an old-time look. Keep the nails at least ¾ inch from the edge of the board to prevent splitting. Orient the nailheads so that the long side is parallel to the length of the board. Predrill pilot holes for best results.

3 **SCREW DOWN THE PLANKS.** Pegging is an alternative look. Some planks come predrilled; if they don't, use a counterbore bit to drill a hole that will match wooden dowel plugs. Screw down the planks, then apply glue to the holes and tap in the plugs.

INSTALLING LAMINATE AND ENGINEERED FLOORING

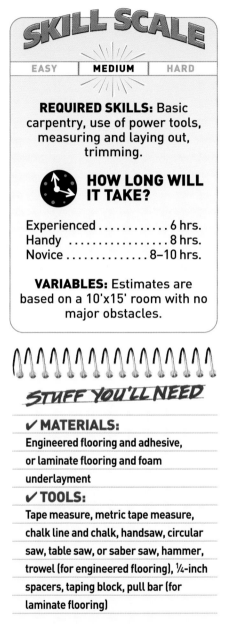
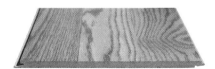

Snap-together laminate

Engineered wood

Laminate and engineered floors have a top layer of flooring material that is bonded in the factory to a layer of plywood. On laminate floors, the top layer is a laminated-plastic-type material. On engineered floors, the top layer is solid wood. The resulting planks are wider than strip-wood floors and, thus, go down more quickly. They are also more stable, and unlike solid wood, can be installed directly over almost any subfloor, including concrete and concrete below grade. Installing over concrete, however, requires a plastic moisture barrier.

On a floating floor, the strips against the wall will need to be at least 2 inches wide if they're going to stay put. (The width doesn't matter on a glue-down installation because the glue holds materials in place.) To make sure the planks in a floating floor will be wide enough, measure the room carefully and divide by the width of a plank. Unless you enjoy dividing fractions by fractions, make the measurements with a metric tape. (You don't have to understand metrics to do this: It just works.) If the remainder is less than 50 mm, the last plank will be less than 2 inches wide.

If you need to trim the first plank, add the calculated width of the final planks to the width of a full plank. Divide by two and cut the first plank to this width. You'll end up with equally sized planks on each side of the room. Once you have the answer, just lay out the cut using the metric tape.

CLOSER LOOK

LAMINATE FLOORS ARE FLOATING FLOORS— which means they are neither glued nor nailed to the subfloor. They're installed over a thin layer of foam cushioning and are held in place by the walls. Engineered floors are usually glued to the subfloor with a mastic, but they can also be nailed down, and in some cases can be installed as a floating floor.

ACCLIMATE THE FLOORING. Place the materials in the room you're flooring two days before you install them. Set the thermostat on its normal setting for the time of year. Put the unopened boxes flat on the floor, or stack them three or four high, log cabin style. After 48 hours, they will have gradually come to the temperature and humidity of the room.

INSTEAD OF TRYING TO CUT FLOORING TO FIT AROUND DOOR MOLDINGS, installers cut away part of the jamb and slip the floor underneath. To do this, put a piece of flooring upside down next to the jamb; if it's a laminate floor, set it on a piece of foam underlayment. If it's engineered flooring, put it on the subfloor you're installing, if any. Put an undercutting saw on the plank and cut at least ½ inch into the jamb. Pop out the waste with a screwdriver or chisel.

Remove the quarter-round molding or shoe mold that's nailed to the baseboard, if any.

FLOORS

Installing laminate flooring

1 **INSTALL A 6 MIL PLASTIC MOISTURE BARRIER OVER CONCRETE.** Overlap the seams as recommended by the manufacturer, then roll out the foam underlayment. Other subfloors need only foam underlayment. Some planks come with the underlayment already attached. If your planks do, you won't need to put more down. Choose the wall you'll start flooring against and roll a single strip of underlayment along it. Roll additional underlayment as you install the planks.

2 **TRIM THE PLANKS IN THE FIRST ROW TO WIDTH IF NECESSARY.** If the last row will be less than 2 inches wide, you'll need to trim the first row to width to create a wider final row. Measure and calculate the width. If you need to trim the first row, add the calculated width of the final row to the width of a plank and divide by two. Cut the plank to this width. To minimize chipping on a table saw, cut the plank face up with a sharp carbide blade. To minimize chipping on a circular saw, run the saw along the bottom of the plank.

3 **CUT THE FIRST PLANK IN THE SECOND ROW TO LENGTH.** While you're at the saw, cut the first plank in the second row to the length called for by the manufacturer. Cutting the plank staggers the ends of neighboring boards and keeps them from aligning. Staggering creates a stronger and more attractive floor. In this case, the manufacturer recommends a plank 32 inches long for the first plank in the second row. Once you've made the cut, temporarily set the plank aside.

4 **PUT DOWN THE FIRST PLANK.** (If you didn't cut the tongue off the planks during earlier trimming, do so now.) It's easiest to assemble the first two rows when they're away from the wall. Start with a full-length plank, positioned with the groove facing into the room. Take the piece you cut to length earlier and put the tongue into the groove in the edge of the first plank.

5 **SNAP THE PIECES TOGETHER.** Different brands interlock differently, so follow the manufacturer's directions. For the brand shown here, lift one edge of the plank off the floor, and slide the tongue into the groove on the other plank. Press the plank flat to snap the pieces together.

6 **PUT DOWN A THIRD PLANK.** Snap the end of the third plank into the end of the first plank, as shown. Put down a fourth plank, snapping the end into the end of the plank two, and leaving a slight gap between it and plank three. To close the gap, kneel on plank one, reach over and lift the far edge of plank three slightly. Pull the plank toward you while pushing down along the groove of plank one. The planks will snap together. Put ¼-inch spacers against the wall and slide the assembled planks against them.

FLOORS

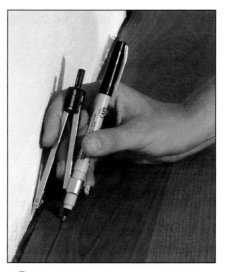

7 **CONTINUE LAYING THE FIRST TWO ROWS ACROSS THE LENGTH OF THE ROOM.** When you get to the far wall, put a spacer against the wall and cut planks to fit in the opening. Put each plank in place, then snap it into the end groove as shown, using a hammer and a pull bar made by the flooring manufacturer.

8 **SLIDE THE ASSEMBLED ROWS AGAINST SPACERS YOU'VE PUT ALONG THE STARTING WALL.** If the gap between the wall and the planks is at any point wider than the molding that will cover it, you will have to trim the board to match the contour of the wall. Set a compass to the space of the largest gap, plus ½ inch. Guide the compass along the wall so that the marker makes a line on the planks.

9 **UNSNAP THE PLANKS AND CUT ALONG THE SCRIBE LINE WITH A SABER SAW** using a laminate blade that is designed to minimize chipping. Reassemble the rows, put spacers against the walls and slide the plank assembly against them. Begin assembling the next rows.

10 **ONCE THE FIRST TWO ROWS ARE IN PLACE, BEGIN THE THIRD ROW.** Cut a plank to length so that the end will fall at least 8 inches from the end of its neighbor in the second row. Put a spacer against the wall, put a plank against the spacer, and snap the plank into the edge of the second row. Work your way across the room, laying a single row. Snap the ends of the planks together first, and then join the sides.

11 **IF A GAP APPEARS ANYWHERE ALONG THE EDGES, CLOSE IT BY TAPPING THE EDGE WITH A BLOCK AND HAMMER.** When you reach the end of a row, cut the piece to fit and put it in place against a spacer as before. Work your way across the room, installing one row at a time. Unroll additional underlayment as needed. Butt underlayment seams, but don't overlap them. Continue across the width of the floor until the space is too narrow for a full plank.

12 **TRIM THE FINAL ROW TO FIT.** Start by assembling a row directly on top of the row just laid. Find a piece of scrap 6 to 10 inches long. If the manufacturer makes the flooring with a bottom lip wider than the top lip, break off the bottom lip. Hold the scrap against the wall, put a pen against the other edge, and pull it along the wall to mark the planks. As before, use a saber saw to trim the planks. Nail quarter-round molding to the baseboard to cover the gap.

Installing a glue-down engineered floor

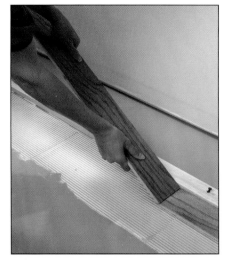

❶ NAIL DOWN A STRAIGHTEDGE AS A GUIDE. Snap a line parallel to the wall—outside walls are usually the straightest and best to use. Add the width of several planks together plus the width of the recommended expansion gap between the flooring and wall. Snap a chalk line this distance from the wall. Nail a straight board on the wall side of the line to use as a guide.

❷ SPREAD A ROW OF ADHESIVE ABOUT TWO PLANKS WIDE ALONG THE STRAIGHTEDGE, using the notched trowel recommended by the manufacturer. The size and spacing of the notches controls the amount of adhesive you put down. Make sure you're putting down the proper amount by pulling up a board every now and then; about 80 percent of the glue should stick to the back of the flooring.

❸ PUT THE TONGUE SIDE OF THE FIRST PLANK AGAINST THE STRAIGHTEDGE, keeping the end away from the wall by the width of the expansion gap. Put the end of the next plank snugly against the end of the installed plank and push the two together. Work your way down the straightedge. Cut the last plank to length accounting for the expansion gap on this end when you make the cut.

Offset end seams on subsequent rows

❹ BEGIN THE SECOND ROW WITH THE CUTOFF FROM THE FIRST ROW. (Offset the board from the end of the board in the first row as required by the manufacturer; cut a new board if necessary.) Work your way down the second row, putting the ends of the boards together, then sliding them into the planks of the first row. Cut the last board to fit, leaving the proper expansion gap.

❺ SPREAD ADHESIVE AND WORK YOUR WAY ACROSS THE ROOM, one row at a time. Clean off excess glue with the recommended cleaner. Trim the first plank in each row as needed to create the proper offset. Always leave the required expansion gap between the ends of the planks and the wall. If a board won't seat against its neighbor, place a piece of scrap against it and tap it into place with a hammer.

❻ REMOVE THE STRAIGHTEDGE AND INSTALL THE LAST ROWS. Once the adhesive dries, remove the straightedge you nailed to the floor earlier. Spread adhesive in the remaining space, and lay flooring one row at a time. Measure and trim the last row as needed, leaving the proper size expansion gap.

Installing carpeting and carpet pad

Unlike vinyl tile or wood flooring, carpet is stretched across the floor like the head of a drum and held in place around the edges by tack strips. They're made of countless tacks, the points of which stick up through the top of the strip and hold the carpet in place.

You'll use two tools in carpet installation that you won't need in any other home improvement job. A knee kicker is a rod with teeth mounted in a head at one end, and a pad mounted on the other. You put the teeth in the carpet and push—don't kick—the pad with your knee to stretch the carpet onto one of the tack trips. The carpet stretcher is a variation of the same tool and is a bit easier on the knee. One end butts against the wall on the side of the room already attached to the tack strip. The other end has teeth that grab the carpet on the other side of the room. By pushing on a lever, you stretch the unattached edge of the carpet over the tack strips. Consider renting these tools rather than buying.

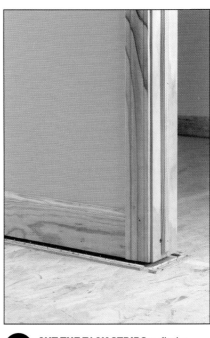

1 **CUT THE TACK STRIPS** to fit the perimeter of the room, including the door areas.

2 **POSITION THE STRIPS WITH THE POINTS FACING THE WALL.** Keep a space equal to the thickness of the carpet between the walls and the strips. Nail the strips to the floor, using concrete nails if installing on a slab.

3 **LAY THE CARPET PADDING OVER THE ENTIRE FLOOR.** Tape the seams together with duct tape, and then staple along them every 10–12 inches. Work toward the tack strips, stretching the pad and stapling as you go. Staple the pad against the edge of the tack strip. Run a knife against the strip to trim the pad.

FLOORS

Installing carpeting and carpet pad (continued)

4 **MEASURE THE ROOM.** Snap chalk lines across the back of the carpet to outline a piece 6 inches longer and wider than the room. Fold the carpet over a piece of scrap wood so that the layout lines face up. Put a straightedge along the lines, and guide a knife along it. Change blades frequently.

If you will need seams choose a carpet that will hide them well.

5 **CENTER THE CARPET IN THE ROOM.** If there are outside corners, make relief cuts so that the carpet lies flat.

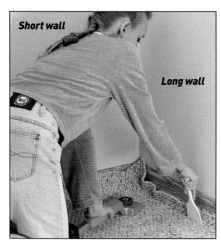

Short wall

Long wall

6 **FACE THE LONG WALL NEAR A CORNER OF THE ROOM.** Put the toothed end of a knee kicker in the carpet about 1 to 3 inches from the wall. Push the padded end with your knee, hooking the back of the carpet over the tack strips in the process. Push down with a plastic broad knife to anchor the carpet. Push, hook, and anchor carpet along about 3 feet of the wall. Repeat on the short wall.

7 **TRIM THE CARPET AS YOU GO.** Set a carpet trimmer to the thickness of the carpet and guide it along the wall to trim the edges of the carpet. Tuck the cut edges into the space between the strips and the wall using a plastic broad knife. Trim and tuck every time you hook a length of carpet over the tack strips.

8 **PUT THE FOOT OF THE STRETCHER AGAINST THE SHORT WALL OF THE STARTING CORNER.** Run the stretcher at about a 15-degree angle toward the opposite corner, as shown in "Closer Look" on the opposite page. Set the head of the stretcher about 6 inches from the wall. Push on the handle to stretch the carpet. Hook and anchor it to about 3 feet of tack strips along both walls of the corner.

FLOORS

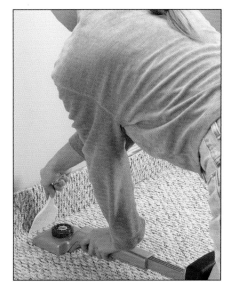

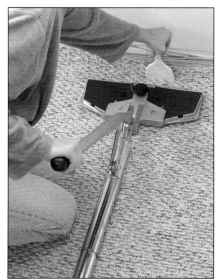

9 **WITH THE KNEE KICKER, PUSH THE CARPET AGAINST THE LONG WALL BETWEEN THE TWO INSTALLED CORNERS.** Anchor with the broad knife. When you're finished, put the foot of the stretcher against the wall, and run it at about a 15-degree angle to the corner, as shown in "Closer Look" below. Stretch the carpet, and anchor about 3 feet along both corner walls.

10 **STARTING IN A CORNER, USE THE KNEE KICKER TO PUSH THE CARPET AGAINST THE SHORT WALL, ATTACHING IT TO THE TACK STRIPS.** Anchor, and then work your way along the short wall, pushing the carpet and attaching it as you go.

11 **POWER STRETCH FROM THE LONG WALL OF THE STARTING CORNER TO THE OPPOSITE LONG WALL,** running the stretcher at about a 15-degree angle. Hook and anchor the carpet over the tack strips near the stretcher head. Move the stretcher along the wall, stretching, hooking, and anchoring the carpet section by section. Power stretch from the short wall of the starting corner, running the stretcher straight across the room. Attach the carpet to the strips, and then work your way across the wall.

CLOSER LOOK

TYPICAL ROOM INSTALLATION

Carpet layers begin by anchoring carpet first in one corner and then in the other corner of a long wall. The rest of the corners are anchored as the job progresses, but the overall picture looks like this: The installer anchors carpet on long wall, followed by the adjoining short wall. The remaining long wall is next, followed by the remaining short wall.

The exact order of work is shown here. Short arrows indicate where you push the carpet with the knee kicker. Long arrows show the angle and starting point of the power stretcher. Once you've attached the carpet near either the kicker or the stretcher, reposition the tool, and work your way along the wall.

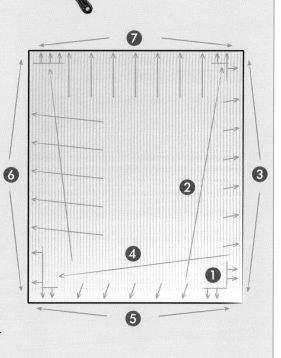

12 **INSTALL A BINDER BAR WHEREVER THE CARPET MEETS OTHER FLOORING.** Nail it to the floor, and push with the kicker to fit over the hooks in the binder bar. When the carpet's in place, put a block of wood over the bar to protect it, and hammer the flange closed.

Carpet retailers carry a wide range of carpet grades, styles, and textures, as well as a choice of pad materials. Carpet fiber has two classes: natural and synthetic. Wool is the primary natural fiber used in carpet. It is commonly used in area rugs and not as commonly used in wall-to-wall carpet.

Synthetic fibers include nylon, polyester, and olefin. Nylon combines superior durability, resilience, appearance, and stain resistance. Polyester is stain-resistant and softer to the touch, but less resilient. Olefin is best suited for indoor/outdoor carpet and commercial carpets. Certain carpet styles, such as berber, combine more than one of these fibers.

Carpet padding increases the durability of the carpet. The best pad is neither the thickest nor the most cushioned. In fact, thin and dense is generally best because it provides the optimal combination of firmness, support, and cushioning. Carpet manufacturers often provide padding specifications; using lesser padding can void the carpet warranty, so follow the recommendations carefully.

CARPET CUTS. Although carpet has a variety of patterns and textures, it comes in two basic types: loop-pile and cut-pile. In loop-pile, the surface of yarn passes through the backing, is looped over, and then returns through the backing. Cut-pile carpet has the tops of the loops trimmed off to create a more plush-feeling carpet. Berber, which salespeople often refer to as a third style, is really a looped carpet made with thicker yarns.

Although durability, stain resistance, and resilience are determined primarily by the type of fiber, texture counts, too.

Match the carpet color to other design elements in the room.

CUT-PILE

Cut-pile includes two styles: saxony and plush. Saxony is dense and has twisted fibers that make it firmer. Plush has longer fibers but they're not as dense, giving the carpet a softer, luxurious feel. Because of the open fibers and cut ends, cut-pile carpets get dirty quicker.

PLUSH

SAXONY

LOOP-PILE

The loops on a level-loop-pile carpet are all the same height, creating a smooth, dense surface that cleans easily. It's wear-resistant and ideal for high-traffic areas. Multilevel-loop has both long and short loops, creating a random, textured pattern. It tends to retain dirt because of the texture, and it wears slightly less well than level-loop. Cut-loop has patterns created by clipping off the top of some of the loops. It's slightly less durable than multilevel-loop.

LEVEL-LOOP

MULTILEVEL-LOOP

CUT-LOOP

BERBER

Berbers were originally a level-loop, light-colored wool rug made from thick yarn. Modern berbers are available in wool, synthetics, or a blend of the two. Berbers are multicolored with one of the colors appearing as flecks against the background color. They tend to have a rugged appearance, with the loops readily visible. Because of its texture, it can be harder to clean than other carpets and should be avoided in high-traffic areas.

FRIEZE

Pronounced "freeze" or "free-ZAY," these carpets have a nubby look produced by twisting the yarn. They may have up to seven nubs per inch; the more twists, the better the carpet is at hiding dirt and the more wear-resistant it is.

FLOORS

Installing baseboard

Installing baseboard requires only two things: a sharp saw and a sharp mind. The joint used to connect two pieces of baseboard is unlike any other joint in woodworking. It's called a cope joint because it's cut with a coping saw; one board is cut to nest into the profile of another.

A simple miter joint for molding work is inadequate. While the joint looks great when installed, changes in the weather cause the wood to expand and contract. Gaps develop and the joint looks sloppy and unfinished.

The cope joint solves this problem. With the two pieces fitting together like jigsaw puzzle pieces, they expand and contract in unison, leaving no gaps.

Installing coped baseboard usually begins on the wall opposite the door. The baseboard runs from wall to wall, with each end cut square. The pieces that meet the first piece are coped to fit it, and then cut square on the other end. On the wall with the door in it, the baseboard is coped in the corner and cut square where it meets the door trim.

Cut the molding a bit longer than the wall it goes against, and then nail it flat to the wall. The extra length ensures a tight joint and holds the molding in place.

If you're putting in a lot of baseboard, consider renting an air compressor and an nail gun that drives finishing nails. They will make the job easier and faster.

FLOORS

A cope joint hides wood expansion and contraction by nesting pieces of molding in the corner.

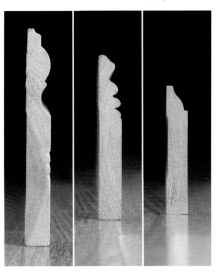

Baseboard molding comes in several basic profiles and varying heights.

Installing baseboard (continued)

1 LAY OUT THE CUT IN PENCIL, USING A SQUARE TO TRANSFER THE MARK TO THE TOP OF THE MOLDING. Put the molding in the chop saw, positioning it so that the cut will result in a board that is too long.

2 START THE CUT, BUT GO NO DEEPER THAN 1/8 INCH INTO THE MOLDING. While holding the molding, slide it along the fence until the saw cut just touches the pencil line.

3 EASE THE SAW INTO THE MOLDING AND FINISH THE CUT. The slower you lower the saw, the smoother it will cut and the better the joint will be.

4 BEGIN ON THE WALL OPPOSITE THE DOOR. Cut a piece 1/16 inch longer than the wall. Put the ends up against the corners, positioning the molding about 1/4 inch above the floor to avoid any irregularities. The piece will bow away from the wall slightly. Push on it to put it into place.

5 NAIL THE BASEBOARD IN PLACE. Drive nails through the bottom of the baseboard into the 2×4 plate that runs along the floor inside the wall. Drive nails through the top into the studs. If the wood is difficult to nail, predrill for the nails. Clip the head off a finishing nail, put it in your drill, and use it like a regular bit.

6 COPE THE BASEBOARD THAT MEETS THE BOARD YOU'VE JUST INSTALLED. Begin with a piece longer than you'll need. Cut a miter on the end you'll be coping. Trace along the edge of the miter with a pencil to outline the profile.

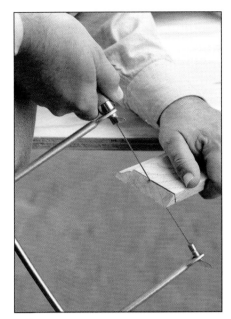

GETTING A TIGHT FIT
Many carpenters, including the pros, wish there was a tool called a "board stretcher," which would magically add length to a piece that was mistakenly cut too short. Well, board stretchers don't exist so experienced carpenters always add about 1/16 inch to the overall length of the wall. Cut the molding to this length by making a square cut at the end opposite the coped joint. Spring the molding in place, and nail as before. For a neater job, some carpenters cut off the tip of the coped piece where it overlaps the top of the mating piece.

7 **CUT ALONG THE PENCIL LINE WITH A COPING SAW.** Angle the saw slightly to create a pointed edge that will fit the other side of the joint snugly. For a smooth cut, use the finest blade you can get and let the saw do the work. Trying to push the saw forward will cause it to jam in the wood.

8 **EVEN THE PROS NEED TO FINE-TUNE A COPED JOINT.** Test-fit your joint and make any necessary corrections by filing with a rat-tail file. Fill in any small mistakes with caulk once the molding is in place. If you make a big mistake, cut off the joint and try again. Stain and finish the baseboard before installation.

Rat-tail files are inexpensive and work well for fine-tuning any mitered or coped cut before installation.

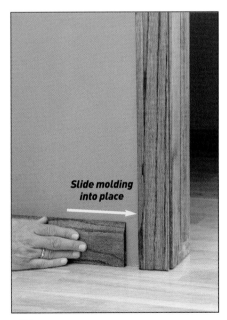

Slide molding into place →

9 **CUT THE MOLDING FOR THE REMAINING WALLS THE SAME WAY:** Cope, measure, cut, and nail. On the fourth wall—which has the door in it—cope the molding in the corners, and cut butt joints where it meets the door trim.

10 **CUT QUARTER ROUND (ALSO CALLED SHOE MOLD) TO FIT ALONG THE BASEBOARD ON THE WALL OPPOSITE THE DOOR.** Like the piece it sits against, it should be 1/16 inch longer than the wall, and both ends should be butt joints. Nail the quarter round to the floor so it won't lift it up and down with the expansion and contraction of the baseboard.

11 **INSTALL THE REST OF THE QUARTER ROUND, FOLLOWING THE PATTERN OF THE BASEBOARD.** Cope the ends that meet the first wall. Cut butt joints in the end of the molding that meets the wall with the door in it. Cut a butt joint where the molding meets the door trim; cope the other end.

Installing baseboard *(continued)*

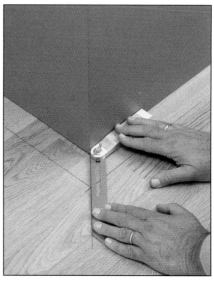

12 OUTSIDE CORNERS ARE MITERED. Start by cutting a couple of sample miters to see how the corners meet. A gap means that the corner isn't a true 90 degrees. If the gap is wider at the wall, the corner is greater than 90 degrees; if it is wider at the point of the miter, the corner is less than 90 degrees.

13 RECUT THE SAMPLES TO CLOSE THE GAPS. To lay out the cut, draw a line parallel to each wall by putting your framing square against the wall and tracing along it lightly with a pencil. Make sure the lines intersect.

14 DETERMINE THE ANGLE OF THE LINE WITH A SLIDING T-BEVEL; set the miter saw to this angle. Cut a trial joint, test the fit, and correct as necessary. Make small angle adjustments without moving the saw itself by slipping a playing card or a bit of sawdust between the molding and the fence of the miter saw.

BUILT-UP MOLDINGS

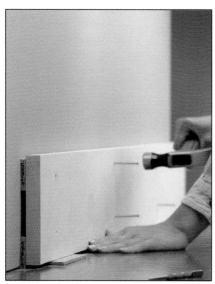

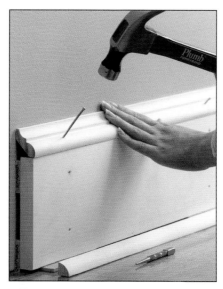

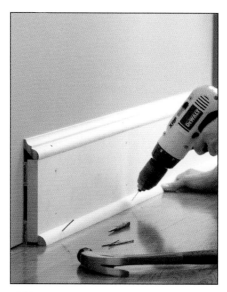

1 SOME BASEBOARDS ARE MADE UP OF SEVERAL MOLDINGS. A typical example begins by cutting and nailing a 1×4 or a 1×6 to the wall. All the joints are butt joints. Sometimes you'll need to nail thinner strips to the wall first so that the cap molding, installed in the next step, will seat properly.

2 NAIL ON A CAP MOLD, cutting and coping the joints as you would for regular baseboard.

3 INSTALL QUARTER-ROUND MOLDING. Cope, miter, and nail it to the wall as you would for any other baseboard. Drilling pilot holes will make nailing more accurate and easier to do. If you're installing a lot of molding, renting an air compressor and a nail gun will save you time and effort.

Thresholds

When a floor meets a doorway, the edge is usually covered by a threshold. It not only provides a graceful edge to the floor, it often serves as a transition to other flooring such as carpet, vinyl, ceramics or hardwood. An old threshold usually has to be removed to make way for new flooring. New flooring often requires a threshold as a transition to the old flooring in the next room. Home improvement centers stock ready-made thresholds. They're traditionally made of wood, although some are made of material similar to that in solid-surface countertops. Either can be worked with simple woodworking tools.

Finish the threshold with the same stain or color you used on the door and frame. It's easier and cleaner to finish the threshold before you install it.

REMOVING A THRESHOLD

1 IF THE THRESHOLD ISN'T TUCKED UNDER THE DOOR STOP, pry it loose with a hammer and metal pry bar. Use the hammer to drive the pry bar underneath the threshold.

2 IF THE THRESHOLD IS TUCKED UNDER THE STOP, remove the nails with a cat's paw. Drive the threshold out from under the door stops with a hammer. If that doesn't work, saw the threshold into two pieces and remove them separately.

INSTALLING A NEW THRESHOLD

1 BEFORE INSTALLING A NEW THRESHOLD, UNDERCUT THE DOOR STOPS. Make the cut by resting a saw on a piece of wood the thickness of the threshold and cutting through the stops, but not into the jambs. Cut the threshold to length with a circular saw or chop saw and slide it under the stops.

2 THRESHOLDS ARE USUALLY MADE OF HARDWOOD, WHICH CAN BEND THE NAILS YOU TRY TO DRIVE INTO THEM. Drill pilot holes by clipping the head off an 8d nail and using the nail as a drill bit. Once you've drilled the holes, drive and set 8d nails to hold the threshold in place.

WE COUNT ON DOORS TO MAKE A GOOD IMPRESSION. This can be accomplished in three ways: Repair and paint or stain; attach new hardware; or replace them. Paint or stain is inexpensive and quick. New hardware offers an old door a new lease on life. Doors that are damaged, warped, or just out of style should be replaced.

If you want a professional-looking job, follow the advice of professional painters and finishers:

- Prep work is the most important part of painting or staining. Prep may take 80 to 90 percent of the total time for a project.

- Always prime whatever surface you're about to paint. Primer seals any stains in the surface below it and improves adhesion of the finish coat.

- The door will never look any better than what's underneath. Scratches, gouges, and discoloration will show right through the most expensive products. Sand, seal, and fill before you apply the finish.

- Apply paint or stain generously. Use enough to get complete, uniform coverage.

- Start with the edges. You can roll extra paint up onto the wider surface and work it into that paint.

- Mask surfaces you don't want to paint or stain and work in well-ventilated spaces. Wear a respirator and rubber gloves as required by manufacturer of the product you're using.

- Keep your work area clean and free of dust.

SECTION 7 PROJECTS

REAL-WORLD SITUATIONS

HANG UPS

Hanging a door successfully depends as much on the opening as it does on the door. If the opening isn't level, plumb, square, and parallel, there's no way to hang a level, plumb, square door in it. Don't assume that, because the existing door works well, a new door also will fit the opening. A door and its opening grow old together; the warps in one often compensate for those in the other. Check the opening carefully, as described below. Anything out of square, plumb, or level may mean trouble, as does any binding or rubbing. Ask a carpenter or a home center or lumberyard salesperson for advice. It may be better to install a prehung door, or you may choose to refinish and repair the existing door.

Analyzing problems in an old door:

Check the header to see if it's level.

Check the top corners of the opening to see if they're square.

Look for gaps to see if the door fits its frame.

Check both jambs with a level to see if they're plumb. Measure from jamb to jamb at the top, middle, and bottom of the door to see if the opening is consistent.

On the left and right sides of the door, **check the wall** with a level to see if both sides are plumb.

Check to see if the **door swings freely**.

DOORS

Door basics

When the time comes to replace an old door, you'll have a choice between a prehung door and what manufacturers call a "slab" door. A prehung door comes attached to hinges and a door jamb; a slab comes with nothing. Neither includes the doorknob and lockset. To install a prehung door, you'll take out the trim and jamb as well as the existing door, and then nail the prehung jamb and door in place. Once everything's ready, add some new trim and you're finished.

Prehung doors sound like a bit of work, but then so is most home improvement. The fact is, hanging a slab door is about as fussy as it gets. Given the choice, most carpenters would prefer working with a prehung door, even though they're perfectly capable of hanging a slab. Follow their lead. The detail work has already been done at the factory.

Prehung and slab doors both come in a variety of styles, some of which are shown here.

COMMON DOOR STYLES

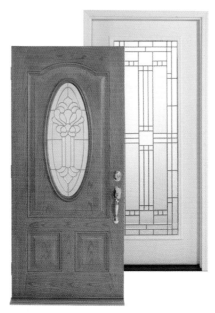

INSULATED EXTERIOR DOORS keep out cold the way old-style wooden doors never could. This "oak" door is really a wood composite with foam insulation inside. The glass in both doors is double-layered to reduce heat loss.

INTERIOR HOLLOW-CORE PREHUNG DOORS have a contemporary look and are available in many stock sizes. Hollow-core doors are lightweight and inexpensive. Six-panel doors (not shown) offer a more traditional look.

HINGED PATIO OR INTERIOR DOORS have an elegant appearance. Weathertight models are used to join indoor and outdoor living areas, while indoor models are used to link two rooms. Because these doors open on hinges, your room design must allow space for them to swing. ▼

DECORATIVE STORM DOORS can improve the security, energy efficiency, and appearance of your entry. A storm door prolongs the life of an expensive entry door by protecting it from the elements.

▲ **SLIDING PATIO DOORS** offer good visibility and lighting. Because they slide on tracks and require no floor space for opening, sliding doors are ideal for cramped spaces where swinging doors do not fit.

THE DOOR HANGER'S TOOL KIT

Below are some basic door tools. For more information see the Tool Glossary on page 544.

BACKSAW

COMBINATION SQUARE

FILES

LOCKING PLIERS

RECIPROCATING SAW

TAPE MEASURE

BLOCK PLANE

COMBINATION WRENCH

HACKSAW

MARKER

SAFETY GLASSES

TIN SNIPS

CAULKING GUN

DRILL

HAMMER AND NAIL SET

PLUMB BOB AND CHALK LINE

SAWHORSE

UTILITY KNIFE

CIRCULAR SAW

DRILL BITS

HOLE SAW

PRY BARS

SCREWDRIVERS

WOOD CHISELS

CLAMP

DUST MASK

LEVEL

RATCHET WRENCH AND SOCKET SET

STUD FINDER

WORK GLOVES

Locksets and latches

Locksets and latches fall into three basic types: passage locksets, which may include a lock but which principally serve as a mechanism to hold the door shut; entry locksets, which include a keyed security lock; and security or dead-bolt locks, which offer a more secure barrier to unauthorized entry but do not include a knob or latch mechanism.

While most modern locksets are more or less interchangeable within their basic types, older passage locksets used a mortise that may not accept a new lock. If you can't repair an older lockset, check the fit of a new one, and if necessary, look for a reproduction. If neither works, you may have to replace the whole door.

Backset is the distance from the center of the doorknob spindle to the edge of the door. The backset on some, but not all, locksets is adjustable. Be sure to buy your replacement with the same backset as the previous unit.

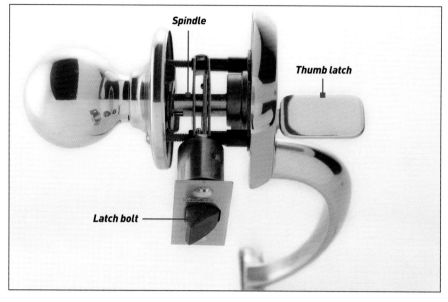

Spindle

Thumb latch

Latch bolt

LOCKSETS OPERATE BY EXTENDING THE LATCH BOLT INTO A STRIKE PLATE (see opposite page) set in the door frame. The latch bolt is moved back and forth by a spindle or connecting rod operated by a thumb latch, handle, or keyed cylinder. If the doorknob or key binds when turned, the problem usually lies in the spindle and latch bolt mechanism. Cleaning and lubricating the moving parts will correct most problems.

A sliding latch bolt (shown above) allows the door to be pushed shut; it can lock automatically, depending on how you set the lock mechanism. A dead bolt, shown below on the security lock, must always be opened and closed with a key or handle.

Types of locksets

OLDER PASSAGE LOCKSETS are easily cleaned and lubricated by loosening the handle setscrew and removing the handles and spindle. Loosen the faceplate screws and pry the lockset from the door. Remove the lockset cover, lubricate the parts, and then reassemble the unit.

MODERN PASSAGE LOCKSETS usually need little maintenance. If necessary, they're cleaned and lubricated by releasing the spring catch and connecting screws, and removing the handles. Remove the faceplate and latch bolt, lubricate the parts, and reassemble.

SECURITY LOCKS, like passage locksets, should be relatively trouble-free. If they need maintenance, remove the connecting screws and cylinders. Remove the faceplate and latch bolt. Lubricate the components and reassemble.

DOORS

Solving door latch problems

When a door fails to latch, the problem is usually one of alignment. The latch bolt, for some reason, fails to drop smoothly into the center of the strike plate.

Determine the direction in which the latch bolt is off-center. If it meets the strike plate above or below center, correct the problem by shimming a hinge to change the angle at which the door hangs. The shim may solve the problem, but it also may make the door bind with the jamb. If the alignment seems fine, but the door won't latch or must be pushed firmly to latch, the door is probably warped. A warped door may indicate a moisture problem. Check the edges of the door to make sure they're properly sealed. Suspending the door between two sawhorses and weighting down the center may counteract the warp, but think about buying a replacement door.

Locksets can be part of a complete decorating scheme; they come in a wide range of styles and prices.

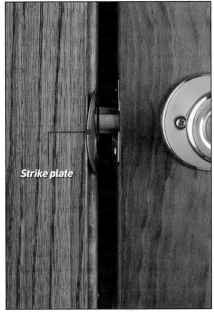

Strike plate

Misalignment with the strike plate will prevent the latch bolt from extending into the strike plate opening. If necessary, you can raise the position of the latch bolt by inserting a thin cardboard shim behind the bottom hinge. Lower it by putting the shim behind the top hinge. If this causes the door to jamb, explore the solutions below.

ALIGNING THE LATCH BOLT AND STRIKE PLATE

1 TIGHTEN ANY LOOSE HINGE SCREWS AND TEST THE DOOR. If the door continues to sag, replace the hinges. If the latch bolt still doesn't catch, fix minor alignment problems by filing the strike plate until the latch bolt fits.

2 CHECK THE DOOR FOR A SQUARE FIT. If the size of the gap between the door and frame changes as it moves from top to bottom or side to side, the door is crooked in its opening. Remove the door and shim either the top or bottom hinge with an index card or playing card to correct the problem.

3 IF THE LATCH AND STRIKE PLATE ARE STILL MISALIGNED, THEY MAY HAVE BEEN INSTALLED INCORRECTLY. Remove the plate and mark where the latch meets the door jamb. Move the strike plate to this point, chiseling away wood behind it if necessary. Fill in gaps around the plate with wood filler, and paint or stain to match.

Freeing a sticking door

Doors stick when the hinges sag, when the door frame shifts, or when humidity causes the door to swell.

If the door seems to sag within the frame, make sure the hinge screws are tight. Once you have tightened the hinge screws, if a door continues to stick, sand or plane the door edge at the sticking point. Avoid doing this during a period of high humidity, as you may remove too much of the surface. Wait for dry weather, test to see if the door is still sticking, then have at it. Varnish or paint the edges of the sanded or planed door to minimize the effects of humidity in the future.

Doors get a lot of attention because they're central to the finished look of a room. When working on a door be careful not to scrape, gouge, or scratch the door itself, and don't damage the finish on the hinges.

1 **IF THE DOOR SAGS** because one of the screws is loose and won't tighten, drive the lower hinge pin out with a screwdriver and hammer. Hold the door in place and drive out the upper hinge pin. Some hinges have a hole in the bottom. On these hinges, put a nail in the hole and tap on it with a hammer to drive the pin upward.

2 **ONCE YOU REMOVE THE DOOR FROM ITS HINGES,** check to see which screws won't tighten, and then remove the hinges completely.

3 **COAT WOODEN GOLF TEES OR DOWELS WITH EPOXY** and then drive them into the worn screw holes. Let the epoxy dry completely and cut off the excess wood.

4 **DRILL PILOT HOLES IN THE NEW WOOD AND REHANG THE HINGE** with the new wood as a base for the screws.

DOORS

Installing a door lock

If you're installing a new lock on your door, chances are it's a security (or dead-bolt) lock. Entrance door and passage locks are usually already in place. If you do find yourself replacing an entrance or passage lock, it's much like installing a dead bolt. Instead of putting in the key cylinders, however, you'll put in the doorknobs. If you're putting in a new door and lock, get a predrilled door—the hole for the knob and latch are already there. Just screw the lock in place.

When you head out to buy a dead bolt, you'll have a few choices. The biggest is how you want to open the door. Single-cylinder locks can be opened from the inside with a thumb latch. Double-cylinder locks require a key from either side.

In most applications, a single cylinder is fine. A key opens it from the outside; a twist of the thumb screw opens it from the inside. But if you have a door with a window, a double cylinder provides more security. Someone breaking the window will still need a key to get in. However, someone needing to get out—in the case of a fire, for example—will also need a key. Most people solve the problem by leaving the key in the inside cylinder; this helps in the event of fire but is useless in preventing break-ins.

All door locks have what is called a "setback"—the distance from the edge of the door to the center of the knob or cylinder. The two standard setbacks are 2¾ and 2⅜ inches. If you're drilling the holes yourself, a lock with either setback is fine, and neither has an advantage over the other. If the hole is predrilled, measure the setback and get a lock that matches. If you arrive at the store only to discover you forgot the measurements, good news. Both locks and dead bolts are available with an adjustable setback.

WORK SMARTER

INSTALL THE LOCKSET FIRST
If hanging a door from scratch, install the lockset while the door is on the sawhorses. That way you won't have a swinging door to contend with while you're drilling holes.

DOORS

① MEASURE TO FIND THE LOCK LOCATION. Tape the cardboard template, supplied with the lockset, onto the door. Use a nail or awl to mark the center of the cylinder on the face and the latch bolt on the edge of the door.

② BORE A HOLE FOR THE LOCK CYLINDER WITH A HOLE SAW AND DRILL. To avoid splintering the door, drill through one side until the drill bit just starts to come out the other side. Remove the hole saw and then complete the hole from the opposite side of the door.

③ USING A SPADE BIT, DRILL TO BORE THE LATCH BOLT HOLE from the edge of the door into the cylinder hole. Keep the drill perpendicular to the door edge while drilling.

Installing a door lock *(continued)*

4 **THE PLATE ON THE BOLT MECHANISM NEEDS TO BE INSET SO THAT IT'S FLUSH WITH THE EDGE OF THE DOOR.** Lay out the recess by putting the bolt in its hole. Line up the plate and screw it into the door. Trace around the plate with a utility knife. Remove the plate from the door.

5 **CUT THE OUTLINE OF THE RECESS BY HOLDING A CHISEL WITH THE BEVEL SIDE FACING THE INSIDE OF THE RECESS.** Tap the butt end lightly with a mallet or hammer until the cut is as deep as the plate is thick. To help gauge the depth, measure back from the cutting edge of the chisel by the thickness of the plate, and draw a line on the chisel.

6 **TO HELP REMOVE THE WASTE, MAKE A SERIES OF PARALLEL DEPTH CUTS** ¼ inch apart across the recess while holding the chisel at a 45-degree angle. Drive the chisel with light mallet blows to the butt end of the chisel.

7 **CUT OUT THE WASTE CHIPS** by holding the chisel at a low angle with the bevel side toward the work surface. Striking the chisel with a mallet will drive the chisel too deep; push the chisel by hand to make the cut.

8 **INSERT THE LATCH BOLT IN THE EDGE HOLE.** Insert the lock tailpiece through the latch bolt mechanism, and test-fit the cylinders. If the tailpiece is too long, snap it at the indentations by bending it with one set of pliers while holding it with a second set.

9 **PUT THE STRIKE PLATE IN PLACE AND TRACE AROUND THE HOLE.** Mark the center. Drill the latch bolt hole with a spade bit. Install the strike plate using the retaining screws provided with the lockset. Trace around it with a knife, and cut a recess for it the same way you cut one for the bolt. Screw the plate in place.

Removing an entry door

Before you can install your new entry door unit, you must clear away the old door and frame. Removing an old door is a fairly easy task, requiring more muscle than skill, and not too much muscle, if you take your time and proceed systematically.

With the exception of the interior trim, you probably plan to discard the old pieces, so it's OK if you damage them. Make the removal process as easy on yourself as you can. If you have a reciprocating saw with a metal-cutting blade, use it to cut through any nails that can't readily be pulled out, then hammer the remaining nail shanks flush with the rough opening. You can also saw the door frame and pry it out in pieces if you have to.

SKILL SCALE

| EASY | **MEDIUM** | HARD |

REQUIRED SKILLS: Basic carpentry skills.

HOW LONG WILL IT TAKE?

Experienced . . . . 30 min.
Handy . . . . 45 min.
Novice . . . . 1 hr.

VARIABLES: Condition of the old door and manner of attachment will influence how long removal will take.

STUFF YOU'LL NEED

✔ **MATERIALS:**
Scrap wood

✔ **TOOLS:**
Pry bar, utility knife, reciprocating saw

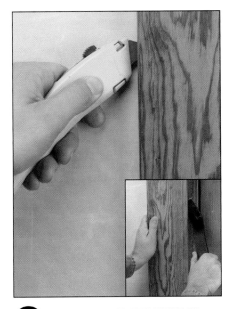

1 **FIRST USE A UTILITY KNIFE TO SCORE BETWEEN THE MOLDING AND THE WALL,** and then use a pry bar (see inset) and hammer to gently remove the interior door trim. Protect the wallboard or plaster by placing a thin piece of scrap wood under the pry bar. Save the trim to reapply after the new door is installed.

2 **TO PREVENT THE FACE OF THE TRIM FROM SPLINTERING,** remove any remaining finishing nails by pulling them from the back with a hammer. You can also drive the nails beneath the surface of the trim and fill the holes.

3 **USE A UTILITY KNIFE TO CUT AWAY THE OLD CAULK** between the exterior siding and the brick molding on the door frame.

4 **PRY AWAY AND DISCARD THE OLD DOOR JAMB AND THRESHOLD.** Cut stubborn nails with a reciprocating saw.

Making an opening for a door or window

The first step in cutting an opening for a door or window is to buy the door or window, then read the directions. What you're looking for is the size of the rough opening—the distance between the pieces of framing that support the door or window. It will be slightly larger than the size of the door or window.

The opening for doors, for example, is usually 2 inches larger than the door size (but follow the directions for your door). This leaves room for two ¾-inch door jambs, plus ½ inch of wiggle room that you'll fill with shims.

See page 237 for full-size examples of how door and window openings are framed.

See page 237 for full-size examples

SKILL SCALE

EASY	**MEDIUM**	HARD

REQUIRED SKILLS: Basic carpentry and framing skills, accurate measuring and working with tools.

⏱ HOW LONG WILL IT TAKE?

Experienced . . . . .Variable
Handy . . . . .Variable
Novice . . . . .Variable

VARIABLES: You will never know what kind of issues you will run when you start removing materials. Give yourself extra time to complete the job.

STUFF YOU'LL NEED

✔ MATERIALS:
2×6, ½" plywood for header; 8d nails; 16d nails

✔ TOOLS:
Hammer, pry bar, screwdriver, jack posts, short lengths of 2×6, utility knife, circular saw, stud finder, square, level, tape measure

① **REMOVE THE TRIM WITH A PRY BAR AND HAMMER, THEN PROTECT THE FLOOR WITH DROP CLOTHS.** Cover interior doorways with plastic to confine dust. Shut off power and water that may run through the wall. Remove electrical cover plates and heating duct covers if they are located in the area to be removed.

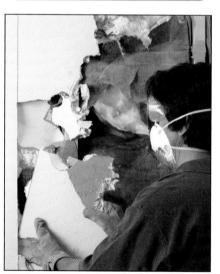

② **MARK THE AREA OF THE WALL YOU WILL REMOVE.** Put on safety glasses and a dust mask. On drywall, cut along the layout line with a utility knife. On plaster, cut the line with a circular saw, cutting through the lath but not into the studs. Remove the plaster or drywall surface with a hammer and pry bar.

Double top plate

③ **ALL EXTERIOR WALLS ARE LOAD-BEARING,** so you will need to provide support for the floor and roof above while you work. Begin by using a stud finder to find the joists nearest the area you're opening. Brace them with jack posts and a 36-inch 2×6, which is long enough to span the joists. Interior walls that have a double top plate (see inset) are also load-bearing and will need the same support.

④ **REMOVE THE STUDS.** (First relocate wires and pipes that are in the way.) Cut them at top and bottom with a reciprocating saw or push the studs from side to side and pry them out with a pry bar. You may be able to reuse some of the material for jack or cripple studs when you frame the opening.

DOORS

5 **LAY OUT THE FRAMING ON THE SOLEPLATE.** Start by drawing lines marking the edges of the rough opening. Measure 3 inches outside the opening, and draw a line marking the outside edge of the king stud you'll use to help frame the opening. See page 237 for what your finished opening will look like.

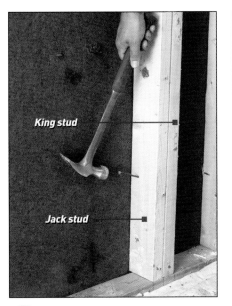

King stud

Jack stud

6 **TOENAIL THE KING STUDS IN PLACE, WITH FOUR 8d NAILS AT EACH END.** (Face-nail with 16d nails; toenail with 8d.) Then cut a jack stud long enough to reach from the soleplate to the top of the rough opening. Nail it to the king studs you just installed.

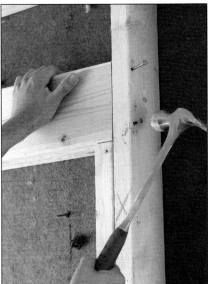

7 **ON NON-LOAD-BEARING WALLS, NAIL A 2x4 HEADER ACROSS THE TOP OF THE TRIMMERS.** On load-bearing walls, nail a built-up header in place. (See Making Headers, page 342.) Cut short pieces of 2×4 to fit between the top of the header and the top plate. Nail pieces with 16d nails and toenail them in place with four 8d nails.

Ⓐ

Ⓑ

8 **Ⓐ IF FRAMING A DOOR,** cut through and remove the soleplate. **Ⓑ IF FRAMING A WINDOW,** mark the bottom of the rough opening on the jack studs. Cut a rough sill to fit snugly between the jack studs, and wedge it in place. Make sure it's level and toenail it in place. Cut cripple studs to fit between the sill and soleplate—one under each end, and one every 16 inches.

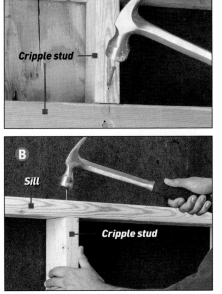

Ⓐ Cripple stud

Ⓑ Sill

Cripple stud

9 **NAIL THE CRIPPLE STUDS IN PLACE.** Ⓐ For doors toenail cripple studs between the header and the top plate every 16 inches. Ⓑ For windows install cripple studs every 16 inches between the sill and the soleplate and the header and the top plate.

Window opening

Door opening

10 **WHEN YOU'RE READY TO INSTALL THE DOOR OR WINDOW, REMOVE THE WALL SECTION BEHIND IT.** Start by drilling through the wall at each corner of the rough opening. Put the blade of a reciprocating saw in one of the holes and cut along the trimmer until you reach the next hole. Continue until you've cut out the sheathing.

DOORS

Making headers

A header is a wooden beam that provides support for the framing above it. It spans a doorway or window in a load-bearing wall—and all outside walls are load-bearing. On a non-load-bearing wall, you won't need a header over the doorway: A single 2×4 laid flat is enough. (Some interior walls are load-bearing; to determine, see page 236, Removing a Wall.)

Headers are built up to be as wide as the surrounding framing. In 2×4 framing, for example, the header is a sandwich of two 2×4s on edge, with ½-inch plywood in the middle. The "real" dimensions of 2×4s are 1½ inches by 3½ inches, so the built-up beam is 3½ inches thick and fits perfectly in place.

If the thickness of the header is determined by the surrounding framing, the width depends on the application. Codes vary, but generally speaking, the solid wood in a header for an opening up to 4 feet long should be 2×4s. From 4 to 6 feet, the lumber should be 2×6s. (Beyond that, you should call a carpenter.)

When you make a header, cut a piece of ½-inch plywood to the same width as the 2×, and then cut all three to length. Make a sandwich, and nail it together with 16d nails at 16-inch (or 24-inch if that is your stud span) centers along the edges.

The section of wall that supports a header is framed a bit differently from the rest of the wall. The header fits between two "king studs," which run floor to ceiling. The header sits on top of two "jack studs," which are nailed to and supported by the king studs. In practice, you'll install both the king and jack studs before you put the header in place. (See page 237 for a diagram of king and jack studs.)

Because codes vary, don't drive a nail until you've talked with your local building inspector. You must get a permit anyway. Ask a few questions, and get some advice while you're at the permit office.

LOAD-BEARING WALL

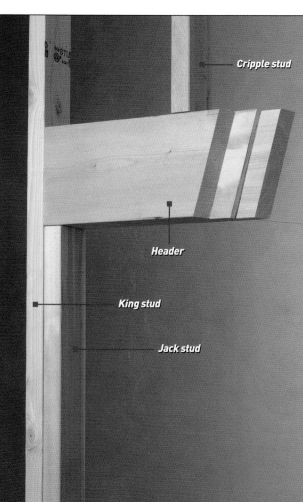

Cripple stud

Header

King stud

Jack stud

NON-LOAD-BEARING WALL

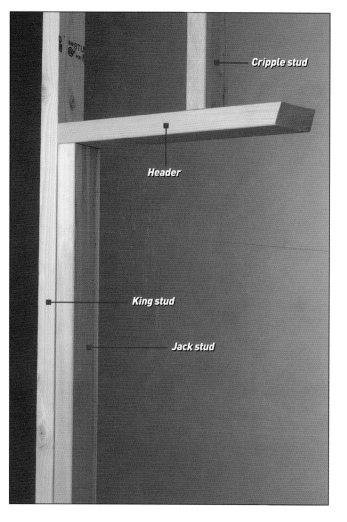

Cripple stud

Header

King stud

Jack stud

Installing a prehung interior door

Installing a prehung door is easier and faster than starting from scratch because most of the difficult operations have already been completed. All that's left is to pop off the trim from the existing opening and remove the jambs. This may sound and look like major work, but all it takes is time and muscle. Once the jamb is out, putting in the new door is a matter of shims and a few finishing nails.

1 REMOVE THE EXISTING DOOR. Start by loosening the trim with a stiff putty knife, then use a pry bar and a block of wood to remove the trim without damaging the wall. The head and side jambs are usually nailed together. It's easier to remove them from the opening at the same time. Pry the side jambs away from the studs. Then pry down the head jamb.

3 SHIM THE JAMB PLUMB, LEVEL, AND STRAIGHT. The door frame is slightly smaller than the opening it fits in to allow for adjustments. Slip shims under the side jamb until the head jamb is level. Then shim between the side jambs and the studs to fill in the spaces between them. On the hinge side, start with the bottom and top of the jamb. Then shim between the hinges and the studs, positioning the shims so that about half the shim is above the hinge. (This will help you later when nailing.) Make sure the jambs are plumb. On the latch side, shim at roughly the same places and at latch level.

If you're installing over carpet, remember to account for the thickness before you hang the door. You may have to trim the bottom in order for the door to swing properly.

2 SLIDE THE PREHUNG DOOR UNIT INTO THE ROUGH OPENING. Put the door in the opening and slide it until the jamb is flush with the wall. Make sure that the door opens in the desired direction, and into the room you want it to swing into. Remove and reposition, if necessary.

Installing a prehung interior door *(continued)*

Stuff you won't need

Most prehung doors have packing that you should remove before you put up the door. Wrappers and plastic banding are obvious, but you also may find a plastic plug in the lock mortise. (This kept the door from swinging open during shipping.) The strip of wood across the bottom of the opening is there to keep the legs (vertical pieces) from coming loose during shipping. Pull it off before you hang the door.

4 **NAIL THE DOOR FRAME TO THE STUDS.** Drive #8 finishing nails through the frame, through the shims, and into the studs. Drive two nails through each shim about an inch from each edge of the jamb, with one about ½ inch above the other. Before driving the nails home, open and close the door, and make any necessary adjustments. When you're happy with the way it works, drive and set the nails.

5 **NAIL THE TRIM TO THE JAMB AND STUDS.** Drive #6 finishing nails through the trim and into the studs behind the wall, spacing the nails about 16 inches apart. Trim any exposed shims by scoring them with a knife and then breaking along the line. Cut and install trim on the second side of the door.

Installing split-jamb interior doors

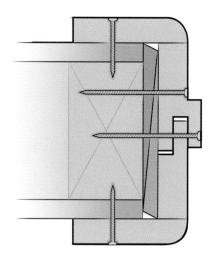

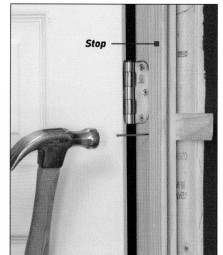

Stop

SPLIT-JAMB PREHUNG DOORS WORK WELL in situations where the rough frame is wider than a standard opening. They have a two-piece jamb that sandwiches the wall. One added advantage of a split-jamb door is that the casing is already attached, so no mitering is necessary.

1 **SEPARATE THE TWO HALVES OF THE JAMB.** Set the "slip" (or unhinged) side in the room where it will be installed. Put the hinge stop side in the opening. Tack through the casing near the top. Block and shim near the hinges on both jambs and above the jamb. Plumb and square the unit. Nail through the jamb (not the stop) into the frame with 6d finishing nails.

2 **CUT THE SHIMS FLUSH WITH THE FIRST HALF OF THE JAMB.** Inset the other slip of the door into the first half and gently push it into place until the casing reaches the wall. Use 6d finishing nails to nail through both halves of the jamb right in the center of the stop. Nail the casing to the wall with 4d finishing nails.

Installing molding for interior doors

When installing door trim, some carpenters begin with the legs (vertical pieces); others prefer to hang the top trim first. Installing the top first has the advantage of offering precise control over the most finicky part of the installation—the miters. Once the top trim is up, install the legs one at a time, positioning each so that the miter is perfect. If you install the legs first, you'll have to fit the top trim on both miters simultaneously. Unless both miters are perfect and the legs perfectly parallel, you're bound to get gaps you can't close.

Lay out the reveal. The door trim is never flush with the edge of the jamb; typically it sits back from the edge by about ⅛ inch. The space, or reveal, leaves enough room for the hinge barrel and provides a margin of error if the jamb dips.

The frame on a prehung door is likely to have a layout line on it that marks the edge of the reveal. If you work on an unmarked door frame, set a combination square to ⅛ inch, and guide it and a pencil along the frame. Mark the reveal on both sides and above the door.

Getting the trim to fit is the last step in hanging a door. The molding around a door is one of the most visible finish elements in a room.

❶ MEASURE AND MITER THE TOP TRIM. First cut a 45-degree miter on one end of the top trim piece; hold it in place to mark the inside point of the second miter cut. Lay out the cut with a combination square, and cut it with a miter box.

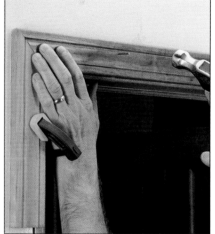

❷ NAIL THE TOP TRIM IN PLACE. To help position the trim, miter two scrap pieces of molding, and clamp them in place along the sides of the door frame. Cut and place the top trim and adjust as necessary to get a tight miter. Nail the top trim into the jamb. (Leave at least ⅛ inch of the nails exposed in case you need to adjust the piece later.) Use #6 finishing nails for the jambs and #8 finishing nails through the trim and into the studs.

Installing molding for interior doors *(continued)*

3 **MITER THE LEGS.** Mitering a piece to fit can be tricky. Make it easy on yourself by mitering the legs before you square them off. Then place the legs against the frame so they're upside down. This leaves the miter on the floor and the full length of the trim extending toward the ceiling. Mark where the top trim touches the leg and cut the leg square at the mark.

Leave a little extra length on the legs to ensure a good fit. Fine-tuning for a tight fit makes the finished door look great instead of just good.

4 **NAIL THE LEGS TO THE DOOR FRAME.** Start at the top, holding the leg so the miter closes tightly, and drive a #6 finishing nail through it and into the jamb. Work down the leg, flexing it if necessary so that it aligns with the line that marks the reveal. When you're satisfied, drive #8 finishing nails into the framing behind the wall. Repeat on the opposite leg, and then set all the nails. To keep the corners tight, predrill and drive a #6 finishing nail at an angle up through the edge of the leg, through the miter, and into the header molding.

WORK SMARTER

HIDE THE NAIL

Hide nails by driving them into one of the grooves in the molding. After you set the nail, fill the hole with glazing putty if you paint. If you stain, stain and varnish before you put up the molding, as shown. After the trim is up, fill the nail holes with colored wax sticks sold in paint departments. Pick a stick that matches the stain and rub it across the nail hole until it is filled.

The Victorian approach

Victorian molding took a more decorative—and simpler-to-install—approach toward doors. Plinth blocks were installed at the bottom trim and rosette blocks at the top corners. Molding was then cut square to fit between the blocks.

An advantage of this approach is that you have no miter joints to cut; another is that it adds Victorian style.

Plinth blocks, rosettes, and reversible pilaster trim are available in packaged kits. Install the end blocks first with construction adhesive; then crosscut lengths of trim to fit between blocks.

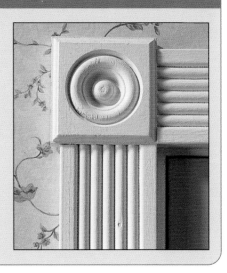

Installing a prehung entry door

STUFF YOU'LL NEED

✔ **MATERIALS:**

Drip edge, wood shims, casing nails, silicone caulk

✔ **TOOLS:**

Tin snips, hammer, carpenter's level, pencil, pry bar, circular saw, wood chisel, nail set, caulking gun, handsaw

A new steel entry door—with energy-efficient insulation and weather stripping, easy-to-maintain baked enamel primer coat, and a wide variety of styles—can greatly enhance the comfort, security, and appearance of your home.

Because replacement steel entry doors are prehung with jambs, brick molding, and hardware (except locksets), installing them need not be a difficult project. Insulated steel entry doors can be heavy, though, so you may want to line up a helper before you begin.

Entry doors are also made of wood or fiberglass. Talk to your door supplier about the door most appropriate for your situation.

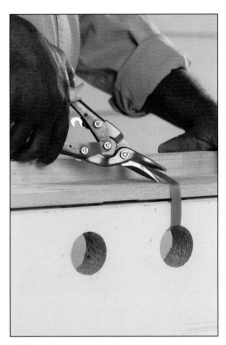

1 **PREPARE THE ROUGH OPENING, IF NECESSARY, AND REMOVE THE NEW DOOR AND FRAME FROM THEIR PACKING.** Leave in place the retaining brackets that hold the door closed while you're working on it. Measure both the door and rough opening to make sure the door is the right size.

2 **TEST-FIT THE DOOR AND FRAME, CENTERING THEM IN THE ROUGH OPENING.** Use a level to make sure the door is plumb. If necessary, shim under the lower side jamb until the door is plumb. Adjust as necessary to keep the doorjambs square with each other. Double-check to make sure the door is centered.

3 **TRACE THE OUTLINE OF THE BRICK MOLDING ONTO THE SIDING.** If you have vinyl or metal siding, be sure to enlarge the outline to make room for the extra trim required. Remove the door and frame after finishing the outline.

DOORS

Installing a prehung entry door *(continued)*

4 **PUT ON YOUR SAFETY GLASSES AND CUT ALONG THE OUTLINE DOWN TO, BUT NOT INTO, THE SHEATHING.** Start the cut with the blade clear of the siding, and then lower the moving blade into it. Stop just short of the corners to prevent damaging the siding that will remain. Finish the corners with a sharp wood chisel.

5 **TO PROVIDE A MOISTURE BARRIER, CUT A PIECE OF DRIP EDGE TO FIT THE WIDTH OF THE ROUGH OPENING,** then slide it underneath the siding at the top of the opening. Do not nail the drip edge.

6 **CHECK THE FIT OF THE DOOR AND ENLARGE THE OPENING AS NECESSARY.** Remove the door and apply several thick beads of silicone caulk to the bottom of the doorsill. Caulk underneath the spots where the bottom of the jamb and brick molding will be.

7 **CENTER THE DOOR UNIT IN THE ROUGH OPENING** and push the molding tight against the sheathing.

8 **CHECK THAT THE DOORJAMB ON THE HINGE SIDE IS PLUMB;** shim underneath it as necessary to correct any problems. Temporarily screw the hinge jamb in place by driving two #8 3-inch drywall screws through it: One about 2 inches above the top hinge and the other about 2 inches from the center hinge. Loosen the screws if necessary to bring the jamb back into plumb.

TOOL TIP

SQUARE TALK ON LEVELS
Levels are a carpenter's best friend, especially if they're used properly. Here are some tips to keep your projects plumb.

- Always use the longest level that will fit into your work space. Low spots and high spots will be more apparent and you'll get a more accurate reading.

- Use a level that allows you to adjust the vials that hold the bubbles so you can keep the level true.

- Be precise. Make sure the bubble is centered between the lines on the vial when you're taking a reading. A little bit off can become a significant problem over two or three feet.

9 **GO INSIDE THE HOUSE THROUGH ANOTHER DOOR AND PLACE PAIRS OF WEDGE-SHAPED CEDAR SHIMS TOGETHER TO FORM FLAT SHIMS,** and insert them into the gaps behind the hinges and between the jamb and framing to stabilize the jamb. Cedar shims are preferable to pine because they are more weather-resistant.

10 **REMOVE THE RETAINING BRACKETS** installed by the manufacturer; open and close the door to make sure it works properly.

11 **REMOVE TWO OF THE SCREWS ON THE TOP HINGE AND REPLACE THEM WITH LONG ANCHOR SCREWS** (usually included with the unit). These anchor screws will penetrate the framing members to strengthen the installation. DO NOT use longer screws than the manufacturer calls for on doors with sidelights—the screws might break the glass.

12 **ANCHOR THE BRICK MOLDING TO THE FRAMING MEMBERS** with 10d galvanized casing nails driven every 12 inches. Use a nail set to drive the nailheads below the surface of the wood.

13 **IF YOUR DOOR HAS AN ADJUSTABLE THRESHOLD,** adjust it for a tight seal as directed by the manufacturer.

    NOTE: If you make it too high, it will make the door difficult to open and eventually could damage either the door or the weather stripping.

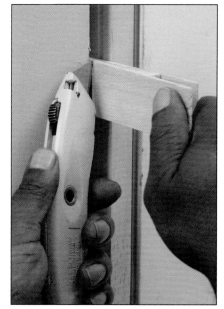

14 **CUT THE SHIMS** flush with the framing using a utility knife.

Installing a prehung entry door *(continued)*

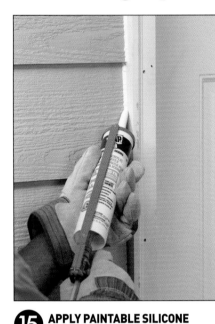

15 **APPLY PAINTABLE SILICONE CAULK AROUND THE ENTIRE DOOR UNIT.** Fill all nail holes with caulk. Finish the door as directed by the manufacturer.

16 **REPLACE THE CASING ON THE INSIDE OF THE DOORJAMB.** If the trim was damaged during removal, cut and install new casing.

17 **INSTALL A NEW DOOR LOCK.** First, insert the latch through the hole for it in the door. Then insert the lockset tailpieces through the latch bolt, and screw the handles together by tightening the retaining screws.

If you're replacing an entry door you can replace the trim you removed or put on an entirely new style of interior trim to match your room decor.

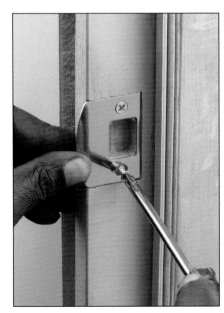

18 **SCREW THE STRIKE PLATE TO THE DOORJAMB AND ADJUST THE PLATE POSITION TO FIT THE LATCH BOLT.** Avoid damage to the screw heads by using a hand screwdriver.

Sidelights

Some doorways have windows, called sidelights, immediately to one or both sides of the opening. If you have sidelights, you can leave them in place as we did here, as long as they aren't part of a prefabricated frame. If you'd like to install sidelights where there aren't any, get a prefabricated door with attached sidelights. You'll have to enlarge the rough opening to make room for the sidelights, so look before you leap. Make sure you want to—and can—do the carpentry. Take a look at page 340, Making an Opening for a Door or Window, to see what's involved. Start framing when you have the new door on site.

DOORS

Installing a storm door

A storm door, as simple as it is, provides many benefits to your home. It can add years to the outward finish and surface of your entry door, it helps to insulate and weatherproof your entry door, it provides additional security, and it improves the appearance of your house, all at the same time.

When you buy your storm door, look for a model that has a solid inner core, low-maintenance finish, and a seamless outer shell. You can find a storm door to complement just about any house style. Look closely at your current door, however. If it juts out beyond the trim by even the slightest amount, you'll have a bit of extra carpentry to do. Take off the trim and replace it with a new layer of wood thick enough so that the door no longer juts out. Nail the trim to the new layer of wood.

Storm door frames allow for a small degree of accommodation to your existing door opening, but it is important to measure the opening carefully. Find the dimensions from the inside edges of the entry door's brick molding. Subtract approximately ¼ inch from the width of the opening to arrive at a suitable storm door size. Any difference in opening size can easily be adjusted and compensated for when you install the storm door frame.

Most storm doors are made so that you can install the same door with the hinge on either the left or the right. Some manufacturers require you to choose either a left- or right-handed door when you order. When you install your storm door, install it so the hinge is on the same side as those on the entry door. It makes getting through the door a lot easier—especially if you have groceries in your arms.

Storm doors, because of the large amount of glass combined with weather stripping, can cause sunlight to produce considerable heat buildup in the space between the storm door and the entry door. In the winter, this additional heat can be beneficial. But not all storm doors have screens, and the summer heat buildup from a glass storm door can actually damage the plastic trim on entry doors. As a result, some manufacturers recommend avoiding certain types of storm doors. Check with the maker of your entry door to verify it is compatible with the storm door that you have in mind. Ask the salesperson for advice when you buy your new storm door.

DOORS

1 INSTALLATION VARIES SLIGHTLY FROM ONE MANUFACTURER TO ANOTHER. Some brands require installing the drip cap (the top part of the storm door frame) first; others install the cap later. Install the drip cap now if the directions that came with your door say to. If not, follow the manufacturer's directions.

2 FIND THE FRAME PIECE, CALLED A Z-CHANNEL BECAUSE IT REMOTELY RESEMBLES A "Z," THAT'S MARKED FOR THE HINGES. Most doors are made so you can hang them with the hinges on either the left or right, using the same channel. Put the channel against the opening on the hinge side, and mark the top with tape.

3 SUBTRACT ⅛ INCH FROM THE DISTANCE BETWEEN THE DOORSILL AND THE TOP OF THE OPENING. Draw a cutoff line this distance from the top of the Z-channel. If the sill slants, follow the manufacturer's directions. Cut along the line with a hacksaw.

Installing a storm door (continued)

4 **POSITION THE CHANNEL AGAINST THE HINGE SIDE OF THE DOOR** so that it extends about ⅛ inch above the top of the door. (This ensures that when closing, the top of the door will clear the drip cap.) Screw the Z-channel to the door hinges, which usually come installed on the door.

5 **SET THE DOOR IN THE DOORWAY WITH THE Z-CHANNEL TIGHT AGAINST THE TOP.** Check with a level to make sure it's plumb. Have a helper drive a couple of screws to hold the channel; check to make sure that the door opens and closes freely. Adjust if necessary, and install the remaining screws.

6 **INSTALL THE DRIP CAP, IF YOU HAVEN'T YET.** Position it so that there's an even ⅛-inch gap between it and the top of the door. If the door seats against the weather stripping and closes without hitting the drip cap, drive the remaining screws. If not, make the necessary adjustments before driving the screws.

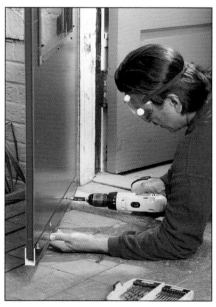

7 **CUT THE LATCH-SIDE Z-CHANNEL AS IN STEP 3.** Put it in the opening, tight against the drip cap. Adjust it so there's a gap between the channel and the door's edge; the amount varies between brands. Screw it in place. For a gap of more than ¼ inch, the directions may require you to cut a filler strip to close it.

8 **ATTACH THE SWEEP TO THE DOOR'S BOTTOM.** A sweep is either a wide strip or a U-channel with weather stripping across the bottom. Read your door's directions carefully: Some require installation of the strip before you hang the door. Position the sweep so its weather stripping touches the sill; screw it in place.

9 **MOUNT THE DOOR HANDLE FOLLOWING THE MANUFACTURER'S DIRECTIONS.** Depending on the model, the holes may be predrilled, or you may have to drill them yourself. Mount a hydraulic door closer on the door. Most are adjustable so that you can control how quickly the door closes. Follow the manufacturer's directions to make any adjustments.

Installing a hinged patio door

STUFF YOU'LL NEED

✔ **MATERIALS:**
Door assembly, drip edge, caulk, shims, 2-inch galvanized roofing nails, 10d casing nails, fiberglass insulation

✔ **TOOLS:**
Screwdriver, 4-foot level, circular saw, chisel, caulking gun, utility knife, gloves, dust mask, safety glasses, ear protection

Patio doors dramatically incorporate an outdoor deck or patio into your living space, creating an easy flow of traffic into and out of your house. If you're installing a door in a new location, the first step is to cut and frame a rough opening in the wall. (See Making an Opening for a Door or Window, page 340.) If you're simply replacing a door, start with Step 1 below.

INSTALLATION TIPS:

● **To simplify installation,** buy a patio door with the door already mounted in preassembled frames. Install the patio door so that it is level and plumb, and anchor the unit securely to the framing to prevent the possibility of bowing and warping.

● **Yearly caulking and touch-up painting** will help prevent moisture from warping the jambs.

● **The doors may be removed** if you're installing the frame without help. Reinstall the doors after you have placed the frame in the rough opening and nailed at opposite corners. Adjust the bottom rollers on a sliding door after the installation is complete.

● **To remove a hinged door,** remove the hinge pins. On sliding doors, remove the stop rail found on the top jamb of the door unit.

KEEP IT SIMPLE
If you are installing a door in an existing opening, see if you can find a new door that will fit without having to reframe the rough opening. It'll save you time and money.

1 REMOVE THE OLD DOOR. Lift the doors out of their tracks and set them aside. Remove all framing down to the rough opening. If installing a door in a new location, remove the necessary interior wall surfaces, then frame the rough opening for the patio door. Finally, remove the exterior surfaces inside the framed opening. For more information, see page 340.

2 TEST-FIT THE NEW DOOR UNIT. Center the unit in the rough opening. Check to make sure that the door is plumb. If necessary, shim under the threshold to level the door. Have a helper hold the door in place while it is unattached.

Installing a hinged patio door (continued)

3 **TRACE THE OUTLINE OF THE BRICK MOLDING OR NAILING FIN ONTO THE SIDING.** Remove the door unit.

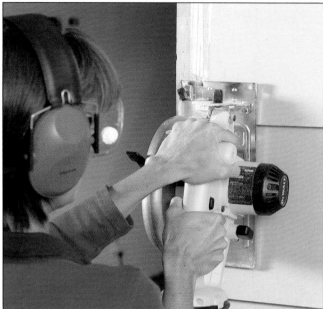

4 **CUT THE SIDING.** Wear ear protection and safety glasses. Using a circular saw, cut the siding along the outline, just down to the sheathing. Stop just short of the corners to prevent damage to the siding that will remain. Finish the cuts at the corners with a sharp wood chisel. Be careful of kickback and of wiring inside the wall.

5 **CHECK THE OPENING FOR SQUARE.** Measure diagonally from inside corner to inside corner. If the measurements on both diagonals are equal, the frame is square. If the diagonals differ by more than ¼ inch, the door will be too far out of alignment. Shim at the sides, directly under a jamb, to correct the problem.

6 **CUT A DRIP EDGE.** For extra protection from rain, cut a piece of drip edge to fit the width of the rough opening, and then slide it between the siding and the existing building paper at the top of the opening. Do not nail the drip edge.

7 **CHECK THE FLOOR OR SUBFLOOR.** In some cases, removing an old door also removes part of the floor or subfloor. If so, cut a piece of pressure-treated wood the same thickness as the interior floor to fit the opening. Put it in place and check to see whether it's level. If necessary, level the surface with shims every 4 inches.

8 **INSTALL THE SHIMS.** Put the shims in place and apply two or three beads of caulk.

9 **NAIL THE PATCH** in place with galvanized roofing nails.

10 **CAULK THE THRESHOLD.** Once you've prepared the subfloor, get ready to install the door. Apply beads of caulk along what will be the edges of the door threshold. Underneath on the threshold or deck, apply a bead of caulk positioned so that it will seal the end grain of the jambs and brick mold.

11 **CAULK THE FINS.** Some doors have metal fins that you nail through to hold the door against the house. Others have a piece of molding known as "brick mold" that extends beyond the door frame; you nail that to the house. Caulk the back of the fins or molding before positioning. You'll nail them in Step 14.

Installing a hinged patio door *(continued)*

12 **LIFT THE DOOR INTO PLACE.** Remove any packaging from the door and lift it in place carefully so that you don't accidentally smear the caulk onto an exposed part of the floor.

13 **CHECK FOR SQUARE.** Double-check the diagonals to make sure the door has remained square. If the diagonals differ by more than ⅛ inch, shim as necessary to bring the door back into square.

WORK SMARTER

SHIM THE THRESHOLD
Metal thresholds need a solid surface under them. Gaps, or an out-of-level floor, will cause the threshold to bend when you step on it. Many manufacturers specify that you support the bottom of the threshold with a solid surface that runs the entire length of the threshold. If you need to shim under such a threshold, you can still use individual shims, as long as you don't leave spaces between them. Once you've installed the threshold, start any necessary shimming at one end. Install the first shims on each side of the threshold. Install the next two shims snugly against them. Work your way to the center, checking the threshold with a level as you go.

14 **NAIL THE FINS OR BRICK MOLD TO THE SHEATHING NEAR THE TOP CORNERS OF THE DOOR.** Use 2-inch galvanized roofing nails.

15 **SHIM THE SIDES OF THE DOOR.** Drive the shims just far enough to make them snug. Double the shims, if necessary, or trim a few inches off the thin end in order to have a shim thick enough to do the job. Shim behind each hinge and behind the latch strike as well. Do not shim around the top of the door.

16 **NAIL THE DOOR IN PLACE AND TRIM THE SHIMS.** Double-check for square and level, and make any necessary corrections. Then drive 2-inch galvanized finishing nails into the doorjamb, through the shims, and into the frame. Trim the shims by scoring them with a knife and then snapping off the excess.

17 **INSULATE AROUND THE DOOR.** To reduce drafts, use a shim to stuff scraps of fiberglass insulation into the voids around the frame. Wear safety glasses, gloves, and a dust mask when working with insulation. Wash work clothes separately from general laundry.

18 **ATTACH THE EXTERIOR MOLDING.** If your door is surrounded by brick mold, drive 10d casing nails through it every 12 inches, attaching the molding and door to the house. If your door has a nailing fin, drive the nails specified by the manufacturer through the holes in it; cover the fin with molding.

19 **CAULK THE SILL.** Caulk completely around the sill nosing and the brick mold or metal trim. Press the caulk into cracks with a damp finger or with an inexpensive caulking tool. As soon as the caulk is dry, paint the sill nosing. Finish the door and install the lockset as directed by the manufacturer.

Installing a garage door

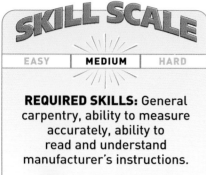

SKILL SCALE

EASY	**MEDIUM**	HARD

REQUIRED SKILLS: General carpentry, ability to measure accurately, ability to read and understand manufacturer's instructions.

HOW LONG WILL IT TAKE?

Experienced . . . . 5 hrs.
Handy . . . . 8 hrs.
Novice . . . . 12 hrs.

STUFF YOU'LL NEED

✔ **MATERIALS:**
Garage door assembly, shims, rear track hangers, nails

✔ **TOOLS:**
Sawhorses, hammer, level, utility knife, drill, two wrenches, tape measure, locking pliers or C-clamps

Garage doors are made of wood, metal, or fiberglass. They can be highly decorative or very plain. Whatever the style, they all depend on a good set of springs to make them work. The springs provide the lift that opens the door, as well as the resistance that keeps it from crashing down on your head.

If the door has extension springs, like the door shown here, getting the proper tension on the springs is simple and safe for the homeowner. If the door has torsion springs, which are essentially huge window-shade rollers, leave the job to a pro. These springs need to be wound up, and losing control of them can be dangerous. (Fortunately, most doors made for residential use are on extension springs, and any style you do find on torsion springs is likely to be available in extension springs.)

Installation of garage doors varies both from brand to brand and situation to situation. The instructions here are typical, but pay close attention to the directions that come with your door. It's the largest moving part of your home, and, pretty face or not, safe installation requires attention to detail.

SAFETY ALERT

TORSION SPRINGS ARE DANGEROUS

On some garage doors a tightly wound spring called a torsion spring runs over the top of the door and helps open and close it by counterbalancing the weight. These springs are always under tension and are extremely powerful. An unplanned release can cause serious injury if you don't know how to remove them safely. Instead of attempting to remove one yourself, get a garage door professional to do the removal or installation.

PARTS OF A TYPICAL ROLL-UP DOOR

ROLL-UP GARAGE-DOOR COMPONENTS INCLUDE:

- **A** stud pulley
- **B** clevis pulley
- **C** tension spring
- **D** front track brace
- **E** track
- **F** track bracket
- **G** door lock
- **H** lock bar
- **I** roller hinge
- **J** cable anchor

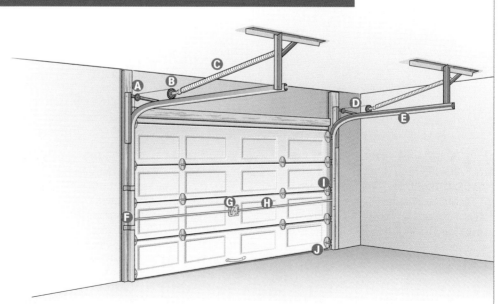

1 **PUT THE DOOR PANELS ON A PAIR OF SAWHORSES** to make working on them easier. Slip the weather stripping into its channel, screw it in place if so directed, and trim off the excess with a knife.

2 **SET THE FIRST PANEL IN THE OPENING.** Check for level and shim as necessary. Hold it in place by driving nails into the door framing at an angle so that the upper portion of the nail traps the door. Do not drive nails through the door.

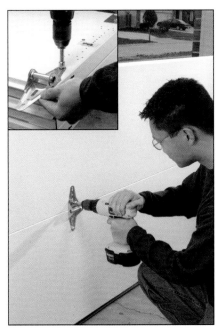

3 **STACK THE REST OF THE PANELS.** Hold them in place with bent-over nails. Attach one side of the hinges along the edges and middle of the door before you stack them. (See inset.) Attach the top rollers to the top edges of the panel.

4 **INSERT ROLLER SHAFTS INTO THE HINGES AS DIRECTED BY THE MANUFACTURER.** If any are held in place by special brackets, install them now too. If a separate bracket holds the rope you use to close the door, install it now.

5 **INSTALL THE TRACKS AROUND THE ASSEMBLED DOOR.** Begin by slipping the straight tracks over the lower wheels in the door. Put the mounting brackets against the wood framing, positioning them so that there is about ⅝ inch to ⅞ inch between the door and track. Temporarily bolt the brackets in place. (You will need to adjust them later.)

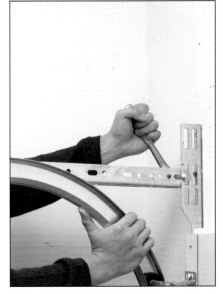

6 **ASSEMBLE THE CURVED, J-SHAPED TRACKS NEXT.** Each side has a track that bolts to two angle irons, which are joined at 90 degrees. Assemble the pieces on the floor, then slip them over the door rollers. Temporarily support the back end with a ladder or board if necessary. Position the track so it's level and plumb, shimming from the ladder as necessary.

Installing a garage door (continued)

This bolt will also stop the door from running off the back of the track

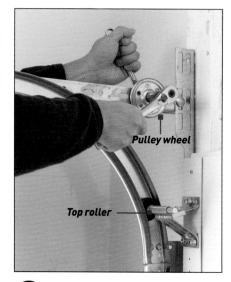

Pulley wheel

Top roller

7 **INSTALL THE REAR TRACK HANGERS.** (You'll need to purchase these separately.) The track hangers must support the full weight of the door, so they must be attached securely to a rafter or joist. Measure the distance between the back end of the J-shaped tracks and the nearest rafter. Cut the track hangers to length, if necessary, as directed by the manufacturer and attach them to the joist or rafter.

8 **ATTACH THE TRACK TO THE HANGER.** The rear track hangers hold the track level and square to the door. Check by comparing two diagonal measurements: one from the top left-hand corner of the door to the rear right-hand horizontal track and the other from the right front to the left rear. Adjust the tracks until the measurements are within ½ inch; temporarily fasten the hangers.

9 **ADJUST THE TOP ROLLER AND ATTACH THE PULLEY WHEEL.** Some doors will have a top roller that adjusts to keep the door tight against the jamb. Attach the front pulley wheels to the horizontal angles as directed by the manufacturer. Now you are ready to roll up the door for the first time. Remove the nails before you raise the door.

1 *Lock pliers to track*   **2** *Attach spring*   **3** *Attach S-hook*

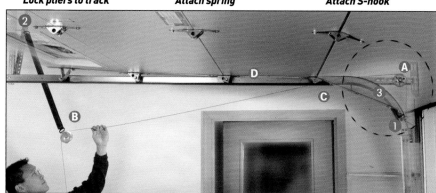

10 **RAISE THE DOOR ABOUT 4 FEET, PROP IT OPEN,** and look to see whether the spacing between the door and track is between ⅝ inch and ⅞ inch along the entire track. If not, lower the door and correct the problem by repositioning the track hanger on the joist. Once the tracks are properly aligned and the door opens smoothly from top to bottom, permanently fasten the tracks and hangers.

11 **A CABLE CALLED THE LIFT CABLE CONNECTS THE SPRING AND DOORS.** Carefully raise the door to the fully open position. **1** Attach locking pliers or C-clamps to the track to keep the door in place. **2** Attach the spring to a hook installed in the rear hanging bracket then attach one end of the cable to the bottom of the door, as directed by the manufacturer. Thread the cable around **A** the front pulley and around **B** the spring pulley, and attach the end to **C** an S-hook, using the hardware provided. **3** Attach the S-hook to **D** the horizontal track support, leaving the same amount of slack in each cable, as directed by the manufacturer.

RELEASE THE DOOR AND TEST IT TO MAKE SURE IT CLOSES GENTLY ON THE FLOOR. If it comes down with a crash, increase the spring tension, either by moving the S-hook forward on the horizontal track support or by adjusting the cable where it attaches to the S-hook. If the door won't close all the way, decrease the spring tension.

Adjusting an out-of-balance garage door

With time, the cables and springs on a garage door stretch, and the door can become dangerously out-of-balance. The usual problem is a door that closes too quickly—endangering your feet, your children, or anything else in its path. The door can also open too quickly, which can damage the door or your shoulder. A properly balanced door remains stationary when it's opened 3 to 4 feet. When you open or close it, it should come to a gentle stop. If it slams down, or closes and then reopens slightly, you'll need to adjust the spring tension.

SAFETY ALERT

BE CAREFUL OF THE SPRINGS
Springs can cause injury if released suddenly. Prop the door open to relieve tension on the springs before you attempt to remove them.

1 BEGIN WITH THE DOOR ABOUT 3 FEET ABOVE THE GROUND. Move it up and down until you find the point where the door remains stationary when you release it. If that point is more than 4 feet or less than 3 feet above the ground, you need to balance the door.

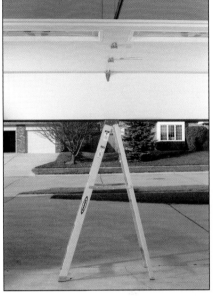

2 MAKE ALL ADJUSTMENTS WITH THE DOOR OPEN. This takes the pressure off the door springs. Prop the door open with a ladder to make sure the door won't close accidentally while you're working on it. If your ladder isn't tall enough, attach C-clamps in the door track to hold the door in place.

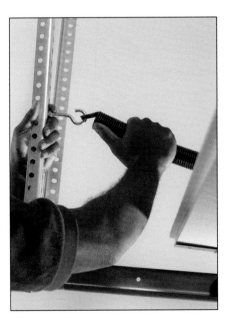

3 MAKE SURE THE SPRING IS COMPRESSED COMPLETELY, AND THEN REMOVE IT FROM THE TRACK HANGER. If the door was closing too quickly, move the spring to the next higher hole on the bracket. If it was opening too quickly, move it to the next lower hole. Move both springs and retest the balance.

4 CLOSE THE DOOR AND CHECK WITH A LEVEL TO MAKE SURE THE DOOR COMES DOWN EVENLY ON BOTH SIDES. If it doesn't, adjust the spring tension on each side of the door until it does.

5 IF YOU NEED TO MAKE FINE ADJUSTMENTS, YOU CAN ADJUST THE LIFTING CABLE INSTEAD OF THE SPRING. The cable is attached to the door and runs to an S-hook that attaches to the track support. With the door propped open, take the S-hook out of the support and tighten or loosen the cable as needed.

Installing a garage door opener

GARAGE-DOOR OPENER COMPONENTS INCLUDE: Ⓐ The power unit activated by a transmitter, key, or auxiliary switch. The Ⓑ rail guides and supports the Ⓒ traveler, which connects the door-opener chain to the Ⓓ support arm, which is attached to the garage door. The manual Ⓔ safety release disengages the trolley from the garage-door arm and allows manual operation of the door in the event of a power failure. The Ⓕ header bracket secures the rail above the door and supports the idler assembly and pulley that guides the chain drive. The Ⓖ interior auxiliary switch allows garage-door opener operation from inside the garage.

Almost any garage door opener you buy will open any garage door in America. The chain drive opener is the best-selling opener on the market. A motor pulls a chain, the chain pulls a carriage, and the carriage pulls a cable that opens the door.

The direct drive opener (shown here) works basically the same way except that the carriage travels along a large, threaded rod (like a huge bolt) instead of the door being pulled by a chain. Direct drive openers are slightly more expensive but quieter. They work best in warmer climates and tend to bog down in freezing climates.

HOMER'S HINDSIGHT

REMOVE THOSE LATCH BARS

I helped my son-in-law install an opener for his old manual garage door. When I left, I reminded him to leave the latch handle but remove the locking bars. As usual, he forgot. On a rainy day a few months later his kids locked the door while they were playing in the garage. He was outside in his car trying to get the door open with the remote until he burned the motor out. Now I kid him that since he must have wanted a manual garage door from the beginning why did we go to all that trouble.

1 **ASSEMBLE THE CARRIAGE TUBE.** This tube runs from the power unit to the front wall of the garage. The carriage, which raises and lowers the door, travels along it. It's usually shipped in sections—assemble them as directed, making sure to seat the pieces securely. Measure to verify the assembled length matches that required by the manufacturer. Make any necessary adjustments.

DOORS

2 **MOUNT THE CARRIAGE ON THE FRONT OF THE POWER UNIT, FOLLOWING THE MANUFACTURER'S DIRECTIONS.** Attach the rail clamps, which will later connect to a bracket on the wall above the door. On some doors you'll install switches and wiring at this point.

3 **SLIP THE CARRIAGE OVER THE TUBE.** Different makes and models attach differently, so follow the manufacturer's directions.

4 **MOUNT THE HEADER BRACKET, WHICH HOLDS THE CARRIAGE TUBE TO THE WALL ABOVE THE DOOR.** The exact location depends on the type of door, so follow the directions supplied by the manufacturer. Lift the power unit and set it on top of a stepladder.

5 **HANG THE POWER UNIT FROM THE CEILING.** Most units hang from angle irons and metal straps that have holes drilled in them at regular intervals. Bolt the angle irons to a rafter (or rafters) with lag screws. Attach the straps to the irons with hex-head screws, and attach the straps to the power unit with the hardware provided. Open the door several times to make sure it doesn't hit the opener while moving.

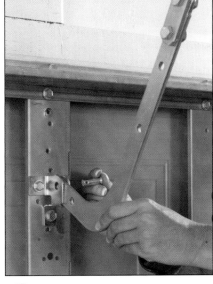

6 **THE DOOR IS OPENED BY ONE ARM THAT LIFTS IT AS THE CARRIAGE TRAVELS ALONG THE TUBE.** Before you can attach the arm, you must attach the bracket that connects it to the door. The exact location varies, depending on the door. Follow the manufacturer's instructions.

7 **BY LAW, ALL UNITS HAVE A SAFETY DEVICE THAT SHUTS DOWN THE MOTOR IF SOMETHING IS IN THE PATH OF A CLOSING DOOR.** The safety device is usually a light beam and sensor. Mount one on each side of the door as directed. Plug the unit into its socket. Test the operation and make any necessary corrections. (See Safety Testing a Garage Door Opener, page 365.)

Adjusting and maintaining a garage door opener

ADJUST THE CHAIN TENSION TO ELIMINATE A SAGGING CHAIN. If the chain sags more than ½ inch below the rail, it may bang against the rail and cause undue wear on the drive sprocket. Tighten the chain until it rests ½ inch above the base of the rail, but be careful not to overtighten.

ADJUST THE LIMIT SCREWS IF THE GARAGE DOOR OPENS MORE THAN 5 FEET BUT FAILS TO OPEN COMPLETELY. Unplug the opener and locate the open-force adjustment screw on the power unit. Turn the screw clockwise. Plug in the opener, run it through a cycle, and adjust as necessary to open the desired amount.

CHECK THE ALIGNMENT OF THE SAFETY REVERSING SENSORS AS RECOMMENDED BY THE MANUFACTURER AND ADJUST AS NECESSARY TO MAINTAIN PROPER OPERATION. The sensors must face each other across the garage door opening in order to function properly.

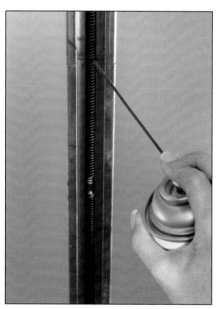

CLEAN AND LUBRICATE THE DRIVE CHAIN AND TRACK OF THE AUTOMATIC DOOR OPENER. Instead of using grease, use a light penetrating oil so it doesn't collect dirt and grit.

KILL THE POWER
Always disconnect power to the garage door opener prior to making adjustments.

CHANGING FREQUENCIES
When you push the button on the opener's remote control, it transmits a frequency-coded message to the door. Send the right message and the door opens. Send the wrong one and the door stays put. Some remotes transmit the same message each time. Others transmit a randomly changing message, or "rolling code," making it harder for someone else's remote to open your door.

How much harder? Depending on the maker, a single-code opener may be preset to one of as many as 3.6 million codes. By listening in with a special decoder, however, a clever thief can record your code, reprogram an opener, and drive right into your garage.

A more secure option is a rolling-code opener, which may have as many as 16 billion codes to choose from, and the code changes randomly each time the door opens. A rolling code is virtually impossible to crack, and if you're at all worried about security, it's a feature you'll want in a new opener. If you have an existing single-code opener, ask about kits that will convert it to rolling code.

If you have a car with a built-in garage door remote, it will probably work with a rolling-code door. Follow the directions for programming it carefully—you may have to press the button several times before the reprogramming takes effect.

Safety testing a garage door opener

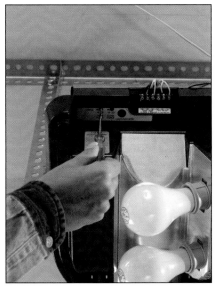

PERIODICALLY TEST THE CLOSE-FORCE SENSITIVITY SETTING OF THE GARAGE DOOR OPENER. Place a board 1 inch or thicker on the garage floor in the center of the doorway, then trigger the opener to close the door. When the door comes in contact with the board, the opener should strain slightly, then reverse and open the door. If the pressure is too great or too slight, you'll need to make adjustments.

ADJUST THE CLOSE-FORCE SENSITIVITY if the opener is either auto-reversing too easily or striking an obstacle too hard. Unplug the power unit and adjust the close-force screw according to which solution is required.

TEST THE CLOSE-FORCE SENSITIVITY BY HAND after you have used the board method mentioned above. This will allow you to physically determine the amount of pressure the opener is exerting in case the door comes in contact with people or pets. Stand in the center of the doorway and trigger the opener to close the door. As the door is closing, hold the bottom of the door in your hands and exert pressure to stop the door. Determine if the pressure to trigger the auto-reversing is too much or too little and make the necessary adjustments on the close-force sensitivity screws.

TEST THE SAFETY REVERSING SENSORS BY PLACING YOUR HAND IN THE SENSOR BEAM AS THE GARAGE DOOR IS CLOSING. The garage door mechanism should automatically reverse and open the door. If it doesn't, check the wire connections. Check the sensor alignment and clean the sensor lenses. Retest.

8 WINDOWS

WINDOWS ARE INTRICATE PIECES OF WORK. They've evolved over the centuries to give us a view and still keep the outdoors outside. Movable frames, complex joinery, and the physics of letting in light while keeping out the cold and bugs make them complicated units that present challenges when it comes to installation, maintenance, and repair.

Windows take a real beating—ultraviolet rays, temperature changes, moisture, and stray baseballs all take their toll. But they are such an integral part of a home that they deserve special attention and care.

Regular window maintenance pays off in long service and saves energy, and the beauty windows add to both the interior and exterior of your home is certainly a bonus.

- During the winter water builds up on the inside of the window when moist air hits cold glass. Installing storm windows, which have small drainage holes at the bottom, prevents this buildup.

- Clean the windows frequently to prevent debris from building up on the surfaces or the glass.

- Maintain the glaze on the outside of older wooden windows. Moisture seeps in between the glaze and the panes of glass. When it dries out, the glaze breaks away and the moisture will cause paint failure and wood rot.

- Follow the manufacturer's maintenance recommendations for vinyl-clad windows.

- Replace broken glass immediately.

- Weatherproof, weatherproof, weatherproof.

SECTION 8 PROJECTS

REAL-WORLD SITUATIONS

GETTING TO KNOW YOU

When you deal with window installations or make repairs, it helps to be able to speak window to the retailer or installer. Knowing the parts will save you time and energy when you're in the store. The word "sash," like the garment, has gone largely out of style. Most people would call the sash the window, or perhaps the window frame. But window installers need to be precise. Sash survives, as do several other words that the do-it-yourselfer should know.

    Double-hung window: A window like the one shown here with two sashes, which you raise and lower to open and close the window.

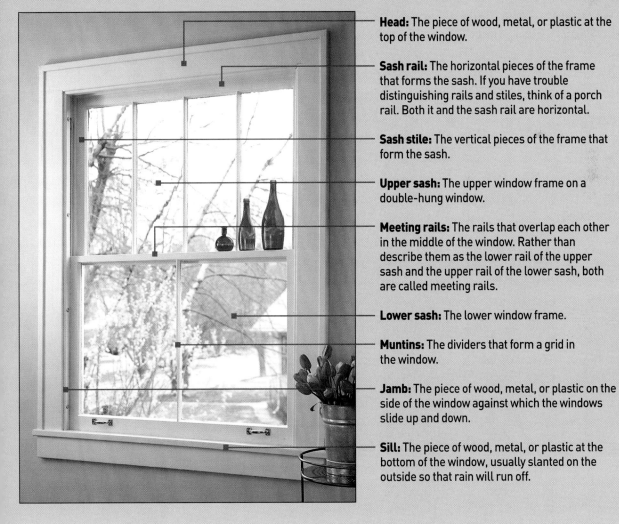

Head: The piece of wood, metal, or plastic at the top of the window.

Sash rail: The horizontal pieces of the frame that forms the sash. If you have trouble distinguishing rails and stiles, think of a porch rail. Both it and the sash rail are horizontal.

Sash stile: The vertical pieces of the frame that form the sash.

Upper sash: The upper window frame on a double-hung window.

Meeting rails: The rails that overlap each other in the middle of the window. Rather than describe them as the lower rail of the upper sash and the upper rail of the lower sash, both are called meeting rails.

Lower sash: The lower window frame.

Muntins: The dividers that form a grid in the window.

Jamb: The piece of wood, metal, or plastic on the side of the window against which the windows slide up and down.

Sill: The piece of wood, metal, or plastic at the bottom of the window, usually slanted on the outside so that rain will run off.

WINDOWS

Window basics

Choosing windows used to be a matter of deciding on double-hung, fixed, or casement windows. Now you're faced with U-factors (heat loss), SHGC (solar heat gain coefficient), VT (visible transmittance), argon, and krypton.

When buying windows, consider the following:

● **Without any bells and whistles,** the insulating value of a double-glazed window is about one-third greater than that of a single-glazed window.

● **A low-E coating is a microscopic layer of metal on the inside face of the glass** that reduces heat transmission. Because it also reflects incoming light and the resulting solar heat, manufacturers have developed low-E coatings for high, low, or moderate solar gain.

● **Sealing a gas between the layers reduces heat flow even more.** Argon is efficient and cheap. Krypton is a better insulator, but more expensive.

● **Frames can be made of wood, hardboard, aluminum, or vinyl.** Wood is strong and light but needs maintenance, as does hardboard. Aluminum is an ineffective insulator, but frames with added foam core work well. Vinyl is maintenance-free and somewhat of an insulator.

FOLLOW THE ENERGY STAR. So now what? Look for an Energy Star sticker, which lists government performance standards for each of three climate zones: Northern, where heating is a primary energy concern; Central, where heating and cooling are both concerns; and Southern, where cooling is the major concern.

Energy Star labels rate windows for efficiency. Ratings are based on the following:

● **U-factor is the rate of heat loss.** The lower the U-factor, the better a window insulates.

● **SHGC stands for solar heat gain coefficient.** It's rated on a scale of 0 to 1 and the lower the number, the less solar heat the window transmits.

People living at the equator would prefer a lower number.

● **VT stands for visible transmission**—the amount of light that gets through—and is rated on a scale of 0 to 1. The higher the number, the more light you'll have.

● **AL stands for air leakage, a measure of how much air slips past the weather stripping.** The lower the leakage, the better the window, but manufacturers say leakage is not as important a concern as U-factor or SHGC.

Once you know the standards and what they mean, look at the **Energy Performance** section of the label. Compare the factors you think are important with what the manufacturer says the window does.

If you're wondering if this research is worth the work, consider this: Top-notch windows can cut a Boston homeowner's heating bill by 30 to 40 percent. An Albuquerque homeowner can save between 6 and 32 percent in air-conditioning costs.

Window maintenance tips

CLEANING AND LUBRICATING

CLEAN THE TRACKS ON WINDOWS AND DOORS WITH A HAND VACUUM AND A TOOTHBRUSH TO KEEP THEM OPERATING SMOOTHLY. Dirt buildup is particularly a problem on storm window tracks. Aluminum and vinyl tracks can be washed with soap and water.

ONCE THE WINDOW TRACK IS CLEAN, COAT IT WITH WAX OR SOAP. Wax, being waterproof, will last longer. For windows with metal edges that run on metal tracks, you'll find a variety of lubricants: penetrating oils, silicone sprays, and powdered graphite. Some cleaners containing solvents may damage vinyl-clad windows; test them on a hidden part of the window first.

CLEAN WEATHER STRIPPING BY SPRAYING IT WITH A HOUSEHOLD CLEANER AND WIPING AWAY THE DIRT. Soap will wash paint off vinyl weather stripping, metal, or plastic runners. If paint is causing the edge of a wooden window to bind, you will have to remove the window and sand it smooth.

FREEING A STUCK WINDOW

IF A WINDOW IS PAINTED SHUT, YOU CAN OFTEN BREAK THE PAINT FILM by putting a block of wood against both the sash and the stop. Strike the block with a hammer in the direction of the stop to free the window.

IF A HAMMER AND BLOCK OF WOOD WON'T BREAK THE PAINT FILM, cut the film with a tool known variously as a sash saw, window opener, or paint zipper. Put the teeth into the crack between the window stop and sash, and slide it along the sash to cut the paint.

Newer aluminum or vinyl windows have spiral counterbalances to keep them from crashing down when open. You can adjust the spring tension by turning screws in the track insert. Adjust until the window travels easily but won't slip down when put in place.

Replacing broken sash cords

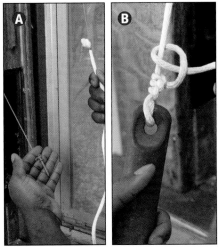

1 **OLDER WINDOWS HAVE SASH WEIGHTS AS COUNTERBALANCES.** If the cord holding them breaks, pry off the window stops and remove the lower sash. Cut both cords, and then pry the cover off the weight pocket in the lower end of the window channels. Remove the weight and cut off the cord.

2 **TIE A PIECE OF STRING TO A SMALL NAIL AND THE OTHER END TO A NEW SASH CORD. Ⓐ** Drop the nail over the pulley at the top of the window channel and into the weight pocket. Tie this end of the rope to the weight Ⓑ and pull the cord to raise the weight against the pulley.

3 **REST THE BOTTOM SASH ON THE SILL.** While holding the sash cord firmly against the side of the window, cut the cord 3 inches beyond the hole in the sash. Knot the sash cord, and wedge the knot in the hole. Replace the pocket cover, put the sash back in place, and reattach the stops.

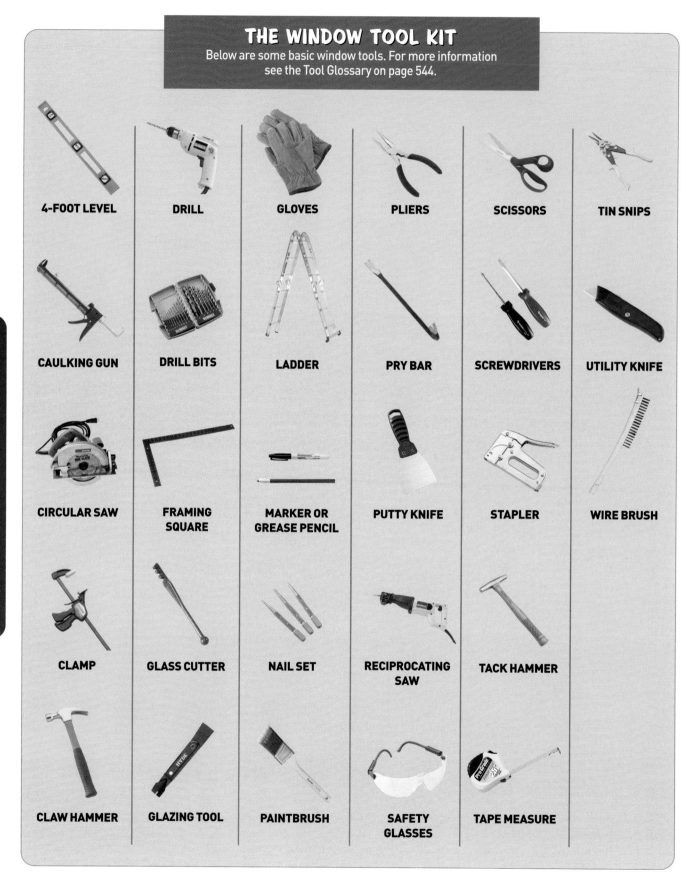

THE WINDOW TOOL KIT

Below are some basic window tools. For more information
see the Tool Glossary on page 544.

4-FOOT LEVEL

DRILL

GLOVES

PLIERS

SCISSORS

TIN SNIPS

CAULKING GUN

DRILL BITS

LADDER

PRY BAR

SCREWDRIVERS

UTILITY KNIFE

CIRCULAR SAW

FRAMING SQUARE

MARKER OR GREASE PENCIL

PUTTY KNIFE

STAPLER

WIRE BRUSH

CLAMP

GLASS CUTTER

NAIL SET

RECIPROCATING SAW

TACK HAMMER

CLAW HAMMER

GLAZING TOOL

PAINTBRUSH

SAFETY GLASSES

TAPE MEASURE

REPAIRING A BROKEN WINDOWPANE

Fepairing broken windows is messy but not hard. Chances are you'll have to repair at least one.

Put on a pair of stout leather gloves, remove the broken pane, and measure for a new one. Cut the glass yourself or have a home center or hardware store cut the glass to size. The replacement should be 1/16 inch to 1/8 inch smaller than the opening.

Glazing is the messy part. Traditional compound is a puttylike substance; a modern variation is caulklike. If you're adept with caulk, this is the route to go. Rest the nozzle (which is square) on the window frame and on the glass, and caulk away. By pulling the trigger gently and taking your time, you'll get a flat bead that slopes from muntin to windowsill at the perfect angle. If your timing is a little off, you'll get some extra caulk here and there, which can be difficult to clean up.

Traditional putty has more body and takes direction better. Bed it firmly in the channel, and then create the slope by pulling a putty knife or glazing tool along it. A glazing tool is a bit easier to use. It has two short wings, mounted at an angle to each other, and a short center slot that you rest on the muntin as you work. About all you have to do is keep the angle constant. Whether you use a putty knife or a glazing tool, keep the angle high so that just the tip of the knife travels along the putty. Wipe the tool clean before you start the next side.

Paint the putty channel before you install the glass and apply the glaze or caulk. Dry wood will pull the moisture out of the putty and it won't stick.

The National Glazing Code requires that shatter-resistant panes be used in applications such as doors and sidelights. Let the salesperson know what the glass is for so that you purchase the right type. And if you're replacing glass in a factory-built window, you may not be able to do so by following the directions below—especially if the glass is double- or triple-paned. The major manufacturers recommend you call your distributor to get the parts you'll need for repairs. In some cases you'll need to replace the entire sash.

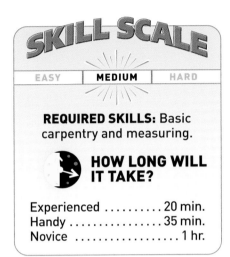

SKILL SCALE

EASY	**MEDIUM**	HARD

REQUIRED SKILLS: Basic carpentry and measuring.

HOW LONG WILL IT TAKE?

Experienced .... 20 min.
Handy .... 35 min.
Novice .... 1 hr.

STUFF YOU'LL NEED

✔ MATERIALS:
Glass, glazing points, glazing compound or caulk, paint

✔ TOOLS:
Framing square, glass cutter, heat gun, putty knife, glazing tool, marker or grease pencil, gloves

REPAIRING A BROKEN WINDOWPANE
Cutting glass

1 **ALTHOUGH IT'S EASIEST TO HAVE THE STORE CUT GLASS TO SIZE,** you can do it yourself. Make sure you have at least 1/2 inch or so between the edge and your cut. Smaller cuts are extremely difficult. Put the glass on a flat surface padded with several layers of newspaper.

2 **DRAW A LINE WITH A MARKER OR A GREASE PENCIL,** indicating where you want the cut. A framing square will help ensure a square cut.

3 **MAKE A SINGLE, FIRM PASS ALONG THE LAYOUT LINE** using a glass cutter guided along a straightedge. The cutter will score the glass, rather than cut through it. Put the scored line along the edge of the framing square, and then tap along the scored line with the butt end of a glass cutter to snap it free.

REPAIRING A BROKEN WINDOWPANE
Installing new glass

1 **MOST WINDOWS CAN BE REPAIRED WHILE THEY ARE STILL IN THE FRAME,** but if you're removing the window for other repairs, it's a bit easier to work on a table or workbench.

Start by putting on heavy leather work gloves and removing the loose pieces of broken glass.

2 **SOFTEN THE OLD PUTTY WITH A HEAT GUN, BEING CAREFUL NOT TO SCORCH THE WOOD.** Scrape away the soft putty with a putty knife and remove the remaining glass. Small pieces of metal that hold the glass in place—called glazing points—probably remain in the frame. Pry them out with a putty knife or pull them out with pliers. Wire-brush the channel to completely remove the old putty, and sand the grooves to clean them.

3 **PAINT THE BARE WOOD WITH AN OIL-BASED PAINT,** or coat it with linseed oil, so that the new putty will stick. (Bare wood pulls the moisture out of the putty, making it too dry to adhere.)

4 **PUT A THIN BEAD OF GLAZING COMPOUND IN THE CHANNEL THAT HOLDS THE GLASS.** Press the replacement pane into the compound, bedding it. Press in new glazing points every 10 inches with the tip of a putty knife or glazing tool. Avoid pushing the glazing points toward the glass; the pressure may break the pane.

5 **IF USING A PUTTYLIKE GLAZING COMPOUND, ROLL A BALL OF IT BETWEEN YOUR FINGERS TO MAKE A LONG THICK NOODLE.** Press the noodle against the glass and the side of the channel. Set it firmly with the tip of a putty knife or glazing tool. If using a caulklike glazing compound, put it in a caulking gun and poke a hole in the seal. (The nozzle is already shaped and need not be cut open.) Move the tip along the glass, applying even pressure to the trigger. (See inset.)

6 **SMOOTH THE GLAZING COMPOUND WITH A GLAZING TOOL OR WET PUTTY KNIFE.** Position the notched end of the glazing tool so that one edge rests on the glass and the other rests on the wood and pull to the corners. Let the compound dry as directed on its container; clean away excess, then paint.

Replacing a screen

REPLACING A SCREEN IN A WOODEN FRAME

1 ON A WOODEN FRAME, PRY UP THE SCREEN MOLDING WITH A SCRAPER OR PUTTY KNIFE. If the molding is sealed with paint, cut through the paint film with a putty knife to free the molding. Remove the old screen and put the new material in place, leaving it oversized so that you'll have excess to pull on to tighten the screen.

2 STAPLE THE NEW SCREEN IN ONE CORNER AND STRETCH THE SCREEN TIGHT ACROSS TO THE NEAREST CORNER. Staple every few inches between the two corners. Stretch the screen tight to one of the remaining corners, staple it, and then work back toward the previously stapled corner, driving staples every few inches. Repeat with the remaining corner.

3 NAIL THE SCREEN MOLDING BACK IN PLACE WITH WIRE BRADS. Cut away the excess screen with a utility knife.

REPLACING A SCREEN IN AN ALUMINUM FRAME

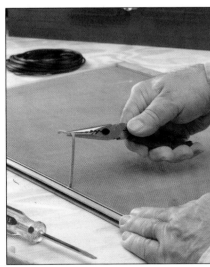

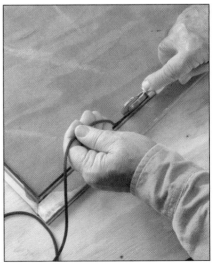

1 PRY AND PULL THE VINYL SPLINE FROM THE GROOVES AROUND THE EDGE OF THE FRAME with a screwdriver and pliers. Keep the old spline if it's still flexible; if not, buy a new one.

2 PUT THE NEW SCREEN FABRIC OVER THE FRAME SO THAT IT OVERLAPS THE RETAINING GROOVES. Trim the corner as shown so that excess material won't interfere with installing the screen.

3 USE A SPLINE ROLLER TO PRESS THE SPLINE AND SCREEN INTO THE GROOVES. Keep the screen tight as you advance the spline. Cut away the excess screen with a utility knife.

Window and glass door security

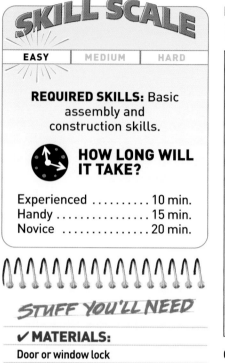
To delay and, ideally, deter thieves, you need more than the standard window or patio door latch. Because you may need to exit through locked windows and doors yourself in an emergency, keep the key near the lock, but hidden from outside view. When possible, buy all latches from the same manufacturer so that the keys will be interchangeable.

If local fire code permits it, further improve security by replacing single glazing with polycarbonate or wire-embedded glass. In some cases, you may even want to install security shutters, a grill, or a security gate.

Windows and doors that are considered fire or emergency exits may not be allowed by law or fire codes to have locks that require separate keys. Make sure before you install them.

LOCKS FOR SLIDING WINDOWS

CASEMENT WINDOWS CAN BE CLOSED WITH A DOOR-BOLT-LIKE DEVICE that operates with a key. Screw the lock to the window and slide the bolt into a metal cup that mounts in the sill.

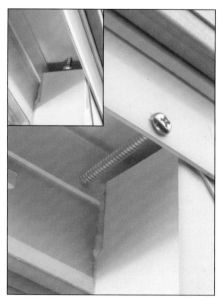

DRIVE A SCREW INTO THE TOP OF THE UPPER TRACK TO KEEP THIEVES FROM LIFTING A GLIDING WINDOW OUT OF ITS TRACK (see inset). To keep the window from sliding, drive a screw horizontally through the track.

SEVERAL COMPANIES MAKE LOCKS FOR SLIDING WINDOWS. On this one, a stop slips over the window track. Turn the lever one way to lock the window; turn it the other to allow it to slide. Other locks use a thumbscrew instead of a lever.

A KEY TRACK STOP IS A LOCKING STOP THAT YOU CAN ATTACH ANYWHERE ON THE TRACK. You can position it to lock the window shut, or so that the window opens only a certain amount, allowing for ventilation and safety.

DOUBLE-HUNG WINDOW LOCKS

ON DOUBLE-HUNG WINDOWS, YOU CAN INSTALL A LOCKING PIN that goes through one sash and into the next to keep intruders from lifting the sash. Some pins screw through a hole you drill, while others drive in and out with a special key that comes with them.

VENTILATING LOCKS SCREW TO THE SIDE OF THE TOP SASH AN INCH OR SO ABOVE THE MEETING RAIL. When the pin is positioned as shown, it allows you to open the window until the pin strikes a plate screwed to the other sash. Slide the pin around the corner and you can raise the window the full amount.

A HINGED WEDGE LOCK NAILS IN THE WINDOW TRACK OF A DOUBLE-HUNG WINDOW. Choose a position for the wedge that lets you open the window enough to get fresh air. When the wedge is in place, the window will only rise up to it (see inset). When you swing the wedge out of the way, the window opens freely to any height.

PATIO DOOR LOCKS

A KEYED TURNBUCKLE REPLACES THE NORMAL LATCH, SO YOU'LL NEED A KEY TO OPEN THE WINDOW. A child-safety latch also replaces the original latch. It's similar to the childproof caps on medicine but easier to use. In order to open the window, a child has to be able to squeeze a lever while turning the latch.

REINFORCE THE LOCK ON A PATIO DOOR WITH A SECURITY BAR. Screw the hinged side to the doorjamb and the locking saddle to the other jamb. Swing the bar into the saddle to lock the door; lift it out to allow the door to open. You can also set the bar so that the door will open partway.

A KEYED PATIO DOOR LOCK SCREWS TO THE SIDE OF THE DOOR. When you want to lock the door, put the bolt into a hole you've drilled into the door frame. Unlock and lower the bolt to open the door.

Removing a window

WINDOWS

Almost any window can be repaired. Sometimes, however, it's more work than it's worth. A window may be so badly deteriorated, or leak so much heat, that the most economical option is to replace it.

Before replacing the window, do two things: Of course, remove the old window. But before you do that, make sure you really want to remove the window.

If you live in an old Victorian house, a farmhouse sitting on a few acres, or an original New England saltbox, for example, replacing windows should be a last resort. A new window will call attention to itself and damage the charm, and possibly the resale value, of the house. Better to thoroughly caulk, weather strip, and add storm windows.

Sometimes, of course, you simply need a new window. Whether the house is new or old, the new window should match the old as closely as possible. If you can't find a good match on the shelf, talk to the store about custom-made windows. These often cost only a little more than ready-made.

1 **USE A UTILITY KNIFE TO CUT THROUGH THE PAINT WHEREVER TRIM MEETS THE WALL,** both inside and outside the house. This will keep paint from chipping or drywall from tearing when you remove the trim. Pry off all the trim with a pry bar. Put a piece of scrap wood under the pry bar to keep from damaging the wall surrounding the window.

2 **OLDER DOUBLE-HUNG WINDOWS HAVE SASH WEIGHTS** that keep the window from crashing down. Remove the weights by cutting the cord that runs to them. Hang onto the cord, raise the weights, and remove them. Fill the void with fiberglass insulation.

3 **PRY OFF THE EXTERIOR MOLDINGS.** If you have to pry against the siding, protect it by putting a block of wood between it and the pry bar.

4 **CUT THROUGH THE NAILS ATTACHING THE WINDOW TO THE FRAMING.** If the window has nailing fins, pry loose any siding covering them. With a claw hammer or pry bar, pull out the nails that run through the fins into the sheathing. Remove any shims, and slide the window out of the opening.

Installing a window

STUFF YOU'LL NEED

✔ **MATERIALS:**
Window, wood shims, drip edge, casing nails, fiberglass insulation, silicone caulk

✔ **TOOLS:**
Hammer, 4-foot level, circular saw, drill and bit, nail set, utility knife, caulking gun

MEASURE ALL WINDOWS
You might think it's safe to assume that all your windows are the same size and that if you've measured one you've measured them all. However, it's best to measure each rough opening to be sure that the window will fit properly and that you won't have a hole in your wall while you wait for the correct replacement. Mark the opening and the window to match correctly.

Replacement windows are available in various shapes, styles, colors, and construction types. They are commonly made of wood, aluminum, or vinyl. Each manufacturer's product has its own specific installation instructions, but on the whole, window units are installed in the same manner.

Prehung windows come complete with finish frames, and you can insert them in one piece into the rough opening left by the old window. Measure the rough opening and be sure to purchase a new window unit to fit.

You'll need to custom-order most windows, and delivery can take several weeks. It's risky to remove the existing windows before the replacements are on-site. Between manufacturer's delays, bad weather, wrong orders, and shipping problems, it's difficult to guarantee an exact delivery date. If you're in a hurry, you could wind up with a big hole in the side of your house and no cover for it.

The bottom line: Keep the old windows in place until the new ones have arrived and you have inspected them for damage and verified their size.

As important as windows are to the security, appearance, and energy efficiency of your home, you'll be pleasantly surprised by the simplicity of installing them. You'll need to rent scaffolding to safely install windows on upper levels of your home. Windows are awkward to handle so it's generally a good idea to find a helper when you're working above the first floor.

The basics of installing new windows are pretty similar from manufacturer to manufacturer, but there will be differences. Follow instructions carefully.

1 REMOVE THE EXISTING WINDOW OR WALL SURFACE AND THEN TEST-FIT THE WINDOW, centering it in the rough opening. Support the window with wood blocks and shims placed below the horizontal jambs. Make sure the window is plumb and level, and adjust the shims if necessary.

2 CLAMP OR HOLD THE MOLDING IN PLACE, THEN TRACE AROUND IT.
If you have vinyl or aluminum siding, you may need to install something called a J-channel to hold the trim. This usually requires trimming away a bit more siding. If a J-channel is required it will be called for and explained in the manufacturer's instructions.

Installing a window *(continued)*

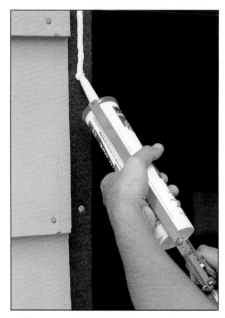

3 **CUT THE SIDING ALONG THE OUTLINE.** Use a circular saw adjusted so the blade depth equals the thickness of the siding. Start the cut with the toe of the saw plate on the siding, but with the blade and heel of the plate above the surface. Slide the saw guard back, start the saw, and ease the blade into the wood. To avoid splintering, stop before the corner. Complete the corner cuts with a sharp chisel.

4 **CUT A LENGTH OF DRIP EDGE TO FIT OVER THE TOP OF THE WINDOW,** and then slide it between the siding and the building paper.

Wear ear and eye protection when working with power tools.

5 **YOUR WINDOW WILL EITHER HAVE A PIECE OF MOLDING, CALLED BRICK MOLD, AROUND THE OUTSIDE, OR A NAILING FIN.** If it has brick mold, apply a continuous bead of caulk around the opening. If it has a nailing fin, apply the caulk to the back of the fin.

6 **INSERT THE WINDOW INTO THE OPENING** and push the brick mold or nailing fin tight against the sheathing.

7 **CHECK TO SEE HOW MUCH ADJUSTMENT WILL BE NECESSARY** to level and plumb the window unit.

8 **IF THE WINDOW IS PERFECTLY LEVEL, TACK IT IN PLACE.** On a window with brick mold, do this by predrilling and then driving 16d casing nails partway into the top corners of the molding. If the window is uneven, correct it by shimming below the side jambs and then tacking in place.

Nailing fins

On windows with nailing fins, drive 2-inch roofing nails into the holes at the upper corners and partway into the framing. Leave enough of the nail exposed so that you can remove it if you have problems later in the installation.

9 **PLACE SHIMS TOGETHER SO THAT THEIR COMBINED THICKNESS WILL FILL THE OPENING BETWEEN THE JAMBS AND FRAMING.** Despite the nails you just put in, the window will still move somewhat. Use the shims to center the window in the opening.

10 **MEASURE THE DIAGONALS OF THE WINDOW FOR SQUARE.** If they are equal, the window is square. If not, adjust the shims until the window is square. Always recheck for level and square after you adjust the shims.

Instead of handling large windows by yourself, have a helper around. It's easier, faster, and much safer.

11 **IF THE WINDOW HAS A BRICK MOLD, PREDRILL HOLES IN IT AND DRIVE 16d NAILS THROUGH IT AND INTO THE FRAMING.** If the window has a nailing fin, nail through it into the framing. In either case, start at the corners and space the remaining nails as recommended by the manufacturer. Drive all nailheads below the wood surface with a nail set.

Vinyl replacement windows

Removing and replacing a window is a big carpentry job, even if it's not difficult. If you're unsure of your skills or you simply don't have time for the job, consider a vinyl replacement window.

A replacement window fits in the jamb that holds your existing window. To install one, you'll pull out the old window, plus moldings, stops, etc., until you're left with just the sill and jambs. Some replacement windows sit in a frame that you simply slide between the jambs—window and all—and then screw in place. Others are designed so that you'll attach tracks to the jambs and then slip windows into the jambs. The first option is easier but reduces your view by the thickness of the frame holding the window. The second option involves a few more pieces, but they're thinner, improving your view.

Replacement windows are custom-built to your specifications. Building them can take a few weeks, so keep any old windows in place until the new ones arrive. Stop by the millwork department of your home center and ask what measurements they'll need to place the order. (They should have a form with clear directions.)

Because the window frames are vinyl, they're energy-efficient. Some windows are better insulated than others, however, and some have better glass than others. Read the brochures and make sure you get what you want. For definitions of terms, see Window Basics, page 368.

Installing a window *(continued)*

12 **A WINDOW WITH A NAILING FIN OFTEN HAS A SPECIAL-ORDER MOLDING** that you apply over it. Install as directed by the manufacturer.

13 **FILL THE GAPS BETWEEN THE WINDOW JAMBS** and the framing members with loosely packed fiberglass insulation. Wear work gloves, safety glasses, and a dust mask when handling insulation.

14 **TRIM THE SHIMS FLUSH WITH THE FRAMING** by scoring them with a utility knife and then snapping off the excess.

15 **APPLY PAINTABLE SILICONE CAULK AROUND THE ENTIRE WINDOW UNIT** and fill the nail holes with caulk. When the caulk dries, paint to match the trim on the rest of your house.

Installation variation: Masonry clips

Use metal masonry clips when a masonry or brick surface prevents you from nailing brick molding in place. The masonry clips hook into precut grooves in the window jambs and attach to the jambs with utility screws. After positioning the window unit in the rough opening, bend the masonry clips around the framing members.

Anchor the masonry clips with utility screws. You can also use masonry clips in ordinary lap siding installations to avoid making nail holes in the smooth surface of the brick moldings. For example, windows precoated with polymer-based paint can be installed with masonry clips so that the brick moldings are not punctured by nails.

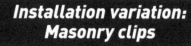

WINDOWS

Installing a storm window

Before you install storm windows, you'll have to buy them, and before you buy them, you'll have to know what size you need. Begin by measuring what's called the clear opening. When measuring the width, measure from jamb to jamb, as shown in the illustration. When measuring the height, measure from the sill to the top jamb. You'll also want to note the spot where the top and bottom sashes meet. Measure from the top jamb down to the bottom of either sash. When you select your storm windows, you should make sure the top and bottom sashes meet at the same point as those on the window they'll cover. Take all three measurements with you to the store.

Once you're there, you may discover that storms don't come in the exact size you need. Within reason, this is OK. The skirt or "fins" around the window are made to be easily trimmed. Depending on the window, you may have as much as 2 inches that you can trim. Owners of older homes, however, may find that their windows are simply a nonstandard size. For them, the only alternative is to custom-order a window.

Each storm window has a small hole (called a weep hole) in the bottom fin that allows trapped moisture to escape. A little heat gets out too, but not enough to worry about. Trapped moisture causes the paint to flake and the wood to rot. Check periodically to make sure the hole isn't plugged.

Storm windows cut energy costs significantly, but they are most efficient when installed over every window.

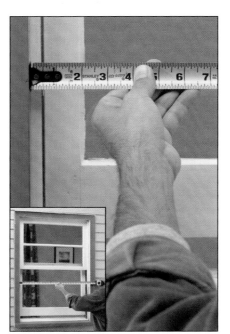

1 **LOOKING AT THE WINDOW FROM THE OUTSIDE, FIND THE NARROW STRIPS OF WOOD NEAR THE EDGES.** These are called blind stops, and the window slides up and down behind them. Measure the distance from the outside of one stop to the outside of the other (see inset). Then measure the distance from the sill to the outside edge of the top stop. Get a window designed to fit this size opening.

2 **TRIM THE STORM WINDOW, IF NECESSARY,** to fit it in the opening. Use tin snips to cut along the lines stamped in the fins of the window. Cut equal amounts off each side. If the window is too tall, trim the bottom only, where the cut will be less visible.

Installing a storm window (continued)

3 **APPLY A BEAD OF CAULK ALONG EACH OF THE BLIND STOPS.** Leave the sill uncaulked, however, to allow moisture trapped between the windows to escape.

4 **PUT THE WINDOW IN THE OPENING** with the bottom resting on the sill. Tilt the window into place.

5 **HAVE A HELPER HOLD THE WINDOW WHILE YOU DRILL HOLES** for screws near the edge of the fins. The exact size and spacing depends on the manufacturer. Drive screws through the holes and into the wood behind them to hold the window in place. If the small weep hole at the bottom of the window is plugged by dirt, clean it out with a small finishing nail.

Installing a skylight

Skylights come in many shapes and sizes. Installation varies in complexity, from installation in roofs directly over rooms to installation in attics and crawlspaces. Some systems refract light through tubes, bringing natural light to almost any area of the home.

Skylights provide natural light to interior areas that normally would receive a minimal amount of outside light. They connect people to the environment and can help save on energy bills by cutting down on the use of interior lights. Installing a skylight requires carpentry skills, confidence when working on the roof, and the willingness to cut a hole in your roof. Lay out a skylight from the bottom up—beginning at the ceiling, working up to the attic floor, and then finally up to the roof. You then install a skylight from the roof down—cutting the holes, putting in the skylight, framing the shaft, and then finally cutting the hole in the ceiling.

Begin by deciding roughly where you want the skylight, and whether you want an opening that's splayed, offset, or perpendicular. Outline the opening on the ceiling with painter's masking tape—the easily removable blue kind—and move it around until you're sure of its position.

Next drive 16d nails through the corners of the outline so that you can see them from the attic. Use strings to transfer the layout to the roof, and then stop and look. If pipes, heating runs, plumbing vents, or other obstructions are present, you must either move them or move the skylight. (It's easier to move the skylight.)

Once you have decided on the location, and once you have marked it on the roof, install the skylight. Then work your way back down—drop lines from the roof to the attic floor to lay out the bottom of the light shaft. Check to see whether the corners are still over the nails you drove through the masking tape outline. If not, drill holes from the attic down to mark the proper location, and cut away the ceiling. Frame the opening, and then build the light shaft above it.

WINDOWS

Do you really want to work up on the roof?

Before you decide to install a skylight on your own, take the gumption test that follows. Give yourself two gumption points for each task you're willing to do. Score one skill point for each task you know how to do, and another skill point for each task you've actually done. If

you're unwilling to do any one of the tasks, or if the score is anything less than a tie, hire a pro.

1. Any skylight wider than 13¾ inches requires a cut through a roof rafter. Once you make the cut, you'll have to reframe that section of the roof—doubling up rafters on both sides of the opening, and framing in double headers above and below the opening.

2. The hole you cut in the ceiling requires similar treatment.

3. You'll need to lay out the opening on the ceiling, the attic floor (if any), and the roof, keeping all carefully aligned.

4. To create the opening, you'll need to go up to the roof and cut through the shingles and plywood. The easiest way is to make a plunge cut with a circular saw: Rest the toe of the saw on the roof, start the saw, and lower the spinning blade into the roof.

5. Once you've made the cuts, the plywood will still be nailed to a center rafter: You'll need to pry it loose while balancing yourself on the roof.

6. Skylights weigh between 40 and 110 pounds and must be hauled up to and installed from the top of the roof.

7. To prevent leaks, you'll need to put in felt paper, flashing, and shingles. You'll also need to insulate to prevent condensation and heat loss.

8. A skylight that isn't square in its opening may leak and probably won't open correctly. You'll need to shim from below, but measuring is most accurately done from above.

9. The light shaft between the roof and the room below has to be framed, drywalled, taped, and finished. Most likely, at least one of the walls will have to slope.

Getting the shaft

Unless you want to look from the ceiling into the attic, you'll need a light shaft between the roof and the room below. The shaft can be a piece of ductlike tubing, as shown at right, or it can be framed and built almost as if it were a small room the same size as the skylight and perpendicular to it. You can splay one or more of the walls so that the shaft is wider than the skylight, letting in more light. Or you can make the shaft any size you choose and angle it down so that the opening is offset from the skylight.

A splayed opening is the most typical for a couple of reasons: Unless the skylight is rather large, a shaft the exact size of the opening is difficult to drywall, tape, and finish. As for offsetting the opening, very few situations require it. Roofs are big and flat: It's usually fairly simple to find a spot that's more or less above the opening you want in the ceiling.

The easiest way to lay out a splayed shaft is with string. The wall on the lowest end of the skylight is plumb, as are the two sidewalls. Lay them out with the help of lines and a plumb bob. The wall on the high edge of the skylight is perpendicular to the roof. Lay it out with string too, moving the string until a framing square indicates that the string is perpendicular to the roof, and then marking where the string hits the floor. Double-check for square with the 3-4-5 triangle method.

Lay out other shafts with string too. Lay out a perpendicular shaft by simply dropping a plumb bob from the corners of the opening and marking where it meets the floor. If the shaft is offset, decide on the size of the ceiling opening, and follow the manufacturer's directions when marking the opening on the roof. Stretch strings between the corners on the floor and the corners on the roof to outline the shaft.

CABINETS, COUNTERTOPS, SHELVING, AND STORAGE

EFFICIENT STORAGE CREATES ORDER IN THE HOME. Carefully placing everyday and rarely used items is important throughout the house, whether it's in the kitchen, garage, laundry room, or your closets. Whatever you need to store and wherever you need to store it, easy access and organization are keys to well-run working and living spaces. Certain areas of the house, such as the kitchen, bathroom, and closets, are constantly in use. In these spaces good organization and easy access is essential. Tennis rackets, seasonal clothing, golf clubs, and air hockey games may go through cycles of use. They need to be more accessible at some times than at others. Here's how to make storage decisions:

- Take an inventory of your belongings. What items do you need access to every day? Once a week? Once a

month? Never, but for sentimental reasons you just can't bear to see them go? Also take into account the needs of different family members.

- Review your lifestyle and the patterns of use and movement that make up your daily life. Do you have room to pursue ongoing projects and hobbies? Do all the cleaning supplies fall to the floor when you open the utility closet ? Do you even have a utility closet?

- Tour your house and take a hard look at the existing storage areas. Are they big enough? Deep enough? Easy to access? Then look around for underused areas that could potentially become storage with a little carpentry or a trip to a home center or a store that specializes in storage solutions.

SECTION 9 PROJECTS

REAL-WORLD SITUATIONS

STORAGE SOLUTIONS ARE BIG BUSINESS

Home centers, hardware stores, discount chains, and even antiques shops are into storage solutions in a big way. Other stores specialize in every conceivable type of off-the-shelf storage you can imagine. Of course, some types of storage can only be custom-made, such as built-to-order kitchen cabinetry or built-in bookshelves and closets, or even additions to your living space. But it's worth a shopping trip or two to see what's available ready-made before you decide to start swinging a hammer. Here's a room-by-room look at storage issues and solutions:

Kitchens. Cabinets are the storage unit of choice in kitchens. But while they're wide and deep, a large volume of useful space is lost in the rear. Sliding and staggered shelving, door racks, lazy Susans, tilt-out bins, drawer dividers, and pullout trays with dividers make maximum use of space.

Bathrooms. Adequate storage in most bathrooms is nonexistent, partly because most bathrooms are too small to accommodate storage areas. One area of opportunity is the medicine cabinet. Consider installing the largest ready-made unit you can fit or have one custom-made to the room specifications. Install the largest vanity you can and add rolling trays as well as interior shelving. Home centers and discount chains offer a multitude of ready-made storage solutions for small bathrooms.

Closets. Custom shelving and rods with storage for folded and hanging clothes, as well as shoes, can be supplemented with a wide variety of flexible wire closet products that are easily customized and installed.

Living spaces. Foyers, hallways, and living, dining, and family rooms lend themselves to built-in closets, bookcases, and entertainment units. Also consider furniture to enclose televisions and stereo equipment.

Laundry rooms. Stacking washers and dryers maximize laundry room space, as do cabinets with pullout or pull-down ironing boards. Consider stacked recycling bins on sliders and wire containers for supplies. Open cubicles and cabinets work well for holding items that are in transition from one part of the house to another.

Garages and basements. Consider open shelving, hooks to suspend bicycles and tools, workbenches with pegboard wall attachments for tools and materials, rolling containers, and plastic storage boxes that stack. Ready-to-assemble wardrobes provide storage for seasonal clothing.

Cabinet and countertop basics

Cabinets come in a wide variety of shapes, finishes, and styles. Like cars or appliances, quality and durability are about what you see and what you don't.

WHAT YOU DON'T SEE. All cabinets are boxes made of either medium-density fiberboard (MDF), particleboard, or plywood. MDF and particleboard are made of ground wood pressed with glue into sheets. The ground wood is larger in particleboard than in MDF, making it somewhat stronger. Plywood is made of thin sheets of wood glued together so that the grain in one layer is perpendicular to the grain in the next, making it the strongest of the three choices. It's also the most water-resistant and the most expensive.

WHAT YOU DO SEE. MDF is often covered with a smooth, white or wood-grained resin called melamine. It's a cheap, cleanable finish, but not as durable as similar-looking laminates—thicker sheets of plastic glued in place.

MDF, plywood, and particleboard can be veneered, and once they are, it's hard to tell them apart. You'll probably have to ask to find out, but don't take "solid wood" for an answer. Technically, all three are "solid wood," as is a board made of one piece of solid wood.

You'll hear a lot of talk about framed versus frameless cabinets. (See above.) The difference is more important to the person building the cabinets than it is to the person buying them. Once installed,

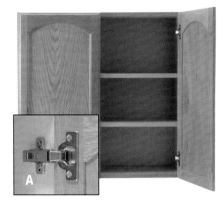

Ⓐ FRAMELESS CABINETS, sometimes called European-style, lack face frames. Contemporary-looking cabinets are almost guaranteed to be frameless, and more styles have become available as frameless cabinets have gained popularity. Most framed and frameless cabinets look virtually alike.

Ⓑ FRAMED CABINETS have openings that are completely surrounded by face frames made of vertical stiles and horizontal rails. Door hinges are attached directly to these frames. This is the classic cabinetmaker's approach to construction, and most framed cabinets are traditional-looking.

both are equally durable. Frameless cabinets are easier to build; thus, they cost somewhat less. Keeping frameless cabinets square during installation is fussier than it is with framed cabinets. The hardware on frameless cabinets lets you adjust the position of the doors, making it easier to align the tops of the doors than it is on a framed cabinet.

Most cabinets, including custom-built, are frameless these days, as are almost any off-the-shelf systems.

Ⓐ *Bare plywood*

Ⓑ *Bare MDF*

Ⓒ *Bare particleboard*

Ⓓ *MDF with melamine*

Breaking the cabinet code

If you look through a catalog of kitchen cabinets, you'll find all sorts of codes, such as **BBD1824D3**, used for description. So once you know what you want, how do you crack the ordering code? First, you need to know that two elements are standard and don't appear at all. Wall cabinets are always 12 inches deep. Base cabinets are always 34½ inches high. So this is how the code **BBD1824D3** breaks down:

● The first character denotes the general type: W=wall; T=tall; B=base; V=vanity; D=desk. **(B)**

● The next one or two characters refer to the specific type of cabinet: BB=blind base; BC=blind corner; BD=base with drawers; C=corner. **(BD)**

● The next two digits are the unit's width in inches. **(18)**

● The next two digits are either the height of a wall cabinet or, in this case, the depth of a base cabinet. **(24)**

● The last one or two characters identify anything nonstandard about

the unit. D=diagonal corner unit; GD=glass doors; D3=three drawers. **(D3)**

● An R or an L anywhere in the code would indicate the location of the door hinges.

So **BBD1824D3** is a 3-drawer base cabinet measuring 18 inches wide, 34½ inches high, and 24 inches deep.

THE CABINETMAKER'S TOOL KIT

Below are some basic cabinetmaking tools. For more information see the Tool Glossary on page 544.

BACKSAW

CLAMP

DEAD-BLOW HAMMER

HOLE SAW

PLUMB BOB

SAFETY GLASSES

BELT SANDER

CLAW HAMMER

DRILL

LEVEL

PNEUMATIC POWER NAILER

SAWHORSE

CABINET TEMPLATE

COMBINATION SQUARE

DRILL BITS

LINE LEVEL

POWER MITER SAW

SCREWDRIVERS

CAULKING GUN

COMPASS

DUST MASK

MITER BOX

PRY BARS

STUD FINDER

CHALK LINE

COPING SAW

EAR PROTECTION

NAIL SET

ROUTER

TAPE MEASURE

CIRCULAR SAW

COUNTERSINK BIT

FRAMING SQUARE

PAINTBRUSHES

SABER SAW

UTILITY KNIFE

Replacing cabinet hardware

Much of a cabinet's appearance depends on its hardware. Replacing a cabinet's Early American knobs with wooden ones gives it a Shaker look. Replacing them with bin pulls can give it a Victorian look. Putting on hammered metal pulls can steer a cabinet toward the Mission style.

Any of the above, done poorly, can make a mess out of the finest cabinet. To do the job right you must consider two things: fit and appearance. Fit is the simplest: When you remove a piece of hardware, you have to replace it with one that requires the same mounting holes, or one that is big enough to cover the old holes.

Look is a different issue. Mission furniture was almost always oak, and it can be hard to make maple, cherry, or walnut fit the bill. Shaker furniture was plain and unadorned. Most Victorian cabinets would have a hard time passing for Shaker no matter what hardware you put on them.

But it's your house, and who left the art critics in charge, anyway? If you like the way the hardware looks, it's the right hardware. First do a little reading about the look that you're trying to create. Then check stores, mail-order catalogs, and old house magazines to see what's available. Try a knob on a door and a drawer, and live with it for a while. If it works, install the rest.

1 **BEGIN BY REMOVING A SAMPLE PIECE OF THE CABINET'S HARDWARE.** To remove a drawer handle, open the drawer and remove the bolt or bolts that go through the drawer front and into the handle. Then open a door and remove the bolt or bolts holding the handle.

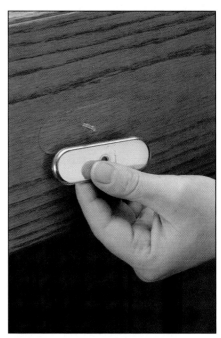

2 **DOOR OR DRAWER HANDLES MAY HAVE PLATES, CALLED ESCUTCHEONS, BEHIND THEM.** They may be made of brass, porcelain, or contrasting wood, and are held in place with brads. Depending on the door, you may be able to pull the brads with a brad puller or small "cat's paw." If not, work a narrow putty knife under the center of the escutcheon and pry. When prying, always make sure the end of the knife is under the escutcheon. Putting it elsewhere will leave a visible mark.

3 **IF ANY OF THE HARDWARE HAD TWO BOLTS HOLDING IT IN PLACE,** you need to know the distance from the center of one bolt to the center of the other. Special templates, like the one shown here, help you measure the distance or lay out new holes. If you can't get a template, measure the distance between the center of the bolt holes. Accuracy to the nearest ⅛ inch is sufficient here.

4 **TAKE THE HARDWARE AND THE MEASUREMENTS TO THE STORE.** Most hardware comes in a few different sizes. Find something you like, and then find the size that matches your center-to-center measurements. Double-check by measuring and by holding the old hardware next to the new hardware to compare the spacing for the bolts.

5 **BUY A SAMPLE PIECE OF HARDWARE AND INSTALL IT TO MAKE SURE IT FITS PROPERLY.** If the new bolts aren't the right length, you can usually substitute the old bolts or buy replacements in the store's hardware section. Live with and use the new hardware for a few days to make sure you really like it. When you're sure, buy and install the rest of the hardware.

BE CAUTIOUS WHEN BUYING THIN HANDLES SUCH AS THESE "WIRE" PULLS. Their base is so narrow that they can actually slip through oversized or worn bolt holes. They also can expose much of the wood covered by the old pull. Even after refinishing the surface, you may see the silhouette of the old hardware.

SURFACE-MOUNT PULLS, SUCH AS THIS ONE, FREE YOU FROM HAVING TO WORRY ABOUT THE DISTANCE BETWEEN THE OLD BOLT HOLES. Its broad surface covers the bolt holes and often the silhouette of the old hardware.

Replacing cabinet doors and drawers

If a close look tells you that your doors and drawers are a wreck but the cabinets are in good shape, replacing or upgrading them may be smarter than putting $20,000 into a new set of cabinets. The trick is to find doors and drawer fronts in a matching finish, and to hang the doors. Begin by looking at the hinges: Traditional hinges look like small house door hinges. Hanging doors on them requires some intermediate cabinetmaking skills. If they're European hinges, such as those shown below, hanging doors on them is much easier—as long as the holes are predrilled in the proper places.

The parts on ready-to-assemble cabinets—the ones that come in a box—are usually interchangeable. Hinge holes are uniform from unit to unit. However, replacement doors on custom cabinets, even if factory-built, may not be uniform.

Buy replacement doors and drawer fronts from the company that made the cabinets in the first place. Hang samples to see what problems you may run into.

Complete do-it-yourself cabinet refacing is another option. (The extra work comes in applying self-stick veneer over the face frames.) While it may cost more, you can save time by getting custom-made drawer and door fronts that come with fasteners guaranteed to fit your cabinets.

1 **REMOVE AN OLD DOOR FROM THE CABINET.** European-style hinges have a big, round or square piece, called a hinge cup, that fits in a matching hole in the door. The base that mounts on the cabinet is usually T-shaped and often has sliding parts so that you can move the door up or down to bring it into alignment with other doors. Remove the screws holding the cups in place and take the doors off the cups.

2 **DRAWERS ARE USUALLY BOXES WITH DECORATIVE FALSE FRONTS SCREWED OVER THE FRONT OF THE BOX.** Remove the screws to remove the false front. If the front isn't removable, you'll have a hard time replacing it. Consider a complete refacing job, in which custom fronts and minor drawer alterations make the upgrade possible.

3 **PUT THE HINGE CUP IN THE HOLE IN THE DOOR AND SCREW IT IN PLACE.** Slide the arm of the hinge over the base piece inside the cabinet and tighten the screw. Close the door and see how it sits on the cabinet. If the door juts out from the cabinet or binds when it closes, loosen the screw you just tightened, slide the arm along the base piece, and retighten. Slide the arm away from the back of the cabinet to help fix binding doors; push it toward the back of the cabinet to help fix doors that jut out when closed.

4 **PUT A COUPLE OF PIECES OF DOUBLE-SIDED TAPE ON THE NEW DRAWER FRONT TO HELP YOU POSITION IT.** Close the drawer and bring the new front up to it. Align the edges so that an equal overhang exists on each side and so that the gap between the drawer bottom and door top is constant; then push the drawer front against the tape. Open the drawer carefully, clamp the false front to the box, as shown above, and then screw the new false front in place.

Cabinet refacing

abinet refacing not only involves replacing the doors and drawer fronts but also refacing the cabinet exteriors. It's a real kitchen overhaul and, therefore, a notch up from simply replacing doors and drawer fronts. Not only do you have more choices of doors and drawers—you veneer over the frames as well, giving your kitchen an entirely new look.

While some companies will reface cabinets for you, this can be nearly as expensive as buying new cabinets. Work with a company that will help you do it yourself. They'll custom-build doors and drawer fronts in any style and finish you like, and provide you with matching self-stick veneer. All of the techniques are basic, allowing you to do your entire kitchen in a weekend or two.

Many do-it-yourself refacing suppliers work with home improvement centers. Others are available online. The job starts with measuring—find out from the home center which measurements they need.

Parts are custom-made to your specs, so expect to wait three or four weeks before they're ready.

The peel-and-stick veneer goes on the face frames first. It's easy to align because you apply it oversized and then trim it with a knife to fit. You can cover exposed cabinet sides with plywood to match, or with a panel that matches your doors. Once you've dressed up the cabinets, hang the doors, which come with new, adjustable, European-style hinges. The matching drawer fronts screw in place.

If you're unsure whether to reface or replace, look at it this way: If you're keeping the countertop, reface the cabinets. If you're replacing the countertop, also replace the cabinets. Your choice will result in a project that is either a little harder or a little more expensive.

Old doors or drawers can be dressed up with peel-and-stick veneer sold especially for cabinet refacing. The strips on the right are applied to the faces and trimmed to size .

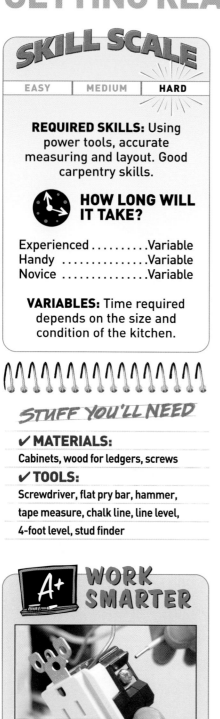

SKILL SCALE

EASY	MEDIUM	HARD

REQUIRED SKILLS: Using power tools, accurate measuring and layout. Good carpentry skills.

HOW LONG WILL IT TAKE?

Experienced . . . . .Variable
Handy . . . . .Variable
Novice . . . . .Variable

VARIABLES: Time required depends on the size and condition of the kitchen.

STUFF YOU'LL NEED

✔ **MATERIALS:**
Cabinets, wood for ledgers, screws

✔ **TOOLS:**
Screwdriver, flat pry bar, hammer, tape measure, chalk line, line level, 4-foot level, stud finder

WORK SMARTER

UPGRADE WIRING AND PLUMBING NOW

Like it or not, toasters, blenders, and coffeemakers come with 4-foot cords. Put GFCI outlets every 8 feet along the counter, and you'll always be able to reach one. Replace any old or faulty plumbing. There'll never be a better time because you're making a mess anyway.

It's the little things that make a house a home and the little things can ruin a cabinet installation too. Doors that won't close, drawers that won't stay closed, countertops that run uphill—they're all signs of a hasty installation. Unless you want to spend the rest of your life looking at a bad job that saved you a little time, prepare properly.

First, avoid installing a kitchen the week before the holidays or any major events. This job will take time. Second, realize that the expected delivery date may change. Wait until the new cabinets arrive before tearing out the old ones.

Once your cabinets arrive, have a place where you can assemble them. Line them up as they'll go in the kitchen. Inspect the finish; look for dings, dents, and broken pieces. Be sure the color and patterns of adjacent cabinets look good together. If necessary, order replacements; you'll probably wait as long as you did for the first shipment. Once everything has arrived and is assembled, working, and damage-free, move everything out of the kitchen: appliances, tables, chairs, sinks, rugs, pots, pans, dishes, and pictures. Then, and only then, should you start to remove the old cabinets.

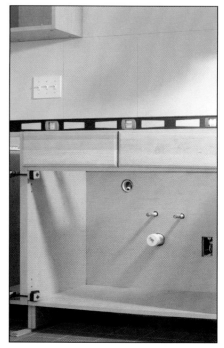

Installing cabinets involves making a proper plan, applying basic and intermediate carpentry skills, and being flexible about delivery schedules.

CLOSER LOOK

REMEMBER THE DISHWASHER

If you're putting in a new floor, build up the floor underneath the cabinets to the height of the finished floor. If you don't, you may discover that you need more room to slip the dishwasher underneath the counter. The thicker the new floor, of course, the greater the problem. Ask your flooring dealer how thick the finished floor will be. Include the thickness of the flooring material itself, plus any subfloor, mortar, underlayment, or other material that you'll put down. Once you have the answer, ask your cabinet dealer how far the cabinet toe-kick will be from the wall.

You'll probably need to apply a couple layers of plywood to get the right thickness. Combine various thicknesses to get what you need. Stack the sheets up and measure them—plywood is often a bit thinner than it claims to be.

Once you have the right thickness, cut the plywood to width on a table saw (or have the store do it for you). Give yourself a margin of error and cut each layer about ¼ inch narrower than the distance from toe-kick to wall. The floor will hide the gap. Nail the plywood to the floor so that you have a sturdy surface.

Resist the obvious shortcut of simply installing the floor first. Vinyl will compress under the weight of the cabinets. Ceramic tile grout lines will fall in the wrong place. Wood is guaranteed to get damaged, as is carpet.

Removing old cabinets

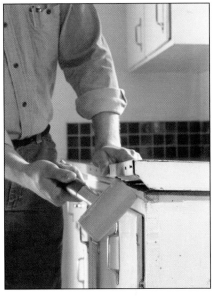

1 PREPARE THE SPACE. Before you begin removing the old units, clear out the shelves, drawers, and underneath the sink. If you are saving the floor, protect it with ¼-inch plywood or kraft paper. Start with the base cabinets.

2 REMOVE THE SINK. Shut off the electricity and the water. Loosen the sink and remove it from the counter. Disconnect any electrical connections beneath the sink or in the cabinets.

3 BEGIN REMOVING THE COUNTERTOP. This is real demolition, but resist the impulse to just rip things out. Determine how the the countertop is attached; remove screws or nails you can reach. Use a heavy hammer to begin loosening the countertop.

4 PRY UP THE COUNTERTOP using a flat pry bar. Start in a corner and work your way along the length until the top is free. Cut the top into manageable pieces and remove debris as you work. (For more information on removing different kinds of countertops, see page 394.)

5 REMOVE DOORS AND DRAWERS. Pull the drawers out of their slots and remove the doors from the base frames. If you're going to reface, start at an open end and begin removing the base cabinets. First determine how they are attached to the wall and to each other. Remove debris as you work.

6 REMOVE THE WALL CABINETS. Remove the cabinet doors, then strip the cabinets from the walls. Once the area is clear, perform any wiring or plumbing upgrades, such as adding outlets and switches, drains and supply risers, or dishwasher hookups. Repair wall or ceiling damage and paint before you begin installing new cabinetry and fixtures.

CABINETS, COUNTERTOPS, SHELVING, AND STORAGE

Removing countertops

Removing an old countertop is easiest if you're removing the cabinets too. It's usually a matter of taking out a couple of screws and perhaps doing some work with a pry bar.

If you want to keep the cabinets, however, work carefully. Cabinets that you've just destroyed while removing the counter will be unusable. The labor you'll have to do depends on what you find. And what you find depends on when the kitchen was put in and how inventive the installer was. Almost any cabinet could have anything holding it in place; but fortunately, a look at the surface tells you what's usually underneath.

SAFETY ● ALERT

LINOLEUM COUNTERTOPS
In the 1930s and 1940s, linoleum, which often contained asbestos, was used for countertops. Quite a few are still around, most of them in need of replacement. The countertops were usually built in place, a layer at a time. First the installer topped a cabinet by nailing (or perhaps screwing) on a plywood counter. The plywood was covered with linoleum and then trimmed with a metal edge. Taking the countertop off usually results in breaking it, thus releasing cancer-causing asbestos fibers into the air. If you have a linoleum countertop, contact your state health department for information on removing it.

Resist the impulse to whack away with that sledgehammer and pry bar when you're taking out old countertops. You just want to remove the material, not destroy the kitchen. Work carefully and learn as much as you can about what you're getting into before you start.

Countertop removal procedures

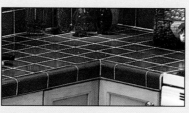

Laminate countertops are made of a thin layer of material glued to a piece of plywood or chipboard. They're usually screwed to a corner block on the end cabinets. Remove the screws and try lifting. If the countertop doesn't budge, look for screws recessed into the bottom of the top front cabinet rail. If the cabinet has a top (most don't) or rails that run along the top (many do), look for screws that run through and into the counter. If the counter goes around a corner, a cleat spans the seam or, more likely, miter clamps. Unscrew and pry off any cleats. Loosen the heads of boltlike clamps until the clamps fall out. Once you've removed all the screws, the counter should lift easily off the cabinets.

"Solid surface" countertops are made of a single, thick layer of plastic resin. They're heavy and are usually supported by three top rails that run the length of the cabinets. The counter is usually attached to the rails with dabs of silicone caulk, and the backsplash is usually silicone-caulked to the wall. Miters are either chemically "welded" or held together by miter clamps, which you should remove. Run a utility knife along the top of the backsplash to score the wall and prevent it from tearing when you remove the counter. It's almost impossible to remove the counter by prying it off the rails without damaging the cabinet. Pry gently—and if it looks, sounds, or feels like trouble, crawl inside the cabinet and cut through the support rails with a small backsaw.

Tile countertops sit on a cement backerboard, which is attached to a plywood substrate. If the cabinet is built to modern standards, 1×6 supports at the top of the cabinet run the length of the counter. The plywood is screwed to the 1×6 from below; remove the screws. Recruit as much help as you can to slide the countertop off—it will be heavy. If the countertop wasn't installed to modern standards, the nails or screws attaching it may be covered by the tiles. The only way to remove such a countertop is to break it. Nothing works well, but try a 3-lb. sledgehammer with a short handle.

Butcher-block countertops work well on islands and as cutting blocks, but water will damage them elsewhere in the kitchen. If you have one you want to remove, it's probably bolted to the cabinet, usually into supports at the top of the cabinet. Some supports have slots in them for the bolts, allowing the bolt to travel back and forth as the countertop expands and contracts with changes in weather. Other supports have an oversized hole instead of a slot. In either case, you should find a bolt every couple of feet along the length and every foot across the width. Remove the bolts and lift or slide the countertop to remove it.

INSTALLING KITCHEN CABINETS

Look in the average silverware drawer and you will understand the importance of planning ahead. Stores that sell cabinets usually have a designer who can help solve storage problems as well as create an efficient work flow around the sink, stove, and refrigerator.

Because cabinets are standard sizes, you can make a floor plan and then choose your cabinets. You'll have two broad choices: framed or frameless. Think of a picture frame glued to the front of a box, and you have a framed cabinet. The frame stiffens the box, and the doors are hung from it. Frameless cabinets, of course, lack the picture frame. The doors are hung directly on the side of the box, using special adjustable hinges. While they're just as strong as framed cabinets once installed, they do flex a little during installation. It's easier to put things in and take things out of a frameless cabinet because you don't have to work around that center post.

Once you've chosen between the two, choose from the countless styles—modern, traditional, country, French provincial, and more.

Even if design requires help from the pros, installation can be a do-it-yourself job. The difficult part is keeping everything perfectly level and perfectly aligned while setting it on a floor that probably is neither. Start by removing all the cabinet doors and drawers: They only make the unit heavier and easier to damage. Get a good 4-foot level and use it constantly. Start with the wall cabinets—they're much easier to hang before the base cabinets are in place. Begin in a corner—about the only way to make sure the cabinet is properly positioned. Once the wall cabinets are up, install the base cabinets. Unlike the wall cabinets, which you installed one at a time, you'll put all of the base cabinets in place and double-check everything before screwing anything to the wall.

Two kinds of corner cabinets—blind and diagonal—are available. The following steps show how to install both.

Think of traffic patterns and electric and plumbing outlets before finalizing your cabinet plan.

Installing wall cabinets

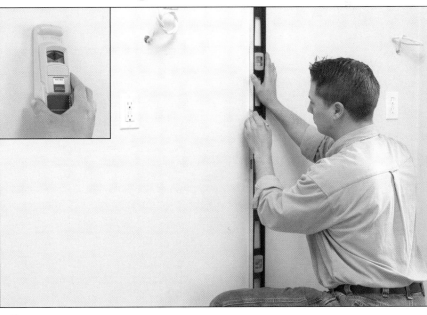

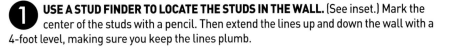

1 **USE A STUD FINDER TO LOCATE THE STUDS IN THE WALL.** (See inset.) Mark the center of the studs with a pencil. Then extend the lines up and down the wall with a 4-foot level, making sure you keep the lines plumb.

Installing wall cabinets *(continued)*

Transfer level line to wall and extend around room

2 **LOCATE HIGH SPOTS IN THE FLOOR.** Begin by placing a straight 2×4 on the floor against the wall and placing a 4-foot level on top of it. Shim the low end of the 2×4 until you get a level reading. Transfer the top of the level line to the wall and extend it around the room. The point at which the distance between the line and floor is smallest is the high spot. This is the point from which you will begin laying out the cabinets. Mark it with an X.

3 **MARK THE TOP OF THE BASE CABINETS ON THE WALL.** Begin at the high point on the floor and measure up 34½ inches, the standard height of a base cabinet before the counter is added. Extend a level line around the room at this height (see inset).

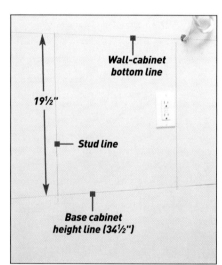

Wall-cabinet bottom line

19½"

Stud line

Base cabinet height line (34½")

4 **MARK THE BOTTOM OF THE WALL CABINETS** by drawing a level line 19½ inches above the top line of the base cabinets that you drew in the last step. Then mark all of the cabinets on the wall with a pencil and level to double-check your layout. (See "Work Smarter," right.)

A+ WORK SMARTER

LAY OUT THE COMPLETE JOB
Lay everything out on the wall with a pencil and level so that you know what goes where, and mark where each cabinet should be. A 15-inch cabinet looks much like an 18-inch cabinet—until you get to the end of the row and you notice a 3-inch gap you hadn't counted on. Drawing the cabinet outlines on the wall is one way to check your work as you go.

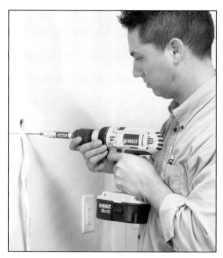

5 **INSTALL THE UPPER CABINETS FIRST.** It is easier to install them before the base cabinets are in place. Temporarily drive a couple of long screws into the studs along the line marking the bottom of the upper cabinets to help support them while you're installing. Some installers screw a board, called a ledger, along the entire length of the wall to hold the cabinets. The ledger works as long as the wall is flat and plumb. If it's not, you'll need to shim behind the cabinets to align them, and the ledger would get in the way.

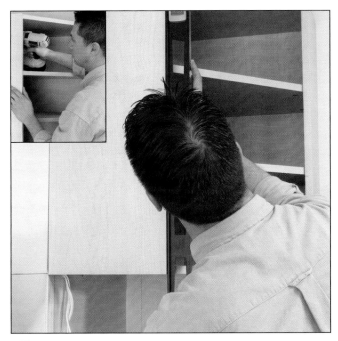

6 **START INSTALLATION WITH A CORNER WALL CABINET.** Place the cabinet on the screws or ledger. If the cabinet isn't plumb, slip shims between the cabinet and wall at the stud lines and adjust as necessary. Drill and countersink two holes in each of the mounting rails inside the cabinet and drive 2½-inch drywall screws through the holes. (See inset.)

7 **WITH A HELPER, REST THE NEIGHBORING CABINET ON THE SCREW OR LEDGER AND LINE UP THE FRONT WITH THE CABINET YOU JUST INSTALLED.** Clamp the two cabinets together. Check for level and plumb, and shim between the wall and cabinet as necessary.

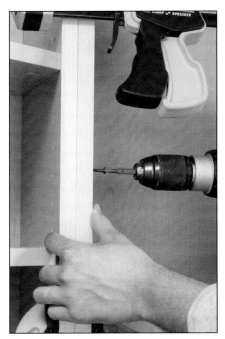

TOOL TIP

EFFICIENT COUNTERSINKING
Screws you use to install the cabinet have to be countersunk so that their heads are below the surface of the wood. You'll also need to drill a pilot hole the same diameter as the screw so that the screw won't split the mounting rail. Get a combination bit, which bores both holes in one operation. Use a bit holder that allows you to change bits without having to open the chuck.

8 **ON FRAMELESS CABINETS, SUCH AS THE ONES SHOWN HERE, DRILL THE HOLES FOR CONNECTORS** (a screw-and-sleeve set found at most stores that sell cabinets). Screw the cabinets together. On framed cabinets, drill holes for 1¼-inch drywall screws in the recesses for the hinges to hide them.

9 **DRILL AND COUNTERSINK TWO PILOT HOLES THROUGH EACH OF THE MOUNTING RAILS, CENTERING THE HOLES OVER THE STUDS.** (On some wall cabinets, the mounting rails are inside the cabinet. On others, they are hidden by the back.) Drive 2½-inch drywall screws through the holes and into the studs.

Installing wall cabinets *(continued)*

10 **HANG THE REST OF THE CABINETS THE WAY YOU HUNG THE FIRST ONES, CHECKING FOR LEVEL AND PLUMB AS YOU GO.** Once all the wall cabinets are in place, remove the ledger screws you installed in Step 5. Trim any visible shims flush with the cabinet using a utility knife.

11 **IF YOU HAVE A SLIGHT GAP BETWEEN THE BACK OF THE LAST CABINET AND THE WALL, COVER IT WITH A STRIP OF MOLDING.** Cut a piece as long as the cabinet; stain and finish it to match. Nail it in place with a brad gun, and fill the holes with a putty made by the cabinet manufacturer to match the cabinet finish.

A valance that bridges two sections of wall cabinets over a sink or stove presents an opportunity to add accent or task lighting.

12 **IF YOU HAVE A GAP BETWEEN THE SIDE OF THE CABINET AND AN END WALL OR APPLIANCE, CUT A FILLER STRIP TO CLOSE IT.** The cabinet distributor usually sells these strips. Scribe the strip with a compass (see inset) and cut along the line with a saber saw. Slip the strip in place and attach it with drywall screws.

13 **A VALANCE IS A DECORATIVE PIECE THAT CONNECTS TWO WALL CABINETS ABOVE A SINK.** Have someone help you hold the valance in position; drill and countersink pilot holes into the side of the cabinets on each side, and attach the valance with drywall screws. (See the finished installation on page 384.)

Installing base cabinets

1 **PUT THE CORNER CABINET—IN THIS CASE, A BLIND CORNER CABINET—IN PLACE.** (Leave a space between the cabinet and wall as required by the manufacturer.) Shim to align it with the top-of-cabinet line you drew on the wall. Check for level and plumb, and shim as necessary. You'll install a toe-kick later, which will cover the shims. The counter and cabinets will hide the other shims.

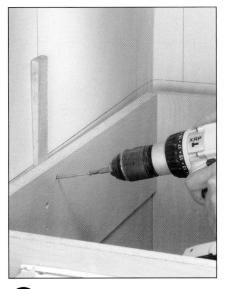

2 **DRILL AND COUNTERSINK PILOT HOLES INTO THE BACK OF THE CORNER CABINET.** Drill one hole at each stud, through any shims. Drive screws partway into the wall. Check for level again, shim as necessary, and drive the screws home.

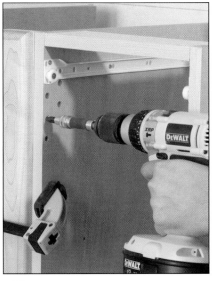

3 **SET THE NEIGHBORING CABINET IN PLACE,** install doors or drawers, and verify that they'll open. If necessary, attach a filler strip between the cabinets. You can usually order the fillers at the same time as your cabinets. Clamp the filler flush with the front of the cabinet. Drill and countersink pilot holes into the edge of the filler and screw the filler to the cabinet.

WORK SMARTER

LEAVE EXTRA ROOM FOR BLIND CABINETS

Don't be blindsided by blind corner cabinets. All are designed to sit away from the wall in order to keep the doors and drawers from hitting neighboring doors and drawers. Most require mounting some kind of spacer on the side. **Read the manufacturer's installation directions carefully.** Because you removed the doors and drawers during installation, you usually don't realize you've made a mistake until you hang the doors. By then, you've usually installed the entire kitchen, and fixing the problem will require taking apart about half of it.

4 **CHECK THE SECOND CABINET FOR LEVEL AND PLUMB,** and shim at the floor or wall if necessary. You will now begin assembling the row of base cabinets, making any cutouts for plumbing or wiring, as in Step 5.

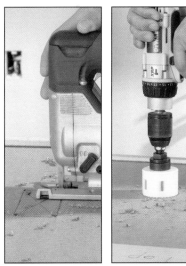

5 **BEFORE YOU INSTALL THE SINK CABINET, DRILL AND CUT HOLES FOR ANY WIRING AND THE PIPES.** Measure how far they are from the adjoining cabinet. Subtract the thickness of the side of the sink cabinet, and mark the pipe locations on the cabinets. Drill at the marks with a spade bit or hole saw to cut holes for the pipes.

Installing base cabinets *(continued)*

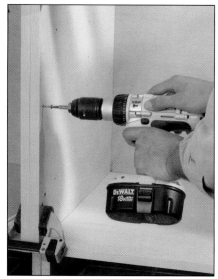

6 **INSTALL THE REST OF THE CABINETS, CHECKING FOR LEVEL AND PLUMB; SHIM AS YOU GO.** When all the remaining cabinets are in position, step back and check for level and plumb before you screw any in place.

7 **WHEN ALL CABINETS ARE IN THE PROPER PLACE, DRILL AND COUNTERSINK PILOT HOLES.** Attach the cabinets to the studs with at least two screws in each mounting rail. Attach them to each other with at least four drywall screws.

8 **ONCE ALL THE CABINETS ARE SCREWED IN PLACE, INSTALL A TOE-KICK TO COVER THE GAP ALONG THE BOTTOM.** This is often a two-step process: First nail a plain ¾-inch filler strip in place; then attach a thinner piece that is finished to match the cabinet. Drill pilot holes and drive 4d finishing nails through the toe-kick into the cabinets.

Installing a kitchen island

1 **BEGIN BY MARKING WHERE THE INSIDE EDGES OF THE CABINET WILL BE ON THE FLOOR.** To do this, put the island in position and trace around it, marking the outside corners on the floor. Remove the island. Measure in from the lines by the thickness of the island's sides, and draw lines marking the inside edges of the cabinet.

2 **CUT SHORT PIECES OF 2x4 TO USE AS CLEATS.** Screw these to the floor at the edge of each individual cabinet.

3 **WITH A HELPER, LIFT THE ISLAND OVER THE CLEATS AND SET IT IN POSITION.** Check for level and shim as necessary. Nail it in place with a power nailer, or drill pilot holes and drive finishing nails through the base and into the cleats.

Countertop basics

Laminate

Ceramic tile

Marble

Solid-surface

Two types of countertops are available for the do-it-yourselfer: tile and prefabricated laminate. You'll learn how to install these countertops in this section.

Other choices—granite, solid-surface, metal, concrete, soapstone, and slate—should be installed by professionals. Some, such as granite, are difficult to install, and you probably lack the skills and equipment to complete the job. Others, like solid-surface, can't be installed by the homeowner without voiding the warranty.

Despite these limitations, you can still consider some of the ritzier counters.

Here's a brief comparison of countertop materials:

Laminate: Generally the least expensive of the lot, it's low-maintenance and durable. Prefab counters called postform are made for do-it-yourself installation. Home centers, kitchen suppliers, and local cabinetmakers can supply countless custom variations.

Ceramic: As tough as they come, it's easy to clean, although the grout can be a nuisance, and it's moisture- and heat-resistant. You can do it yourself or hire a pro.

Solid-surface: Durable and available in many styles and colors, it can be special-ordered with a built-in sink. It looks like it would make an ideal chopping board, but knife marks ruin its surface. Avoid sanding away dings, dents, and stains, unless you want a big divot in the middle of the counter.

Stone: Cost-competitive with solid-surface, stone is beautiful and durable, cleans easily, and stands up well to water. Marble, however, can stain and is not recommended in the kitchen or around sinks. Granite is the best all around but should be sealed to protect it from oil stains.

Butcher block: A wood counter is beautiful but hard to protect from scratches, water, and hot pans. Coat it occasionally with mineral oil. It's about the only finish that's considered "food safe," but it isn't as durable as other countertop options.

Installing countertops

If your cabinets have lived on long after your countertop died, it's possible to fix the problem without ditching the cabinets.

As always, there's a catch: If you want solid stone, such as granite, or a wood solid surface, don't do it yourself. Let the pros come to the house, do the work, and give you a guarantee. (Some solid surface manufacturers will void the warranty if the installation isn't done by a certified professional.) But if you like laminates and don't mind using a saber saw, you can do the work yourself. Go to the home center, and look at the "postform" counters. Postform counters come with a pre-attached backsplash, plus a sheet of laminate that starts on the top of the backsplash and continues around the counter's rounded front edge. You'll find several varieties and lengths, as well as counters with precut miters and counters that are square on both ends. The ends come unfinished and are later covered by an iron-on piece of laminate.

If your cabinets require a nonstandard countertop length, you'll need to have one custom-made. The built-in backboard on postform counters makes them almost impossible to trim.

1 TAKE ACCURATE MEASUREMENTS OF THE CABINET LAYOUT and draw a plan on a piece of graph paper. Plan for a 1-inch overhang at any exposed end, and subtract 1/16 inch from pieces that will butt against an appliance, such as a range or refrigerator, to allow for easy installation and removal.

WORK SMARTER

WHEN TO HIRE A PRO
If two counters come together in a corner, verify that the corner is square. Start by marking 3 feet from the corner on one wall, and 4 feet from the corner on the second wall. If the distance between the marks isn't 5 feet, your corner is out of square. Prefab counters are made to fit in square corners, and cutting a new miter is hard, even for a pro. Have the counter custom-made and professionally installed. The cabinetmaker will solve the problems right in the shop, and the installer knows how to solve the ones that crop up during installation.

If you're considering installing a prefab U-shaped counter, you're considering one of the hardest installations. Not only must both outside corners be perfectly square, any irregularity along the wall will affect how the counter sits against the other walls. Hire a pro.

2 PUT THE COUNTERTOP UPSIDE DOWN ON THE SAWHORSES AND CLAMP IT IN PLACE. If either end of the counter will be exposed once installed, you'll need to put laminate on the end. End cap kits are available from home stores that sell countertops; the kits contain everything you'll need, including battens that you glue underneath the counter to build the ends up to the proper thickness. Begin by gluing the battens in place and fasten with finishing nails or screws.

3 THE END CAP IS OVERSIZED—PUT IT OVER THE BATTEN SO THAT IT COVERS THE EDGE OF THE COUNTERTOP. The end cap is backed with a heat-sensitive glue. Press the end cap against the end of the counter, using an iron set at medium heat, for the time suggested by the manufacturer. (If the iron is too hot, it will damage the laminate.) Wipe off excess adhesive while it's still hot.

4 ROUT THE END CAP FLUSH WITH THE COUNTERTOP USING A SMALL ROUTER CALLED A LAMINATE TRIMMER. Work carefully and hold the trimmer flat on the end cap—tipping the router will cut into the surface of the counter.

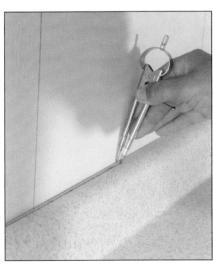

5 SET THE COUNTERTOP ON THE CABINETS, CLAMP IT IN PLACE, AND CHECK IT FOR LEVEL. Shim it if necessary. Typically, you'll have small gaps between the wall and backsplash; fill them later with caulk. If the gaps are large, however, you'll have to sand the countertop's edge so that it fits against the wall. Set the span of a compass to the size of the largest gap between the backsplash and the wall. Mark what you'll have to remove by pulling the compass along the wall.

6 REMOVE THE COUNTERTOP AND CLAMP AND PLACE IT BACK ON THE SAWHORSES. Use a belt sander to sand the backsplash to the line you drew with the compass. This will eliminate any gaps between the countertop and the wall.

7 TO HOLD PIECES TIGHTLY TOGETHER AT THE CORNERS, most counters have grooves that hold joint-fastening bolts that span the seam. You'll get the best seam where two pieces of countertop meet if you join them before you put them on the cabinet. Start by gluing them together with the glue from a miter-clamp kit. If the kit has no glue, apply a thin bead of silicone caulk to the edge of both pieces and paint the rest of the edges heavily with wood glue. Then press the edges together.

Installing countertops *(continued)*

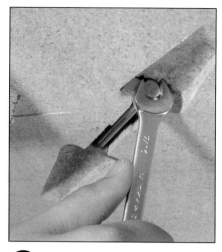

8 **MAKE SURE THE ENTIRE SURFACE IS FLUSH AT THE SEAM ALONG THE FRONT EDGE OF THE COUNTER.** Adjust as necessary and tighten the nearest miter clamp. Wipe away any excess glue. Standing behind the backsplash, push the countertops up and down as necessary to make the seam flush along the back of the counter. Tighten the miter clamp nearest the backsplash.

9 **LOOK AT THE REST OF THE SEAM.** If one side is higher than the other, tap the countertop with a dead-blow hammer like the one shown here. If you use a regular hammer, protect the countertop with a piece of wood. Once the seam is level, tighten the remaining miter clamps.

10 **FASTEN THE COUNTERTOP TO THE CABINETS BY SCREWING UP THROUGH THE TOP OF THE CABINETS.** If your cabinets have no tops, screw through the front rail and through any blocks built into the cabinet for that purpose. **SEAL THE SEAM BETWEEN THE BACKSPLASH AND WALL** with a silicone caulk that matches the color of the countertop.

Sink cutout

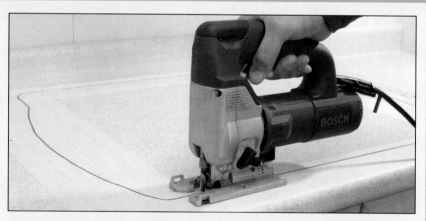

All sink manufacturers supply a cutting template, or directions for making one, with their sinks. Set the countertop across a pair of sawhorses. Position the template on the countertop, following the manufacturer's instructions. Tape it in place and trace the outline with a pencil. Mark separate holes for the faucets, if necessary.

Clamp the countertop to the sawhorses and drill a ½-inch starter hole inside the outline with a spade bit. If other holes are necessary for faucets or other fixtures, drill them with a hole saw. Fit a saber saw with a laminate blade, which has special teeth to minimize chipping. Insert the blade into the starter hole to begin the cut.

Cut carefully along the outline. Once you've cut along part of the outline, screw a drywall screw into the gap left by the saw cut to keep the cutout from vibrating. If the backsplash interferes with the cut, change to a regular blade, turn the counter over, and continue the cut from the bottom to avoid chipping.

HOMER'S HINDSIGHT

DON'T SCREW UP

Check, countercheck, cross-check, and double-check the length of every screw before you drive it through the cabinet and into the countertop. One lousy screw that's wrong spells disaster. A really good installer I know got a long screw in his pouch by mistake. He was in a hurry and not paying attention so he drove the screw right through the top of the laminate counter. An expensive mistake because all you can do at that point is ask the dealer to order some matching seam-fill and hope you can hide the damage. Seam-fill comes in a small, plastic tube. It's designed to help hide bad seams, but it can hide other mistakes too. Squeeze some on, work it flush using a small and flexible putty knife, and let it dry.

Tiling a countertop

EASY | **MEDIUM** | HARD

REQUIRED SKILLS: Basic carpentry, tile layout, tile cutting and fitting.

HOW LONG WILL IT TAKE?

Experienced . . . . .Variable
Handy . . . . .Variable
Novice . . . . .Variable

VARIABLES: Length of job will depend on complexity of tile layout and size of counter.

STUFF YOU'LL NEED

✔ MATERIALS:

Ceramic tiles, edge tiles or edge bead, mortar, grout, grout sealer, scrap 2×4, ¾-inch exterior-grade plywood, 4-mil plastic sheeting, backerboard, backerboard screws, 1¼-inch drywall screws, 3-inch fiberglass tape, tile spacers

✔ TOOLS:

Drill with ⅛-inch masonry bit and phillips bit, tape measure, utility knife, notched trowel, drywall tape knife, tile cutter or wet saw, tile nippers, level, rubber grout float, burlap

Installing a ceramic-tile countertop creates a beautiful, long-lasting, and functional work surface. Like floor tile, countertop tile is permanently installed using mortar adhesive and grout. Most tiles are countertop material—glazed, quarry, mosaic, or even stone tiles, such as slate or granite. You have your choice of many sizes and shapes of tile, but be aware that different sizes affect the finished appearance. Smaller tiles require more grout lines that may stain or degrade with use. Larger tiles are more appropriate for floors. Midsize tiles (4 to 6 inches) are ideal for countertops.

The surface below the countertop tile may be more important than the surface beneath a tiled floor. Carefully follow the steps involved in preparing the substrate (the surface below the tile) to avoid problems.

BUYER'S GUIDE

TILING TERMS

- **Mortar** is a mixture of sand and portland cement.

- **Dry-set mortar** is a specially formulated mixture for application over backerboard.

- **Latex Portland cement mortar** has a latex additive that makes the mortar more flexible, and is best suited for countertops. You'll find two types—one is a powder to which a liquid latex additive is added; the other is a powder containing dry latex resin to which water is added. Both do the job equally well.

- **Backerboard** is a rigid panel that provides a sound substrate for setting tile. Depending on the manufacturer, backerboard can be made of cement, fiber cement, gypsum, plywood, or plastic. Fiber cement panels do not require fiberglass mesh to bind the material into a panel. Although several thicknesses are available, ¼ and ½ inch are commonly used for both walls and floors in residential construction. Follow the manufacturer's recommendations for installation.

Designer Tip

A BALANCED APPROACH

The tiles around your sink look best when they are the same width on all sides. The time to solve this problem is while you're laying them out. On a straight counter, lay out the tiles so that the first one is centered over what will be the center of the sink and work toward the ends. If the counter is L-shape, however, lay out the tiles with a full tile in the corner, as shown in Step 10 on page 407. If placing the tile there creates problems at the sink, reposition the sink opening before you cut it to make sure you have equal widths all around the sides.

Tiling a countertop *(continued)*

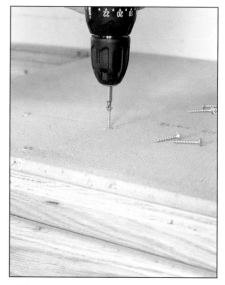

1 **INSTALL A PLYWOOD SUBSTRATE.** The base cabinets form the structural support for the countertop. Install ¾-inch exterior-grade plywood cut to fit. Screw it in place with 1¼-inch drywall screws, shimming as necessary to ensure a flat surface.

2 **CUT OUT PLYWOOD FOR THE SINK.** New sinks often come with a template or measurements. (If you are reusing the old sink, measure the opening after you remove it.) Position the template. Make sure the new faucet will clear the wall behind the counter. Mark the cutout. Drill a ⅜-inch starter hole inside the cutout near one of the corners; then cut with a saber saw.

3 **INSTALL BACKERBOARD.** Cut it to fit by scoring and snapping. Cut sink curves freehand on both faces. Finish curves by snapping material away with pliers. Leave a ⅛-inch gap between pieces for mortar. Predrill screw holes every 6 to 8 inches. Remove the pieces and staple on a 4-mil plastic moisture barrier. Apply mortar on the plastic with a ¼-inch notch trowel. Reposition the pieces and install them with backerboard screws.

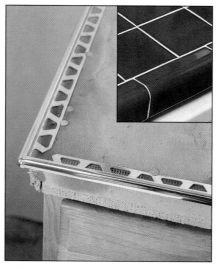

4 **TAPE AND FILL SEAMS.** Reinforce exposed edges of the backerboard with three layers of fiberglass tape. Then apply a 3-inch-wide layer of latex Portland cement mortar to fill the gaps between sheets of backerboard. Lay a strip of fiberglass mesh tape across the gap. Press the tape firmly into the mortar with a 4-inch taping knife.

5 **APPLY AN EDGE BEAD.** Apply a stainless steel decorative edge by bending it around the corners and nailing it into the backboard with galvanized nails. An alternative is to use ceramic edge trim for a softer look. (See inset.)

6 **CUT THE TILES TO SIZE.** Use either a score-and-snap-type tile cutter or a wet saw to make straight cuts in the tile. Mark the tile with a felt-tip pen and position it against the fence on the tile cutter. Hold the tile firmly and slide the scoring wheel across the tile in a continuous motion. Reposition the tool with the pressure plate flat against the face of the tile and press down to snap the tile.

Larger tiles (12"×12") can vary slightly in thickness and size even if they're from the same box, so be sure to compensate for differences when you lay out the tile.

7 **DRY-FIT THE TILES.** Tiles vary widely from the size they're supposed to be. To avoid surprises, lay out the entire countertop before applying mortar. Lay all the full tiles first, then cut the others to fit. In countertops with a sink, adjust the layout to ensure the tiles are even on each side of the sink. On an L-shape countertop, start with a full tile at the inside corner. Use tile spacers to maintain even spacing. Leave a ⅛-inch gap between perimeter tiles and the wall.

8 **CUT THE TILES AROUND THE SINK.** Cutting curves or notches is more challenging than straight cuts. (See inset.) Mark the cut with a felt-tip pen. Gradually nip off small pieces of tile with tile nippers to reach the mark. Sand or smooth with a file if necessary.

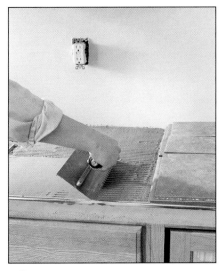

9 **SPREAD THE MORTAR.** Mix the mortar according to the label directions. Spread an even coat of mortar with a notched trowel. The mortar instructions will specify the appropriate notch size, which is determined by the size of the tile. Hold the trowel at a consistent angle (about 45 degrees) and drag it against the backerboard surface.

10 **LAY THE TILES IN THE MORTAR.** Start laying the full tiles at the more critical areas of the layout—around the sink or at an inside corner of an L-shape counter. Work from front to back, placing as many of the full tiles as possible. Press each tile into the mortar with a slight twisting motion. Use tile spacers to keep the tiles aligned. To level the set tiles, place a straight piece of 2×4 on its edge across the tile, then tap gently on it. Check for flatness with a 2-foot level.

11 **LAY PARTIAL TILES AT THE PERIMETER AND AROUND THE SINK.** When all the full tiles are in place, set the partial tiles and any tiles cut to fit around the sink. Use the spacers between cut tiles and full tiles. Let discrepancies in spacing end at the wall—the backsplash or trim will hide any flaws.

Tiling a countertop *(continued)*

 WORK SMARTER

TILING THE BACKSPLASH

The section of wall against the countertop covered with countertop material is called a backsplash because it protects the wall from splashes, bumps, and spills. You can make the backsplash a few inches high, or run it to the cabinets above, as shown at right. Whatever method you use, put up backerboard before you tile. Follow the same procedure as for the countertop: Put mortar directly on the wall, put backerboard over it, and screw it to the studs. Leave spaces between the edges, fill with mortar, and cover with fiberglass tape.

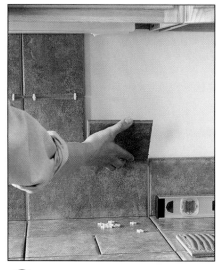

12 TILE THE BACKSPLASH, running the tiles from the counter to the bottom of the wall cabinets, or stopping after a single row. If you're only applying a single row, use bullnose tile, which has a finished edge. If the backsplash wall contains electrical outlets, cut tiles around them and add box extension rings (available in the electrical department) to bring the outlets flush with the tiles.

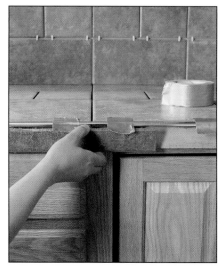

13 TILE THE EDGE. If using edge bead, cut the tiles so that they bridge the grout lines on the main countertop, as shown. Apply grout. Put the tiles tightly against the bead and tape them in place to hold them while the mortar dries. If using edge tiles, it's unnecessary to tape them because part of the tile sits on the countertop. Space edge tiles so the grout lines between them match those on the counter.

14 GROUT THE TILE. After the tile has completely set (check the mortar instructions), pull out the spacers and apply the grout. Mix the grout following the manufacturer's directions. Spread grout across the counter with a rubber grout float. Work the grout into the joints by moving the float diagonally across the tile. Once all the joints are filled, remove excess by wiping diagonally with a wet sponge (see inset). Rinse the sponge frequently in clean water. Sponge off the excess grout from the surface of the tile and leave the grout slightly depressed in the joints. Let the grout dry, then rub the tiles with cheesecloth to remove the haze left by the grout.

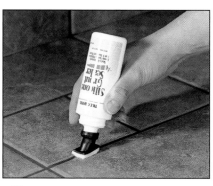

15 SEAL THE GROUT. Because grout is prone to staining, seal it with a silicone grout sealer after it has cured completely—about 30 days, or as recommended by the manufacturer. Apply the silicone grout sealer to the grout lines with a foam brush or applicator, let it soak in for a few minutes, and wipe away the excess.

GOOD IDEA

TILING OVER PLASTIC LAMINATE

You can lay tile over a plastic laminate countertop as long as there are no loose areas, and as long as the edges are square. (Rounded-over edges, or "waterfalls," between the backsplash and counters can't be tiled.) Edges that have lifted should be glued down with construction adhesive and clamps. Then screw down cement backerboard and follow the steps on these pages. Tiling over an existing countertop will make counter edges thicker and may affect sink and faucet installation.

Grout is available in different colors to coordinate or contrast with the color of the tile.

Adding a closet

SKILL SCALE

EASY	MEDIUM	**HARD**

REQUIRED SKILLS:
Intermediate carpentry skills, using power tools.

HOW LONG WILL IT TAKE?

Experienced . . . . 3 days
Handy . . . . 4 days
Novice . . . . 5 days

VARIABLES: Time is based on building a 2'×4' closet. Larger closets will take longer to frame and drywall.

STUFF YOU'LL NEED

✔ **MATERIALS:**

2×4 lumber, drywall, prehung door, 8d and 10d nails or 2½- and 3-inch drywall screws for framing, 6d and 8d nails for trim, toggle bolts, shims, metal corner bead, joint compound, drywall tape, paint, primer

✔ **TOOLS:**

Tape measure, framing square, combination square, chalk line, plumb bob and line, miter saw, small backsaw, hammer, 4-foot level, drill with drill and screwdriver bits, screwdriver, clamps, utility knife, 6-, 8-, and 12-inch drywall knives, coping saw, paint roller or paintbrush

GOOD IDEA

UP TO CODE

In most municipalities, adding a closet is considered a major renovation. Check with your building officials to see if you need to obtain a building permit.

Before you start measuring hangers and making plans, the minimum depth you'll need for a closet is 24 inches. If you're hanging coats instead of suits and dresses, plan on a minimum of 28 inches. As for length, allow 48 inches per person.

This, of course, is the inside dimension. The outside dimension is an extra 4½ inches for each wall—3½ inches for the studs and another ½ inch on each side for the drywall. If you have the space, get out your tape measure and start making plans. Putting the closet in the middle of a long wall, for example, is sure to look like the afterthought that it is. Tucking it into an unused corner of a large room, or along the entire length of a windowless wall, on the other hand, will make the closet seem like part of the overall scheme.

Building a closet in a room with a finished ceiling is a bit different than building one in an unfinished room. It's no longer possible to build the wall flat on the floor, and then roll it up in place without wedging it at an angle between the floor and ceiling. Instead, you'll have to nail a plate to the floor and one to the ceiling, then measure and cut the studs to fit between. (For more information on framing the door opening, see page 237.)

Note that when the time comes to draw layout lines, you should start on the ceiling. This simplifies aligning the floor

WORK SMARTER

CLOSET LIGHTING

Plan ahead for closet lighting. Get a recessed fixture—code no longer lets you install a bare bulb above the shelf, where the heat can start a fire. Install the fixture before the new walls get in your way. Consider covering up the holes you'll have to chop by screwing a new drywall ceiling right over the old one. Run wiring for the switch before you drywall the new walls, and shop around for a switch. Ask about one that turns the light on and off automatically as you open and close the door.

---

and ceiling plates because you can transfer the lines to the floor with a plumb bob. If you find overhead layout confusing, by all means, start your layout on the floor. When you need to transfer lines to the ceiling, keep moving the string until the plumb bob is over the right spot on the floor.

On average you'll want the closet bar 63 inches off the floor for dresses or about 72 inches off the floor if you're storing a collection of ballroom gowns. Either of these heights works for suits, blouses, and skirts, but if you drop the bar down to 45 inches, you can install a lot of shelf space, or even another bar, above it. It's also an appropriate height for a kid's closet when they're from about 6 to 12 years old. Drop down to 30 inches for younger children.

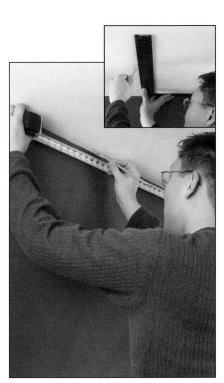

1 BEGIN BY LAYING OUT THE SHORTEST WALL OF THE CLOSET. Measure along what will become the back wall to what will be the outside edge of the new wall. Measure back the thickness of the drywall, ½ inch, and use a framing square to draw a line marking the outside edge of the ceiling plate. Draw a second line marking the inside edge of the ceiling plate.

Adding a closet (continued)

2 **MEASURE AND LAY OUT A FRONT CLOSET WALL PARALLEL TO THE EXISTING BACK WALL.** This assures that the closet depth won't change because of an out-of-kilter corner. Once you've located the front edge of the wall, measure back by the thickness of the drywall to lay out the plate. Draw a second line laying out the inside edge of the plate.

3 **USE A PLUMB BOB TO TRANSFER THE LINES FROM THE CEILING TO THE FLOOR.** Begin by hanging the plumb bob from what will be the outside corner of the plates. When it stops swinging, mark the spot on the floor immediately below it. Repeat to mark the inside corner, and then mark the inside and outside edges of where the plates meet the wall.

4 **CUT THE PLATES TO LENGTH.** One ceiling plate and one soleplate will be the full length of the closet wall; the others will be shorter than their walls by 3½ inches—the width of the adjoining plates. Lay the long plates side by side, and lay out studs 16 inches apart, on center. Repeat on the shorter plates.

5 **BUY A PREHUNG DOOR BEFORE DOING THIS STEP.** Find the rough opening required—it will be listed on the installation directions that come with the door. Lay out the opening on the plates. Each side of the opening requires two studs—one that runs floor to ceiling, and one that runs to the top of the rough opening. (See Step 15 photo.) For now, just lay out the edges of the rough opening.

6 **THE BEST WAY TO MATCH TRIM TO THE EXISTING TRIM IS TO REUSE AS MUCH OF IT AS YOU CAN.** Cut along the edge of any baseboard or other trim that you will have to remove—this breaks any paint seal between it and the wall. Pry the molding loose, protecting the wall with a piece of scrap wood as you pry, as shown. If the molding seems reluctant to come off, try driving the nails that are holding it all the way through the molding and into the wall.

7 **NAIL THE PLATES TO THE FLOOR, DRIVING NAILS EVERY 2 FEET.** Use common nails long enough to extend through the subfloor and into the framing; 10d nails are usually adequate.

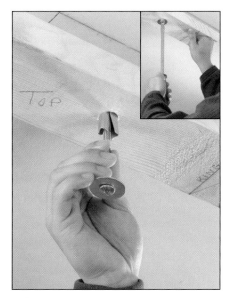

8 **UNLESS A JOIST JUST HAPPENS TO FALL IN THE RIGHT PLACE,** only the ceiling plate that runs perpendicular to the joists will have any framing above it. Nail or screw this plate into the joists that cross it. (If the ceiling is plaster and lath, be sure to screw it to avoid cracking the plaster.)

9 **ATTACH THE OTHER TOP PLATE WITH TOGGLE BOLTS.** Begin by drilling holes in the plate that are big enough to slip the folded toggle through. Put the plate in place and trace through the holes to mark the ceiling. Remove the plate and drill holes in the ceiling for the toggles. Secure the plate to the ceiling by tightening the toggles (see inset) and toenail it into the other plate.

10 **FIND THE STRAIGHTEST STUDS FOR FRAMING THE DOOR.** Measure back 3 inches from the marks you made for the rough opening and make a second mark. This will be the outside edge of the king stud, the one that runs from ceiling to floor. Measure, cut to length, and nail it in place, leaving a 1½-inch space between the edge of the rough opening and the nearest face of the stud. The jack stud gets nailed into this space later. (See page 237.)

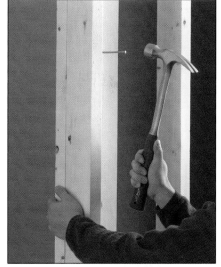

11 **BECAUSE THE DISTANCE BETWEEN THE PLATE MAY VARY SLIGHTLY, MEASURE FOR LENGTH EACH OF THE REMAINING FULL-LENGTH STUDS ONE AT A TIME.** Cut them to length and toenail them to the plates with 8d nails. Nail the studs nearest the existing walls to the framing inside them. If there is no framing directly behind the new studs, attach them to the wall with toggle bolts, the same way you attached the plate to the ceiling.

12 **FRAME THE CORNER TO CREATE A STRUCTURE THAT LOOKS LIKE THIS.** Begin by nailing a stud in place at the end of either one of the walls that forms the corner. Nail spacers to it, and nail a full-length stud to the spacers. Once you've nailed in the spacers and both studs, begin work on the adjacent wall by nailing a full-length stud in place.

13 **NOW THAT ALL THE FULL-LENGTH STUDS ARE IN PLACE, GO BACK TO THE CLOSET OPENING.** Cut the jack studs to length—they will be as long as the rough opening is high. Clamp both jack studs to the king studs, and verify with a level that the top of one stud is level with the other. Adjust as necessary and nail in place.

Adding a closet (continued)

14 **CUT A 2x4 TO FIT ACROSS THE OPENING.** Put it in place and nail down through it to secure it.

15 **TO SUPPORT THE SPACE ABOVE THE DOOR,** you will need to place cripple studs at 16-inch centers between the top plate and the 2×4 across the opening. Lay out the locations and measure to see if the length varies. Cut the studs to length and nail in place. (See page 237 for general information on framing openings.)

16 **RUN ANY WIRING THAT YOU'LL WANT FOR THE CLOSET.** If you want a light, put the switch for it near the door and position it ½ inch beyond the framing to account for the thickness of the drywall. By law, closet lights must be recessed into the ceiling to prevent an accidental fire.

17 **COVER THE INSIDE AND OUTSIDE OF THE CLOSET WITH DRYWALL.** (It's easiest if you prime it first, and then start hanging on the inside of the closet.) Cut any necessary openings for switches and receptacles, and screw the drywall in place. Put a metal corner bead on the outside corner and tape and finish the drywall with joint compound. For more on working with drywall, see Installing Drywall, page 245.

18 **HANG THE DOOR FOLLOWING THE INSTRUCTIONS THAT COME WITH IT.** Start with the jamb on the hinge side, shimming as necessary until the jamb is straight and plumb. Shim the other side so that it is plumb and so that there's a gap about the thickness of a nickel between the door and the door jambs. Level and shim the top, leaving the same-size gap. For more on hanging doors, see Installing a Prehung Interior Door, page 343.

19 **TRIM AROUND THE DOOR AND THEN INSTALL BASEBOARD.** If you saved the old baseboard, it will match up best with the baseboard already on the wall. For a tight fit, cope the joint—cut the piece going in so that it nests with the piece on the wall. Find the profile by mitering the closet molding and then cutting along the edge with a coping saw, as shown. Practice on a scrap first. See page 264 for more on coping.

Making bookshelves

Rabbet joint
Top

Dado joint
Shelf

Dado joint
Base

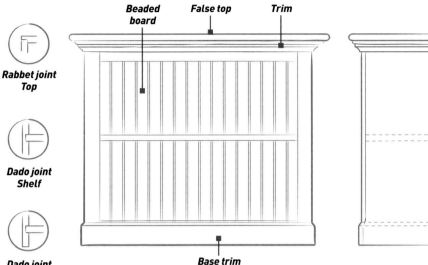

This bookshelf is simple to build and will teach you the basics of cabinetmaking. The project involves making a case with a single shelf and a false top with moldings and trim, such as wainscoting, for the back to add decorative appeal. You'll use hand tools and power tools, such as a router, a table saw, and a power miter saw. You will learn to cut rabbets (open channels along the edges and top of the bookshelf to hold the back) and dados (grooves cut across the sides to secure the shelves). You'll also learn to apply moldings, trim, and finishes that will guarantee professional looking results. Use the drawing (above) and the cut list (right) as your guides throughout the project.

Cabinetmaking demands careful thought and patience, as well as following a few basic rules.

● The more accurately you measure and mark, the more successful the result. Measure twice, cut once, and always check for square.

● Nails make ideal clamps when you're putting in shelving or molding, but you'll have to fill the holes. If you're staining, test the filler in advance to make sure it takes stain: Some fillers show up as a white blotch on the surface.

● Apply glue to both surfaces for a strong joint. If you fail to do so, the dry piece will pull the moisture out of the glue before it can penetrate both

CUT LIST

2 sides at ¾" × 10" × 30"
1 top at ¾" × 10" × 35¼"
1 bottom at ¾" × 10" × 35¼"
1 shelf at ¾" × 9⅝" × 35¼"
1 false top at ¾" x 11" x 38"
2 stiles at ¾" × 2½" × 30"
1 rail at ¾" × 2½" × 31"
1 rail at ¾" × 3⅜" × 31"

MOLDING

2 side pieces, cut to fit
1 front piece, cut to fit

BASEBOARD

2 side pieces, cut to fit
1 front piece, cut to fit

BACK

Wainscoting, cut to fit

surfaces. Apply glue from a squeeze bottle and spread with a plumber's acid brush or with your finger. Have a damp rag nearby to clean your hands and the cabinet.

● Clamp pieces together with the shelf laying on its face. As you're clamping, verify that pieces are lying flat, and check to make sure the shelf is square.

● When mitering molding, cut the pieces square and several inches longer than you need. Then miter an end, still leaving the piece long. Hold the piece in place and mark the final length on the back, then cut at the mark. It's much more accurate than measuring.

Making bookshelves (continued)

Router jig Ⓑ

Final depth

❶ CUT THE TOP, BOTTOM, AND SIDE PIECES TO SIZE ON A TABLE SAW, then rout rabbets for the back. Use a handheld router with a ⅜-inch rabbet bit (shown above) to rout a ⅜-inch-deep rabbet along the top, bottom, and one long edge of each side piece. Make the cut in three passes until the final depth of ⅜ inch is reached. At the start and end of the cuts, the bearing will roll around the corner, leaving a dip. To avoid this, clamp a piece of scrap wood to each end.

❷ CLAMP THE SIDES OF THE BOOKCASE TOGETHER. Ⓐ Make sure the ends are aligned and the rabbeted edges are to the outside. Draw layout lines for the shelf dados (grooves) with a carpenter's square and sharp pencil.

MAKE A JIG TO ROUT THE DADOS.
Ⓑ Screw a piece of 1×3 to a piece of ¼-inch plywood. Guide a router with a ¾-inch-diameter bit along the edge of the 1×3, routing a groove in the plywood. Make a second pass, cutting all the way through the ply.

❸ ALIGN THE EDGE OF THE JIG WITH THE EDGE OF THE SHELF DADO. Clamp it in place and square it up. Leave the ¾-inch bit in the router and guide the router along the 1×3, routing a shallow dado. Rout to the same depth as the rabbets in two more passes. Reposition the jig and rout a dado for the bottom. Also cut the rabbet for the case top with the jig—a rabbeting bit won't make a big enough cut. Start by positioning the jig cut to a groove along the top edge of the board. Rout the rabbet in three successively deeper passes.

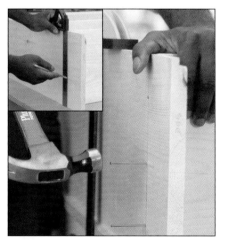

❹ CLAMP THE SHELF TOGETHER TEMPORARILY AND FIX ANYTHING THAT KEEPS IT FROM FITTING TOGETHER CORRECTLY. Remove the clamps and apply glue to the shelf edges, the rabbets along the top, and the dados, but not to the back rabbets. Clamp the case together. Check to make sure the case is lying flat. If not, the final shelves will be twisted.

❺ NAIL THE CASE TOGETHER. Mark nailing layout lines on the outside of the case with a combination square (see inset). The layout line should fall in the center of the dado so that the nails are driven into the center of the shelf. Remove the clamps, if necessary, and nail the case together with 6d finishing nails. Drive the nails straight and level so that they don't pop through the top or bottom of the shelf, then reclamp.

❻ CHECK THE CASE FOR SQUARE BY MEASURING DIAGONALLY FROM CORNER TO CORNER. If the two measurements are equal, the case is square. If not, loosen the clamps and tilt them so that they are angled slightly in the direction of the longer diagonal. Retighten the clamps and check the diagonals with every half-turn. Stop tightening when the diagonals are equal. Remove the clamps when the glue is dry.

7 **TO ADD A WAINSCOT BACK ,** cut all pieces to length. Nail the first piece to the shelf and rabbets. Nail the next piece so that the tongue goes halfway into the groove of the first piece, giving the board room to expand in humid weather. Install the rest of the boards, spacing and nailing them the same way. Cut the last piece to width, if necessary.

TO ADD A PLYWOOD BACK B, cut a piece of plywood to fit, then nail at the perimeter. Mark a line across the shelf and nail the back to the shelf.

8 **RIP THE FACE FRAME PIECES TO WIDTH ON A TABLE SAW AND CUT ONE END OF EACH PIECE SQUARE.** Put the stiles (verticals) on the case and mark the length with a knife. Cut to length along the knife line. If you're staining, glue and clamp the stiles in place. If you're painting, you can glue and nail them in place.

9 **INSTALL THE RAILS.** Once the stiles are in place, hold the square end of the rail against one of them, while a helper marks the other end with a knife to show where to cut. Cut to length. Glue and nail the top and bottom rails in place if you are painting. Glue only if you are staining. (See "Work Smarter," below.)

CABINETS, COUNTERTOPS, SHELVING, AND STORAGE

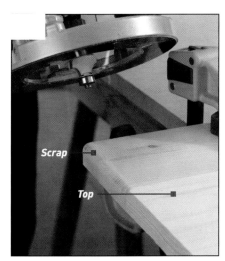
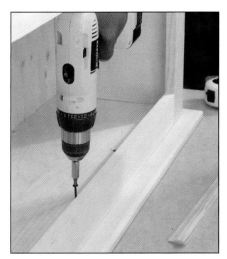

10 **MAKE THE FALSE TOP.** Cut the false top to length and round over the front and sides with the router. Clamp a piece of scrap lumber to the table and butt the top against the scrap so that the router won't dip around the back corners. Clamp the top to the table. Insert a ¼-inch round-over bit and run the router around the edges.

11 **SCREW THE TOP TO THE CASE.** Set the top on the case and line up the overhangs on the front and sides, making sure the back of the top is flush with the back of the case. Screw the top on with 1¼-inch #8 drywall screws.

A+ WORK SMARTER

MAKING MOLDING STAY PUT
If the molding keeps slipping while you're trying to nail it, you're not alone. Pros usually solve the problem by using a pneumatic brad gun—a handy tool but an expensive solution if you're only making one shelf. There are, however, a couple of other things you can do to help yourself. First, predrill a nail hole in the molding, using a nail as a drill bit. (Clip off the head for a smoother job.) If you then position the molding correctly, the first blow of the hammer drives the nail into the perfect spot on the cabinet. If you're still having trouble, predrill and then brush the back of the piece lightly with contact cement. Stick the molding in place while the contact cement is still slightly wet and hold it briefly until the glue dries. Nail it in place.

Making bookshelves (continued)

12 **INSTALL THE TOP MOLDING ON THE FRONT.** Cut a piece of molding for the front 3 inches longer than the front of the cabinet. Miter one end and line the miter up with a corner of the cabinet. Mark and cut the other side. When the piece fits exactly, glue and nail the molding in place with 3d finishing nails.

13 **INSTALL THE TOP MOLDING ON THE SIDES.** Mark and cut the side molding in the same manner as the front. Cut the miter first, then mark the other end and cut it square. If a gap appears where the moldings meet in the corner, roll a screwdriver across it (see inset), forcing the fibers together to close the gap.

14 **INSTALL THE MOLDING ON THE BOTTOM OF THE CASE.** The molding for the bottom is stock baseboard mitered and attached in the same manner as the top molding. Once all the molding is in place, set the nails below the surface with a nail set, and fill the holes with a paintable or stainable filler, depending on how you will finished the piece.

15 **SAND AND FINISH.** Once the bookcase is sanded, sealed, and all the nail holes are filled, you have the option of applying stain or paint. Supporting the unit on blocks while you apply the finish means not having to move it while you're working and will make the job easier.

SAFETY ALERT

FIRE HAZARD

The heat and fumes from rags soaked with stain or finish can cause fire by spontaneous combustion if kept in a closed container. Hang them unfolded on an outside line until completely dry, and then throw them out.

BUYER'S GUIDE

CHOOSING STAINS AND FINISHES

There are two types of stains: those that use pigment and those that use dye. Dye stains penetrate more deeply into the wood, but most stains available to consumers are pigment-based. Water-based stains offer many color options and easy cleanup. You'll also find combinations of stain and polyurethane in one can. Water-based polyurethanes are environmentally friendly but more expensive than oil-based versions. Shellac and varnish are also finishing alternatives.

Installing wire shelf storage systems

N o one has ever been known to have enough closet space. Short of renting a mini-storage for your out-of-season clothes, wire shelf organizers are one solution that won't cost a fortune, and which vastly improves your chances of finding your shoes.

Wire organizers are made by various companies and in a variety of styles. They are all basically systems of wire shelves, baskets, drawers, and supports that quickly screw together to increase available storage. They're not just for closets, either: you can buy soda-pop can holders for the kitchen; rake, shovel, and long-handled tool holders for the garage; and adjustable-height shelves for any room in the house.

Most manufacturers sell prepackaged organizers for specific needs, like the guestroom closet or kitchen pantry. They also sell individual shelving and drawer items that you can mix and match to create your own organizer. Check out their websites. Some manufacturers provide a design-it-yourself website, or may even have their designers design a storage system to meet your needs.

1 MARK THE LOCATION OF THE STUDS ON THE WALL. You can do this with a stud finder or by knocking on the wall with your knuckles and listening for the spots where the wall no longer sounds hollow. Once you find the first stud, measure to find the others—the center of one stud will be either 16 or 24 inches from the center of the neighboring studs.

Cutting wire shelves

If your closet is somewhere between two standard shelf lengths, you have two choices. You can install a shelf that doesn't reach all the way across the closet, or you can buy a longer shelf and cut it to size. Cut the shelf with either bolt cutters or a hacksaw, rounding the desired length down to the next lower full inch. Make the cut so that the cut wires extend far enough from the crosspiece to hold a plastic shelf end cap which will avoid cuts and snags.

2 IN THIS SYSTEM, SHELF STANDARDS ARE ATTACHED TO A PIECE CALLED A HANG TRACK, which runs parallel to the ceiling and screws in place. You can hang it at any height, as long as you screw it into the studs. For the strongest installation, run the hang track across the top of the wall. Screw it into the top plate, a piece of framing that runs the length of the wall and extends about 1½ inches below the ceiling. Screw into the plate through the middle of the track with a #12 pan-head screw, or as directed by the manufacturer.

Installing wire shelf storage systems *(continued)*

3 **LEVEL THE HANG TRACK BEFORE DRIVING THE REST OF THE SCREWS.** If the ceiling is out of level, it may interfere with leveling the track. If so, drop the entire track ½ inch and reinstall.

4 **HANG THE SHELF STANDARDS FROM THE TRACK.** Generally speaking, the standards should be no more than 24 inches apart, though manufacturer's recommendations may vary. Wherever possible, put each directly over a stud so that you can screw directly into it. Before screwing a standard in place, verify that it is plumb and draw a line along it. Screw it in place along the line, using the screws the manufacturer recommends.

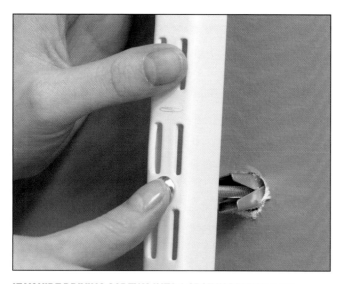

IF YOU'RE DRIVING SCREWS INTO A SPOT IN DRYWALL OR PLASTER WITHOUT FRAMING BEHIND IT, BUY THE APPROPRIATE-SIZE TOGGLE BOLTS. The nut, which comes with the bolt, has wings that fold flat. Drill a hole that the folded nut will just fit through. Put the nut and bolt on the standard. Fold the wings and slip the nut through the hole. When you let go, the wings will pop open so that the nut can't come back out of the hole. Pull gently on the bolt as you tighten to keep the nut from spinning.

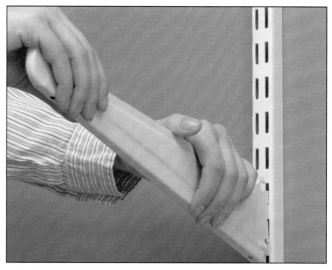

5 **ONCE THE STANDARDS ARE IN PLACE, INSTALL THE HANGER BARS.** These go in the same way adjustable shelf hangers do. Put small arms on the back of the hanger into the slots in the standard. Push down until they snap in place. If your closet will include baskets that hang from the shelves, make sure you've allowed enough space for them.

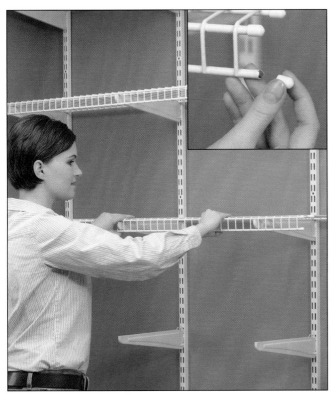

6 **PUT THE SHELVES ON THE HANGER BARS, MAKING SURE THEY ARE FIRMLY IN PLACE.** Put end caps on the exposed ends of each shelf. (See inset.)

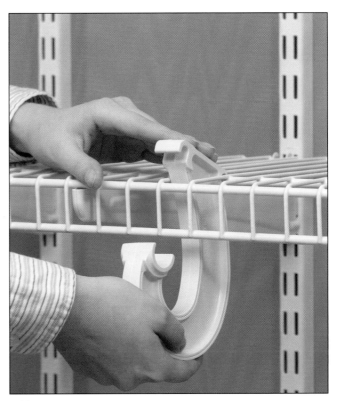

7 **IF YOU WANT TO HAVE A CLOTHING BAR IN THE CLOSET, HANG A BAR SUPPORT FROM THE SHELF.** The design varies from manufacturer to manufacturer. The ones in this closet slip through the space between the wires and then lock in place.

8 **YOU CAN ALSO INSTALL HANGING BASKETS FROM THE SHELVES.** Clip them to the wire shelf and, if desired, hang additional ones below.

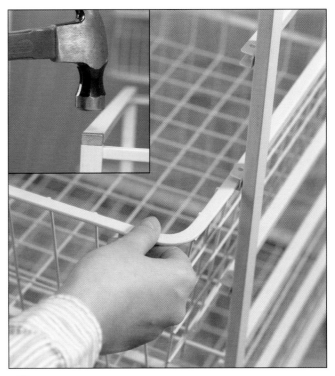

9 **FLOOR-BASED BASKET UNITS SLIDE IN AND OUT LIKE DRAWERS** and usually hang on a wire frame that snaps together. Tap the frame together (see inset) and then slide the baskets into the runners.

10 INSULATION AND WEATHERPROOFING

INSULATION HAS COME A LONG WAY SINCE THE DAYS OF STUFFING MUD AND STRAW WATTLE BETWEEN THE BEAMS. And heat has come a long way from the open fireplace and Franklin stove. But the central truth remains: You need both heat and insulation to stay warm.

The furnace gets most homeowners' attention. When it's not happy it groans, bangs, whines, and even goes on strike. Insulation, meanwhile, sits quietly in the attic. We ignore it, tending to the moans and whistles of the monster in the basement. If we understood the moans, however, we might pay more attention to the insulation—the furnace is telling us that it can't keep up; the job is more than it can handle.

And more likely than not, the long-term solution is in its silent partner, insulation. Older homes, built in the days of low-cost energy, lack the insulation they need to keep heat in the house. If you're cold, or if you're heating bill is through the roof, start at the roof. An uninsulated attic accounts for 40 percent of lost heat. Unrolling insulation in an unfinished attic is simple enough; in an attic with a floor, you might want to consider blow-in insulation. In this chapter you'll learn the ins and outs of insulation and its cousin, weather stripping. Such installations are among the simplest jobs a homeowner can do. Do them—your furnace will thank you.

REAL-WORLD SITUATIONS

ENERGY LOSS IS EXPENSIVE

Unless your house has the proper weather stripping, caulking, and storm windows, 20 to 50 percent of the money you spend is going to heat the great outdoors. Solutions are generally simple, low-tech, and with the possible exception of storm doors and windows, fairly inexpensive. However, a house should never be completely airtight. Even with extensive weatherproofing, that's not a problem in older homes but newer homes need to "breathe" to avoid health and structural problems. If you want to know how your house rates, do a quick inventory:

● Verify that the seams between the house and window or door moldings are sealed with caulk.

● Check windows for weather stripping. Windows should have weather stripping on the top, bottom, and sides. Double-hung windows should have weather stripping between the two sashes.

● Look for broken or loose windowpanes. If the putty around the windows is cracked or missing, replace it.

● Check the storm windows. If you have none, get them. If you do have them, make sure the weep hole on the bottom of the frame is open. A clogged hole traps moisture, causing fogged windows, paint failure, and rot.

● Check all exterior doors. They should be weatherstripped on both sides and at the top. There should be a sweep across the bottom to prevent air leakage at the threshold.

● Look for leaks around openings in the foundation or siding. Typical suspects include plumbing and gas pipes, wiring, telephone lines, and TV antenna wires or cable. Caulk and seal any openings you find.

● Verify that you have foam gaskets behind the switch and receptacle plates on exterior walls. Switches and outlets are notorious for leaking air. Gaskets solve the problem, for the most part, and are easy to install.

● Keep the fireplace flue closed when not in use.

● Check the amount of insulation in your attic, and compare it to the chart on page 436. Get more insulation if you need it. Check the insulation under crawlspaces too. It can fall down, leaving you with an extremely cold floor. Wall insulation is harder to check. Try a full energy audit, which will include inspection of the wall insulation and more. Check the Yellow Pages or with your power company to find someone who does audits.

Insulation and weatherproofing basics

Whether you live in a warm or a cold climate, adequately weatherizing and insulating your house has many benefits. Most importantly, you save money. Even in homes with average insulation, heating and cooling costs account for more than half of the total energy bill. And because most insulating and weather-stripping products are relatively inexpensive, an investment in them can be recovered through energy savings in a short period of time.

A well-insulated house not only saves money, it's easier on the environment because it uses less energy. By reducing energy use, you help reduce pollution and slow the depletion of natural resources. In an average home in a cold climate, it is estimated that reducing energy usage by only 15 percent can save the equivalent of 500 pounds of coal each year. And finally, a tightly sealed, well-insulated house eliminates drafts and cold spots, creating a more comfortable home for you to enjoy.

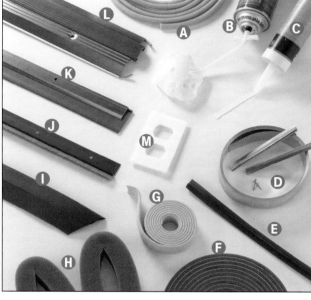

TIGHTEN UP THE HOUSE WITH A VARIETY OF PRODUCTS (above): **A** foam backer rod which is stuffed into a wide crack that will be caulked, **B** expandable foam, **C** silicone caulk, **D** metal tension strip, **E** tube gasket, **F** open cell foam, **G** closed-cell foam, **H** air-conditioner weather stripping, **I** garage door gasket, **J** bristle door sweep, **K** vinyl door sweep, **L** threshold, and **M** foam gasket for outlets.

FASTENERS (below) include **A** screws, **B** common nails, **C** construction adhesive, and **D** finishing nails. Seal cracks with a bead of **E** silicone caulk.

THE THREE TYPES OF INSULATION YOU'RE MOST LIKELY TO ENCOUNTER ARE FIBERGLASS, CELLULOSE, AND RIGID FOAM.
A Fiberglass comes in rolls and bats that you stuff between the framing of the house. **B** Insulation stays are used to support fiberglass in ceilings and crawlspaces. **C** Cellulose is blown in place and works well when you need to fit a lot of insulation in narrow spaces, such as between the joists of existing attics. Rigid foam comes in three types—**D** polyisocyanurate, **E** molded expanded polystyrene (MEPS), **F** extruded polystyrene (EXPS).

MEPS is the foam from which coffee cups and coolers are made. It has an R-value of R-4 per inch. (See "How Much is Enough?" on page 423.) EXPS is more common in building, has a hard, flat surface, and has an R-value of R-5 per inch. Polyisocyanurate is a closed-cell foam with an insulating gas trapped in the cells. The R-value is between R-7 and R-8 per inch, but it drops slightly as the gas escapes naturally. The indoor surfaces of all foam boards must be covered with drywall to meet fire code.

Insulation is measured in R-values—the ability to withstand heat transfer. In a cold climate, you'll want R-38 in the roof, R-19 in the wall, and R-22 in the floor. In moderate climates, you'll want R-26 in the roof, R-19 in the wall, and R-11 in the floor. A map on page 436 will help you identify your needs. Here's a look at the R-values of common insulation:

Fiberglass
3½"	R-13
5¼"	R-21
7¼"	R-25
10"	R-30
12"	R-38

Molded Expanded Polystyrene
1"	R-4
1½"	R-6
2"	R-8

Extruded Polystyrene
1"	R-5
2"	R-10

Polyurethane and Polyisocyanurate
1"	R-7 to R-8

Cellulose
1"	R-3.4 to R-3.8

THE INSULATION AND WEATHERPROOFING TOOL KIT

Below are some basic insulating and weatherproofing tools. For more information see the Tool Glossary on page 544.

CAULKING GUN	DRILL	GLOVES	MASK	SAFETY GLASSES	STUD FINDER
CLAW HAMMER	DRILL BITS	HANDSAW	PUTTY KNIFE	SCISSORS	TACK HAMMER
CIRCULAR SAW	FLAT PRY BAR	INSULATION BLOWER	RECIPROCATING SAW	SCREWDRIVERS	TAPE MEASURE
COMBINATION SQUARE	FRAMING SQUARE	LADDER AND STABILIZER BAR	SABER SAW	STAPLER	UTILITY KNIFE

INSULATION AND WEATHERPROOFING

Evaluating your home's energy efficiency

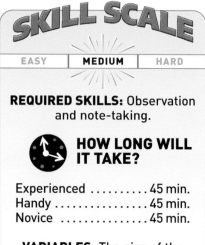

SKILL SCALE

EASY	MEDIUM	HARD

REQUIRED SKILLS: Observation and note-taking.

HOW LONG WILL IT TAKE?

Experienced .... 45 min.
Handy .... 45 min.
Novice .... 45 min.

VARIABLES: The size of the house and the number of windows will greatly affect the time required.

Leaks through small cracks around windows and doors are responsible for 30 to 40 percent of the heat that leaks out of your house. Before you tackle more extensive—and more expensive—insulating jobs, track down and fix these smaller problems. Companies will do this for you using infrared detectors and other sophisticated equipment, but while they may do a slightly more dramatic job, you'll be able to figure out on your own where the problems are.

Start outside by looking at places where two different materials meet: walls meeting windows, water spigots, pipes, or phone lines. These are the areas where leaks occur. Try slipping a sheet of paper between the two surfaces, or look for light leaking through. Either indicates a space. Check for rattling—a window or door that rattles in its frame is loose, and loose equals leakage. Finally, do what's called a depressurization test. Wait for a cool, windy day and close up the house as tightly as you can. Turn on any fans, such as bath or kitchen vents, that move air outdoors. Check for leaks with a smoking match or burning incense stick as described below.

Once you've checked 10 or 20 windows, it can be difficult to remember which of them needed to be fixed. Mark any leaks as soon as you find them, using a piece of red tape. It's guaranteed to nag you into fixing the problem.

STUFF YOU'LL NEED

✔ **TOOLS:**
Thermometer, incense sticks, paper

CHECK FOR LEAKS AROUND WINDOWS AND DOORS on a cool, windy day. Close and lock all the windows and doors, and turn off the furnace. To help encourage leaks, turn on all the fans, such as those in bathrooms or cooking hoods. Move a smoking incense stick around the doors and windows. If the smoke flutters, you have a leak.

TO LOCATE THE LIKELY SOURCE OF A LEAK, look at existing weather stripping and caulking. Look for signs of deterioration, such as crumbling foam or rubber; hardening of flexible products, such as felt or foam rubber; or damaged or torn metal stripping. Replace the products as needed. Most weather stripping products will last only a few years, so expect this to be a seasonal chore. When caulking, instead of filling the gap, apply the caulk so that it spans the gap and grabs onto the adjoining surfaces.

LOOK FOR CONDENSATION, FROST, OR ICE BUILDUP ON THE INSIDE SURFACES OF INTERIOR WINDOW SASHES. Such conditions indicate that you need storm windows or that air is leaking around the ones you have. Also check for condensation, frost, or ice buildup on storm windows. This indicates that warm, moist air is escaping and that the seal between the interior window and the storm window needs attention.

EVEN IF THE WINDOW IS WELL-SEALED, AIR CAN LEAK AROUND AND THROUGH AN AIR-CONDITIONER. Put foam air-conditioner weather stripping around the edges of the air-conditioner, and put a vinyl fabric cover over the outside of the air-conditioner at the first sign of cold weather.

MEASURE THE TEMPERATURE IN DIFFERENT PARTS OF A ROOM. Differences of more than 1 or 2 degrees indicate that the room is poorly sealed or that air movement inside the house is poor. Update weather stripping around doors and windows, then measure temperatures again. If the differences still exist, you may have an airflow problem with your heating system. Often, your public utility company will provide information about airflow problems and how to correct them.

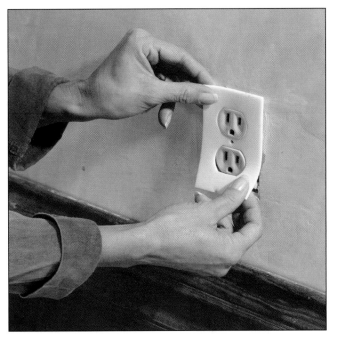

A SURPRISING AMOUNT OF COLD AIR SEEPS IN AROUND OUTLETS AND SWITCHES. Seal the leaks by slipping an inexpensive foam gasket between the faceplate and the electrical connection.

WEATHERPROOFING YOUR HOME

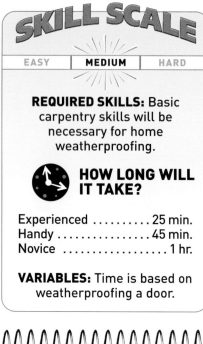

SKILL SCALE

EASY	**MEDIUM**	HARD

REQUIRED SKILLS: Basic carpentry skills will be necessary for home weatherproofing.

HOW LONG WILL IT TAKE?

Experienced . . . . 25 min.
Handy . . . . 45 min.
Novice . . . . 1 hr.

VARIABLES: Time is based on weatherproofing a door.

STUFF YOU'LL NEED

✔ **MATERIALS:**
Silicone caulk, expandable insulating foam, weather stripping, wood filler

✔ **TOOLS:**
Hammer, putty knives, screwdriver, pry bar, wood chisel, handsaw, tape measure, staple gun, caulking gun

A+ WORK SMARTER

MINIMIZE HEAT LOSS
Cover window wells with plastic window-well covers to minimize heat loss through your basement windows. Measure the widest point of your window well and note whether the front edge is rectangular or semicircular in design. Most covers have an upper flange designed to slip under the siding. Fasten the cover to foundation walls with masonry anchors and weigh down the bottom flange with stones or gravel. Caulk around the edges for extra weather protection.

Weatherproofing is the process of fixing unwanted leaks. While your doors and windows are designed to keep the cold out and the heat in, they cannot be airtight. In order to open and close, they need room to move—small gaps around the edges though which air quite easily seeps. In an average house, these cracks account for as much air as you'd lose through a 2-foot-diameter hole. Given the low cost of weather stripping and the ease of installation, you'll get a quick return on your investment. Of the many types available, the metal, foam-filled vinyl tubes, plastic V, and closed-cell vinyl foam have been found the most effective and easiest to install. Metal is the most durable, lasting from 10 to 20 years. Plastic V weather stripping lasts from 2 to 10 years. Foam-filled vinyl has a life expectancy of 5 to 10 years.

Sealing out also means you're sealing air in. Beware of carbon monoxide or other inside air problems.

CAULK AROUND THE DRYER VENT, WINDOWS, EXHAUST FAN VENTS, and any other fittings mounted to the sides of your house. Fill any cracks larger than ½ inch with expandable foam or foam "backer rods" before caulking.

SEAL BETWEEN BASEBOARDS AND FLOORBOARDS. Remove the base molding and spray in expandable insulating foam. This not only prevents drafts, it helps stop insects from entering your living areas. Be aware that a little foam goes a long way. It will expand too much if you overuse it.

INSULATE AROUND SPIGOTS, TELEVISION CABLE JACKS, TELEPHONE LINES, AND OTHER ENTRY POINTS TO YOUR HOUSE with expandable insulating foam. Trim off the excess with a utility knife, but avoid cutting into wires when trimming around electrical lines.

Weatherproofing an entry door

1 **ADJUST THE DOOR IF IT HAS FALLEN OUT OF ALIGNMENT.** Reset and shim hinges to even out the gaps around the door, making the door easier to weather strip. Adjust strike plates and latches to keep doors snug in their frames.

2 **WITH TIN SNIPS, CUT METAL TENSION STRIPS TO FIT IN THE DOOR JAMB.** Tack the strips in place and open them slightly to create a tight seal. If using vinyl Vs, cut them with scissors and fold them lengthwise along the seam. Remove the adhesive backing and stick the weather stripping in place.

3 **TO CREATE A DOUBLE SEAL, PUT TUBE GASKETS WITH METAL BACKING ON THE OUTSIDE OF THE DOOR.** Cut them to length with tin snips, and screw or tack them in place so that they are snug against the door.

4 **OPTION A: SCREW A BRISTLE SWEEP TO THE BOTTOM OF THE DOOR.** Sweeps help keep air from leaking under the door, and you can attach one without trimming the door. Sweeps also are available on rollers to compensate for an uneven floor.

OPTION B: ATTACH A NEW DOOR BOTTOM WITH AN INTEGRAL SWEEP on the inside and a drip edge on the outside. This may require you to adjust your threshold height or plane the bottom of the door slightly. If you plane the door, seal the wood by painting it before you attach the sweep.

5 **FIX ANY CRACKS IN DOOR PANELS** or around sidelight panels with wood filler or caulk.

INSULATION AND WEATHERPROOFING

Weatherproofing an entry door threshold

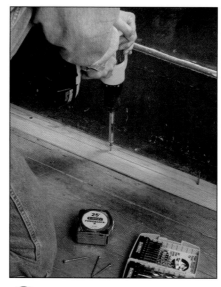

1 **OLDER THRESHOLDS LACK THE BUILT-IN WEATHER STRIPPING THAT NEWER ONES HAVE.** To replace an old threshold, protect the floor, cut through the threshold with a handsaw, then pry out the pieces. Clean out the area beneath it.

2 **MEASURE THE OPENING FOR THE NEW THRESHOLD AND CUT IT TO FIT.** Make sure the threshold will slope away from the house when installed, shimming it if necessary. Lay a bead of caulk along the bottom of the threshold, then screw it in place through the area that will be underneath the gasket.

3 **CUT AND INSTALL THE GASKET.** Test to see how the door closes over the new threshold. If the fit is too tight, cut or plane the door as necessary.

Weatherproofing other door types

SEAL THE JAMB CHANNELS WITH CLOSED-CELL VINYL FOAM (not to be confused with foam rubber, which is less effective). If the door doesn't have thermal glass, buy clear plastic sheeting made to fit over the inside of windows, and use a hair dryer to shrink it until tight.

ATTACH A NEW RUBBER GASKET TO THE BOTTOM OF A GARAGE DOOR IF THE OLD ONE HAS DETERIORATED. Weather stripping for the top and sides of the door is sold separately.

A STORM DOOR DECREASES ENTRY-DOOR HEAT LOSS BY ABOUT 50 PERCENT. For directions on installation, see Installing a Storm Door, page 351.

TEST LATCHES AND ADJUST AS NEEDED. A properly functioning storm-door latch draws the door tightly and securely into the frame and holds it in place. A loose door lets air in around the edges.

ADD A WIND CHAIN IF YOUR STORM DOOR DOES NOT HAVE ONE. Wind chains prevent doors from blowing open and off the hinges. Set the chain so that the door will not open more than 90 degrees. You can temporarily disconnect the chain if you ever need to open the door farther.

ADJUST DOOR-CLOSER TENSION TO CLOSE THE DOOR SECURELY. The tension on most closers is adjustable so that you can set the door to close without slamming. Most closers also lock in place to hold doors open when necessary, making it much easier on the people delivering your new couch.

WEATHERPROOFING YOUR HOME
Weatherproofing windows

① CUT METAL OR VINYL V-STRIPS TO FIT IN THE SASH CHANNELS. Cut them long enough to extend at least 1 inch beyond the sash ends when the window is closed. Cut vinyl with scissors; cut metal with tin snips.

② REMOVE THE ADHESIVE BACKING AND STICK THE VINYL IN PLACE. Tack metal strips in place, driving the tacks flush so that the window sash will not snag on them. Flare out the open ends of the metal V-channels with a putty knife to create a tight seal with the sash.

③ WIPE DOWN THE UNDERSIDE OF THE BOTTOM SASH WITH A DAMP RAG AND WAIT FOR IT TO DRY; then attach self-adhesive closed-cell vinyl foam to the edges of the underside. The surface must be at least 50 degrees for self-adhesive strips to stick.

4 **SEAL THE GAP WHERE THE TOP SASH MEETS THE BOTTOM SASH.** For double-hung windows, raise the bottom sash completely to the top, and then lower the upper sash a couple of inches. This reveals the lower rail, which is normally hidden. Seal with V-channel weather stripping. If the top sash is stationary, tack tubular gasket to the outside of the lower sash so that it compresses slightly against the top sash when the window is locked shut.

5 **APPLY PAINTABLE CAULK AROUND BOTH THE INTERIOR AND EXTERIOR WINDOW TRIM.** Smooth with a wet finger.

POLYETHYLENE SHEETING KITS PROVIDE A QUICK WAY TO WEATHERPROOF A WINDOW WITHOUT STORMS. They come with nailing strips and nails. Installation is a matter of cutting the plastic and then attaching it with the nailing strips. Polyethylene is cloudy, however. While you might not mind it over a bathroom window, you probably want to avoid putting it over a picture window in the front of your house.

INTERIOR PLASTIC SHEETING IS A CLEAR SHRINK-WRAP PRODUCT THAT IS ALSO AVAILABLE IN KITS. It's even easier to install than polyethylene. Tape the plastic to the inside of the window with double-stick tape; then warm it with a hair dryer to remove the wrinkles. Once installed, it's virtually invisible and easy to remove.

Weatherproofing other window types

STEEL WINDOWS, WHICH WERE POPULAR ABOUT 40 YEARS AGO, can best be sealed with closed-cell foam adhesive tape.

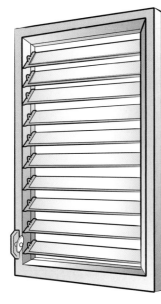

JALOUSIE WINDOWS ARE NOTORIOUSLY LEAKY. Cover them with polyethylene sheeting.

USE THE SAME STRATEGY ON METAL-CLAD AND VINYL-CLAD WINDOWS AS ON WOOD-FRAME WINDOWS, but use only self-adhesive weather-stripping products that will not puncture the cladding.

Tips for weatherproofing storm windows

CREATE A TIGHT SEAL BY CAULKING AROUND THE WINDOW. Rope caulking, a puttylike material sold in strips, will fit nicely along the gap between the storm and the house and can be easily pressed into place.

THE WEEP HOLE AT THE BOTTOM OF THE WINDOW LETS MOISTURE OUT so that it doesn't condense on the window. Check to see that the hole isn't plugged. If it is, clean it out with a small nail. If there's no weep hole, create one by poking a nail through the caulk at the bottom of the window.

INSTALLING SOFFIT AND ROOF VENTS

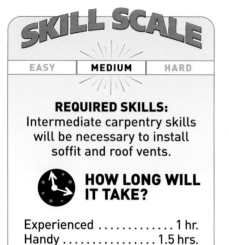
Proper air circulation is essential for effective insulation. If you have inadequate venting, warm, moist air that escapes through the insulation condenses in the cold, attic air. This trapped moisture can cause wood rot, mildew, and water damage. You can also have exterior roofing problems, along with higher cooling costs in the summer.

A balanced circulation system will have 1 square foot of venting for every 150 square feet of attic. (Change this to 1 in 300 square feet if the insulation has a vapor barrier.)

You should have an equal amount of soffit intake and roof exhaust vents. Check for blockages of airflow in your attic vents, baffles, and roof vents. Also verify that attic insulation doesn't block any vents.

Vents range from static open units to thermostatically controlled electric fan units. The type of vent you purchase will depend on the amount of air you need to move, the size of your attic, the scope of the project you wish to undertake, and of course, your budget!

HOMER'S HINDSIGHT

SOFFIT BLUES

I love insulation, it saves me money. So, I've put in a lot of it over the years and advise my neighbors to so the same. A lady from across the street told me she insulated the attic but she was having trouble with mildew and wood rot. I told her she probably needed some soffits to promote air flow and that they were so easy to install I'd give her a hand. After we finished she added more insulation but later told me the soffits weren't doing their job. I was baffled. We crawled back into her attic and found that the new insulation was covering the soffits. "What you need now are some baffles to keep the soffit vents free," I told her. "Does it ever end with home repair?" she asked. I had to say no, it really doesn't. Of course, we had to remove the new insulation to put in the baffles but now the attic is vented and her utility bills have taken a dive.

Effective insulation requires ventilation

Sufficient airflow is critical to proper roof-system ventilation.
Airflow prevents heat buildup in your attic and helps protect your roof from damage caused by condensation or ice. A typical ventilation system has vents in the soffits to admit fresh air that flows upward through the baffle beneath the roof sheathing and exits through roof vents.

Measure attic space to determine the number of vents per cubic foot. If there is no vapor barrier, you'll need 1 square foot of vent for every 150 square feet of attic space. You'll need 1 square foot of vent per 300 square feet of attic if there is a barrier. Either way, you'll need several vents for adequate circulation. Distribute them evenly throughout your attic.

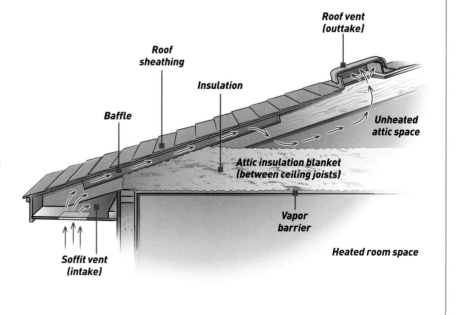

Roof vent (outtake)

Roof sheathing

Insulation

Baffle

Unheated attic space

Attic insulation blanket (between ceiling joists)

Vapor barrier

Heated room space

Soffit vent (intake)

SOFFIT-VENT OPTIONS

ADD SOFFIT VENTS TO INCREASE AIRFLOW INTO ATTICS. Make sure there is an unobstructed air passage from the soffit area to the roof before you install new soffit vents. Do not cover the vents with insulation.

CONTINUOUS SOFFIT VENTS PROVIDE EVEN AIRFLOW INTO ATTICS. They are usually installed during new construction, but they can be added as retrofits to unvented soffit panels.

ROOF-VENT OPTIONS

ROOF VENTS ARE ONE WAY TO GET AIR OUT OF THE ATTIC, and installation is fairly simple.

A POWERED ROOF VENT (inset) has a thermostat-controlled fan that will increase air circulation; one of these may be all the venting your house needs.

CONTINUOUS RIDGE VENTS INCREASE AIR CIRCULATION DRAMATICALLY and are much less noticeable than traditional roof vents. Because these span the entire length of the ridge, they provide more consistent air circulation than other vents. Ridge vents are best installed during roof construction but can be retrofitted.

GABLE VENTS, LIKE ROOF VENTS, INCREASE CIRCULATION without calling attention to themselves. Because you don't need to climb on the roof to install them, they're ideal when the roof is too steep for comfort.

Installing a soffit vent

1 **FROM INSIDE THE ATTIC, CHOOSE AND MARK A PLACE FOR THE SOFFIT VENT THAT ALLOWS THE AIR TO FLOW FREELY.** Drill through the soffit to enable you to spot the location from outside. If you're unable to get near enough to the wall because of the roof slope, locate the joists with a stud finder, as shown here, and position the vent between them.

2 **TRACE AROUND THE VENT ON THE SOFFIT.** Be sure the vent will fall between rafter ends or nailer strips.

SAFETY ALERT

SECURE YOUR LADDER
Use a secure platform (ladder or scaffolding) when working at aboveground elevations.

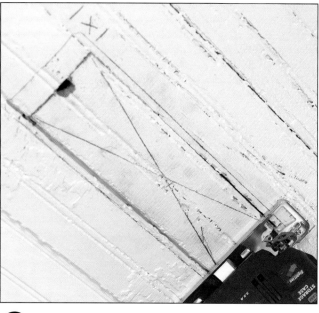

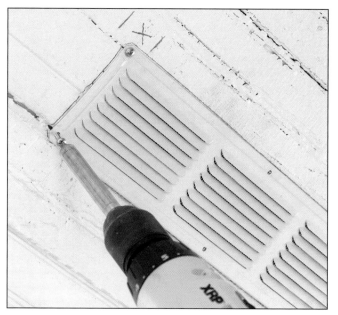

3 **CUT THE VENT OPENINGS ¼ INCH INSIDE THE MARKED LAYOUT LINES** (or as directed) to leave room for fastening the vent covers. Use a saber saw.

4 **INSTALL THE SOFFIT VENTS** and fasten them with stainless-steel screws or galvanized wood screws.

Installing a roof vent

① DRIVE A NAIL THROUGH THE ROOF FROM INSIDE TO MARK THE POSITION OF THE VENT HOLE. Locate roof vents as high as possible on the roof, but below the ridge line, and on the least visible slope of the house. Place the vent between rafters to avoid cutting through a rafter. Locate turbine vents close to the ridge with a minimum clearance of 8 inches to the ridge line. Using the nail as a center point, draw a circle with a diameter equal to the vent's opening.

② REMOVE THE SHINGLES JUST ABOVE AND TO THE SIDE OF THE CUTOUT AREA THAT WILL BE COVERED BY THE FLANGE AT THE BASE OF THE VENT. Do not remove shingles below the vent cutout—they will be covered by the flange. Hammer the centering nail back through the roof. Drill a pilot hole with a spade bit at each corner of the cutout area; then use a reciprocating saw to cut the vent hole.

③ APPLY ROOFING CEMENT TO THE UNDERSIDE OF THE FLANGE. Slide the top edge of the flange under the shingles immediately above the hole you cut. Center the vent over the hole.

④ NAIL THE VENT IN PLACE with galvanized roofing nails. Nail the base at the top, sides, and bottom. Cover the nail holes and the seam between the base and the roof with roofing cement. Leave the bottom edge exposed.

INSULATION AND WEATHERPROOFING

Insulating an attic

Older homes in particular can be poorly insulated, and when they are, both heat and heating bills go through the roof. Even homes in the mildest climates should have about 9 inches of fiberglass insulation. Homes in northern areas—Buffalo, Des Moines, and Duluth, for example—should have more than 12 inches of fiberglass, according to the United States Department of Energy.

Insulating an attic is relatively easy if it has no floor: You simply roll in the insulation. If your attic has a floor, you'll want to apply blow-in insulation. Blow-in is available as either fiberglass or loose-fill cellulose. The manufacturers of each type trumpet the advantages of their product, but in short, the tune goes like this: Blow-in cellulose provides more insulation than fiberglass. Fiberglass, however, is less prone to settling, which reduces the efficiency of the insulation over time. Cellulose turns into a gooey mess when wet; fiberglass temporarily loses its insulating ability, but it does recover once it's dry.

The amount of insulation you need may determine which kind you get. Find your location on the map below to determine which zone you're in. The chart tells you the R-value your insulation should have. The R-value is printed on insulation packages—the higher the R-value, the greater the insulation.

Incidentally, if you have a whole-house fan, slip some insulation over the louvers during the winter.

WORK SMARTER

VAPOR BARRIER SAVVY

When the warm, moist air hits the cold, outdoor air, water vapor condenses and collects in the wall or ceiling, where it causes all sorts of problems. Because of this, roll or batt insulation comes with a facing that acts as a vapor barrier. In most parts of the country, you install the facing toward the occupied part of the house. In some areas of the South, however, you should install the barrier facing the home's exterior. Check local codes. Two vapor barriers are actually worse than one, so if you're adding insulation on top of insulation that already has a barrier, use insulation without a facing.

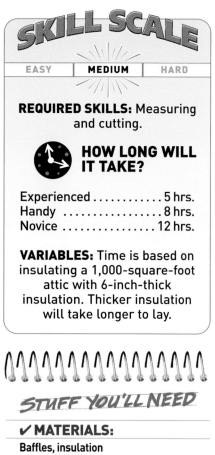

SKILL SCALE

| EASY | **MEDIUM** | HARD |

REQUIRED SKILLS: Measuring and cutting.

HOW LONG WILL IT TAKE?

Experienced . . . . 5 hrs.
Handy . . . . 8 hrs.
Novice . . . . 12 hrs.

VARIABLES: Time is based on insulating a 1,000-square-foot attic with 6-inch-thick insulation. Thicker insulation will take longer to lay.

STUFF YOU'LL NEED

✔ **MATERIALS:**

Baffles, insulation

✔ **TOOLS:**

Tape measure, utility knife and extra blades, straightedge, particle-resistant dust mask, safety glasses, gloves

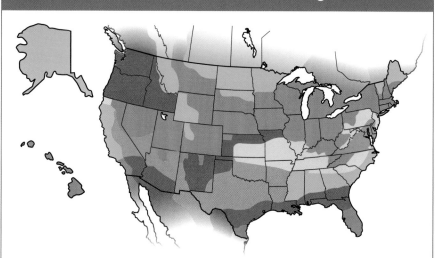

How much insulation is enough?

Insulation zone	Ceilings below ventilated attics		Floors over unheated crawl		Exterior walls[a] (wood frame)		Crawl space walls[b]	
	Gas, oil, or heat pump	Electric resistance	Gas, oil, or heat pump	Electric resistance	Gas, oil, or heat pump	Electric resistance	Gas, oil, or heat pump	Electric resistance
1	R-49	R-49	R-19	R-19	R-11	R-11	R-19	R-19
2	R-38	R-49	R-19	R-19	R-11	R-11	R-19	R-19
3	R-38	R-38	R-19	R-19	R-11	R-11	R-19	R-19
4	R-38	R-38	R-19	R-19	R-11	R-11	R-19	R-19
5	R-30	R-38	R-19	R-19	R-11	R-11	R-19	R-19
6	R-30	R-38	(c)	R-19	R-11	R-11	R-19	R-19
7	R-30	R-30	(c)	(c)	R-11	R-11	R-19	R-19
8	R-19	R-30	(c)	(c)	(c)	R-11	R-11	R-11

(a) For new construction, R-19 is recommended for exterior walls. Jamming a R-19 batt into a 3½-inch cavity will not yield R-19 because compression reduces the R-value.

(b) Insulate crawl space walls only if the crawl space is dry all year, the floor above is not insulated, and all ventilation to the crawl space is blocked.

(c) Thermal response of existing space for cooling benefits does not suggest additional insulation.

INSULATING WITH FIBERGLASS

1 **INSPECT YOUR EXISTING INSULATION BY MEASURING ITS DEPTH.** Measure the distance between the joists so that you can buy insulation that is the right width—standard widths are 15 inches or 23 inches.

2 **ADEQUATE INSULATION REQUIRES PROPER VENTING, WHICH IS USUALLY SUPPLIED BY VENTS IN THE SOFFIT.** Blocking vents allows moist air to collect in the attic, causing wood rot and mildew. To avoid this, install rigid plastic foam vents, called baffles or rafter vents. Put one end over the soffit vent, and staple the baffle in place.

3 **MEASURE AND CUT TO LENGTH THE PIECES OF INSULATION YOU'LL NEED.** Work in a well-ventilated area to keep to a minimum the amount of fiberglass dust raised. Cut the insulation with a sharp utility knife guided by a straightedge. Have a solid work surface beneath the insulation and apply lots of pressure.

4 **PUT THE INSULATION BETWEEN THE JOISTS, STARTING AT AN EXTERIOR WALL** and working toward the entry to the attic. If working in an uninsulated attic, get insulation with a vapor barrier and install the barrier facedown. (See "Work Smarter," page 436.) If you're applying insulation over existing insulation, get insulation without a facing.

5 **THE NATIONAL ELECTRICAL CODE REQUIRES A 3-INCH GAP BETWEEN INSULATION AND ANY ELECTRICAL LIGHTS OR FIXTURES.** Check to see if your local code is stricter. Nail wooden barriers around the light to keep the insulation away from it, then cut the insulation to fit.

6 **IF THE EXISTING INSULATION FILLS OR NEARLY FILLS THE CAVITY BETWEEN THE JOISTS,** you can still add more insulation by rolling it across the top of the joists, perpendicular to them.

INSULATION AND WEATHERPROOFING

Installing loose-fill insulation

Short of tearing off the walls, blow-in, loose-fill insulation is the only way to insulate a house built before the days of adequate insulation. You can buy fiberglass or cellulose loose-fill. Put the insulation in a blower located outside the house and stretch a hose to the area you're insulating. The hose usually has a switch that lets you turn the machine on and off from wherever you're working. Have a helper working outside to refill the blower with insulation.

SKILL SCALE

EASY	**MEDIUM**	HARD

REQUIRED SKILLS: Basic carpentry skills are needed to install loose-fill insulation.

HOW LONG WILL IT TAKE?

Experienced . . . . 3 hrs.
Handy . . . . 4 hrs.
Novice . . . . 5 hrs.

VARIABLES: Time is based on installing loose-fill insulation in a 20'×30' attic.

STUFF YOU'LL NEED

✔ **MATERIALS:**

Cellulose insulation, staples, foam

baffles, fiberglass insulation

✔ **TOOLS:**

Tape measure, hand stapler, drill and

bits, insulation blower, safety glasses,

dust mask, gloves, pry bar

BLOWING IN ATTIC INSULATION

1 **PREVENT THE INSULATION FROM BLOCKING SOFFIT VENTS** by installing a rigid plastic foam baffle above each vent. If you have a continuous soffit vent, install a baffle in every third space between rafters.

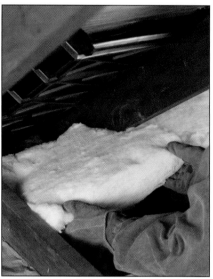

2 **ONCE THE BAFFLES ARE IN,** block off each vent to prevent it from filling with insulation and causing moisture problems by cutting sections of fiberglass insulation and stuffing them between the joists directly in front of the soffit.

3 **IF THE ATTIC HAS A FLOOR, REMOVE A BOARD** to give you access to the bays between the joists. Insert the blower hose the entire length of the bay, and back it out as the space in front of it fills with insulation. (Drill through the floor if it's plywood.) If the attic has no floor, put down pieces of plywood and walk along them as you spray the insulation in place.

4 **POUR AND SPREAD INSULATION BY HAND, ESPECIALLY NEAR ELECTRICAL FIXTURES.** Electrical codes require that you keep insulation at least 3 inches from heat-producing fixtures, such as recessed ceiling lights. Nail 2× blocking between the joists, positioning it to keep the cellulose away from the fixture.

BLOWING LOOSE-FILL INTO A WALL

1 DRILL ACCESS HOLES EQUAL TO THE DIAMETER OF THE BLOWER'S FILLER HOSE. If you drill the holes from outdoors, remove a piece of siding first. Pick a piece slightly above the level of the interior floor and drill holes through the sheathing. On the top floor, remove the fascia or soffit instead of the siding.

2 FILL THE BIN WITH INSULATION. Wearing safety glasses, a mask, and gloves, fill the bin to the level recommended by the manufacturer.

Buy an extra bag or two of insulation just in case. You can always return the unopened ones when you're finished.

3 USE A TAPE MEASURE TO CHECK FOR HORIZONTAL OBSTRUCTIONS, SUCH AS FIRE BLOCKS IN THE FRAMING, THAT MIGHT BLOCK THE INSULATION. If the tape hits an obstruction, first make sure it's not electrical and then drill an access hole several inches above it. When you insulate, fill the bay from both the original hole and the new one.

4 ONCE THE HOLES ARE DRILLED, INSERT THE FILLER TUBE and push it to within 18 inches of the top of the wall. Blow in the insulation, retracting the tube as the bay fills. When you've insulated the entire wall, plug the holes. Although plastic, foam, and wooden plugs are available, plastic is typically the best choice. Replace the trim or siding. (See inset.)

TIME SAVER

KNOW YOUR BLOWER

You can usually find insulation blowers where you buy your insulation, and you may be able to use a blower at no additional charge. Ask the salesperson to demonstrate how the blower works, and check that all of the fittings, attachments, and hoses are included.

A+ WORK SMARTER

MOISTURE MATTERS

Most insulation requires a vapor barrier on the side that is warm in the winter. You won't need a vapor barrier in the attic as long as you have 1 square foot of ventilation for every 150 square feet of insulation. If you have less ventilation than that, paint the ceiling below the insulated area with vapor-retarding paint. Paint the walls only if the winter temperature typically drops below -15° F. Before you insulate, look closely for peeling paint, which may be a sign of existing moisture trouble. If the situation seems to get worse after you insulate—or if you see signs of trouble elsewhere—a coat of vapor-retarding paint on the inside wall should solve the problem.

INSULATION AND WEATHERPROOFING

Insulating basement walls

An insulated basement makes the space more comfortable and helps keep upper floors warmer too.

Rigid foam is available in both urethane and polystyrene (plastic foam) in thicknesses from ½ inch to 2 inches. Urethane is more expensive but is easier to work with and is the better insulator.

Both are flammable and must be covered by ½-inch drywall. If you like the look of wood paneling, apply it over the drywall. If you don't want to install drywall, build a regular 2×4 stud wall and insulate with fiberglass between studs.

EASY	**MEDIUM**	HARD

REQUIRED SKILLS: Basic carpentry skills will be necessary to insulate your basement.

HOW LONG WILL IT TAKE?

Experienced . . . . 2 hrs.
Handy . . . . 2.5 hrs.
Novice . . . . 3 hrs.

VARIABLES: Time is based on insulating an 8'×25' wall.

STUFF YOU'LL NEED

✔ MATERIALS:

Fiberglass insulation, 1×3 furring strips, construction adhesive, 6-mil poly, insulation stays or chicken wire, rigid insulation, tape, 3d nails, drywall, 1-inch drywall screws, drywall tape and compound

✔ TOOLS:

Particle-resistant dust mask, utility knife, caulking gun, hammer, circular saw, straightedge, drill and screwdriver bit, level

1 **BEFORE YOU INSULATE ON THE WALLS, INSULATE THE SPACES BETWEEN THE JOISTS ABOVE THE FOUNDATION.** Wearing a mask and protective clothing, use a utility knife to cut fiberglass insulation to fit between the joists; pack loosely in place. Compressing insulation will reduce its ability to do its job.

2 **TAPE A PLASTIC VAPOR BARRIER TO THE WALL TO KEEP OUT MOISTURE** that may seep into the basement. The furring strips you will add in the next step will hold the plastic in place permanently.

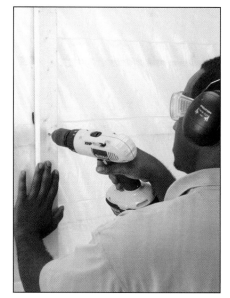

3 **NAIL 1x3 FURRING STRIPS BOTH HORIZONTALLY AND VERTICALLY OVER THE VAPOR BARRIER.** The verticals bridge irregularities in the wall; the horizontals at the top and bottom support the edges of the drywall. Nail or screw the horizontal strips in place first then install the verical strips on 16 inch centers just as you would regular wall studs.

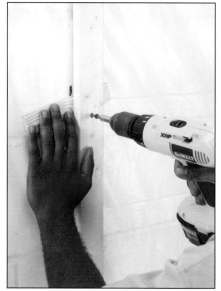

4 **SHIM THE VERTICAL STRIPS AS NECESSARY TO MAKE THE WALL PLUMB AND FLAT.** Check the vertical grid of 1×3s with a straightedge, and shim as necessary to make sure they form a flat surface. Also use a level to make sure the furring strips are plumb. Cut the insulation panels to fit snugly between them as shown in Steps 5 and 6.

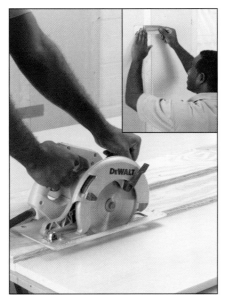

5 CUT THE PANELS TO FIT BETWEEN THE 1x3s. Make a jig to simplify the job. Begin by screwing a wide board to a narrow board. You'll guide the saw edge away from the blade along the narrow board's edge, rather than trying to follow a drawn line.

6 TO USE THE JIG, CLAMP IT IN PLACE WITH THE WIDE EDGE ON THE LAYOUT LINE. Guide the saw along the narrow edge. Once you've cut the panels, tape them in place until you put up the drywall. (See inset.)

7 SCREW THE DRYWALL IN PLACE, AND TAPE AND FINISH IT. If you're going to apply paneling over the drywall, leave the drywall unfinished and untaped and nail the paneling over it with 3d nails.

INSULATING A CRAWLSPACE

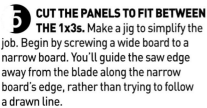

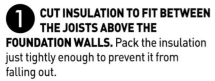

1 CUT INSULATION TO FIT BETWEEN THE JOISTS ABOVE THE FOUNDATION WALLS. Pack the insulation just tightly enough to prevent it from falling out.

2 INSTALL FIBERGLASS INSULATION BETWEEN FLOOR JOISTS OVER CRAWLSPACES OR UNHEATED BASEMENTS. Make sure the vapor barrier faces up, and install insulation stays (shown here) or chicken wire to hold the insulation in place.

3 CUT PIECES OF INSULATION LONG ENOUGH TO DRAPE FROM THE MUDSILL, down the wall, and a couple of feet onto the floor. Hold in place by putting a 1×3 over it and tacking both to the mudsill, driving the nails enough to anchor the insulation while compressing it only slightly. Lay a 6-mil vapor barrier on the dirt floor, anchoring it with a few bricks.

11 EXTERIOR

MAINTAINING THE EXTERIOR OF YOUR **HOME** is equally as important as keeping the interior systems in prime working order. After all, the exterior shells protect your family and your most valuable possessions. Whether you're repairing the siding, the gutters, or the roof itself, you need to apply the same pride and determination that goes along with improving and maintaining the interior.

As you make decisions about an exterior project, whether it's fixing the gutters, repairing siding, or redoing your roof, it's important that you evaluate yourself carefully in terms of what you feel confident about accomplishing.

Take into consideration that working outside is harder and potentially more dangerous than working inside. In some cases you'll be working on ladders or scaffolding, and no safety shortcuts are allowed. Nothing is wrong with hiring a pro to do work you're not comfortable doing. And if that's the route you choose, by studying these pages you'll be far more qualified to get the job done right.

That being said, the skills required to do a lot of exterior work are, for the most part, basic and within the grasp of most handy homeowners. If you take your time, plan well, and get advice and professional help as necessary, you can have the satisfaction of a job well-done. You'll save money that otherwise would go toward paying a contractor's labor bills, plus you'll have control of the job from beginning to end.

SECTION 11 PROJECTS

REAL-WORLD SITUATIONS

WORKING OUTSIDE

The scale of exterior jobs requires careful planning and even more careful execution. Do your research and estimate materials carefully. Understand the project thoroughly before you start and make sure all the tools and materials are in place when you begin. Big exterior projects are almost always easier with some extra hands. If you can't round up volunteers, consider hiring day labor to help out as necessary.

- **Addressing safety issues goes along with working on scaffolding, roofs, and ladders.** Know how to set up and use ladders and scaffolding properly.

Work safely in the air; if you get tired, stop. Rent a safety harness and wear protective gear as necessary. Always have someone else at the work site when you're working above ground. If you're at all uncomfortable with heights, hire a pro.

- **The weather is always a factor.** While you can't predict what's coming with 100 percent accuracy, it's common sense to consider it. Unexpected rain can delay completion and cause damage to projects in progress. Alternately, several days of blistering heat can be dangerous to your health, especially if you're working on a roof. Work early in the morning and late in the afternoon if possible. Always drink plenty of liquids and protect yourself from the sun as much as possible.

- **You're often dealing with heavy materials and sometimes unfamiliar tools.** Stretch your legs and back for a break. Read the instructions and practice with tools you're not familiar with before you climb ladders or scaffolding. Nail guns and air compressors, for instance, are real timesavers but they take some getting used to. If you're renting tools, the clerk can show you the ropes.

- **You're dealing with disposal of substantial quantities of materials.** Rent a large trash receptacle while you're removing old shingles or siding. A messy work site invites accidents, and there's no point in ruining your lawn to make the roof pretty and leakproof.

Exterior maintenance basics

Every hour of every day, paint is peeling, shingles are curling, gutters are sagging, and decks are rotting all over America. It's called entropy—the natural tendency of things to break down over time—and it's hard at work on the exterior of your house.

When entropy visits, its effects are right there for all to see. Without regular maintenance, your house will quickly begin to deteriorate and soon take on a shabby appearance.

While the demands of exterior maintenance are persistent, the skills required are basic. When the exterior of your house is well-maintained, it's safe, it functions properly, and it's right out there for everyone to see and admire.

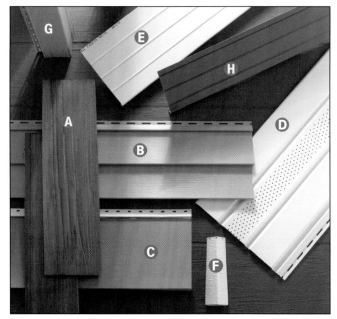

SIDING COMES IN A LOT OF MATERIALS, SHAPES, AND SIZES INCLUDING, Ⓐ wood, Ⓑ vinyl, and Ⓒ aluminum. All the options mean you may have more choices than you might think when you're considering updating your exterior. Ⓓ Soffits, Ⓔ fascia, and Ⓕ siding corner cap made of plastic or aluminum minimize painting, but if you have structural problems under the eaves or behind the siding, you'll have to fix them before you do repairs or apply new materials. Also pictured are edging for roofing: Ⓖ Rake edge, Ⓗ drip edge.

FASTENERS YOU'LL USE FOR EXTERIOR MAINTENANCE INCLUDE Ⓐ nails, Ⓑ screws, and Ⓒ construction adhesive. Ⓓ Pre-mixed stucco and Ⓔ a caulklike stucco patch for cracks simplify stucco repairs.

GOOD IDEA

HANG ON TO THE EXTRAS
Store leftover gutters, roofing, hardware, and other materials in a safe place. Being prepared to replace or repair items by having materials on hand will save you a trip to the store.

TOOL TIP

RENTING SAFETY
Many tools make exterior home repair easier; many others make the work safer and the job go more smoothly.

If you're working from a ladder, rent one that will reach where you need to reach. Add ladder stabilizers for more stability and to distance the ladder from the gutter system, preventing damage to the gutters.

Ladder jacks, used with two or more extension ladders, allow you to work from a plank without having to use scaffolding. You can use either wooden or aluminum planks with ladder jacks.

Big projects may require the use of scaffolding. This takes a little longer to set up but makes a much more secure and stable platform to work from. You may want to use aluminum planking to provide a work platform that is less bouncy than conventional wooden planks.

If you're working just a few feet off the ground, a standard ladder is fine. Use a fiberglass or wooden ladder if working around power lines or performing electrical repairs.

THE EXTERIOR MAINTENANCE TOOL KIT

Below are some basic exterior maintenance tools. For more information see the Tool Glossary on page 544.

BROOM	**CIRCULAR SAW**	**DRILL BITS**	**HOLE SAW**	**ROOF JACK**	**TAPE MEASURE**
CAULKING GUN	**CLAW HAMMER**	**FLAT PRY BAR**	**JIGSAW**	**ROOFING KNIFE**	**TIN SNIPS**
CHOP SAW	**DRILL**	**HACKSAW**	**LADDER WITH STABILIZER**	**SIDING REMOVAL TOOL**	**TROWEL**

Preventing water infiltration problems

PROPER GRADING WILL HELP KEEP WATER AWAY FROM THE FOUNDATION AND OUT OF THE BASEMENT. If water is building up in the basement, haul in dirt and slope the ground around the foundation away from the house. If the basement still collects water, talk to a contractor about interior or exterior foundation drains.

IMPROPERLY MAINTAINED GUTTERS WILL FAIL TO DIRECT WATER WHERE YOU WANT IT TO GO. Backups and clogs in gutters may cause roof leaks. Water on the ground below the gutters can seep into the basement or damage paint and wood below.

DOWNSPOUT EXTENSIONS DIRECT GUTTER WATER AWAY FROM THE FOUNDATION and help to dissipate runoff along the grade.

REPAIRING GUTTERS

SKILL SCALE

EASY	**MEDIUM**	HARD

REQUIRED SKILLS: Average carpentry skills will be necessary when repairing gutters.

HOW LONG WILL IT TAKE?

Experienced .... 1 hr.
Handy .... 1.5 hrs.
Novice .... 2 hrs.

VARIABLES: Time is based on two people repairing a 20-foot section of gutter.

BUYER'S GUIDE

EVALUATING GUTTERS

Gutters have been made of nearly everything—wood, copper, vinyl, galvanized steel, and aluminum.

Because of their cost, wood and copper are seldom used today. Until recently, most new gutters were aluminum. Enameled aluminum gutters are available in several colors and are lightweight and corrosion-resistant.

Vinyl gutters are becoming more popular because they are durable, available in several colors, and easy to install. Sections and fittings are precolored and come in standard sizes that basically snap together.

Galvanized-steel gutters are often the lowest-priced of all systems and usually have an enameled finish. Unless they're painted frequently, however, galvanized gutters have a shorter life than the alternatives.

All gutters slope toward the downspouts to allow water to drain properly. Follow the manufacturer's recommendations.

Gutters prevent the water that falls on your roof from collecting near your foundation. Houses without gutters usually have a distinct "drip line" where the water that has fallen from the roof edge has eroded the soil below. Where entrances or walkways pass under a roof edge, gutters prevent water from sheeting off the roof directly onto people below.

Because gutters are subject to some of the harshest natural elements—wind, water, ice, and sunlight—damage from corrosion and physical stress is almost inevitable. When that happens, leaks and water damage can quickly follow.

Corrosion in a gutter system typically occurs from the inside out. If your gutters are beginning to leak as a result of corrosion, the prognosis is not good. Patching may provide a temporary solution, but now would be an excellent time to start shopping for a new gutter system.

Sometimes even when the gutter system itself is sound, the gutter supports have broken or pulled away from the house. If the gutters are sagging, water that would normally flow toward one of the downspouts will pool at the low spot and then spill over the side of the gutter.

If leaves are a problem, put plastic mesh gutter guards over the gutter. The mesh comes in a roll. Trim it to width if necessary and then slip it into the top of the gutter. Clean your gutters twice a year to avoid blockages.

STUFF YOU'LL NEED

✔ MATERIALS:
Gutter mesh cover, silicone gutter adhesive/caulk, sheet metal screws, rivets, rubber gaskets, plastic roofing cement

✔ TOOLS:
Pliers, wire brush, paintbrush, rivet gun, pry bar, hacksaw, hammer, putty knife, scissors, caulking gun, screwdriver

REPAIRING GUTTERS
Fixing sagging gutters

IF YOUR GUTTERS ARE HELD IN PLACE WITH BRACKETS, BEND THE BRACKETS SLIGHTLY WITH A PAIR OF PLIERS TO CORRECT THE SAG. Pour a bucket of water into the gutter to check whether you've fixed the problem. If the water collects in a puddle, rebend and retest until it runs into the downspout.

IF YOUR GUTTERS ARE HELD IN PLACE BY SPIKES AND FERRULES, A LOOSE SPIKE IS CAUSING THE SAG. Find the spike and remove it. (See page 448, Step 1.) Replace it by running a 7-inch galvanized screw through the ferrule. (You can buy screws made specifically for the job, but any galvanized screw will do.)

EXTERIOR

Repairing leaky metal gutters

1 **PATCHES WON'T STICK TO RUSTY OR DIRTY METAL.** Clean the area around the leak with a wire brush and water. Once the area has dried, scrub it with an abrasive pad. Wash off all grit; let the gutter dry.

2 **PATCH SMALL HOLES BY APPLYING PLASTIC ROOFING CEMENT OVER THE HOLE.** Feather the cement out on the surrounding area and flatten out any steep edges created by the cement that would interfere with the water flow.

Use caution when working on elevated spaces!

IF THE LEAKS ARE LARGER THAN NAIL HOLES, USE TIN SNIPS TO CUT A STRIP OF FLASHING. The flashing should be the same material as the gutter. If the gutter is made of galvanized steel use galvanized steel, if aluminum use aluminum—mixing metals can cause corrosion. The flashing strip should be big enough to cover the hole and the area around it. Bend the strip to match the shape of the gutter and embed the flashing in the cement. Feather out the cement around the edges of the repair.

Repairing leaky joints

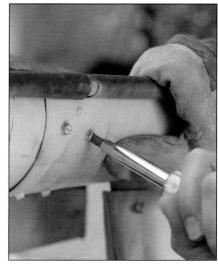

1 **PIECES OF METAL DOWNSPOUT ARE SCREWED TO EACH OTHER AND TO THE GUTTER.** Remove the screws (or other connecting hardware) at the joint and disassemble it. You may need to remove other gutter or downspout sections near the leaky joint before inserting new sections.

2 **CLEAN ANY CAULK OR ADHESIVE FROM BOTH PARTS OF THE JOINT USING A STIFF WIRE BRUSH.** Replace rubber gaskets on vinyl or PVC (poly vinyl chloride) gutters.

3 **APPLY SILICONE CAULK TO ONE OF THE PARTS THAT FORMS THE JOINT,** then reassemble the gutter system by pressing the two parts together. Verify that the uphill section is always on top of the downhill section. Resecure fasteners or connectors.

Replacing a section of metal gutter

1 **REMOVE THE SCREWS AND CONNECTORS FROM THE DAMAGED AREA OF THE GUTTER.** If you are prying out nails or spike-and-ferrule fasteners, put a piece of scrap wood across the opening to keep from crushing the gutter. Pull gently so that you maintain your balance when the spike comes out.

2 **LEAVE THE SCRAP IN PLACE TO KEEP THE GUTTER FROM BENDING.** Cut out the damaged area by cutting through the gutter on each side of the damage.

3 **CUT THE REPLACEMENT SECTION OF THE GUTTER** so that it is 4 inches longer than the removed section.

Make sure your ladder is on solid footing before starting.

4 **APPLY PLASTIC ROOF CEMENT OR GUTTER REPAIR COMPOUND** on the 2 inches of gutter nearest the cuts. Set the new section in place so that the uphill section of gutter is on top of the downhill section at each joint.

5 **DRILL PILOT HOLES FOR RIVETS.** Connect the two sections with rivets driven by a pop riveter.

6 **DRILL PILOT HOLES FOR SPIKE-AND-FERRULE FASTENERS THROUGH GUTTERS,** leaving the spacer blocks in place. Insert spikes in the front of the gutter, slip on the ferrules, and then drive the spikes into the fascia until the heads are flush with the gutter. Remove the spacers once you've hung the gutters.

EXTERIOR

Installing a vinyl gutter system

Vinyl is a bit easier to use than metal: You won't cut your fingers on the edges or have to try to squeeze a piece just right to get it to slip into another one.

Like metal gutters, vinyl gutters must slope from one end or the other so that water will flow down them. Unlike metal gutters, a fair amount of expansion and contraction occurs with changes in temperature.

Each manufacturer approaches slope and expansion differently, so follow your product's instructions carefully.

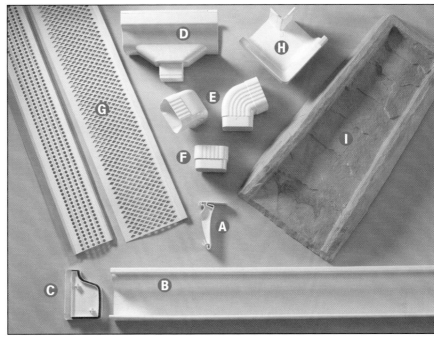

SNAP-TOGETHER GUTTER SYSTEMS are assembled from preformed parts. Typical parts include **A** gutter hangers, **B** gutters, **C** endcaps, **D** gutter drop outlets, **E** elbows, **F** downspout diverters, **G** gutter guards, **H** inside and outside corners, and **I** splash blocks that sit under the downspouts and help divert water away from the foundation.

ASSEMBLING AND HANGING VINYL GUTTERS

① AT THE END OF THE GUTTER RUN FARTHEST FROM THE DOWNSPOUT, measure down ½ inch (or as directed by the manufacturer) from the eaves and make a mark. At the other end, measure down at least ½ inch plus ⅛ inch for every 10 feet of gutter in the run. Snap a chalk line between these two points.

② WHILE THE GUTTER IS STILL ON THE GROUND, ASSEMBLE AS MUCH AS YOU CAN. Install the end cap, corners, and outlets. Put hanging hooks on the gutters, spacing them every 2 feet.

Installing a vinyl gutter system *(continued)*

ASSEMBLING AND HANGING VINYL GUTTERS

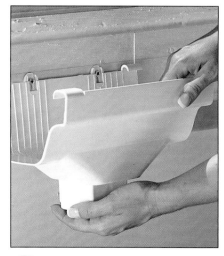

3 **WITH A HELPER, HOLD THE GUTTER IN PLACE.** Starting at the middle, screw the hanging hooks into the chalk line on the fascia. Vinyl expands and contracts, so after screwing each hook in place, make sure the gutter will move in its brackets. If not, the hook is either too high or low. Reposition it as needed.

IF THE GUTTER GOES AROUND AN INSIDE OR OUTSIDE CORNER, START AT THE CORNER. Put a corner piece, instead of an end cap, on the first piece of gutter you install. Hang the rest as described previously and on this page.

4 **ATTACH THE DROP OUTLET TO THE LAST SECTION OF GUTTER BEFORE HANGING.** Then measure for the piece that extends to the corner. Cut a piece to length and put it in the drop outlet. Attach the hangers and hang the drop outlet on them.

5 **JOIN THE SECTIONS USING THE APPROPRIATE CONNECTORS,** and adjust for expansion according to the manufacturer's directions.

6 **INSTALL ELBOWS AS NEEDED.** Sometimes an elbow directs the flow to the side and into another elbow, as shown here; if the the roof overhangs the wall, the elbow will direct the flow toward an elbow against the wall. Assemble the elbows and the piece between them. Measure from the lower elbow to a point 6-8 inches above the ground and cut a downspout to this length. Test fit the entire assembly.

7 **ATTACH THE DOWNSPOUT TO THE HOUSE.** Mark a spot a few inches above the end of the downspout and move the spout out of the way. Screw a hanger to the house at the mark. Attach the downspout to the hanger and attach an elbow and a section of downspout to direct the flow away from the foundation.

EXTERIOR

REPAIRING SIDING

Although a large number of siding materials are available today, repair choices are simple and basic. Fortunately, you can make most repairs yourself. Before you do, however, repair the problem that caused the damage—it's usually water. Check behind the siding for dampness and water damage, and if you find any, look for the leak that caused it. If the problem isn't behind the wall, the damage could be caused by a leaking gutter or a dripping faucet, among other things. If the source isn't obvious, wait until it rains, and then look for the source.

SAFETY ALERT

ASBESTOS SIDING

Asbestos can be found in some older types of siding. If you have or think that you have asbestos siding, check with your state department of environmental affairs or your local health department. They can tell you how to find a certified professional to test the siding material and, if necessary, remove and dispose of it.

You can also contact the EPA (Environmental Protection Agency) at www.epa.gov/lead or 800/ 242-LEAD (800/ 242-5323) for more information.

Fix damaged siding immediately. The longer you wait, the more extensive the damage and the more difficult the repair.

Common siding types and problems

Wood board-and-batten siding usually will require repair due to weathering or water damage. It is relatively easy to repair. Pry off the battens, replace the boards, and replace the battens.

Cedar shakes are traditionally single, hand-split tapered boards that vary in length and are rough in texture. Cedar shingles are similar but are machine-sawn. Repair them by removing and replacing the damaged shingles or shakes.

Wood lap siding is the likeliest type of siding to need repairs due to splitting, weathering, and water damage. Luckily, it is one of the easiest to remove and replace.

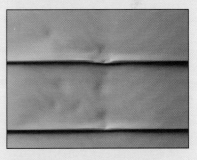

Aluminum or metal siding is somewhat susceptible to damage from hail and the occasional foul ball, but replacement is quite easy with the proper tools.

Vinyl siding can be difficult to repair, depending on the damage. Always check your warranty information before making any repairs to avoid inadvertently voiding the manufacturer's warranty.

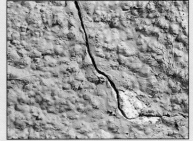

Stucco siding repairs can usually be handled by the homeowner with a little practice and the proper tools and materials. Silicone stucco caulk and stucco patches can make your home look new and stop further damage.

Repairing wood siding

Wood siding is subject to deterioration from weather. Some varieties of wood, cedar and redwood for example, are less susceptible to rot and are therefore more desirable as siding. Composite materials, such as hardboard, resist rot but are vulnerable to moisture unless treated and sealed. Sun damage is likely to be greater on the south and west walls.

Siding standards have varied over the years. If you're replacing siding on an older house, you may find it difficult to locate a suitable match. A building materials supplier may be able to special-order replacement siding or suggest a specialty siding source in your area.

SKILL SCALE

EASY	**MEDIUM**	HARD

REQUIRED SKILLS: Average carpentry skills will be necessary to repair wood siding.

HOW LONG WILL IT TAKE?

Experienced . . . . .Variable
Handy . . . . .Variable
Novice . . . . .Variable

VARIABLES: Damage may be more extensive than it first appears.

STUFF YOU'LL NEED

✔ **MATERIALS:**
Epoxy wood filler, wood spacers, siding material, siding nails, building paper, paintable exterior caulk

✔ **TOOLS:**
Putty knife, flat pry bar, hammer, shingle puller or hacksaw, circular saw, keyhole saw, jigsaw, hand stapler

EXTERIOR

TIPS FOR REPAIRING WOOD SIDING

1 **FILL SMALL HOLES IN WOOD SIDING BY CUTTING OUT THE DAMAGED AREA WITH A CHISEL.** Once you've removed all the rotten wood, use a putty knife to fill the area with an epoxy wood filler. Prime and paint to match the existing color.

2 **TO PATCH LARGER HOLES, REMOVE THE DAMAGED SIDING.** Start by driving spacers between the damage and the siding above it. Gradually pry up a wide area on either side of the damaged area to avoid splitting or cracking the old wood.

3 **PRY OUT THE NAILS HOLDING THE DAMAGED SIDING IN PLACE.** If you're worried about damaging a piece of siding that neighbors the damaged area, slip a scrap of wood between the pry bar and siding. Remove the piece of damaged siding.

4 **CUT REPLACEMENT SIDING BOARDS TO FIT, LEAVING AN EXPANSION GAP OF 1/16 INCH AT EACH END.** The expansion gap is essential. Without some breathing room the new siding could warp or buckle.

5 **USE OLD SIDING AS A PATTERN FOR TRACING CUTOUTS** around wall openings, fixtures, or obstructions. Prime and seal the cut ends on the house and the replacement boards and let the pieces dry thoroughly before you install them.

6 **REPLACE DAMAGED BUILDING PAPER BEFORE ATTACHING THE NEW SIDING.** Cut the replacement paper so that it overlaps the repair area by at least 4 inches. Make a cut in and remove the existing building paper. Tuck the top edge of the patch through the cut and staple in place.

7 **NAIL NEW SIDING BOARDS IN PLACE USING THE SAME NAILING PATTERN AS ON THE ORIGINAL BOARDS.** If you're replacing more than one board, begin with the lowest boards and work up. Align the bottom with the bottom of neighboring pieces.

8 **SET THE SPIGOT IN PAINTABLE SILICONE CAULK, THEN PAINT THE NEW SIDING.** For a color match, take a piece of the old siding to a store with a computer color-matching system (or an old pro who's really good). Brush the new paint over the old and dry with a hair dryer to check the color match.

Repairing wood siding *(continued)*

REPLACING SHINGLES OR SHAKES

1 SPLIT DAMAGED SHINGLES OR SHAKES WITH A HAMMER AND CHISEL and wiggle them from side to side to remove. The shingle directly above the one you're removing will hide the nails. Remove them by slipping a shingle puller over them or cut them flush with the surface with a hacksaw.

2 SPLIT NEW SHINGLES OR SHAKES TO FIT, ALLOWING A ¼-INCH-WIDE EXPANSION GAP. Starting with the lowest row, position the replacements. Nail near the top with aluminum or zinc-coated nails. When you loosely nail the top row in place, slip the top of the replacements under the row above, with the bottom edges ½ inch below the old shingles.

3 TAP THE SHINGLES INTO ALIGNMENT, hiding the nails in the process.

Stain the new shingles to match the weathered color, not the original.

REPLACING DAMAGED BOARD-AND-BATTEN

1 REMOVE THE BATTENS ON EACH SIDE OF THE DAMAGED PANEL. Remove the damaged panel. Replace the underlayment if necessary. Find a replacement panel that matches neighboring material.

2 CUT A REPLACEMENT BOARD TO FIT, LEAVING A ⅛-INCH GAP ON EACH SIDE BETWEEN THE NEW BOARD AND THE OLD. Prime or finish the edges and back of the new board and let it dry.

3 NAIL THE REPLACEMENT BOARD IN PLACE. Caulk the joints between the new and old boards, then reattach the battens. Prime and paint or stain to match.

EXTERIOR

Repairing vinyl and metal siding

Repairs to vinyl and aluminum siding arc a bit trickier than those to wood. The replacement pieces have to match the originals exactly, and finding them sometimes proves harder than the actual repair. Your best option: Once you've removed the damaged panel, take it to a home center or show it to a reputable contractor, who will probably be able to identify the manufacturer. If neither can supply you with the materials you need, contact the manufacturer and ask to be put in touch with a dealer near you.

SKILL SCALE

EASY	MEDIUM	HARD

REQUIRED SKILLS: Average carpentry skills will be necessary to repair vinyl and metal siding.

⏰ HOW LONG WILL IT TAKE?

Experienced . . . . 1hr.
Handy . . . . 2 hrs.
Novice . . . . 2.5 hrs.

VARIABLES: Weather and the amount of repair needed will affect the time for the project.

STUFF YOU'LL NEED

✔ MATERIALS:
Replacement siding, panel adhesive, caulk, aluminum nails, roofing cement

✔ TOOLS:
Siding removal tool, pry bar, slot cutter, hammer, tin snips, roofing knife, pliers, file, caulking gun

PATCHING VINYL SIDING

1 **REMOVE AND INSTALL VINYL SIDING WITH THE HELP OF A SIDING REMOVAL TOOL,** available at home centers. Find the top of the damaged panel and slip the tool between it and the panel above. Slide the tool along the seam, pulling out and slightly downward.

3 **INSERT THE NEW PANEL (OR PANELS) IN THE REPAIR AREA, STARTING AT THE BOTTOM.** Secure panels with the same fasteners used originally. For the last panel, force the fastener in with a pry bar slipped under the lap above. Lock the panels together with a siding removal tool. (See inset.)

Nailing slots

2 **LIFT THE PANEL ABOVE THE DAMAGED AREA OUT OF THE WAY BUT DO NOT REMOVE IT.** (The panels are flexible enough to lift away easily.) Use a pry bar to loosen and remove nails securing the damaged panel or panels. Remove the damaged panel(s).

Let that vinyl breathe

Vinyl siding expands and contracts even more than wood siding. A series of nailing slots run across the top of the panel. Drive the nail into the center of the slot and let it stick out 1/8 to 1/4 inch so that the vinyl can move. Driving the nails tight will cause buckling. Avoid stretching the panel to maximum width when you nail, which will limit it's ability to contract and expand.

Trimming a piece to fit removes the elongated nail holes; however, don't nail directly into the paneling, even if the trim looks as if it will cover up your work. Use a nail hole slot punch to add holes wherever you need them.

EXTERIOR

Repairing vinyl and metal siding *(continued)*

REPLACING ALUMINUM SIDING

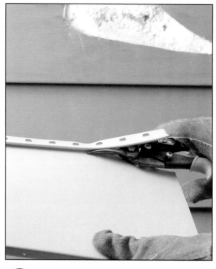

① **CUT OUT THE DAMAGED SECTION USING A ROOFING KNIFE AND TIN SNIPS.** Make the top cut about ¼ inch from the top of the damaged piece. Avoid making cuts on the vertical seam between two pieces. Pull downward to remove the piece from the wall.

② **USING AN EXTRA PIECE OF SIDING, CUT A PATCH 1 INCH LONGER THAN THE HOLE.** Trim off the fastener along the top of the piece so that it will lie flat, but leave the bottom lip intact. If replacing more than one piece, trim the fastener off the top piece only. File any rough edges smooth.

③ **TEST-FIT THE PATCH.** If the pieces don't fit well, straighten out the S-curve along the bottom of the patch with pliers. Apply construction adhesive on the siding near the edges of the patch and around the damage. Put the patch over the repair area. Tap the bottom edge with a 2×4 scrap and a hammer to snap the piece in place. Paint to match the existing siding.

REPLACING ALUMINUM END CAPS

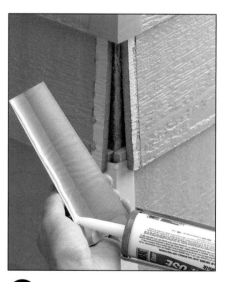

① **SOMETIMES DAMAGED CORNER CAPS COME OFF EASILY.** If the cap is pinned tightly under the cap above, however, pry out the bottom of the damaged cap, cut along the top of the cap, and remove it.

② **LOCATE MATCHING REPLACEMENT CAPS AND THEN ATTACH THEM WITH ALUMINUM NAILS.** Start at the bottom if replacing more than one cap.

③ **TRIM THE NAILING TAB OFF THE TOP REPLACEMENT CAP AND THEN APPLY PANEL ADHESIVE TO THE BACK.** Snap the cap over the bottom lips of joining siding courses. Seat the cap in the construction adhesive, aligning it properly.

Repairing stucco

Patching damaged stucco can be difficult because no stucco repair is invisible. It's almost impossible to match the texture and color, but it's important that you try. More important is a tight seal with adjacent materials. Cracks and holes in stucco let water into the walls, and the problems that result will be far worse than a mismatched patch.

Prior experience with masonry tools will give you a distinct advantage when attempting to match a particular stucco texture. Stucco pigments can be obtained at masonry supply stores and are meant to be mixed with the final coat. When pigmenting stucco, keep in mind that the color is likely to change as the stucco dries. For the best match, take the time to experiment with stucco and pigment proportions until you find a tint that matches the existing stucco wall when dry.

Make necessary repairs to the underlying structure before you begin. Plan on building up your repair in layers over several days, allowing the stucco to cure between applications.

FILL MINOR CRACKS WITH SPECIALTY STUCCO CAULK PRODUCTS. These caulks do not harden fully, maintaining a flexible bond between cracks. Stucco caulks are not available in colors, so the repair area will be plainly visible. You can, however, paint over a caulk strip to match the color of your stucco.

EXTERIOR

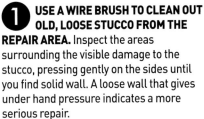

1 **USE A WIRE BRUSH TO CLEAN OUT OLD, LOOSE STUCCO FROM THE REPAIR AREA.** Inspect the areas surrounding the visible damage to the stucco, pressing gently on the sides until you find solid wall. A loose wall that gives under hand pressure indicates a more serious repair.

2 **FILL THE HOLE WITH PRE-MIXED STUCCO PATCH USING A TROWEL.** Apply the stucco in two or three thin layers, letting each layer dry completely between applications.

3 **SMOOTH OUT THE FINAL COAT TO MATCH THE SURROUNDING TEXTURE** using a trowel; then dab with the straw ends of a whisk broom to blend in the texture of the repair.

REPAIRING FASCIA AND SOFFITS

Carpenters originally created fascia and soffits to solve the problems of exposed rafters and open eaves. Fascia are nailed to the cut ends of rafters and prevent water from being drawn back along the overhang and inside the walls. They also provide an even surface to which you can attach gutters.

Soffits close off the underside of the rafters, preventing birds and other critters from nesting under eaves or getting into the attic. Properly vented, soffits allow air into the attic, helping to solve moisture problems and increases shingle life, thus extending the life of the roof.

Maintenance is essential to the soundness of your fascia and soffits. Solve problems before they affect the structure of your house. Repaint peeling surfaces and replace missing or rotted pieces as soon as you notice them.

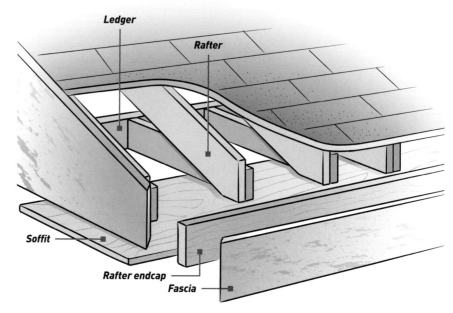

Ledger

Rafter

Soffit

Rafter endcap

Fascia

SKILL SCALE

EASY	**MEDIUM**	HARD

REQUIRED SKILLS: Average carpentry skills will be necessary.

HOW LONG WILL IT TAKE?

Experienced ....Variable
Handy ....Variable
Novice ....Variable

VARIABLES: Time depends on condition of existing soffit.

STUFF YOU'LL NEED

✔ **MATERIALS:**
Galvanized nails or screws, fascia material, soffit materials, silicone caulk, primer, paint or stain, 2×2 nailing strip

✔ **TOOLS:**
Pry bar, hammer, ladder, nail set, jigsaw, caulking gun, drill and driver, circular saw, paintbrush

FASCIA AND SOFFITS WORK TOGETHER TO CLOSE OFF THE AREA BENEATH THE ROOF EAVES. The fascia covers the rafter ends while providing a surface for attaching gutters. Soffits prevent birds from nesting under your eaves and often have vents to bring fresh air into your attic space. (See page 432.)

(See page 432.)

SAFETY ALERT

WORK SAFELY OUTSIDE
Always use a GFCI-protected cord if working with power tools outside to minimize the potential for a shock.

INSTALLING FASCIA COVERS AND SOFFITS

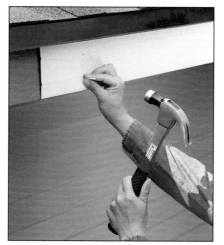

VINYL OR ALUMINUM FASCIA COVERS HELP REDUCE MAINTENANCE ON WOODEN FASCIA. They are not, however, a substitute for repairs. Fix any rot or other damage before installing covers. Then nail the covers directly to the existing fascia. If you have or want soffits, get fascia with a channel designed to hold them.

THE QUICKEST WAY TO INSTALL SOFFITS IS TO INSTALL FASCIA COVERS WITH CHANNELS DESIGNED TO HOLD THEM. Hang matching channels on the house. Cut soffits to fit, angle them up into the opening, and drop them in place. Make sure you've repaired areas covered by the new soffits before you hang them.

Replacing a section of fascia

1 **REMOVE GUTTERS OR TRIM, EXPOSING THE ENTIRE DAMAGED SECTION OF FASCIA.** Be extremely careful when handling gutters and long moldings. If they hit nearby power lines, the shock can kill you. Long pieces also can make you lose your balance. Plan to be near the middle of the piece when you finally pry it loose.

2 **PRY THE FASCIA LOOSE WITH A FLAT PRY BAR, THEN REMOVE IT.** Fascia usually is nailed at every rafter end, except when it is attached directly to another fascia at the edge of the roof.

3 **MARK OFF THE DAMAGED AREA OF FASCIA BY DRAWING CUT LINES THAT WILL FALL IN THE MIDDLE OF THE RAFTERS.** Set the saw to cut at a 45-degree angle and cut out the damaged area of the soffit.

Ladder stabilizers, shown in Step 1, help keep the ladder from tipping and hold it away from the gutter and fascia.

Mitered end

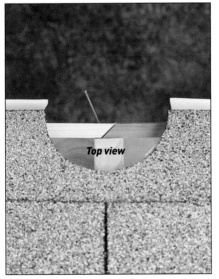

Top view

4 **NAIL OR SCREW THE ORIGINAL PIECE OR PIECES OF FASCIA IN THEIR ORIGINAL POSITIONS,** leaving a gap where you cut out the damage. Measure the gap, then subtract 1/8 inch to allow for expansion. Cut the new board to this size with the saw still set at 45 degrees. Prime the back and ends of the board.

5 **POSITION THE REPLACEMENT BOARD WITH AN EXPANSION GAP OF ABOUT 1/16 INCH AT EACH END.** Nail it in place, driving the nail at an angle through the miters.

6 **REPLACE THE FASCIA MOLDINGS, THEN SET THE NAILHEADS AND FILL THE NAIL HOLES WITH CAULK.** Prime and paint or stain to match the existing fascia. Reinstall the gutters after the paint or stain dries.

Repairing plywood soffits

1 **REMOVE ANY MOLDING HOLDING THE SOFFIT IN PLACE.** In order to remove the soffit, it sometimes helps to cut out the damaged area. Find the rafters on either side of the damaged area and draw a line along the rafter edge closest to the damage. Drill entry holes for a jigsaw and then cut along the lines.

2 **PUT A PRY BAR INTO THE CUT YOU JUST MADE AND PRY TO REMOVE THE DAMAGE.** Move slowly and pry gently so that you maintain your balance. When you've removed the damage, get a helper on a second ladder. Pull on the soffit with your hands to remove it as your helper supports the far end.

3 **REMOVE ANY OF THE DAMAGED SOFFIT THAT REMAINS ON THE OTHER SIDE OF THE CUTOUT.** In all, you'll need to remove enough soffit to reveal the seam between the damaged section and its neighbors. Damage is likely to be anyplace where water has been running through a plywood edge.

4 **MEASURE THE SIZE OF THE HOLE CAUSED BY REMOVING THE DAMAGED SECTION OF SOFFIT.** Cut a piece of exterior plywood to fit the opening. (Most home centers will cut a section of plywood for a small fee.) If the damaged section had vents, cut matching ones in the replacement panel. Prime the entire panel and let it dry.

5 **PUT THE REPLACEMENT PANEL OVER THE OPENING AND SCREW IT TO THE RAFTERS** with 1¼-inch galvanized deck screws. Reinstall any molding that helped hold the panel in place.

6 **FILL NAIL HOLES, SCREW HOLES, AND JOINTS WITH PAINTABLE SILICONE CAULK.** Paint the replacement panel to match the rest of the soffit, then reinstall any vent covers that you removed.

EXTERIOR

Repairing length-run tongue-and-groove soffits

1 REMOVE ANY MOLDING OVER THE BOARDS, THEN LOCATE THE RAFTER ON EACH SIDE OF THE DAMAGE by looking for nails in the fascia. Drill entry holes for a jigsaw, positioning them to avoid the rafter. Put the jigsaw blade in one of the holes and cut away the damage.

2 PUT YOUR FINGER IN ONE OF THE HOLES AND PULL DOWN ANY PIECES THAT WILL COME LOOSE. Remove the rest of the scrap. Cut and install 2×2 nailing strips at each edge of the opening in the soffit, screwing them to the rafters.

3 CUT REPLACEMENT TONGUE-AND-GROOVE BOARDS USING BOARDS THE SAME THICKNESS AS THE ORIGINALS. Begin installing the new boards next to the siding, nailing them to the nailing strips.

Repairing width-run soffits

4 TRIM THE UPPER LIP FROM THE LAST BOARD, THEN POSITION IT IN THE OPENING. Nail it in place, fill the nail holes, and paint the replacement board to match the soffit. Replace the soffit vents, if necessary. Prime and paint.

1 PUT A METAL CUTTING BLADE IN A JIGSAW, AND CUT ALONG THE FASCIA WITH THE SAW to free the damaged section (width-run soffits are usually inserted into grooves in the fascia and may be nailed through the groove). Remove support moldings and pry out the damaged soffit boards.

2 CUT REPLACEMENT BOARDS TO LENGTH AND PRIME BOTH SIDES AND ENDS. Insert the strips into the groove in the fascia. When you get to the last board, cut off the upper lip so that you can install it. Reattach the support molding, caulk the nail holes, and paint the boards to match the existing soffits.

EXTERIOR

Roofing basics

It's a whole lot wiser and more economical to fix your roof before it leaks than to procrastinate. If you do you may find you will then have to fix your roof, ceiling, interior walls, and flooring. The best way to ensure that you won't have to go back up on the roof anytime soon is to buy the highest-quality roofing materials you can afford.

Asphalt shingles are the shingle of choice, and installation is well within a homeowner's skill. Asphalt shingles are either tab or architectural. Tab shingles are the ones that took America by storm in the 1950s. Architectural shingles are essentially tab shingles with a fancier bottom edge.

Top-notch architectural shingles are guaranteed for 40 years, sometimes longer if the manufacturer's installation instructions are strictly followed. They're thicker than low-cost shingles so they resist curling and cupping and generally withstand more abuse from weather extremes.

If you happen to have asbestos roof shingles, hire a professional to do the removal and repair.

If you're doing your own work and you're comfortable working with sheet metal, you can buy galvanized steel or aluminum in bulk rolls and custom-cut it to fit. Otherwise, you'll have to spend a little more for prefabricated flashing.

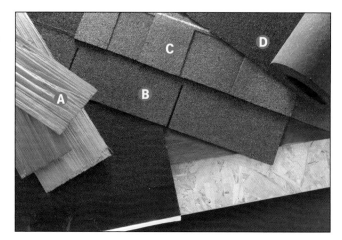

THE VARIETY OF ROOFING SHINGLES IS WIDE. Ⓐ Cedar shakes are split from wood (cedar shingles are sawn); Ⓑ 3-tab shingles are the most common shingle; the textured look of Ⓒ architectural shingles comes from laminating small pieces of shingle to a solid shingle base; Ⓓ roll roofing, designed for roofs with a low slope, goes on quickly but is less durable than other materials.

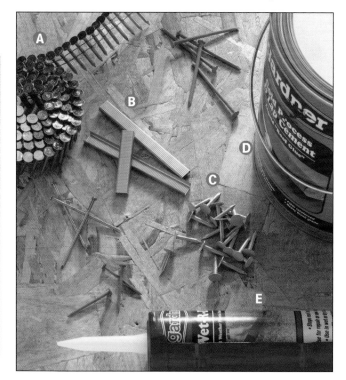

ROOFING REQUIRES A VARIETY OF FASTENERS. Ⓐ Coil nails fit in a nail gun. Use Ⓑ staples in a hand or hammer stapler. Nail down shingles with Ⓒ hot-dipped galvanized roofing nails. Roofing cement comes in Ⓓ a can and Ⓔ a tube; it is used to seal seams and help hold down flashing.

FLASHING KEEPS WATER FROM LEAKING IN WHERE TWO PARTS OF THE ROOF MEET. Ⓐ Vent flashing goes around the plumbing stack that comes out of the roof; use Ⓑ step flashing along chimney edges. Ⓒ Prefab valley flashing goes in the valley where two sloping roofs meet. Cut custom replacement flashing from Ⓓ roll flashing. Ⓔ Gutter aprons and Ⓕ drip edges are used to protect the edges of the roof.

SAFETY ALERT

WEAR THE RIGHT GEAR
Roofs are slippery, especially once you've stripped them down to the plywood. Wear the right shoes. Sneakers with flat rubber soles that will grab and hold are great but seem to attracts nails. Steel-toed work boots may not be as comfortable but they prevent injuries.

Put your tools in a tool belt when working on the roof. Tools set on the roof will obey the laws of gravity and quickly end up on the ground—or someone's head.

THE ROOFER'S TOOL KIT

Below are some basic roofing tools. For more information see the Tool Glossary on page 544.

AIR COMPRESSOR	**DRILL**	**HAMMER STAPLER**	**PRY BAR**	**SAWHORSE**	**TROWEL**
CAULKING GUN	**DRILL BITS**	**KNEE PADS**	**PUSH BROOM**	**STRAIGHTEDGE**	**UTILITY KNIFE**
CHALK LINE	**EAR PLUGS**	**LADDER WITH STABILIZER**	**ROOFING KNIFE**	**TAPE MEASURE**	**WHEELBARROW**
CHISELS	**FLAT PRY BAR**	**MAGNETIC SWEEP**	**ROOFING SHOVEL**	**TARPS**	**WIRE BRUSH**
CIRCULAR SAW	**FRAMING SQUARE**	**PITCHFORK**	**SAFETY GLASSES**	**TIN SNIPS**	
CLAW HAMMER	**GLOVES**	**PNEUMATIC POWER NAILER**	**SAFETY HARNESS**	**TOOL BELT**	

Architectural shingles are solid shingles without water lines like those found on three-tab shingles. Architectural shingles have a textured appearance. They are available with longer warranties than three-tab shingles; however, installation of both types is the same.

Cedar shakes and shingles are wooden. Split shakes, such as the ones shown here, are thicker and last longer. Installation is generally done by professionals.

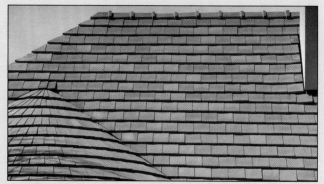

Clay, or terra-cotta, comes in a variety of shapes: flat tiles, shaped tiles, and the Spanish barrel-shaped tiles. Terra-cotta dates from Roman times but became popular in North America in the 19th century. It's available in its natural, red-clay color, as well as yellow, green, and blue glazed tiles. The tiles were originally made by hand. Makers formed the barrel-shaped tiles by spreading clay over their thighs. Original tiles not only bear the shape of the maker's leg, the surface often contains a handprint made hundreds of years ago by a now-anonymous craftsperson.

Properly installed, slate roofs are said to last 150 years. In some parts of the country, slate was once standard utilitarian roofing, as likely to be found on a barn as on a fancy Victorian home. Today, however, slate is hard to get and expensive. If you're in the market for a new slate roof, have a pro install one (they're very heavy). To repair an existing roof, find an experienced slate roofer and ask what can be done.

BUYER'S GUIDE

METAL ROOFING

Metal roofing comes in three broad categories: standing-seam roofing, panel roofing, and look-alikes including tile, cedar, or slate. Traditional standing-seam metal roofing has large ribs that are crimped or soldered together; panel roofing looks somewhat like it but screws down. Metal roofing is durable and long-lasting, but with the exception of screw-down panels, installation requires special training and is usually left to professionals.

EXTERIOR

Getting ready for a roofing project

SAFETY HARNESSES ARE A WISE CHOICE

Talk to any roofer and you'll hear tales of falls from high places. Because of the danger involved, OSHA now requires professional roofers to wear harnesses, and if people who walk on roofs every day of their lives need harnesses, so do you.

The kind of harness you want is called a fall-arrest harness, as opposed to a rescue, suspension, or positioning harness. You'll need at least a 25-foot lifeline with a shock-absorbing lanyard (strap) and a roof anchor.

The harness slips over your body and legs and has a ring on the back for the lanyard. The lanyard has a shock-absorbing core that stretches to reduce the shock that occurs when the lifeline stops a fall. The lifeline is a heavy-duty rope, one end of which attaches to the lanyard, the other end to the roof anchor. The roof anchor attaches to the peak of the roof with heavy-duty nails.

A good harness system will cost you as much as a good nail gun, but unlike a nail gun, it's required by OSHA and will save your life. Check the Yellow Pages to see if you can rent a harness, but if you have to buy, do so. If you do rent, get printed instructions for using the harness. If your home center doesn't carry harnesses, check with a roofing distributor or look on the Web and in the Yellow Pages. Buy all the components from the same manufacturer to make sure they work as designed. Ask about kits that include everything you need.

WORK SMARTER

HIRING A PRO?

If you've decided not to do the job yourself, get a reliable roofer. Ask contractors you've worked with for names. Ask the roofers for references and phone numbers, and follow up on the quality of their work.

Verify that the roofer is licensed and bonded, and ask for proof. Discuss who will handle disposal of the old roof. Have the roofer take out the permit so that you won't be responsible for insurance.

Get two or three estimates for time and cost. As a rule, it will take two or three workers about a day to strip the average roof, and another day or so to apply shingles.

Measuring for roofing

The first thing you should consider if you're thinking about roofing is getting up on the roof to measure it. It can be done from the ground, and pros do it all the time, but it's much simpler to do it on the roof. It's also the acid test: How willing are you to climb up to the ridge or walk over to the edge and peer over? If you're nervous about climbing up to measure, or if you get up to the roof and freeze (as many a good soul has), hire a pro.

Start measuring by drawing a picture of your roof—not necessarily to scale—and then divide it into a series of rectangles and triangles. Climb up on the roof, watching out for loose shingles that could send you tumbling. Measure the height and width of each rectangle, and multiply them to get the square footage. Multiply the base and height of the triangles, then divide by two to find the area of triangular sections of the roof. Mark your measurements on your sketch and then do the math. Add 10 percent for gables and 15 percent for hips.

When you get to the retailer, tell the salesperson how many square feet you need. The experts can convert into the standard roofing measurement of "squares" and tell you how many bundles you need. If you're curious, a "square" is 100 square feet, and a bundle covers about one-third of that, depending on the shingle. A 30×30 roof is 900 square feet, or nine squares, and requires 27 bundles of shingles. Have them delivered.

CLOSER LOOK

PNEUMATIC NAIL GUNS

Nail guns make quick work out of driving the roughly 400 nails you'll need for every 100 square feet of shingles. Use a coil-fed roofing nailer for roof work. One coil of nails is about enough to do a bundle of shingles. A box of coils will

fasten approximately 2,000 square feet of shingles. Use 1¼- inch nails for shingles, 1⅝-inch nails for roof caps, and 1¾-inch nails when reroofing by adding a layer of shingles.

If you're using only one nail gun, power it with a small compressor. Multiple nailers will require a compressor with at least a ½-horsepower motor and a 10- to 20-gallon storage tank. You'll also need *a lot* of hose. Have your retailer or rental agency help you match the amount to the size and height of your roof.

If you're only going to use the gun once, rent instead of buying. Whatever you decide, oil and maintain the gun as directed by the manufacturer.

Identifying roofing problems

A working roof and gutter system usually goes unnoticed. If they are working properly, they provide adequate air circulation and venting, protection against the elements, and proper drainage of rain and snow.

If you find problems with the roof, such as leaks, worn sections, missing shingle parts, or cupped or bowed shingles, replacing your roof may be a better idea than trying to repair it. Depending on your location, codes will allow either one or two layers of new shingles over the original roof. Beyond that you will need to strip away the old roof and start over.

FLASHING AROUND VENT PIPES often cracks, letting water into the attic and even down into the wall. Look for faulty repairs, such as this one done with roofing cement, as well as actual cracks.

BUCKLED AND CUPPED SHINGLES generally indicate a moisture problem. Tear off the old shingles, repair the problem, and reroof.

WEAR OCCURS AS SHINGLES AGE. If the majority of shingles are damaged or worn, tear off and replace them.

DAMAGED OR DETERIORATED SHINGLES are a main cause of roof leaks. These shingles are damaged beyond repair and a new roof is the only solution. In cases of minor or localized problems you need only replace the damaged shingles.

DETACHED OR LOOSE FLASHING often can be replaced or reattached. Clean out the old caulk or roof cement and replace it with fresh sealant.

LEAKS OFTEN OCCUR AT CHIMNEYS when flashing fails. Look for the kind of gaps that occur in other types of flashing, as well as repairs that use lots of roofing cement or patches. Any patch is temporary and is a sure sign that if you don't need a new roof now, you soon will.

Protecting yourself and your house

As any roofer will tell you, no matter how hard the roofing job, getting rid of the old shingles and nails is worse. To save your back, follow these suggestions:

- Put a large trash receptacle or flatbed truck next to the house and throw the shingles in it instead of on the ground.

- Put a tarp on the ground wherever the shingles will land.

- Protect bushes and shrubs with plywood and tarps.

- Protect windows by leaning plywood against them.

- Pick up stray nails and debris as you work (there will be lots) with a heavy-duty "sweep" magnet (also called a release magnet), available in the roofing department or from a tool rental store.

- Always have another person around when you work above ground in case of an emergency.

- Wear shoes with soles that nails cannot penetrate.

- Wear a tool apron to keep tools from sliding off the roof.

PROTECT YOUR HOUSE AGAINST DAMAGE FROM DISCARDED ROOFING MATERIALS.
Hang large tarps over the side of the house. Protect your landscape against falling debris by setting plywood sheets against the house and over windows. Protect gardens and yard elements with plastic tarps. Load shingles in a wheelbarrow and then a truck or large trash receptacle. If you can put it next to the house, throwing debris directly into it will make the job easier.

USE ROOF JACKS

1 NAIL TWO ROOF JACKS ON A STEEP ROOF AFTER SHINGLING THE FIRST FOUR COURSES. Drive two 12 or 16d common nails into each jack, and nail it firmly into a rafter. Nail into the section of a shingle that will be covered and so that the jack doesn't interfere with the nailing pattern. Run another set of jacks along the bottom of the roof to catch falling tools—or falling workers.

2 SHINGLE NORMALLY OVER THE TOPS OF THE ROOF JACKS, then insert a board across the two jacks to form a safe support for yourself and your tools. Continue your work at the new level.

3 DETACH A ROOF JACK BY HITTING THE BOTTOM OF THE JACK toward the ridge and sliding it upward off the nails. Slip a pry bar under a shingle and use it to finish driving in the hidden nails left from the roof jack.

Repairing damaged roofs

If damage is limited, try short-term fixes by replacing shingles and applying roofing cement. Damaged or missing shingles are obvious; cracks or separated joints in the flashing can be harder to locate. When tracking the source of a leak, remember that water, having penetrated the roofing, often flows down the sheathing or, once through the sheathing, down a joist before finally dripping onto the ceiling below. Inside damage tells you nothing about outside entry. If you can get into the attic or crawlspace and if the roof joists are exposed, try to locate the actual entry point from below before going up on the roof. Use reference points, such as chimneys, ventilation pipes, windows, or valleys, to help you pinpoint the site once you're on the roof.

While you're up there patching shingles that have already leaked, survey the roof for other problem areas.

SKILL SCALE

EASY	MEDIUM	HARD

REQUIRED SKILLS: Average carpentry skills will be necessary to repair a damaged roof.

HOW LONG WILL IT TAKE?

Experienced . . . . 20 min.
Handy . . . . 25 min.
Novice . . . . 30 min.

VARIABLES: Time is for repairing one shingle.

STUFF YOU'LL NEED

✔ **MATERIALS:**
Roofing cement, roofing nails, shingles

✔ **TOOLS:**
Ladder, claw hammer, caulking gun, flat pry bar, wood chisel, shingle puller, tool belt

MAKING REPAIRS WITH ROOFING CEMENT

REATTACH BUCKLED SHINGLES WITH ROOFING CEMENT. Also use roofing cement to patch any cracks or other minor shingle problems.

REFRESH DETERIORATED ROOFING CEMENT AROUND FLASHING IF THE SEAL IS BAD. Joints around flashing or skylights are the most common places leaks can occur.

REPLACING ASPHALT SHINGLES

1 **TEAR OFF THE UPPERMOST SHINGLE NEEDING REPAIR BY GRASPING THE SIDES AND WRIGGLING IT LOOSE.** If you're replacing multiple shingles, start with the highest one. Remove all damaged shingles this way. Be careful not to damage surrounding shingles in good condition.

2 **REMOVE OLD NAILS WITH A PRY BAR.** If you cannot pry them out, drive the nails flat into the sheathing with a hammer. Patch any holes in the building paper with roofing cement.

③ INSTALL NEW SHINGLES ON LOWER COURSES following the normal shingle installation procedure shown on the bundle wrapper.

④ COAT THE TOP OF THE LAST SHINGLE above the seal line with roofing cement.

⑤ SLIP THE LAST SHINGLE INTO PLACE UNDER THE OVERLAPPING SHINGLE. Depending on the arrangement of the shingles, you may be able to drive a couple of nails into the shingle by gently lifting overlapping tabs of other shingles. If not, press the shingle down firmly to seat it in roofing cement.

Gravity always wins, so wear a tool apron and use it to hold your tools while on the roof. Loose tools are guaranteed to slide off.

REPLACING WOODEN SHAKES

① SPLIT THE DAMAGED SHINGLE WITH A HAMMER AND CHISEL AND REMOVE THE SHINGLE PIECES. Use a shingle puller to remove hidden nails. Slip the shingle puller under the shingle above, catch a nail, and hammer on the flat part of the handle to pull or cut the nail. Check the building paper for damage and repair or replace as necessary. (See Step 6 on page 453.)

② TRIM A NEW SHINGLE TO FIT, LEAVING ABOUT ⅜ INCH CLEARANCE ON EITHER SIDE FOR EXPANSION. Push the shingle in place until the lower edge is about an inch below the edge of the neighboring shingles. Drive nails into the top of the replacement shingle.

③ TAP THE BOTTOM EDGE OF THE SHINGLE, AS SHOWN, TO DRIVE IT INTO PLACE. The nails will bend slightly, hiding them under the shingle above. If the shingle splits when you try this, cut a new one, spread roofing cement on the upper half, and slide it in place under the shingle above.

Roof tear-off and repair

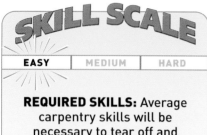

STUFF YOU'LL NEED

✔ **MATERIALS:**

Exterior-grade plywood, 2½-inch galvanized screws, 8d ringshank nails

✔ **TOOLS:**

Roofing knife, flat pry bar, roofing shovel or pitchfork, circular saw, claw hammer, broom, drill and driver bit

HOMER'S HINDSIGHT

DON'T GET RAINED OUT

When I was getting ready to tear off my old roof, I gathered all the equipment I needed, rounded up a couple of friends, and even rented a dump truck. If only I had checked the weather forecast, everything would have been perfect. My advice: Have a couple of tarps on hand in case of rain.

WHAT'S UP ON THE ROOF?

Ridge

Hip

Valley

Rake

Eave

EAVE: *The bottom edge of the roof.*
HIP: *A line running from the eave to the ridge formed where two sloping sections of roof meet. Found on roofs with more than two main faces.*
RAKE: *The side edge of the roof, which runs from eave to ridge or hip.*
RIDGE: *The line across the top of the roof, formed where two main faces of the roof meet.*
VALLEY: *A trough formed by two sections of roof meeting at an angle.*

A new roof can go over an old roof. Depending on local code, it can even go over two layers of roof. (See page 483 for information on roofing over an old roof.)

Tearing off an old roof is hard work. Roofing materials start out heavy and seem to gain weight as the day goes on. Gathering the torn-up shingles once they hit the ground is even more work, so before you tear off the first shingle, borrow or rent a truck and park it under the eaves. Shovel the old shingles off the roof and directly into the truck. It will keep nails out of your lawn mower and your back out of traction.

Find help if you can—this would be an excellent time to call in old favors. Before you let anybody on your roof, though, check your insurance coverage. And if the pitch of your roof is steep, make certain that each worker is secured by roofing jacks or a safety harness. Helpers who discover their fear of heights can still clean up and act as emergency "watchers."

1 **START AT THE TOP OF THE ROOF AND REMOVE THE OLD SHINGLES IN SECTIONS.** Keep the roofing shovel (shown) or pitchfork tight against the plywood sheathing or lumber decking so that you can peel the shingles off in large chunks instead of individually. If you are saving your gutters, be careful not to ruin them during tear-off.

EXTERIOR

REMOVE FLASHING FROM ROOF VENTS, SKYLIGHTS, AND DORMERS. Some flashing such as that used on skylights is reusable. Chimneys should have two layers of flashing, some of which may be reusable. The rest, including the boot (a waterproof fitting) that goes around vent pipes, valley flashing, and dormer flashing should be removed and replaced. **REMOVE THE SHINGLES ACROSS THE RIDGE.** Remove the ridge with a pitchfork or roofing shovel last to protect the peak in case of rain.

3 **PRY OUT ANY REMAINING NAILS.** A ripping hammer with a flat claw like this one is specifically designed for pulling nails. Once you've pulled the nails, sweep the roof completely: It must be free of protruding nails and completely clean before you can move to the next step, which will be sheathing or shingling, depending on the roofing material you choose. Clean up stray nails from the yard using a release magnet, available at most rental centers.

REPLACING DAMAGED SHEATHING

1 **SHEATHING CAN BE MADE OF EITHER PLYWOOD OR SOLID WOOD.** While plywood is shown here, the procedure is the same for solid wood. Use the nail holes to help locate the rafters. Outline an area to cut out that is larger than the damaged area, cutting ends that are directly above the centers of the rafters. Set your circular saw to cut through the sheathing but not into the rafters, then make the cutout.

2 **IF THE RAFTER IS SPLINTERED OR DETERIORATED BENEATH THE SHEATHING,** screw or nail a 2×4 cleat to the side to provide a surface to attach the new sheathing. The new sheathing should be the same thickness as the old—generally ½-inch. In some areas ⁷⁄₁₆-inch material is suitable as a replacement.

3 **CUT NEW SHEATHING FROM EXTERIOR-GRADE PLYWOOD, MATCHING THE THICKNESS OF THE OLD SHEATHING.** (Use solid wood to replace solid wood.) Cut the patch to allow a ⅛-inch expansion gap on each side. Nail the patch in place with galvanized 8d ringshank nails driven into the rafters and spaced 6 inches apart.

Applying underlayment

SKILL SCALE

EASY	**MEDIUM**	HARD

REQUIRED SKILLS: Average carpentry skills will be necessary to apply roofing underlayment.

HOW LONG WILL IT TAKE?

Experienced .... 10 min.
Handy .... 15 min.
Novice .... 20 min.

VARIABLES: Time is for laying one roll of underlayment.

STUFF YOU'LL NEED

✔ MATERIALS:

Eave drip cap, rake drip cap, underlayment, ice-dam barrier underlayment, hot-dipped galvanized roofing nails, roofing cement

✔ TOOLS:

Safety glasses, claw hammer, tin snips, chalk line, roofing knife, hand roller, tape measure, pry bar

In roofing, underlayment means rolls of 15- or 30-pound roofing felt (felt soaked in asphalt). Check with the manufacturer of your shingles and use the underlayment they specify. Underlayment is a must—not an option—for a good roof. Using the wrong materials can void the warranty.

Here's why: The roof is a system of layers designed to keep out water. The shingles do the basic job of shedding and channeling rain. The underlayment is a final barrier to moisture penetration.

Application begins at the bottom of the roof and works its way up. Each strip overlaps the previous one by a few inches. Any water flowing down from the top of the roof is directed over the seam instead of into it.

In cold climates, heat leaking from the house often melts snow on the upper part of the roof; the water refreezes when it reaches the colder eaves, and the resulting slush and water (called an ice dam) can be forced up under the shingles. Proper insulation and venting help prevent this (see pages 432–439), but you should also install an ice-dam barrier underlayment over the section of roof covering the first 2 feet of the attic and in the valleys. It applies much like roofing felt but is heavier and self-adhesive. For more on installation, see "Preventing Ice-Dam Damage" on page 473.

Measure the slope of your roof with a level and tape measure. If the slope is between 2 and 4 inches per foot, apply a double layer of roofing felt at the bottom, and overlap courses by 19 inches instead of by the amount shown here. For a roof with a slope of less than 2 inches per foot, use roll roofing (see page 484).

Applied correctly, underlayment offers a degree of protection in case it should rain before you shingle. And if the roof has problems, you'll have peace of mind that comes from knowing that its underlayment is solid.

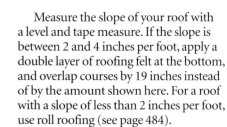

WORK SMARTER

USE THE RIGHT EDGING

The metal trim along the eave (bottom) of the roof is different from that which runs up the side of the roof. The bottom trim is called **gutter apron** and directs water into the eave trough. **Drip** or **roof edge** is narrower and runs along the side of the roof to support the ends of the shingles. Underlayment goes over the gutter apron and under the roof or rake edge (see Step 7).

① NAIL A STRIP OF EAVE DRIP EDGE ALONG THE BOTTOM OF THE ROOF. If you need more than one strip, overlap the ends of neighboring strips by 2 inches. Use tin snips to miter the end that will butt against the drip edge covering the rake, or edge, of the roof (see Step 7).

② UNROLL ROOFING FELT, ALSO CALLED UNDERLAYMENT, ALONG THE BOTTOM EDGE OF THE ROOF. The felt should overlap the eave drip edge by about ⅜ inch. Staple or nail the felt in place. If you nail, use 1-inch hot-dipped galvanized roofing nails, even though they will poke through the sheathing below.

③ ROLL OUT THE NEXT COURSE OF ROOFING FELT, overlapping the existing paper or ice-dam barrier by 4 inches. Fasten the felt with staples or with hot-dipped galvanized roofing nails.

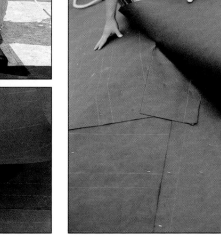

4 WORK YOUR WAY UP THE ROOF DECK WITH ROOFING FELT, OVERLAPPING COURSES BY 4 INCHES.
When a roll runs out, start a new one, overlapping the ends by 12 inches. Roll felt across valleys from both sides, extending it 36 inches on both sides of the valley. **WHEN YOU COME TO AN OBSTRUCTION, CUT A HOLE IN THE FELT** that will slip over it if possible. Otherwise roll the roofing felt up to the obstruction, then resume the course on the other side. Cut a patch extending 12 inches on each side of the obstruction, fit it over the obstruction, and nail it into place.

5 AT RIDGES AND HIPS, WRAP 6 INCHES OVER THE TOP AND NAIL OR STAPLE IN PLACE. Staple every 3 inches along the edge.
NOTE: If you are installing roll roofing (see page 484) cut a strip of felt 12 inches wide, snap a chalk line 6 inches on each side of the ridge or hip; spread a 2-inch-wide strip of roofing cement just inside the lines. Set the underlayment so that the outside edges anchor in the roofing cement.

6 IF THE ROOF HAS A DORMER OR SIDEWALLS, START AT THE SIDEWALL. Tuck the roofing felt under the siding to create an unbroken seal at the roof and wall joint.

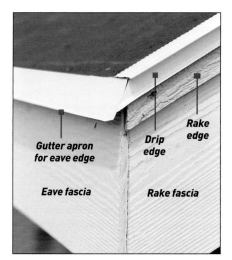

Gutter apron for eave edge

Drip edge

Rake edge

Eave fascia

Rake fascia

7 NAIL A STRIP OF DRIP EDGE OVER THE RAKE EDGE THAT COVERS THE UNDERLAYMENT, STARTING AT THE BOTTOM AND WORKING TOWARD THE RIDGE. Overlap joining strips of drip edge by 2 inches. Miter the ends of drip edge where they meet at eaves. (Rake and eave drip edges are different. Make sure you get the proper amount of each kind.)

Preventing ice-dam damage

In areas of the country with rough winters, roofers often install an ice-dam barrier. (This heavy-duty, self-adhesive, waterproof sheet of underlayment prevents melting snow from getting under the shingles when it runs into ice at the bottom of the roof). To be effective the ice dam has to extend at least 24 inches up the outside of the roof, measuring from the interior attic wall. (The eaves must be covered but exclude them when you measure.) Measure up the roof from inside the attic to determine how many courses of ice-dam barrier to lay down.

Apply the ice-dam barrier along the bottom edge of the roof. Ideally the strip should run the length of the roof with no cuts. For longer runs, cut the barrier into manageable lengths. Peel off about 2 feet of the backing on the underside to expose a contact adhesive. Put the sticky side face down on the roof, overhanging the drip edge by about ⅜ inch. Press the barrier onto the roof with your hands, nail across the top every 18 inches, and roll the edges with a hand roller. Work your way across the roof, peeling off the paper, pressing, nailing, and rolling as you go.

Overlap seams by 6 inches, nail every 6 or 8 inches, and roll the seam with the hand roller.

(The manufacturer may also recommend applying the barrier along the rake edges of the roof; if so, follow the directions for installation.)

INSTALLING FLASHING

If you have experience working with sheet metal and have the equipment necessary to do so, you can make your own flashing from rolls of metal sold as roll flashing. Avoid using anything less than 26-gauge galvanized steel, even if working with aluminum is easier.

You'll probably get better results with prefabricated flashing, sold in lengths that are already creased and shaped. If necessary, trim them to length with a pair of tin snips.

Custom sheet-metal fabricators can also cut and form your flashing to fit. Carefully measure chimneys, dormers, and roof slope to ensure a watertight seal.

Valley flashing is applied before the shingles go up. Other types are applied while you apply the shingles.

A proper job of flashing around chimneys, dormers, vent pipes, valleys, and skylights is the most important action you can take to avoid leaks.

INSTALLING FLASHING
Valley flashing options

EXTERIOR

TO MAKE TRADITIONAL METAL FLASHING, bend your own from rolls of flashing material. Make the bend by folding the metal along a straightedge. Metal flashing provides a sturdy base when laying shingles for a closed valley. (See "Closer Look" on page 480.) Prefab metal flashing is easier and more durable when laying an open valley.

ROLLED, SELF-ADHESIVE FLASHING MEMBRANES ARE GUARANTEED TO LAST AS LONG AS THE SHINGLES YOU PUT OVER THEM. Cut the roll into pieces 6 to 10 feet long. Starting at the bottom of the roof, fold the flashing in half lengthwise. Remove a half-width of the backing covering the adhesive, center the fold in the valley, then stick the membrane to the roof. Remove the rest of the backing and adhere the remainder of the membrane. Install the next piece the same way, overlapping the first piece by at least 6 inches.

PREFABRICATED METAL FLASHING HAS A PEAK THAT DEFLECTS WATER FLOW AWAY FROM THE WEAK SPOT IN THE BOTTOM OF THE VALLEY. It's most commonly used when shingling an open valley and required for shakes or wooden shingles. (See page 481.) Install the flashing from the bottom of the roof up, centering the peak over the valley. Attach the flashing by nailing along, but not through, the edges. For extra protection, cover the nail with plastic-based asphalt roofing cement. Trim the edge of the flashing flush with the eaves at the bottom of the roof. When you shingle, trim the shingles to end short of the peak in the flashing.

Installing flashing around a chimney

Every chimney is different, which makes flashing one a bit of a custom job. Chimneys generally are not attached to the house framing so that the inevitable shifts and settling will not damage them. Consequently, the chimney area is a prime place for leaks and water damage. Protecting the chimney requires a two-part flashing solution.

First, attach base and step flashing to the roof around the entire base. Then mortar counterflashing (sometimes called cap flashing) into the chimney itself to protect the base flashing and still allow for movement. Counterflashing must be installed around the entire chimney and overlap at least 3 inches.

If your chimney is not mounted on the peak, install a "cricket" at the high end of the chimney to keep water flowing down and debris from gathering. A cricket is simply a small roof constructed of two triangles of exterior-grade plywood and mounted to the roof deck, creating a small peak. It is flashed and shingled in the same manner as the rest of the roof.

1 USE A PRY BAR TO REMOVE THE OLD FLASHING (SAVE IT TO USE FOR PATTERNS). Flashing a chimney involves installing base flashing, step flashing up the sides of the chimney, top flashing, and counter flashing (cap flashing) over the top of the step flashing. First, remove all the old flashing around the chimney, then continue shingling and flashing around the chimney, working up the roof. Wear gloves when working with flashing; the edges are sharp.

2 INSTALL THE CRICKET AT THE TOP SIDE OF THE CHIMNEY BEFORE LAYING UNDERLAYMENT AND SHINGLES. Use the existing cricket if possible. If not, make a new one to fit on the ridge side of the chimney. The edges of the cricket should extend to the edges of the chimney so that water and debris will flow cleanly around it. The peak of the cricket should be at least 6 to 8 inches from the deck and should be supported by 2×4 or 2×6 framing underneath. Apply underlayment and staple in place. (See inset.)

3 CUT A PIECE OF FLASHING TO GO AROUND THE BOTTOM OF THE CHIMNEY out of 10- or 12-inch galvanized metal. If you can, use the old piece as a pattern. It should wrap around the corners of the chimney as shown. Bend it so it will cover both the chimney and the roof, then cut in from the edges so that you can wrap the single piece around the chimney. Nail it to the roof with one nail at each edge and cement it to the chimney with roofing cement.

4 CONTINUE SHINGLING AND FLASHING AROUND THE CHIMNEY. Before you install the final shingle next to the chimney, insert a piece of 5"×7" step flashing. Put roofing cement on the chimney half and align the first piece of the flashing with the bottom edge of the first row of chimney shingles. Nail it to the roof with two nails, one at the top and one at the bottom. Cover with roofing cement, nail the final shingle in place. Continue shingling, lining up the bottom of the flashing with the bottom of the shingle to create the 2-inch overlap.

Installing flashing around a chimney (continued)

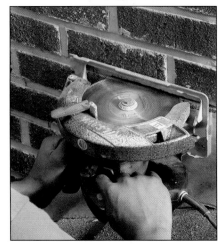

5 **YOU MAY BE ABLE TO USE THE EXISTING GROOVES IN THE CHIMNEY FOR COUNTERFLASHING.** If not, cut along a mortar joint using a circular saw with a masonry blade to make a groove at least 1½ inches deep to hold the counter flashing.

6 **INSTALL COUNTERFLASHING.** If possible, use the old piece of counterflashing as a pattern. If you cut a new groove, make a cardboard template. The flashing should overlap at least 3 inches. Cut the flashing with tin snips. Bend the edge and put it in the groove. Set it with pre-mixed mortar in a caulking gun. (See inset.) Bend the counterflashing down to cover the step flashing.

7 **SHINGLE AND FLASH THE CRICKET.** After installing the underlayment continue shingling up the roof, covering the peak of the cricket as you would the peak of the roof. Finish with hip shingles and add flashing, starting at the peak of the cricket and working down to the base of the chimney. Install the counter flashing around the entire chimney as described next.

Cut the counterflashing in one piece to follow the pitch of the cricket.

8 **CUT NEW COUNTERFLASHING FOR THE CRICKET.** Use the old piece of counterflashing as a pattern to make the new one, if possible. If you cut a new groove, make a cardboard template. Cut out the new flashing with tin snips, put it in the groove, and seal with mortar. Bend the counterflashing into place.

Bending and shaping rolled flashing

CUT AND BEND SMALL PIECES OF FLASHING, SUCH AS CHIMNEY FLASHING, ON A FLAT SURFACE WITH A STRAIGHT EDGE. A sawhorse or workbench works well. Sometimes you can form the piece freehand, as shown here. Other times, it may help to put in a row of nails as a stop. Position the nails to hold the piece so that the bend is directly over the straight edge. Clamp the piece to be bent in 2×4s or 2×6s for long bends.

USE OLD FLASHING AS A TEMPLATE FOR REPLACEMENT FLASHING. This is especially useful for reproducing complicated flashing, such as chimney flashing. Flatten out the old piece, trace around it with a grease pencil or marker, and cut along the lines with tin snips.

INSTALLING FLASHING
Installing flashing around vent pipes

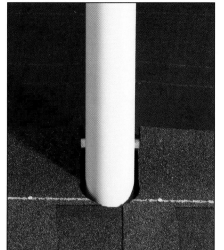

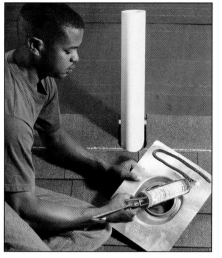

1 VENT PIPE FLASHING GOES ON OVER THE SHINGLES INSTEAD OF SITTING ON THE UNDERLAYMENT. Shingle as explained on page 478 until you get to the first shingle that meets the vent pipe. Cut a notch in a shingle, fit it over the pipe, and set the entire shingle in plastic-based asphalt roofing cement.

2 BUY A PREFORMED FLASHING FLANGE DESIGNED TO FIT AROUND THE VENT PIPE. Position it so it lies flat on the roof and mark the top of the flange on the underlayment with a pencil. Apply plastic-based asphalt roofing cement to the flange bottom and along the pencil line on the underlayment. Slip the flange over the pipe and press it in place.

3 CONTINUE LAYING SHINGLES, CUTTING THEM TO FIT AROUND THE PIPE and setting them in plastic-based asphalt roofing cement (see inset). Apply the shingles to cover the upper edge of the flashing, but leave the lower edge exposed so that water and debris run off the surface.

INSTALLING FLASHING
Installing step flashing around a dormer

THIS DORMER HAS YET TO BE SIDED. If working on a dormer that already has siding, remove the lowest piece. Apply roofing cement to the side of the dormer. Set the flashing in the cement. Work your way up the roof, always positioning the upper piece so that it overlaps the piece of flashing below.

1 FLASH AROUND A DORMER AS YOU'RE SHINGLING IT. Shingle as you normally would, bringing the shingles to a point just below the dormer. Lift the existing counterflashing and slip new flashing underneath it. **NAIL THE LOWER EDGE OF THE FLASHING IN PLACE.** This can be done with either a pneumatic nailer or with a regular hammer and nails.

2 COVER THE FLASHING ALONG THE FRONT OF THE DORMER WITH SHINGLES. Apply roofing cement along the lower edge of the flashing. Trim the shingles to fit and set them in the cement. **STEP-FLASH THE SIDES** starting at the bottom of the dormer and working up the roof. (See Installing Flashing Around a Chimney on page 475.)

ROOFING WITH ASPHALT SHINGLES

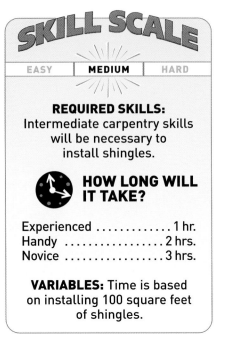

STUFF YOU'LL NEED

✔ **MATERIALS:**
Shingles, roofing nails, plastic-based asphalt roofing cement, roofing felt

✔ **TOOLS:**
Roofing knife, tape measure, chalk line, claw hammer, roofing hammer, framing square, caulking gun, pneumatic nailer

CLOSER LOOK

THREE-TAB VS. ARCHITECTURAL SHINGLES
Three-tab shingles are the shingles that most of us grew up with; two slots cut through the colored part of the shingle divide it into thirds. The shingles in this project are *architectural* shingles, which install the same way but look different and last a little longer. Instead of slots, they get texture from tabs that are laminated to a solid shingle. The extra thickness helps give the shingle its longer life.

Shingling begins, not surprisingly, with something called a starter strip, which is immediately covered up completely by the first course of shingles. If you look at a piece of shingling, you'll see why. Each shingle is 36 inches long and 12 inches wide. At the lower end are three tabs coated with a layer of fine stone. Just above the tabs are dabs of black sealant, which softens in warm weather and binds the layers of shingles together. Between the tabs is a space about ⅜ inch wide. If it weren't for the starter strip, water would flow down through these gaps and onto the tar paper, which would quickly wear out. Having a starter strip underneath the first course solves the problem.

Years ago the starter strip was simply a row of shingles installed with the tabs facing the peak of the roof. This method is no longer used.

These days the general opinion is that you should cut the tabs off the starter strip and throw them out. Put the rest of the shingle on with the cut edge overlapping the eaves and gutter apron. While anyone can see that this is a lot more work, it's less obvious that this results in a better roof. The cutting brings the self-sealing adhesive closer to the lower edge of the roof. When you put the first course over the starter strip, the adhesive helps seal the lower edge of the roof.

The roof shown here is a hipped roof. The process is exactly the same on a more traditional shed roof except that on a hipped roof the end shingle is trimmed at an angle. On a shed roof, the end shingles are cut in a straight line.

ROOFING WITH ASPHALT SHINGLES
Asphalt shingle basics

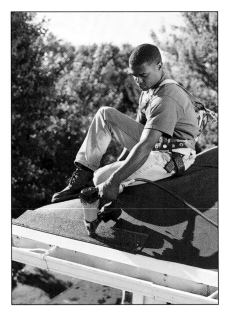

① **BEGIN A STARTER STRIP BY CUTTING THE TABS OFF A SHINGLE WITH A ROOFING KNIFE;** then cut 6 inches off one end. Position the trimmed shingle on the roof with the cut edges overlapping the rake (edge) and eave (bottom) by ½ to ¾ inch. Nail the shingle on the roof with four galvanized roofing nails, positioned 3 to 4 inches from the eaves. (See Step 7, page 473.)

② **CUT THE TABS OFF ANOTHER SHINGLE AND PUT THE FULL LENGTH ON THE ROOF.** Butt it against the first shingle and nail it in place with galvanized roofing nails spaced 12 inches apart. Continue cutting and installing along the roof until you have installed the starter strip from one side to the other.

EXTERIOR

3 PUT A SHINGLE ON THE ROOF SO THAT THE LOWER EDGE OVERLAPS THE GUTTER APRON at the eaves no more than ¾ inch. (As shown in Step 4.) Measure from the edge of the roof to the top of the shingle and snap a chalk line this distance from the edge along the entire roof. Do not use red chalk because red pigment will stain roofing materials.

4 APPLY THE FIRST SHINGLE OF THE FIRST COURSE. Begin at the edge and start with a full shingle. Position the shingle to overhang the eaves and rake edges by ¾ inch. Nail the shingle in place with four nails.

5 ONCE THE FIRST SHINGLE IS ON, MOVE TO THE FIRST SHINGLE OF THE SECOND COURSE. This helps align the shingles properly and means you don't have to move across the roof for every shingle. Cut 6 inches off the end of a shingle. Align the bottom edge of the shingle with the top of the cutouts in the first shingle. Nail it in place according to the manufacturer's directions.

6 WITH TWO SHINGLES IN PLACE, START THE THIRD COURSE. Cut 12 inches off the end of a shingle. Align the edge with the edge of the roof, and align the bottom with the top of the cutouts in the shingle below. Nail it in place. Continue up the roof to the sixth course, trimming each shingle to be 6 inches narrower than the one below it. (After the sixth course, you will apply a full-length shingle along the edge of the roof.)

7 RETURN TO THE LOWER EDGE OF THE ROOF to reach the space next to the first shingle you installed. Butt a full-length shingle next to it and nail it in place.

8 WORK YOUR WAY UP THE ROOF, NAILING A SINGLE FULL-LENGTH SHINGLE NEXT TO EACH OF THE SHINGLES ALREADY IN PLACE. After you've completed the sixth course, nail a full-length shingle in place to start the seventh course. Measure and snap a chalk line across the top to make sure the row is straight. Snap a line every seven rows so that you can correct any errors before they get too serious.

Asphalt shingle basics *(continued)*

9 **CONTINUE WORKING DIAGONALLY UP AND ACROSS THE ROOF.** All the shingles are full-length, except those applied near the edge. Trim these shingles so that each is 6 inches narrower than the one below. When the rake shingle is only 6 inches wide, start the pattern over, applying a full shingle above it.

10 **WHEN YOU REACH THE FAR EDGE OF THE ROOF, TRIM THE SHINGLES.** On a straight-edged roof, trim the shingles so that they are just long enough to overlap the rake by no more than ¾ inch. On a roof like the one shown here, trim them using a utility knife. Hooked blades will make cutting easier.

11 **FINISH SHINGLING ALL THE WAY UP TO THE RIDGE, ADDING FLASHING AS NEEDED.** When you reach the top, trim the shingle flush with the ridge. When you shingle the other side of the ridge, overlap the shingle on the ridge and nail it in place.

Some companies provide premade ridge caps. Check to see if they're available for the shingles you're installing.

Shingling hips and ridges

Sealing tab

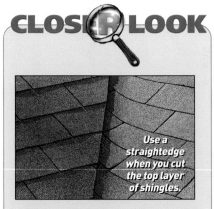

1 **CUT 12-INCH-SQUARE HIP CAPS FROM REGULAR SHINGLES.** Then trim them further so that they taper at one end to 10 inches. Snap a chalk line parallel to the hip and 6 inches away from it on each side of the ridge. Attach each side of each cap with one roofing nail, 1 inch from the edge, just above the sealing tab. Overlap the caps by 1 inch.

2 **WHEN TWO HIPS MEET, CUT A 4-INCH V OUT OF THE MIDDLE OF A HIP SHINGLE.** Nail it in place and cover the nailheads with roofing cement. Shingle ridges as you would hips, working from each end toward the middle. **AT THE MIDPOINT OF THE RIDGE, BUTT THE NEIGHBORING RIDGE CAPS.** Cut 1 inch off the narrow end of the final cap shingle, and nail over the butted caps. Cover nailheads with roofing cement.

CLOSER LOOK

Use a straightedge when you cut the top layer of shingles.

LAYING A CLOSED CUT VALLEY
Lay a closed cut valley over either metal roll flashing or heavy-duty valley liner, as described on page 474. Then lay the shingles to overlap, and cut back the upper layer to create a roof that looks like the one above. Offset the cut 2 inches from the center of the valley so that the bulk of the water won't run directly over the seam, and snap a chalk line from top to bottom for the trim. Insert a piece of flashing between the shingles when you trim the top to avoid cutting the layer underneath.

Laying a valley with architectural shingles

1 A VALLEY MADE WITH ARCHITECTURAL SHINGLES BEGINS LIKE ONE MADE WITH 3-TAB SHINGLES. Start on one side of the valley and shingle normally. Continue shingling well across the valley, but avoid driving nails into the flashing below.

2 LINE THE VALLEY WITH A ROW OF SHINGLES. Lay out the position by snapping a chalk line that runs from the top to the bottom of the valley, positioned so that it is about 2 inches above the low point of the valley. Lay a row of shingles up the valley with the bottom edge of the shingle on the chalk line.

3 LAY SHINGLES FOR THE ADJOINING ROOF STARTING AT THE VALLEY. Position the first shingle of each row so that its lower corner lines up with the lower edge of the shingles going up the valley. Lay the row, and then come back to the valley and lay the next row the same way. Continue to the top of the dormer. The completed valley of shingles is shown in the inset above.

Laying a metal open valley

A METAL OPEN VALLEY IS WIDER AT THE BOTTOM THAN AT THE TOP BECAUSE IT CHANNELS MORE WATER AT THE BOTTOM OF THE ROOF. The heart of the valley is 20-inch-wide noncorroding prefab metal flashing. Make sure that you don't drive any nails through the flashing as you lay the roof.

1 COVER THE VALLEY WITH AN ICE-DAM BARRIER, WORKING FROM THE BOTTOM OF THE ROOF UP and overlapping the ends by 6 inches if you use more than one piece. Center metal flashing in the valley and drive nails along the edges to hold it. (See inset.) Strike two chalk lines to create a space 6 inches wide (3 inches on each side of the center of the flashing) at the peak and tapering $\frac{1}{8}$ inch per foot to the eave of the valley on each side.

2 SHINGLE TO THE EDGE OF THE LINE. Trim the last shingle of the bottom row so that it follows the chalk line. Clip off the top corner. Spread roofing cement from the outer edge of the flashing up to the chalk line (see inset), press the shingle into position, then nail it in place. Nail the ice-dam barrier, avoiding the metal. Work your way up the roof, following the standard roofing pattern.

EXTERIOR

Roofing a dormer

1 **SHINGLE ALONG THE ROOF IN NORMAL PATTERN, FLASHING AROUND THE DORMER** and butting shingles against it as you go. For more information, see Installing Step Flashing Around a Dormer, page 477. Snap a chalk line to lay out the first full row of shingles that will cross the roof above the dormer. Apply a row of shingles along this line.

2 **SHINGLE ONE OF THE SIDE ROOFS THAT FORMS THE DORMER.** Start at the bottom and work your way up as if it were a section of the regular roof. Start near the main roof, and shingle it and the valley from the bottom up. (For more information on valleys, see pages 474 and 481.) If the dormer has three roofs like this one, stop the shingles when they touch the corner formed by the front roof. If the dormer has two roofs, shingle to the end and trim as you would on the main roof.

3 **SHINGLE THE OTHER SIDE ROOF.** Use the same technique as in Step 2 but continue shingling so that the shingle overlaps the front roof, if any, and the ridge. Fold the shingles over and nail them in place.

4 **IF THE DORMER HAS A FRONT ROOF, SHINGLE IT FROM THE BOTTOM UP.** Shingle over any shingles from the second side roof (on the right in this photo). Wrap the shingles around onto the first side roof (on the left in the photo). When you have run courses up the peak to the ridge install cap shingles to cover the hips and top of the dormer. Cap shingles are single tabs (see inset).

5 **CUT AND INSTALL THE CAP SHINGLES.** Cut a group of shingles into single tabs. starting at the front of the dormer, wrap a tab over the peak and nail it as shown. Put a second tab over the first so that it covers half the tab. Nail it in place and continue working your way back to the main roof. Tuck the last single tab under the row that you installed in Step 1. If the dormer has a front roof, cover the ridges on each side of it with single tabs and then cover the peak.

6 **MAKE SURE THE ROWS ON ONE SIDE OF THE DORMER ALIGN WITH THOSE ON THE OTHER.** Start on the finished section of the main roof and measure the distance from the row you installed in Step 1 to the row you want to install. Transfer the measurement to the unfinished side of the roof, as shown here, and snap a chalk line. Lay a row along the line and repeat until you reach the row from which you're measuring.

EXTERIOR

Reroofing over an existing roof

SKILL SCALE

EASY	MEDIUM	HARD

REQUIRED SKILLS:
Intermediate carpentry skills will be necessary to install shingles.

🕐 HOW LONG WILL IT TAKE?

Experienced .... 1 hr.
Handy .... 2 hrs.
Novice .... 3 hrs.

VARIABLES: Time is based on installing 100 square feet of shingles.

Lucky you. If you're reading this, your roof currently has only one or two layers of shingles and they are worn, but basically sound and in good repair.

Reroofing differs only slightly from installing a new roof. Think about it: The underlying surface is not smooth. It is, in fact, shingled. The successive courses of shingles are stacked on top of each other, like flat little stairs. Another stairlike layer on top would make for a somewhat ragged roof.

Fortunately, the solution is simple: Fill in the first step. Cut shingles lengthwise, making them just wide enough to cover the bottom row of tabs on the existing roof, and nail them over the tabs. This fills in the first step. From here on, it's smooth sailing. Shingle as you would a regular roof. Each new shingle fills in the step for the shingle that follows.

Make sure the nails are long enough to go at least ¾ inch into the roofing deck.

WORK SMARTER

THREE-TAB SHINGLES
Shingles applied over an old roof don't last as long as those applied over a roof from which the existing shingles have been removed. That's one reason the shingles shown here are 3-tab instead of thicker, longer-lasting, and more expensive architectural shingles. If you're going to buy the best, strip off the old roof first. If you're going to roof over the existing roof, you'll still get a solid roof, but the shingles won't last quite as long as advertised.

If your home is the same age as your neighbor's and you see your neighbor roofing, take a second and inspect your own roof.

1 TRIM ENOUGH OFF THE TOP EDGE OF THE STARTER SHINGLES SO THAT EACH SHINGLE FITS PERFECTLY OVER THE TABS OF THE EXISTING FIRST COURSE. Then cut 6 inches off the *end* of the first shingle so that ends won't align with those of the existing shingles. Nail the starter shingles in place along the entire bottom of the roof. **COVER THE STARTER SHINGLES WITH FULL-WIDTH SHINGLES,** positioning them so that they hang no more than ¾ inch over the edge of the roof or gutter apron.

2 BUTT SUCCESSIVE COURSES AGAINST THE BOTTOM OF EXISTING COURSES. Apply the remaining shingles as you would during a new installation (see pages 478–482). Remove damaged flashing as you install shingles and replace it with new flashing, shimming it to the proper height with shingles. Seal seams around flashing with roofing cement.

3 TEAR OFF OLD HIP AND RIDGE CAPS AS YOU APPROACH THE TOP OF THE ROOF. Waiting to remove the old hips and ridges is added protection in case it rains. Replace hip and ridge caps with new shingles after all other shingling has been completed.

Installing roll roofing

Roll roofing is commonly used for garages, outbuildings, storage sheds, and lean-tos that have more gradual roof pitches. It is normally sold in rolls. Flattened out in precut strips of 18 feet or less, it is fairly easy to install by yourself. Roll roofing is generally made of the same material as asphalt shingles except that you can cut it into strips according to your needs.

Generally roll roofing is installed as shown in this project because it is more resistant to wind damage. Another method is to install roll roofing is to overlap half of each preceding course with each subsequent course, nail the top edge of each course, and cement the remaining edges. This results in a more appealing roof because there are no exposed nails covered with roof cement, but depending on wind conditions, it can be less durable.

(see pages 472–473)

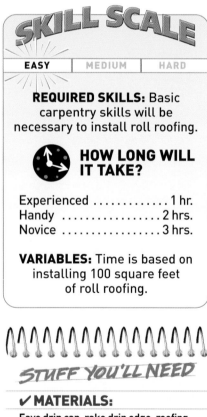

SKILL SCALE

EASY	MEDIUM	HARD

REQUIRED SKILLS: Basic carpentry skills will be necessary to install roll roofing.

HOW LONG WILL IT TAKE?

Experienced	1 hr.
Handy	2 hrs.
Novice	3 hrs.

VARIABLES: Time is based on installing 100 square feet of roll roofing.

STUFF YOU'LL NEED

✔ **MATERIALS:**
Eave drip cap, rake drip edge, roofing nails, lap cement, roof cement

✔ **TOOLS:**
Broom, roofing knife, tape measure, chalk line, hammer or nail gun, trowel, straightedge (for trimming)

EXTERIOR

1 SWEEP THE ROOF DECK CLEAN AND INSTALL GUTTER APRON, RAKE DRIP EDGE, AND UNDERLAYMENT (see pages 472–473). Unroll the roofing material on the ground and let it flatten. Cut a full-width strip long enough to overlap the eave and rakes by about ⅜ inch. Reroll the material and take it to the roof.

2 TROWEL ROOFING CEMENT ONTO THE UNDERLAYMENT. Apply the layer no more than ⅛ inch thick. Thicker layers can cause the roof to blister.

3 PUT THE ROLL ROOFING IN PLACE, ENSURING THAT IT COVERS THE DRIP CAP. Walk along the roofing material to seat it firmly in the roofing cement.

Roofing cement is messy and sticks permanently to clothes. To save your clothes, buy a disposable work suit and toss it when you're done.

4 DRIVE NAILS ALONG THE EAVES AND RAKE EDGES EVERY 3 INCHES. Use hot-dipped galvanized roofing nails long enough to penetrate the deck ¾ inch. On a deck ½ inch thick, use nails long enough to go through the deck and extend ¼ inch beyond it. Drive the nails about 1 inch from the edges, but stagger them slightly to avoid splitting the wood below.

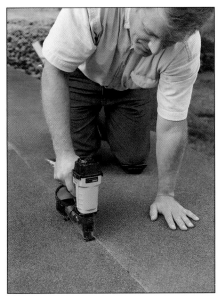

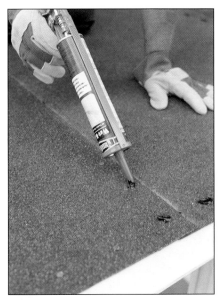

5 **THE NEXT COURSE OVERLAPS THE FIRST BY 2 INCHES.** Snap a chalk guideline marking both the upper and lower edges of the course. Trowel roof cement onto this area and unroll the roofing into it. Seat by walking along the roofing as before. Nail the top edge with nails spaced approximately 18 inches apart.

6 **NAIL THE LOWER EDGE AND ENDS OF THE STRIP, DRIVING THE NAILS ON 3-INCH CENTERS.** Stagger the nails slightly, placing them at least ¾ inch above the seam. Apply roofing cement, lay subsequent courses, and nail up to the top of the roof.

7 **SEAL THE NAIL HOLES BY COVERING THEM WITH ROOFING CEMENT.** A roof cement caulk, such as that shown here, works well and can be applied with a caulk gun.

REPAIRING A ROLLED ROOF

8 **IF A PIECE OF ROOFING IS TOO SHORT, APPLY A SECOND PIECE THAT OVERLAPS THE ENDS OF THE FIRST BY AT LEAST 6 INCHES.** Apply roofing cement to the entire overlap and push the top piece into the one below. Drive a row of nails spaced 4 inches apart through both layers; drive a second row through both layers spaced 4 inches from the first.

FOR SMALL HOLES OR PUNCTURES, clean out the damaged area and fill it with roof sealer or roof tar.

FOR LARGER HOLES, CUT OUT THE DAMAGED AREA AND REPLACE IT WITH A SECTION OF ROOFING MATERIAL. Replace the underlayment too if it's damaged. Overlap the existing roof by 2 inches on the top and bottom and 6 inches on the edges. Cement and nail as you would when applying new roofing material.

GAS, OIL, OR ELECTRIC: WHICH WAY TO GO? Each type of heat has its pros and cons. Gas heat proponents point out that gas burns more cleanly and that it has historically been less expensive than oil or electricity. The oil heat fan club replies that oil burns 400 degrees hotter than gas, giving you more heat faster, and that new, high-tech oil furnaces burn as cleanly and efficiently as gas.

Radiant electrical heat is the most expensive of the three to run, but it installs quickly in additions and renovations and doesn't require the large initial investment of a gas or oil furnace. An air-source heat pump is relatively inefficient at heating compared to other systems but is a good source of summer air-conditioning.

Ground-source heat pumps take their heat from well or lake water that is generally warmer than the outdoor air. Such pumps are extremely efficient but more expensive to install.

If your furnace is working, the cost of changing to another fuel source wipes out any savings. If you need a new furnace, the most economical and best heat source varies from region to region. Talk to your gas, oil, and electric companies. Ask about cost, maintenance, and reliability of fuel delivery. Also ask about the cost of getting oil tanks, running new gas lines or similar needs. And make sure you inquire about the cost of getting rid of the old furnace and ducting.

SECTION 12 PROJECTS

REAL-WORLD SITUATIONS

RUNNING HOT AND COLD

When making heating and cooling decisions there are two considerations: first, the source—oil, gas, or electric; second, the delivery system—forced air or radiant (including radiators and baseboard heaters). Because either delivery system can have any source, we'll look at factors one at a time: first oil, then gas, followed by forced air, hot water, and, finally, a heat pump.

Once you've read about furnaces, you'll learn how to do routine furnace maintenance. Most people avoid maintenance, but it's something you must do. Cleaning alone will prevent many future problems.

On oil furnaces, maintenance is often covered by a service contract you have with the supplier. Do the jobs you're comfortable with, but keep the contract. Some of the services it provides for are less routine, and some of them create a huge mess if you lack the proper equipment. While gas suppliers usually don't offer service contracts, the routine work is simple and clean enough that you should be comfortable with giving it a try.

In addition to learning about furnace repair and maintenance, you'll learn how to install a window air-conditioner, an evaporative cooler, a new heat vent, auxiliary gas and electric heaters, and a hot-water baseboard heater.

Putting in a furnace or replacing an existing one requires experience in determining the right-sized unit, matching it to the existing venting, putting in new vents, and troubleshooting the air flow. Hire a professional.

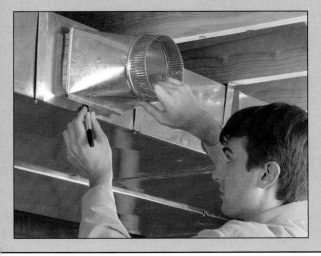

How an oil furnace works

O n a modern oil furnace, when the furnace starts, a pump draws oil through a filter and forces it inside the firing assembly. There the oil is pumped through a nozzle, creating an oil spray. A transformer on top of the assembly provides power to an electrode that sparks and ignites the oil spray. One of two systems ensures that the oil has ignited—an electric eye senses the flame, or a sensor in the chimney notes a rise in temperature. If the sensors detect nothing, the furnace shuts down.

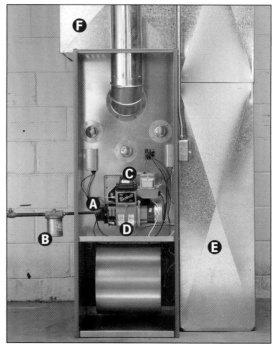

Ⓐ Oil pump

Ⓑ Filter

Ⓒ Firing assembly

Ⓓ Transformer

Ⓔ Cold-air return

Ⓕ Plenum

How a gas furnace works

O n a modern gas furnace, when the temperature falls below the one the thermostat is set to, a call for heat goes to the furnace, which turns on the igniter. The igniter is usually what's called a hot surface igniter, a piece of metal that glows bright red when electricity is fed to it. After about 20 seconds, the igniter is warm enough to open a valve, letting gas flow into the furnace. The gas flows through a pipe called a manifold and then into tubelike burners attached to it. Each burner has an adjustable opening, called an air port, that mixes air with the gas to control how efficiently the gas burns. The burner ends inside a firebox, which heats up to provide heat for the house. The heat is distributed through either a forced-air or hot-water system (discussed later in the chapter). When the house reaches its set temperature, the thermostat cuts off the gas. The fire goes out until the thermostat calls for more heat. Older furnaces have a constantly burning pilot light instead of a hot surface igniter. On these a thermocouple monitors the heat created by the pilot. If the pilot goes out, the thermocouple notices a drop in temperature and shuts off the flow of gas.

If natural gas isn't piped to your home, you can use propane, or bottle gas, instead, though you'll need to change the nozzle in the burner to do so. Talk to your propane dealer to see what's involved in having a bottle-gas system installed.

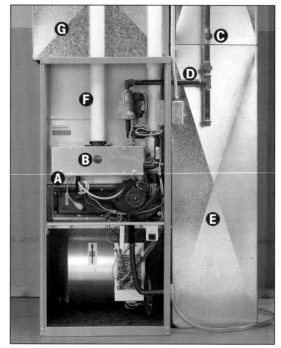

Ⓐ Igniter

Ⓑ Observation window

Ⓒ Gas shutoff valve

Ⓓ Gas line

Ⓔ Cold-air return

Ⓕ Vent pipe

Ⓖ Plenum

How a forced-air system works

I f air vents deliver heat to the rooms in your house, you have a forced-air system. Oil or gas is heating up inside the furnace, and a small fan is sending the air throughout the house. In addition to the fan, you'll want to understand a few important controls.

Once the thermostat hanging on your wall tells the furnace to send heat, the furnace starts a fire in the firebox. Before the heat reaches you, two more controls must do their jobs.

The first is the blower relay, which turns the fan off and on. The thermostat, operating at 24 volts, is connected to one side of the relay. The fan, connected to the other side, operates at 110 volts. With the help of the relay, the 24-volt thermostat starts (and later stops) the 110-volt blower.

Meanwhile, the fan-and-limit control is monitoring the heat of the air as produced by the flame. The fan-and-limit control prevents the fan from starting until the firebox reaches a prescribed temperature usually around 115°F (46°C). When the air does start flowing, the fan pumps it into a large central vent, called a plenum, to which all other vents are attached. The air flows through the house and then returns to the furnace through the cold-air return. Without the return vents, the furnace would heat dank basement air and send it through the house. With no cold-air vent pulling air back out of the rooms, they would become slightly pressurized and resist the new hot air coming out of the vents. So the return vents allow the flow of air that maintains comfort.

When the house warms up and the thermostat turns off the heat, the fan-and-limit control is still monitoring the firebox. When most of the residual heat has been pumped into the house, the control lets the fan turn off. When the thermostat calls for heat again, the cycle starts over.

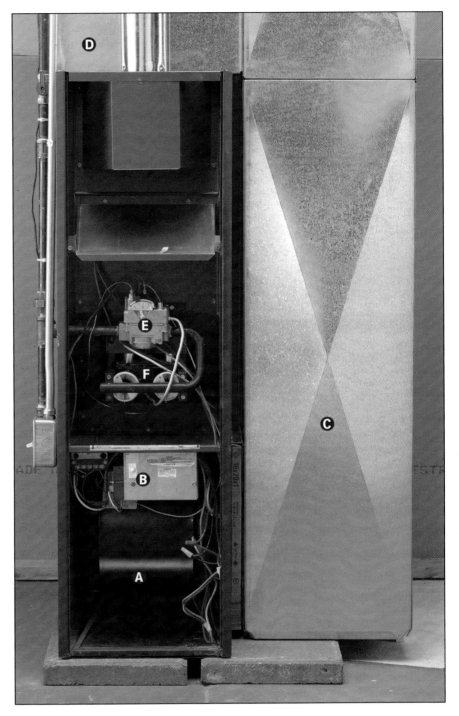

Ⓐ *Fan motor assembly*

Ⓑ *Safety switch*

Ⓒ *Cold-air return*

Ⓓ *Plenum*

Ⓔ *Pilot control*

Ⓕ *Burners*

HEATING, VENTILATION, AND AIR-CONDITIONING

How a hot-water heat system works

How a hot-water heat system works

When the thermostat calls for heat, the furnace starts a fire in the boiler of a hot-water system. While it's heating, a thermometer called an aquastat measures water temperature. When the temperature reaches a set point, the aquastat activates a switch and the circulator starts pumping water through the convectors—baseboard units that have largely replaced radiators.

The circulator is really a three-part device. First is the electrical motor, which provides power once the aquastat turns it on. Second comes the coupling, a clutch that connects the motor to the last element, the pump. If any of the three fails, water won't flow, no matter how hot the boiler gets.

Fortunately, the aquastat is watching the system for this very situation. If the water in the boiler gets too hot, it shuts down the furnace before too much pressure can build up in the boiler.

Because water expands as it warms, some pressure buildup is inevitable. During routine operation—when the pump is working and the water temperature is neither too high nor too low—expanding water flows into an expansion tank. As the water flows into the tank, it compresses the air inside and creates the pressure that the system needs to run once the water has reached its final density.

Ⓐ *Burner*

Ⓑ *Manifold*

Ⓒ *Pilot control*

Ⓓ *Expansion tank*

How a heat pump works

If you've ever stood outside by a window air-conditioner, you've probably noticed that the air coming out of it is hot. If you were to turn the air-conditioner around so that the controls were outside, it would take the heat out of the outside air and pump it inside. Simply stated, a window air-conditioner is a heat pump: It takes the heat from inside the house and pumps it outside.

Unlike a window air-conditioner, the big heat-pump systems that heat your house in the winter and cool it in the summer have a **reversing valve** in them. They comprise two units, one inside the house and one outside.

When you call for heat, refrigerant is pumped outdoors first, where it absorbs whatever heat is there, turning it to a gas in the process. It flows through a compressor, which turns it into a liquid, and the resulting heat is released through coils inside the house to the fan and duct system.

When you call for air-conditioning the process is reversed. The refrigerant absorbs heat inside the house and releases it outside.

Depending on where you live, a heat pump can be based on air source, ground source, or water source. In an air-source pump the outdoor coils are exposed to the air. In a ground-source pump the coils are underground. In a water-source pump the coils are cooled by water from a lake, well, or stream.

Each type has its advantages. Although air source is the least expensive, it is prone to frosting over and, thus, requires a small defrosting unit on the outside coils. Ground source is more efficient because the ground is warmer than the air during the winter. The compressor works less, so it's likely to last longer; however, the installation is considerably more expensive. A water-source pump can have coils on the bottom of a body of water or it can get water from a well. Once the water has done its job, a water-source heat pump sends it back to its source or into the

sewer, depending on local regulations. Because water source has the same advantages and disadvantages as ground source, choosing between the two is usually a matter of finding which one costs less and has a reliable supplier in your area.

Ⓐ *Reversing valve*

Ⓑ *Coils*

Ⓒ *Capacitor*

Ⓓ *Contractor*

Ⓔ *Refrigerant lines*

Window air-conditioner maintenance

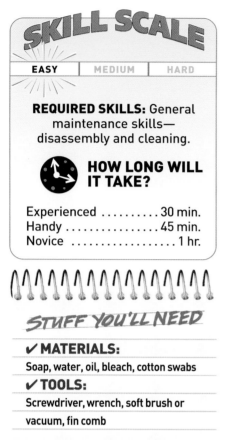

SKILL SCALE

EASY	MEDIUM	HARD

REQUIRED SKILLS: General maintenance skills—disassembly and cleaning.

HOW LONG WILL IT TAKE?

Experienced . . . . 30 min.
Handy . . . . 45 min.
Novice . . . . 1 hr.

STUFF YOU'LL NEED

✔ **MATERIALS:**

Soap, water, oil, bleach, cotton swabs

✔ **TOOLS:**

Screwdriver, wrench, soft brush or vacuum, fin comb

Air-conditioners are basically plug and play: You buy them, put them in the window, plug them in, and turn them on. There's not much more to it than that.

But neatness counts, and when it comes to air-conditioners, cleanliness is next to, well, efficiency. Dirty coils or filters can increase the cost of cooling a room. In some cases, the dirt can keep you from getting the room as cool as you want it. In the worst case, dirt causes ice to form on the coils, reducing efficiency to the point where you'll be paying good money to keep the room just as hot as it was.

As you might suspect, cleaning involves little more than soap and water. Begin by removing the air-conditioner from the window. Check the owner's manual to see how much disassembly you'll have to do to get to the filter, the front coils, and the rear coils. If you don't have the manual, remove the front of the unit to get started, and unscrew or unsnap other parts as necessary.

Once you have access to the guts, vacuum, brush, or wash as directed below. If the motor requires it, squirt in a little oil.

Proper maintenance, even if it's just cleaning, can prolong the life of your air-conditioner. No matter what you do, however, it eventually may break down. The problem can be as simple as a faulty thermostat or as complicated as a broken compressor. Diagnosis can be difficult, and many repairs require someone licensed to recycle ozone-damaging refrigerant. If a problem crops up that maintenance won't solve, check the Yellow Pages for a reputable repair person.

In colder climates, cover the air-conditioner during the winter. Better yet, remove it entirely during the months it goes unused.

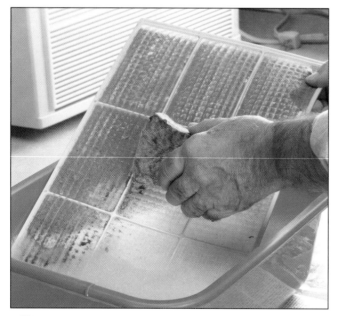

1 **CLEAN THE AIR FILTER.** This is a removable sponge sheet about ⅛ inch thick. On some air-conditioners you can remove a panel to get to it. On others you'll have to remove the entire front of the air-conditioner. Remove the filter; wash it in soap and water. Let it dry and then reinstall it.

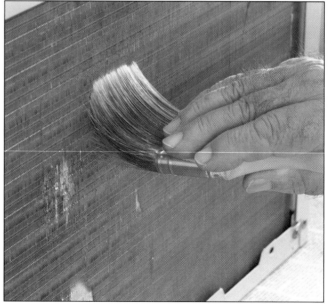

2 **CLEAN THE EXTERIOR FINS ONCE A YEAR.** The fins are on the back side of the air-conditioner and may be covered by a protective grill. Dirt can plug the openings enough to seriously affect the ability of the fins to dissipate the heat the air-conditioner expels from inside the house. Remove the protective grill and either brush the fins gently with a soft brush—a clean paintbrush works well—or vacuum to remove the dirt.

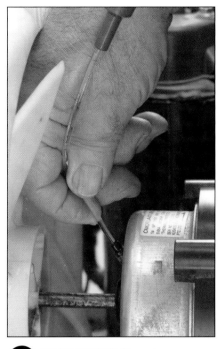

③ STRAIGHTEN THE FINS. If the fins are bent they restrict airflow and fail to dissipate heat properly. Straighten them with a fin comb, available at home centers or from heating and air-conditioning suppliers. Put the comb between an undamaged section of fins and comb gently through damaged fins to straighten them.

④ OIL THE MOTOR. Many air-conditioner fan motors contain oil ports. If yours does, oil the motor twice a year: once before the season starts and once when it ends for the year. Some motors are sealed at the factory and need no oil.

⑤ VACUUM THE PARTS AND CLEAN THE TRAY. A shallow tray at the bottom of the unit collects water that condenses on the coils. Remove the tray and wash it thoroughly in a solution of half water and half bleach.

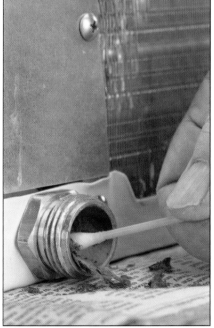

⑥ CLEAN THE DRAIN HOLE. The water in the tray drains through a hole in the tray and out a hose somewhere in the back of the unit. Use a cotton swab or a piece of dowel to clean both the hole and the stem.

BUYER'S GUIDE

BE COOL

When you buy an air-conditioner, get the right size. A bigger air-conditioner isn't necessarily better: It costs more to buy, costs more to run, and cools the room unevenly.

The output of an air-conditioner is measured in British thermal units, or Btus. Your air-conditioner needs to produce about 20 to 30 Btus per square foot of a room. The Department of Energy says you'd need a 5,000 Btu air-conditioner for a room with 150 square feet of living space. If the room were a sunny kitchen you might need 9,500

Btus. Check the department's website for more information.

Once you've settled on the size of an air-conditioner, look into its efficiency. Look for an EER—energy efficiency ratio, which is the ratio between cooling power and energy draw—of 10 or higher. New air-conditioners are up to 70 percent more efficient than the old ones. Start by looking for the Energy Star label, an indication that the unit is eco-friendly. Then check the yellow Energy Guide label for the EER.

If you replace or add a window air-conditioner, make sure the electrical circuit has the proper amperage and voltage to handle the unit. Bigger units often require 220-volt service, a separate circuit, and a special receptacle.

Installing a window air-conditioner

N ot long ago installing an air-conditioner was a hard, sweaty, two-person job. In fact, if you still have an old air-conditioner, it may have been more recent—perhaps yesterday.

Whether you're installing a brand-new unit, a hand-me-down, or old faithful, start with the window. Most air-conditioners are designed for double-hung windows. If you have another kind of window, you have two choices, neither of which is desirable: Replace the window or install a through-the-wall air-conditioner. (Replacing windows is covered in Section 8 on page 377. Follow the directions that come with a through-the-wall unit. Also, pages 340–342 provide more information on creating a rough opening.)

Before installing the air-conditioner, make sure the window is sound. Repair any rot and damage. If the paint is peeling, repaint. Ideally, the window you choose should be near the center of the room and shaded from the afternoon sun. If you must choose between one or the other, choose shade.

Put the air-conditioner in a window near an outlet, or install a new outlet. You want it close to the power source because power drops and the temperature rises as electricity runs through an extension cord. Given the power that an air-conditioner draws, using an extension cord can result in a dangerously hot cord driving a sadly underpowered unit.

Older units have a mounting frame supported, perhaps, by a mounting bracket that holds the air-conditioner in the window. Newer air-conditioners are lighter and more efficient. The mounting frame is built-in; and except on heavier units, the mounting bracket has disappeared altogether.

SAFETY ALERT

SECOND STORY
Air-conditioners can be heavy, and their shape makes them awkward to handle. Be especially careful when installing them on upper stories. Have a watcher on the ground below and a helper to hold the unit in the window.

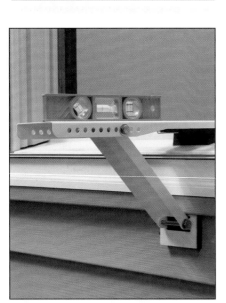

1 INSTALL THE MOUNTING BRACKETS, IF ANY. Heavy and older air-conditioners may have a bracket that screws to the windowsill. Screw it in place using sheet-metal screws on a metal frame and wood screws on a wood or vinyl frame. Put a level across the bracket and sill, and adjust the bracket as needed to level it.

2 PUT THE AIR-CONDITIONER IN THE FRAME OR WINDOW. If there is a frame, move the accordion panels aside and slide the air-conditioner in. If the frame is built-in, open the window a bit wider than necessary to make it easier to put the air-conditioner in place. Close the window to hold it in place.

3 SLIDE THE ACCORDION PANELS BACK IN PLACE SO THAT THEY ARE TIGHT AGAINST THE AIR-CONDITIONER. Secure the mounting frame and panels as directed by the manufacturer. If you're driving screws in a new location, drill pilot holes first, using a bit slightly smaller than the diameter of the screw.

4 **IF THE INSTALLATION KIT THAT CAME WITH YOUR UNIT CONTAINS ANGLE BRACKETS, SCREW THEM TO THE UPPER SASH AS DIRECTED.** The brackets keep the weight of the air-conditioner from forcing the window open. If there aren't any brackets, buy and install ones that are similar to that shown here.

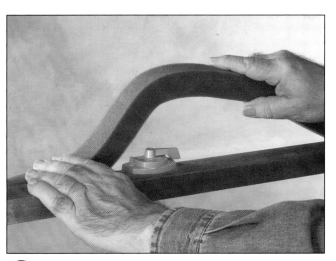

5 **BECAUSE THE LOWER SASH IS PARTIALLY OPEN, THERE IS A LARGE GAP BETWEEN IT AND THE WINDOW.** Fill the gap with the foam weather stripping that came with the unit or buy some at a home improvement center.

Installing an evaporative cooler

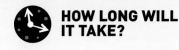
Evaporative coolers, known as swamp coolers, use water, air, and a fan to cool houses in areas with low or no humidity. They work on the same principle as a wet towel: Wrap a wet towel around yourself, and as the water evaporates, it takes with it the heat of your body. Before you know it, you get cold.

An evaporative cooler blows air through a water-soaked pad, cooling it via the wet-towel principle and then blowing it into your house. The drier the surrounding air, the greater the evaporation and the cooler the final product is. Consequently, swamp coolers are more popular in drier climates, such as Arizona, where manufacturers say the cooled air may be as much as 30 degrees cooler than the outside air. On the East Coast, where the air is much more humid, the air produced may be only 10 degrees cooler than the outside air.

Whatever the results, the evaporative cooler has a significant advantage over the refrigerant-powered air-conditioner: It's economical to run. A swamp cooler uses about one-quarter of the electricity an air-conditioner uses.

Whole-house units are mounted on the roof, a job beyond the capability of most homeowners. Installing a window-mounted unit, however, is simple. The actual cooler is a box-shaped unit that hangs outside the window. A cool-air vent extends through the window and, from inside the house, it looks much like a refrigerant air-conditioner.

Installing an evaporative cooler (continued)

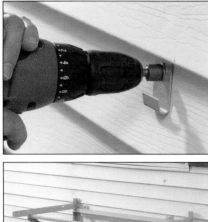

1 **INSTALL THE HANGERS AND SUPPORT ASSEMBLY.** Following manufacturer's instructions, mount the hangers then assemble and install the support brackets. Build up the outside windowsill as directed to support the cool-air vent that goes through the window.

If the cooler is hung from from the top by chains follow the manufacturer's instructions for assembly and installation.

2 **SET THE COOLER ON THE SUPPORT ASSEMBLY.** Put the cooler in the window, resting the vent on the sill. Attach the cooler to the brackets as directed by the manufacturer.

GOOD IDEA

MAINTAINING AN EVAPORATIVE COOLER
Manufacturers recommend routine maintenance three times a year: at the start of the cooling season, at the end of the season, and midway through the season. Maintenance includes oiling the blower shaft and other bearings, checking the belt tension, and checking the water supply lines for leaks. Also clean the water pump by removing and washing it with a mild detergent. (Most pumps are easy to remove.)

In addition, replace the cooling pads at the beginning of and midway through the season. Drain the unit at the end of the season.

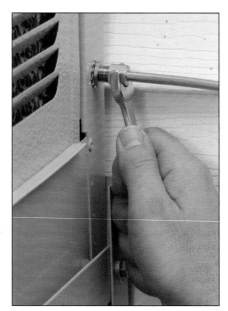

3 **RUN A WATER LINE TO THE COOLER.** Put in a cutoff valve that you can drain in the winter. On slab construction, run the pipe from the cutoff up through the attic and then down the outside wall. If you have a basement, run the pipe through the rim joist and then outside the house to the cooler. The cooler has an overflow drain line that you attach to a hose. Run the hose on the ground, well away from the foundation.

4 **INSTALL THE COOL AIR VENT** that directs air from the unit into the house. Plug in the cord attached to the vent that runs through the window. Use any grounded 120-volt circuit inside the house.

MAINTAINING AN OIL FURNACE

In numerous cases, your oil supplier includes a yearly oil burner tune-up in the price that you pay for oil. If someone else is willing to do the dirty work, before you pick up the screwdriver, pick up the phone.

If you're going to do the work yourself, remember that what you're taking apart is essentially a large campfire. Like a campfire, a furnace is relatively easy to take apart. Getting everything back in exactly the same place, shape, and order, however, requires both skill and caution. The electrodes—which spark to start the fire that warms you—need to be filed to a point. They also need to be spaced the proper distance from each other and from the nozzle that shoots the oil into the furnace. Look over Steps 8 through 10 on page 501 to see how it's done. If it looks like more than you want to tackle, hire a pro for the entire job.

Routine maintenance not only improves the efficiency of your furnace,

it may also correct some problems. Cleaning or replacing the nozzle may cure a pulsating, thumping, or rumbling furnace. A smoky furnace may be caused by a dirty nozzle or a dirty fan, both of which are discussed in this section. If maintenance doesn't solve a problem, call a pro. Smoke, in particular, may indicate a cracked firebox and the presence of deadly carbon monoxide in your home.

STUFF YOU'LL NEED

✔ **MATERIALS:**
Electric-motor oil, pie pan filled with sand or cat litter, paint thinner or kerosene, oil filter, nozzle (depending on furnace), electrodes (if damaged)

✔ **TOOLS:**
Screwdriver, shop vacuum with brush, open-ended wrenches, metal file, toothbrush, tape measure

MAINTAINING AN OIL FURNACE
Replacing the oil filter

1 **THE OIL FILTER KEEPS DIRT FROM ENTERING THE FURNACE FUEL LINE.** It should be replaced once a year as part of a routine furnace tune-up. Start by closing the oil supply valve, which is usually at the bottom of the oil tank. Fill a disposable pie pan about halfway with cat litter, then set it under the filter. Unscrew the bolt on the top of the filter, remove the canister, and let the oil drain into the pan.

2 **INSIDE THE CANISTER IS A DISPOSABLE FILTER CARTRIDGE.** Loosen the bolt on top of the canister and disassemble it. Remove and replace the filter, then remove and replace the gasket on the lip of the filter canister or lid. Reattach the canister.

3 **REPLACING THE FILTER ALLOWED AIR TO ENTER THE FUEL LINE**—air that you must get back out. Loosen the bleeder valve on the filter top by turning it counterclockwise. Reopen the oil supply valve. Air will rush out the bleeder valve as oil begins to flow into the canister. When the air has been purged, oil will begin to come out the bleeder valve. Close it at this point.

HEATING, VENTILATION, AND AIR-CONDITIONING

MAINTAINING AN OIL FURNACE
Cleaning and oiling the fan

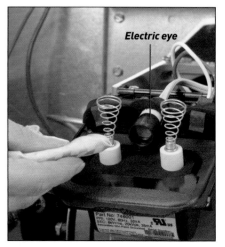

Electric eye

1 LOCATE THE FIRING ASSEMBLY BY FOLLOWING THE OIL LINE INTO THE FURNACE. Nearby you'll find a motor for the firing assembly fan. If it has oil ports, drop in 2 to 5 drops of SAE 10 nondetergent electric-motor oil. If no ports exist, the motor is sealed and needs no oil.

2 CLEAN THE FIRING ASSEMBLY FAN. This fan forces air into the combustion chamber. Dirt on it can keep the burner from getting enough air, resulting in a smoky furnace. To clean the fan, remove the transformer on the top of the firing assembly, usually a matter of loosening a few screws. Put the brush attachment onto a shop vacuum and vacuum the fins on the fan to clean them.

3 CLEAN THE SENSOR. Oil furnaces have an electric eye (above) that senses whether the flame is lit and shuts down the motor if it isn't. If the glass over the sensor is dirty, clean it by wiping it with a clean, dry cloth.

MAINTAINING AN OIL FURNACE
Removing the firing assembly

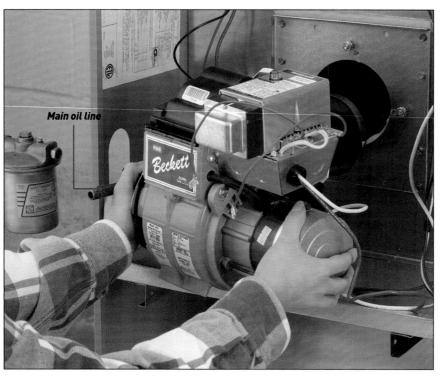

Main oil line

1 REMOVE THE ASSEMBLY. Turn off the oil supply to the firing assembly with the oil cutoff valve. Turn off the furnace at the circuit breaker box. Disconnect the oil line to the pump. Unbolt the unit from the furnace, remove any wires that will impede removal, and pull the unit out. Turn the unit around to expose the pump.

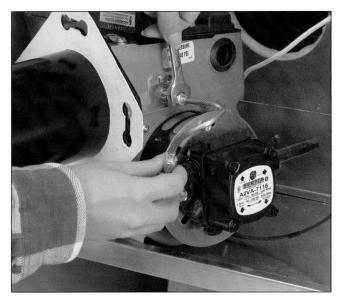

2 DISCONNECT THE COPPER OIL LINE. Remove the copper oil line from the pump and body of the unit with a wrench and set it aside.

Maintain the oil filter and strainer in your furnace as you do in your car.

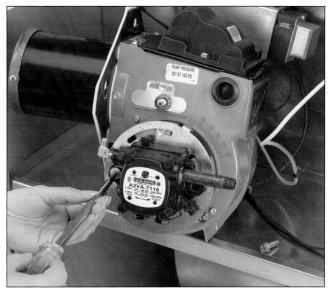

3 REMOVE THE PUMP FROM THE UNIT. The pump is usually attached to the unit with screws. Remove them with a screwdriver and set them aside. Put all the parts you remove in a safe place so that you can easily find them later. Slide the pump carefully out of the assembly.

MAINTAINING AN OIL FURNACE
Cleaning the strainer

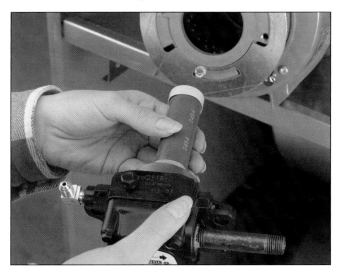

1 THE PUMP STRAINER IS A SECONDARY FILTER INSIDE THE PUMP. Clean it annually; a clog can result in a pulsating flame or no flame at all.

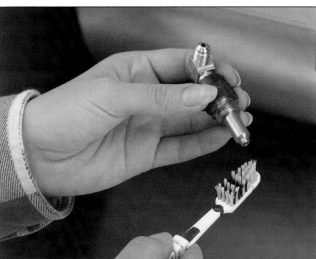

2 REMOVE THE STRAINER AND WASH IT WITH A SOFT BRUSH AND KEROSENE, paint thinner, or clean fuel oil. Replace the gasket and reinstall the strainer.

Maintaining the firing assembly

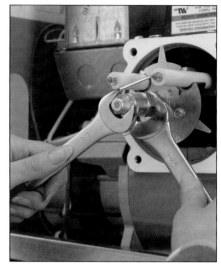

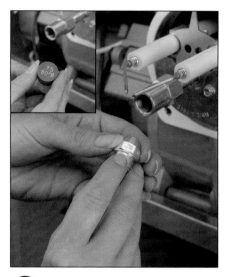

1 **THE FIRING ASSEMBLY IS THE HEART OF THE FURNACE.** A nozzle shoots a fine mist of oil into the combustion chamber, a fan blows air into the chamber, and electrodes produce a spark to start the flame. Remove the oil line that runs from the firing assembly to the pump. Loosen the bolts that hold the assembly in place. Pull the assembly out, twisting as necessary to avoid bumping the electrodes against the rest of the furnace. Remove the housing around the nozzle, if any.

2 **REMOVE THE NOZZLE.** Nozzles are designed to shoot a certain volume of oil per hour in a particular spray pattern. The volume and pattern vary from furnace to furnace. A clogged nozzle can seriously affect furnace performance. To remove the nozzle, put one wrench on the hex nut on the oil line and another on the nozzle. Hold the oil line steady while turning the nozzle to remove it.

3 **INSPECT THE NOZZLE TO FIND OUT THE SIZE AND SPRAY ANGLE,** which are usually stamped on the hex end of the nozzle. If the nozzle is rated less than 1.5 gallons per hour (gph), replace it. The new nozzle container will also indicate the size of the nozzle (see inset). Make sure the new nozzle matches the old.

4 **IF THE NOZZLE IS RATED MORE THAN 1.5 GPH,** you can clean it. First unscrew the strainer, a small basketlike device at the back of the nozzle. Disassemble the nozzle by putting a screwdriver inside and backing out the locknut. Turn the piece on end, allowing the piece inside the nozzle to slide out.

5 **SOAK ALL THE NOZZLE PARTS IN PAINT THINNER.** Brush the nozzle opening with an old toothbrush—a metal brush will damage the nozzle. Clean grooves with a piece of stiff paper. Return the parts to the jar of thinner and let them soak while you check and clean the electrodes.

6 **LOOSEN THE SCREW THAT HOLDS THE ELECTRODES IN PLACE.** The electrodes take power from the transformer and produce a spark to ignite the oil at the beginning of the heating cycle. An electrode consists of a wire encased in a porcelain sleeve. If the sleeve has any cracks, replace it with exactly the same make and model.

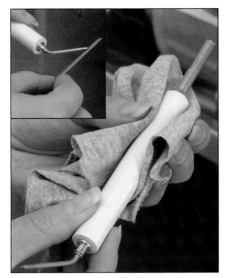

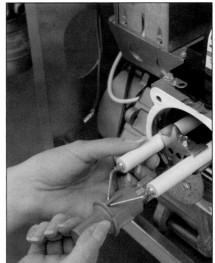

7 **CLEAN THE ELECTRODES.** Wipe the porcelain with a rag and paint thinner. If the sleeves are OK, file the ends of the electrodes into sharp points. (See inset.)

8 **REASSEMBLE THE NOZZLE.** Remove the nozzle parts from the paint thinner, rinse them with water, and let them dry. Thread the nozzle finger-tight and tighten a quarter-turn with the wrenches.

9 **ALIGN THE ELECTRODES.** Adjust the electrodes using a caliper, available at home centers and heating supply stores. Tighten the screw just enough so that the electrodes can turn and move back and forth but will hold their position. Using the caliper, set the distance between the electrode tips according to the manufacturer's specifications. Also set the forward and backward alignment. The alignment chart at left lists typical settings. Double-check them against those given by the manufacturer of your furnace. When the electrodes are set correctly, tighten the screw to hold them firmly in place.

Alignment chart

Spray angle:	Electrode tip to nozzle center:	Electrode tip extends beyond nozzle by:
45 degrees	½ inch	¼ inch
60 degrees	⅝ inch	¼ inch
70 degrees	⅝ inch	⅛ inch
80 degrees	⅝ inch	⅛ inch
90 degrees	⅝ inch	0

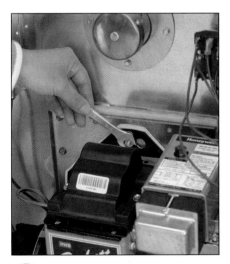

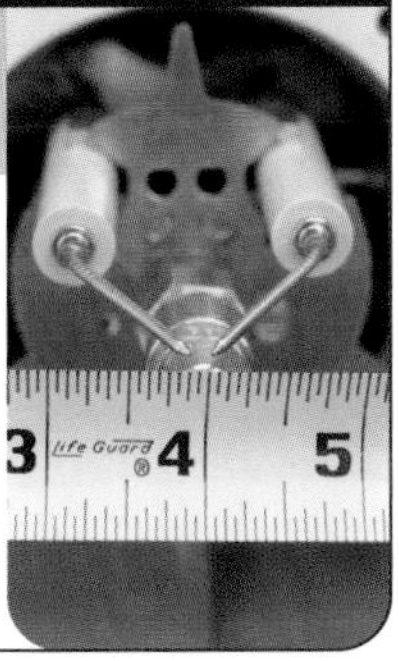

10 **PUT THE FIRING ASSEMBLY BACK IN PLACE.** Once the assembly is in place, reattach the oil line. Double-check all the connections before you test the furnace.

11 **YOU'RE ABOUT READY TO FIRE UP THE FURNACE.** Turn the oil back on at the oil cutoff valve near the filter. Turn the power back on at the circuit breaker box.

GOOD IDEA

PRIME TIME
Before you can run the furnace, you may need to prime the pump. If so, put the end of the oil line—which you disconnected to remove the firing assembly—over a bucket. Turn the power to the furnace back on, and have a helper turn the thermostat to its highest setting. Let oil pump from the line for 10 to 15 seconds, and then have the helper turn the thermostat back down. Reconnect the oil line.

MAINTAINING A GAS BURNER

SKILL SCALE

EASY	MEDIUM	**HARD**

REQUIRED SKILLS: Basic mechanical skills, using common tools, the ability to follow directions.

HOW LONG WILL IT TAKE?

Experienced . . . . .Variable
Handy . . . . .Variable
Novice . . . . .Variable

VARIABLES: You may need all or none of the materials, depending on what's wrong with the furnace.

SAFETY ALERT

SHUT OFF THE GAS VALVE
Always turn off the gas before working on your furnace. To do this, follow the gas line from the furnace back to a red-handled valve. This is the manual cutoff valve. To shut off the gas, turn the handle so it's perpendicular to the pipe (shown). Wait 5 minutes before doing any work.

I n a gas furnace, burning fuel heats air or water, which is then distributed throughout the house. Because gas burns more cleanly than oil, the yearly service is less demanding. Problems could be as simple as relighting the pilot on some models or, on others, replacing the igniter, a piece of high-resistance metal that lights the furnace without the use of a pilot.

While homeowners can easily maintain gas furnaces, repair or installation of gas lines is best left to professionals.

Dirt that builds up in the burners can result in a yellow flame or in delayed ignition. Avoid a service call by cleaning the burners once a year.

In addition to a vacuum, you'll need either the owner's manual or an inquisitive mind: No two furnaces are built exactly alike. You can attach the burners any number of ways, so the directions here have to be general.

- If you must figure out the system on your own, trace the gas line to the burners and carefully examine the fittings and brackets along the way. Take particular note of the burners—how they are aligned and how they are held in—so that once you get them out, you'll get them back in correctly, with no extra pieces.

- If the pilot fails to stay lit when you release the control knob, relight it and look at the color of the flame. If it's mostly yellow the pilot's not getting

STUFF YOU'LL NEED

✔ **MATERIALS:**
Dish soap, thermocouple, igniter, long lighter or match

✔ **TOOLS:**
Wrench, screwdriver, multimeter, leather work gloves, shop vacuum

enough oxygen and probably not producing enough heat to trigger the thermocouple. The nozzle may be clogged and needs to be cleaned. If the flame is mostly blue, check the thermocouple.

- The hole in the pilot's nozzle is sized to produce a flame of the right size, height, and temperature to activate the thermocouple. If it is too big it can cause the thermocouple to fail or it can burn other components. When cleaning the nozzle, first try blowing through it and if that doesn't work, use a wire brush or replace the nozzle.

Begin any maintenance or repair by turning off the gas at the manual valve and the power at the circuit breaker box.

A+ WORK SMARTER

THE ORDER OF BATTLE
When tracking a problem, always try the easiest and most obvious solution first. With a gas furnace:

- First, make sure the pilot is lit.

- Second, clean the nozzle.

- Third, check the thermocouple. If you find ash buildup on the tip of the thermocouple, it needs to be cleaned or replaced.

- Ash buildup is also an indication that the burners are in need of cleaning as well. Cleaning and reassembly of the thermocouple is easier with the burners out of the furnace, so you might as well clean them at the same time.

MAINTAINING A GAS BURNER
Checking for leaks

Bubbles indicate leaks.

GAS LEAKS USUALLY OCCUR WHERE TWO PIPES MEET. If you suspect a leak, test the joint with slightly diluted dish soap. Brush the soap on at all the joints. Bubbles indicate a leak. If you discover one, immediately turn off the gas at the meter.

Adjusting the air shutter

Most furnaces allow you to adjust the burner flame to make sure it is burning at the correct temperature. Turn the thermostat up to start the furnace, then remove the burner access cover so that you can look at the flame.

Loosen the lock screw, turn the shutter, and watch the flame. It will change colors and size. To achieve the correct setting, turn the shutter until the flame turns blue with a green core. (A yellow flame like the one shown here is starved for air. A blue flame with a dark blue center is getting too much air.) Once the flame is the right color, turn the shutter until the flame lifts away from the burner. Then turn the shutter back the other way until the flame reseats itself on the burner.
Tighten the lock screw and repeat the process on the remaining burners.

MAINTAINING A GAS BURNER
Lighting the pilot

1 **OLDER FURNACES HAVE A CONSTANTLY BURNING PILOT LIGHT THAT IGNITES THE FURNACE WHEN YOU NEED HEAT.** The furnace won't work if the pilot goes out. To check it, take the access cover off the furnace and look for the gas control knob. If your furnace has a pilot, the knob will turn to three positions: Off, On, and Pilot.

2 **TURN THE KNOB UNTIL THE ARROW IS POINTING AT THE WORD "PILOT."** Push the knob (or the button next to it) down to start the flow of gas.

If the pilot won't light, check the circuit breaker or fuse box to make sure the furnace is getting power.

3 **HOLD A LONG MATCH, OR A LONG-NOSE BUTANE LIGHTER** designed for the fireplace, up to the pilot nozzle to light the pilot. Once the flame is lit, hold the knob down for about a minute, then release it. If the pilot stays lit, turn the knob back to the On position. If it goes out, try again, holding the button for a longer period of time. If the flame still goes out, the nozzle may be dirty; clean it as explained below.

MAINTAINING A GAS BURNER
Cleaning the pilot

1 **CHECK THE FLAME.** If it's burning mostly yellow, it needs more oxygen to produce enough heat to trigger the thermocouple. The nozzle may have become clogged with debris and, thus, may need to be cleaned.

2 **TURN OFF THE GAS AND DISCONNECT THE PILOT LINE FROM THE BRACKET HOUSING THE BURNER.** The pilot line feeds gas to the burners. Once the line is disconnected, remove and clean the nozzle.

3 **THE NOZZLE IS USUALLY HOUSED IN A BARREL-SHAPED PART OF THE PILOT BRACKET.** It's either a threaded piece that twists out of the bracket or a loose piece that you can shake out. Remove the nozzle and gently blow through it to remove debris, clean it gently with a small brass brush, or replace it with a new nozzle.

MAINTAINING A GAS BURNER
Checking the thermocouple

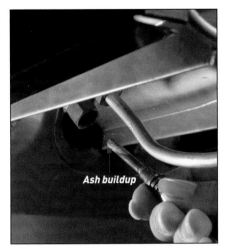

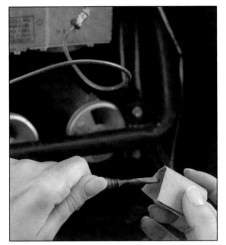

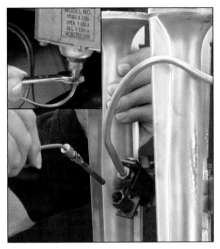

1 **THE THERMOCOUPLE IS THE THINNER OF THE TWO TUBES RUNNING TOWARD THE PILOT LIGHT.** If the flame is mostly blue the thermocouple could be the problem; clean or replace it. Remove the nut at the end nearest the pilot and pull the thermocouple out of the bracket.

2 **GENTLY CLEAN THE END OF THE THERMOCOUPLE.** Ash and other debris can build up on the end of the thermocouple, inhibiting its ability to fire the furnace. Before replacing it try cleaning it gently with fine-grit sandpaper. Replace it and retest the flame. If it fails to light or is the wrong color, replace the thermocouple.

3 **IF THE THERMOCOUPLE IS BAD, TURN OFF THE PILOT** and cut off the gas at the manual shutoff valve. Turn off the power at the circuit breaker or fuse box. Let the thermocouple cool, remove it by loosening the nut with a wrench. (See inset.) Remove the thermocouple and take it to a dealer for a replacement. Install the new thermocouple and relight the pilot.

MAINTAINING A GAS BURNER
Cleaning the burner

1 **TURN OFF THE ELECTRICITY AT THE BREAKER BOX AND SHUT OFF THE GAS AT THE MANUAL VALVE.** Wait 5 minutes and remove the furnace access panel; then remove the access panel that covers the burners. The burners are tubes with an opening along the side to let in air. Remove the tubes as recommended by the manufacturer.

2 **IN MOST CASES YOU'LL HAVE TO REMOVE A GAS PIPE,** called the manifold, that runs along the back of the burners. Look to see whether this is necessary, and if so, loosen the union where the pipe enters the gas control box until the line is free of the union. Lift the manifold to remove it, being careful not to hit the igniter.

3 **REMOVE ONE OF THE ROUND, TUBELIKE BURNERS.** Clean it with a brush attached to a shop vacuum, and then put it back in place. Look to see how it locks in place—some burners have locking tabs—and then position it as necessary. Clean the other tubes one at a time; on some furnaces each tube is designed for a specific location.

MAINTAINING A GAS BURNER
Cleaning the burner (continued)

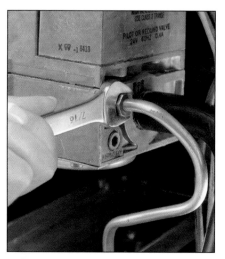

④ WHEN YOU'VE FINISHED VACUUMING ALL THE BURNERS, REPLACE THE MANIFOLD. Check the alignment, then screw the bracket holding the manifold back in place. If you've disconnected the gas line feeding the burners, reattach it.

⑤ RECONNECT THE GAS LINE TO THE MANIFOLD. After the burners are fully seated in their channels (or channel), use a screwdriver to reconnect the gas line.

⑥ REATTACH THE PILOT LINE TO THE CONTROL BOX. Once the gas line is reattached to the control box, turn the gas back on and test the furnace. You may have to readjust the air shutter to get the proper flame on the pilot.

MAINTAINING A GAS BURNER
Checking and replacing the igniter

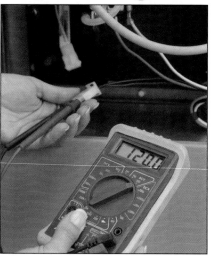

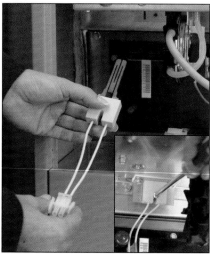

① THE IGNITER HAS REPLACED THE PILOT LIGHT ON NEWER FURNACES. If your furnace has an igniter but won't fire up, watch the igniter as someone turns up the thermostat. If you can't see the igniter glowing like this through the observation window, you may need to replace it.

② IF THE IGNITER ISN'T GLOWING, REMOVE THE COVER THAT HOUSES THE OBSERVATION WINDOW. Unplug the wires going into the igniter. Put a lead in each of the igniter wires that lead back into the furnace. Set a multimeter to read AC volts and turn the thermostat up enough to start the furnace. If the meter reads around 120 volts, the igniter is faulty. If there is no power, the control box may be bad; call a service person.

③ TO REPLACE THE IGNITER, LOOSEN THE SCREW IN THE BRACKET THAT ATTACHES IT TO THE FURNACE. Replace it with an identical igniter and reattach it to the furnace. When you handle the igniter, hold it by the porcelain part or by the bracket: Touching the surface that heats up may shorten its life. Reattach the wires, then screw the igniter in place (see inset). Turn up the thermostat to test it before reattaching the cover.

MAINTAINING A FORCED-AIR FURNACE

STUFF YOU'LL NEED

✔ **MATERIALS:** Filters, household oil, masking tape

✔ **TOOLS:** Vacuum cleaner, wrenches, framing square, needle-nose pliers, multimeter

HOMER'S HINDSIGHT

ON AND OFF

When we left for vacation I turned my furnace down to 55 degrees to save energy. When I got back I turned it up to our usual temperature. The furnace started turning on and off and the house wasn't getting warm. I poked around but couldn't figure out the problem so I called a repair person who said that the furnace was probably fine. Turning on and off was it's way of catching up and expelling all the cold air from the system.

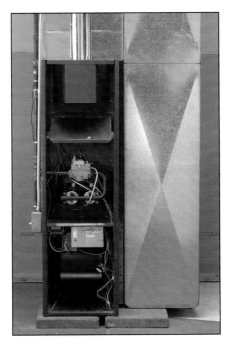

If you know anything about fans, you know most of what there is to know about forced-air heat: When the furnace is ready, the fan turns on. If the fan doesn't turn on, you're going to get cold.

If you see a fire in the firebox but the fan doesn't kick on, the next few pages should help you diagnose and repair the problem. (If there's no fire in the firebox, see Maintaining an Oil Furnace, page 497 or Maintaining a Gas Burner, page 502.) On older furnaces, the problem may be a broken fan belt. Newer furnaces have direct-drive fans, so the problem is going to be in one of the controls or in the motor itself. All you'll need to find the problem is a relatively inexpensive multimeter (a meter that tests AC and DC voltage, as well as resistance—see Step 2, page 506) and someone willing to run back and forth to turn up the thermostat.

Add water for better breathing— Installing online humidifiers

Furnaces dry out the air in your home, causing dry skin, scratchy throats, and respiratory irritation. Dry air also causes wood to shrink, warping boards and ruining furniture joints.

Installing an online humidifier can help solve the problem. Humidifiers come in three basic types: spray, drum, and flow-through.

● **Spray humidifiers** spray water into the airstream of your furnace. They're the least expensive but produce less humidity.

● **Drum humidifiers** have a large, water-absorbent rotating drum partially submerged in a pool of water. Air blowing across the top adds moisture to the heated air.

● **Flow-through humidifiers** work on the same principle as drum humidifiers, but water drips across a pad through which air is blown. They're more efficient, and the amount of moisture added to the air can be precisely controlled. They have a drain line, which connects to a drain into the house plumbing system.

All three types need a water source, usually a simple plumbing job. A valve is attached to an existing pipe. PVC or flexible copper tubing supplies water to the humidifier.

All three mount on one of the furnace's main ducts. A spray humidifier mounts on the plenum and sprays water into the warm airstream. Using a template supplied with the unit, you'll cut a hole in the plenum with a pair of tin snips. The humidifier bolts or screws in place.

Drum and flow-through humidifiers generally mount on the cold-air return duct using a vent that pipes humid air to the plenum. Once again, use a template and tin snips.

All three types are controlled by a humidistat—a thermostat-type device that measures humidity in the air. You can mount the humidistat directly in the air vent or as a separate wall-mounted control in the room of your choice. The humidistat, motors, and other controls all require electricity. This requires minimal wiring— usually just tapping into one of the connections in the furnace.

HEATING, VENTILATION, AND AIR-CONDITIONING

Understanding furnace filters

The sole purpose of a dust filter is to pull dust out of the air. How thorough you want to be about it is largely a matter of preference and budget. Whichever filter you settle on, however, replace or clean it as directed by the manufacturer. A dirty filter won't do any damage to your furnace in the short run. Trying to force air through a clogged filter, however, is like trying to force water through a brick. It's inefficient and will quickly wipe out all the savings your high-tech furnace is supposed to deliver. The simplest filter is the oldest, most economical, and least efficient: spun glass. When it gets dirty you toss it out. Fiber filters are essentially spun plastic. They're as efficient as glass, but washable. If you want to remove the most dust from the air, get a media filter or an electrostatic filter. One's disposable, the other recyclable, and both are efficient at pulling dust out of the air. Last, and most expensive, is the electrostatic precipitator—the electrical version of the electrostatic filter. It removes just about everything except the air but requires professional installation.

TYPES OF FILTERS

SPUN GLASS. These are the least expensive filters, the kind that were common on furnaces through the 1970s. They remove 10 to 15 percent of the dust in the air, enough to protect the fan but not much more. Replace these filters monthly. Of all the filter types, they allow the most dust to get through.

FIBER. This is a washable version of the spun-glass filter. It is no more effective; the benefit is that you can wash it instead of replacing it.

MEDIA. These are spun-glass filters with a pleated fiber core. They remove between 45 and 90 percent of the dust in the air. Like spun-glass filters, they are disposable—though some are good for as long as three months. If your furnace will accept two filters at once, you can extend the life of a media filter by putting a spun-glass filter in front of it.

ELECTROSTATIC. Electrostatic filters are layered to form an electrostatic charge that pulls dust out of the air and into a foam filter. Because the charge is permanent and the filter is plastic, you can clean it instead of throwing it out. Electrostatic HEPA (High-Efficiency Particulate Air) filters will remove 99 percent of the pollutants in the air. Clean these filters every 3 months.

ELECTROSTATIC PRECIPITATORS. These are similar to electrostatic filters except that a power source supplies the charge. Precipitators restrict airflow, so they usually include a small booster fan; installation is complicated and best left to a pro. These filters will filter down to 0.001 micron, which makes them efficient enough to remove smoke and similar pollutants from the air. They use about as much power as a small lightbulb. Clean these filters every 3 months.

MAINTAINING A FORCED-AIR FURNACE
Removing and cleaning a filter

Part of maintaining your furnace and its efficiency is keeping the filter clean. With some disposable filters, you'll simply remove the old one and put in the new one. With other filters, you'll vacuum and wash the filter and then reuse it. In either event, removal is the same. Take off the furnace access panel and set it aside. In older furnaces, the filter lifts in and out of a groove. In newer furnaces, a flexible metal arm jams in place to hold the filter. The arm usually tucks behind a flange near the access panel. To remove the filter, lift up on the arm and swing it forward once it clears the flange.

CLEANING A REUSABLE FILTER. Remove the filter, vacuum it, then rinse thoroughly with water with a hose or in a bathtub. You can reinstall the filter while it's still wet.

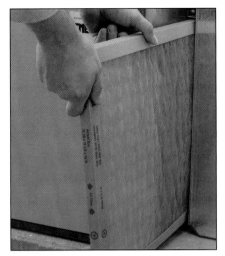

REPLACING A DISPOSABLE FILTER. Remove the filter and replace it with one that is the exact size and shape of the one you are replacing.

MAINTAINING A FORCED-AIR FURNACE
Maintaining the fan motor

OILING THE MOTOR. Not all furnaces need to be oiled; many have permanent bearings that are sealed at the factory. To find out whether your blower needs oiling, remove the access panel and look at the blower motor. Those that need oiling will have small holes at either end of the motor. Put a couple of drops of household oil (usually 10W, nondetergent) through the holes.

TIGHTENING THE FAN BELT. If the fan runs off a belt (not all of them do), push down on the belt at a point midway between the motor and the fan. **The belt should flex about 1 inch.** If it doesn't, loosen the locknut on the bracket that holds the motor and turn the second nut to tighten or loosen the belt. Retighten the locknut once the belt is properly tensioned. If the adjustment bolt is frozen, apply penetrating oil until it turns easily. Replace cracked or stretched belts, and apply belt dressing for longer belt life.

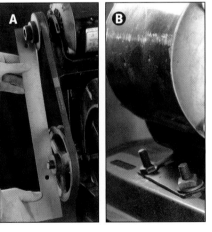

ALIGNING THE MOTOR AND FAN PULLEYS. For the quietest and most efficient operation, the pulleys on the motor and on the fan should be in line with each other. **Ⓐ** To check the alignment, put a straightedge, such as a level or framing square, against the sides of both pulleys. A triangular space between one of the pulleys and the straightedge means they aren't aligned. To correct this, loosen the nuts or bolts that hold the motor bracket to the mounting bar. Once loosened, the motor should slide along the bar. **Ⓑ** Position the motor so that the pulleys are aligned and retighten the nuts or bolts.

Tracking fan or motor problems

I f the blower fan pumps no air into the vents, you have at least two problems. The first is that you're cold. The second is a bit harder to track down. In order to figure out where the problem is, trace the circuit from the thermostat through the other controls and finally to the motor. Do what the pros do—check the obvious first.

THE THERMOSTAT. The thermostat hanging on your wall is nothing more than a big switch. When the temperature falls below the point at which you've set the thermostat, its switch flips and the furnace comes on. When the temperature rises to the set point, the switch flips the other way and the furnace turns off. Verify that the thermostat is set to On and is turned up, and that the wires are properly connected. If the thermostat has batteries check them as well.

THE BLOWER RELAY. With the help of the blower relay, the 24-volt thermostat can start and stop the 110-volt blower.

THE FAN-AND-LIMIT CONTROL. The fan-and-limit control senses when the firebox is hot enough to send air through the ducts and into the house. Even if the thermostat and blower relay say it's time for the blower to kick on, nothing happens until the fan-and-limit control says the furnace is hot enough. When the thermostat and blower relay are ready to turn off the blower, the fan-and-limit control lets that happen only when most of the residual heat has been pumped into the house. If the fan were to turn on at the same moment the thermostat started the flame in the box, the air it blew would still be reasonably cold. And if the fan shut off the minute the flame stopped, a lot of hot air would remain in the furnace, doing no one any good.

Diagnosing fan and motor problems

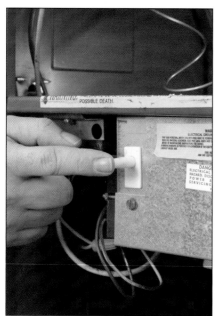

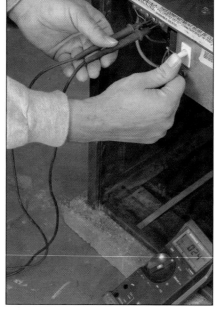

CHECK THE SAFETY SWITCH AT THE FURNACE. After you've checked the thermostat upstairs, head for the furnace. Make sure the access panels are in place and that they have depressed the push-button safety switch. Remove the panels and push the safety button down. If the furnace fires but the fan doesn't, test the thermostat. If the furnace doesn't fire, see the sections on oil furnaces and gas burners for more information.

TEST THE THERMOSTAT. Find the blower relay, one side of which is connected to the thermostat. Set a multimeter to the 50 volts AC range. Put one of the leads on the terminal labeled G—this is one of the blower wires. Put the other on C, which is one of the transformer terminals. Set the thermostat as high as it will go. The furnace should light, the meter should read about 24 volts, and the blower should start up in a few seconds. If not, replace the thermostat.

TEST THE RELAY. Turn the power to the furnace off at the circuit breaker box. Set a multimeter to the ohmmeter setting. Put the leads on the relay's G and C terminals again. The readout should be 0 when you touch them and 1 when you separate them. If not, the relay is faulty. Label the wires so that you'll know where each goes, then remove and replace the relay.

TESTING THE FAN-AND-LIMIT CONTROL

1 **TO TEST THE BLOWER,** look to see whether the fan-and-limit control has a button or switch on it labeled something like "summer/winter" or "auto/manual." Push or flip the switch to the summer or manual position. Restore power to the furnace. If the blower is working, it will turn on immediately, indicating that the fan-and-limit control needs to be replaced. If the motor starts, the problem is with the motor or its capacitor (see page 512).

2 **IF THE RELAY AND THERMOSTAT ARE FINE BUT THE MOTOR WON'T START,** test the fan-and-limit control. The control is often enclosed in a small metal box. Turn the power off at the circuit breaker or fuse box and remove the fan-and-limit control cover.

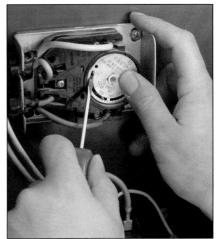

3 **IF THERE IS NO SWITCH,** test the motor by changing the control's settings. As you look at the dial, you'll notice either two or three sliding tabs and a numbered scale. Hold the dial firmly and move the two tabs at the lowest setting as far clockwise as you can. Restore power to the furnace. If the motor is working, it will turn on immediately, indicating that the fan-and-limit control needs to be replaced. You'll also need to replace the fan-and-limit switch.

REPLACING THE FAN-AND-LIMIT CONTROL

1 **IF YOUR TESTS HAVE SHOWN THAT THE FAN-AND-LIMIT CONTROL IS BAD, YOU WILL NEED TO REPLACE IT.** Label the wiring. Put a piece of tape next to each terminal, identifying it. Put a piece of tape on each wire identifying where it came from. Then remove the wires from their terminals.

2 **WITH A PAIR OF PLIERS, GRAB ONE OF THE GROMMETS SURROUNDING THE WIRING THAT COMES INTO THE CONTROL.** Squeeze the grommet and slide it out of the bottom of the control. If there is a second set of wires, remove it in the same way.

3 **REMOVE THE SCREWS ATTACHING THE CONTROL TO THE FURNACE.** A sensor tube extends into the firebox. Pull the control out until the tube clears. Take the control with you and get an identical replacement. You may have to reset the sliding tabs to match the settings on the old control. Don't move the dial. If there is a third tab on the dial, do not reset it.

If you repair or replace the fan-and-limit control switch, make sure the settings match those specified by the manufacturer.

Diagnosing fan and motor problems (continued)

TESTING THE CAPACITOR

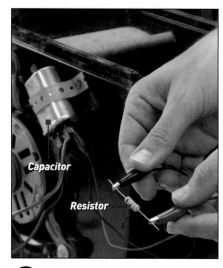

Capacitor

Resistor

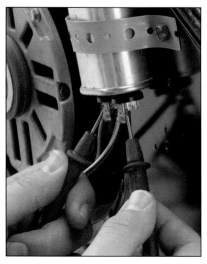

1 IF YOUR TESTS UP TO NOW SHOW THAT THE CONTROLS ARE WORKING, even though the motor isn't, either the motor or the capacitor that helps start it is defective. The first step in checking them is turning off the power at the circuit breaker box and at the furnace itself. Remove the motor access panel and set it aside. Locate the capacitor, usually located above the motor itself.

2 DISCHARGE THE CAPACITOR. The blower motor has a capacitor to help it start. It charges up like a battery and discharges instantaneously to give the motor unit extra starting power. Until discharged, capacitors can give you a dangerous shock (see "Safety Alert," below).

3 TEST THE CAPACITOR WITH THE OHMMETER ON YOUR MULTIMETER. Resistance should drop as the battery in your meter charges the capacitor. On a meter with a needle, the needle should quickly rise as the capacitor discharges, and then fall. On a digital meter the initial reading should be one, then it should fall to zero and rise back to one. If no change occurs, replace the capacitor.

SAFETY ALERT

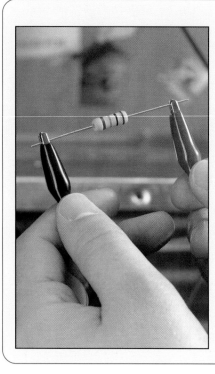

DISCHARGING CAPACITORS SAFELY

Capacitors store an electrical charge to boost the power to an electric motor, allowing it to achieve full torque immediately. The electrical charge remains in the capacitor until it's discharged, so even though the power is turned off the capacitor is still live. Obviously you could be shocked, so make sure the capacitor is discharged before you continue working on the furnace. Make a discharger from parts available at an electronic supply store: a 20,000-ohm, 5-watt resistor and two leads with alligator clips on both ends.

HERE'S THE PROCEDURE:

1 Turn off the main power at the breaker panel.

2 Clip the two leads to the resistor, as shown.

3 Carefully clip the other ends of the leads to the terminals on the capacitor and wait about 15 seconds while it discharges.

4 Test the capacitor with an ohmmeter by placing a probe on each terminal. Resistance should drop as the battery in the meter charges the capacitor.

MAINTAINING A FORCED-AIR FURNACE
Replacing the fan motor

1 **IF YOUR THERMOSTAT, RELAY, FAN-AND-LIMIT CONTROL, AND CAPACITOR** have all passed their tests, the problem is the motor. Make sure the power is off, then mark the wires and terminals with tape. Loosen and remove the bolts in the mounting bracket. Then pull the motor forward to slide it out of the track.

2 **IF THE BLOWER IS DIRECT-DRIVE, IT WILL HAVE COME OFF WITH THE MOTOR.** Loosen the setscrew on the blower to free the blower shaft. Then turn the fan so that it is motor-side up and disconnect the green ground wire, if there is one.

Have someone help you remove the motor—it can weigh up to 50 pounds.

3 **UNBOLT THE BRACKETS HOLDING THE MOTOR INSIDE THE FAN.** Pull the motor out and undo the collar bolts holding the front of the motor to the bracket. Remove the motor and replace it with an identical one.

4 **REPLACE THE REPAIRED UNIT.** Slide the motor assembly into its slot and reattach the necessary wiring. Turn on the power at the breaker box and test the unit.

MAINTAINING A HOT-WATER HEAT SYSTEM

Even if you'd rather not think about working on furnaces, you can do a few simple jobs to keep a hot-water system running well. Oiling the pump, a simple matter of dropping a bit of oil in the right places, can keep the motor from failing. Letting trapped air out of the system, or "bleeding" it, removes large air bubbles that keep warm water from running throughout the entire system. It's not usually part of a furnace tune-up, but it's simple, makes a big difference, and is more fun than something this important should be.

A good dusting should be part of your maintenance program. Dust buildup on the pump motor keeps it from running efficiently. Dust buildup on the fins inside the baseboard keeps heat from leaving the system and getting into the room.

Air is both a friend and an enemy in a hot-water system. The expansion tank, located near the furnace, needs air. As the boiler heats the water, the water expands and needs a place to go. The expansion tank contains a cushion of air that compresses as the water comes in and expands as the water cools.

Put the same air in a pipe, radiator, or baseboard heater and you've got trouble: The water can't get by it. Every radiator or baseboard downstream of the bubble goes cold. Since it's almost impossible to keep air out of the lines, hot-water systems have what are called bleeder valves. In essence, they are tiny faucets attached to the radiator or baseboard. When you turn the faucet when the heat is on, trapped air is forced out through the valve. Once it's gone, water flows out the valve, and you turn it off. Bleed the system at the beginning of the heating season, starting at the top of the house and working your way down.

Steam heat removes a great deal of humidity from the air and can cause dry skin and itchy throats. A humidifier can help balance the moisture content of the air in your home.

Hot-water systems combine the worlds of plumbing, electrical, and HVAC.

TWICE A YEAR OIL THE MOTOR THAT RUNS THE CIRCULATOR. On most furnaces the motor is a separate unit attached to the side of the circulator. Look for three oil ports: one on the front of the funnel-shaped bearing housing, and one each at the front and back of the motor. The port on the bearing housing will probably be an oil cup. Those on the motor may have plastic feeder tubes that help you get oil inside the port. Oil with a few drops of household oil. If you can't find oil ports, don't worry. Some motors are permanently sealed and don't need oil.

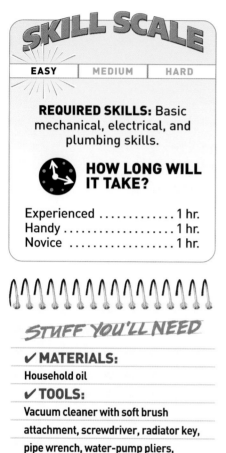

CLEAN THE CASING WITH A SOFT BRUSH ATTACHED TO A VACUUM. Run the brush over the holes in the motor casing and in the bearing housing to remove dust that makes operation less efficient.

Bleeding baseboards and radiators

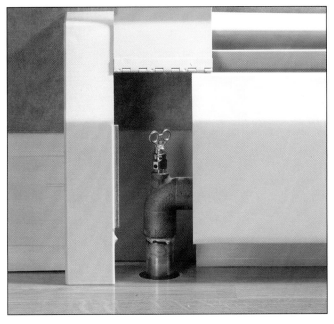

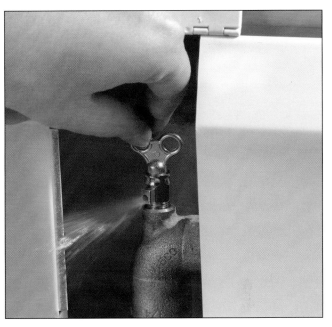

BASEBOARD HOT-WATER HEATERS, called convectors, have a slightly different bleeder, located under the cover that shields the fins. As you look at the baseboard, you'll see a door at each end. Open the doors and look for the bleeder.

ON SOME UNITS, THE BLEEDER WILL BE NEAR OR ON TOP OF THE CUTOFF VALVE. On other units it will be at the opposite end. The valve has a small spout on one side that releases the air. Looking for the spout is an easy way to find the valve. Once you find it, you'll see a screw or knob on top that operates the valve. Open the valve until water runs out, then close the valve.

RADIATORS are usually relics of a steam-heat system that has been converted to hot water. Steam traveled through the pipes under its own pressure. Hot water needs to be pumped but can be produced with considerably less energy. Steam radiators need bleeding too. The valve is on the side near the top of the radiator and operates with a removable key, available from most HVAC retailers. Be careful: If your system is still steam, it will be hot enough to scald you when it comes out of the valve.

BASEBOARD FINS COLLECT DUST QUICKLY, compromising the efficiency of the system. Once a year, slide or snap the cover off the front of the baseboard. Clean the fins by wiping them with a soft brush attachment on your vacuum.

Repairing a waterlogged expansion tank

SKILL SCALE

EASY	MEDIUM	HARD

REQUIRED SKILLS: Basic mechanical and plumbing skills.

HOW LONG WILL IT TAKE?

Experienced . . . . 1 hr.
Handy . . . . 1 hr.
Novice . . . . 1 hr.

VARIABLES: Replacing a tank will take considerably longer than draining and refilling a waterlogged tank.

When the boiler heats water in the system, the water expands. Unless it has a place to go, you've got trouble. Fortunately, the expansion tank is there. Located near the furnace, the expansion tank is basically a tank partially filled with air. The expanding water flows into the tank, relieving pressure on the system. As the water flows into the tank, it compresses the air inside and creates the pressure that the system needs to run once the water has reached its final density. Sometimes an older tank gets waterlogged—the air inside leaks out and the tank fills entirely with water. This probably won't happen if you have a newer tank. In new tanks, the air is sealed into one side of the tank by a diaphragm. As the pressure in the system increases, it pushes against the diaphragm to compress the air. As the pressure drops, the air expands, pushing the diaphragm back into its original position.

Your expansion tank is probably located a few feet away from the furnace and may be hung from the ceiling. To find it, just follow the warm pipes coming out of the furnace.

Draining your expansion tank should be part of your yearly maintenance schedule.

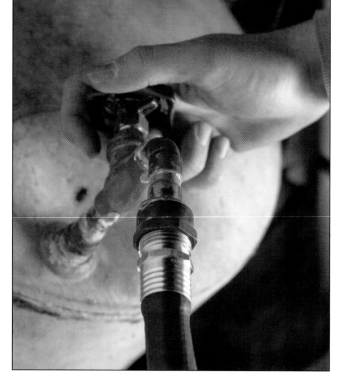

OLDER TANKS HAVE A DRAIN VALVE YOU SHOULD OPEN ONCE A YEAR to prevent waterlogging. Start by tracing the pipe that runs from the furnace to the tank, and then close the valve between the two. Put a hose on the tank's drain valve and open the valve.

WHEN THE WATER STARTS DRAINING, OPEN THE AIR VALVE. This may be located on the side of the tank or on the drain valve, or it may be a small cap on the valve between the furnace and the tank. Open the valve or unscrew the cap to let air into the tank as it drains. Close the drain and air valve once water stops running and reopen the valve between the furnace and the tank. The tank will automatically refill to the proper level.

NEWER TANKS HAVE A DIAPHRAGM THAT SEALS THE AIR IN ONE PART OF THE TANK, separating it from the water. When the pressure in the heating system increases, it pushes against the diaphragm, compressing the air and letting more water into the tank. Because the air is sealed in, diaphragm tanks are less likely to become waterlogged. If the tank does become waterlogged, your heating technician can pump more air into the tank, which usually fixes the problem (and is often part of the yearly furnace maintenance). If the problem remains, it's likely that the diaphragm is broken. (You can't repair a broken diaphragm; consequently, some service people prefer nondiaphragm tanks.) If you need a new tank, look at the one you have and write down the brand and model number. Talk over the issue of diaphragm versus nondiaphragm with your supplier and have a replacement on hand before you start the repair. You'd hate to be standing by the furnace midwinter with no heat and a replacement tank on back order.

Have a helper around when you're replacing an expansion tank. It can be heavy and trying to do it yourself is not worth an injury.

MAINTAINING A HOT-WATER HEAT SYSTEM
Replacing an expansion tank

Expansion tank valve

Pipe to expansion tank

① SHUT OFF POWER TO THE FURNACE AND LET IT COOL DOWN FOR SEVERAL HOURS. Close the valve between the furnace and the expansion tank and drain it as described on page 516. Once the tank is empty, put a pipe wrench on the fitting between the expansion tank and the valve and disconnect by turning the pipe with water-pump pliers. If the pipe suspends the tank, get a helper to hold it while you work.

② ONCE THE TANK IS DISCONNECTED, REMOVE IT. The tank may be heavy—another reason for a helper.

New expansion tanks are smaller but just as effective as older models.

③ INSTALL YOUR REPLACEMENT TANK. Reconnect the pipes and fittings you removed in Step 1 to the valve using Teflon plumber's tape. Support the pipe with the pipe straps, adjusting as necessary. Wrap Teflon tape around the threads of the pipe that leads into the tank and screw the tank onto the fitting to install it. Turn on the valve to restore water flow and check for leaks.

Testing and fixing an aquastat

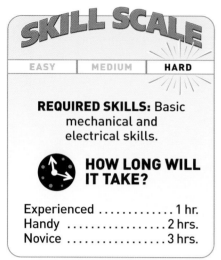

SKILL SCALE

EASY	MEDIUM	**HARD**

REQUIRED SKILLS: Basic mechanical and electrical skills.

HOW LONG WILL IT TAKE?

Experienced . . . . 1 hr.
Handy . . . . 2 hrs.
Novice . . . . 3 hrs.

An aquastat is simply a thermostat (not to be confused with the thermostat upstairs) that measures water temperature in the boiler and activates a switch when the temperature reaches a certain point. A hot-water heat system has at least two aquastats. One turns the burner off to keep the boiler temperature from getting too hot. The other keeps the circulator from pumping water through the radiator unless it's hot enough to do some good. On some furnaces the aquastats are individual units. On others the aquastats are housed in the same box and share a sensor that passes through the furnace wall and into the boiler. What an aquastat looks like inside the box depends on the make and model. If there are two dials, one controls the boiler temperature while the other controls the circulator temperature. Both temperatures are allowed to vary below the setting by a preset amount. If there are three dials, one controls the boiler temperature, the second controls the circulator, and the third sets the amount the two are allowed to vary.

Aquastats are usually mounted on the furnace but are sometimes found on a pipe leading from the circulator.

TESTING AN AQUASTAT

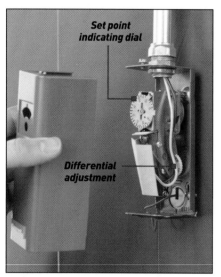

Set point indicating dial

Differential adjustment

1 REMOVE THE COVER ON THE AQUASTAT. Testing an aquastat is a matter of resetting the dials and watching what happens. On this furnace, there are two aquastats (one for the burner and one for the circulator) mounted in different locations. On other furnaces, both aquastats may be housed in the same box. The larger aquastat dial controls the set point—the temperature at which it will turn off the burner or pump. The smaller dial controls the differential, or number of degrees below the set point at which the burner or circulator will come on.

2 TURN THE WALL THERMOSTAT UPSTAIRS TO ITS HIGHEST SETTING. If the furnace is functioning correctly it should turn on. If not, test the burner (set point) aquastat on the furnace—the one set to the highest temperature—by lowering the setting to less than 100°F (38°C). If the aquastat is working, the burner should go off. Return the burner aquastat to its original setting. If the aquastat is working, the burner should go back on within 10 minutes. If the aquastat fails at either setting, replace it.

Make a note of the original settings before you adjust them.

3 RUN A SIMILAR TEST ON THE CIRCULATOR AQUASTAT. First raise the temperature setting to higher than 100°F (38°C). If the aquastat and circulator are both working, the circulator will go on. If not, find the source of the problem by putting a multimeter set to 120 V AC across the aquastat terminals labeled C1 and C2, which lead to the circulator. If you get no reading, the aquastat is defective. If you get a reading, check the circulator (pump) motor as described on page 520. Once you've tested the setting, reset the aquastat to lower than 100°F (38°C). The circulator should go off. If not, replace it.

REPLACING AN AQUASTAT

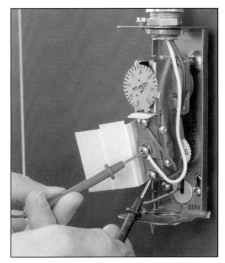

1 **TURN OFF THE POWER AT THE CIRCUIT BREAKER BOX AND AT THE EMERGENCY CUTOFF SWITCH.** Make sure the power is off by putting a meter or voltage tester across the two terminals labeled Line. Double-check by putting one lead on a piece of bare metal inside the box and the other lead on first one line terminal and then the other. If the light comes on or the meter gives you a reading other than zero, you've turned off the wrong breaker. Do not work on the furnace until your meter or voltage tester tells you that you've turned off the correct breaker.

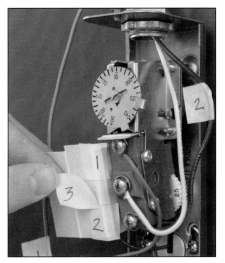

2 **DISCONNECT THE WIRES LEADING TO THE AQUASTAT ONE AT A TIME.** Mark each wire with a piece of tape showing which terminal the wire came from.

When replacing parts, bring the old ones with you to the store. It'll save you time and frustration.

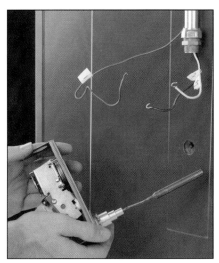

3 **REMOVE THE AQUASTAT.** In most cases, including this one, the aquastat fits on the surface of the furnace and has a sensor that fits into a well inside the boiler. Remove the screws holding the aquastat in place and remove it from the furnace. On rare occasions the aquastat is mounted on a pipe leading to a baseboard or radiator. If so, remove the screws holding it in place. Take the aquastat to a dealer and buy a replacement that matches.

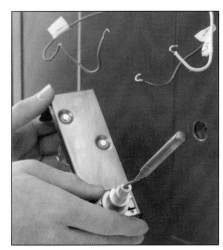
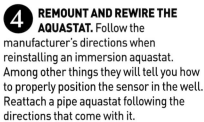

4 **REMOUNT AND REWIRE THE AQUASTAT.** Follow the manufacturer's directions when reinstalling an immersion aquastat. Among other things they will tell you how to properly position the sensor in the well. Reattach a pipe aquastat following the directions that come with it.

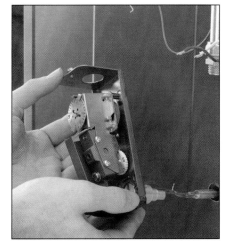

5 **IN SOME CASES THE EXISTING WELL MAY NOT MATCH THE REPLACEMENT AQUASTAT.** Make sure you've got the correct aquastat and replace the well. Drain the boiler using the pressure-relief valve, then follow the manufacturer's directions for installing a new well. Put the sensor in the well as directed and reattach the aquastat.

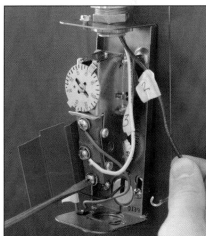

6 **REATTACH THE WIRES USING THE LABELS TO MAKE SURE** each one is attached to the correct terminal. Set the dials on the new aquastat to match the pretesting settings on the old one.

HEATING, VENTILATION, AND AIR-CONDITIONING

HEATING, VENTILATION, AND AIR-CONDITIONING 519

Testing and replacing the pump motor

EASY	MEDIUM	**HARD**

REQUIRED SKILLS: Basic mechanical and electrical skills.

HOW LONG WILL IT TAKE?

Experienced . . . . 1.5 hrs.
Handy . . . . 3 hrs.
Novice . . . . 4 hrs.

VARIABLES: Refitting a replacement coupler on the motor shaft can be frustrating.

STUFF YOU'LL NEED

✔ **MATERIALS:**
Wire nuts, masking tape (for marking electrical leads), coupler spring assembly

✔ **TOOLS:**
Multimeter, allen wrench, open-ended or adjustable wrench, gloves

If you're reading these pages, you're either extremely curious or extremely cold. If curiosity brought you here, you're just interested in the way things work. If a failed motor brought you here, it means that no matter how hard the furnace is working, the heat isn't reaching the rest of the house.

You should have already tested the aquastat, which controls when the pump motor turns on. (If you haven't, see page 518.) If you have, the problem is probably in your motor or very close to it. Traditionally the pump (known technically as a circulator) is a three-part assembly: motor, bearing housing, and pump. Inside the bearing housing a safety device called the coupler acts as a once-and-done clutch. If the pump jams, the coupler breaks the connection between the motor and pump so that the motor won't burn itself out. Once the coupler goes into action, though, it's broken. You'll have to replace it.

Have someone turn the heat way up while you're standing next to the pump. If the motor comes on but the pump doesn't run, the problem is most likely the coupler. Replacing the coupler is a simple matter, but usually only a temporary cure. Whatever caused the coupler to break in the first place is likely to act up again. Unless you fix the core problem, sooner or later the new coupler will break.

If the coupler's intact and further tests indicate the motor or pump is broken, talk to your HVAC supplier about a combination pump, motor, and coupler sold as a single unit. Service people love them, and they're considerably less expensive than the traditional assemblies. Installing one is a matter of loosening a few bolts, putting the assembly in place, then retightening the bolts.

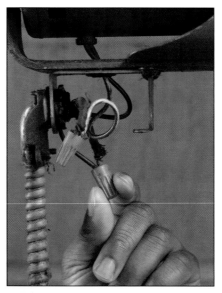

1 **TURN OFF THE POWER AT THE BREAKER BOX AND EMERGENCY CUTOFF SWITCH.** Make sure the power is off by putting a meter across the line terminals of the aquastat. Remove the cover from the junction box on the pump motor. Gently remove the wire caps on the wires and double-check to make sure no power is going to them. Label the wires with pieces of tape so that you'll know how to put them back together.

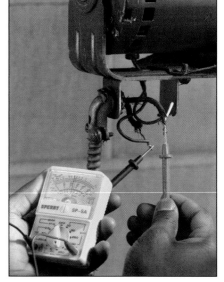

2 **TEST THE MOTOR BY SETTING A MULTIMETER TO RX1** and putting a lead on each of the motor wires. The meter needle should swing or the readout change to indicate continuity. If you get no reading, replace or repair the motor. Talk to your supplier about replacing the motor and bearing assembly with a less expensive (but reliable) unit that combines the two.

HEATING, VENTILATION, AND AIR-CONDITIONING

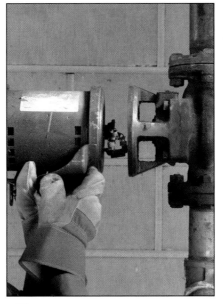

3 **IF THERE IS CONTINUITY THE MOTOR IS PROBABLY USABLE.**
The problem may be the coupler, the spring-loaded device between the motor and pump that protects the motor if the pump jams. The coupler is located inside the bearing housing, the funnel-shaped piece between the motor and pump. Look inside for the setscrew on the pump end of the assembly and loosen it.

4 **REMOVE THE BOLTS HOLDING THE MOTOR TO THE BEARING ASSEMBLY.** Slide the motor and coupler off the pump shaft.

Motors can be heavy and awkward; have a helper handy in case you need assistance.

5 **LOOK AT THE COUPLER AND SPRINGS TO CHECK FOR BROKEN PARTS.** If there are any, remove the setscrew holding the coupler to the motor and replace the coupler. If the coupler appears to be intact and you are still not getting heat, call a service technician.

6 **SLIDE THE MOTOR AND COUPLER BACK ONTO THE PUMP SHAFT.** The motor is heavy and it can be difficult to get the spring assembly back over the shaft. Enlist a helper to support the motor while you wrestle the assembly into place.

7 **REATTACH THE MOTOR TO THE BEARING HOUSING.** Tighten the setscrew attaching the coupler to the pump shaft and rewire the motor. Turn on the furnace. If the motor doesn't come on by the time the thermometer on the side of the furnace reaches the temperature on the aquastat, call a service technician.

GOOD IDEA

A SHORT-TERM SOLUTION IF THE PUMP FAILS

If the pump motor fails at 2:30 a.m. and the baby's crying and the pipes are freezing as you try to figure out what to do—you're having a bad night. But as long as the boiler is firing, there may be a short-term solution. You still must repair the pump but, in the meantime, try turning up the thermostat all the way. Hot water will still move slowly through the system of pipes and radiators without the pump by natural convection and cold water will return to the boiler. The thermostat won't control the temperature until you've repaired the pump. But the house will be warmer and the pipes less likely to freeze.

MAINTAINING A HEAT PUMP

Most heat pump manufacturers delight in telling you that a heat pump is not a household appliance, implying strongly that you ought to keep your hands off. They're probably right, but then a heating system that cost you several thousand dollars probably shouldn't break down at the first frost.

Where's the middle ground? There's no question that routine maintenance is up to you. At the very least it's your job to change or clean the filters once a month. In winter shovel snow or ice away from the outdoor unit. In summer wash it down with soap and water.

Beyond that, talk with your repair person. Find out what a maintenance package costs and check your warranty to see whether you can do the sorts of things described in this part without voiding the warranty. You'll be surprised at what you can do and how much you can save.

STUFF YOU'LL NEED

✔ **MATERIALS:**
Household oil, germicidal cleaner for coils, bleach, disposable air filter (if applicable), necessary replacement parts

✔ **TOOLS:**
Screwdriver, wrenches, or both; shop vacuum with brush attachment; 20,000-ohm, 5-watt resistor; two wire leads with alligator clips at each end; multimeter

MAINTAINING A HEAT PUMP
Outdoor maintenance

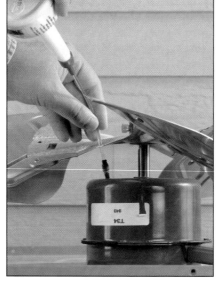

1 **BEFORE YOU CAN DO ANY MAINTENANCE, YOU'LL NEED TO TURN OFF THE POWER** at the circuit breaker or fuse panel and at the cutoff switch outside the home.

2 **TAKE OUT THE SCREWS OR BOLTS THAT HOLD THE FAN COVER IN PLACE.** Remove the screws or bolts holding the casing around the unit and take off the casing.

OIL THE FAN MOTOR. Look for oil ports on the fan motor. If they exist, squeeze in a couple drops of household oil.

3 **DIRT IN THE COILS CAN LOWER A HEAT PUMP'S EFFICIENCY BY AS MUCH AS ONE-THIRD.** Most manufacturers recommend flushing out the dirt with a garden hose, spraying as best you can from the inside toward the outside. While you're cleaning, scrub the fan, taking care not to bend the blades. Check to see if any of the fins are bent. If so, straighten them with a fin comb.

Indoor maintenance

The indoor end of the heat pump looks much like any forced-air furnace but with no flame. Instead of fire, the furnace has a series of coils that look similar to those on the outside. The purpose of the coils is different: The outdoor coils are either absorbing or giving off heat, depending on whether the pump is heating or cooling; the indoor coils are bringing the air blown across them to the desired temperature. The coils and the filters that clean the air that goes across them need regular maintenance.

Maintenance is largely a matter of keeping things clean. Like the air filters on any other forced-air furnace, those on a heat pump must be cleaned regularly. Dirty filters drastically reduce the efficiency of a furnace. Having spent the money for an efficient furnace, it would be a shame to send all that heat up the stack.

Despite the filters, dust and dirt are likely to build up on the inside coils. This will be less than what you find in the outside coils, so don't even think of hosing it down. Do the job with a vacuum cleaner. The best time is at the beginning and end of the heating season. During cooling season, dust may stick to condensation on the coils.

Heat pumps can develop that classic smell you get when you first turn on the air-conditioner in a motel room. A germicidal cleaner for coils, applied according to manufacturer's recommendations, will help to clear the air.

Underneath the coils you'll find a drain pan that collects water that drips from the air-conditioner coils. A clogged drain hole spells trouble, so as long as the unit is open, take a look and clean it out as necessary.

Once you're done with the furnace, walk around the house to make sure the vents are open and aren't blocked by rugs or furniture. Blocked vents mean that the compressor has to run longer to bring a room to the desired temperature. Excessive use costs money and shortens the life of the compressor and valves.

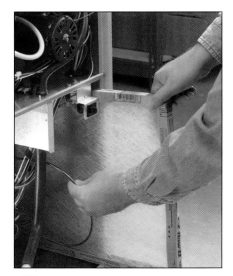

1 **DOUBLE-CHECK THAT THE POWER IS STILL OFF,** remove the access panel, and look for the filter or filters. You'll find them near the coil. Pull out the springlike retaining arm and remove the filter. Vacuum and wash reusable filters with the hose; replace disposable filters.

2 **DIRT ON THE COILS NOT ONLY REDUCES EFFICIENCY,** it can also be the source of dirt, spores, and odors that get blown through the house. Turn off the power, put a soft brush on a shop vacuum, and thoroughly vacuum and brush the coils. Wash the coils with a germicidal cleaner designed for indoor coils. Vacuum the blower wheel on the fan.

3 **STANDING WATER IN THE DRAIN PAN IS A SIGN THAT THE DRAIN HOLE IS PLUGGED.** Mop up the water and unplug the drain hole. Rinse with a mixture of 1 part household bleach to 4 parts water. Put the filters back in and put the access panel in place. **CLEAN THE BASE PAN AT THE BOTTOM OF THE UNIT,** and make sure none of the drain holes are plugged. Replace the cover.

GOOD IDEA

GET PROFESSIONAL HELP
Heat pumps are extremely sophisticated furnaces. Simple maintenance is a matter of having the time. But the best way to guarantee the system won't crash when you need it most is to check and maintain the refrigerant system. This requires a pro.

A pro will check everything, one of the most important being the refrigerant level. The technician will visually check for leaks, monitor temperature in different parts of the system, and perhaps take a couple of readings with a gauge. If the test shows that the coolant level is low, recharging the system is in order, a task that only a licensed technician can do. Have a local HVAC company make a yearly inspection for refrigerant and other problems. You'll save yourself a cold and sleepless night.

Diagnosing a pump that won't start

Not all heat pump repairs are the do-it-yourself type. Any problem with the compressor, for example, requires a technician licensed to work with refrigerants. About all you can do on your own is wreck the pump and ruin earth's ozone layer.

The homeowner with a basic knowledge of electricity can fix motor problems, but before you do anything or call anyone, check the obvious. Is the power on, both at the circuit breaker and at the external cutoff? Are the thermostat wires all connected and is the thermostat set to the right temperature? If the compressor is warm it may be temporarily overloaded. Let it cool and try again.

If none of the suggestions above and none of those below solve the problem, call a technician. It may be the compressor, or it could be any one of several circuits that need a professional's expertise.

Discharging capacitors can be dangerous. For more information on discharging them safely, see page 512.

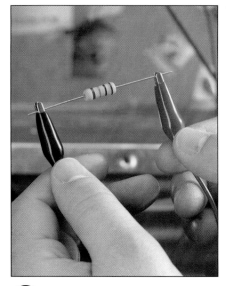

1 **IF YOU'VE RULED OUT THE OBVIOUS, THE PROBLEM MAY BE IN THE MOTOR CIRCUIT.** Remove the covers to the outdoor unit and test the capacitor, which stores energy to help the motor start. Make a capacitor discharger from two leads and a 20,000-ohm, 5-watt resistor. (See page 512.) Put a lead on each of the capacitor terminals and leave them there for about 10 seconds. This releases the stored energy and the circuit is safe to work on.

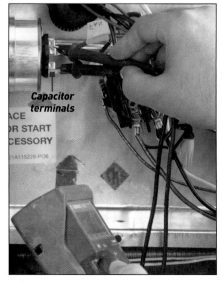

Capacitor terminals

2 **TO TEST THE CAPACITOR,** set the ohmmeter on your multimeter to RX1. Put a meter lead on each side of the discharged capacitor. A digital meter will show resistance rise and then fall. On analog meters the needle should move across the scale and then back. If it doesn't, replace the capacitor.

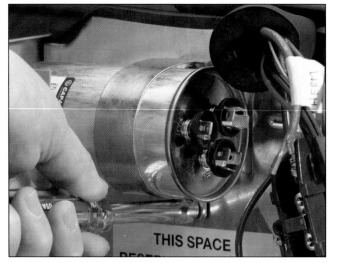

THIS SPACE

3 **BEFORE YOU REPLACE THE CAPACITOR, DISCONNECT THE WIRES,** labeling them and marking the corresponding terminals too. Unscrew the screws holding the bracket in place and take out the capacitor. Replace it with an identical model.

4 **IF THE CAPACITOR CHECKS OUT, TEST THE MOTOR WINDINGS.** Set the ohmmeter to RX100. Put one of the probes on the compressor discharge piping. Put the other on the R (run) terminal, then on the S (start) terminal, and finally on the C (common) terminal. If the meter moves when the probes are at any of these points, the motor windings have short-circuited and you'll need to replace the motor.

MAINTAINING A HEAT PUMP
Diagnosing ice buildup on outside coils

Some ice buildup on the outside coils is normal—so normal that the system actually has a defrost cycle. The problem usually occurs when the outdoor temperature drops below the boiling point of the coolant—around 15°F (-9.4°C). The temperature drop causes the coolant to liquefy and act as a refrigerant on the outdoor coils. To prevent this, a defrost cycle kicks in at about 28°F (-2°C). The heat pump temporarily runs backward, melting the ice. The auxiliary heat source in the house kicks on, and both you and the outdoor coils are warm.

Sometimes, however, things go wrong. This may be something like a faulty valve, which requires a trained technician who can work with refrigerants. But just as often, it's a problem you can solve yourself.

Simple maintenance chores on a regular schedule will save you money and keep you warm.

1 **IF ICING OCCURS, FIRST CHECK THE THERMOSTAT.** Make sure it's set to heating, not cooling, and that the room temperature is above 55°F (13°C). If not, reset the controls as needed and the problem will likely go away. Then go outside and make sure the outdoor coil isn't blocked by snow or leaves.

2 **CLEAN THE AIR FILTER.** A dirty or clogged filter will keep the fan from blowing enough air over the indoor coils to warm them adequately. When the refrigerant makes the trip back outside, it can't give off enough heat to defrost the coils. No matter how clean you think the filter is, take it out, and vacuum and wash it (or replace a disposable filter). Put parts back in place, and if nothing else, you've eliminated the filter as a problem.

3 **THE REVERSING VALVE, FOUND IN THE OUTSIDE UNIT,** is responsible for running the system in defrost mode and must be replaced professionally. You can, however, diagnose and fix the solenoid and the needle valve that controls it. To check the solenoid, turn off the power, remove the cover, and look for a valve that has six tubes going into it. The solenoid coil is attached. Remove the wires going into it and put the ohmmeter leads where the wires were. If the reading isn't between zero and infinity, you'll need to replace the coil.

4 **TO REPLACE THE COIL, REMOVE THE NUT HOLDING IT IN PLACE** and slide it off its stem. Slide an identical replacement coil over the stem and tighten the nut over it. Reattach the wires.

Installing an electric baseboard heater

An electric baseboard heater can get heat into a cold part of the house. But head for the breaker box first because a new heater requires a new circuit, and you want to make sure you have room for it. You will need at least one empty spot on the panel. Two are better. If there's no room for an extra circuit, find another way to heat the cold spot. Code requires an electric heater to have its own circuit, and even if it didn't, combining it with an existing circuit would overload the breakers every time the heat came on.

Two open slots will let you put in a 240-volt heater, which, because it draws less current, wastes less electricity. Always go with a 240-volt heater, if possible. If you only have space for a 120-volt circuit, make sure you buy a 120-volt heater. Putting a 240-volt heater on a 120-volt circuit is dangerous and won't give you enough heat anyway.

You can hang electric heaters against drywall, wallpaper, wood paneling, particleboard, chipboard, and tongue-and-groove panel. Putting a baseboard heater against soundproofing board, pegboard, or ceiling tile is a fire hazard.

The directions here are for a 240-volt heater, which is both the most efficient and the most common. Wiring for a 120-volt heater is slightly different. Follow the directions that come with the heater.

STUFF YOU'LL NEED

✔ MATERIALS:
240-volt electric heater, 10/2 cable, wire caps, electrical tape, thermostat and junction box, cable clamps, breaker or breakers

✔ TOOLS:
Drill and bits, drywall saw, utility knife, fish tape, screwdriver, wire stripper, needle-nose pliers, stud finder

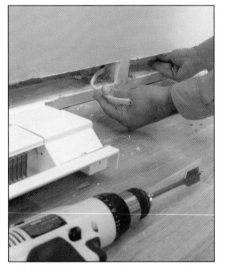

① CHOOSE A SPOT UNDER A WINDOW FOR THE HEATER. If you're using a heater with a built-in thermometer, run 10/2 cable from the heater to the breaker panel. The wires need to run *through* the wall—you can't leave them exposed, and you can't tuck them between the heater and the baseboard. Remove materials and drill holes for the cable through studs along the path. Fish the cable, leaving about 2 feet extra at the heater. Run the cable to the panel, leaving the cable long enough to drape to the floor once it reaches the panel. Wait to connect it.

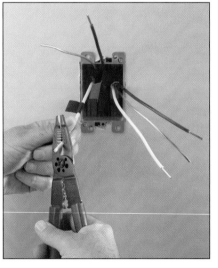

IF YOU'RE USING A WALL-MOUNTED THERMOSTAT, THE CABLE FROM THE BREAKER PANEL WON'T RUN DIRECTLY TO THE HEATER. Run the cable to where the thermostat will be, instead, and run a second length of cable from there to the heater. Feed both through a junction box and install it, marking the wires so that you know which is which.

② IT'S EASIEST TO WIRE THE HEATER BEFORE YOU MOUNT IT ON THE WALL. Remove the knockout in the back of the heater by giving it a sharp blow with the blade of a screwdriver. Put in a connector—a type of clamp required by code to prevent the edge of the box from accidentally shorting out the cable. Strip about a hand's length of the outer insulation off the cable. Fish it through the connector and tighten the clamp around the end of the outer insulation.

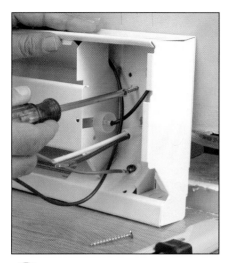

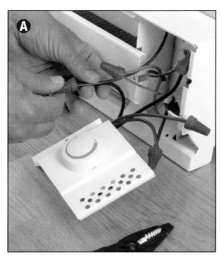

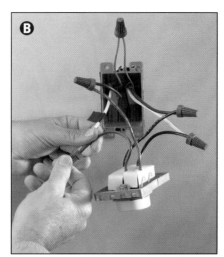

❸ FIND AND MARK THE STUDS BEHIND THE HEATER. Line up the holes in the back of the heater with the studs. Push any extra cable inside the wall, then screw the heater in place as directed by the manufacturer. (Accessing the screw holes sometimes involves removing a part or two.) What you do next depends on what type of thermostat is being used. (See Options **Ⓐ** and **Ⓑ** at right.)

OPTION Ⓐ IF YOU'RE USING A BUILT-IN THERMOSTAT, WIRE IT AS DIRECTED. Usually the incoming black and white supply wires connect to two red wires on the thermostat. The two black wires on the thermostat connect to the two black heater wires that were twisted together. On a 240-volt circuit like the one shown here, the white wire is hot, and code requires you to mark it with a piece of black tape as a reminder.

OPTION Ⓑ IF YOU ARE USING A WALL-MOUNTED THERMOSTAT, it must be a 240-volt, double-pole thermostat. A regular thermostat, designed to run at 24 volts, will burn up if connected to 240 volts. Necessary to meet code, a double-pole switch shuts off power to both 120-volt lines that make up the 240 volts going to the heater. Wire the thermostat as directed. The black and white wires coming from the panel are usually connected to the two red thermostat wires. The black wires coming out of the thermostat are connected to the white and black wires that run to the heater. Connect the bare ground wires to each other and to the thermostat ground wire, if there is one.

When the white wire is hot, code requires you to mark it with black tape as a reminder.

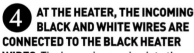

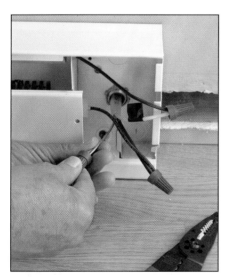

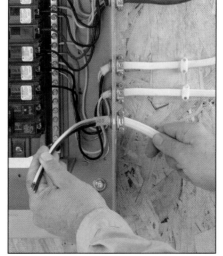

❹ AT THE HEATER, THE INCOMING BLACK AND WHITE WIRES ARE CONNECTED TO THE BLACK HEATER WIRES. The bare wire coming into the heater is connected to a green ground screw in the heater. Mark the white wire with black tape to show anyone working on it in the future that the wire is hot.

❺ TURN OFF THE POWER TO THE ENTIRE HOUSE. Punch out a new knockout in the side of the breaker box. Install a connector for the cable. Feed the cable through the connector to the slots for the new breakers. Mark the cable at the connector. Remove and strip the outer insulation back to the mark, put it back through the connector, and tighten it. Wrap a piece of black tape around the insulation of the white wire to show that it's hot.

❻ A 240-VOLT CIRCUIT REQUIRES TWO BREAKERS. To install, put the tab on one end of the breakers under the notch for it. Bring the other end down onto the other tab and press until it snaps into place. Screw the black wire into one of the breakers; screw the white wire into the other and mark it with a piece of black tape. Screw the bare ground wire to the ground bus bar (see page 183, Step 7).

Adding a hot-water baseboard heater

REQUIRED SKILLS:
Basic mechanical and carpentry skills.

🕐 **HOW LONG WILL IT TAKE?**

Experienced . . . . 5 hrs.
Handy . . . . 8 hrs.
Novice . . . . 12 hrs.

VARIABLES: Some older systems have cast-iron pipe rather than copper. Leave cast-iron work to the pros. If you're working on copper, the success of the job depends on your ability to sweat (solder) copper pipe. If you've never done it before, this isn't the place to start. There are a lot of joints, and a leak in the wrong one can ruin a floor or ceiling.

STUFF YOU'LL NEED

✔ **MATERIALS:**
Hot-water baseboard heater, Type M pipe, reducer elbows or tees, other fittings as needed, pipe supports, plumbing solder, flux

✔ **TOOLS:**
Pipe cutter, propane torch, tape measure, drill and bit

Getting hot-water baseboard heat into an addition or a cold room is an issue of real estate as much as it is a plumbing issue. As always, the three things you need to worry about are location, location, and location. First, plan to put the new baseboard heater where you'll find the coldest air—on an outside wall, preferably under a window. Second, decide where the couch is going to go before you pick your spot. Hiding the baseboard heater with furniture blocks off much of the heat. Third, look at the floor framing underneath the intended location and adjust the position as necessary to avoid hitting the joists. If the finished floor has yet to be installed, make sure there will be a minimum of 1 inch between the bottom of the heater and the finished floor so that air can flow through the heater.

As for plumbing, baseboard pipe is either ½- or ¾-inch-diameter copper. Check what you have in the house and buy a baseboard heater to match. (Many are convertible and will fit either size pipe, but don't count on it without

checking.) Instead of using regular plumbing pipe (Type L), use Type M copper pipe, the standard in heating. It's a low-pressure pipe with a thinner wall and costs less than Type L. When you buy the baseboard heater, get one that says it's complete, meaning that the pipe and heating fins are inside the case. You'll have to purchase the cutoff valve, bleeder, and end panels separately; get panels with doors so that you can access the bleeder and cutoff valves when necessary.

Leaks are both a problem and a real possibility. Even the pros test for them, though they usually test with pressurized air before turning on the water. You probably don't have a pressure tester on hand, so you'll have to test with the furnace on and water running through the pipes. Know in advance where all the cutoff valves are.

Layout of the pipes depends on the size of the baseboard heater, so buy the heater before you start. Take the measurements of the room with you and talk to a salesperson about getting the proper size baseboard heater.

① **AVOID FLOOR JOISTS WHEN CHOOSING THE LOCATION FOR THE NEW HEATER.** Slip a cutoff valve on the in-feed side of the baseboard. Slip a bleeder valve on the other end and position the baseboard against the wall. Screw the heater in place, mark the floor underneath the center of each fitting, and remove the heater. Drill holes through the marks that are at least ⅜ inch larger in diameter than the pipe you'll be using.

② **REASSEMBLE THE HEATER AND TEST-FIT ALL THE PIPE BEFORE SOLDERING.** Attach the elbow to the riser. (Make it a few inches longer than you will need.) Drop the riser down the hole. Attach the elbow to the valve. Friction hold the pipes in the fittings while you are installing the run below. **NOW TURN THE FURNACE OFF AND OPEN THE VALVE TO DRAIN THE BOILER.** What you do next depends on how the existing plumbing is run. (See Options **Ⓐ** and **Ⓑ** above right.)

OPTION Ⓐ IF THE WATER FLOWS IN A LARGE LOOP THROUGH ALL THE BASEBOARD HEATERS, you'll see risers going up through the floor at each end of the baseboard heater, with no main supply pipe in between. In this kind of system, cut through the main supply pipe opposite the new supply riser. Put on a reducer elbow that steps down from the size of the main to the size of the riser. Cut through the line opposite the return riser and add a reducer elbow.

Make sure the pipes are dry before soldering them.

OPTION Ⓑ IF THERE ARE TWO PARALLEL PIPES WITH A PIPE RUNNING FROM EACH INTO EACH OF THE BASEBOARDS, one pipe is supplying water and the other is returning it to the furnace. (The return line goes into the boiler at a lower point than the supply line.) Cut the supply line opposite what will be the new supply riser; cut the return pipe opposite the new return riser. On one end of the cut, put a reducer tee that steps down from the pipe diameter to the riser diameter. Then cut each pipe again so that it will fit into the other end of the tee.

③ RUN PIPE FROM THE FITTING TO THE RISER. If the pipe will run through joists, drill holes ⅜ inch larger than the pipe diameter. If the pipes run parallel to the joists, support them with pipe hangers spaced every 4 feet. (See inset.) Make sure the pipe is level, adjusting the supports as necessary.

A+ WORK SMARTER

FITTINGS HAVE TO FIT

Fittings are designed to fit just so far, and no farther, over a pipe. Knowing how far is important when you're splicing into existing systems or connecting into a fixed object. Fortunately, the solution is simple. The end of a fitting holds a length of pipe equal to the pipe's diameter. A ¾-inch fitting holds a ¾-inch length of pipe at each end. A ½-inch fitting holds a ½-inch length of pipe at each end. If in doubt, just put a small ruler or tape inside the fitting. The fitting will house a length of pipe equal to the distance from the end of the fitting to the point inside where it steps down to a smaller diameter.

Adding a hot-water baseboard heater *(continued)*

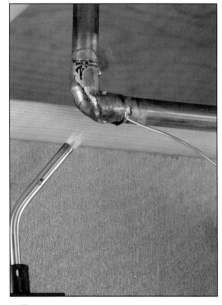

4 **MARK EACH RISER TO LENGTH.** You can measure the length of the riser, but it's as effective to do it by eye. Slip an elbow on the run to the riser to help determine where you will make the cut.

5 **CUT THE RISER TO LENGTH WITH A PIPE CUTTER.** Connect the riser to the run with the elbow, and you're ready to solder the entire system together.

For more information on soldering see page 93.

6 **DOUBLE-CHECK THAT ALL THE PIPES ARE THE CORRECT LENGTH.** You don't want to solder a joint that's under pressure because the pipe's too long. Clean and solder the joints one by one. Once you've soldered the pipe and elbow going into the baseboard heater, install the end caps on the baseboard.

7 **AT THIS POINT, THE PLUMBING'S DONE, BUT ALL YOUR PIPES ARE FILLED WITH AIR.** To get rid of it, find pipes that enter the furnace and go into the boiler. One carries water out to the baseboard heaters, and the other returns it to the boiler. Open the drain valve on the return (lower) pipe. Turn on the furnace and turn up the heat until the circulator starts running. Air will begin to rush out of the open drain valve. Wait until water begins to come out and then close the valve. Bleed each of the baseboard heaters as described on page 515.

Dry sweat

When you solder a fitting to a pipe, the pipe must be dry. Even a trickle of water running through the pipe will cool it enough to prevent a successful job. Steam coming out of the fitting is a good indication that it's too wet to solder. Drain the system and flex pipes downward to drain them before soldering on new fittings. If you can't stop a trickle, roll a piece of soft, white bread into a ball (no crusts), and stuff it into the pipe before soldering. Once you turn the water back on, the moisture will cause the bread to dissolve.

Adding a forced-air heat run

When it comes to adding a run of ducting and register to a cold room, there's very little a pro can do that you can't do on your own.

The first thing you need to know is that you should use rigid duct as much as possible. You'll find several different diameters of rigid duct; measure the room you're heating and install the recommended size. Flex duct—flexible plastic duct lined with a metal coil—may be easy to install and works well in certain situations but sags and turns can severely restrict airflow and sometimes deliver no heat at all.

Elbows also restrict airflow but are absolutely necessary. An adjustable, round metal elbow is built like a piece of lightweight armor and adjusts from straight to 90 degrees. Rotate the ends to get the desired angle.

Duct work is held together with sheet metal screws and sealed to prevent loss of air through joints and seams. Sealing the joints and seams properly can result in significant savings on heating and air-conditioning bills. Even though it's called duct tape, duct tape is not an efficient or long-lasting solution and should be not be used as a sealing agent.

Duct mastic, which is a water-based, flexible sealant that can be applied by brush or with gloved hand, is the sealant of choice of the U.S. Department of Energy for efficiency and durability.

Foil-backed tape with a rubber-based adhesive is also acceptable but somewhat less durable and versatile in application.

Support rigid ductwork with metal plumber's tape that nails to the framing. If you need to use short lengths of flex duct, support it with supports sold for that purpose.

You can install a special fitting with a damper in the duct run between the boot and the starter collar to help regulate air flow.

① BEGIN AS CLOSE TO THE PLENUM AS YOU CAN. Ideally, install the vent on the top of the plenum next to the furnace (see page 489) but that isn't always possible and you may need to come off an existing duct. Put a starting collar on the duct and trace a cutout line around it.

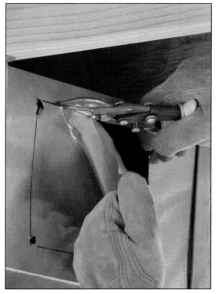

② CUT A HOLE ALONG THE LAYOUT LINES. If the duct is sheet metal, make the cut with tin snips. If it's a flat, rigid fiberglass panel with a metal facing, cut it with a jigsaw. Apply duct mastic and place the fitting in the hole. Bend back the fingers to hold it in place and insert sheet metal screws through the lips of the collar.

Adding a forced-air heat run *(continued)*

3 **INSTALL THE REGISTER BOOT NEXT, TRACING AROUND IT ON THE FLOOR TO LAY OUT THE HOLE YOU'LL CUT.** Start the cutout by drilling a ½- or ¾-inch hole. Put the blade of your jigsaw in the hole, and then cut along the lines to create the opening. (See inset.) Put the boot inside the opening and nail it in place with a couple of roofing nails. Screw a register over the boot and into the floor.

4 **CUT, TEST FIT, AND AND TEMPORARILY ASSEMBLE THE RUN OF DUCT TO CONNECT THE STARTER COLLAR TO THE REGISTER BOOT.** Use as much rigid duct as possible, and as few elbows and as little flex duct as possible. Cut rigid duct with tin snips. Cut flex duct with a flex-duct tool. Support duct with plumber's tape nailed to the rafters every 4 feet and within 6 inches of any connection. Don't let flex duct sag more than ½ inch per foot.

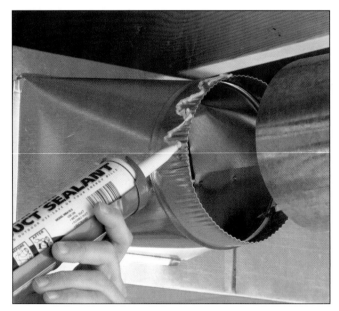

5 **SEAL THE JOINTS BETWEEN SECTIONS WITH DUCT MASTIC.** Begin on the metal ductwork by sliding the joint partially apart and covering the exposed surface with duct mastic. Reseat the joint and screw it together with two sheet-metal screws.

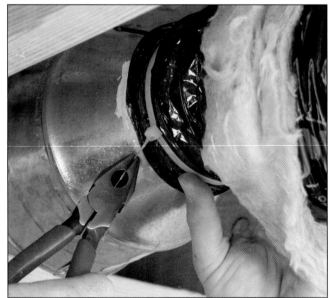

6 **IF YOU'VE USED FLEX DUCT, ROLL BACK THE INSULATION AND THE OUTER LINER OF PLASTIC.** Use mastic to coat the metal that the flex duct fits over. Slide the inner plastic over the mastic and attach it with a compression strap. Put the insulation and outer layer over the takeoff and attach it with a second compression strap. Stretch the duct to full length so that it's as smooth as possible. Attach the other end using mastic and compression straps.

Installing auxiliary gas heaters

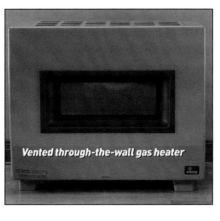
Vented through-the-wall gas heater

Through-the-wall gas heaters reach places your main system can't. The three basic types are vent-free, vented, and direct-vent. Check local codes for the kinds of auxiliary gas heaters approved for use in your area.

A **vent-free heater** is the simplest to install and the most efficient. It actually hangs on the wall. Because its high-efficiency burner produces almost no fumes and doesn't require a chimney or vent, it's a perfect choice for an area that's used occasionally. The U.S. Department of Energy warns against operating one for more than two hours a day. It also recommends leaving the window open about ½ inch to provide a constant source of fresh air.

A **vented heater** has an exhaust vent that directs the fumes outside. As long as you use the appropriate vent pipe, the vent can go through the wall or roof, but it must go nearly to the roof peak. Like a vent-free heater, it needs a constant source of fresh air. Most frame construction allows plenty of outside air to get in the house, but you may need to install registers to get fresh air into the room. The unit must also stand at least 6 inches from the wall because air flows to the flame from the back.

The vent on a **direct-vent heater** is a pipe within a pipe. The core pipe acts like a chimney; the outer section pulls fresh air in from outside. Because the fumes go outdoors, and because it has an external air supply, the direct-vent heater is a smart choice for a part of the house that gets more than a few hours' use a day.

All three types have optional fans that help to better distribute the heat.

Whichever heater you install, you must leave installation of the gas pipe and vent to a trained professional. However, you can do much of the work yourself.

Installing a vent-free gas heater

1 MEASURE THE ROOM TO DETERMINE THE PROPER SIZE FOR THE HEATER. A small room may not contain enough air for a large heater, so begin by figuring out the volume of the room. Multiply its length by its width by its height (all measured in feet). Multiply by 20 to see how large a heater (measured in British thermal units, or Btus) it can support. A 7'×10' room with an 8-foot ceiling would need an 11,200-Btu heater (7×10×8×20 = 11,200 Btus). The BTU rating of a heater is listed on its box. A heater producing 10,000 Btus/hour will probably work well in this space, but one producing 20,000 Btus/hour would require additional venting—usually just a register that passes through to another room. Follow the directions in the owner's manual.

Installing a vent-free gas heater *(continued)*

② **CHOOSE A SPOT ON THE WALL FOR THE HEATER.** It's best to put the heater in the coldest spot, usually under a window. Heaters also require certain clearances between the objects in the room and the heater's top, bottom, and sides. Check the owner's manual and choose the spot with clearances in mind. If the unit has a fan, make sure you put the heater near an outlet. This type of heater usually hangs from a wall bracket that comes with it. Draw a level line on the wall, indicating its position. The owner's manual will tell you how far from the floor it should be.

③ **FIND THE STUDS IN THE WALL WITH A STUD FINDER.** Line the mounting bracket up with the level line, moving it if possible so that it will be screwed into a stud. Temporarily tape it in place. Trace around the screw holes to mark their location on the wall. If the screws will miss the studs, drill for anchors—they're usually included with the heater—and put them in the wall. Screw the bracket in place. If there is a thermostat bulb, position it as directed in the owner's manual and hang the heater on the wall. Drive additional screws as directed. Have your gas company or a plumber connect the gas line.

Installing a vented heater

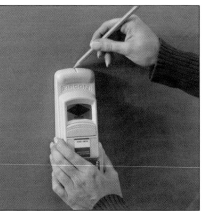
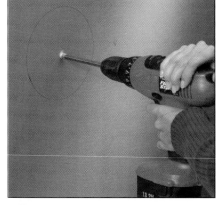

① **CHOOSE A SPOT ALONG AN OUTSIDE WALL FOR THE HEATER.** Allow for manufacturer's clearances and the vent that will run through the wall. Find the studs near where the heater will be located. Position the heater in relation to the studs as directed. You'll want it to be near an outlet if it has a fan. If there is an outlet or switch in the wall cavity through which the vent will pass, choose a new spot to avoid cutting through any wires. With a noncontact voltage tester, double-check that there are no wires near where you'll be cutting.

② **LAY OUT THE HOLE FOR THE VENT WITH EITHER THE TEMPLATE OR THE DIMENSIONS** supplied by the manufacturer. To make sure that the hole you cut through the outside of the house aligns with the hole on the inside, drill a ⅜-inch-diameter locator hole through the center of what will be the vent hole and out through the siding of the house. Lay out the outside hole by centering the template over the locator hole.

③ **CUT OUT THE LAYOUT LINE.** Follow the line as closely as possible. The wall plates are large enough to cover almost any mistake. Once you've cut the inside opening, cut the outside opening. Have a qualified heating technician install the vent and gas line, using Type-B, double-walled vent pipe and allowing the proper clearance. The pipe must extend at least 3 feet beyond the roof and 2 feet above anything within 10 feet, including higher sections of the roof. The top of the pipe must have a cap to prevent back drafts.

Installing a direct-vent heater

The heart of a direct-vent heater is a sealed combustion box. Air for the fire comes in from an outside vent; any fumes that are produced go directly back out. In a properly operating system, room air never mixes with the fire. This not only eliminates fumes, it eliminates a problem common to other heaters: room air that has already been heated at least partially. If room air is used to feed the fire, some of it will go up the chimney, taking heat with it.

The vent that takes air to and from the combustion chamber is a pipe within a pipe. While you can place the heater yourself, have a pro install the vent to make sure no fumes work their way into the house.

The unit will be most effective when it's placed as close as possible to the coldest part of the room, even if this means moving a power source.

1 POSITION THE HEATER AS DIRECTED IN THE OWNER'S MANUAL. As with vented heaters, choose the location based on wiring that may be in the way, a nearby power source for the fan (if necessary), and location of the studs.

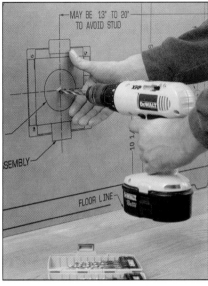

2 LAY OUT THE VENT USING THE TEMPLATE OR MEASUREMENTS IN YOUR OWNER'S MANUAL. Make sure the inside and outside holes align by drilling a locator hole first. Center the template on the locator hole to lay out both the inside and outside holes.

3 UNLIKE VENTED HEATERS, DIRECT-VENT HEATERS CAN GO THROUGH THE WALL without having to run up to the roof. Some manufacturers make a telescoping vent that adjusts to the thickness of the wall. Other types of vent must be cut to length, with the inner pipe being cut slightly longer than the outer pipe. While you can cut the vent pipe, have your heating technician install it and the cap that goes over it.

4 DIRECT-VENT HEATERS VARY DEPENDING ON THE MANUFACTURER: Some screw directly to the wall, some have mounting brackets, and others sit on the floor. Install the heater as directed.

5 HAVE A HEATING TECHNICIAN INSTALL BOTH THE VENT AND THE GAS LINE, using black iron or steel gas line, Type-B vent, and the appropriate cap to prevent back drafts.

BUILDING CODES in the United States (U.S.) and Canada are similar, and most of the directions in this book meet code on either side of the border. There are differences, however, and sometimes what meets code in the U.S. doesn't make the grade in Canada, or Canadian codes offer alternatives that wouldn't meet specifications in the U.S.

The biggest differences are in the plumbing and electrical codes. Canadian codes permit the use of ABS plastic pipe for drain and waste lines. U.S. code allows primarily PVC, but ABS is acceptable in certain parts of the country. Canadian electrical code calls for a separate service-panel bus bar for the ground wire, and for a ground screw on all receptacle and switchboxes boxes (metal or plastic). U.S. code generally requires neither.

UNIFORM DIFFERENCES. Neither country has a monopoly on conflicting code authorities. The National Housing Code of Canada (NHC) sets uniform standards, but provinces, cities, and towns can set local standards. As a result, your local code may vary from what's described here.

You can purchase full-length copies of the relevant codes but they can be expensive and difficult to wade through. Most of the material deals with commercial installations. Smaller, more distilled handbooks are available to buy or borrow from libraries that emphasize residential installations.

In Canada, as in the U.S., the only way to be sure you're meeting code is to ask your local building inspector while the job is still in the planning stages. Which begs the question: If it's your house and you're doing the work yourself why should a city inspector come around and tell you what to do?

COLLECTIVE WISDOM. Codes and inspections are a sort of collective wisdom based on the experience of the construction trades, fire and police departments, and manufacturers. Those lessons have been incorporated into building codes. They exist to prevent house fires and injury from shocks and to keep all the systems in your home running effectively.

MEETING NATIONAL, PROVINCIAL, AND LOCAL CODES. Your local building department will often require you to get a permit and have the work approved by one of its inspectors. Inspectors and building departments use the national code references as the basis for most of their regulations. However, local standards often supplement or modify these basic rules. You'll find an overview of most common code requirements on the following pages. However, the list is not complete and you may need other sources of information.

COORDINATING THE TASKS. If you are building an addition to your house or gutting walls to remodel a kitchen or bathroom, you'll need to juggle carpentry, plumbing, and wall and floor finishing. Whether you do all or some of the work yourself, it's important that the various jobs are coordinated so that workers do not get in the way of each other and so that inspectors can see what they need to inspect. Here's an example of a properly phased installation:

❶ Install framing or gut the walls.

❷ Run the rough plumbing, install electrical cable and boxes, and then call in the inspector.

❸ Cover the walls with drywall, and paint.

❹ Install the finish plumbing and electrical, and have it inspected.

HOMER'S HINDSIGHT

DO YOUR HOMEWORK

Meeting with an inspector can seem like an annoyance especially when you've been around home improvement as long as I have. Fact is, anyone can benefit from an inspector's expertise. Recently, I showed a guy a rough sketch and an even sketchier materials list for a project I was in a hurry to complete. I admit it was kind of a mess. He wasn't happy about but he looked it over anyway and pointed out a dangerously overloaded circuit I was planning to install. I was glad he took a look.

Working with an inspector

Inspectors usually work with professional electricians who know codes and what is expected at inspections. Inspectors usually have a tight schedule and can't take time to educate you about what is needed. Their job is to inspect, not to help you plan your project. Take these steps to ensure that the inspections go smoothly.

● Before scheduling an inspection, ask the building department for printed information about your type of electrical project. Make neat, readable, and complete drawings and provide a list of the materials.

● When you present your plans, accept criticisms and directives graciously. It usually does no good to argue—and the inspector does know more than you do. Make it clear that you want to do things the right way. Take notes while the inspector talks to you so you can remember every detail of what needs to be done.

● Be clear on when the inspections will take place and exactly what needs to be done before each inspection. Before calling for an inspection, double-check that everything required is complete—don't make the inspector come back again. Don't cover up wiring that the inspector needs to see. If you install drywall before the inspection, you may have to rip it out and reinstall it after the inspection.

● Some building departments limit the kinds of work that a homeowner can do; you may have to hire a professional for at least part of a job. Others will let you take on advanced work only if you can pass an oral or written test.

General construction

BASEMENT INSULATION. In Canada, the inside of basement walls must be treated with a damp-proofing product (usually a paint-on product) before insulation is installed. The insulation goes against the damp-proofing, and is then covered by a vapor barrier. In the U.S., polyethylene sheeting is attached to the wall instead.

CRAWL SPACE INSULATION. Insulation must go down the wall, but stop no less than 2 inches (50 mm) above the floor. In the U.S., insulation continues to the floor and runs partway across it.

DOOR JAMBS. To help a door withstand forced entry, Canadian code requires solid wood blocking at lock height on both the lock and hinge side of the door.

FLOOR JOISTS. Generally speaking, replacement joists should be the same width as the old ones. Both Canada and the U.S. set standards, however, on how long an unsupported span of joist can be. The span varies based both on the width of the joist, and how far apart the joists are spaced. Generally speaking, Canadian code requires shorter spans than those allowed in the U.S. If you suspect the joists supporting your floor aren't wide enough, talk with your local building inspector.

HEADERS. Although construction of headers is the same in both Canada and the U.S., allowable spans for load-bearing headers are slightly different. Allowable spans also vary with the number of floors the header supports, and the amount of snow likely to build up on the roof. In areas with milder weather, a header made of two 2×4s (38×89 mm), with ½-inch (12-mm) plywood in between can span a door opening as wide as 40 inches (1.01 meters), considerably more than in the U.S. A 2×8 (38×184 mm) beam built the same way can span an opening of up to 68 inches (1.75 mm) slightly less than in the U.S. Check with your local building authority on how snowfall, number of floors, and the wood species you're using will affect requirements.

LINTELS. See "Headers."

SMOKE ALARMS. Smoke alarms must be placed on every floor, must be interconnected, and must be powered by the home's electrical system. Battery-operated smoke alarms are acceptable only in homes with no power.

WOOD FLOORING. Standard wood-flooring thicknesses are different in the U.S. and Canada, as are the nailing patterns. In Canada, the size and spacing of nails depends on the thickness of the flooring. In the U.S., the nailing pattern also depends on the width of the flooring. Whether in the U.S. or Canada, follow the manufacturer's instructions, and check with your local building authority for specifics.

- **5⁄16-INCH-THICK (7.9-MM) FLOOR:** 1½-inch-long (38-mm) nails spaced at a maximum of 8 inches (200 mm).

- **7⁄16-INCH-THICK (11.1-MM) FLOOR:** 2-inch-long (51-mm) nails spaced at a maximum of 12 inches (300 mm).

- **¾-INCH-THICK (19-MM) FLOOR:** 2¼-inch-long (57-mm) nails spaced at a maximum of 16 inches (400 mm).

Metrics and you

The metric system has taken most of the world by storm— with the exception of all of the United States and some of the building trades. In Canada, you'll find that some trades have converted completely to metric, while others still use the old English measurements. When you get right down to it, it doesn't really matter: The guy at the lumberyard is going to hand you exactly the same sheet whether you order 19-mm plywood or ¾-inch plywood.To make it easy to compare sizes, however, we've included both English and metric measurements on these pages where applicable. When you go to the store, use whichever measurement is more commonly used for the items you're buying.

Metric conversions

U.S. Units to Metric Equivalents			Metric Units to U.S. Equivalents		
To Convert From	Multiply By	To Get	To Convert From	Multiply By	To Get
Inches	25.4	Millimeters	Millimeters	0.0394	Inches
Inches	2.54	Centimeters	Centimeters	0.3937	Inches
Feet	30.48	Centimeters	Centimeters	0.0328	Feet
Feet	0.3048	Meters	Meters	3.2808	Feet
Yards	0.9144	Meters	Meters	1.0936	Yards
Square inches	6.4516	Square centimeters	Square centimeters	0.1550	Square inches
Square feet	0.0929	Square meters	Square meters	10.764	Square feet
Square yards	0.8361	Square meters	Square meters	1.1960	Square yards
Acres	0.4047	Hectares	Hectares	2.4711	Acres
Cubic inches	16.387	Cubic centimeters	Cubic centimeters	0.0610	Cubic inches
Cubic feet	0.0283	Cubic meters	Cubic meters	35.315	Cubic feet
Cubic feet	28.316	Liters	Liters	0.0353	Cubic feet
Cubic yards	0.7646	Cubic meters	Cubic meters	1.308	Cubic yards
Cubic yards	764.55	Liters	Liters	0.0013	Cubic yards

To convert from degrees Fahrenheit (F) to degrees Celsius (C), first subtract 32, then multiply by ⅝.

To convert from degrees Celsius to degrees Fahrenheit, multiply by ⅖, then add 32.

Plumbing

PVC AND ABS PIPE.
Canadian code allows the use of both PVC and ABS pipe in drain and water systems. ABS is the most commonly used in Canada. Procedures for attaching fittings and installing PVC and ABS are similar. They are both easy to cut, lightweight, and rigid; however, ABS has a slightly shorter lifespan and can become brittle over time. The key difference is the nature of the adhesives, which are not interchangeable. PVC does not require a primer but you must use a specified cleaner prior to applying the adhesive.

You may find yourself in a situation where you need to join PVC and ABS. If so, special transition fittings are available to make the hookup.

ABS pipe and fittings

3" 90° long sweep elbow

Cleanout and plug

3" Y fitting

3" cap

Reducer

3" pipe

3" coupling

3" 45° elbow

End outlet with vertical tee

DOUBLE BOWL SINKS CANNOT DRAIN THROUGH A CENTER TEE IN CANADA. In Canadian systems, the drainpipe from one of the sinks runs straight down, through the trap, and then straight down into the rest of the DVW system. The drainpipe from the second sink connects with the first drain through a vertical tee located above the trap. (On center-tee systems, the pipes from the sinks meet midway between the two sinks, and then run down through the trap.)

P-TRAPS: ALL DRAINS IN CANADA MUST USE A P-TRAP, WHICH KEEPS SEWER GASES FROM BACKING UP INTO THE HOUSE.
The trap serves as a safety device by preventing noxious gases from backing up the sewer pipe and entering the house. Sewer gases not only pose a health hazard, they can also be explosive. The curved portion of the trap holds standing water. Every time the drain is used, water is flushed through the trap and is replaced with fresh water. Solids will adhere to the trap over time and eventually clog the drain or possibly damage the trap—which means it's time to install a new one.

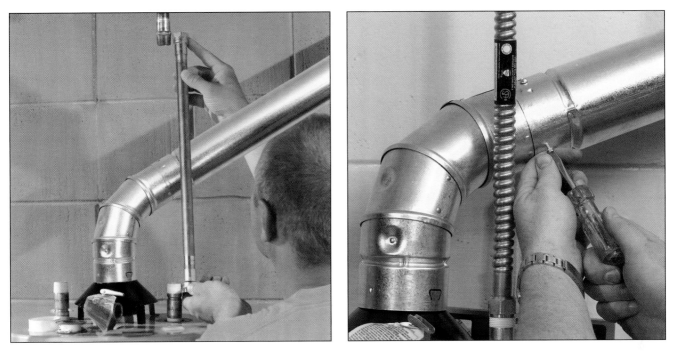

WATER HEATERS. Both rigid and flexible copper supply pipe as shown above can be used to hook up the hot and cold lines in some areas. Check with local provincial codes. Rigid copper pipe remains the most common installation. Flexible gas supply must be used from the gas line to the unit. In areas subject to earthquake, the hot water heater must be attached to the house framing.

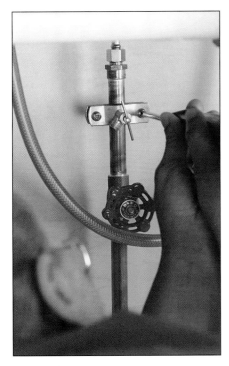

THE SADDLE TEE SHOWN ABOVE CANNOT BE USED to tap into an existing pipe in Canada. It does not meet code. You must use a compression tee as shown at right for the job.

Installing a compression fitting

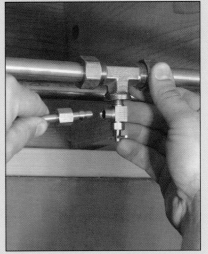

1 **INSTALL THE VALVE.** The kit may come with a saddle tee but they don't always meet code so you should use a compression tee instead. Installing the compression tee follows the same steps as installing a shutoff valve. (See page 98.)

2 **CONNECT THE TUBING TO THE VALVE.** Insert the tubing into the valve and tighten the nut. Use an adjustable wrench to connect the compression fitting. (See page 98 for connecting compression fittings.)

Electrical

2 **40-VOLT AND 120-/240-VOLT CIRCUITS.** The shape of the plug and receptacles on these circuits differs in the U.S. and Canada. The wiring is the same. Four-conductor wiring—two hot, a neutral, and a ground—is required by most, but not all, local codes.

BREAKERS. Half-size breakers do not meet code in Canada.

CABLE COLOR. Canadian cable is available with a solid red jacket. Red-coded cables are used for wires that run directly from the service panel to an outlet.

GFCI-OUTLETS. GFCI outlets are not required along kitchen countertops in Canada. See "Kitchens" for other differences.

GROUNDING LIGHT FIXTURES AND CEILING FANS. Light fixtures must be grounded in both Canada and the U.S. In Canada, however, the ground wire must run to a separate grounding bus bar in the service panel. (In the U.S., it runs to the common bus bar.) Connect the circuit's ground wire to the fixture's ground wire, if it has one. If not, connect the circuit's ground wire to a screw on the mounting strap.

GROUNDING METAL ELECTRICAL BOXES. Devices such as switches and receptacles, as well as the boxes that house them, must be connected to the service-panel ground bus. There is a screw, generally in the back of the box, for the ground wire. Connect this screw and the screw on the body of the device

to pigtails. Attach both pigtails to the circuit's ground wire.

GROUNDING PLASTIC ELECTRICAL BOXES. Plastic boxes in Canada have a ground screw in them, even though plastic is not a conductor. An internal connection in the box connects the screw to the body of the device (a switch or outlet) that the box houses. The connection grounds exposed metal parts of the device, protecting you should they become energized. (The ground screw in a metal box provides the same protection.) When you're wiring, connect both the ground screw in the box and the ground screw on the receptacle to a pigtail. Attach the pigtails to the wire running to the service panel's ground bus.

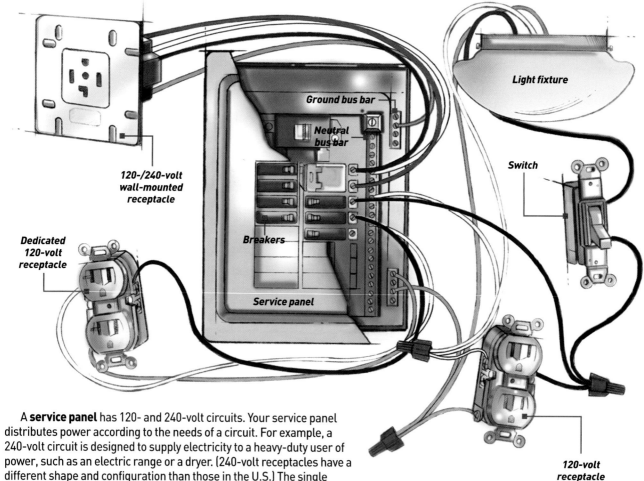

120-/240-volt wall-mounted receptacle

Ground bus bar

Neutral bus bar

Light fixture

Switch

Dedicated 120-volt receptacle

Breakers

Service panel

120-volt receptacle

A **service panel** has 120- and 240-volt circuits. Your service panel distributes power according to the needs of a circuit. For example, a 240-volt circuit is designed to supply electricity to a heavy-duty user of power, such as an electric range or a dryer. (240-volt receptacles have a different shape and configuration than those in the U.S.) The single receptacle on a dedicated 120-volt circuit might feed a refrigerator or a large microwave, while another 120-volt circuit feeds a series of receptacles and switched overhead light fixtures.

Depending on local code and the manufacturer, some switches may not have a grounding wire.

NOTE: In some service panels you may find that the neutral feed wire is not white. If that's the case, strips of white tape may have been added to differentiate between the neutral and hot feeds.

GROUNDING SWITCHES AND RECEPTACLES. Switches and receptacles have a green ground screw, which should be connected to the circuit's ground wire via a pigtail. A second pigtail should run from the ground wire to the ground screw on the box. The wiring inside the box is the same in the U.S. and Canada. In Canada, however, the ground wire runs to a ground bus bar in the service panel. In the U.S., it usually runs to the common bus bar.

GROUNDING SERVICE PANELS. Canadian code requires three separate bus bars in a service panel: a hot bus, neutral bus, and a ground bus. (Boxes in the U.S. have only two bus bars: hot and neutral.) All ground wires in the circuit run back to the service panel and are connected to the ground bar.

KITCHENS. Canadian code requires at least one 15-amp circuit for lighting. Space receptacles above countertops no more than 4 feet apart. Receptacles above a countertop must be split-circuit, meaning that the upper outlet must be on one circuit, while the lower outlet is on another circuit. (There is no requirement for GFCI receptacles above counters because the outlets on a GFCI cannot be split.) Many local Canadian codes require dedicated circuits for dishwashers and refrigerators. A microwave must have a single 20-amp circuit.

U.S. code requires a 15-amp circuit for lighting, two 20-amp circuits for receptacles, and separate circuits for the dishwasher and refrigerator. Receptacles above counters must be no more than 4 feet apart and must be GFCI.

ELECTRICAL CODES YOU MAY ENCOUNTER

Here's a quick summary of codes that are typical for household wiring projects. Follow them as you work up your plans and write your materials list.

These guidelines should satisfy most requirements, but keep in mind that your local codes might have different requirements. You probably will want to exceed requirements in order to provide your family with sufficient and safe electrical service.

The more you communicate your specific plans and techniques to your inspector, the less chance that you will have to tear out and do the job over again. It's better to be set straight by your inspector when the job is still on paper.

CABLE TYPE	Most locales allow NM (nonmetallic) cable for all installations where the cable runs inside walls or ceilings. Some areas require armored cable or conduit. If the cable will be exposed, many local codes require armored cable or conduit.
WIRE GAUGE	Use #14 wire for 15-amp circuits and #12 wire for 20-amp circuits.
PLASTIC AND METAL BOXES	Many locales allow plastic boxes for receptacles, switches, and fixtures; but some require metal boxes. Boxes must be flush with the finished drywall, plaster, or paneling. Make sure boxes are large enough for their conductors (page 170).
RUNNING CABLE	NM and armored cable must be run through holes in the center of studs or joists so that a drywall or trim nail cannot reach it. Most codes require metal nail guards as well. Some inspectors want cable for receptacles to be run about 10 inches above the receptacles. NM cable should be stapled to a stud or joist within 8 inches of the box it enters. Once the cable is clamped to a box, at least ¼ inch of sheathing should be visible in the box, and at least 8 inches of wire should be available for connecting to the device or fixture.
CIRCUIT CAPACITY	Make sure usage does not exceed "safe capacity" (pages 150–151). Local codes may be stricter.
LIVING ROOM, DINING ROOM, FAMILY ROOM, AND BEDROOM SPECS	Space receptacles every 12 feet (4 meters) along each wall and 6 feet (2 meters) from the first opening. If a small section of wall (between two doors, for example) is more than 3 feet (1 meter) wide, it should have a receptacle. For most purposes, use 15-amp receptacles. For convenience, rooms should have at least one light controlled by a wall switch near the entry door. However, pull chains for ceiling lights are acceptable. The switch may control an overhead light or one outlet of a receptacle, into which you can plug a lamp. Make sure the box you attach ceiling fans to can support the additional weight.
HALLWAY AND STAIRWAY SPECS	A stairway must have an overhead light controlled by three-way switches at the bottom and top of the stairs. If a hallway is more than 10 feet (3 meters) long, it must have at least one receptacle.
KITCHEN SPECS	Above countertops, space receptacles no more than 4 feet (1.22 meters) apart. Codes call for split-circuit receptacles above a countertop, which cannot be GFCI. Install one 15-amp circuit for lighting. Many codes require split receptacles on 15-amp circuits in kitchens and dedicated circuits for the dishwasher and refrigerator. A microwave must have a single 20-amp circuit.
BATHROOM SPECS	Any GFCI receptacle should be on its own circuit. Install the lights and fan on a separate 15- or 20-amp circuit.
GARAGE AND WORKSHOP SPECS	Install a 15-amp circuit for lights and a 20-amp circuit for tools. Install two 20-amp circuits if you have many power tools. Many areas require GFCIs in garages. Check your local code.

Electrical (continued)

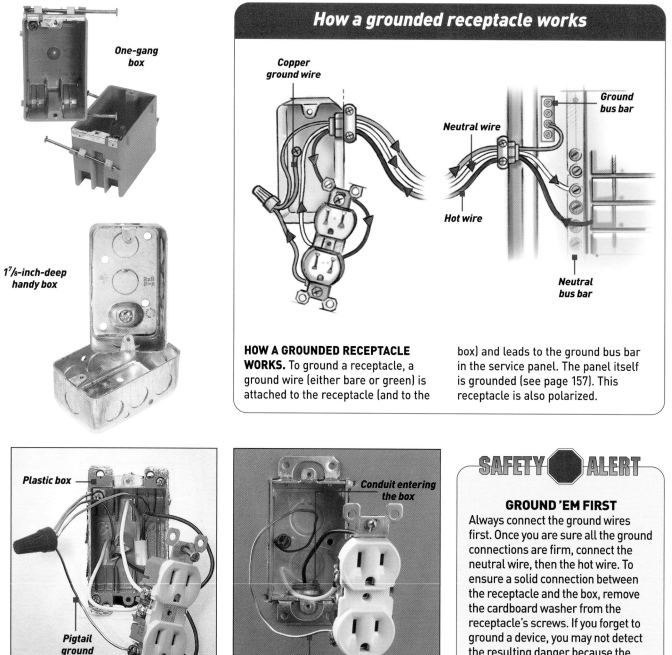

One-gang box

1⁷⁄₈-inch-deep handy box

How a grounded receptacle works

Copper ground wire

Neutral wire

Hot wire

Ground bus bar

Neutral bus bar

HOW A GROUNDED RECEPTACLE WORKS. To ground a receptacle, a ground wire (either bare or green) is attached to the receptacle (and to the box) and leads to the ground bus bar in the service panel. The panel itself is grounded (see page 157). This receptacle is also polarized.

Plastic box

Pigtail ground

Conduit entering the box

Ground

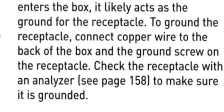

SAFETY ALERT

GROUND 'EM FIRST
Always connect the ground wires first. Once you are sure all the ground connections are firm, connect the neutral wire, then the hot wire. To ensure a solid connection between the receptacle and the box, remove the cardboard washer from the receptacle's screws. If you forget to ground a device, you may not detect the resulting danger because the ungrounded device or fixture will work just fine.

CABLES IN A PLASTIC BOX. Because plastic boxes do not conduct electricity, the receptacle must be grounded by attaching it to the bare ground wire in the cable. Check that bare copper grounding wires are spliced together and are attached to the grounding screw of the receptacle with a pigtail ground wire.

CONDUIT IN A METAL BOX. If conduit enters the box, it likely acts as the ground for the receptacle. To ground the receptacle, connect copper wire to the back of the box and the ground screw on the receptacle. Check the receptacle with an analyzer (see page 158) to make sure it is grounded.

Roofing

ICE-GUARD UNDERLAYMENT. Canadian code requires that, where used, ice-dam underlayment extend from the eave 36 inches (900 mm) up the roof. U.S. practice is to have underlayment extend 24 inches (609 mm) from the inside face of the exterior wall.

ROOFING NAILS. Canadian code says the nails should go a minimum of ½ inch (12 mm) into the roof deck. U.S. standards call for nails a minimum of ¾-inch long (19-mm), which pass all the way through the deck, and protrude a minimum of ¼ inch (6 mm) beyond it.

ROOFS WITH LOW SLOPES. In Canada, shingles on roofs with a slope less than 1:3 must be set in a band of asphalt cement. The band must be 8 inches (200 mm) wide. When laying the starter row, the asphalt cement goes directly on the underlayment. In subsequent rows, it's applied to the section of shingle that will be covered by the row above. Space the rows so that each shingle overlaps two-thirds of the shingle below instead of the usual half shingle.

In the U.S., practice requires extra underlayment instead of close spacing of the shingles. Start at the bottom of the roof with a 19-inch-wide (482-mm) strip of underlayment. Cover it entirely with a 36-inch-wide (914 mm) strip. Cover the 36-inch strip with another 36-inch strip that starts 17 inches (432 mm) from the bottom of the roof. Subsequent strips are 36 inches wide, and overlap the one below by 19 inches. Space shingles normally. Instead of a band of adhesive, hold 3-tab shingles down with two dabs of asphalt cement. Use three dabs on architectural shingles.

VALLEYS. In Canada, open valleys are required on all but very steep roofs (those with a slope of 1 in 1.2).

Heating, ventilation, and air-conditioning

Canadian code requires a ventilation system that brings fresh air into the house. While this can be a separate system, it can also be built into the furnace. If so, a vent pipe runs from outdoors into the return air plenum. Vent size, the need for a fan, and how the vent is attached varies, depending on the size of the house and the furnace. Consult local building authorities for specifics.

TOOL GLOSSARY

4-IN-1 TOOL
A multipurpose tool for cleaning and deburring copper pipe before soldering.

ABRASIVE STONE FILE
A file used to finish custom cuts on ceramic tile.

ACID FLUX BRUSH
Used to apply flux to copper fittings.

ADJUSTABLE WRENCH
A wrench with an adjustable head to accommodate various sizes of nuts and bolts.

ALLEN WRENCHES
Hexagonal wrenches used in conjunction with screws or bolts with recessed hexagonal heads.

BACK SAW
Fine-toothed handsaw that cuts on the back stroke. Used for precise cuts on molding and trim.

BALL PIEN HAMMER
A hammer with a flat face for driving and pounding on one end and a rounded surface on the other, used for shaping metal.

BAR CLAMP
(HAND SCREW)
An adjustable clamp used to secure materials and hold them in place. Comes in several lengths.

BASIN WRENCH
A specially designed wrench for removing or installing mounting and coupling nuts on faucets.

BASIN WRENCH
(PLASTIC FITTINGS)
A plumbing tool used to remove plastic fittings on plumbing fixtures.

BELT SANDER
A heavy-duty sander used to remove grain and thickness on wood.

BEVEL GAUGE
An adjustable measuring tool used to copy and mark angles for cutting.

BLOCK PLANE
A small hand plane used to shave, smooth, and shape wood.

BRUSH AND ROLLER SPINNER
Used to spin excess water out of brushes or roller covers after cleaning.

BRUSH AND TOOL EXTENDER
An extension pole with a clamp used to hold paint brushes or other tools to get to hard to reach places. Clamp is adjustable.

C-CLAMP
A screw-operated clamping device. Comes in several sizes.

CABINET TEMPLATE
Used to mark holes for attaching cabinet hardware.

CARBIDE DRILL BIT
(ADJUSTABLE)
An adjustable carbide drill bit used for cutting precise access holes in ceramic tile.

CARBIDE GRIT ROD SAW
A hand tool used for cutting ceramic tile.

CARPENTER'S LEVEL
A straightedge with leveling bubbles available in several lengths. Used to determine horizontal or vertical planes.

CARPENTER'S PENCIL
A large flat pencil with a wide lead used for marking.

CAT'S PAW (PRY BAR)
A steel bar used to remove nails or to pry pieces apart.

CAULKING GUN
A tool used to hold tubes of caulking or adhesives for applications such as sealing seams and bonding materials.

CHALK LINE
A chalk-filled container used to mark long straight lines for cutting or alignment. Also used as a plumb bob.

CIRCUIT TESTER
(NEON)
Used to test for the presence of electricity in a circuit.

CIRCULAR LEVEL
Used to determine level on horizontal surfaces.

CIRCULAR SAW
A hand power tool primarily used for crosscutting and ripping wood materials to length and width.

CLAW HAMMER

A hammer that comes in various weights with a face for driving nails and curved tines on the other for prying and nail removal.

CLOSET AUGER

An auger designed specifically to remove clogs in toilets without damaging the toilet.

COLD CHISEL

A steel chisel with a tempered edge used for cutting steel and for removing ceramic tile. Available with rubber safety handles.

COMBS

Made of plastic or rubber, used to apply decorative finishes to surfaces.

COMBINATION SQUARE

A layout tool with a sliding handle used for marking lines at both 90 and 45 degrees.

COMBINATION WRENCH

A wrench with an open and boxed end. The boxed end provides more control and less slippage.

COMPASS (SCRIBING)

An adjustable tool used to transfer contours from one surface to another with a pin on one leg and pencil clamp on the other.

CONTINUITY TESTER

An instrument that tells whether a device is capable of carrying electricity.

COPING SAW

A fine-toothed, thin-bladed sawblade mounted in a C-shaped frame used to cut precise outlines in wood.

COPPER FITTING BRUSH

Deburrs and cleans debris from the interior surface of copper pipe and fittings.

COPPER TUBE DEBURRER

Removes burrs and debris from the exterior of copper pipe in preparation for soldering.

CORDLESS REVERSIBLE SCREWDRIVER

Light-weight, battery-operated screwdriver. Useful for small assembly projects.

COUNTERSINK BIT

A combination drill bit used to set screws flush to or below the surface of the wood.

DIAGONAL CUTTING PLIERS

Wire cutting tool with diagonal blades that provide extra leverage. Also used to remove nails and staples.

DOUBLE BOX-ENDED RATCHET WRENCH

The box ends allow for more control when removing or installing nuts and bolts. The wrench comes in various sizes.

DOUBLE OPEN-ENDED WRENCH

Used to tighten or loosen nuts and bolts. Usually sold in sets with wrenches in graduated sizes.

DRAIN AUGER (DRILL DRIVEN)

A power-driven auger used to remove clogs from drain and waste lines. Not to be used in toilets or other fragile fixtures.

DRAIN AUGER (HAND SNAKE)

A manual drain auger used to remove clogs in drain and waste pipes. Not for use in toilets.

DRAIN AUGER (HAND SPINNING)

A hand-turned drain auger used to remove clogs from drain and waste lines. Not for use on toilets.

DRILL BIT EXTENSION

Extends the reach of a standard drill bit.

DROP CLOTH

Large canvas or paper/plastic sheet used to protect surfaces or objects during work sessions.

DRYWALL HAWK

A metal platform with a spindle handle used to hold joint compound or plaster while applying them to surfaces.

DRYWALL JOINT KNIFE

A flat-bladed knife used to apply joint compound and to finish seams.

DRYWALL SANDER

Finely-meshed, plastic screens attached to an extension pole, allowing finish sanding of drywall joint compound.

DRYWALL SAW

A coarse-bladed handsaw used to cut openings for fixtures in drywall.

DRYWALL SCREW BIT WITH DEPTH GAUGE

A bit with a stop used to set screws the proper depth in drywall without damaging the surface.

DRYWALL TAPING KNIFE

A flat-bladed, flexible knife used for finishing and smoothing joint compound on drywall.

Tool glossary *(continued)*

DUAL CARTRIDGE RESPIRATOR

A canister-style respirator with replaceable cartridges that filter particulate matter or solvent vapors.

DUST MASK (LATEX)

A mask worn to protect from particulate exposure while applying latex paint, usually by spraying.

DUST MASK (LEAD)

Particle mask with special filters to protect wearer from lead paint particles and fumes.

DUST MASK (SANDING)

A mask used to protect mouth and nose from particulate matter such as sawdust. Will not filter toxic matter or fumes. Use carefully.

EAR PLUGS

Foam inserts to protect hearing by reducing high-frequency and high-decibel noise from power tools and machinery.

EAR PROTECTION (MUFF)

Protects ears and hearing by reducing high-frequency and high-decibel noise from power tools and machinery.

ELECTRIC DRILL (CORDED)

A general purpose, variable-speed drill with a ⅜-inch chuck used for drilling holes in wood, metal, and other materials.

ELECTRIC DRILL (CORDLESS)

A battery-operated general purpose electric drill. Generally the higher the battery voltage, the more powerful the drill.

ELECTRICAL TAPE (BLACK)

A plastic tape used by electricians to insulate and secure wiring connections. Used in conjunction with wire nuts.

ELECTRICAL TAPE (COLORED)

Various colors used by electricians to mark and identify wires.

EMORY CLOTH

An abrasive material sold in rolls used to clean and prepare copper fittings for soldering.

EXTENSION POLE

A telescoping rod with a threaded end designed to accept paint rollers or brushes. For ceilings and other hard-to-reach places.

FELT MARKER

Marking tool for surfaces that resist pencil lines such as tile or metal. Generally leaves a permanent mark.

FILES

Hand-held tools with teeth or ridges used to shape, scrape, and otherwise finish wood, plastic, or metal.

FISH TAPE

Use to run cable through finished walls and pull wires through conduit.

FLAT PRY BAR

A tool used to remove nails or to assist in demolition.

FOAM BRUSHES

Economy level paintbrushes that come in various sizes. Primarily for single-use applications.

FRAMING HAMMERS

Long-handled, heavy-weight hammers with a striking face and straight tines used in rough carpentry.

FRAMING SQUARE (CARPENTER'S)

A flat piece of steel with legs at 90 degrees for measuring and layout. A framing square is essential for general carpentry.

FUSE PULLER

A plastic plier designed specifically to remove fuses from electrical boxes.

GFCI EXTENSION CORD

An extension cord with a GFCI outlet.

GLASS SCRAPER

A hand tool with replaceable blades used to remove paint from windows after painting trim.

GLAZING TOOL

A multipurpose tool with a flat blade on one end and a notched blade on the other used to remove and apply glaze to windows.

GREASE PENCIL

Marking tool for surfaces that resist pencil lines such as tile or metal. The mark can be removed.

GROUT BAG

A canvas or plastic tube with a nozzle on the end used to apply grout to seams.

GROUT FLOAT

A masonry tool used to apply grout to seams in ceramic tile.

GROUT SAW

A fine-toothed saw with an offset handle used to remove grout from seams.

HACKSAW

A saw with interchangeable blades designed specifically for cutting metal pipe or tubing.

HAMMER DRILL

An electric drill that also pulses the drill bit forward and backward. Use to drill holes in concrete and masonry.

HAMMER STAPLER

A staple gun used like a hammer to set staples, primarily used when applying underlayment to decking.

HANDSAW

A wood-cutting tool. Blades for handsaws are designed for cross-cutting and ripping lumber.

HOLE SAW

A cutting bit used with a drill to cut large diameter holes. Cuts wood, plastic, ceramic tile, and a variety of other materials.

HOT-GLUE GUN

A hand tool that distributes adhesive to surfaces using heat to melt sticks of glue.

INSULATION BLOWER

Rental unit with hopper to hold insulation and blower motor. Flexible tubing guides insulation into closed spaces.

KEYHOLE SAW

A handsaw with interchangeable blades used for cutting holes in drywall and trimming soft woods such as pine.

KNEE PADS

Worn to protect the knees while kneeling on hard surfaces.

LASER LEVEL

Laser levels project horizontal beams on surfaces to mark level.

LATEX GLOVES

Used to protect hands while working with paint.

LEATHER GLOVES

Used to protect hands when working with rough edged materials. Will not protect hands from liquids or other solvents.

LINE LEVEL

A level that attaches to mason's string to set horizontal planes over longer distances.

LOCKING PLIERS

Combination pliers and clamp. Comes in various sizes.

MALLET HAMMER

A hammer with a head of hard rubber. Used in applications where a steel hammer might mar the material.

MARGIN TROWEL

Masonry tool used to spread adhesive in tight or awkward places such as corners.

MASON'S STRING

Heavy-gauge string woven not to stretch. Used to set finish heights and widths for masonry, carpentry, and deck installation.

MASONRY DRILL BITS

Drill bits especially designed for use with a power drill to bore holes in masonry and brick.

MITER BOX (HAND)

An inexpensive miter box for cutting simple angles and miters in wood.

MORTAR MIXING PADDLE

A paddle that attaches to an electric drill used to mix mortar for tile installation.

MUD PAN

A long plastic pan used to mix and hold mortar or other compounds during application.

MULTITESTER (VOLTAGE)

Used to test electrical equipment for flow and/or presence of current through the circuit.

NAIL HOLE SLOT PUNCH

Used to cut slots in vinyl siding when replacing pieces.

NAIL MAGNET

Used to remove nails and other metal objects from worksites such as lawns and landscaping after a roofing project.

NAIL PULLER

A tool designed to give extra leverage when removing large nails or fasteners.

NAIL SET

Used to set nail heads below the surface of a material prior to finishing. Also referred to as nail punches.

NEEDLE-NOSE PLIERS

Used for reaching into enclosed areas and to bend or hold wire or small hardware. Also has cutting blades in the plier joint.

Tool glossary *(continued)*

NITRILE GLOVES

Hand protection for those allergic to latex.

NON-ABRASIVE SCOURING PAD

Used for general cleaning when abrasive materials such as steel wool would damage surfaces.

OFFSET DOUBLE BOX-END WRENCH

Offset box-end wrenches are used to get into tight places.

ORBITAL SANDER

A power sanding tool with an orbital action to reduce sanding marks on wood. Can be used with or against the grain.

OVERHEAD MITER BOX

A hand miter box with the miter saw mounted in a support bracket for more precise cutting.

PAD SANDER

A finishing sander with a vibrating action to reduce sanding marks on wood.

PAINTBRUSH COMB

Used to remove dried or caked paint from the bristles of paintbrushes.

PAINTBRUSH (DISPOSABLE)

An inexpensive bristle style brush primarily for one-time use.

PAINTBRUSHES (BRISTLE)

Good quality bristle paintbrushes are used for finish painting and to guarantee smooth, even surfaces.

PAINTBRUSHES (DETAIL)

Paintbrushes in various shapes and sizes used for detail work or decorative painting.

PAINT BUCKET

A plastic or disposable cardboard paint bucket ranging in size from 1 quart to 5 gallons. Used for holding and mixing paint.

PAINT CAN OPENER

An inexpensive specialty tool designed specifically to open paint cans without damaging the lid.

PAINT CAN POURING SPOUT

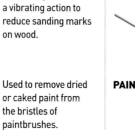

Attaches to the lip of a standard paint can to limit spills while pouring paint.

PAINT MITT

A wool or synthetic glove used to apply paint to irregular surfaces such as fences, grillwork, or gates.

PAINT MIXER

A rod with a paddle on the end, used with an electric drill to thoroughly mix large quantities of paint.

PAINT PAD

A foam pad attached to a handle used to apply even coats of paint. Alternative to a brush.

PAINT ROLLER AND CAGE

Used to apply paint to large surfaces. Rollers come in a variety of materials and thicknesses for different applications.

PAINT ROLLER CAGES

Used to hold paint rollers for application. A cage with at least 5 rods has the most reliable tension on the roller.

PAINT ROLLER GRID

Allows clean and even loading of paint on the roller when using a five-gallon bucket.

PAINT ROLLER (HOT DOG)

A foam roller used to apply smooth, brush-mark free paint to surfaces such as trim and doors.

PAINT SCRAPER

A tool designed to ease removal of old paint from surfaces in preparation for new applications.

PAINT TRAY LINER

A disposable plastic liner designed to fit in paint trays. Speeds cleanup.

PAINT TRAY (METAL)

A tray with a well at one end to hold paint and a sloped incline designed to apply paint evenly to a paint roller.

PAINT TRAY (PLASTIC)

A tray with a well at one end to hold paint and a sloped incline designed to apply paint evenly to a paint roller.

PAINTER'S MASKING DISPENSER

Dispenser that applies masking tape to masking film or paper for masking surfaces such baseboards in continuous application.

PAINTER'S TAPE

A low-tack tape used to protect surfaces while painting. Low-tack tape removes easily without leaving traces of adhesive.

PAINTER'S TOOL (5-IN-1)

A multi-purpose painter's tool designed to open paint cans and clean roller covers. Also used to help with repair and preparation.

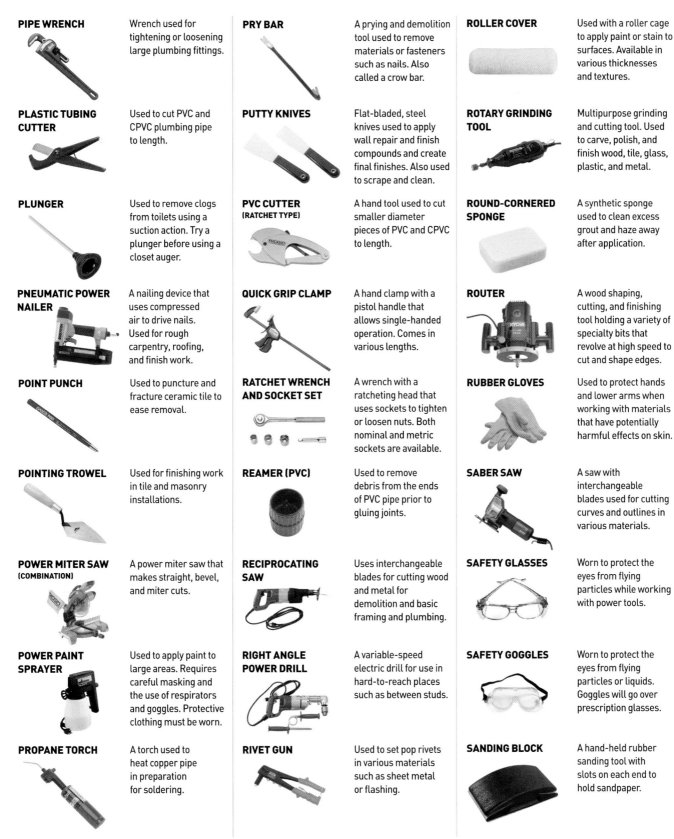

PIPE WRENCH
Wrench used for tightening or loosening large plumbing fittings.

PLASTIC TUBING CUTTER
Used to cut PVC and CPVC plumbing pipe to length.

PLUNGER
Used to remove clogs from toilets using a suction action. Try a plunger before using a closet auger.

PNEUMATIC POWER NAILER
A nailing device that uses compressed air to drive nails. Used for rough carpentry, roofing, and finish work.

POINT PUNCH
Used to puncture and fracture ceramic tile to ease removal.

POINTING TROWEL
Used for finishing work in tile and masonry installations.

POWER MITER SAW (COMBINATION)
A power miter saw that makes straight, bevel, and miter cuts.

POWER PAINT SPRAYER
Used to apply paint to large areas. Requires careful masking and the use of respirators and goggles. Protective clothing must be worn.

PROPANE TORCH
A torch used to heat copper pipe in preparation for soldering.

PRY BAR
A prying and demolition tool used to remove materials or fasteners such as nails. Also called a crow bar.

PUTTY KNIVES
Flat-bladed, steel knives used to apply wall repair and finish compounds and create final finishes. Also used to scrape and clean.

PVC CUTTER (RATCHET TYPE)
A hand tool used to cut smaller diameter pieces of PVC and CPVC to length.

QUICK GRIP CLAMP
A hand clamp with a pistol handle that allows single-handed operation. Comes in various lengths.

RATCHET WRENCH AND SOCKET SET
A wrench with a ratcheting head that uses sockets to tighten or loosen nuts. Both nominal and metric sockets are available.

REAMER (PVC)
Used to remove debris from the ends of PVC pipe prior to gluing joints.

RECIPROCATING SAW
Uses interchangeable blades for cutting wood and metal for demolition and basic framing and plumbing.

RIGHT ANGLE POWER DRILL
A variable-speed electric drill for use in hard-to-reach places such as between studs.

RIVET GUN
Used to set pop rivets in various materials such as sheet metal or flashing.

ROLLER COVER
Used with a roller cage to apply paint or stain to surfaces. Available in various thicknesses and textures.

ROTARY GRINDING TOOL
Multipurpose grinding and cutting tool. Used to carve, polish, and finish wood, tile, glass, plastic, and metal.

ROUND-CORNERED SPONGE
A synthetic sponge used to clean excess grout and haze away after application.

ROUTER
A wood shaping, cutting, and finishing tool holding a variety of specialty bits that revolve at high speed to cut and shape edges.

RUBBER GLOVES
Used to protect hands and lower arms when working with materials that have potentially harmful effects on skin.

SABER SAW
A saw with interchangeable blades used for cutting curves and outlines in various materials.

SAFETY GLASSES
Worn to protect the eyes from flying particles while working with power tools.

SAFETY GOGGLES
Worn to protect the eyes from flying particles or liquids. Goggles will go over prescription glasses.

SANDING BLOCK
A hand-held rubber sanding tool with slots on each end to hold sandpaper.

Tool glossary *(continued)*

SANDING SPONGE — A synthetic sponge with coarse and fine surfaces used with water to smooth and finish drywall.

SCRATCH AWL — A tool used to scratch cutting marks into various surfaces. Also may be used as a hole punch.

SCREW GUN — A variable-speed hand tool designed to set screws. Primarily used to install drywall, metal stud walls, and sheet metal duct work.

SCREWDRIVERS (INSULATED) — Screwdrivers with insulated handles used in electrical work.

SCREWDRIVERS (SLOTTED AND PHILLIPS) — Used to set screws in various materials. Available for various screw heads such as slotted and Phillips.

SEAT DRESSING TOOL — Used to reset the valve seat in a compression faucet.

SEAT WRENCH — A specialty wrench used to install the valve seats in compression faucets.

SIDE-CUTTING PLIERS (LINEMAN'S) — A heavy-duty, square jawed pliers with insulated handles used for cutting and bending wire.

SIDING REMOVAL TOOL — Used to remove vinyl siding for replacement or repair.

SLEDGE HAMMER — A hammer with identical striking surfaces used for demolition and to move heavy objects into final position.

SLIDING COMPOUND POWER MITER SAW — A compound miter saw that slides on tracks to allow cutting and mitering of larger pieces of material.

SLIP-JOINT PLIERS — General purpose pliers used to hold and bend objects.

SPADE DRILL BITS — Drill bits for drilling holes of various diameters usually up to 1½ inches in wood.

SPECIALTY BRUSHES — Paintbrushes of various sizes and configurations used for finish and decorative painting.

SPLIT FOAM ROLLER — A foam roller designed to apply paint to acoustical ceilings without damaging the application.

SPRAY BOTTLE — Used primarily with water to mist and dampen surfaces for cleaning, preparation, or application of latex paint.

SPUD WRENCH — Specially designed plumbing tool to remove or tighten very large nuts by grabbing the lugs on the nut.

SQUARE NOTCHED TROWEL — A mason's trowel notched on two edges of the blade used to apply adhesive to surfaces. Comes in a variety of notch sizes.

SQUEEGEE — Comb with notched rubber edge used in decorative painting to create a combed effect on surfaces.

STAPLER (MANUAL) — A hand stapling tool accommodating various lengths of staples.

STIPPLING BRUSH — Has many long, soft bristles to lift some of the wet glaze off the wall for a decorative painting technique.

STRAIGHTEDGE — A long metal ruler used as a guide for making straight cuts in wallpaper and vinyl tile.

STRAINER LOCKNUT WRENCH — A special tool to ease removal of the locknut on a sink strainer.

STRAP WRENCH — An adjustable wrench that grips larger sizes of pipe for fitting or removal.

STUD DRIVER — A tool powered by a bullet-like cartridge used to drive special nails into concrete or other hard surfaces.

STUD FINDER — An electronic tool that senses the presence of metal in walls to locate studs.

T-SQUARE — A combination straightedge and T-square used primarily to measure and cut materials for drywall installation.

TACK HAMMER

A small hammer with a striking face on one end and a magnetic tip on the other. Used to drive small nails.

TAPE MEASURE (RETRACTABLE)

A handheld measuring tool with a retractable blade used for determining incremental dimensions.

TILE CUTTER (SLIDING)

A tool used to cut ceramic tile. The tile is scored and then snapped by pressing down the lever.

TILE NIPPERS

A cutting and shaping tool used to custom-fit ceramic tile around obstacles.

TILE SCORER

A knife with two pointed blades used to score ceramic tile.

TIN SNIPS

Heavy-duty scissor-like cutting tool for metal such as flashing or ducting.

TORPEDO LEVEL

A level used to level and/or plumb short pieces of material.

TRY SQUARE

A smaller version of a carpenter's square. Used for checking and/or marking 90 degree angles.

TUBING CUTTER

Used to accurately cut various kinds of metal tubing, primarily copper, to length while keeping tubing perfectly round.

UTILITY KNIFE

Multipurpose cutting tool with interchangeable razor blades. Used for general cutting, trimming, and fitting.

UTILITY KNIFE (HOOKED BLADE)

A utility knife with a hooked blade used to cut flooring and roofing materials. Also called a roofing knife.

V-NOTCHED TROWEL

A mason's trowel used to apply adhesive to surfaces that will receive tile.

WALLPAPER BROADKNIFE

Used to apply and smooth wallpaper.

WALLPAPER BRUSHES AND ROLLER

Used to apply wallpaper paste and to smooth and seal seams.

WALLPAPER SCORING TOOL

A hand tool used to score wallpaper to ease removal.

WALLPAPER SPONGE

A synthetic sponge used to clean and smooth wallpaper and to remove excess water or paste.

WALLPAPER STRIPPER

A hand tool with an interchangeable blade used to remove wallpaper without damaging the wall surface.

WATER HEATER ELEMENT WRENCH

Makes the job of removing the electrical element in a water heater easier.

WATER LEVEL

Used with a battery-powered electronic sensor to define level over long distances.

WATER-PUMP PLIERS

A multipurpose gripping tool with adjustable ridged jaws for secure contact. Tape jaws to prevent damage to fixtures.

WATER TRAY

A long plastic tray used to hold wallpaper while soaking in preparation for application.

WET SAW

A table-style circular saw for cutting ceramic tile with a special blade and lubricating system using water.

WIRE BRUSH

A wooden handled brush with stiff wire bristles used to clean and prepare surfaces for finishing or bonding.

WIRE STRIPPER, COMBINATION

A multipurpose tool for cutting and stripping insulation from wire prior to connecting.

WIRE STRIPPERS

Pliers with graduated cutting notches. Used to strip insulation from various gauges of wire without damaging the wire itself.

WOOD CHISELS

A wood shaping and finishing tool with an angled cutting edge. Used with or without a mallet or hammer to remove precise amounts of wood.

INDEX

INDEX

ACKNOWLEDGEMENTS & RESOURCES

Page 84
Sink: #7162.001
  Chandler Americast Single Bowl Kitchen Sink
Faucet: #4205.100.025
  Combi Faucet
  Chrome and White
American Standard
800/ 524-9797, ext. 199
www.americanstandard-us.com/press

Page 192
Chandelier
Elkhorn Designs
165 N Center St.
Jackson, WY 83001
307/ 733-4655
www.elkhorndesigns.com

Pages 256–260
Wheatland wall tile: #5207
Daltile
800/ 933-TILE (800/ 933-8453)
www.daltile.com

Page 278
Flooring Materials:
  Marble tile
Renaissance Marble and Tile
Des Moines, IA

Pages 304–305
Desert Parquet Flooring
  American Home Series (AHS) 100
Bruce Hardwood Floors
16803 Dallas Pkwy.
Addison, TX 75001
800/ 722-4647
www.bruce.com

Pages 314–315
Medallion: #305-30 in lead and SBS
Border: #130-RO Rose© in lead
Historic Floors of Oshkosh, Inc.
920/ 582-9977
www.oshkoshfloors.com

Page 323
Illustration by permission of The Carpet and Rug Institute
Dalton, GA 30722-2048
www.carpet-rug.com

Pages 330, 347–348
Exterior Door: StaTru Plus Entry System 3/0x7/0 K1 Door Unit
Stanley Door Systems
7300 Reames Rd.
Charlotte, NC 28216
704/ 921-3503
800/ 521-2752
www.stanleyworks.com

Page 332
Insulated Exterior Door: Prefinished wood grain fiberglass entry door (Golden Oak), D58
Insulated Exterior Door: StaTru Plus Steel entry door (Patina), L19
Stanley Door Systems
7300 Reames Rd.
Charlotte, NC 28216
704/ 921-3503
800/ 521-2752
www.stanleyworks.com

Decorative Storm Door:
  All Seasons Door HD 300 Colonial Triple Track
EMCO Enterprises
2121 East Walnut St.
Des Moines, IA 50317
www.allseasonsdoors.com
www.forever.com
800/ 933-3626

Pages 351–352
Storm Door:
  All Seasons Door HD 200 Triple Track Bronze
EMCO Enterprises
2121 East Walnut St.
Des Moines, IA 50317
www.allseasonsdoors.com
www.forever.com
800/ 933-3626

Pages 353–357
Patio Door: Proline 6ft. White Hinged Patio Door and Screen
Pella Windows
102 Main St.
Pella, IA 50219
www.pella.com
888/ 84-PELLA (888/ 847-3552)

Pages 358–360
Garage Door
Clopay Building Products
312 Walnut St.
Cincinnati, OH 45202
Consumer Hotline:
800/ 2-CLOPAY (800/ 225-6729)
www.clopaydoor.com

Pages 362–363
Genie Garage Door Opener
www.geniecompany.com

Pages 366, 377–380
Proline Tilt DH, White Windows, Screens, Mullion Kit
Pella Windows
102 Main St.
Pella, IA 50219
www.pella.com
888/ 84-PELLA (888/ 847-3552)

Page 375
Patio door lock
Franklin Manufacturing
516/ 694-1800

Page 384
Cabinet Hardware:
Cup pull: #424
Knob satin/chrome: #412
Amerock Corp.
4000 Auburn St.
P.O. Box 7018
Rockford, IL 61125-7018
www.amerock.com
800/ 435-6959

Pages 384, 397–400
Cabinets:
Hartford Natural Maple
Mills Pride
www.millspride.com

Pages 385, 417–419
Wire Shelf Storage System:
8' wide closet, Superslide
ClosetMaid
www.closetmaid.com

Pages 388–389
Cabinet Hardware:
Ceramic Pull with Brass Finial:
    #10312
Southwest Pull:
    Verdigris Finish, #31252
Southwest Pull:
    Verdigris Finish, #63511
Southwest Backplate:
    Verdigris Finish, #31294
Polished Brass Cup Pull:
    3", #10676
Rockler Woodworking
    and Hardware
4365 Willow Dr.
Medina, MN 55340
www.rockler.com
800/ 279-4441

Page 391
Cabinet Refacing
Kitchen Solvers
515/ 252-6146

Pages 423, 439
Insulation Blower
Krendl Manufacturing
419/ 692-3060
www.krendlmachine.com

Pages 442, 478–480
Traditional Series Shingles:
Supreme® shingles:
    Estate gray
Owens Corning
www.owenscorning.com
800/ GET-PINK (800/ 438-7465)

Pages 449–450
TuffFlo Vinyl Gutter System
GSW Thermoplastics
www.gswthermo.com

Page 458
Soffit and Fascia
ASHLAND-DAVIS
www.certainteed.com

Pages 463, 465, 543
Roofing harness assembly:
DBI/Sala Full Body Harness:
    Delta No-Tangle Harness,
    #1102000
Rope Grab:
    Rope Lifeline Assembly,
    #1202790
Lanyard:
    EZ Stop® III Shock Absorbing
    Lanyard, #1224006
General Fire and Safety
    Equipment Co., Inc.
3210 NE 14th St.
Des Moines, IA 50316
www.assehawk.org/gfs.html
515/ 265-3206

Page 463
Air Compressor:
2 HP, 6 gallon Pancake
    Compressor, #CF2600
Porter-Cable Professional
    Power Tools
4825 Hwy. 45 North
P.O. Box 2468
Jackson, TN 38302-2468
www.porter-cable.com

Pages 478–485
Roofing Coil nailer: RN175
Porter-Cable Professional
    Power Tools
4825 Hwy. 45 North
P.O. Box 2468
Jackson, TN 38302-2468
www.porter-cable.com

Page 481
Laying a valley with
    architectural shingles—
Architectural Series Shingles:
    Oakridge® 25 Shingles:
        Estate gray
Laying a metal open valley—
Traditional Series Shingles:
    Supreme® shingles:
        Aspen gray
Owens Corning
www.owenscorning.com
800/ GET-PINK (800/ 438-7465)

Pages 484–485
Roll Roofing: black
Owens Corning
www.owenscorning.com
800/ GET-PINK (800/ 438-7465)

Page 495
Evaporative cooler:
Master Cooler #MW5500
    window cooler
AdobeAir
www.adobeair.com
602/ 257-0060

Page 533
Auxiliary Gas Heater: RH50B
Empire Comfort Systems
www.empirecomfort.com
800/ 233-0255

Page 535
Direct-Vent Heater: DV40E
Empire Comfort Systems
www.empirecomfort.com
800/ 233-0255

Skilled Technicians
Arends Production Services
Set Construction
Tim Arends
www.arends.com

Quality Ceramic Tile
Tiling a Wall
Roger Jaqua
Des Moines, IA

Ned Davis
Wallpapering
Des Moines, IA

Steve Covington
Roofing
Ames, IA

Denny Nielson
Pella Windows
Pella, IA

Todd Armstrong
Dan's Overhead Doors
Des Moines, IA

Todd Fuson
Garage Door Installation
Indianola, IA

Randy Rogers
Exterior Painting
Minneapolis, MN

Kane Powell
Cabinet Installation,
    Paradigm Installations
Des Moines, IA

Lawrence L. Gilmer
Builder, Skilled Technician
612/ 823-8454

Evan Parker
HVAC
Central Iowa Heating
    and Cooling
Des Moines, IA

Production Crew
Tim Arends
Set Construction
Arends Production Services
www.arends.com

Cameron Sadeghpour
    Digital Helm

Janet Dady and Molly Branco
    Production Coordinators

Adam Albright, Jason
Wallsmith, Lou Lyle, Dallas
Hallam, and Mike Faas
    Assistants

Ann Holtz and Susan Strelecki
    Stylists

John Halstrom
    Second Photographer

Cindy Cohrs
    Prop Runner

Ellen Boeke and Ann Holtz
    Project Managers

ACKNOWLEDGEMENTS & RESOURCES

Raynard Alexandria
Los Angeles, CA

Dave Alleyne
Davie, FL

Allen Applebaum
Willow Grove, PA

Mary Ann Barish
Bensalem, PA

Stafford Barker
Los Angeles, CA

Rick L. Brazil
Manteca, CA

Carl Cady
Phoenix, AZ

Derek Clarke
Scottsdale, AZ

Derek Cleveland
Monrovia, CA

Susan Curtis
Thousand Oaks, CA

Bill Dame
Robbinsville, NJ

Danny Dana
Sacramento, CA

Roy Davis
Mesa, AZ

Ruth M. Drosdick
Greensburg, PA

Timothy Dunkowski
Williamsville, NY

Thomas Fellerer
Fridley, MN

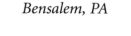

Many thanks to the employees
of The Home Depot®, whose
"wisdom of the aisles" has made
Home Improvement 1-2-3® the
most useful book of its kind.

Denyse M. Ferguson
Atlanta, GA

Jay Fields
Brooklyn Park, MN

Diane R. Fisher
West Berlin, NJ

Terry Flanagan
Lawrenceville, GA

Marcus Frederickson
Lakewood, CO

Michael J. Gardaphe
Pompano Beach, FL

Sandy Golay
Mesa, AZ

Bill H. Grimm
Mesa, AZ

Robert Guth
Bridgeport, CT

Ed Hard
Marietta, GA

Pat Hines
Burnsville, MN

Ted Hoffman
Douglasville, GA

Bruce Hudson
Cape May, NJ

Wayne Hunyadi
Louisville, CO

Gary Isakson
St. Louis, MN

Josephine Jackson
Bronx, NY

John Lee Johnson
Phoenix, AZ

Neal C. Johnson
Plymouth, MN